"十二五"国家重点出版项目

国家出版基金项目

国家出版基金项目
NATIONAL PUBLICATION FOUNDATION

中国医学院士文库

曾毅院士集

ZENG YI YUANSHIJI

曾 毅 主 编

人民军醫出版社

PEOPLE'S MILITARY MEDICAL PRESS

北 京

图书在版编目(CIP)数据

曾毅院士集/曾　毅主编 . —北京:人民军医出版社,2014.11
(中国医学院士文库)
ISBN 978-7-5091-7723-5

Ⅰ.①曾… Ⅱ.①曾… Ⅲ.①曾毅—生平事迹 Ⅳ.①K826.2

中国版本图书馆 CIP 数据核字(2014)第 262337 号

策划编辑:李玉梅　于晓红　　文字编辑:陈　鹏　　责任审读:余满松
出版发行:人民军医出版社　　　　　　经销:新华书店
通信地址:北京市 100036 信箱 188 分箱　　邮编:100036
质量反馈电话:(010)51927290;(010)51927283
邮购电话:(010)51927252
策划编辑电话:(010)51927300—8746
网址:www.pmmp.com.cn

印刷:北京天宇星印刷厂　　装订:胜宏达印装有限公司
开本:850mm×1168mm　1/16
印张:26.25·彩页 13 面　字数:1162 千字
版、印次:2014 年 11 月第 1 版第 1 次印刷
印数:001—930
定价:230.00 元

曾毅院士

内容提要

　　《曾毅院士集》是《中国医学院士文库》的分册之一。本书由五部分组成。第一部分奋斗历程，介绍了院士的主要经历和事业发展的宝贵经验；第二部分学术贡献，包括院士的主要学术论文、学术著作以及学术年表等，反映了院士在理论创新和技术进步方面的主要成果及其价值；第三部分大师风范，记载了院士在培养人才和团队建设上为人师表的生动事例；第四部分社会影响，汇集了社会各界对院士学术成果和先进事迹的评价和赞誉；第五部分人生风采，以丰富的图片资料展示了院士在不同时期工作、讲学、国际交流、社会活动和业余生活等方方面面的风采。全书充分诠释了曾毅院士的学术成就、学术思想和学术风范，可供广大医学工作者，特别是从事疾病预防控制、病毒性疾病和肿瘤研究的科研人员、临床医务工作者学习、借鉴。

编著者名单

主　　编　曾　毅

主编助理　李红霞

编　著　者　（以姓氏笔画为序）

王　辉　邓　洪　左建明　叶树清　叶景荣　冯　霞
司静懿　皮国华　朱义鑫　刘　畅　刘纯仁　刘育希
刘彦仿　刘振声　刘新蕾　汤敏中　许丽艳　纪志武
李　杨　李红霞　李来云　李恩民　吴映成　岑　山
余双庆　沈　健　沈淑静　张　伟　张芦光　张建坤
陆圣经　陈伟平　陈志坚　陈敏华　邵一鸣　苗学谦
周　玲　庞　英　郑裕明　赵文平　钟建明　姚庆云
唐伟平　龚翠红　章　东　韩日才　曾　毅　谭碧芳
滕智平

（以英文字母为序）

BAYLIS Sally A　BORNKAMN GW　BOUVIER Guy
DAY Nicholas E　DEGOS Laurent　Desgranges C
de The Guy　HUANG Doll P　HUBERT A　IEE Kun
ITO Yohei　JAIO B　James A. Lautenberger　JAN MG
KOSHIMIZU Koichi　Lei yi-ing　LI Er-koe
LITTLER Edward　MORGAN AJ　OHIGASHI Hajme
OHSHIMA Hiroshi　OOKA Tadamasa　Poirier S
POISSON A　ROWE M　TUPPIN P　Wolf H

《中国医学院士文库》编委会办公室

主　　任　余化刚

成　　员　李　勇　唐　泽　曾　星　姚　磊　杨越朝　张卫民　任淦平

《中国医学院士文库》出版工作小组

项目组长　姚　磊

项目统筹　黄春霞

项目设计　姚　磊　齐学进　石　虹

组稿策划　姚　磊　杨越朝　齐学进　曾　星　黄春霞　徐卓立　郝文娜
　　　　　高爱英　杨磊石　程晓红　李玉梅　黄建松　秦速励　丁　震
　　　　　王显刚　马　莉　王海燕　于晓红　张　晶　郭　威　焦健姿
　　　　　杨德胜　梁紫岩　管　悦　郭　颖　李　欢　路　弘　纳　琨
　　　　　曾小珍　马凤娟　池　静　任海霞　王久红　王　琳　崔玲和
　　　　　张怡泓　郭伟疆　杨　淮　于　哲　张利峰　张忠丽　高玉婷
　　　　　张　田　崔晓荣　严雪梅　刘　立　王灵芳　晋　桦

编校审读　余满松　周晓洲　黄栩兵　杜云祥　杨磊石　张宇辉　谢秀英
　　　　　吴铁双　陈晓平　王三荣　卢紫晔　高　磊　陈　鹏　王　璐
　　　　　韩　志　黄维佳　刘新瑞　袁朝阳　郁　静　陈　娟　侯小芳
　　　　　赵晶辉　李　昆　刘婉婷　纳　琨　李　欢　王显刚　于晓红
　　　　　高玉婷　王久红　王灵芳　严雪梅　杨　芳　焦健姿　任海霞
　　　　　邓　艳　梁雅慧　陈　卓　王红健　魏　新　杨善芝　王月红
　　　　　程晓红　晋　桦

出版保障　刘　平　陈琪福　程晓红　成智颖　张国深　秦新利　徐敬东
　　　　　周晓冰　冯亚莉　吴朝洪　陶　金　晋　桦　王爱英

《中国医学院士文库》

序

　　《中国医学院士文库》作为国家出版基金重点支持的大型出版工程，要为中国科学院和中国工程院的每一位医学界院士出版一个分册。组织这项出版工程的目的，是要将我国两院医学院士的学术成就、学术思想及治学精神广泛传播、系统传承和长久留存，它对于提升我国的医学科学技术水平与创新能力，进而为党的十八大提出的建成人人享有健康的小康社会提供重要的医学科技支撑，具有重要的时代意义和科学价值。参与这项出版工程的医学界两院院士都是我们国家的精英，在他们身上集中反映了爱国主义的精神和高尚的职业道德。每一位院士都有各自闪亮的人生经历、鲜明的个性风格、独到的学术创新。出版《中国医学院士文库》，对中国医学院士这个优秀群体进行集中全面的反映，这对弘扬科学精神和人文精神、促进医学文化传承创新、提升全行业的职业道德建设水平，包括对青年一代医学工作者的教育，都具有不可替代的重要意义。

　　承担《中国医学院士文库》这一国家出版基金项目的人民军医出版社，在国家卫生部和总后卫生部的支持下，于2012年2月组织召开了《中国医学院士文库》编委会工作会议，正式启动了这一工程。在京的近二十名两院医学院士，国家卫生部、总后卫生部领导，中华医学会、中国医师协会、中华口腔医学会等学术机构的领导，共一百多人出席了会议。当时我很感慨，这项工程得到这么多院士、专家、领导的拥护，有这么多医学界的领军人物相聚一堂，共商《中国医学院士文库》编写出版事宜，这在当代医学出版史上是极为罕见的。参加会议的时候，我想起了古人的《兰亭集序》。在公元350年左右，"群贤毕至，修禊事也"，留下了千古名篇。抚今追往，我当时非常高兴，随口吟出了"中华人民共和国，六十三年，岁在壬辰，早春之初，会于'京西'，研讨编著两书事宜也。群贤毕至，少长咸集。此地既无崇山峻岭，茂林修竹，又无清流激湍，映带左右。引以为医界群英，列坐左右，各抒己见，亦足以畅叙幽情，立于史册……"以表达内心的感慨。我深深地觉得，我们今天编写医学院士文库这部书，也一定会有历史意义的，也完全称得上是新中国医学界的一次盛世修典，是前追古人、后慰来者、造福当代、功德无量的一件大好事。

在编写《中国医学院士文库》过程中，各位院士付出了巨大的努力，克服了许多困难，各相关单位给予了大力支持，许多同志提供了具体帮助。经过大家的共同努力，各分册正陆续完稿并相继出版。我相信，这部巨著一定能取得成功，一定能达到预定的目标，一定能发挥重要作用。

在本书出版之际，我要再一次向为此书出版付出辛勤劳动的各位院士表示深深敬意！向支持本书出版的各有关单位和各界人士表示衷心感谢！

2012 年 12 月

《中国医学院士文库》

序

　　新中国成立以来，医学科学事业取得了举世瞩目的伟大成就，除了政府的高度重视、广大医务工作者的辛勤努力外，一代代医学前辈给我们留下的宝贵知识遗产功不可没。承前启后，继往开来，是每一个时代应负的责任。中国科学院、中国工程院两院医学院士均为公认的学术领军人物，他们的高尚医德、严谨医风、精湛医术，已成为我国医学界的宝贵财富。将这些名家大师们的思想和科研成果，进行深入挖掘、系统总结和传承，从而得以造福后世，是我们这一代人义不容辞的历史责任。

　　人民军医出版社组织出版《中国医学院士文库》，充分体现了这种高度的历史责任感和文化自觉。在国家和军队有关部门及中华医学会和中国医师协会、中华口腔医学会的积极参与下，特别是在各位院士的全力支持下，《中国医学院士文库》终于呈现在大家面前。《文库》从文化出版与医疗卫生这两个行业的结合点上，准确地把握住了军地医务人员对弘扬医德医风、提升医疗技术的深层需求和期待，广大医务人员可以从中领略、学习到我国医学界名医大家不畏艰辛的奋斗历程、科学严谨的治学风范、勇于创新的学术精神、开阔深刻的思维品质。

　　党的十八大提出要"多谋民生之利，多解民生之忧"，"为群众提供安全有效方便价廉的公共卫生和基本医疗服务"。要实现这个目标，既需要一批服务保障体系完善、让老百姓放心的基层医疗卫生机构，更需要一支医德医风高尚、业务素质过硬的医药卫生人才队伍。我相信，这套凝聚着各位医学院士智慧和心血的著作，一定会受到广大医务人员的欢迎和喜爱，一定会在加强各级医疗机构能力建设，提升医务人员职业素养、增进职业操守、加快职业成长方面，发挥应有的作用。

卫 生 部 部 长
中华医学会会长

2013 年 2 月

《中国医学院士文库》

序

由人民军医出版社承担的《中国医学院士文库》这一国家出版基金重点支持的大型出版项目，在国家卫生部、总后卫生部和中华医学会、中国医师协会和中华口腔医学会的大力支持下，今天终于与读者见面了。我对《中国医学院士文库》的出版，由衷地感到高兴并表示热烈的祝贺！

党的十八大正式把文化建设纳入中国特色社会主义"五位一体"的总体布局，开启了向社会主义文化强国的伟大进军。《中国医学院士文库》这个国家级重点出版项目，既是大型出版工程和科技推广工程，同时也是医学文化建设工程。组织推出这种高水平的出版成果和精品力作，正是医学出版界与医学界携手落实党的十八大精神的实际行动，也是文化大发展大繁荣在医疗卫生行业得以贯彻落实的具体体现。

组织出版《中国医学院士文库》是对当代医学宝库进行挖掘、传承和积淀的必要举措。新中国成立60年来特别是改革开放以来，中国当代医学呈现出快速发展和全面繁荣的良好局面，取得了一批具有国际先进水平的重要成果，涌现出一大批以医学院士为代表的医学科学大家和临床医学大师。把这些大家、大师的宝贵经验进行系统总结、深入挖掘、整理建档，使当代最优秀的医学发展成果得以"藏之于名山，传之于后世"，既是充实丰富当代医学宝库的需要，也是使其传之后世造福后人的需要，更是我们这一代人义不容辞的责任所在。

医生是一个特殊的职业。医生的人品、医品、才品，直接关系着患者的健康与生命。长期以来，民间流传着"不为良相，便为良医"之说，形象地反映了人们对医生这个职业的极高期许和特殊要求。在价值多元、学术浮躁、急功近利的社会风气有所抬头的情况下，我们推出《中国医学院士文库》这个出版项目，为军地的广大医务工作者如何做人，如何行医，如何成才，如何提高职业操守、业务本领和临床操作能力，提供了为之效仿、为之学习的典范，对于促进医务人员成长与发展，必将起到积极有益的影响和作用。

《中国医学院士文库》作为国家级出版项目，它体现的是国家意志，代表的是国家水平。全国人大常委会韩启德副委员长亲自担任这个项目的名誉主任委员，对这个项目给予了高度关注和悉心指导。国家卫生部陈竺部长多次过问项目的详细情况，并担任编委会的主任委员。国家卫生部、中华医学会、中国医师协会、中华口腔医学会给予了全力支持和多方帮助，并对组织机构、编委会和专家组人选，多次予以指导和把关。特别是组成了有近40名德高望重院士参加的编委会，这在我们国家的医学出版史上是极为罕见的。承担这个项目具体组织出版工作的人民军医出版社，科学规划、周密安排、精心组织实施，确保了这一高难度大型项目的顺利推进和完成。《中国医学院士文库》的出版，既是各位院士智慧和心血的结晶，也是国家卫生部、中华医学会、中国医师协会、中华口腔医学会悉心指导的结果，是军地携手、通力合作、群策群力的结果。

我相信，这部倾注了上百名院士和领导大量心血的巨著，一定会受到全国广大军地医务工作者的欢迎和喜爱，一定会成为一部功在当代、惠及后人的传世之作，一定会在中华医学宝库中长久地发挥它应有的重要作用。

总后勤部卫生部原部长
中国医师协会会长

2012 年 12 月

目　录

第一部分

奋斗历程

曾毅院士成长大事记

曾毅院士是我国著名的病毒学和肿瘤学专家,中国疾病预防控制中心性病艾滋病预防控制中心首席科学家,中国科学院院士,法国国家医学科学院外籍院士,俄罗斯医学科学院外籍院士,美国马里兰大学人类病毒研究所兼职教授,博士,博士后导师。获国务院政府特殊津贴。

主要成长经历

1929 年 3 月生于广东揭西县。

1943 年初中毕业,考入广东梅县东山中学读高中。

1946 年考入上海复旦大学商学院,1 年后又考入上海医学院。

1952 年毕业于上海第一医学院,留校参加国家高级师资培训班。

1953 年任广州华南医学院(现中山大学医学院)微生物教研室助教,开始对钩端螺旋体、恙虫病和立克次体等的研究工作。

1956 年调入北京中央卫生研究院微生物系病毒室从事病毒研究工作。

1956—1960 年在黄祯祥教授领导下开展了脊髓灰质炎病毒、肠道病毒和麻疹病毒等的研究。在国内首次应用人羊膜细胞培养病毒;系统开展了脊髓灰质炎病毒型别的流行病学调查;对肠道病毒进行了分离鉴定和抗体测定;首次参加脊髓灰质炎病毒减毒活疫苗的免疫工作并获得成功。首次在国内建立麻疹病毒血凝抑制试验测定抗体的方法并应用于麻疹疫苗效果的测定。

1961 年率先在国内开展了肿瘤病毒研究,明确了 EB 病毒与鼻咽癌的关系(1973 年),确立了鼻咽癌血清学诊断指标和系列方法,使鼻咽癌发生的可能性预测提前至发病前的 $18\sim20$ 年,从而将早期诊断率从 $20\%\sim30\%$ 提高到 $80\%\sim90\%$,挽救了很多患者的生命;在国际上首次建立了高分化和低分化鼻咽癌细胞株,发现高分化癌细胞带有 EB 病毒基因和抗原;发现组织相容性抗原(HLA)与鼻咽癌发病有关的易感基因和抵抗基因,鼻咽癌高发区的某些中草药、植物和食物带有肿瘤多肽抗原(TPA)等促癌物,人鼻咽部的厌氧杆菌能产生促癌物丁酸;在国际上首次证明在促癌物 TPA 和丁酸的协同作用下,EB 病毒感染的人胎鼻咽部黏膜组织能诱发裸鼠 T、B 细胞淋巴瘤和人鼻咽癌,为 EB 病毒诱发人鼻咽癌提供了直接证据,同时也提供了研究鼻咽癌病因多因素和作用机制的模型;研究的 EB 病毒疫苗,2011 年获国家药监局批准,正在进行临床试验,证明 EBV LAMP 2 疫苗能提高鼻咽癌患者的特异性细胞免疫。1980 年中央电视台拍摄的"与魔鬼打交道的人"翔实记录了曾毅及其科研团队在 EB 病毒的研究中所做的工作和成果。

1969 年曾毅在肿瘤医院建立肿瘤研究组,1971 年在林县建立实验室。

1974 年赴英国格斯拉斯哥 MRC 病毒研究所做客座研究员,学习深造肿瘤病毒的研究理论和技术。回国后任职于中国医学科学院和中国预防医学科学院病毒病预防控制所继续从事病毒研究工作。

1981年出任中国预防医学科学院病毒病预防控制所副所长。

1983年晋升为研究员,同年12月出任中国预防医学科学院病毒病预防控制所所长。

1984年在国内率先进行了艾滋病毒(HIV)的研究,通过流行病学调查和实验室研究证明1982年HIV随血液制品从美国传入中国,1983感染中国第一个公民。指出:艾滋病毒在我国有传播的潜在危险。

同年曾毅获得"对国家有突出贡献的中青年科学家"称号,并升任中国预防医学科学院副院长。

1985年与浙江医科大学协作从使用过进口凝血Ⅷ因子制剂的9人中发现4例感染了病毒。

1986—1987年赴法国国家科学研究中心为客座研究员,从事HIV的研究。1990年,法国电视台专程来华拍摄题为"Hope from China"的纪录片,报道了曾毅院士的工作精神和研究成果,高度评价早期诊断在防治癌症的重要意义,在法国电视台播放两次,获得好评。

1987年报告分离出我国第一株HIV病毒,进行了HIV-1分子流行病学的研究,研制和发展了HIV病毒系列检测试剂,如简单易行的酶免疫法和最终确诊的快速蛋白印迹法。快速诊断试剂盒获卫生部批准使用,制备试剂供应全国。

为加强艾滋病的检测和防治工作,经卫生部批准中国预防医学科学院病毒病所成立了"全国艾滋病检测中心"。

1989年与云南省有关部门合作,对滇缅边境瑞丽市的毒瘾者开展了HIV感染普查,发现了大批HIV感染者。经与相关部门协同,积极采取了防治措施和知识普教,为阻止艾滋病在我国的蔓延做了大量工作。

研制的治疗艾滋病的中药2008年经国家药监局批准,已进入临床试验阶段;2013年研究的多载体序贯和重复应用的HIV疫苗,有两种已获得国家药监局临床试验许可,正在进行临床试验。为我国艾滋病的预防提供了有效手段。

1992年出任中国预防医学科学院院长。在任职期间,曾毅院士坚持一线科研工作,首次研究了人类T淋巴细胞白血病病毒Ⅰ型(HTLV-1病毒)在我国的分布及其与成年人T淋巴细胞白血病及神经系统疾病的关系;研究人疱疹病毒(HHV-8病毒)在我国的流行分布及其与卡波西肉瘤和艾滋病的关系;研究人乳头瘤病毒(HPV)与宫颈癌的关系;证明食管癌有HPV16或18型等病毒,HPV18 E6E7单独或与促癌物、致癌物、放射等因素协同作用能诱发正常胎儿食管上皮细胞癌变;表明HPV在食管癌发生中起重要作用,正在研究多种新型HPV疫苗;首次应用人乙肝病毒与黄曲霉毒素共同作用诱发人胎肝细胞癌变并建立了细胞株。

2006年英国Belly-Martin基金会授予曾毅院士"艾滋病防治贡献奖"。

2008年中华医学会授予曾毅院士"中华预防医学会公共卫生与预防医学发展贡献奖"。

2012年美国马里兰大学人类病毒研究所授予曾毅院士"公共卫生终身成就奖"。

现任(2014年)的主要职务

中国疾病预防控制中心病毒病预防控制所院士研究室主任

北京工业大学生命科学与生物工程学院名誉院长

北京工业大学学术委员会副主任

国家性病艾滋病预防控制中心首席科学家

中国合格评定国家认可委员会(CNAS)资深顾问和生物安全专业委员会主任

中华预防医学会名誉会长

全球病毒网络中心(Global Virus Network)科学顾问委员会执行委员

中国全球病毒网络中心主任

全球华人公共卫生协会副会长

至 2014 年曾担任的主要职务

中国预防医学科学院病毒病预防控制所副所长、所长

中国预防医学科学院副院长、院长

北京工业大学生命科学与生物工程学院院长

中国预防性病艾滋病基金会会长

中华医学会常务理事

中华预防医学会会长

三届国务院学位评审组成员

卫生部科技评审委员会副主任

世界卫生组织全球顾问委员会委员

世界卫生组织肿瘤专家顾问委员会委员

国际微生物联盟执行委员

联合国亚太地区艾滋病与发展领导论坛指导委员会执行委员

第二部分

学术贡献

一、曾毅院士主要学术成就和学术思想

肿瘤病毒和艾滋病病毒的研究及其防治领域的开拓者

邵一鸣　周　玲

中国疾病预防控制中心病毒病所

曾毅院士是国际权威的病毒学和肿瘤防治学专家。新中国成立之初,他毕业于上海医科大学,留校从事微生物学和病毒学教学研究工作不久后,到我国最高医学研究机构中国医学科学院病毒病学研究所,致力于医学研究和传染病防治工作。在六十多年漫长岁月中,所在机构根据国家需要历经了中国预防医学科学院和中国疾病预防控制中心的建立和发展,曾毅的研究随之从急性传染病,扩展到肿瘤病毒和艾滋病病毒等尖端医学研究领域,在丰富多彩的科学生涯中攀登着一座又一座医学科学高峰。

开展肿瘤病毒研究,并将成果应用于指导临床诊疗

在 20 世纪 50 至 60 年代,曾毅根据实验观察到鸡白血病病毒、多瘤病毒、乳头瘤病毒等可引起很多动物肿瘤的现象,提出人的肿瘤也可由病毒引起。他从 70 年代起开展研究人的肿瘤病毒,包括 EB 病毒、HPV 和成人 T 细胞白血病病毒等。他系统地研究了 EB 病毒在鼻咽癌发生和发展中的作用,创造性地将国际上的分子病毒学技术与现场流行病学调查相结合,建立了简易的 EB 病毒 EA/IgA 和 VCA/IgA 抗体检测试剂盒,并获得卫生部的生产许可证,辅以临床和病理活检的鼻咽癌早期诊断技术。该技术体系经研究验证后,大规模应用于广西鼻咽癌流行调查,显著提高了鼻咽癌的早期诊断率和治愈率,挽救了许多病人的生命。用病毒血清学指标诊断癌症是肿瘤病毒学和肿瘤诊断学领域中的一项创举,是将基础研究成果应用于指导临床诊疗的"from bench to bedside"理想设计,是转化医学的成功案例。

在鼻咽癌的病毒病因学研究领域,曾毅也通过多学科合作的研究方式,开展大规模现场病因学调查研究,结合实验室研究成果,提出了以 EB 病毒为病因,环境致癌和促癌因素起协同作用,遗传易感性为基础的鼻咽癌多病因学说。这一学说在鼻咽癌的病因学领域中占有重要的学术地位,促进了肿瘤病毒学研究的不断深入。在 EB 病毒疫苗研究领域,曾毅与德国 H. Wolf 教授合作进行了 EB 病毒膜抗原疫苗(EBVMA)的研制;他还与英国 Rickinson 院士合作进行了 EB 病毒潜伏膜蛋白(EBV-LMP)疫苗的研制。在国家"863"项目的资助下,主持研制了具有自主知识产权的含有 EBV-LMP2 腺病毒疫苗,获得国家药监局 I 期临床批件,于 2013 年完成了临床的所有

观察试验及总结报告,正在申报II期临床试验批件。该疫苗为鼻咽癌的免疫治疗和预防带来了福音。

在我国最早开展艾滋病血清流行病学研究

20世纪80年代初,一个来势凶猛的新发传染病—艾滋病在美国被发现。作为肿瘤病毒学家,曾毅立即在国内建立相关研究的实验室和技术方法,紧密追踪该领域的国际研究进展。1983年法国科学家Montagmier首次报道发现艾滋病病毒,1984年曾毅在国内进行艾滋病病毒筛查,开展了我国最早艾滋病血清流行病学研究。1985年,曾毅首次在国内报道了4例HIV感染病例。之后,曾毅的实验室承担起我国艾滋病诊断、培训、技术支持和艾滋病诊断试剂的研发工作,有力地支持了我国早期的艾滋病诊断和血清学检测和研究工作。在艾滋病免疫治疗方面,曾毅在国际上首次提出了"HIV多载体疫苗序贯和重复免疫"作为艾滋病治疗性疫苗的策略。多载体中的基因疫苗加痘苗病毒载体疫苗(DNA+MVA)获得国家药监局的批准,正在开展I期临床试验。曾毅还在申请腺病毒(AD)载体疫苗临床批文,推动DNA+MVA+AD联合疫苗进入临床研究。曾毅还与其夫人李泽琳教授合作,开展了从中药筛选抗艾滋病病毒成分的研究,经过二十多年的不懈努力,研制的中药复方ZL-1已经国家药监局批准,正在进行临床试验。

积极推动我国预防医学研究的发展

作为中科院院士,曾毅不仅是我国的科学泰斗,还是我国疾病防治机构和学术团体的负责人和社会活动家。在他担任中国预防医学科学院院长、中华预防医学会会长期间,对推动我国预防医学研究,促进传染病防治工作开展和防治人才培养都发挥了积极的推动作用。以艾滋病防治为例,曾先生在不同历史时期不断呼吁政府加强艾滋病的防治工作和对艾滋病科研的投入。他还不断到全国各地开展科普宣传和政策演讲,亲自参与包括举办艾滋病防治知识巡展等活动。在担任艾滋病基金会会长期间,他与社会各界人士交朋友,采取各种形式募集资金,支持艾滋病防治宣传活动和对艾滋病弱势群体和孤儿的救助。我国艾滋病防治工作能有今天的进步和发展,离不开像曾院士这样的我国一批著名科学家的努力推动。从曾院士身上,我们看到的是我国老一辈科学家的优良品质、创业精神和对祖国人民的责任感。他们是我们国家的科技脊梁,创造出两弹一星功勋和人均寿命翻番的伟业,当年支撑着年青的共和国攻坚克难,巍然屹立于世界的东方,今天推动着中华民族一天天走向繁荣富强。

二、曾毅院士代表性学术论文

Establishment of an Epithelioid Cell Line and a Fusiform Cell Line from a Patient with Nasopharyngeal Carcinoma[①]

Laboratory of Tumor Viruses of Cancer Institute, Laboratory of Tumor Virusce of Institute of Epidemiology, Department of Radiotherapy of Cancer Institute, and Laboratory of Cell Biology of Cancer Institute. Chinese Academy of Medical Sciences Laboratory of Electron Microscope, Department of Microbiology, and Laboratory of Pathogenesis, Chuny Shan Medical Colloge Chinese Academy of Medical Sciences

[SUMMARY] An epithelioid cell line and a fusiform eell liue were established from a tumor biopsy from a patient with nasopharyngeal carcinoma whieh was histologieally diagnosed as a well differentiated squamous cell carcinoma. Based on studies of the cell growth pattern, ehromosome analysis, heterotransplantation, and electron microscopy, these two cell lines were considered to be squamous carcinoma cells, and the fusiform cells might have originated from the epithelioid cells. There were many round cells on top of the epithelioid and fusiform cell sheets, many of which became continuously detached into the medium. Cultures initiated from these floating round cells grew into their original epithelioid or fusiform forms. No lymphoblastoid cell line could be established after cultivating these two cell lines for more than one year.

No EB virus particle or early antigen could be detected in these two cell lines by means of electron microscopic examination and indirect immunofluoresccnce test.

INTRODUCTION

The serological relationship between nasopharyngeal carcinoma (NPC) and EB virus was first demonstrated by old et al. in 1966 using immunodiffusion test[1]. It was shown subsequently by indirect immunofluorescence test that NPC patients had various antibodies to EB virus, and the antibody spectra and titers were clearly referable to total tumor burden[2-8]; furthermore, EB virus DNA and nuclear antigen (EBNA) have been demonstrated regularly in epithelial tumor cells of NPC[9-16]. All the above rusults indicate a close association of EBV with NPC.

Extensive attempts have been made in establishing a permanent epithelial cell line from NPC patients in order to investigate further the relationship between EBV and NPC but no successful results have been reported[16-18]. In our laboratory, we have succeeded in establishing an epithelioid cell line and a fusiform cell line from a patient with NPC. These cell lines have been maintained in culture for 19 months and subcultured for more than 80 times. This paper deseribes the establishment and the characteristics of these cell lines.

MATERIALS AND METHODS

The tissue used for cultures was obtained from a tumor biopsy from a 58-year-old woman with NPC on August 13, 1975. The patient had severe headache, tinnitus, and epistaxis. Clinical examination showed the presence of a tumor in the nasopharynx whice had invaded the base of skull, with compression signs of cranial nerves (Ⅲ, Ⅳ, Ⅵ, Ⅸ, Ⅻ), and with metastases to the lymph nodes on both sides of the neck. The soft tissue tumor mass on the posterior wall of nasopharynx was also confirmed on orentgeuography, X-ray film of the base of the skull showed suspected bony destruction of the left side of the external plate of pterygoidal process of sphenoid. Tumor biopsy revealed a well-differentiated squamous cell carcinoma (Fig. 1).

The tumor specimen was cut into approximately 0.5-1.0 mm pieces. Minced tumor fragments were placed on the surface of flasks which had been pretreated with rat tail collagen to aid the attachment of explants. RPMI 1640 medium supplemented with 40% of calf serum, 100 units of penicillin, and $100\mu g$ of streptomycin per ml were added to the flasks at the opposite side of the explants. The cultures were incubated at 37℃ for 3 hr in an incubator with 5% CO_2 in air, and the flasks were turned over to allow the medium to cover the explants. The medium was changed twice a week. Subcultures were made by dispersing the cells with 25% trypsin; 0.2% versene solution.

---

① First appeared in Chinese in the note form in Kexue Tongbao, p. 143, No. 3, 1977.

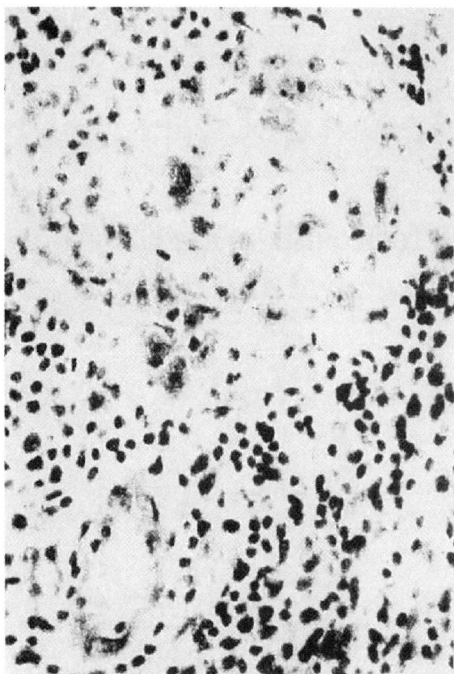

Fig. 1　Patient with NPC, histologic section from nasopharyngeal carcinome. HE stain (× 100)

COURSE OF ESTABLISHMENT OF PERMA-NENT CELL LINES

Epithelioid cells began to outgrow around the tissue frag-ments in two of five flasks on the 10th day of cultivation, after which the cell sheet increased in size gradually. Attempts to transfer the epithelioid cells by dispersing part of the cell sheet with trypsin. Versene (0.25% ： 0.02%) or by scraping cells with eapillary pipette failed. The first successful subculture was made by trypsin: versene 11 weeks after cultivation. Thereafter the cells were successively transferred once every week. Thus an epithelioid cell line designated as CNE was es-tablished. The epithelioid cells were polygonal in shape with the nuclei varying in size. Some multi-nucleated giant cells and cytoplasmic vacuoles were present (Fig. 2). In old cultures some cells frequently had part of the cytoplasm protruded and finally detached from the cell sheet as dead cells. At the 12th passage a few fusiform cells appeared among the epithelioid cells and gradually increased in number (Fig. 3). The fusiform cells were isolated as an independent line and designated as CNF. There were many round cells on the top of both cell sheets, especially on the fusiform ones. Many of them became continuously detached into the medium. Cultures initiated from the floating round cells reeovered their original epithelioid or fusiform cell morphology. No lymphoblastoid cell line could be established after long-term cutivation without transfer up to the 7th month, and no fibroblast cells appeared during the course of establishment of cell lines.

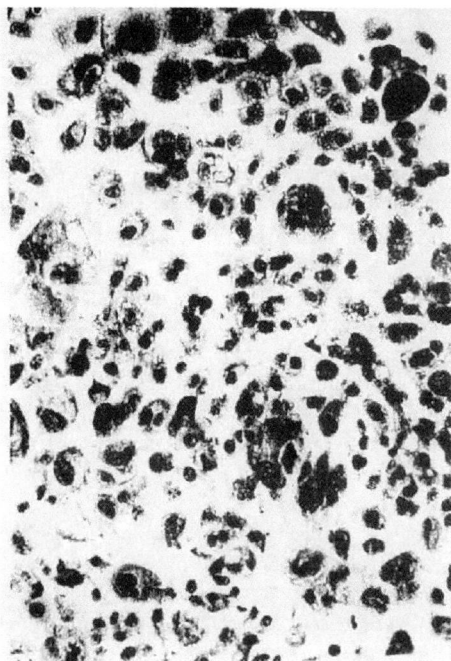

Fig. 2　Epithelioid cells, 7th passage, Giemsa stain (×200)

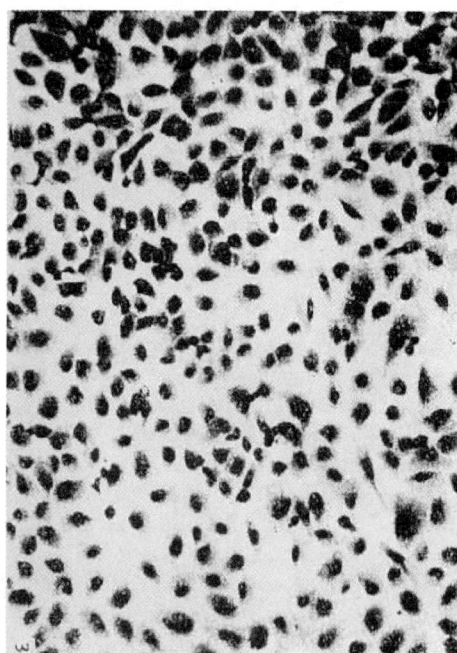

Fig. 3　Epithelioid cells, 12th passage. Giemsa stain (×100)

The CNE and CNF cells were dispersed by trypsin: versene (0.25% : 0.2%) and inoculated into separated dishes with 5ml of medium containing 40, 20 and 10 cells respectively. Ten days after cultivation at 37℃ in 5% CO_2, the typical clones of the epithelioid and fusiform cells were isolated from dishes at terminal dilutions (Figs. 4&5). This procedure was repeated twice. The clonal epithelioid and fusiform cell lines thus obtained were designated as CNEC and CNFC respectively (Figs. 6&7). The epithelioid cell sheet was not as readily dispersed by trypsin: versene (0.25% : 0.02%) as fusiform cell sheet unless the concentration of versene was increased to 0.2%.

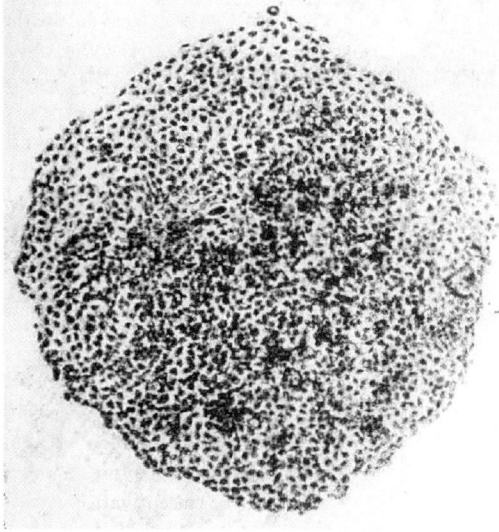

Fig. 4　Clone of ONE cell line. Giemsa stain (× 40)

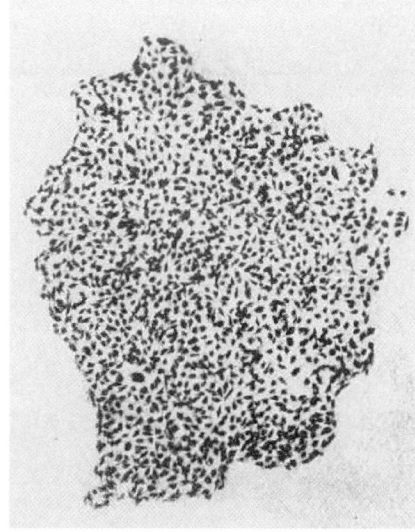

Fig. 5　Clone of CNF cell line. Giemsa stain (× 40)

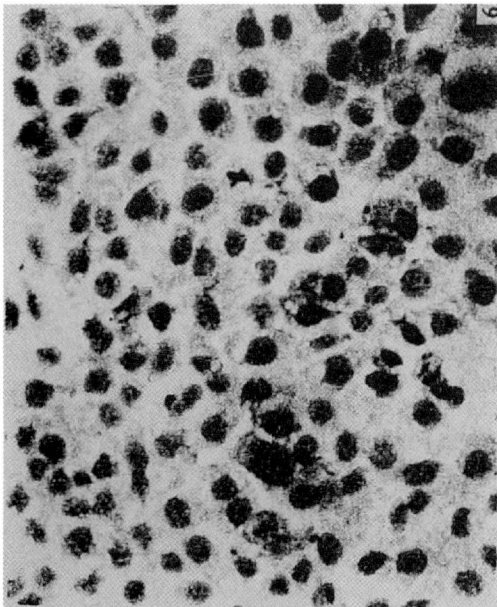

Fig. 6　Clonal cell line of epithelioid cells (CNEC). Giemsa stainn (× 200)

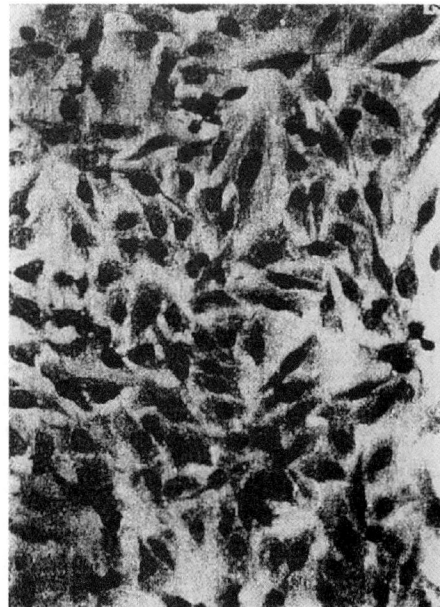

Fig. 7　Clonal cell line of fusiform cells (CNFC). Giemsa stain (× 200)

GROWTH CURVE, SATURATION DENSITY, AND PLATING EFFICIENCY

Monolayer cells of CNE and CNF cell lines were dispersed with trypsin and versene (0.25% : 0.02%), 30ml flasks were plated with 1×10^5 cells in 3.5ml of complete RPMI 1640 medium. Cell cultures were kept at 37℃. The medium was changed and the cell counting from 2 flasks was performed every 3 days for 12 days. The effect of different concentrations of calf serum on the growth of both cell lines was studied. As shown in Fig. 8, the growth curves of CNE and CNF cell lines were similar in media with 20% and 40% of calf serum. The cell number increased logarithmically on the 6th-9th day, reaching more than 20 times of that originally seeded. The growth rate of both cell lines in medium containing 5% of calf serum was slower. The cell number on the 12th day was 14-15 times of that originally seeded.

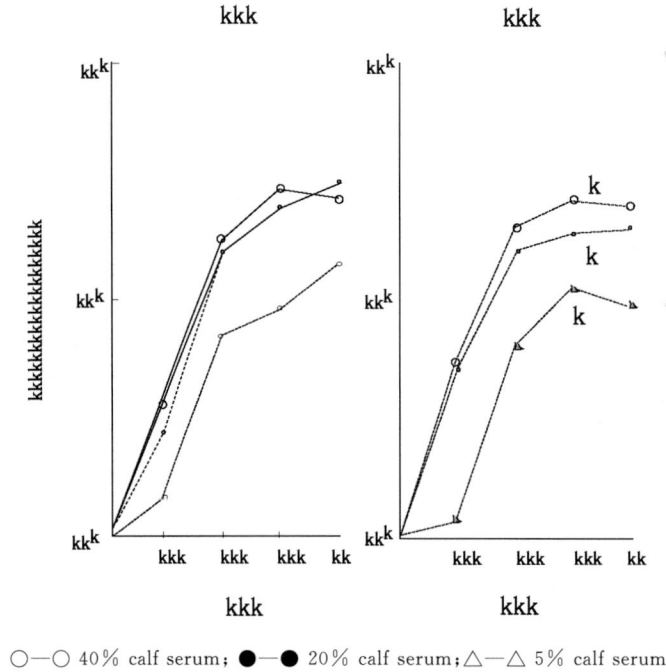

○—○ 40% calf serum; ●—● 20% calf serum; △—△ 5% calf serum

Fig. 8 Growth curves of CNF and CNE cell lines

The value where two successive harvest showed no increase in cell number was taken as saturation density. The saturation densities of CNE and CNF cell lines were $2.13 \times 10^5/cm^2$ and $2.26 \times 10^5/cm^2$ respectively.

All suspension was diluted in RPMI 1640 medium and 200 cells in 5ml of complete RPMI 1640 medium were plated in 6cm dishes. After 10 days of incubation at 37℃ in 5% CO_2, the colonies were stained with the Giemsa stain and counted. The number of colonies was calculated from the average of 5 dishes. The plating efficiencies of CNE and CNF cell lines were 22% and 52% respectively. The colonies of CNE cell consisting of epithelioid cells were uniform in size with regular margin, whereas the colonies of CNF consisting of fusiform cells showed variable size with irregular margin.

ASSAY OF AGGLUTINATION BY CONCANAVALIN-A

2×10^5 cells of CNE, CNF, CNEC, and CNFC cell lines in 3ml of complete RPMI 1640 medium were plated into separate flasks and incubated at 37℃ for 24 hours. After washing twice with PBS lacking calcium and magnesium, the cells were dispersed with versenc (0.02%), washed again with PBS, and then suspensed in PBS containing calcium and magnesium at a concentration of 4×10^5 cells per ml. 0.1ml of concanavalin-A at different concentrations in PBS was mixed with 0.1ml of the cell suspension in 100mm × 12mm tubes at room temperature for 30 minutes. The aggregates were scored under inverse microscope in a scale from-to ＋ ＋ ＋ ＋. As shown in Tab. 1, cells of all four lines could be agglutinated by 4μg of concanavalin-A, and the size of the aggregates increased with the increasing concentrations of concanavalin-A.

Tab. 1　Characteristics of Nasopharyngeal Carcinoma Cell Lines

Cell Line	Morphology	Typsin: Versene (0.25%: 0.02%)	Saturation Density (10^5 cells/cm^2)	Plating Effieiency (%)	Concana-valin-A Agglu-tination	Heterotrans-plantation	Chromosome Aberration	Electron Microscopic Examination		Immuno-logical Test	
								Cell	EBV	CF Antigen	EA
CNE	Epithelioid	Rather difficult to disperse	2.13	22	+	Poorly dif-fereutiated squamous carcinoma	Aneuploidy	Squamous carcinoma	−	−	−
CNEC	Epithelioid	Rather difficult to disperse			+		Aneuploidy				−
CNF	Fusiform	Rather easy to disperse	2.26	58	+	Poorly dif-ferentiated squamous carcinoma	Ancuploidy	Squamous carcinoma	−	−	−
CNFC	Fusiform	Rather easy to disperse			+		Aneuploidy				−

CHROMOSOME ANALYSIS

Cell liues of the CNE (51st passage), CNEC (20th passage), CNF (34th & 38th passages), and CNFC (16th passage) were treated with colchicine (final concentration 0.02μg/ml) for 2-4 hours during the logarithmie growing phase. The chromosome preparation was made according to an air-dried technique. 100-200 metaphase plates of ench line were counted and chromosome aberrations also recorded. The detailed data are summarized in Tab. 2 and Fig. 9.

Tab. 2　Chromosome Aberrations of Nasopharyngeal Carcinoma Cell Lines

Cell Line	Dicentric	Tricentric	Tetracentric	Fragmental	Minute	Superfragmental	Different Types of Aberration in Some Cells
				Type and %			
CNE	5	0	0	2	3	0	0
CNEC	2	0	0	2	3	1	1
CNF	22	0.5	0.5	7	2	2	2
CNFC	54	0	0	11	4	0	0

Chromosome numbers of these cell lines showed a wide distribution with a mode between hypotriploid and hypotetraploid (Fig. 10). Although the stemline of the CNEC and CNF cell lines was not formed, yet cells with chromosomes numbering over 100 appeared frequently. In the CNE cell line the mode accumulated between hypertriploid and hypotetraploid with a stemline of 80 chromosomes. For the CNFC cell line, a stemline of 70 chromosomes was noted at the 16th passage.

Various types of chromosome aberration, such as the dicentric, mulitcentric, fragmental, minute, and superfragmental, were observed in different cell lines. Furthermore, different types of aberration may be noted in the same cells (Fig. 10). About 2%-5% of chromosome aberrations occurred in the CNE and CNFC cell lines. Besides other types of chromosome aberration, dicentric chromosome was most frequently encountered in the CNF cell line, accounting for 22% of all types. The dicentric, fragmental, and minute types of chromosome aberration were frequently observed in the CNFC cell line, 54% of them were classified as the dicentric type. The reason why such a high incidence of unstable chromosome aberrations appeared in the CNF and CNFC cell lines remains to be studied.

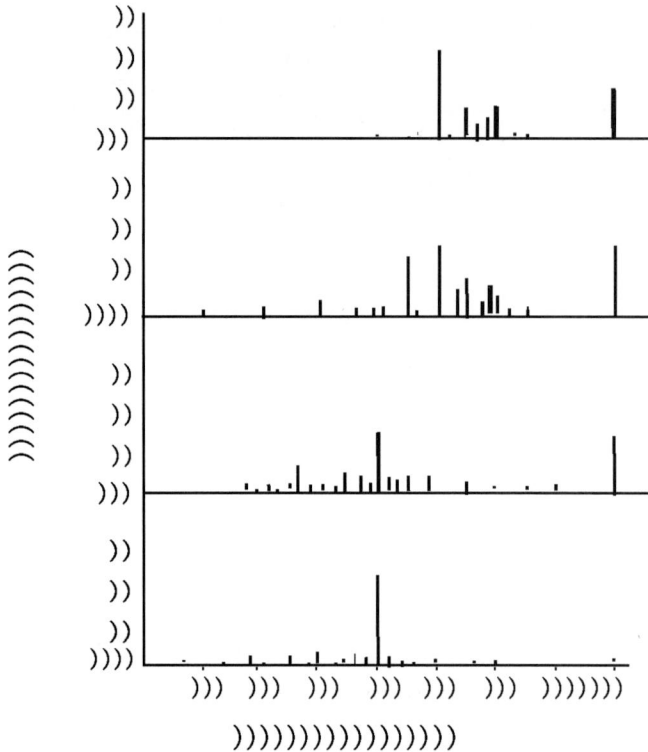

Fig. 9　Comparison of the distribution of chromosome number of 4 cell lines of nasopharyngeal carcinona

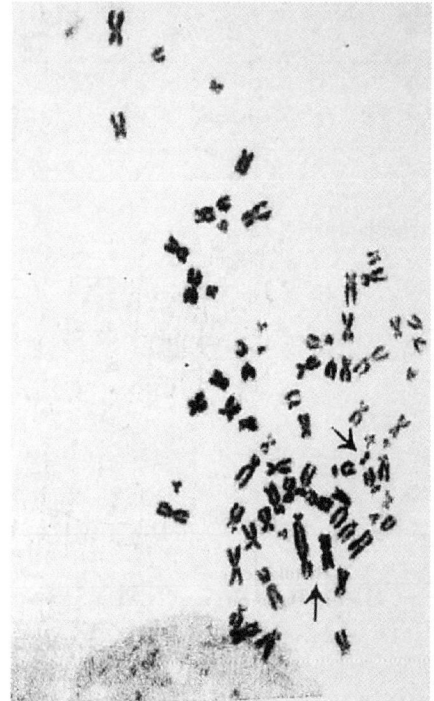

Fig. 10　Chromosome aberration in the CNF cell line. Dicentric and fragmental chromosome

HETEROTRANSPLANTATION

0.1ml each of the CNE (33rd passage) and CNF (19th passage) cell suspension were transplanted subcutaneously into newborn rats. Anti-thymocyte serum (0.4ml) was given on the day of transplantation and subsequently on the 3rd, 5th, and 8th days. 11 days after implantation the animals were sacrificed. The tumors measured 0.5-0.7cm in diameter and were examined histologically. Anti-thymocyte rabbit serum with titer of 1 : 640 was prepared in this laboratory. As shown in Tab. 1, the transplantability of CNE and CNF was 77% and 100% respectively. Histologically, these tumors were poorly differentiated squamous carcinoma(Figs. 11&12)

ELECTRON MICROSCOPIC EXAMINATION

CNE and CNF cells were scraped off with a rubber policemand and centrifuged at 1000 r/min for 1-2 minutes. Cell pellets were fixed in 5% gluteraldehyde followed by osmie acid, then embedded in butyl methacrylate. Thin-section specimens were stained with uranyl acetate and lead citrate, and examined under electronmicroscope.

Electronmicroscopy showed that the CNE cells maintained typical features of epithelial cells, including desmosomes, tonofibrils, keratohyalin granules and membrane coating granules (Fig. 13). The CNF cells were polymorphic; some of them contained minute desmosomes and tonofilaments, but not as typical as those seen in CNE cells. The ratio of nucleus to cytoplasm of CNF cells was larger, and more endoplasmic reticula, free ribosomes, and mitochondria were seen in the cytoplasm (Fig. 14). It is rather difficult to identify the nature of some fusiform cells, so CNF cells are temporarily classfied as poorly differentiated carcinoma cells.

It is of particular interest that some round cells without the characteristic features of epithelial cells were seen in the CNE cell line. These round cells contained large nuclei and some vacuoles, and were rich in the ribosome in cytoplasm. The nature of these cells remains to be identified (Fig. 15).

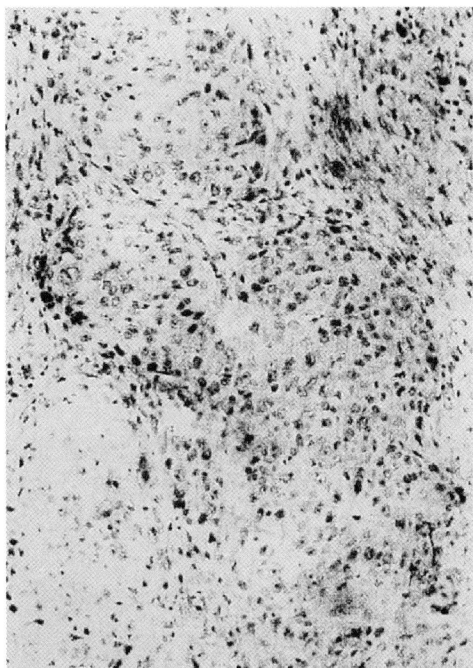

Fig. 11 Histologic section of transplanted tumor in newborn rat, CNE, 33rd passage. HE stain (× 125)

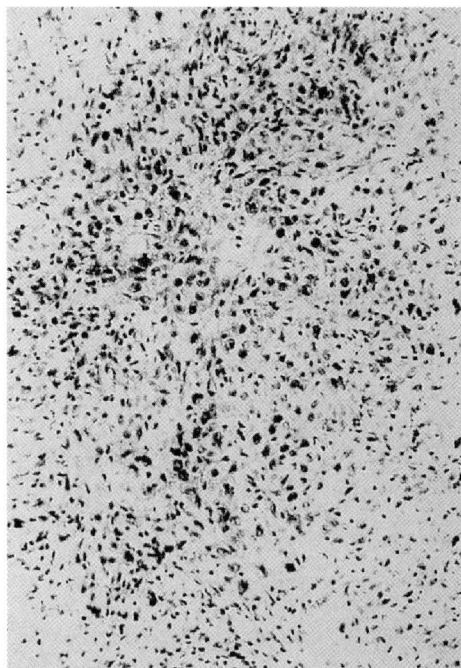

Fig. 12 Histologic section of transplanted tumor in newborn rat, CNF, 19th passage. HE stain (× 125)

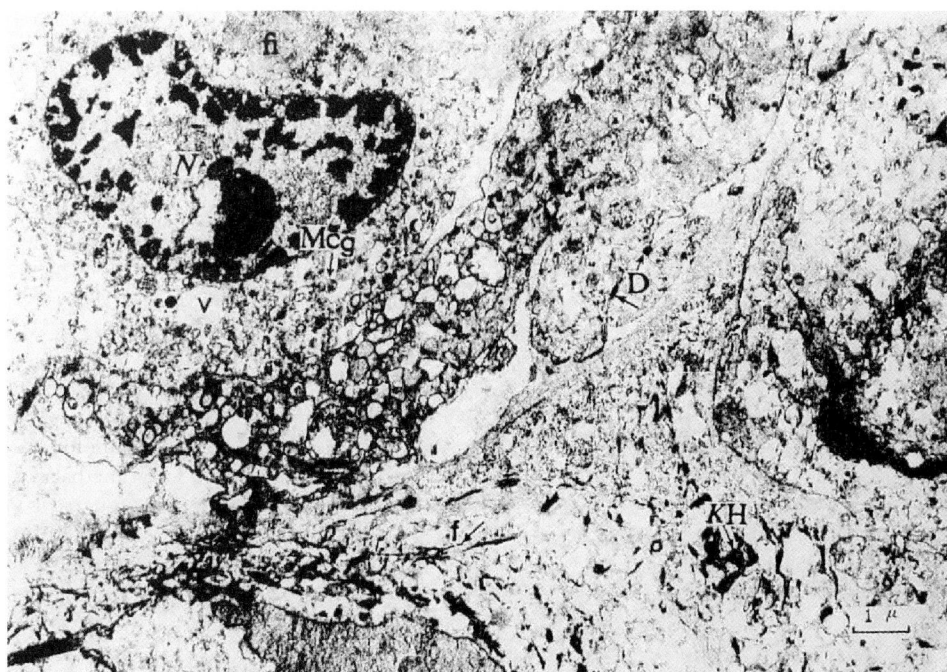

Fig. 13 Ultrastructure of CNE cell line, 38th passage: D-desmosome, f-tonofibril, f_1-tonofilament, KH-keratohyalin granule, Mcg-membrane coating grmule, V-vesicle (×5000)

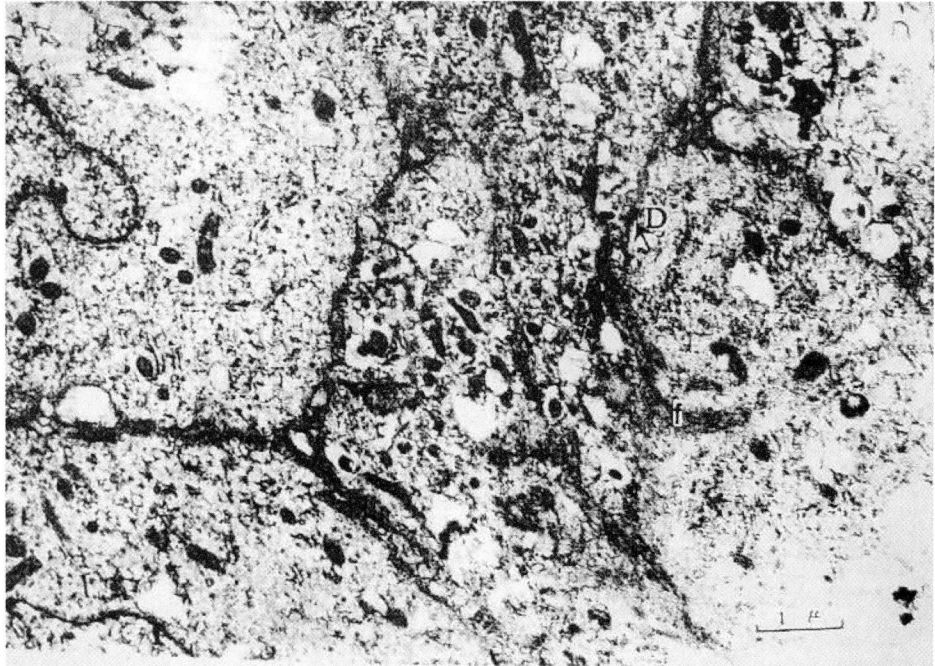

Fig. 14　Ultrastructure of CNF cell line, 24th passage: D-desmosome, f-tonofibril(× 14000)

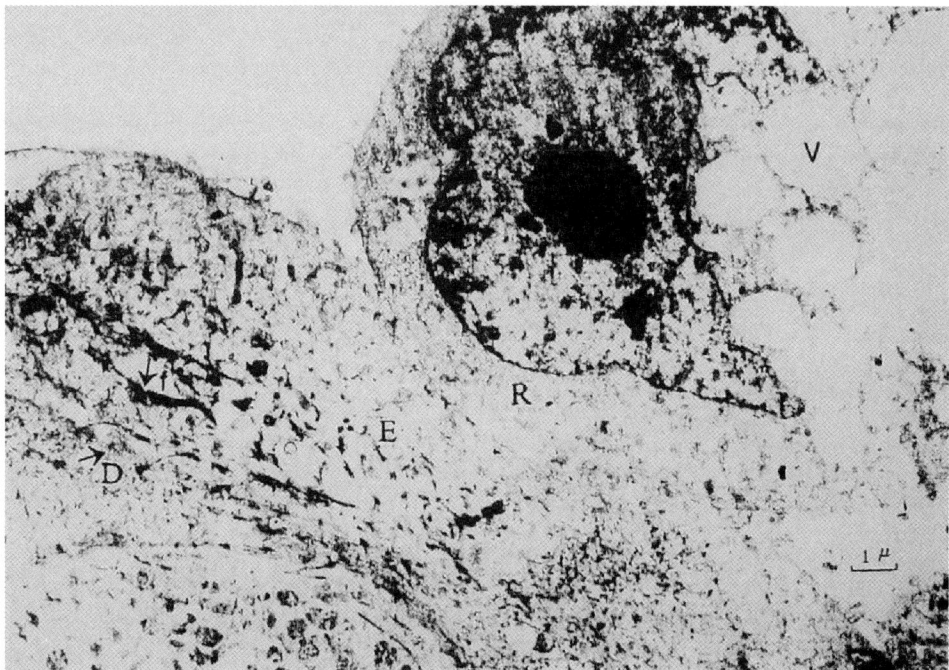

Fig. 15　Ultrastructure of CNE cell line 38th passage, a round cell with epithelial cell characteristics: D-
desmosome, f-tonofibril, R-ribosome, V-vesicle(×7800)

No virus could be found in CNE and CNF cells treated or untreated with INDR (30μg/ml).

DETECTION OF EBV SPECIFIC ANTIGEN

1. Complement Fixation Test

A 5% suspension of CNE and CNF cells in veronal buffered saline was sonicated and centrifuged at 27000g for 30 minutes. The supernatant was used as antigen and tested with strong EBV positive serum from an NPC patient by microcomplement fixation test. The results were negative.

2. Indirect Immunofluoresccnce Test

The CNE, CNEC, CNF, and CNFC cells growing on coverslips were treated with IUDR (50μ/ml) in complete RPMI 1640 medium for 6 days. They were examined for EBVsecific early antigen (EA) by indirect immunofluorescence test. No early antigen could be found in these lines.

DISCUSSION

Based on studies of the cell growth pattern, chromosome analysis, heterotransplantation, and electronmicroscopy, the CNE cell line had the characteristics of epithelial cells and was confirmed to be squamous carcinoma cells. The fusiform cells could not be seen in cultures of the epithelioid cell line until the 12th passage. The CNF cell line also had some characteristics of epithelial cells and formed poorly differentiated squamous cell carcinoma in animals treated with antithymocyte serum. Therefore, the fusiform cells probably originated from the epithelioid cell line. Contamination by other malignant epithelial cell line could be ruled out, because no other epithelial cell line was present in our laboratory.

Many round cells were observed on the top of monolayer or multilayers of the both cell lines, and became continuously detached into the medium. These floating cells, after seeding into another flask, Could grow into their original epithelioid cell or fusiform forms. Since many patients with nasopharyngeal carcinoma had lymph node metastases in the neck region in the absence of notable tumor in the nasopharynx when they first came to the outpatient clinic, the easy detachment of cancer cells from the original tumor might be similar to the phemomenon as observed in tissue culture. No EB virus particle or early antigen could be detected in these two cell lines either treated or untreated with IUDR. These cell lines were established from an NPC patient with well differentiated squamous cell carcinoma. This might be similar to the results as reported by Klein et al. [14], who could not demonstrate EBV, DNA, and EBNA in the well-differentiated squamous carcinoma cells of NPC transplanted in nude mice. But Liang Po-chiang et al. [19] reported that nasopharyngeal carcinomas showed, during their course of development, a definite tendency to change their histological pattern, and did so in a definite sequence, i.e. from highly differentiated type toward poorly differentiated type and from poorly differentiated type toward undifferentiated type. Even in the same biopsy specimen of the primary growth, different parts of the tumor revealed different histologic patterus. Our two cell lines formed poorly differentiated squamous cell carcinoma in immunosuppressive animals. Whether there are viral genome and its expression in these two cell lines or not needs further study by other methods.

REFERENCES

[1] Old LT, et al. Proc Nat Acad Sci(USA),1966, 56: 1699.

[2] de Schryvei A, et al. Clin Exp Immunol, 1969,5: 443.

[3] Henle W, et al. In Comparative Leukemia Rcsearch (ed. Dutcher R M), Basel: Karger,1969, 706.

[4] Henle G, et al. Int J Cancer, 1971, 8:272.

[5] Henle W, et al. Cancer Res, 1973, 33:1419.

[6] Henle W, et al. J Nat Cancer Inst, 1973, 51:361.

[7] Henderson BE, et al. Cancer Res, 1974, 34:1207.

[8] de-The G, et al. Int J Cancer, 1975, 16:713.

[9] Zur Hausen H, et al. Nature (London), 1970,228: 1056.

[10] Zur Hausen H, et al. Int J Cancer, 1974, 13:657.

[11] Nonoyama M, et al. Proc Nat Acad Sci (USA),1973, 70:3267.

[12] Wolf H, et al. Nature, 1973, 244:245.

[13] Huang DP, et al. Int J Cancer, 1974, 14:580.

[14] Klein G, et al. Proc Nat Acad Sci. (USA),1974, 71:4737.

[15] Degrange C, et al. Int J Cancer, 1975, 16:7.

[16] Trumpet PA, et al. Int J Cancer, 1976, 17:578.

[17] de-The G, et al. Int J Cancer, 1970, 6:189.

[18] de-The G, In Oncogenesis and Herpes Virus, eds. Biggs PM, et al. Lyon. 1972, 275.

[19] Liang PC, et al. Chinese MJ, 1962, 81:629.

[In 《Scientia Sinica》1978, 21(1): 127-134]

Application of an Immunoenzymatic Method and an Immunoautoradiograhic Method for a Mass Survey of Nasopharyngeal Carcinoma

Zeng Yi, Liu Yuxi, Liu Chunren, Chen Sanwen, Wei Jihneng, Zhu Jisong and Zai Huijong

Institute of Virology, Chinese Academy of Medical Sciences; Cancer Institute, Chinese Academy of Medical Sciences; People's Hospital of Guangsi Zhuang Autonomous Region; Cancer Control Office of Zangwu County; and Institute of Atomic Energy, Academia Sinica-Beijing, People's Republic of China

[SUMMARY] The frequency of IgA antibody to virus capsid antigen (VCA) of EB virus was tested by an immunoenzymatic method among adults in a mass serological screening of the general population of 6 communes in South China, as a guide toward early detection of nasopharyngeal carcinoma. Sera from 56 patients already recognized as having nasopharyngeal carcinoma (NPC) also were tested. The screening was conducted with sera fom 56,584 persons age 30 years and older in Zangwu County in the Guangsi Zhuang Autonomous Region. IgA antibody to VCA was found in 96% of the NPC patients tested; the geometric mean antibody titer for this group was 1 : 41. The antibody also was detected in 117 of the persons surveyed in the mass screening, and among these, the geometric mean antibody titer was 1 : 21. 20 of the antibody-positive persons were diagnosed by clinical and pathological examination as having NPC. 18 of these cases were diagnosed soon after the initial tests in June-September, 1978, and an additional 2 were diagnosed only after follow-up examinations 10 months after the first blood sample was taken. All of the persons who are in the antibody-positive group but exhibit no detectable tumors are to be reexamined periodically.

Addition to the immunoenzymatic method, an immunoautoradiographic method was also used in tests with sera from 12,328 persons in one of the communes. IgA antibody to VCA of EB virus was detected in 25 subjects by the immunoenzymatic test and in 69 by immunoautoradiography. Thus the immunoautoradiographic method appears to be more sensitive. However, sera from the 18 NPC patients detected by serological screening were positive by both methods. The results indicate that both methods are simple and sensitive, and that serological screening is valuable in the early detection of NPC.

[Keywords] Nasopharyngeal carcinoma; EB virus; VCA antibody; IgA antibody; Immunoenzymatic method; Immunoautoradiographic method

INTRODUCTION

Nasopharyngeal carcinoma (NPC) is one of the common malignancies in South China. A close association of EB Virus with NPC has been demonstrated by serological, virological and molecular biological studies. It is of interest that IgA antibody to EBV-related antigen is greatly elevated in sera of NPC patients[1]. Detection of IgA antibody has also been carried out in our laboratories by immunofluorescence, immunoenzymatic and immunoautoradiographic methods[2-5]. The frequency of antibody detection in sera from patients with NPC was over 90%, that from patients with other malignancies was less than 4%, whereas sera examined from normal persons have given negative results. Therefore, detection of IgA antibody is useful in the diagnosis of NPC and might be valuable for mass surveys to detect potential NPC patients among the population in areas at high risk for NPC. This paper reports the application of immunoenzymatic and immunoautoradiographic methods for the detection of IgA antibody to viral capsid antigen (VCA) of EB virus, in sera from the general adult population in a high-risk area for NPC.

Zangwu County is located in the eastern part of Guangsi. The population is 474,705 persons (male 244,747, female 229,958), of whom 99. 6% are of Han ethnic background, while the others are of Zhuang, Yao, and other minority ethnic groups. The county is divided into 14 rural communes and one urban commune. From 1971 to 1977, the yearly mortality rate from NPC was 10. 18/100,000. A clinical mass survey of NPC had been conducted in persons aged 15 years and older from December 1977 to March 1978, with a detection rate of 51. 5/100,000. If all ages were included, the prevalence rate would be 29. 96/100,000. In the 6 communes included in this report, the yearly incidence rate of NPC for 1975,1976, and 1977 was 15. 6, 14. 8, and 15. 8, respectively, per 100,000. Of the total NPC patients,91. 4% were age 30 years and over. The population of these 6 communes totals 177,022 persons. Sera were collected from 56,584 persons age 30 years and over (90. 4% of the age group). The sex and age distribution of the persons examined was similar to that of the general population.

MATERIALS AND METHODS

Sera

The sera, collected by pricking the ear lobe, were stored at $-15°$. Venous blood specimens were then obtained from persons who were antibody-positive in the initial screening, and also from patients suspected or proven to have NPC.

Immunoenzymatic Method[4]

Cell smears were prepared from B95-8 cultures, fixed in acetone and used in the indirect immunoenzymatic method with peroxidase-conjugated anti-human IgA antibody. Sera diluted to 1 : 2. 5 and 1 : 5 were added to separate wells of slides. The slides were incubated at 37 for 30 min in a humid atmosphere, and washed 3 times with phosphate-buffered saline (PBS). Peroxidase-conjugated antihuman IgA antibody in appropriate dilution was added to the slides. The slides were incubated for 30 min, washed 3 times with PBS, and flooded with diaminobenzidine and H_2O_2 for 10 min. Positive and negative serum controls were included in each experiment. Slides were examined under the light microscope. A serum was considered positive if the cells in the well that contained the 1 : 2. 5 dilution showed brown color characteristic of this test. Venous blood specimens from suspected NPC patients and from persons antibody-positive in the initial screening were tested in further dilutions. The highest dilution of serum still positive for IgA antibody to VCA was considered as the antibody titer of that serum.

Immunoautoradiographic Method[5]

Sera diluted 1 : 160 and 1 : 640 were added to separate wells. After incubation at $37°$ in a humid atmosphere for 30 min, slides were washed 3 times with PBS containing 1% calf serum. 0. 7ml of ^{125}I-labeled antihuman IgA antibody in appropriate dilution was added on each slide. The slides were incubated at $37°$ for 30 min, washed 3 times with PBS containing 1% calf serum and left to air-dry. They were then coated with nuclear emulsion, slowly dried, and kept in the dark at room temperature for 24h. Slides were developed in D-19 for 15 min, placed in fixing reagent for 10 min, washed and left to air-dry, and then were examined under the light microscope. A serum was considered positive if the cells in the well that contained the 1 : 640 dilution showed black granules typical of this test. Venous blood was further tested in selected instances as described under Immunoenzymatic Method, above.

Clinical and Pathological Examination

The antibody-positive persons were examined by nasopharyngoscope. Biopsies were taken from the following antibody-positive persons: (1) those diagnosed clinically as NPC patients or suspected of having NPC; (2) those having some lesions in the nasopharynx, such as hyperplasia or a residue of adenoidal tissue, rough mucosa, local congestion or inflammation; (3) those without lesions in the nasopharynx but with high antibody titer.

RESULTS

Immunoenzymatic Method

i. Detection of IgA Antibody to VCA in Sera from Patients with NPC. Among patients with NPC that had developed and had been identified before the serological mass survey, 96% have IgA antibody to VCA, with a geometric mean titer (GMT) of 1 : 40. 5.

ii. Detection of IgA Antibody to VCA in Sera from the General Population. Among 56,584 persons age 30 years and older in the general population studied, 117 were found to have IgA antibody to VCA. The prevalence rates of antibody in different communes varied from 125/100,000 to 290/100,000, with an average rate of 207/100,000 (Tab. I).

Tab. I　Results of IgA-VCA antibody screening

Commune No.	Number of persons examined	Number positive	Antibody prevalence (per 100,000)
1	7,430	11	148
2	7,780	15	193
3	11,380	33	290
4	12,075	26	215
5	12,328	25	203
6	5,588	7	125
Total	56,584	117	207

The antibody titers among the antibodypositive individuals ranged from 1∶2.5 to 1∶1,280(Tab. Ⅱ). In this group of 117 persons，91(78%) had antibody titers of 1∶10 or more；63 (54%) were at levels of 1∶20 or above；and 38 (32%) had titers of 1∶40 or higher. Among 52 patients with NPC already diagnosed before the serum was taken，47 (90%) had antibody titers of 1∶10 or higher；for 38 (73%) the antibody titers were 1∶20 or more；and for 31 (60%)，the antibody levels were 1∶40 or more. The GMT for the previously recognized patients was twice that calculated for the 117 antibody-positive persons who were discovered in this survey, 1∶46 vs. 1∶21.

Clinical and Pathological Examination，and Antibody Titers by Two Methods

Biopsies were taken from 74 of the 117 persons who were antibody-positive. 19 of these subjects were diagnosed clinically and pathologically as having malignant tumors；these included 18 NPCs and 1 skin basal-cell carcinoma of the face. Of 18 patients with NPC，7 were in stage Ⅰ, 4 in stage Ⅱ, 5 in stage Ⅲ, and 2 in stage Ⅳ (Tab. Ⅲ). The 7 patients considered to be in stage Ⅰ had no subjective symptoms，and the early pathological changes—such as rough and nodular mucosa—could only be found after careful examination. All of the NPC patients，except 1 with undifferentiated carcinoma，showed poorly differentiated squamous carcinoma. All of these sera were antibody-positive by both the immunoenzymatic method and the immunoautoradiographic method. The GMT for these newly discovered patients was rather high—1∶109 by the immunoenzymatic method，as compared with 1∶46 for the persons previously recognized as having NPC（Tab. Ⅱ）.

Tab. Ⅱ Distribution of anti-VCA antibody in NPC patients previously diagnosed and in persons found antibody-positive in serological screening

Antibody titer (reciprocal)	Patients with NPC previously diagnosed		Persons found antibody-positive in serological screening	
	number positive	% positive	number positive	% positive
2.5	0	0	10	9
5	5	10	16	14
10	9	17	28	24
20	7	13	25	21
40	6	12	11	9
80	9	17	9	8
160	8	15	9	8
320	6	12	4	3
640	2	4	3	3
1,280	0	0	2	2
Total	52	100	117	100
Geometric mean titer	1∶46		1∶21	

Prevalence Rate and Incidence Rate of NPC

There were 74 NPC patients in the 6 communes studied，among them the 18 patients who were first detected by this serological mass survey；this constitutes an NPC prevalence rate of 42/100,000—higher than that detected by the clinical mass survey conducted from November 1977 to March 1978 (32.2/100,000). The comparative data are shown in Tab. Ⅳ. Cases detected in 1978 totaled 37，including the 18 first identified as a result of this serological survey，yielding an incidence rate for 1978 of 20.9/100,000—higher than that reported for 1975—1977 (which was 14.8 to 15.8 per 100,000).

Immunoautoradiographic Method

Detection of IgA antibody to VCA in sera from the general population in commune No. 5 was done by immunoautoradiography in addition to the immunoenzymatic testing used in the overall study (Tab. Ⅴ). Of 12,328 persons age 30 years and older in this commune，69 were positive for IgA antibody to VCA when tested by the immunoautoradiographic method. This constituted an antibody prevalence rate of 560/100,000—considerably higher than that detected in this same population by use of the immunoenzymatic method，which revealed only 25 antibody-positive persons—a rate of 203/100,000. However, for 2 patients in this commune who already had NPC classed in stage I and confirmed by pathological examination, the antibody was detected by both methods. The immunoautoradiographic antibody titers ranged from 1:640 to 1:40,960, with a GMT of 1:748.

Tab. Ⅲ　NPC patients found in serological mass survey

Case number	Sex	Age years	Clinical stage	Pathological diagnoses	Antibody titer[1]	
					IE	IR
23	male	31	I		10	640
30	male	47	I		160	2,560
38	male	44	I	NPC:poorly differentiated carcinoma	20	2,560
41	male	58	I		40	640
75	male	39	I		320	10,240
67	female	68	I	NPC:undifferentiated carcinoma	1,280	40,960
32218	male	36	I		80	640
70	female	54	II		160	2,560
33	female	52	II		80	10,240
31	male	59	II		80	640
63	female	33	II		160	2,560
36	male	50	III	NPC:poorly differentiated carcinoma	640	40,960
28	female	59	III		1,280	10,240
72	male	40	III		80	640
73	male	51	III		40	10,240
74	female	83	III		160	10,240
29	male	59	IV		160	640
71	male	38	IV		10	640
42	male	77		skin basal cell carcinoma	20	2,560

[1] IE=Immunoenzymatic method; IR=immunoautoradiographic method.

Tab. Ⅳ　Comparison of NPC prevalence rates detected as a result of clinical and serological mass surveys

Commune No.	Number of patients with NPC	New NPC patients	Total	Prevalence rate by serological mass survey (per 100,000)	Prevalence rate by clinical mass survey[1] (per 100,000)
1	12	9	21	57.7	30.2
2	15	2	17	48.9	43.1
3	8	5	13	46.8	28.8
4	11	1	12	31.0	28.5
5	5	0	5	19.6	31.5
6	5	1	6	43.0	50.2
	56	18	74	42.0	32.2

[1] Clinical mass survey carried out from December 1977 to March 1978.

Tab. V   Detection of VCA-IgA antibody in persons of age 30 years and older in commune No. 5

Method	Number tested	Number positive	Antibody prevalence (per 100,000)	Patients with stage I NPC
Immunoautoradiographic method	12,328	69	560	2
Immunoenzymatic method		25	203	2

Resurvey of the IgA Antibody-Positive individuals

Aside from the 18 NPC patients and 1 patient with skin basal cell carcinoma detected by pathological examination among the 117 IgA antibody-positive persons as reported above, the rest—98 persons—were reexamined in April 1979. 29 biopsies were obtained from the persons suspected to have NPC and from persons having high titers of IgA antibody to VCA. Among them, 2 NPC patients in stages I and II were diagnosed pathologically in this follow-up, 10 months after the first blood samples were taken. The antibody titer in the patient in stage I maintained the same level, 1 : 10, but in the patient in stage II the titer increased from 1 : 20 to 1 : 1,280. Taken together with the above, 20 NPC patients have been diagnosed among the 117 persons who were discovered in the 1978 screening to be positive for IgA antibody to VCA of EB virus.

DISCUSSION

The results obtained for patients with NPC in the field study are in accordance with our previous reports[2-5]. Of 56,584 persons of age 30 years and over in the general population, 117 had IgA antibody to VCA. Among these 117 persons, 74 were biopsied in the first survey and 18 (24%) were diagnosed by clinical and pathological examination as having NPC. 7 cases without subjective symptoms were in stage I, and 4 were in stage II. In the second survey which took place 10 months later, 2 additional NPC patients were diagnosed. These results indicate that NPC patients—including early cases not recognized clinically—could be identified by the immunoenzymatic method. The early diagnosis of NPC means a more favorable outcome of radiotherapy. It is expected that periodic follow-up for the remaining antibody-positive persons without detectable tumors will reveal more NPC cases. Such studies not only are important for early detection of NPC, but also should help to clarify the relationship between EB virus and NPC.

Tests were conducted by both immunoenzymatic and immunoautoradiographic methods for detection of IgA antibody to VCA, in the sera from 12,328 persons age 30 years and older in one of the communes studied. Positive results were obtained in 25 and 69 cases, respectively. So it appears that the immunoautoradiographic method is more sensitive than the immunoenzymatic method. However, sera from the 18 NPC patients detected by this serological mass survey gave positive results by both methods. The results indicate that both methods are simple, sensitive and specific, and that antibody screening is valuable in the early detection of NPC.

REFERENCES

[1]   Henle, G. and Henle, W.: Int. J. Cancer 17:1-7(1976).
[2]   Laboratory of Tumor Viruses of Cancer Institute, et al.: Acta microbiol. sin. 18: 253(1978).
[3]   Zeng Yi, et al.: Chinese J. Oncol. 1: 2(1979).
[4]   Liu Yuxi, et al.: Chinese J. Oncol. 1: 8(1979).
[5]   Liu Chunren, et al.: Kexue Tongbao 24: 715(1979).

[In 《Intervirology》1980, 13: 162-168]

Development of an Anticomplement Immunoenzyme Test for Detection of EB Virus Nuclear Antigen(EBNA) and Antibody to EBNA

Pi Guo-hua, Zeng Yi, Zhao Win-ping, Zhang Qin

Department of Tumor Virus. Institiute of Virology Chinese Academy of Medical Sciences, Peking, Rep. of China

[SUMMARY] An anticomplement immunoenzyme test was developed by conjugating anti-human C3 antibody with horeseradish peroxidase. EBNA could be detected by this test in all cell lines related to EB virus, as well as in nasopharyngeal carcinoma cells, but not in unrelated cell lines. Antibody to EBNA could also be detected. The test is sensitive and does not require a fluorescence microscope which makes it particularly suitable for mass survey.

INTRODUCTION

Nasopharyngeal carcinoma(NPC) may be detected at an early stage by serological mass surveys and follow-up studies(Zeng et al. 1979a, 1979b, 1980), but there remains a large number of VCA-IgA antibody-positive persons with no evidence of NPC. EBNA and EBV DNA are regularly found in NPC cells(Wolf et al. 1973, 1975; Huang et al. 1974, 1978; Klein et al. 1974; Desgranges et al. 1975).

Detection of EBNA in nasopharyngeal cells from VCA-IgA antibody-positive individuals and NPC-suspected persons might be of help for early diagnosis of NPC. Reedman and Klein(1973) developed on anticomplement immunofluorescence test for the detection of EBNA. This test requires fluorescence microscopy and hence is not convenient for field surveys. We have, therefore, developed an anticomplement immunoenzymetic test.

MATERIALS AND METHODS

1. Cell lines
Raji, Namalwa, B95-8, CNE, CFN, S-H and Vero cell lines were used.

2. NPC specimens
Exfoliated cells were obtained from the nasopharynx of NPC patients by negative pressure suction.

3. Sera
Sera were obtained from 5 NPC patients and normal individuals.

4. Anticomplement immunoenzyme test(ACIE)
Anticomplement(anti-C3) serum was prepared by immunizing rabbits with human complement C3 absorbed on inulin. Briefly, 1g of inulin was washed 3 times with barbital buffer, pH 7. 6. Forty ml of fresh human serum from 6 persons were added to the inulin drop by drop. After mixing, the mixture was incubated in a waterbath at 37℃ for 1h, with shaking every 5 min. The inulin-C3 complex was then washed 7 times with barbital buffer. Barbital buffer(19ml) was added to the pellet of inulin-C3 complex and the preparation was stored at-30℃. Five ml of inulin-C3 complex was emulsified with an equal amount of complete Freund's adjuvant and injected subcutaneously int 10 sites in the back and into the enlarged lymph nodes of rabbits, which had received BCG in the footpads 10 days previously. Two further injections of inulin-C3 complex in incomplete Freund's adjuvant were given at 10-day intervals. Bleedings were taken 10 days after the last injection. The titer of anticomplement C3 antibody was 1：16-1：64 by double immunodiffusion.

The method used for labeling the anticomplement antibody was the horseradish peroxidease technique described by Avrameas(1969). Briefly, 5 mg of lyophilized horseradish peroxidase(HRP, Boehringer, Grade I), was dissolved in 1ml of 0. 3mol/L $NaHCO_3$ and treated for 1h at room temperature with 0. 1ml of flurodintrobenzene in ethanol. One ml of 0. 06mol/L sodium periodate was added and kept at room temperature for 30 min. The reaction was stopped with 1ml of 0. 16 mol/L ethylene glycol and the solution was dialyzed overnight at 4℃ in carbonate/bicarbonate buffer, 0. 01moL/L pH 9. 5. Five mg of anti-human C3 IgG in 1 ml carbonate/bicarbonate buffer, pH 9. 5 was mixed with the activated HRP for 3h at room temperature. Then 5mg of $NaBH_4$ was added to the mixture overnight at 4℃. The solution was dialyzed in PBS. Horseradish peroxidase antibody conjugate was stored at －30℃.

Some of the normal human sera were negative for EBV antibody. These were given by Drs. de-The and Desgranges to be used as sources of complement. There was no antinuclear antibody in these sera. The balanced salt solution(BSS) was used as diluent. The cells were treated with 0.4% KCl at 4℃ for 15 min, and smears were made. After drying in air the cells were fixed with cold acetone.

The reference NPC sera containing antibody to EBNA together with normal human serum with complement (final dilution 1 : 10) were then added to the smears, and the slides placed in a humidified chamber at 37℃ for 1h. After washing 3 times with BSS, the anti-C3 antibody conjugate(1 : 10) was added and the slides were kept at 37℃ for 30 min. The smears were again washed 3 times with BSS, stained with diaminobenzene and H_2O_2, and examined under a light microscope. Nuclei with brown coloration were considered positive for EBNA.

5. Anticomplement immunoflrorescence test(ACIF)

EBNA was also detected by ACIF as described by Reedman and Klein(1973).

RESULTS

1. Detection of EBNA in different cell lines

Raji cells were examined by both ACIE and ACIF. As shown in Figs. 1 and 2, the EBNA was detected in as many Raji cells by ACIE as by ACIF. After inactivation of complement in the NPC reference sera and normal human sera at 56℃ for 30 min, no EBNA could be detected in Raji cells(Tab. 1, Fig. 3).

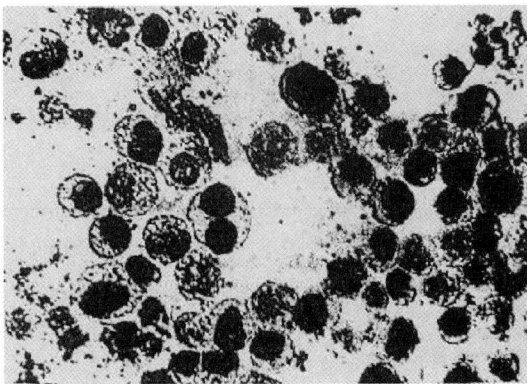

Fig. 1 Raji cells, EBNA-positive(ACIE) ×66

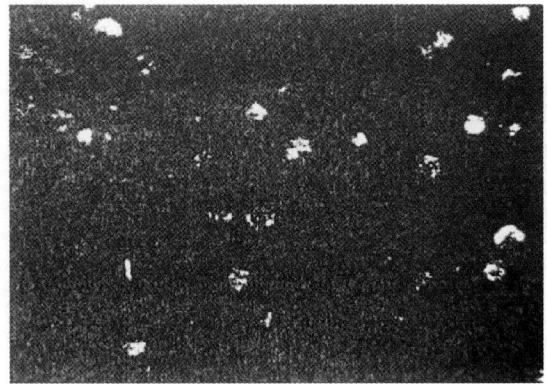

Fig. 2 Raji cells, EBNA-positive(ACIF) ×66

Tab. 1 Detection of EBNA in different cells

	Cells	Sources	EBNA	VCA-IgA antibody
Cell lines	Raji	Burkitt's lymphoma	+	
	Namalwa	Burkitt's lymphoma	+	
	B95-8	EBV transformed marmoset lymphoblastoid cells	+	
	CNE	Well differentiated NPC cells	−	
	CNF	Well differentiated NPC cells	−	
	Vero	Green monkey kidney cells	−	
	S-H	Peripheral blood cells, epithelial cells	−	
Nasopharyngeal	No. 1	Poorly differentiated NPC cells	+	1 : 20
carcinoma	No. 2	Poorly differentiated NPC cells	+	1 : 80
cells	No. 3	Poorly differentiated NPC cells	+	1 : 80
	No. 4	Poorly differentiated NPC cells	+	1 : 1280
	No. 5	Undifferentiated NPC cells	+	

EBNA was demonstrated in Namalwa and B95-8 cells which are related to EB virus, but not in unrelated cells, i. e. CNE, CNF, S-H and Vero cell lines.

2. Detection of EBNA in nasopharyngeal carcinoma cells from NPC patients

EBNA-positive carcinoma cells were found in exfoliated cells from 5 NPC patients by both ACIE (Fig. 4, Tab. 1) and ACIF. All these patients were diagnosed histologically as poorly or undifferentiated NPC.

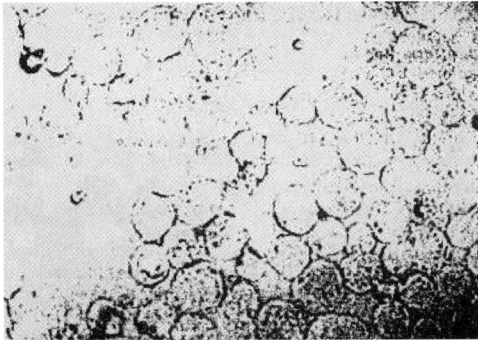

Fig. 3　Raji cells After inactivation of complement
EBNA-negative × 66

Fig. 4　EBNA-positive nasopharyngeal carcinoma cells (ACIF) × 66

3. Detection of antibody to EBNA

Antibody to EBNA was detected in sera from 5 NPC patients with titers of 1 ∶ 1280, 1 ∶ 1280, 1 ∶ 1280, 1 ∶ 320 and 1 ∶ 20, and from 5 normal indivduals with titers of 1 ∶ 1280, 1 ∶ 1280, 1 ∶ 320, 1 ∶ 80 and 1 ∶ 20, respectively.

DISCUSSION

The results of the present study show that EBNA could be detected in all cell lines related to EB virus, but not in unrelated lines, and that antibody to EBNA could also detected by the ACIE test. This test is as sensitive as the ACIF test and much more convenient for field studies. EBNA was also found in nasopharyngeal carcinoma cells. The significance of this finding requires further study.

ACKNOWLEDGEMENTS

We would like to thank Drs. de-The and Desgranges for the human serum negative for EBV antibody and the fluorescence-labeled anti-human C3 antibody, and Dr. S. C. Shen for the exfoliated cells from NPC patients.

We are also grateful to Prof. C. H. Huang, Institute of Virology Beijing, China for critical reading and revision of the manuscript.

REFERENCES

[1] Avrameas S, Immunochemistry, 1969, 6, 43
[2] Desgranges C, Wolf, H. de-The, G. Shanmugaratman, K. Ellouz, R. Cammoun, N. Klein and G. Zur Hausen, H. Int J Cancer, 1975, 16, 7
[3] Huang D P Ho, J H C, Henle W. and Henle, G. Int J Cancer 1974, 14, 580
[4] Huang, D P Ho, J H C, Henle, W. Henle, G. Saw D. and Lui, M. Int J Cancer, 1978, 22, 266
[5] Klein G, Giovannella, B C, Lindahl T, Fialkow PJ, SinS. Nail Acad Sci. USA, 71, 4737
[6] Reedman B M, Klein G, Int J Cancer, 1973, 11, 499
[7] Wolf H, Zur Hausen H, Becker Y, Nature, 1973, 244, 245
[8] Wolf, H, Zur Hausen H, Klein G, Becker Y, Henle G hemle W. Med Microbiol Immunol, 1975, 161, 15
[9] Zeng Y, Liu Yx, Liu CM, Chen SW, Wei JN, Zhu JS, Zei HG, Chin J Oncol, 1979a, 1, 2
[10] Zeng Y, Liu YX, Wei JN, Zhu JS, Cai SL, Wang PZ, Zhong JN, Li RC, Pan WJ, Li EJ, Tan BF, Acta Acad Med Sin, 1979b, 1, 123
[11] Zeng Y, Liu YX, Liu CN, Chen SN, Wei JN, Zhu JS, Zai HJ, Intervirology 1980, 13, 162

[In 《Journal of Immunologycal Methods》 1981, 44∶73-78]

Inhibitory Effect of Retinoids on Epstein-Barr Virus Induction in Raji Cells

ZENG Y, ZHOU HM, XU SP

Institutes of Virology and Materia Medica, Chinese Academy of Medical Sciences, Beijing, China

[SUMMARY]   Induction of Epstein-Barr virus(EBV) early antigen after treatment with various combinations of croton oli and n-butyrate was markedly inhibited by retinoids 7901, 7902 Ro 10-9359 AND Ro 11-1430. Possible administration of retinoids to virus capsid antigen IgA antibody-positive individuals in high-risk areas for masopharyngeal carcinoma to prevent EBV activation and development of this cancer is discussed.

[Keywords]   Retinoid; Croton oil; n-Butyrate; Epstein-Barr virus; Early antigen

INTRODUCTION

Yamamoto et al.[1] first reported that retinoic acid interferes with Epstein-Barr virus(EBV) early antigen(EA) induction in Raji cells treated with 12-O-tertradecanoyl-phorbol-13-acetate. Ito et al[2,3] also reported that increases in EBV EA and virus capsid antigen(VCA) in Raji and P3HR-1 cells treated with croton oil and n-butyrate were markedly inhibited by retinoic acid and retinoids. Although treatment of experimental animals with vitamin A and retinoids inhibits tumors[4-8], vitamin A is highly toxic after long-term administration and cannot be used clinically. However, synthesis of vitamin A derivatives with low toxicity has been accomplished. Such retinoids, made in China and abroad, were tested for inhibitory effect on EBV induction in our laboratory for possible use in the prevention of nasopharyngeal carcinoma(NPC).

MATERIALS AND METHODS

1. Retinoids, croton oil and n-butyrate

Retinoids 7901 and 7902 were made at the Institute of Materia Medica of the Chinese Academy of Medical Sciences, Beijing, and retinoids Ro 10-9359 and Ro 11-1430 were gifts from Dr. Scott. Hoffmann-La Roche Inc. Nutley, N.J. All were dissolved in dimethylsulfoxide and stored at -30℃. Croton oil was dissovled in ethanol and stored at -30℃, whereas n-butyrate was dissolved in RPMI 1640 medium and kept at 4℃.

2. EA Induction and Inhibition

The method used has been described by Ito et al.[2,3]. Briefly, Raji cells were cultivated in RPMI 1640 medium containing 20% calf serum, crolon oil(50-500ng/ml), and n-butyrate(4mmol/L), and were then incubated at 37℃ for 2 days. For inhibition tests, retinoids were simultaneously added to the medium as mentioned above, and the Raji cells were cultivated for 2 days at 37℃. EA-positive cells were detected in smears by immunoenzymatic means[9].

RESULTS

1. Induction of EA in raji cells by croton oil and n-butyrate

Varying concentrations of croton oit and 4mmol/L n-butyrate were used to examine EA induction in Raji cells. As shown in Fig. 1, 47% of the cells were EA-positive when 500ng/ml croton oil and 4mmol/L n-butyrate were used; however, activity decreased with decreasing conocentrations of the oil. Only 3% of the cells appeared to be EA-positive when treated with 500ng/ml croton oil alone, and only 1% of the cells were EA-positive when 4mmol/L n-butyrate was used alone.

2. Effect of Various Concentrations of Ratinoid 7901 on EA Induction in Raji Cells

Treatment of Raji cells with retinoid 7901 effectively inhibited EA induction by croton oil(250 ng/ml) and n-butyrate(4mmol/L). At a 10μmol/L concentration of retinoid, EA induction was inhibited by 84%. The percent inhibition at 1, 0. 1 and 0. 01μmol/L was 63, 60, and 15%, respectively; no suppression of EA induction was observed at 0. 001μmol/L(Fig. 2).

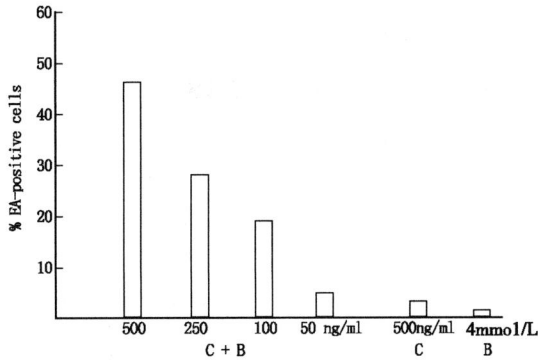

Raji cells were treated with varying concentrations of croton oil(50-500ng/ml) and n-butyrate(4mmol/L) for 48h. C = Croton oil; B = n = butyrate.

Fig. 1 Induction of EA by croton oil and n-buty-rate in Raji cells.

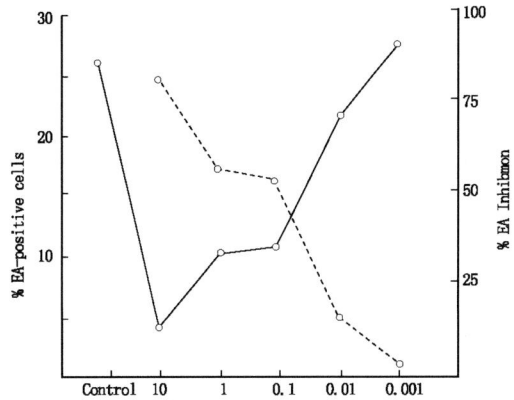

Raji ceels. Raji cells were treated with croton oil(250ng/ml) and n-butyrate(4mmol/L) for 48h. ○-○ = % EA-positive cells; ○-----○ = % EA inhibition

Fig. 2 Inhibitory effect of retinoid 7901 (0.001-10μmol/L) on EA induction in Raji cells.

3. Inhibitory effect of different fetinoids on EA induction

Retinoids 7901, Ro 10-9359 and Ro 11-1430 produced similar inhibitory effects on EA induction, but had no inhibitory effect at a concentration of 0.01μmol/L. Retinoid 7902, however, was more effective and exhibited some inhibitory effect at concentrations as low as 0.01μmol/L(Tab. 1).

Tab. 1 Comparison of the inhibitory effect of different retinoids on EA induction

Retinoid concentration μmol/L	% EA-positive cells			
	Ro 10-9359	Ro 11-1430	7901	7902
10	2.6	4.2	4.3	0
1	10.4	11.3	10	1.2
0.1	11	13.4	11	6.7
0.01	30	26	23	15.3
0.001	31	32	27.3	22
Control	27	27	27	27

4. Effect of Retinoid 7901 on Epstein-Barr Nuclear Antigen(EBNA) in Raji Cells

Raji cells were cultivated in growth medium containing retinoid 7901(10μmol/L). After 5-10passages, EBNA was still present in the cells and EA could be induced by treatment of the cells with croton oil and n-butyrate.

DISCUSSION

EA induction in Raji cells treated with croton oil and n-butyrate, as described by Ito et al[2,3]. provides a good model for examining and identifying inducers of EBV antigens. The present study further confirmed that EA induction by croton oil and n-butyrate could be inhibited markedly by retinoids 7901, 7902, Ro 10-9359 and Ro 11-1430 and that retinoid 7902 was more effective than the others. Since retionid 7901 has a lower toxicity than Ro 10-9359 [unpublished data]. which has been used in clinical trials, it appears that retionid 7901 could also be used clinically. The toxicity of retinoid 7902 is now under study.

Mass serological surveys carried out since 978 in Zangwu County in the Guangsi Zhuang Auto nomous Region of China[9,10], have shown that the frequency of IgA antibody to EBV VCA increased with increasing age, and have enabled detection of NPC at an early stage. Follow-up studies detected additional new NPC cases[11]. These data indicate that the presence of VCA IgA antibo dy is closely related to the development of NPC; however, a large number of normal individuals also are antibody-positive. Our previous workt[12] demonstrated that the level of complement fixing antibody to EBV in sera from patients over 20 years of age in areas of high risk for NPC was significantly higher than that in indivduals in low-risk areas. Thus, it appears that EBV infection is more active in persons in high-risk NPC areas. Because vitamin A and its derivatives have shown effective inhibition of EBV induction and antitumor effect, administration of retinoids to VAC IgA antibody positive individuals might prevent EBV activation and possibly NPC.

ADDENDUM

Since submission of this paper, Lin et al. [Virology 111:294-298, 1981]. have reported inhibition by retinoic acid of EBV DNA induced in P3HR-1 cells by phorbol ester. It should be noted that the P3HR-1 cells are producers, whereas the Raji cells used in this report are nonproducers.

ACKNOWLEDGMENTS

We thank Prof. Y. Ito(Kyoto, Japan) for providing the unpublished data concerning the methods for induction and inhibition of EBV antigens and Prof. C. H. Huang(Beijing) for critically reading the manuscript.

REFERENCES

[1] Yamamoto N, Bister K, zur Hausen H. Retinoic acid inhibition of Epstein-Barr virus induction. Nature, Lond, 1979, 278: 553-554.

[2] Ito Y, Kishishita M, Morigaki T, Yanase S, Hirayama T. Induction and intrevtion of EB virus antigens in human lymphoblastoid cell lines: a simulation model for study of cause and prevention of nasopharyngeal carcinoma and Burkitt lymphoma. Dusseldorf NPC Symp, 1980.

[3] Ito Y, Kishishita M, Yanase S. Induction of Epstein-Barr virus antigens in human lymphoblastoid P3HR-1 cells with culture fluid of Fusobacterium nucleatum. Cancer Res, 1980, 40:4329-7330.

[4] Bollag W. Therapeutic effects of an aromatic retinoic acid analog on chemically induced skin papillomas and carcinomas of mice. Eur J Cancer,1974, 10:731-737.

[5] Bollag W. Prophylaxis of chemically induced epithelial tumors with an aromatic retinoic acid analog(Ro 10-9359). Eur J Cancer, 1975, 11:721-724.

[6] Felix E L, Loyd B, Cohen M H. Inhibition of growh and developmant of a transplantable murine melanoma by vitamin A. Science, 1975, 189:886-888.

[7] Trown P W, Buck M J, Hansen R. Inhibition of growth and regression of a transplantable rat chondrosarcoma by three retionids. Cancer Treatm Rep, 1976, 60:1647-1653.

[8] Ito Y. Effect of an aromatic retinoic acid analo(Ro 10-9359) on growth of virus-induced papilloma(Shope) and related neoplasia of rabbits. Eur J Cancer, 1981, 17: 35-42.

[9] Zeng Y, Liu YX, Wei JN, Zhu JS, Cai SL, Wang PH, Zhong JM, Li RH, Pan WJ. Serological mass survey of NPC. Acta Acad Med, Sin, 1979, 1:123-126.

[10] Zeng Y, Liu YX, Liu CR, Chen SW, We JN, Zhu JS, Zai HJ. Application of immunoenzymatic method and immunoautoradiographicmethod for the mass survey of nasopharyngeal carcinoma. Chin J Oncol, 1979, 1:2-7.

[11] Zeng Y, Liu Y, Liu C, Chen S, Wei J, Zhu J, Zai H. Application of an immunoenzymatic method and an immunoautoradiographic method for a mass survey of nasopharyngeal carcinoma. Intervirology, 1980, 13: 162-168.

[12] Tumor Control Team of Zhong-shan County(Guangdong et al). A study on the serum level of complement-fixing antibody to EB virus in groups of indivduals of Guangdong Province and Beijing. Chin J Otorhinolar, 1978, 13:23-25.

[In 《Intervirology》1981, 16: 29-32]

Serological Mass Survey for Early Detection of Nasopharyngeal Carcinoma in Wuzhou City, China

ZENG Y[1], ZHANG L G[2], LI H Y[2], JAN M G[1], ZHANG Q[1], Wu Y C[2], WANG Y S[2], SU G R[2]

1. Institute of Virology, Chinese Academy of Medical Sciences, Beijing; 2. Wuzhou Red Cross Hospital, Wuzhou, Guangxi Autonomous Region, People's Republic of China

[SUMMARY]　A serological mass survey was carried out in Wuzhou City of the Guangxi Autonomous Region, China. Sera were collected from 12932 persons between the ages of 40 and 59. The positive rate of VCA/IgA antibody-positive persons was 5.3%, but no EA/IgA antibody was found in sera from VCA/IgA-negative persons. Thirteen and nine nasopharyngeal carcinoma(NPC) patients were detected from the VCA/IgA and EA/IgA antibody-positive persons, respectively. With the present combination method the detection rate of NPC for 12932 persons was 100.5/100 000 nad for 680 VCA/IgA antibody-positive persons it was 1900/100 000. Thus, the rate was twice and 37 times higher, respectively, than the annual incidence rate of NPC in persons of the same age group from 1975-1978 in Wuzhou City. Of 13 NPC patients, 9 were in stageI(70%) and 4 stage 11(30%). Therefore, it is possible to reduce the mortality rate of NPC in Wuzhou City by radiotherapy of NPC patients in the early stage of the disease. The present results further suggest that EB virus is closely associated with NPC.

INTRODUCTION

Serological mass surveys were carried out in 1978-1980 in Zangwu County of Guangxi Autonomous Region(Zeng et al. 1979a, b, 1980a). The results indicate that VCA/IgA antibody screening is valuable in the early detection of NPC.

Our previous data also showed that the EA/IgA antibody is more specific for NPC than the VCA/IgA antibody(Laboratory of Tumor Viruses et al. 1978), and that the anticomplement immunoenzymatic method for the detection of EBNA in nasopharyngeal mucosa of VCA/IgA antibody-positive persons in also specific and sensitive for the detection of NPC(Pi et al. 1981; Zeng et al. 1980b).

In order to detect NPC early and to reduce the mortality rate, a serological mass survey was carried out in Wuzhou City using all the methods mentioned above. Located in the center of Zangwu County, Wuzhou City(population 170 000) has high risk for NPC. The mean annual incidence of NPC was 17/100 000 in 1975-1978. The present first-stage study reports the results of examination of 12932 persons in the 40-to 59-year group.

MATERIAL AND METHODS

1. Sera

Sera were obtained from venous blood of 12932 persons and stored at -20℃ in Wuzhou City, sent to the Institute of Virology in Beijing by air and stored at -20℃.

2. Immunoenzymatic method

B958 cells were used for the detection of VCA/IgA antibody, and Raji cells, with EBV early antigen induced by croton oil(200ng/ml) and n-butyrate(4mmol/L), were used for the detection of EA/IgA antibody. Sera diluted 1:5 and 1:10 were added to cells in separate wells of slides. The slides were incubated at 37℃ for 30 min in a humid atmosphere and washed three times with PBS. Horseradish peroxidase(Grade I)-conjugated antihuman IgA antibody in appropriate dilution was added to the slides. The slides were incubated for 30 min, washed three times with PBS and flooded with diaminobenzene solution and H_2O_2 for 10 min. Positive and negative controls were included in each experiment. A serum dilution of 1:10 showing brown staining characteristic of this test was considered positive and tested with further dilutions.

3. Anticomplement immunoenzymatic method(ACIE)

Reference NPC serum containing antibody to EBNA and normal human serum with complement in a final dilution of 1:10 were added to the smears of desquamated nasopharyngeal cells and the slides placed in a humidifed chamber at 37℃ for 1h. After three washes, anti-C3 antibody conjugate with horseradish peroxidase in 1:10 was added, and the slides were placed at 37℃ for 30 min. The slides were washed again three times, stained with diaminobenzene and H_2O_2 and then examined.

4. Method for collecting cells from the nasopharynx by negative pressure suction(Zhangjiang Medical College, 1976)

Dicaine(1%) was sprayed into the oropharyngeal and nasopharyngeal cavity. Exfoliated cells were collected by an electric suction apparatus. Smears from the silk inside the head of the suction apparatus were prepared on slides. All smears were fixed in cold acetone for 10 min, examined by the ACIE method or stained with hematoxyclin and eosin(H. and E.) for cytological examination.

5. Histological examination

Biopsies were taken from suspected lesions of the nasopharynx, fixed with 10% formalin, stained with H. and E. and then examined.

RESULTS

1. Positive rate of VCA/IgA antibody

As shown in Tab. 1 among the 12932 person in the age group of 40-59 years, 680 were found to have VCA/IgA antibody with a GMT of 1:39, the positive rate being 5.3%(680/12 932). About 70% of these people had VCA/IgA antibody titers from 1:10 to 1:40. The is a tendency for an increase in the antibody-positive rate and in the GMT with increasing age(Fig. 1). In the different age groups the positive rates of VCA/IgA antibody were 4.7%, 5.3%, 5.6% and 6.2%, respectively and the GMT of the antibody 1:33.5, 1:34.6, 1:40 and 1:50, respectively. The frequency of VCA/IgA antibody for males and females was similar, and the rate 1.2:1(Tab. 2). EA/IgA antibody among VCA/IgA antibody-positive and-negative individuals.

No EA/IgA antibody could be detected in sera from 507 VCA/IgA antibody-negative persons, but 30 out of 680 VCA/IgA antibody-positive individuals had EA/IgA antibody. The positive rate was 4.4%(Tab. 3). The antibody titers ranged from 1:10 to 1:640 with a GMT of 1:41.9.

Tab. 1   Distribution of antibody titer and gmt of VCA/IgA antibody

Group	Positive number and positive rate	Distribution of antibody									GMT of VCA/IgA antibody
		10	20	40	80	160	320	640	2560	Total	
Persons examined	Positive No.(%)	198(29)	92(14)	191(28)	46(7)	107(16)	2(0.2)	35(5)	9(1)	680[1](100)	1:39
NPC patients	Positive No.(%)	1(7.7)		3(23.0)		5(38.5)		4(30.8)		13(100)	1:116

Notes: [1]VCA/IgA antibody-positive rate =5.3%(680/12 932)

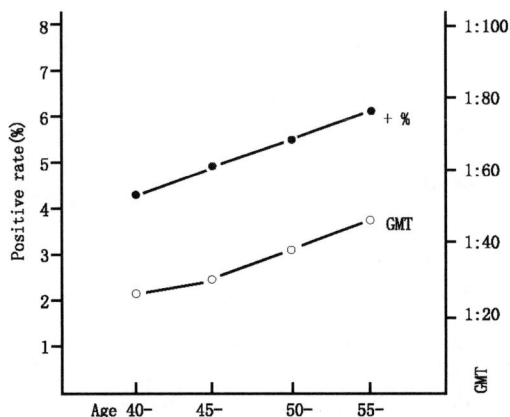

Fig. 1   VCA/IgA antibody-positive rate and GMT in different age groups

Tab. 2   comparison of positive rate of VCA/IgA antibody and detection rate of NPC in males and females

Group	No. of person examined	Positive No.	Positive rate	No. of NPC cases	Detection rate of NPC/100 000
Male	7222	414	5.7	9	124.6
Female	5710	266	4.7	4	70.0
Total	12 932	680	5.3	13	100.5
M:F	1.3:1	1.6:1	1.2:1	2.3:1	1.8:1

Tab. 3 comparison of vca/IgA and EA/IgA antibody

Group	No. of person examined	Positive No. of EA/IgA	Positive rae of EA/IgA(%)
VCA/IgA +	680[1]	30[1]	4.4
VCA/IgA −	507	0	0

Notes: [1] With a GMT of 1:41.9

2. Detection of NPC from the VCA/IgA and EA/IgA antibody-positive persons

Clinical, cytological and histological examinations and the EBNA test were carried out in combination to detected NPC patients from the VCA/IgA and EA/IgA antibody-positive persons. Thirteen NPC cases were finally confirmed histologically (Tab. 4). The frequency of NPC among 680 VCA/IgA antibody-positive persons was 1.9%. Nine out of 13 NPC cases also had EA/IgA antibody. The frequency of NPC among EA/IgA antibody-positive persons was 30%(Tab. 5).

Tab. 4 NPC patients detected by serological mass survey

Case No.	Sex	Age	Histological examination	Clinical stage	Antibody VCA/IgA	EA/IgA
12 660	F	50	Undiff. ca	I	1:10	-
1171	F	46	Poorly diff. ca	I	1:40	-
11 689	M	43	Poorly diff. ca	I	1:40	1:40
361	M	47	Poorly diff. ca	I	1:40	1:40
13 684	F	46	Undiff. ca	I	1:160	1:40
1649	F	42	Poorly diff. ca	I	1:160	—
309	M	50	Poorly diff. ca	I	1:160	1:40
7873	M	57	Poorly diff. ca	I	1:640	1:640
12 735	M	46	Poorly diff. ca	I	1:640	1:40
68	M	50	Poorly diff. ca	II	1:160	-
3433	M	48	Poorly diff. ca	II	1:160	1:40
23	M	50	Poorly diff. ca	II	1:640	1:10
52	M	54	Poorly diff. ca	II	1:640	1:160
GMT					1:144	1:26

Tab. 5 NPC Patients detected from VCA/IgA and EA/IgA antibody-positive person

Group	No. of person examined	No. of NPC	Positive rate of NPC(%)
VCA/IgA +	680	13	1.9
EA/IgA +	30	9	30

The range of VCA/IgA antibody titers for NPC patients was from 1:10-1:640 with a GMT of 1:144, and that of EA/IaA antibody titer for NPC was from 1:10 to 1:640 with a GMT of 1:26(Tab. 4). All NPC patients, except for two with undifferentiated carcinoma, showed poorly differentiated carcinoma. Of 13 patients with NPC, 9 were in stage I and 4 in stage II. The majority of the stage I patients showed no notable tumor, but only some non-specific lesions, such as rough, pale or nodular mucosa.

The detection rate of NPC for 12 932 persons examined was 100.5/100 000, and for males and females it was 124.6/100 000, and 70/100 000, respectively(Tab. 2. Fig. 2). The detection rate of NPC for 680 VCA/IgA antibody-positive persons was 1900/100 000.

DISCUSSION

The positive rate of VCA/IgA antibody was 5. 3%, and the detection rate of NPC among the VCA/IgA antibody-positive persons was 1. 9%. The positive rate of EA/IgA antibody among VCA/IgA antibody-positive persons was 4. 4%, and the detection rate of NPC among the EA/IgA antibody-positive persons was 30%. The difference in the detection rate of NPC between these two groups was 15. 8-fold. These data indicate that only a few VCA/IgA-positive persons eventually become EA/IgA-positive, and that EA/IgA antibody is more specific but not so sensitive for the detection of NPC as VCA/IgA antibody. The test for EA/IgA antibody in serological screening is therefore also valuable for the early diagnosis of NPC, BUT it is necessary to improve the sensitivity of the method. More attention should also be paid to careful and periodic follow-up of the EA/IgA antibody-positive persons.

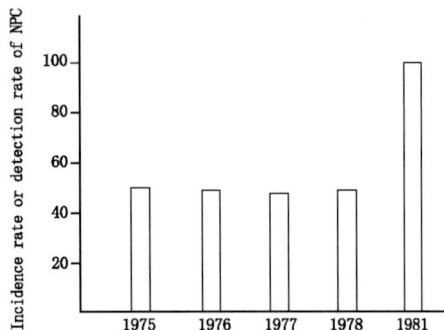

Fig. 2 Comparison of detection rate of NPC for 1981 and incidence rate of NPC for 1975-1978

The detection rate of NPC was 1900/100 000 for 680 VCA/IgA positive persons and 100. 5/100 000 for 12932 persons(age 40 -59) examined. This is 37 times and two times higher, respectively, than the incidence rate(47. 7/100 -50/100)of NPC in the same age group in Wuzhou City(1975-1978)in the retrospective study(Fig. 2). These satisfactory results were obtained by combining all the clinical cytologic -histological data for individuals who were preliminarily screened out by viro-immunological methods. Thus, for example, carcinoma cells with EBNA were found in one case in stage I 2 months before the diagnosis of NPC by cytological and histological examination.

The early diagnosis of NPC means a favorable outcome of radiotherapy. Of 13 NPC patients, 9 were in stage I (70%)and 4 in stage II (30%). Therefore, it is possible to reduce the mortality rate of NPC in Wuzhou City by using the methods mentioned above. The results of the present study further suggest that EB virus in closely associated with NPC. A prospective follow-up study of the whole population is being carried out in Wuzhou City to detect the NPC patients in an early stage and to learn the time sequence: IgA-negative, IgA-positive, NPC and the proportion of NPC which does not get through the IgA-positive step. The positive rate of VCA/IgA antibody is similar for males and females, but the detection rate of NPC for males is higher than that for females. These results agree with the past annual incidence rate for males and females in Wuzhou City, and indicate that there might be some other factors favoring the development of NPC in males.

ACKNOWLEDGEMENTS

We thank Prof. C. H. Huang, Prof C. M. Chu and Dr. de -The for critically reading the manuscript.

REFERENCES

[1] Laboratory of Tumor Viruses of Cancer Institute, Laboratory of Tumor Viruses of Institute of Epidemiology; Department of Radiotherapy of Cancer Institute, Department of Otolaryngology of Beijing Worker-Peasant-Soldier Hospital. Detection of EB virus-specific serum IgA and IgA antibodies from patients with nasopharyngeal carcinoma. Acta microbiol Sin, 1978, 18:253-258.

[2] Pi GH, Zeng Y, Zhao WP, Zhang, QIN. Development of an anticomplement immunoenzyme test for detection of EB virus nuclear antigen(EBNA)and antibody to EBNA. J Immunol Meth, 1981, 44:73-76.

[3] Zeng Y, Liu YX, Lin ZY, Zhen SW, Wei JN, Zhu JS, Zai HJ. Application of immunoenzymatic method and immuno-auto-radiographic method for the mass survey of nasopharyngeal carcinoma. Chinese J Oncol, 1979a, 1:2 -7.

[4] Zeng Y, Liu YX, Lin ZR, Zhen SW, Wei JN, Zhu JS, Zai HS. Application of an immunenzymatic method and an immuno-autoradigraphic method for a mass survey of nasopharyngeal carcinoma. Intervirology, 1980A, 13: 162-168.

[5] Zeng Y, Liu YX, Wei JN, Zhu JS, Lai SL, Wang PZ, Zhong JM, Li RC, Pan WJ, Li EJ, Tan BF. Serological mass survey of nasopharyngeal carcinoma. Acta Acad Med Sin, 1979b, 1: 123-126.

[6] Zeng Y, Pi GH, Zhang Q, Shen SJ, Zhao ML, Ma JL, Dong HJ. Application of anticomplement immunoenzymatic method for the detection of EBNA in carcinoma cells and normal epithelial cells from nasopharynx. Cancer Campaign, Vol. 5. Nasopharyngeal carcinoma. Grundmann et al.(eds). Gustav Fischer Verlag. Stuttgart. New York. 1981, 237-245.

[7] Zhangjiang Medical College, Diagnosis of nasopharyngeal carcinoma by cytological examination of exfoliated cells taken by negative pressure suction. Chinese med J, 1976, 1:45-47.

[In《Int J Cancer》1982, 29:139-141]

Follow-up Studies on Epstein-Barr Virus IgA/VCA Antibody-Positive Persons in Zangwu County, China

ZANG Y[1], ZHONG J M[2], LI L Y[2], WANG P Z[3], TANG H[2], MA Y R[3], ZHU J S[2], PAN W J[2], LIU Y X[4], WEI Z N[3], CHEN J C[2], MO Y K[2], LI E J[3], TAN B F[2]

1. Institute of Virology, Chinese Academy of Medical Sciences, Beijing; 2. Cancer Control Office, Zangwu County; 3. People's Hospital of Guangxi Autonomous Region; 4. Cancer Institute, Chinese Academy of Medical Sciences, Beijing, China

[SUMMARY] Serological mass surveys were carried out in Zangwu County, China, using an immunoenzymatic test. 3533 persons were found to have Epstein-Barr virus(EBV)IgA/VCA antibody among 148 029 persons age 30 years and older who were tested during 1978-1980. Among the IgA/VCA antibody-positive persons, 55 nasopharyngeal carcinoma (NPC)caser were detected. Follow-up studies were carried out yearly on the IgA/VCA antibody-positive persons for 1-3 years, and 32 additional NPC patients were diagnosed. IgA/VCA antibody was detected 8-30 months(average, 13 months) prior to the clinical diagnosis of stage I NPC. There was no marked difference in geometric mean titers of IgA/VCA antibody between the period before onset of NPC and after diagnosis at stage I, but antibody titers were higher during stages II-IV. The NPC detection rates for all persons tested serologically and for IgA/VCA antibody-positive persons, respectively, was 2-and 82-fold the annual incidence of NPC in the general population of the same age group. These data further indicate that serological testing is valuable for the diagnosis of NPC, especially in its early stages, and that EBV may play and important role in the development of NPC.

[Keywords] Epstein-Barr virus; IgA/VCA antibody; Nasopharyngedl carcinoma

INTRODUCTION

148 029 persons aged 30 years or older were screened during 1978-1980 in Zangwu County, Guangxi Autonomous Region, by animmunoenzymatic test[1,2]. 3533 persons were found to have Epstein-Barr virus(EBV)IgA/VCA antibody(≥1∶5). Among these, 55 cases of nasopharyngeal carcinoma(NPC), especially in its early stages, were detected. To study the relationship betwween EBV and NPC, follow-up studies on IgA/VCA antibody-positive person were carried out yearly from 1979 to 1981, anol 32 new NPC cases were detected. The result of this prospective seroepidemiological study are reported here.

MATERIALS AND METHODS

1. Sera
Sera were collected in plastic capillary tubes ty pricking the ear lobe and were stored at -15℃.

2. Immunoenzymatic test
This test was described previously[1]. B95-8 cells and horseradish peroxidase-conjugated antihuman IgA antibody were used for the detection of IgA/VCA antibody.

3. Clinical and histological examination
EBV IgA/VCA antibody-positive persons were examined clinically once a year. Biopsies were taken from suspected NPC cases and from individuals with high IgA/VCA antibody titers(≥1∶80). Sera were again collected and examined.

RESULTS

1. Distribution of EBV IgA/VCA antibody
As shown in Tab. 1, among 148 029 persons tested 3533 persons had IgA/VCA antibody(positive rate, 2.4%). The antibody titers ranged from 1∶5 to 1∶2560 with a geometric mean titer(GMT)of 1∶16. 87% had antibody titers of 1∶5-1∶40, and only 13% had antibody at higher titers(≥1∶80).

2. NPC Patients Detected by Serological Screening
All IgA/VCA antibody-positive persons(3533)were examined clinically and histologically, and biopsies were taken from suspected cases and from persons with high antibody titers(≥1∶80). Among these, 55 cases were diagnosed histologically as NPC(Tab. 2), and 31(57%)of these were in early stages(I and II). The range of IgA/

VCA antibody titers for these NPC patients was from 1 : 10 to 1 : 2560, with a GMT of 1 : 99. 3 cases(62%) had antibody titers of ⩾1 : 80(Tab. 1).

Tab. 1 Distribution of EBV IgA/VCA antibody among NPC patients and normal individuals age 30 years and older in Zangwu County

Item	Antibody titer										Total	GMT
	5	10	20	40	80	160	320	640	1280	2560		
Individuals age 30 years and older												
Number positiver for IgA/VCA antibody	837	967	808	474	335	55	37	10	8	2	3533	1 : 16
Percent positive(%)	23.7	27.3	22.9	13.4	9.5	1.6	1.0	0.3	0.2	0.06	100	
Serological mass survey												
Number of NPC cases	0	4	8	9	12	8	4	4	4	2	55	1 : 99
Percent positive(%)	0	7.3	14.5	16.4	21.8	14.5	7.3	7.3	7.3	3.6	100	
Follow-up study												
Number of NPC cases	0	2	5	4	8	8	2	1	2	0	32	1 : 85
Percent positive(%)	0	6.3	15.6	12.5	25	25	6.3	3.1	6.3	0	100	

3. NPC patients detected by follow -up studies

The IgA/VCA antibody -positive persons were reexamined clinically once a year, and 32 new NPC patients were detected over a 3-year period(Tab. 2). All of the new cases were diagnosed clinically as poorly differentiated squamous cell carcinoma or undifferentiated carcinoma. 21 cases(66%) had IgA/VCA antibody titers of ⩾ 1 : 80. The GMT was 1 : 85(Tab. 1).

Tab. 2 Detection of NPC cases in Zangwu County during 1978 -1980 by serological mass survey and follow -up study

Group	Number of NPC cases					
	carcinoma in situ	stage Ⅰ	stage Ⅱ	stage Ⅲ	stage Ⅳ	total
1978-1980						
Serological mass survey	1	12	19	17	6	55
Follo-up study	0	10	9	11	2	32
Total	1	22	28	28	8	87

As shown in Fig. 1, IgA/VCA antibody was detected 8 -30 months(average, 13 months) prior to the clinical diagnosis of NPC at stage Ⅰ, 10-18 months(average, 14. 4 months) prior to stage Ⅱ, 9 -34 months(average, 17. 3 months) prior to stage Ⅲ, and 12 -24 months(average, 18 months) prior to stage Ⅳ.

There was no marked difference in GMT of IgA/VCA antibody in sera between the period before onset of NPC and the diagnosis made at stage Ⅰ, but antibody titers were higher at stages Ⅱ-Ⅳ(Fig. 2), i. e, when the carcinoma cells metastasized to the cervical lymph nodes.

4. Detection rate of NPC

87 NPC cases were detected among 3533 IgA/VCA antibody -positive persons by serological screening and follow-up studies. The NPC detection rate was 59/100 000 for 148029 persons tested and 2462/100 000 for 3533 IgA/VCA antibody -positive persons. This is 2 -and 82 -fold, respectively, the annual incidence of NPC(30/100 000) in the general population of the same age group in Zangwu County. Similar results were obtained in the city of Wuzhow[3](Tab. 3). These rusults further indicate the close relationship of EBV to NPC.

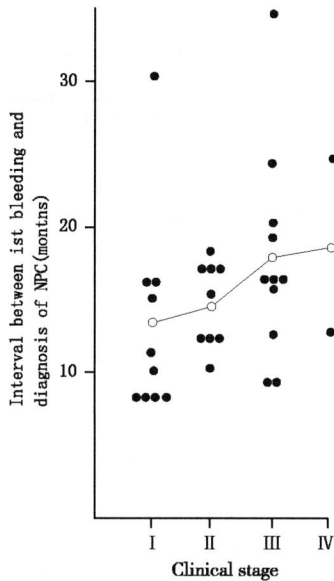

Fig. 1 Follow-up studies on IgA/VCA antibody positive persons.

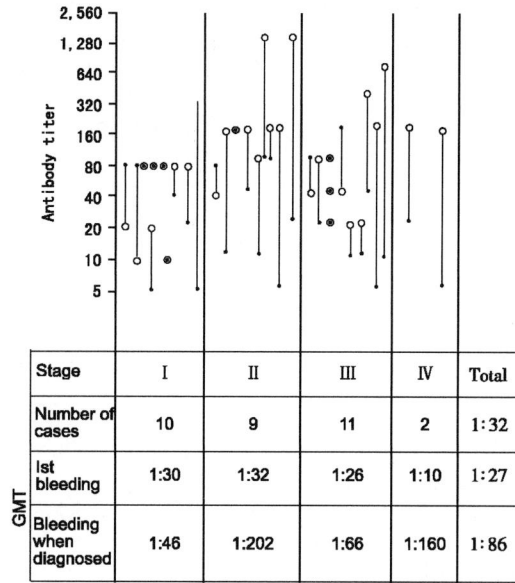

Stage	I	II	III	IV	Total
Number of cases	10	9	11	2	1:32
lst bleeding	1:30	1:32	1:26	1:10	1:27
Bleeding when diagnosed	1:46	1:202	1:66	1:160	1:86

● = First bleeding; ○ = bleeding when diagnosis was confirmed

Fig. 2 Change of titer and GMT of IgA/VCA and body from first bleeding to diagnosis of NPC.

Tab. 3 Comparison of NPC detection and incidence rates

Areas	Number of persons examined	Number positive for IgA/VCA antibody	Number of NPC cases	NPC detection rate among all persons examined	NPC detection rate among IgA/VCA antibody-positive persons	NPC incdence rate per annum
Zangwu County (1978-1980)	148 029	3533	87	59[a](1.96)[b]	2462(82)	30
Wuzhow city(1981)	12 930	680	13	100.5[a](2)	1900(38)	50

Notes: [a] Per 100 000

  [b] Number in parentheses is the detection rate/incidence rate

DISCUSSION

Serological studies indicate that there is a close relationship between EBV and NPC. The detection of IgA/VCA antibody is helpful for the diagnosis of NPC, especially in its early stages[1,2].

The percentage(25.3%)of NPC cases at stage I detected by serological mass surveys was much higher than that(6%)diagnosed in outpatient clinics[4]. 59% of NPC patients diagnosed during follow-up studies were at stages I and II and responded favorably to radiotherapy. 41% of NPC cases were diagnosed at advanced stages(III and IV), because many of the antibody-positive subjects lived in remote areas and clinical examinations were not carried out periodically or the diagnosis was missed at early stages.

IgA/VCA antibody was detected 8-30 months prior to clinical diagnosis of NPC in stage I cases. These results are similar to those reported by Ho et al.[5] and Lanier et al.[6] in their retrospective studies. They found that IgA/VCA antibody was detectable 22-72 months before clinical diagnosis was made in the advanced stages.

How long does IgA/VCA or IgA/EA antibody persist and how many antibody-negative persons become positive? What is the exact proportion of IgA/VCA or IgA/EA-positive and-negative individuals who develop NPC?

These are questions that remain to be answered. More than 25 000 serum samples from normal individuals of age 40 years and older from the city of Wuchow were collected and stored at the Institute of Virology, Chinese Academy of Medical Sciences, Beijing. Careful and periodical follow-up studies on IgA/VCA -or IgA/EA -positive and -negative individuals should answer these questions. Successful intervention against EBV may provide further evidence for the relationship between EBV and NPC. A study of the inhibition of EBV by retinoids is in progress.

Serological diagnosis of NPC is now widely used in China. It is possible to reduce the mortality of NPC through early detection and treatment even though the exact etiological causes have not been elucidated.

The IgA/VCA antibody-positive rate from persons examined in 1978 was low, perhaps due to the grade III, Koch-light horseradish peroxidase(Rz = 0. 62)used. Reexamination of sera from these persons was sone in 1980, using grade I horseradish peroxidase, and a high positive rate was obtained. An additional explanation might be that we were not as skilled at the technique during the first serological screening in 1978.

ACKNOWLEDGMENTS

We thank Prof C H. Huang and Prof. C M. Chu for critical reading of the manuscript.

REFERENCES

[1] Zeng Y, Liu Y, Liu C, Chen S, Wei J, Zhu J, Zai H. Application of an immunoenzymatic method and an immunoautoradiographic method for a mass survey of nasopharyngeal carcinoma. Intervirology,1980,13:162-168.

[2] Zeng Y,Liu YX, Wei JN, Zhu JS, Cai SL, Wang PZ, Zhong JM, Li RC, Pan WJ, Li E J. Tan BF. Serological mass survey of nasopharyngeal carcinoma. Acta Acad Med Sin I,1979,1:123-126.

[3] Zeng Y, Zhang LG, Li HY, Jan M C, Zhang Q, Wa Y C, Wang Y S, Su G R. Serological mass survey for early detection of nasopharyngeal carcinoma in Wuzhow city, China, Int J Cancer, 1982, 29: 139 -141.

[4] Li CC, Chen JJ, Li BJ. Study on precancer ous changes 1. Screening for early detection of nasopharyngeal carcinoma and hyperplastic lesions in nasopharynx. Cancer Chin, 1982, 2:81-83.

[5] Ho J H C, Kwan H C, Ng M H, de-The G. Serum IgA antibodies to EBV capsid antigens preceding symptoms of nasopharyngeal carcinoma. Lancet I,1978,;436 -437.

[6] Lanier AP, Henle W, Benden T R, Henle G, Talbot M L. Epstein-Barr virus-specific antibody titers in seven Alaskan natives before and after diangosis of nasopharyngeal carcinoma, Int J Cancer, 1980,26:133-137.

[In《Intervirology》1983,20:190-194]

Epstein-Barr Virus Early Antigen Induction in Raji Cells by Chinese Medicinal Herbs

ZENG Y[1], ZHONG J M[2], MO Y K[2], MIAO X C[1]

1. Institute of Virology, Chinese Academy of Medical Sciences, Beijing; 2. Cancer Control Office of Zangwu County, Guangxi Autonomous Region, China

[SUMMARY]　Ether extracts of 495 Chinese medicinal herbs from 106 families were studied for Epstein-Barr virus (EBV) early antigen(EA) induction in the Raji cell system. 15 herbs from 10 families were found to have inducing activity. Water extracts of the same herbs also had inducing activity, but it was not as strong. The significance of these herbs in the activation of EBV in vivo and their relation to the development of nasopharyngeal carcinoma are disussed. No EA-inducing activity was found in 73 samples of 14 different foods tested.

[Keywords]　Epstein-Barr virus; Early antigen; Raji cells; Chinese medicinal herbs

INTRODUCTION

Ito and coworkers[1,2] reported that the Raji cell inducing(n-butyrate)system detects most, if not all, of the known promoters derived from Euphorbiaceae plants and their active components, including TPA and related compounds(mezerein and teleocidin). This test system is simple to perform and reproducible. Our previous data[3,4] showed that the geometric mean titer of complement-fixing antibody to Epstein-Barr virus(EBV)in sera from persons aged 20 years and older in highrisk areas for nasopharyngeal carcinoma(NPC)was significantly higher than that from persons of the same age group in NPC low -risk areas, and that the positive rate of IgA/VCA antibody to EBV from normal individuals in NPC high -risk areas increased with increasing age. These data indicate that EBV is more active in persons living in NPC high-risk areas, as a result of the activation of EBV by internal or environmental factors. Therefore, it is necessary to determine whether factors causing activation of EBV are present in foods, Chinese medicinal herbs, etc. As reported here, by using the Raji cell induction system, EBV activtors were found in some of the Chinese medicinal herbs tested.

MATERIALS AND METHODS

1. Cells

Raji cells carrynig the EBV genome were cultivated in RPMI 1640 medium containing 20% calf serum. No spontaneous induction of early antigen(EA)in Raji cells was found. Viability of the cells was checked before and after treatment.

2. Chinese medicinal herbs

495 Chinese medicinal herbs were obtained from pharmacies in Beijing and Zangwu County of Guangxi Autonomous Region.

3. Foods

Peanut oil, pork oil. salted fish, pickles, honey and some dry salt vegetables were tested.

4. Plant Extraction

The method for ether extraction was as described by Ito et al.[1] Briefly, 10g of test material was cutinto small pieces and extracted with 100ml of ether for 72h. The ether solution was then evaporated, and the residual oily extract was used as test substance. Finally, the extract was dissolved in ethanol as a 10mg/ml stock solution and was stored at-10℃. The water extract was made by adding 50ml of distilled water to 5g of test material. After boilling for 10 min and centrifugation at low speed, the supernatant was collected and stored at -10℃ as a stock solution (100mg ml)

5. Experimental Procedure

Raji cells were cultivated in RPMI 1640 medium containing 20% calf serum and 4mmol/L n-butyrate; the test substance was added at varying concentrations. After cultivation at 37℃ for 48h, smears were mede from the cell suspensions and EA-positive cells were detected by the immunoenzymatic test[4]. The test substance was also added to Raji cell suspensions in medium without n-butyrate. Croton oil, Euphorbia lathyris, Euphorbia kansur and tung oil, which were fund to be positive by Ito et al.[1,5] were used as controls(with and without n-butyrate). In each assay 500 cells were counted, and the ratio of EA-positive cells was recorded.

RESULTS

1. EA induction in Raji cells by ether extracts of test materials

495 Chinese medicinal herbs belonging to 106 families and 73 samples of 14 different foods were tested for EBV EA-inducing activity. The results are shown in Tab. 1. Among 495 Chinese medicinal herbs, Daphne genkwa, Stellera chamaejasme, Wikstroemia chamaedaphne, Wisktroemia indica, Edgeworthia chrysantha, Premna fulva and Datura stramonium showed strong activity in inducing EA-positive cells, with the highest positive rates ranging from 43% to 53%. The other 8 herbs(Caesalpinia sappan, Desmodium styracifolium, Sparganium stoloniferum, Tinospora sp, Aleuritopteris argentea, Clematis intricata, Knoxia valerianoides and Angelica pubescens)showed a weaker positive reaction, with the highest positive rate ranging from 1% to 17%. The EA cell-positive rate of 4 mmol/L n-butyrate alone was only 1%. These 15 herbs belong to 10 plant families(Tab. 2). The controls(Euphorbia kansui, Euphorbia lathyris, croton oil and tung oil)belong to the Euphorbiaceae family and showed strong EA -inducing activity, with the highest positive rates ranging from 42% to 53%. Eleven herbs as well as the 4 controls(Tab. 1)also induced EA-positive cells in medium without n-butyrate, but percentage positive was not as high. The other 4 herbs were negative.

Tab. 1   Effect of Chinese medicinal herbs on EBV EA induction in Raji cells

Medicinal herbs	Ether extraction[a]				Water extraction[b]			
	butyrate in assay medium(μg/ml)		without butyrate (μg/ml)		butyrate in assay medium(mg/ml)		without butyrate (mg/ml)	
	10	10	10	10	10	10	10	10
Daphne genkwa	46[c]	45	1	2	15	34	2	1
Stellera chamaejasme	36	46	2	2	2	1	2	1
Wikstroemia chamaedaphne	32	53	1	2	2	20	0.4	1
Wikstroemia indica	42	50	4	2	25	17	1	0
Edgeworihia chrysantha	43	28	1	0	0	0	0	0
Caesalpinia sappan	8	4	0	0	0	0	0	0
Desmodium styracifolium	6	4	0	0	0	0	0	0
Premna fulva	52	42	2	0.4	0.2	0.2	0	0
Sparganium stoloniferum	16	2	0.4	0	0	0	0	0
Datura stramonium	50	25	1	0	1	0	0	0
Tinospora sp	7	3	0.2	0	0	0	0	0
Aleuritopteris argentea	6	17	1	0	0	0	0	0
Clematis intricata	3	2	0.4	0	0.2	0.2	0	0
Knoxia valerianoides	3	1	0	0	0	0	0	0
Angelica pubescens	1	0	0	0	0	0	0	0
Controls								
Euphorbia kansui	28	37	1	1	5	4	1	0
Euphorbia lathyris	30	53	2	2	38	33	4	3
Croton oil	18	40	1	0.4	39	28	2	4
Tung oil	38	42	1	1				

Notes: [a] Stock ether extraction = 10mg/ml; [b] Stock water extraction = 100mg/ml; [c] = Percent EA-positive cells. 4mmol/L n-butyrate alone gave a 1% positive rate

No EA -inducing activity was found in 73 samples from 14 different foods.

Tab. 2　Chinese medicinal herbs having EA -inducing activity from different families

Family	Species
Thymelacaceae	Daphne genkwa
	Stellera chamaejasme
	Wikstroemia chamaedaphne
	Wikstroemia indica
	Edgeworthia chrysanthea
Leguminosae	Caesalpinia sappan
	Desmodium styracifolium
Verbenaceae	Premna fulva
Sparganiaceae	Sparganium stoloniferum
Solanaceae	Datura stramonium
Menispermaceae	Tinospora sp.
Sinopteridaceae	Aleuritopteris argentea
Ranunculaceae	Clematis intricata
Rubiaceae	Knoxia valerianoides
Umbelliferae	Angelica pubescens

2. EA induction in Raji cells by water extracts of test materials

As shown in Tab. 1, EA-inducing activity was also found in water extracts of Daphne genkwa, Stallera chamaejasme, Wisktroemia chamaedaphne, Wikstroemia indica, Premnafulve, Datura stramonium and Clematis intricata, as well as 3 control herbs when the medium contained n -butyrate, but their activity was not as strong as that of ether extracts under the same experimental conditions. The EA cell-positive rate ranged from 0.2% to 25%. Water extracts of the other 8 herbs were negative. Water extracts of 4 herbs from the Tyhmelacaceae family in medium without n-butyrate also showed weak activity.

DISCUSSION

Immunological studies strongly suggest that EBV plays a causative role in the development of NPC. Environmental and genetic factors, and their relationship to EBV, are also considered to be involved in the development of NPC. The present results showed that among 495 Chinese medicinal herbs from 106 families, 15 herbs from 10 families were found to have EA -inducing activity. Daphne genkwa also was found by Ito[5] to have EA-inducing activity. These data extended the work of Ito et al.[1] and confirmed that the Raji cell-inducing system is a useful model for the detection of EBV EA-inducing activity indifferent materials. Some herbs having EA-inducing activity belong to the same family, such as the Thymelacaceae family where 5 species have EA-inducing activity and the Euphorbiaceae family where at least 10 species were found by Ito et al[1]., to have such activity, or they belong to the same group with similar pharmacological action. For example, 5 herbs(Daphne genkwa, Knoxia valerianoides, Euphorbia kansui, Euphorbia lathyris, and croton oil)are all purgative drugs.

Chinese medicinal herbs are usually administered in solution by boiling the herbs in water. Our findings showed that water extracts of herbs also have EA-inducing activity, but not as strong as that of ether extracts. Int et al[6]. reported that n-butyric acid in the culture medium of Fusobacterium nucleatum isolated from the oral cavity and upper respiratory tract was able to induce EBV. n-Butyrate plus extracts of the herbs mentioned above markedly enhanced the induction of EA antigen in Raji cells. For example, the EA cell-positive rate induced by n-butyrate plus water extract of Wikstroemia indica was 25%. This herb is produced in Guangdong, Guangxi, Fujian provinces and others. It is the main component for making tablets for detoxication and antiphlogosis in Guangdong province. The Premna fulva extract is used for treatment of rheumatism. Tung oil is a strong inducer, and people living in NPC high-risk areas come in close contact with tung oil trees. The relationship between activation of EBV by these herbs and the development of NPC needs to be further studied.

ACKNOWLEDGMENTS

We thank Prof. Z W. Xie for identifiction of the Chinese medicinal herbs and Prof. C H. Huang, Prof. C M. Chu, and Prof Y. Ito for critical reding of the manuscript.

REFERENCES

［1］ Ito Y, Yanase S, Fujita J, Harayama T, Takashima M, Imanaka H. Ashort-term in vitro assay for promoter substances using human lymphoblastoid cells latently infected with Epstein-Barr virus. Cancer Lett, 1981,13:29-37.

［2］ Kawanishi M,Sugawara K,Ito Y. Epstein-Barr virus-induced early peptides in Raji and NC37 cells activated by diterpene ester TPA in combination with n-butyrate. Virology, 1981,115:406-409.

［3］ Tumor Control Team of Zhongshan County, Department of Microbiology of Zhongshan Medical College, Laboratory of Tumor Viruses of Cancer Institute,and Institute of Epidemiology of the Chinese Academy of Medical Sciences:A study on the complement fixing antibody to EB virus in groups of normal individuals in Guangdong province and Beijing. Chinese J. ENT, 1978,1:23-25.

［4］ Zeng Y, Liu YX, Liu ZY, Zhen SW, Wei JN, Zhu JS, Zai HJ. Application of immunoenzymatic method and immunoauto-radiographic method for the mass survey of nasopharyngeal carcinoma. Chinese J Oncol, 1979,1:2-7.

［5］ Ito Y. Personal commun,1981.

［6］ Ito Y,Kishishita M,Yanase S. Induction of Epstein-Barr virus antigens in human lymphoblastoid P3HR-1 cells with culture fluid of Fusobacterium nucleatum. Cancer Res, 1980,40:4329-4330.

［In《Intervirology》1983,19:201-204］

Epstein-Barr Virus-Activating Principle in the Ether Extracts of Soils Collected from under Plants which Contain Active Diterpene Esters

ITO Yohei[1], OHIGASHI Hajme[2], KOSHIMIZU Koichi[2], ZENG Yi[3]

1. Department of Micro biology, Faculty of Medicine; 2. Department of Food Science and Technology, Faculty of Agriculture, Kyoto University, Kyoto 606(Japan) and; 3. Institute of Virology, Chinese Acodemy of Medical Sciences, Beijing(China)

[SUMMARY]　Soil samples were collected from the ground under the plants of Euphorbiaceae and Thymelaeaceae known to possess Epstein -Barr virus -activating diterpene esters. In a test system, the ether extracts of such soil samples at a concentration of $20\mu g/ml$ induced Epstein-Barr virus early antigen in approximately 5%-25% of the non -producer Raji cells. These findings suggest a possible interaction between plant -derived diterpene esters and the human system, and provide a new aspect in considering the cause of Epstein -Barr virus -associated diseases, particularly nasopharyngeal carcinoma.

INTRODUCTION

The epstein-Barr virus(EBV)-activating diterpene esters are widely distributed among plants of the Euphorbiaceae and Thymelaeaceae families, many of which are currently used as folk remedies in areas where the EBV-associated diseases, Burkitt's lymphoma(BL) and nasopharyngeal carcinoma(NPC), are endemic[2-4]. The Chinese tung oil tree(Aleurites fordii), a member of Euphorbiaceae, is a popular plant in the southen provinces of China and is cultivated chiefly for an industrial purpose. The plant perse is also used as a herbal drug[6].

While investigating possible routes through which active diterpene esters might gain access to the human system, we came across an idea that such plant constituents could be released into the soil where they are growing and subsequently adsorbed on to the soil particles. These particles may later enter the nasal cavity in the form of soil dust.

Here we report that highly active substances capable of inducing EBV early antigen(EA) in the non -producer Raji cell system[5] cand be extracted from soil samples collected under the Aleurites fordii and other Euphorbiaceae and Thymelaeaceae phants with such activities.

MATERIALS AND METHODS

The EBV genome -carrying human lymphoblastoid Raji cells were cultivated in RPMI 1640 medium containing 10% fetal calf serum, 100 units of penicllin and $250\mu g/ml$ of streptomycin. Under these culture conditions, our Raji subline exerted a spontaneous induction rate of EBV EA of less than 0.01%. The cells were adjusted to a density of 1×10^6 cells/ml and incubated with 4mmol/L n-butyrate and various test extracts. 12 -O-Tetradecanoylphorbol-13 -acetate(TPA) served as a positive control for assessing the activity of the extracts. Assays containing only n-butyrate were used as negative controls.

The soil samples(20g) were collected from the ground under the plants within a distance of 0.5m from the base of the stem and to a depth of 0.2m from the soil surface. The samples were extracted with an equal volume of ether for 20 min at room temperature(20℃). After evaporating the solvent, the crude extracts were weighed and redissolved in dimethylsulfoxide(DMSO) as a stock solution(10mg/ml). The extracts were prepared to a final concentration of 100, 29, $4\mu g/ml$ and tested in the assay system. Cell smears from a 48h culture were prepared on glass slides, airdried, and fixed in acetone at room temperature for 10 min. The activated Raji cells expressing EBV EA were stained with EA(+) VCA(+) serum(titer 1 : 1280) from a patient with NPC using an indirect immunofluorescent method[1]. The NPC serum was used at a dilution of 1 : 40. Untreated cultures served as the controls. In each assay, at least 500 cells were counted randomly and the results were read. The number of viable cells in the culture were determined by the methylene-blue exclusion test.

The n -butyrate and other chemical reagents were purchased from Nararai Chemicals Ltd. Kyoto, Japan. The TPA was obtained from the Chemicals for Cancer Research, Inc. Minnesota, USA. The high-titer NPC serum was a gift of Prof. H. Hattori, Department of Otorhinolaryngology, Kobe University School of Medicine.

RESULTS AND DISCUSSION

An interaction between higher plants involving chemicals which are shed by one species and affect the growth and other biological conditions of the other plant is termed allelopathy[7]. Such chemicals are released from the living plants by rain -wash, root excretion or exudation, decomposition of fallen leaves, flowers, fruits and dead remains of roots. Thus, it is feasible that EBV-activating diterpene esters of Euphorbiaceae and Thymelaeaceae plants may appear in the soil surrounding the organism.

As expected, the ether extracts of soil samples collected from under the plants of the 2 families exerted EBV - activating capacity. Such results are shown in Tab. 1. On the contrary, the extracts of soil samples taken from under the plants without such activity and from randomly selected areas of our university campus and other places showed little or no EBV EA-inducing effect.

In order to carry out a more precise survey of the EBV-activating substance(s) contained in the soil around the plant, we selected a Chinese tung oil tree, growing in the botanical garden of Kyoto College of Pharmacy as a model(Fig. 1). The soil samples were collected in a southerly direction at distances of 0.5, 1.0 and 2.0m from the base of the tree trunk. The data show that the EBV-activationg effect of the soil extracts is highest in the sample from 0.5 m and decreases as the distance from the base increases(Tab. 2). The activity of soil samples from the nearest point(0.5m) is greater than or equal to the positive TPA control(10ng/ml).

Tab. 1 Induction of Epstein-Barr virus EA in human lymphoblastoid Raji cells with extracts of soil samples from under various plants

Soil samples from	Inducing extracts (μg/ml)[a]	EA positive cells (%)	Cell viability (%)	Soil samples from	Inducing extracts (μg/ml)[a]	EA positive cells (%)	Cell viability (%)
Under specines							
(family) of plants							
Ficus elastica	20	0.1[b]	49.1	soil	4	0.1	74.4
Sapium japonica	20	26.5	81.4	(Moraceae)	4	0.1	42.5
(Euphorbiaceae)	4	26.0	86.4	Vinca rosea	20	0.1	61.5
Sapium sebiferum							
(Euphorbiaceae)	20	23.8	77.6	(Apocynaceae)	4	0.1	42.4
Codiaeum uariegatum	20	12.0	55.8	Diospyros kaki(Ebenaceae)	20	0.1	64.7
(Euphorbiaceae)	4	9.8	41.7	Castanea crenata(Fagaceae)	20	0.1	67.9
Euphorbia lathyris	20	3.6	45.4	Control area and material			
(Euphorbiaceae)	4	7.5	51.1	Campus ground	20	0.4	65.9
Daphne odora	20	15.6	49.3	(Kyoto U)	4	0.3	59.3
(Thymelaeaceae)	4	10.5	65.3	Personal garden(Prof T)	20	0.1	86.7
Edgeworthia papyrifera							
(Thymelaeaceae)	20	5.9	73.9	Commercial gardeing	20	0.1	65.2

Notes: [a] Dissolved in DMSO and used with 4mmol/L n-butyrate in the assay[5]; [b] Represents figure less than or equal to 0.1%.

Recently we have observed that the EBV-inducing activity of tung oil can withstand heating at 100℃ for over 6h(data not shown). Such durability may accord with the notion that the EBV-activating principle(s) released into the soil from the plants may persist in an active form for a considerable length of time. Soil particles carrying such principles may be blown up as dust and gain access to the mucous membrane of the nasopharynx, eventually leading to the emergence of malignancy.

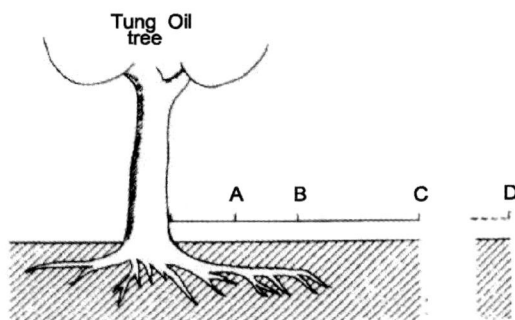

A＝0.5 m，B＝1.0m，C＝2.0m，D＝distant point

Fig. 1　Scheme for collecting soil samples from under Chinese tung oil tree(aleurites fordii).

Tab. 2　Epstein-barr virus activation with ether extracts of soil samples from under the active diterpene esters-containing plant(aleurites fordii)

Soil sample[a]	Concentration of extract(μg/ml)[b]	EA-positive cells(%)	Cell viability(%)
A	100	0.1[c]	9.8
	20	23.0	74.5
	4	3.8	75.5
B	100	0.1	8.1
	20	11.3	79.6
	4	4.3	84.9
C	100	0.1	23.7
	20	6.7	74.5
	4	0.2	68.2
D	20	0.1	80.5
Controls TPA	0.01[b]	21.0	86.7
n-Butyrate	4mmol/L[d]	0.1	70.0

[a] Refer to the codes given in Fig. 1；[b] Dissolved in DMSO and used with 4mmol/L n-butyrate[5]；[c] Represents figure less than or equal to 0.1%；[d] Used alone

ACKNOWLEDGEMENTS

We thank Dr. Katsumi Goto，Kyoto College of Pharmacy for his kind cooperation in collecting soil samples and Mr. Peadar Mac-Gabhan for his assistnce in editing the manuscripth. We also with to thank H. Tokuda and S. Yanase for performing the immunofluorescent tests. This work was supported in part by a grant-in-aid for Cancer Research from the Ministry of Education，Science and Culture of Japan and，by a grant from Japanese Human Cancer Virus Task Force.

REFERENCES

[1]　Henle G，Henle W. Immunofluorescence in cells derived from Burkitt's lymphoma. J. Bacteriol，1966，91：1248-1256.

[2]　Hirayama T，Ito Y. A new view of the etiology of nasopharyngeal carcinoma. Prev. Med，1981，10：614-622.

[3]　Ito Y，Kawanishi M，Harayama T，Takabayashi S Combined effect of the extracts from Croton tiglium, Euphorbia lathyris or Euphorbia tirucalli and n-butyrate on Epstein-Barr virus expression in Human lymphoblastoid P3HR-1 and Raji cells. Cancer Letters，1981，12：175-180.

[4]　Ito Y，Kishishita M，Morigaki T，Yanase S，Hirayama，T，Induction and intervention of Epstein-Barr virus expression in

human lymphoblastoid cells: A siulation model for study of cause and prevention of nasopharyngeal carcinoma and Burkitt's lymphoma. Cancer Campaign,1981, 5:255-262.

[5]　Ito Y, Yanase S, Fujita J, Harayama T, Takashima M, Imanaka H. A short-term in vitro assay for promoter substances using human lymphoblastoid cells latently infected with Epstein-Barr virus. Cancer Letters, 1981, 13:29-37.

[6]　Ito Y, Yanase S, Tokuda H, Kishishita M, Ohigashi H, Hirota M, Koshimizu K. Epstein-Barr virus activation by tung oil. extracts of Aleurites fordii and its diterpene ester HHPA. Cancer Letters, 1983, 18:87-95.

[7]　Muller C, H, Chou CH. Phytotoxins: an ecological phase of phytochemistry. In: Phytochemical Ecology, 1972, 201-216. Editor J B Harborne. Academic Press, London.

[In《Cancer Letters》1983, 19: 113-117]

Comparative Evaluation of Various Techniques to Detect EBV DNA in Exfoliated Nasopharyngeal Cells

Pi G H[1,2], Desgranges C[2], Bornkamm G W[3], Shen S J[1], Zeng Y[1], de-The G[2]

1. Institute of Virology, Chinese Academy of Medical Sciences, Beijing(People's Republic of China); 2. Laboraloire d Epidemiologie el d. Immunouirologic des Tmmerurs, Faculte de Medecine Alexis Carrel. 69372 Lyon Crder 2(France)3. Institute fur Virologie, Zentrum fur Hggiene, Freiburg(Federal Republic of Germang), and4. Zhanjiang Medical College, Zhanjiang(People's Republic of China)

[SUMMARY] Exfoliated epithelial cells from nasopharynx of 27 individuals were collected with a low-negative-pressure suction apparatus. These cells were examined cytologically and stained for Epstein-Barr virus(EBV) nuclear antigen on touch smears by immunoperoxidase. DNA was extraeled from the remaining cells and studied for the presence of EBV sequences by blot and spot hybridization. In the 22 positive nasopharyngeal carcinoma cases(confirmed by clinical, histological and cytological examination) EBV DNA was found with both techniques in 21 cases, while in the 5 cases of chronic inflammation without tumorous cells, no EBV DNA was detected.

[Keywords] Epstein Barr virus; Nasopharyngeal carcinoma; DNA hybridization; Exfoliated cells; China

INTRODUCTION

The presence of the Epstein-Barr virus(EBV) genome in the epithelial tumorous cells of nasopharyngeal carcinoma(NPC) is now well docnmented[16,11,4]. An《outstanding feature》of NPC is also the presence of EBV-specific IgA antibodies in the sera and saliva of the patients[8,9,5].

The presence of these EBV-specific IgA antibodies appears before the tumour is clinically detectable[10]. Recent serological mass surveys in China[17,19] have shown that it is possible to detect early NPC cases, using antivirus capsid antigen IgA antibodies. A proportion of these IgA-positive individuals exhibit EBV DNA and Epstein-Barr nuclear antigen(EBNA) in their nasopharynx[6], believed to represent precancerous conditions.

In the present study, we compared two sensitive techniques for DNA detection(blot versus spot hybridization) on exfoliated cells collected from the nasopharynx by negative-pressure suction[20]. This procedure of cell collection does not traumatize the nasopharyngeal mucosa and allows to have sufficient celluar DNA for spot hvbridization, which is much easier to apply to large numbers of specimens than is blot hybrdization.

MATERIALS AND METHODS

Twenty-seven individuals 22 histologically confirmed NPC cases at different stages of the disease and 5 clinically suspected but histologically unconfirmed NPC. subjects from the Zhanjiang eity of the People's Republic of China were investigated.

1. Specimens collected by negative-pressure suction technique

Exfoliated cells from the nasopharynx were aspira led by negative-pressure suction(30mmHg) with an S-Shaped aspiration device after 10% dicaine had been sprayed into the oropharyngeal cavity, as previously described be the Zhanjiang Medical College[20]. The cells, including small clumps of tiseue eollerted on a silk net in the head of the suction apparatus, could be resuspended in buffer, centrifuged and divided into 3 parts: one part was fixed in 10% formalin, stained with haemalun-eosin and examined cytologically, whilst the remaining two parts were used for DNA extraction and EBNA detection, respectively.

2. Detection of EBV DNA by molecular hybridization

After washing in Hank's solution, exfoliated cells from the second of the three parts collected(see above) were resuspended in 0.05mol/L Tris. pH 8.1, 10mmol/L EDTA and 1% sarkosyl(W/V), and digested with pronase(1mg/ml pre-incubated for 1h at 37℃) for at least 2h at 37℃. After two phenol extractions, the DNA was precipitated by two volumes of ethanol, redissolved in 10mmol/L Tris, pH 7.4 and 1mmol/L EDTA, and digested with RNase(20μg/ml) for 1h at 37℃. After two further phenol extractions, DNA was again precipitated by ethanol and dissolved in 10mmol/L Tris, pH 7.4 and 1mmol/L EDTA.

AGIE = anti-complement immunoenzymatic(test); acif = anti-complement immunofiuorescence(test); EBNA = epstein-Barr nuclear antigen; EBV = Epstein-Barr virus; NPC = nasopharyngeal carcinoma.

3. Blot transfer hybridizalion technique

A total of $16\mu g$ of DNA from each specimen was digested with the restriction endonuclease Pst I(Providencia stuarti, Boehringer Mannheim, Gn. bH) which cleaves four times within the internal EBV repeat[7]. After extraction with cloroform/isoamylalcohol(24/1), the DNA was concentrated by ethanol precipitation and loaded onto 0. 8% horizontal agarose gels and then run for 4-5h at 15-50 V in Tris-acetate buffer(40mmol/L Tris-acetate, pH 7. 8mmol/L EDTA). Bands were visualized on a 254 nm transilluminator(UV prducts, San Gabriel) and photographed with a《Polaroid》camera with a 《 Kodak 》wratten 23A filler. Fragments were transferred to nitrocellulose by the Southern's method[15]. DNA from an EBV-negative cell line. JM[14] was included on each gel as a negative control. As positive controls we used 500 or 50pg B95-8(EBV-transforming virus). EBV DNA(1 or 0. 1 viral genome copy per cell) and an 8-pg internal viral repeat(1 repeat per cell) added to $16\mu g$ JM DNA. The internal repeat (IR) of B95-8 virus DNA cloned in pBR 322[7](IR + pBR 322 = pSL9) was labelled by nick-translation with ^{32}P-dCTP(Amersham; 400 Ci/mmol) as previously described[6].

Hybridization was carried out for 4 days at 42℃ in polyethylene bags in buffer containing 50% formamid, $5 \times SSC(1 \times SSC = 0. 15mol/L$ sodium chloride + 0. 015mol/L sodium citrate),0. 02% bovine serum albumin, 0. 02% polyvinylpyrolidone, 0. 02% Ficoll[3], 20mmol/L sodium phosphate, $200\mu g/ml$ of sheared denatured salmon sperm DNA and 10^6 cpm/ml heat-denatured labelled probe.

The volume of the hybridization reaction was about 0. 1ml/cm^2. Before hybridization, the filters were incubated for 1-2 days at the same temperature with a slightly modified buffer(0. 05 mol/L sodium phosphate, $500\mu g/ml$ salmon sperm DNA and 5 × Denhardt solution) without the labelled prbe. After hvbridzation, blots were washed twice in 2 × SSC and 0. 1% sodium dodecyl sulphate(SDS) at room temperature, followed by 4 washes in 0. 1 SSC and 0. 1% SDS each wash lasting 30 min at 50℃. Blots were exposed to《Kodak Boyal X-omat 》film at-70℃ by using an intensifying screen(Du Pent Cronex lightning-Plus).

4. Spot hybridization

The detection of EBV DNA by the spol technique was first described by Brandsma and Miller[2], by placing the cells directly onto nitrocellulose lillers. With tumour specimens, it is difficult to accurately determine the mumber of cells; so we placed on the filter amounts of 0. 1, 0. 5 and $1\mu g$ of DNA from each specimen and let them dry. After 7 min in 0. 5mol/L NaOH, the lixation was carried out for 10 min in 0. 1mol/L NaOH and 1. 5mol/L NaCl and neutralization was allowed for 2 min in 0. 2mol/L Tris HCl, pH 7. 5 and 2mmol/L EDTA. After two washings in 2 × SSC, the filter was dried for 1h at room temperature and for 2h at 80℃. Hybridization and prebridization were then carried out as for the blot technique, but we observed that a temperature of 50℃ was better as it produced less nonspecific background.

As controls, 7 well-known EBV DNA were used: K3(NPC tumour, positive for EBV), A, B and C(3 tumours for the head and neck, negative for EBV). Raji(a lymphoblastoid cell line, positive for EBV) and JM and Molt(two lymphoblastoid cell lines, negative for EBV).

5. Anticomplement immunoenzymatic(ACIE) test for EBNA detection

The third part of the collected(see above) was treated for EBNA detection. The anti-complement immunoenzymatic(ACIE) test, previouslv described by Zeng et al[8] and Pi et al[12].(a simple modification of the ACIE test described by Reedman and Klein[13], was carried out in the ficld. The anti-complement C3 antiserum was prepared in China by the immunization of rabbits with human C3 adsorbed on insulin(titre of 1/16 to 1/64 by double immunodiffusion).

Labelling of the anti-C3 with horseradish peroxidase was performed as described by Avrameas[1]. EBV-negative French human sera were used as a source of complement, and balanced salt solution(BSS) as diluent. The positive or negative EBNA reference sera and the complement(diluted 1/10) were added onto the smears for 1h at 37℃. After three washings in BSS, the anti-C3 horseradish peroxidase conjugate was added for 30 min at 37℃, washed three times again in BSS, stained with diaminobenzene and H_2O_2 and then examined.

RESULTS

1. Cytological and histological examination

Among the 27 specimens, 22 were confirmed histologically and 24 cytologically as NPC cases(see Tab. 1). The five individuals clinically suspected of NPC(cases 11, 12, 14, 20 and 27) were histopathologically labelled as hyperplasia(cases 11, 14 and 27) or metaplasia(cases 12 and 20).

2. Detection of EBV markers in cell smears

(1) DNA detection

Sufficient cells were obtained by aspiration to yield about $50\mu g$ of cellular DNA, i. e. enough to carry out experiments with different restriction enzymes. By blot transfer hybridization with the laberlled internal EBV repeat (after digestion with Pst I), we obtained 2 major positive bands in 21 of the 22 NPC cases. The quantity of delected EBV DNA was too low in5 of them(cases 1, 17, 19,22 and 26) to be detected by blot hybridzation within 20h exposure, but was seen after 5 days(Fig. 1). No EBV DNA was detected in the 5 non-NPC specimens(cases 11, 12, 14, 20 and 27). For some tumours there were more than 2 major bands, due to partial digestion of both the products and the ragment adjaccnl to the internal repeat which contains part of the internal sequeuces(Fig. 1). On the right-hand side of Fig. 1 can be seen the blots of seven cellular DNA exposed for 5 days, and some of the samples which appeared negative after 20h of exposure(see left-had side of Fig. 1) were now clearly positive.

Tab. 1 Clinical and cytological data compared to EBV markers in exfoliated cells from nasopharyngeal mucosa of 27 Chinese subjects.

Case n°	Clinical stage of NPC	Tumorous cells by cytology	Tumorous eellswith EBNA by peroxidase test(ACIE)	EBV DNA by blot	EBV DNA by spot
8	I	+	+	+	+
15		+	+	+	+
17		+	+	+	−
18		+	+	+	+
3	II	+	+	+	+
6		+	+	+	+
19		+	+	+	−
21		+	+	+	+
22		+	+	+	ND
23		+	+	+	ND
25		+	+	+	+
26		+	+	+	+
1	III	+	+	+	+
2		+	+	+	+
4		+	+	+	+
5		+	+	+	+
7		+	+	+	+
16		+	+	+	+
24		+	+	+	+
9	IV	+	+	+	+
10		+	+	+	+
13		+	+	+	+
11	Non-PC	−	−(∗)	−	−
12	(hyperplasia)	−	−(∗)	−	−
14		−	−(∗)	−	ND
20		−	−(∗)	−	ND
27		−	−(∗)	−	−

Notes:(∗) in these 《chronic inflammation》cases, some epithelial and lymphoid cells were found positive for EBNA + = only positive after 5days of autoradiography. ND = not done

As seen in Fig. 2, the results obtained by spot hybridization usually correlated well with those obtained by blot hybridzation. The use of amounts of 0.1, 0.5 and 1μg of cellular DNA enabled us to obtain a gradient of intensity in spot hybridization which proved useful to distinguish between clearly positive and doubtful cases. For 4 samples(cases 14, 22, 23 and 27) we did not have sufficient cellular DNA to do spot hybridization because we repeated blot hybridization 2 or 3 times in order to be sure of the results.

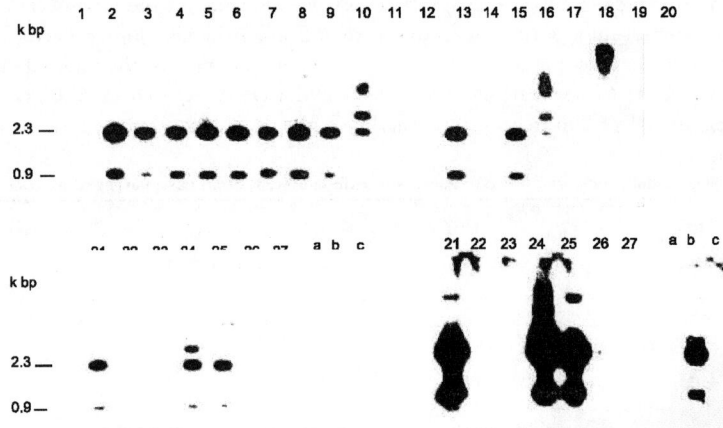

The upper part and the left of the lower part were exposed for 20h and the right of the lower part for five days, respectively, al-70℃ with an intensifying screen. The controls contained 16μg DNA of the EBV-negative cell line JM:
  (a) without viral DNA;
  (b) with one copy of B95-8 DNA per cell;
  (c) with one copy of pSL9 per cell(from left to right)

Fig. 1 Blot hybridization of 16μg of cell DNA collected by aspiration from the nasopharynx of 27 different individuals

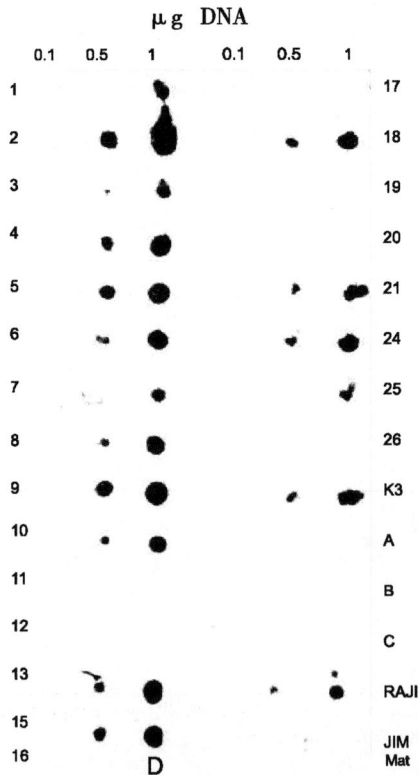

Three different amounts of cellular DNA were spotted onto nitrocclulose(0.1, 0.5, 1μg), The filter was exposed for 20h at −70℃ with an intensifying screen. Cellular DNA of 1 different tumour tissues and of 3 lymphoblastoid cell lines(LCL) was used as control.

  K3＝EBV-positive NPC, A, Band C ＝ EBV-negative head and meck tumours Raji EBA positive LCL. JM and Molt ＝ EBV-negative LCL

Fig. 2 Spot hybridization of the same DNA samples as those in Fig. 4

（2）EBNA detection.

EBNA was detected in the exfoliated cells in all 22 NPC cases(Tab. 1). Positive cells were either isolated or in clumps. Whereas no carcinoma cells were observed cytologically in the 5 cases of hyperplasia and metaplasia, a few lymphocytes in two cases(11 and 14) exhibited EBNA, while in case 27 it appeared as if normal epithelial cells exhibited EBNA.

In this series of specimens, we observed good correlation between the detection of EBNA by the ACIE test and the detection of EBV DNA by spot and blot techniques. Yet in 3 out of the 5《non-NPC》patients where no EBV DNA was detected by blot or spot hybridzation. EBNA was detected in some lymphocytes and possibly in normal epithelial cells.

DISCUSSION

Negative-pressure aspiration of exfolated cells of the nasopharynx provides enough cells to detect both tumorous cells, by cytology, as well as the presence of EBNA and EBV DNA sequences. This simple technique preventing traumatic biopsies, is ideal for epidemiological surveys aimed at screening individuals with anti-virus capsid antigen IgA antibodies who represent the population at highest risk for NPC[19]. The ACIE technique described by Pi et al[12]. is more adapted to the field studies than the ACIE test[13] to detect EBNA in exfolidated nasopharyngeal cells. However, being more sensitive than the ACIE test, the possibility of false positive results needs to be carefully assessed.

The blot hybridization technique is difficult to apply to large numbers of DNA specimens orginating from lield studies, as it is expensive inlime and money. Spot hybridization is much better adapted to explore large numbers of samples, as needed in lield studies. The best approach seems to be to screen samples first by spot hybridzation and then to test the spot-positive specimens by the blot technique. As there are false positive results by spot hybridzation, the second step(blot hybridization) is crtical.

As a probe, we used the cloned internal repeat of B95-8 DNA(pSI, 9 a gift from Dr Hayward), as we assumed that this internal repeal was invariably present within the viral genome. We have shown that 0. 1 copy of the repeat per cell could readily be detected(Bornkamm et al. in press) since a tumour cell usually contains about ten copies or more of the viral genome, and since one viral genome usually carries 5 to 12 repeals it should be possible to detect one such EBV-carrying cell in about 500-2000 cells. Yet by these techniques(spot or blot), it is not possible to distinguish whether the viral genome is in tumorous or normal cells from epithelial or lymphoid origin. As it is difficult to use a short-lived isotope in the lield for epidemiology, this problem might be overcome in the future by labelling probes with precursors copuled covalently with biotin, and the hybrids formed could be identified with avidin or anti-avidin antibodies linked to fluorescein or enzymes.

ACKNOWLEDGMENTS

We thank S. D. Hayward for a gift of pSL9.

Dr G H. Pi was supported by the《Fondation pour la Recherche Medirale》(Paris) and the《Foundation Merieux》(Lyon, France).

This work was financed by《die Deutsche Krebshilfe》(Fruerkennung und I) ifferenzierung Epstein-Barr virus-assozierter Tumoran). the CNBS(GIS 122003) and be National Cancer Institute(contact NO1CP-91035).

REFERENCES

[1] Arbameas S, Coupling of enzymes to protein with gluteraldehyde. Immnnochem, 1969, 6: 43-52.

[2] Brandsma J, Miller G. Nucleic acid and spot hybridization: rapid quantitative screening of lymphoid cell lines for Epstein-Barr viral DNA. Proc nat Acad Sci(Wash), 1980, 77:6851-6855.

[3] Denhardt D T, A membrane filter technique for the detection of complementary DNA. Biochem biophys Res Commun, 1966, 23:611-616.

[4] Desgranges C, Wolf H, de-The G, Shanmcgaratsam, K, Cammoun, N. Ellouz, R. Klein G. Lennert K. Mcnoz N, Zeb Haesen H. Nasopharyngeal carcinoma. X. Presence of Epstein-Barr genomes in separated epithelial cells of tumors in patients from Singapore. Tunisia and Kenya. Int. J Cancer, 1975, 16:7-15.

[5] Desgranges C, de-The G, Ho J H C, Ellouz R. Neutralizing EBV-specific lgA in throat washings of nasopharyngeal carcinoma(NPC) patients. Int J Cancer, 1977, 19:627-633.

[6] Desgranges C, Bornkamm GW, Zeng Y, Wang PC, Zhu J S, Shang M, de-The G. Detection of Epstein-Barr viral DNA internal repeats in the nasopharyngeal mucosa of Chinese with IgA/EBVspecific antibodies, Int J Cancer, 1982, 29:87-91.

[7] Hayward SD, Nogee L, Hayward G.S. Oranization of repeated regions within the Epstein-Barr virus DNA molecule. J Virol, 1980, 33:507-521.

[8] Henle G, Henle W. Epstein-Barr virus-specitic IgA serum antibodies as an outstanding feature of nasopharyngeal carcinoma, Int J Cancer,1976, 17:1-7.

［9］ Ho JHC，Ng MH. Kwan HC，Chan JCW，Epstein-Barr virusspecific IgA and IgG serum antibodies in nasopharyngeal car-cinoma. Brit J Cancer, 1976, 34：655-660.

［10］ Ho JHC，Kwan HC，Ng MH，de-The G. Sernm IgA antibodies to Epstein-Barr virus capsid antigen preceding symptoms of nasopharvngeal carcinoma. Lancel, 1978, 1：136-137.

［11］ Klein G，Giovanella B，C. Lindahi T，Flalrow P J，Singh S，Stehlin J. Direct evidemce for the presence of Epslein-Barr virns DNA and nuclear antigen in malignant epithelial crlls from palienls with anaplaslic carcinoma of the nasopharynx. Proe nat Aced Sci(Wash), 1974, 71：1737-1741.

［12］ Pi GH，Zeng Y，Zhao WP，Zhang QIX. Developmend of an anticomplement immunoenzyme test for detection of EB virus nuclear antigen(EBNA) and antibody to EBNA. J imunol Methods, 1981, 44：73-76.

［13］ Beedman BM. Klein G. Cellular localization of an Epscin-Barr virus-associated complement lixing antigen in producer and non-producer lymphoblastoid cell lines. Int J Cancer, 1973, 11：199-520.

［14］ Schneider U，Sghwenk H C，Bornramm G W. Charaeterization of EBV genome negative《null》and T-cell lines derived from children with acute lymphoblastoid leukemia and leukemic-transformed non Hodgkin lymphoma. Int J Cancer, 1977, 19：621-626.

［15］ Southern E M. Detection of specific sequences among DNA Iragments separated by gel electrophoresis J mol Biol, 1975, 98：503-517.

［16］ Wolf H，Zur Hausen H，Beckenr Y. EB viral genomes in epithelial nasopharyngeal carcinoma cells. Nature(Lond), 1978, 244：245-257.

［17］ Zeng Y，Liu YX，Lin ZB，Zhen SW，Wei JN，Zhe J S，Zai H S. Application of an immunoenzymatic method and an immu-noautoradiogaphic method for a mass survey of nasopharyngeal carcinoma. Intervirology, 1980, 13：162-168.

［18］ Zeng Y，Shen SJ，Pi GH，Ma JI，ZhangQ，Zho ML，Dong HJ. Application of an anticomplement mmunoenzvmatic meth-od for the detection of EBNA in carcinoma cells and normal epithelial cells form the nasopharynx, in：Nasopharvngeal earcinome cancet campaing(Grundmann, et al) vol, 5(pp：237-245). Guslav Fischer. Stuttgart, 1981.

［19］ Zeng Y，Zhan LG，Li H Y，Jan M G，Zhang Q，Wu YG，Wang YS，Su GR. Serological mass survey for early detection of nasopharyngeal carcinoma in Wuzhou city，China. Int J Caancer,1982, 29：139-144.

［20］ Zhangjiang Medical College. Diagnosis of nasopharyngeal carcinome by cytological exmination of exfoliated cells taken by negative pressure suction. Chin med J, 1976, 1：45-47.

［In《Ann Virol》1983，134：21-32］

Detection of Epstein-Barr Virus IgA/EA Antibody for Diagnosis of Nasopharyngeal Carcinoma by immunoautoradiography

ZENG Y[1], GONG C H[1], JAN M G[1], FUN Z[1], ZHANG LG[2], LIH Y[2]

1. Institute of Virology, Chinese Academy of Medical Sciences, Beijing　2. Wuzhou Cancer Research Unit, Wuzhou, Guangxi Autonomous Region, People's Republic of China

[SUMMARY]　An immunoautoradiographlc method was used for the detection of EB virus IgA/EA antibody in sera from NPC patients and other control groups. Ninety-six percent of NPC patients had IgA/EA antibody with a high titer of GMT. The positive rates of IgA/EA antibody in patients with malignant tumours other than NPC and in normal individuals were only 4% and 0%, respectively. Eleven patients histologically diagnosed as having a chronic inflammation and who showed positive for IgA/EA antibody by immunoautoradiography were rebiopsied; six of them were discovered to have squamous cell carcinoma. Fourteen NPC patients had no IgA/EA antibody detected by immunofluorescence and immunoenzymatic testing, but II and six of them had IgA/VCA and IgA/EA antibodies detected by immunoautoradiography, respectively. These data indicate that the immunoautoradiographic method is more sensitive than either the immunofluorescence or immunoenzymatic test for the detection of IgA/EA antibody, and can be used for the detection of NPC in the early stages of development.

INTRODUCTION

The detection of Epstein-Barr(EB) virus IgA/EA antibody cannot used alone for the routine diagnosis of nasopharyngeal carcinoma(NPC), because immunofluorescence testing only reveals this antibody in 50%-70% of NPC patients(Henle and Henle, 1981; Laboratory of Tumor Viruses of Cancer Institute and Institute of Epidemiology, Chinese Academy of Medical Sciences, 1978). IgA/EA antibody can only be detected in IgA/VCA antibody-positive individuals, but not in antibody-negative individuals. The detection rate of NPC among IgA/VCA antibody-positive individuals is 1.9%, and that among IgA/EA antibody-positive individuals is 30%. The difference between these two groups is 15.8 fold(Zeng et al. 1982b). These data indicate that only a few IgA/VCA antibody-positive individuals eventually become IgA/EA antibody-positive and that IgA/EA antibody is more specific, but not so sensitive for the detection of NPC as IgA/VCA antibody. It is therefore necessary to improve the sensitivity of this test for the detection of IgA/EA antibody.

An immunoautoradiographic method was established in our laboratory using ^{125}I-Iabelled anti-human IgA antibody for the detection of EB virus IgA/VCA antibody in sera and saliva(Liu et al. 1979a; Liu et al, 1979b). This test is much more sensitive than the immunoenzymatic test, but rather complicated. The immunoenzymatic test is thus widely used as a routine test for the detection of IgA/VCA antibody in China, but immunoautoradiography which is more sensitive may be useful for the detection of IgA/EA antibody.

MATERIAL AND METHODS

1. Sera

Sera were taken from NPC patients, NPC susected patients, patients with tumors other than NPC and normal individuals, and, stored at-20℃.

2. Immunoautoradiography

Smears of Raji cells treated with croton oil(500ng/ml) and n-butyrate(4mmol/L) were fixed on slide wells with cold acetone. Sear diluted from 1：10 to 1：5120 in four-fold dilutions were added to separate wells. After incubation at 37℃ in a humid atmosphere for 30 min, slides were washed three times with PBS containing 1% calf serum. 0.7ml of ^{125}I-labelled anti-human IgA antibody in an appropriate dilution was added to each slide. The slides were incubated at 37℃ for 30 min, washed three times with PBS containing 1% calf serum and left to air-dry. They were then coated with nuclear emulsion, slowly dried, and kept in the dark at room temperature for 24 h. Slides were developed in D-19 for 15 min, placed in the fixed reagent for 10 min, washed and left to air-dry, and then were examined under the light microscope. Serum was considered positive if the cells in the well that contained the diluted serum showed black granules typical of this test.

3. Immunofluorescance test and immunoenzymatic test

IgA/VCA and IgA/EA antibodies were also detected by the immunofluorescence and immunoenzymatic tests as described by Henle and Henle(1966), and Zeng et al(1982a).

RESULTS

1. Immunoautoradiographic method for detection of EBV IgA/EA antibody

As shown in Fig. 1, there were black granules in Raji cells containing early antigen reacted with IgA/EA antibody positive serum, but no such black granules were found in Raji cells reacted with IgA/EA antibody-negative serum(Fig. 2). The titers of IgA/EA antibody detected by the immunoautoradiographic method were higher than those detected by the immunoenzymatic test(Tab. 1).

Fig. 1　Immunoautoradiography. EB virus IgA/EA antibody positive serum(1000 ✕)

Fig. 2　Immunoautroadiography. EB virus IgA/EA antibody negative serum(1000 ✕)

Tab. 1　comparison of the sensitivity of immunoenzymatic testing and the immunoautoradiographic method

Serum from NPC patients	IgA/EA antibody titer	
	Immunoen-zymatic test	Immunoautorad-iography
7	—	1 : 40
12	—	1 : 40
78	—	1 : 10
3	1 : 10	1 : 40
5	1 : 10	1 : 160
22	1 : 10	1 : 160
13	1 : 20	1 : 640
37	1 : 20	1 : 160
39	1 : 20	1 : 160
10	1 : 80	1 : 2560
56	1 : 320	1 : 2560
51	1 : 640	1 : 10 240

2. Detection of EBV IgA/EA antibody from NPC patients and control by different methods

Sera from different groups were detected by immunofluorescence, and immunoenzymatic testing and by the immunoautoradiographic method. The results are shown in Tab. 2. The positive rate and GMT of IgA/EA antibody detected by immunoautoradiography in the sera from NPC patients were 96% and 1 : 97, respectively. Patients with clinically suspected NP and diagnosed histologically as having a chronic inflammation in the nasopharynx had a positive rate 22% and a GMT of 1 : 9. Seven out of 170 patients with malignant tumours other than NPC were positive(4%) to low titer 1 : 5. 2. All normal individuals were negative. The positive rate and GMT detected by the immunoenzymatic test in these four groups were 80% and 1 : 25. 6, 18% and 1 : 7. 3, 0. 6% and0% and 1 : 5, respectively. In the clinically suspected NPC group(chronic inflammation) biopsies were taken again from 11 IgA/EA antibody-positive individuals and the histological examination showed poorly differentiated squamous cells carcinoma in six of them.

Tab. 2　comparison between the immunoenzymatic and immunoautoradiographic test for detection of IgA/EA

Sera	Number of cases	IE[1]						IR[2]		
		IgA/VCA			IgA/EA			IgA/EA		
		(+)	(%)	GMT	(+)	(%)	GMT	(+)	(%)	GMT
NPC	56	52	(93)	1 : 210	45	(80)	1 : 25. 6	54	(96)	1 : 97
Nasopharyngeal chronic inflammation	50	22	(93)	1 : 12. 5	9	(18)	1 : 7. 3	11	(22)	1 : 9. 0
Tumours other than NPC	170	10	(5. 9)	1 : 5. 3	1	(0. 6)	1 : 5	7	(4)	1 : 5. 2
Normal individual	100	3	(3)	1 : 5	0	(0)	1 : 5	0	(0)	1 : 5

Notes: 1. Immunoenzymatic test; 2. Immunoautoradiographic test

Sera from 14 NPC patients diagnosed histologically but showing negative IgA/VCA and IgA/EA antibody(< 1:10) by the immunoenzymatic test were reexamined by immunoautoradiography, as well as by immunoenzymatic and immunofluorescence testing. As shown in Tab. 3 all of these 14 sera were still IgA/VCA and IgA/EA antibody-negative by the immunoenzymatic and immunofluorescence test, but 11/14 and 6/14 of them had IgA/VCA and IgA/EA antibodies detected by immunautoradiography, respectively.

Tab. 3　Immunofluorescence test and immunoautoradiography por detection of IgA/VCA AND IgA/EA antibodies in 14 NPC patients negative for these antibodies by immunoenzymatic test

Serum sample	Clinical stage	IF		IE				IR	
		IgA		IgG		IgA		IgA	
		VCA	EA	VCA	EA	VCA	EA	VCA	EA
5	I	(−)[1]	(−)	1 : 40	1 : 10	(−)	(−)	1 : 10	(−)
7	I	(−)	(−)	1 : 40	(−)	(−)	(−)	1 : 640	1 : 40
13	I	(−)	(−)	1 : 10	1 : 20	(−)	(−)	1 : 640	1 : 40
15	I	(−)	(−)	1 : 160	(−)	(−)	(−)	(−)	(−)
3	II	(−)	(−)	1 : 640	(−)	(−)	(−)	1 : 40	(−)
12	II	(−)	(−)	1 : 160	1 : 10	(−)	(−)	1 : 640	1 : 40
11	II	(−)	(−)	1 : 10	(−)	(−)	(−)	1 : 2560	1 : 40
14	II	(−)	(−)	1 : 40	(−)	(−)	(−)	1 : 40	(−)
2	III	(−)	(−)	1 : 640	1 : 10	(−)	(−)	1 : 40	1 : 40
8	III	(−)	(−)	1 : 40	(−)	(−)	(−)	1 : 40	(−)
1		(−)	(−)	1 : 40	(−)	(−)	(−)	(−)	(−)

（续　表）

Serum sample	Clinical stage	IF		IE				IR	
		IgA		IgG		IgA		IgA	
		VCA	EA	VCA	EA	VCA	EA	VCA	EA
4		(−)	(−)	1：40	(−)	(−)	(−)	(−)	(−)
6		(−)	(−)	1：40	(−)	(−)	(−)	1：160	(−)
9		(−)	(−)	1：160	(−)	(−)	(−)	1：2560	1：40
Positive rate(%)		0/14 (0%)	0/14 (0%)	14/14 (100%)	14/14 (29%)	0/14 (0%)	0/14 (0%)	11/14 (79%)	6/14 (43%)
GMT		1：5	1：5	1：59.4	1：6.4	1：5	1：5	1：65.6	1：24.4

Notes： $^1 < 1：10 =$ Negative

DISCUSSION

The EBV IgA/EA antibody is more specific for NPC than the IgA/VCA antibody[3], but its positive rate in NPC ptients is not high enough for it to be used as a diagnosis of NPC. By using the immunoautoradiographic method, satisfactory results were obtained. Ninety-six percent of NPC patients had a IgA/EA antibody with a high titer of GMT. The positive rates of IgA/EA atibody in patients with malignant tumors other than NPC and in normal individuals groups were only 4% and 0%, respectively. Out of 11 patients diagnosed histologically as having a chronic inflammation in the nasopharynx and who had IgA/EA antibody detected by immunoautoradiography, six were finally confirmed as NPC after histological examination of the second biopsies. Fourteen NPC patients had no IgA/VCA and IgA/EA antibodies detected by the immunofluorescence and immunoenzymatic test; however, among these 14 patients, 11 had IgA/VCA and six had IgA/EA antibody detected by immunoautoradiography. These data indicate that immunoautoradiography is more sensitive than either the immunoenzymatic test or the immunofluorescence test in the detection of IgA/EA antibody, and that IgA/EA antibody may serve as a specific marker for the detection of NPC. Therefore, for a serological diagnosis or serological mass survey, it is better to proceed first by using the immunoenzymatic or immunofluorescence test for the detection of IgA/VCA antibody. If this antibody is positive, the detection of IgA/EA antibody in the same serum by immunoautoradiography should then be carried out. This will mean that more NPC patients will be diagnosed in the early stages of their disease.

ACKNOWLEDGEMENTS

We thank Professor C. H. Huang for his critical appreciation of the manuscript.

REFERENCES

[1] Henle G, Henle W. Immunofluorescence in cells derived from Burkitt's lymphoma. J Bacteriol,1966, 91： 1248-1256.

[2] Henle G, Henle W. Epstein-Barr virus-specific IgA serum antibodies as an outstanding feature of nasopharyngeal carcinoma. Int, J Cancer,1981, 17:1-7.

[3] Laboratory of tumor viruses of Cancer Institute and Institute of Epidemiology, Chinese Academy of Medical Sciences, Detection of EB virus-specific serum IgG and IgA antibodies from patients with nasopharyngeal carcinoma. Act Microbiologica Sinica, 1978, 18:253-258.

[4] Liu ZR, Shan M, Zeng Y. DaI H J Du R S. Application of immunoautoradiography for detection of IgA/VCA antibody in saliva from patients with NPC. Chinese J Medical Examination,1979a, 2:197-198.

[5] Liu ZR, Shan M, Zeng Y, Han ZS, Dai HJ, Hu YL, Cao GR, Dong WP. Immunoautoradiography and its application in the detection of EBV IgA antibody in NPC patients. Kexue Tongbao, 1979b, 24:715-720.

[6] Zeng Y, Zhang LG, Li HY, Tan MC, Zhang Q, Wang YS, Su GR. Serological mass survey for early detection of nasopharyngeal carcinoma in Wuzhou city, China. Int J Cancer, 1982b, 29:139-141.

[7] Zeng Y, Liu YX, Liu ZR, Chen SW, Wei JN, Zhu JS, Zai HJ. Application of an immunoenzymatic method and an immunoautoradiographic method for a mass survey of nasopharyngeal carcinoma, Intervirology, 1982a, 13:162-168.

[In《Int J Cancer》1983，31：599-601]

Presence of EBV-DNA Sequences in Nasopharyngeal Cells of Individuals without IgA-VCA Antibodies

DESGRANGES C[1], PIG H[2], BORNKAMN G W[3], LEGRAND G W[1], ZENG Y[2], de-The G[1]

1. Laboratory of Epidemiology and Immunovirology of Tumors, Faculty of Medicine Alexis Carrel, Lyon, France　2. Institute of Virology, Chinese Academy of Medical Sciences, Beijing, People's Republic of China 3. Zentrum fur Hygiene, Freiburg in Breisgau, Fed Rep. Germany　4. To whom reprint requests should be sent

[SUMMARY]　Exfoliated nasopharyngeal(NP) cells from 62 normal Cantonese Chinese having IgA/VCA antibodies for more than a year and from 39 similar persons without IgA/VCA antibodies, were tested for the presence of EBV/DNA sequences by spot followed by blot hybridization tests, using the cloned internal repate of B95-8 viral DNA as probe. Thirteen out of 62 specimens from IgA/VCA-positive(21%) and six out of 39 specimens(15.4%) from IgA/VCA-negative individuals were found to contain EBV/DNA sequences. Forty-six cases(20 IgA/VCA-positive and 26 IgA/VCA-negative) were followed a year later for EBV/DNA sequences and EBV serology. Half of the individuals having EBV/DNA sequences in their exfoliated NP cells in 1981 did not have detectable EBV sequences a year later, and to out of 15 negative individuals became EBV/DNA-positive. There was no obvious correlation between EBV/DNA detectability and EBV serology.(We conclude that the best marker for NPC risk remains the increasing IgA/VCA and/or EA antibody titers).

INTRODUCTION

EBV fingerprints are present in undifferentiated carcinoma of the nasopharynx(NPC) in every geographical area, regardless of the NPC incidence level(zur Hausen et al., 1970; Desgranges et al., 1975a, b). Sero-epidemiological surveys in the People's Republic of China by Zeng et al.(1980, 1982) have clearly demonstrated the practical value of the presence of IgA antibodies directed to viral structural antigens(VCA) for early diagnosis of NPC in the highly endemic areas of South China. The detection of IgA/VCA-positive individuals allows most of the NPC cases to be diagnosed at a very early stage of the disease(70% in stage Ⅰ in the latest survey of Zeng et al.,1982), increasing the cure rate by cobahotherapy.

In order see whether the presence of serum EBV/IgA antibodies corresponded to an EBV activity in the nasopharyngeal mucosa, 56 symptomless individuals having serum IgA/VCA antibodies for15 to 18 months were clinically examined and biopsied(de-The et al., 1981). Four early NPC were discovered and 14 further individuals, for whom no histopathological or clinical evidence of NPC was noted, were found to have detectable EBV/DNA sequences and/or EBNA in their nasopharyngeal mucosa(Desgranges et al., 1982). It seemed therefore that the presence of EB viral markers in the nasopharyngeal mucosa could be another critical marker for an immediate risk of NPC.

As it was not possible to biopsy NP mucosa of normal and IgA/VCA-negative individuals, we did not know whether the normal mucosa of these subjects did or did not contain EBV markers. Using a negative pressure apparatus to collect exfoliated nasopharyngeal cells, we compared the presence of EBV markers in exfoliated NP cells from 62 IgA/VCA-positive and 39 IgA-negative individuals from the town of Wuchow, a high-incidence area for NPC in the Guangxi Autonomous Region of the People's Republic of China.

Fifty of these 101 individuals were investigated after 1 year for EBV serology as well as for EBV markers in their nasopharynx.

MATERIAL AND METHODS

1. Selection of individuals, collection of sera and nasopharyngeal samples

Sera from 62 individuals with IgA/VCA antibodies and from 39 individuals without IgA/VCA antibodies for a year, were selected from the on-going seroepidemiological mass survey in Wuchow, aimed at early NPC detection.

IgG and IgA antibodies to VCA and EA in sera were titrated both by the immunoperoxidase test described by Liu and Zeng(1979) in China and in Lyon by the immunofluorescence test according to Henle and Henle(1966) and Henle et al.(1970).

Nasopharyngeal cells from individuals without apparent abnormalities in their nasopharynx were collected with a simple negative pressure suction appartus, as already described by Zeng et al.(1980) and by the Zhanginag Medical College(1976). The cells were collected on a silk net and an aliquot was examined cytologically after Giemsa staining, while the rest was used to extract cellular DNA. The number of cells was sufficient to obtain 50 to 400μg of DNA(Pi et al.,1983).

2. Detection of EBV/DNA sequences in NP cells

DNA extiraction was carried out also already described(Desgranges et al., 1982). In a first step, detection of EBV/DNA sequences was done by "spot gyridization". This technique, introduced by Brandsma and Miller(1980) is an adaptation to eukaryotic cells of the bacterial colony hybridization test of Grunstein and Hogness(1975). As it was difficult to dissociate and evaluate cells from the aspirates, instead of putting a known suspension of cells in dots onto nitrocelulose, we spotted quantified aliquots of extracted cellular DNA(1.0, 0.5 and 1μg) of each sample.

Only the positive and doubtful positive specimens were then reanalyzed by "blot hybridization" as described by Bomkamm et al.(1980, 1983) and Desgranges et al. (1982). As a probe, we used the internal repeat of B95-8 virus DNA cloned in pBR322 and labelled by nick-translation with 32p dCTP and dGTP, as described by Maniatis et al(1975). Hybridization was carried out for 4 days at 45℃ for both the spot and blot hybridizations, as described by Pi et al(1983).

RESULTS

Tab. 1. gives the list and the EBV serological profile of individuals(with or without IgA/VCA antibodies) from whom viral DNA sequences were detected in the corresponding exfoliated cells. Thirteen IgA/VCA-positive individuals out of the 62 tested were positive for viral DNA(21%) while 6 out of the 39 IgA/VCA-negative were also positive for EBV/DNA(15.4%)(Tab. 2). The GMT of the various serological reactivities of both IgA-positive and IgA-negative groups are given in Tab. 2. There was no apparent relationship between the EBV serology and the presence of EBV markers in the NP mucosa. Strangely enough, as seen in Tab. 2, GMT of IgA-positive of negative subgroups IgA/VCA were higher in the individuals with no viral DNA in their mucosa than GMT of IgA/VCA in individuals with detectable viral DNA. These differences were at the border of significance.

Tab. 1　EBV serology of individuals with EBV DNA-positive nasopharyngeal exfoliated cells

Case number	EBV antibodies				
	IgC		IgA		EBNA
	VCA	EA	VCA	EA	
WA 11	640	40	10	<5	160
WA 24	320	80	80	20	80
WA 31	1280	160	320	160	320
WA 44	640	40	80	<5	640
WA 57	640	<5	40	<5	320
WA 59	320	<5	10	<5	80
WB 1	320	<5	10	<5	320
WB 2	160	20	10	<5	80
WB 25	160	<5	10	<5	80
WB 28	640	40	20	<5	320
WB 34	160	20	40	<5	160
WB 58	160	<5	10	<5	40
WB 59	80	<5	10	<5	40
WA 3	320	<5	<5	<5	320
WB 17	80	<5	<5	<5	160
WB 19	80	<5	<5	<5	80

（续 表）

Case number	EBV antibodies				
	IgC		IgA		EBNA
	VCA	EA	VCA	EA	
WB 26	160	40	<5	<5	160
WB 33	160	<5	<5	<5	80
WB 43	320	10	$\leqslant5$	<5	160

Tab. 2　Percentage and geometric mean titers of EBV antibodies of the various groups

		IgG/VCA		IgG/EA		IgA/VCA		IgA/EA		EBNA	
		% +	GMT	% +	GMT	% +	GMT	% +	GMT	% +	GMT
IgA/VCA-positive 62/101	DNA-positive 13/62(21%)	100	304	59	17	100	21	14	<5	100	136
	DNA-negative 49/62	100	413.5	61	16.8	100	25.3	15	<5	100	120.3
	Total 62	100	385	60	16.9	100	24	14.5	<5	100	124
IgA/VCA-negative 39-101	DNA-positive 6/39(15.4%)	100	139.3	33	2.7	0	<5	0	<5	100	142.6
	DNA-negative 33/39	100	261.7	18	7.3	0	<5	0	<2.5	100	139.3
	Total 39	100	260	20.5	7	0	<5	0	<2.5	100	140

All the IgA/VCA-negative samples, positive by spot hybridization, were tested again by blot hybridization(to ensure the specificity) and were found positive by this technique. Fifty individuals(23 IgA/VCA-positive and 27 IgA/VCA-negative) were analyzed a year later(1982). Among the 23 IgA/VCA-positive, 6 were EBV/DNA-positive(26%), while only 2 of the 27 IgA/ VCA negative individuals were found to be EBV/DNA-positive(7.4%).

Among these 50 individuals, 46 were tested 2 years consecutively(26 IgA/VCA-negative, 20 IgA/VCA-positive as observed in1981). Tab. 3 indicates the changes observed in the detectability of viral DNA sequences among IgA/VCA-positive or-negative individuals during the 2-year period. Among the viral DNA-positive, more than half (3/5 IgA/VCA-positive and 1/2 IgA/VCA-negative) become viral DNA-negative. Among the 15 viral DNA-negative IgA/VCA-positive individuals, 2 became viral DNA-positive, but none of the 24 viral DNA-negative-IgA/VCA-negative individuals did so. Tab. 4 gives the changes observed in the detectability of IgA/VCA-antibodies in these two groups. None of the individuals who modified their viral DNA content in exfoliated NP cells exhibited IgA/VCA antibody modifications.

Tab. 3　EBV DNA changes after one year

1981 IgA/VCA	1981		1982	
	Viral DNA	No.of cases	Viral DNA	No.of cases
20 indiv. IgA/VCA-positive	+	5	+	2
			−	3
	−	15	−	3
			−	13
26 indiv. IgA/VCA-negative	+	2	+	1
			−	1
	−	24	+	0
			−	24

Tab. 4　IgA antibody change after one year

	1981		1982	
	No.of cases		No.of cases	%
IgA/VCA-positive	20	+	20	100
		−	0	0
IgA/VCA-negative	20	+	6	23
		−	20	77

DISCUSSION

It was unexpected to observe that the groups of individuals with or without IgA/VCA antibodies both had a number of cases in which EBV DNA sequences could be detected(21% versus 15.4% in 1981; 26% versus 7.4% in 1982). These results suggest that these two markers(presence of EBV/DNA-sequences and IgA anti-VCA antibodies in the serum) are not directly related. We do not yet know if the individuals with detectable EBV DNA-sequences in the nasopharynx have an increased risk of developing NPC, or if this merely reflects a latent stage of EBV in the nasopharynx. To answer this question, the IgA/VCA-negative-EBV DNA-positive individuals will be followed for both the serological changes and the clinical NP abnormalities. These data, however, do not alter the value of IgA VCA for the detection of NPC at an early stage and of individuals at immediate risk of developing the disease(Zeng, 1980, 1982).

From an epidemiological viewpoint, it will be important to assess the rate of sero-conversion to IgA/VCA positivity as well as that of retroversion(from IgA/VCA positivity to negativity) in the Cantonese population. The present study shows that the IgA positivity represents a stable situation after an interval of 1 year. The variations observed in the detectability of viral DNA after a year might reflect a fluctuation in the EBV activity of the NP mucosa or a technical difficulty in detecting viral DNA when only a few copies are present in few cells.

Concerning NPC pathogenesis, these results cannot be properly evaluated until the detected EBV/DNA sequences are localized either in lymphoid or in epithelial cells, intimately mixed in the NP mucosa. Such a study in progress and preliminary results indicate that viral DNA is present in epithelial cells(H. Wolf, personal communication). Pearson(1980), Qualtiere et al.(1982). showed that ADCC activity appears to be the best prognostic marker in NPC patients. Individuals with pre-NPC conditions(characterized by IgA/VCA antibodies, hyperplasia or metaplasia detected by cytology, with or without detectable EBV/DNA, de-The et al., 1982). as well as the individuals with detectable EBV/DNA but without IgA/VCA antibodies, will be tested for ADCC activity. Their clinical follow-up will answer the question of the value of ADCC for charcterizing the individuals at immediate risk for NPC among the above described pre-NPC conditions. The ADCC might have a protective effect by eliminating EBV-infected malignant or pre-malignant epithelial cells.

ACKNOWLEDGEMENTS

The work reported here was made possible through the courtesy and help of the Medical Authorities of the Guang Xi Autonomous Region of the People's Republic of China. This study was financially supported by: Institute of Virology, Chinese Academy of Medical Sciences. Beijing, People's Republic of China; Deutsche Forschungsgemeinschaft(SFB 31), Germany; Centre National de la Recherche Scientifiqus(GIS 410017). France.

REFERENCES

[1] Bornkamm GW, Delius H, Zimber U, Hudewentz J, Epstein M A. Comparison of Epstein-Barr virus strains of different origin by analysis of the viral DNAs. Virol, 1980, 35:603-618.

[2] Bornkamm GW Desgranges C, Gissmann L. Nucleic acid hybridization for the detection of viral genomes. In PA. Bachmann(ed). Current topics in microbiology and immunology, pp. 287-298, Springer-Verlag, Berlin, Heidelberg, New York, 1983.

[3] Branosma J, Hiller G. Nucleic acid and spot hybridization: rapid quantitative screening of lymphoid cell lines for Epstein-Barr viral DNA. Proc nat Acad Sci(Wash), 1980, 77:6851-6855.

[4] Desgranges C Bornkamm GW, Zeng Y, Wang PC, Zhu JS, Shang M, de The G. Detection of Epstein-Barr viral DNA internal repeats in the nasopharyngeal mucosa of Chinese with IgA/EVA-specific antibodies. Int J Cancer, 1982, 87-91.

[5] Desgranges C, Wolf H, de-The G. Shanmugaratnamk, Ellouz R, Cammoun N, Klein G, Zur Hausen H. Nasopharyngeal carcinoma. X. Presence of Epstein-Barr genomes in epithelial cells of tumors from high-and medium-risk areas. Int J Cancer, 1975a, 16:7-15.

[6] Desgranges C, Wolf H, Zur Hausen H, de The G. Further studies on the detection of the Epstein-Barr viral DNA on naso-

pharngeal carcinoma biopsies from different parts of the world. In G. de-The M.A. Epstein and H. zur Hausen(ed). Oncogenesis and herpesviruses Ⅱ. Vol. 2, pp. 191-193. IARC Scientific Publiction No. 1975b, 11, Lyon.

[7] de-The G, Desgranges C, Zeng Y, Wang PC, Bornkamm GW, Zhu JS, Shang M. Search for pre-cancerous lesions and EBV markers in the nasopharynx of IgA positive individuals. In: Grundmann et al(ed). Cancer campaign. Vol. 5, Nasopharyngeal carcinoma, pp. 111-117, Gustav Fischer Verlag Stuttgart. New York, 1981.

[8] de-The G, Zeng Y, Desgranges C, Pi GH. The existence of pre-nasopharyngeal carcinoma conditions should allow preventive interventions. In M J. Simons and K. Shanmugaratnam(ed). The Biology and Nasopharyngeal Carcinoma Report No. 16. Vice technical reports. Series-Volume, 1982: 71, Geneva.

[9] Grunstein M, Hogness D. Colony hybridization. A method for the isolation of cloned NDAs that contain a specific gene. Proc nat Acad Sci(Wash),1975: 72, 3961.

[10] Henle G, Henle W. Immunofluorescence in cells derived from Burkitt's lymphoma. J Bact, 1966,91:1248-1256.

[11] Henle W, HEnle G, Zajac BA, Pearson G. Waubke R, Scriba M. Differential reactivity of human serums with early antigens induced by Epstein-Barr virus. Science, 1970: 169-188-190.

[12] Liu Y X, Zeng Y. Detection of Epstein-Barr virus IgA antibody from patients with nasopharyngeal carcinoma by immunoenzymatic method. Chin J Oncol, 1979, 1:8.

[13] Maniatis T, Jeffrey A, Kleid DG. Nucleotide sequence of the rightward operator of phage. Proc nat Acad Sci(Wash), 1975, 72:1184-1188.

[14] Pearson G R. Epstein-Barr rivas immunolgy. In G. Klein(ed). Viral oncology p. 739, Raven Press. New York, 1980.

[15] Pi GH, Desgranges C, Bornkamm GW, Shen SJ, Zeng Y, de-The G. Comparative evaluation of various techniques to detect EBV DNA in exfoliated nasopharyngeal cells. Ann Vir last Pasteur, 1983, 134E: 21-32.

[16] Qualtiers LF, Chase R, Pearson GR. Purification and biologie characterization of a major EBV induced membrane glycoprotein J Immunol,1982, 129:814-818.

[17] Zeng Y, Liu UX, Liu CR, Chen SW, Wei JN, Zhc JS, Zai HJ. Application of immunoenzymatic method and immuno-autoradiographic method for the mass survey of nasopharyngeal carcinoma. Intervirology, 1980, 13: 162-168.

[18] Zeng Y, Zhang LG, Li HY, Jan MG. Zhang Q, Wc YC, Wang YS, Su GR. Serological mass survey for early detection of nasopharyngeal carcinoma in Wuzhou city. China. Int J Cancer,1982, 29:139-141.

[19] Zhangjiang Medical College. Diagnosis of nasopharyngeal carcinoma by cytological examination of exfoliated cells taken by negative pressure suction Chin Med J, 1976, 1: 45-47.

[20] Zur Hausen H, Schulte-Holthausen H, Klein G, Henle W, Henle G, Clifford P, Santesson L. EBV-DNA in biopsies of Burkitt's tumors and anaplastic carcinomas of the nasopharynx. Natur(Lond), 1970, 228: 1056-1058.

[In《Int J Cancer》1983, 32:543-545]

Early Nasopharyngeal Carcinoma Among IgA/VCA Antibody Positive Individuals Detected by Anticomplement Immunoenzymatic Method

ZENG Yi[1], SHEN Shu -jing[2], DENG Hong[3], MA Jiao-lian[2], ZHANG Qin[1],
ZHU Ji -song[3], CHENG Ji -ru[3]

1. Institute of Virology, Chinese Academy of Medical Sciences, Beijing   2. Zhanjiang Medical College,
Guangedong province   3. Cancer Control Office, Cangwu county, Guangxi Autonmous Region

[SUMMARY]   The anticomplement immunoenzymatic method (ACIE) is used to detect nasopharyngeal carci- noma in EBV IgA/VCA antibody positive individuals in a high risk area. Carcinoma cells with EBNA were found in 4 of the 64 antibody positive individuals. Cytological and histological examinations showed that stage I poorly differentiated carcino- mas were in 4 cases. The intervals between the first bleeding for serology and nasopharyngeal carcinoma (NPC) diagno- sis were 8-9 months. No further evelation of IgA/VCA antibody appeared during this period.

The result of this study confirm the value of anticomplement immunoenzyme for detecting early stage NPC.

INTRODUCTION

Serological mass survey was carried out during 1978 -1980[1-3] in Cangwu county, Guangxi Autonomous Region. Early stage nasopharyngeal carcinoma (NPC) patients can bedetected in IgA/ VCA antibody positive individu- als, but a large number of antibody positive individuals have no evidence of NPC. In order to detect more NPC patients in the early stage, we have perfected a new method using anti -complement immunoenzyme (ACIE) to de- tect EB virus nuclear antigen (EB- NA) in carcinoma cells[4]. Since it is difficult to take biopsies in the early stage, exfoliated cells of the nasopharyngeal mucosaare collected by negative pressure suction apparatus[5] and exam- ined by ACIE for EBNA and cytologically for carcinoma cells. Satisfactory results were obtained in the outpatient clinic[6]. This paper reports use of the ACIE method for detecting early stage NPC from IgA/VCA antibody posi- tive individuals in a high risk area of NPC.

MATERIAL AND METHODS

1. IgA/VCA antibody positive individuals: 64 individuals, found to have IgA/VCA antibodies in 1978 an 1979, but lacking clinical signs of NPC 4 months previously, were included in the study. The IgA/VCA antibody was de- tected by the immunoenzymatic method described by Liu et al.

2. Cell smear: 1% dicaine was sprayed into the oropharyngeal and nasopharyngeal cavities. Exfoliated cells were collected by negative suction apparatus.

Smears were prepared from the silk ball inside the head of the suction apparatus, fixed in cold acetone 10 mi- nutes, examined by ACIE method and HE staining for cytological examination.

3. Histological examination: When positive results were shown by the ACIE method or cytological examina- tion, biopsies were taken to confirm the diagnosis.

4. ACIE test: Reference NPC serum containing EBNA antibody and normal human serum with complement at a final dilution of 1 : 10 were added to the smears and the slides placed in a humidified chamber at 37℃ for 1 hour. After washing with balanced salt solution (BSS) 3 times, anti-C_3 antibody conjugated with horseradish peroxidase at 1 : 10 was added and the slides kept at 37℃ for 30 minutes. The smears were again washed with BSS 3 times, stained with diaminobenzene and H_2O_2 and examined.

RESULTS

As shown in Tab. 1, carcinoma cells with EBNA were found in 4 of the 64 IgA/VCA antibody positive cases. All the 4 cases were also diagnosed cytologically and histologically as having poorly differentiated nasopharyngeal carcinoma (Figs. 1-3).

Tab. 1　NPC patients detected by ACIE method

Case No.	Sex	Age	Clinical examination		Carcinoma cells with EBNA	Cytological examination	Histological examination	IgA/VCA antibody	
			Subjective symtoms	Stage				First bleeding	Diagnosis confirmed
10	M	45	−	I	+	+	+	80	80
12	M	53	−	I	+	+	+	80	20
43	F	38	−	I	+	+	+	80	80
58	F	47	−	I	+	+	+	40	80

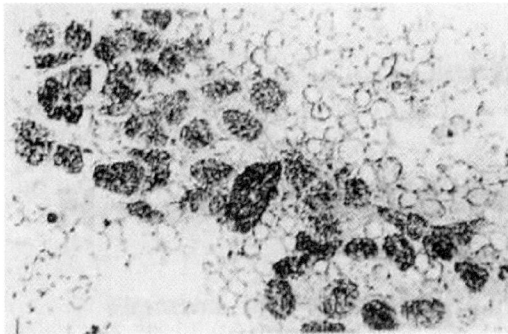

Fig. 1　EBNA positive cells detected by ACIE method (No. 43) × 200

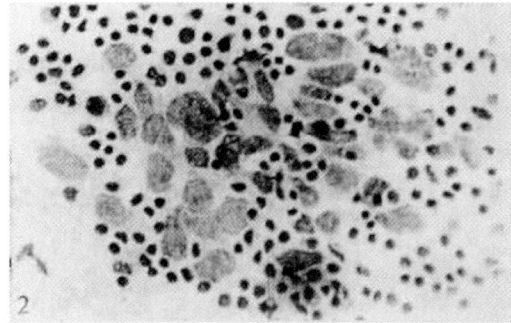

Fig. 2　Carcinoma cells detected by cytological examination (No. 43) × 200

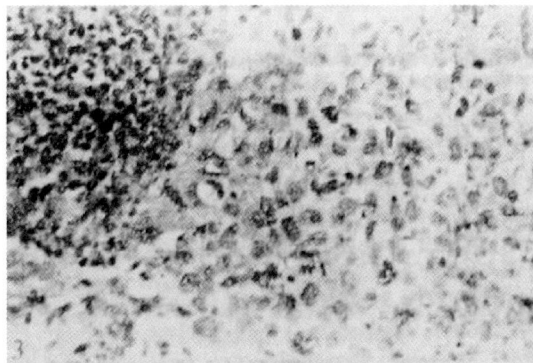

Fig. 3　Carcinoma cells detected by histological examination (No. 43) × 100

Clinical examinations showed that these 4 were Stage I NPC patients without any subjective symptoms. Only rough mucosa on the back roof the nasopharynxes was found in 2 and 0. 5-0. 8cm nodules on the nasopharynxes of the other 2. The intervals between the first serological bleeding and NPC diagnosis were 8 -9 months. No further elevation of IgA antibody occurred in any of the 4 cases during this period.

COMMENT

Our previous results[6] indicated that ACIE method is a sensitive test which successfully detects EBNA in carcinoma cells and can be used in the outpatient clinic. This method was used to detect early NPC in a NPC high risk area. Four Stage I NPC cases without subjective symptoms were detected among 64 IgA/VCA positive individuals, a6. 2% detection rate. The data confirm ACIE as a valuable means of diagnosing NPC and especially for follow-up study of IgA/VCA positive individuals.

ACKNOWLEDGMENT

We thank Prof Huang CH, Prof Chu CM and Dr G de-the for checking this manuscript.

REFERENCES

[1] Zeng Yi, et al. Application of immunoenzymatic method and immunoautoradiographic method for the mass survey of nasopharyngeal carcinoma. Chin J Oncol, 1979, 1:2.

[2] Zeng Yi, et al. Serological mass survey of nasopharyngeal carcinoma. Acta Acad Med Sin, 1979, 1:123.

[3] Zeng Yi, et al. Application of an immunoenzymatic method and an immunoautorediographic method in a mass survey of nasopharyngeal carcinoma. Intervirology, 1980, 13:162.

[4] Pi GH, et al. Development of an anticomplement immunoenzyme test for detection of EB virus nuclear antigen (EBNA) and antibody to EBNA. J Immunol Methods, 1981, 44:73.

[5] Zhanjiang Medical College. Diagnosis of nasopharyngeal carcinoma by cytological examination of ex- foliated cells taken by negative pressure suction apparatus. Chin Med J, 1976, 89:45.

[6] Zeng Yi, et al. Application of anticomplement immunoenzymatic method for the detection of EBNA in carcinoma cells and normal epithelial cells from nasopharynx. XII International Symposium on Nasopharyngeal Carcinoma. Dusseldorf, Fed Rep Germany, Oet, 1980: 23-25.

[7] Liu Y, et al. Detection of EB virus specific IgA antibody from patients with nasopharyngeal carcinoma by immunoenzymatic method. Chin J Oncol,1979, 1:9.

[In 《Chinese Medical Journal》1984, 97(3): 155-157]

HTLV Antibody in China

ZENG Y[1], LAN XY[1], FANG J[1], WANG PZ[2], WANG YR[3],
SUI YE[4] WANG ZT[5], HU RJ[6], HINUMA Y[7]

1. Institute of Virology, China National Centre for Preventive Medicine　2. Zhejiang Medical University
3. Shanxi Tumour Hospital　4. No. 4 Millitary Medical School　5. Institute of Haematology Chines Academy
6. Suzhou Medical College　7. Institute for Virus Research Kyoto university, Kyoto Japan

Sir, Antibody to HTLV (buman T - cell leukarmia - lymphoma virus) has been found in most patients with adult T - cell leukaRmia (ATL) and in 5% - 30% of healthy adults in ATL endemic areas in Japam. We have looked for HTLV antibody in China. We tested 6884 aera from normal indivduals aged 20 years of more in the cities of Beijing and Tianjin and in twenty provinces. 20 sera were from adults from Taiwan province and 25 sera from Japanese living in Beijing 510 sera were from patients with different kinds of leukaemia, including T - cell leukaemia and lymphoma (2 were suspected on cytological grounds of being ATL by Dr M, Hanaoka). Sera known to be positive or negative for HTLV antibody were used as controls. Antibody was detected by indirect immunofluo- resence test with MT- 1 cells target cells.

Of the sera from normal, Chinese adults only I, from a 63-year-old woman living in Nanjing, was anti-HTLV positive(tirre 160). 2 years earlier noe of us (Y. H) had found HTLV antibody in her husband's serum. The husband was Japanese, from Kagoshima, in the southern part of Japan, and had lived in China for 46 years, he died of stomach cancer in 1982. Of the 25 Japanese living in Beijing, only I had antibody to HTLV (titre 80). He is 73 years old from Chibe, Japan; his 70- year-old Japanese wife is antibody negative. All sera from patients with leukaemia were anti-HTLV negative.

850 sera, including the 2 positive sera from normal adulia and sera from leukaemia patients, were simultaneously tested with. MT- 1 and Hu T 102 cells; with identical results.

Thus the only evidence for HTLV in China was in I woman whose Japanese husband had been an HTLV carrier. HTLV antibody was also found in I Japanese, even though he has lived in China for a long time.

This work was partly suppound by a grant from the Japan Society for the Promotion of Science.

[In 《Lancet》1984, 799 -800]

Epstein-Barr Virus Activation in Raji Cells with Ether Extracts of Soil from Different Areas in China

ZENG Y[1], MIAO XC[1], JAIO B[2], LI HY[3], NI HY[4], ITO Yohei[5]

1. Institute of Virology, Chinese Academy of Medical Sciences, Beijing   2. Guangxi Autonomusregional Hospital, Nanning   3. Wuzhou Cancer Unit, Wuzhou   4. Guangxi Botanical Garden of Medicinal Plants, Nanning (China)   5. Department of Microbiology, Faculty of Medicine, Kyoto University, Kyoto (Japan)

[SUMMARY]   Epstein-Barr virus (EBV)inducers were found in soil samples collected from the ground under tung oil trees and other plant species of Euphorbiaceae family growing in southern provinces of China where incidence of an EBV-associated malignancy, nasopharyngeal carcinoma (NPC)is prevalent. In such NPC high risk areas, the positive rate of EBV inducers in soil samples was up to 59.5%. Since many tung oil trees are planted along the roads and rivers of the high risk area, the possible significance of EBV inducers in soil under the trees in the development of malignancy among inhabitants of the area is discussed.

INTRODUCTION

Ito et al.[5] reported that the ether extract of soil samples collected from the ground under plants of Euphorbiaceae and Thymeleaceae families in Japan, which possess Epstein-Barr virus (EBV) - activating diterpene esters, efficiently induced EBV early antigen (EA) in Raji cells. Our previous data[6] also showed that the ether extracts of tung oil and leaves and flowers of the tung oil tree, are all strong EBV inducers. Such trees are planted in abundance along the roads (Fig. 1) and rivers in a high risk area for NPC (Fig. 2). Here we report the detection of EBV inducers in soil samples collected from under the tung oil trees[4] growing in such areas and also in soil samples from under Euphorbiaceae plants in other different areas of the country.

Fig. 1   Tung oil trees (Aleurites fordii) along the main road to Wuzhou City. Indicated by arrows. Photographed, December 5, 1982

Fig.2   Map of NPC incidence in china and places of soil sample collection. ■, 4.00 and over; ▨, 3.99-3.00; ▨, 2.99-2.00; □, below 2.00 per 100 000. (1) Nanning; (2) Rauzhan county; (3) Wuzhou and Zangwu County; (4) Beiing, (H) Hong Kong, (G) Guangzhou. The arrow indicates the Guangxi Zhang Autonomous Region (capital, Nanning). The Western River and Kui River are both in this area. (Modified from a map in: Hirayama, T. and Ito, Y. (1981) Prev. Med.,10:614)

MATERIALS AND METHODS

1. Cells

The human lymphoblastoid Raji cells derived from Burkitt's lymphoma were cultivated in RPMI1640 medium supplemented with 20% calf serum.

2. Soil samples

The samples were collected from the ground under the plants in different places, both from NPC endemic and non-endemic areas, to a depth of 5cm from the surface. Five grams of such soil was extracted with 50ml of ether at room temperature for 7 days. After removing the solution, the ether was evaporated, and the residue was dissolved in ethanol as 10mg/ml stock soulution.

3. Experimental procedure

The synergistic assay method[2] was used. The cells were cultivated with 4mmol/L n-butyrate and the test substance was added at varying concentration After cultivation at 37℃ for 48h, smears were made and the detection of EBV EA - expressing cells was carried out by the immunoenzymic test[7], each assay, 500 cells were counted and the ratio of EBV EA-positive cells was recorded.

RESULTS AND DISCUSSION

As liosted in Tab. 1. The ether extracts of soil samples collected fron under Chinese tung oil trees along the Western River and Kui River in NP high risk areas, i. e. Wuzhou City and Zangwu County of Guangxi Zhan Autonomous Region, showed positive rates of 59.5% and 40%, respectively One of 4 samples from the dock of Western River and one of 3 samples for the bank of Kuiriver in Wuzhou City showed weak activity.

Tab. 1　Induction of EBV EA in Raji cells by extracts of soil samples from Wuzhou city and Zangwu county

Soil samples	Positive sample No.	EBV EA positive cells(%)		
		Ether extract(μg/ml)		
		10	2	0.4
Under tung	15	25.0	14.0	2.6
oil trees along	3	14	11.4	0.6
the road and the	5	10.6	0	0
Western River	8	4.0	3.0	2.0
(11/19+)	11	2.6	0.6	6.0
	2	1.4	2.2	1.4
	1	2.0	0.6	1.0
	14	0	1.8	1.0
	17	0.8	1.2	1.6
	18	1.4	0.6	0.8
	4	1.0	0	0
Under tung oil	35	6.6	9.6	4.6
trees along the	21	8.0	2.8	2.0
road and the	31	2.0	8.0	1.0
Kui River[a]	22	0	4.0	0
(8/20+)	23	8.0	1.6	0.4
	36	2.0	1.0	2.0
	29	2.0	0.4	0.8
	39	0.6	0.8	1.4
From the dock of	41	2.0	0.6	0.8
Western River[a]				
(1/4+)				

（续　表）

Soil samples	Positive sample No.	EBV EA positive cells(%) Ether extract($\mu g/ml$)		
		10	2	0.4
From vegetable garden (1/10 +)	54	1.0	1.0	0.6
From the bank of Kui River[a] (1/3 +)	56	0	1.0	0
Under Codiacum variegatus	76	2.8	8.0	6.0
Codiacum uariegatus	77	8.0	6.0	1.6
Cediacum variegatus	78	2.0	8.0	12.0
Euphorbia milli (4/4+)	80	-	4.0	30.0

Notes: Controls: B (n-butyrate) + C(eroton oil) = 45.7%; B: only =0.4%; C: only =0.8%; Untreated Raji cells =0%. -, not tested.

[a] Rivers in Guangxi Autonomous Region (NPC high risk area).

The EBV-activating substance was also found in the ether extract of soil samples collected from under Euphorbiaceae and other plant families in Guangxi Botanical Garden of Medicinal Plants in Zanning (5/20 positive) (Tab. 2), parks in Beijing (3/24 positive) (Tab. 3) and in Rauzhan County (8/44 positive) (Tab. 4). Ho et al.[1] and our previous work showed that the marine population living in boat has a much higher incidence rate of NPC than the land dwellers. There are a lot of tung oil trees along the roads and rivers of the NPC high incidence area, and much rain in southern part of China. It may be assumed that the soil particles adsorbing EBV inducer substances can easily go to the river after raining. The boat people drink water from those rivers throughout their life. Thus, the high incidence of NPC among the boat people could be related to the drinking water possibly containing EBV inducers. However, more direct evidence based on extensive epidemiological studies needs to be found. Such studies are now being carried out.

Alternatively, some Chinese medicinal herbs can enhance the transformation of lymphocytes by EBV [Hu and Zeng, unpublished data]and the EBV genomes are present in normal epithelial cells. The soil dust containing EBV inducer may be inhaled by the inhabitants of the district and reach the nasopharyngeal mucosa membrane to act on the EBV geonme as inducer or on such genome-harboring epithelial cells as promoter, eventually leding to the malinant transfromation of the cells. Since many of the EBV inducers are tumor promoter[3], such an assumption is valid not only for NPC but also for other malignan tumors. Further studies are necessary.

Tab. 2　Induction of EBV EA in Raji cells by extracts of soil samples from Beijing

Soil samples under	Positive sample No.	EBV EA positive cells (%) Ether extract($\mu g/ml$)		
		10	2	0.4
Euphorbia milli	1718	0	3.0	10.6
Stellera chamaejasme	1717	7.6	1.0	0.4
Angelica pubes (3/24+)	1716	0.8	0.2	0

Notes: Controls: B+C=15.4%; B=0.5%; C=0.6%; untreated Raji cells =0%

Tab. 3　Induction of EBV EA in Raji cells by extracts of soil samples from Nanning

Soil samples under	Positive sample No.	EBV EA positive cells（%）		
		Ether extract（μ/ml）		
		10	2	0.4
Euphorbia heterophylla	2117	15.6	9.6	11.7
Sapium sebiferum	2129	0.9	5.5	5.0
Euphorbia milli	2131	0	3.8	7.6
Euphorbia cochinchinensis	2120	0.8	32.4	28.2
Croton tiglium(5/20＋)	2125	30.0	36.2	31.0

Notes：Controls：B＋C＝28.9%；B＝1.4%；C＝1.4% untreated Rali cells ＝0%

Tab. 4　Induction of EBV EA in Raji cells by extracts of soil samples from Kauzhan county

Soil samples	Positive sample No.	EBV EA positive cells（%）		
		Ether extracts （μg/ml）		
		10	2	0
Under				
Tung oil tree	2279	11.2	7.0	3
Tung oil tree	2273	15.0	12.7	5
Tung oil tree	2285	21.2	11.1	3
Tung oil tree	2278	15.4	5.3	-
From[a]				
Zhenan	2264	18.7	8.9	2
Tianho	2261	14.1	21.4	11
Siba	2260	13.1	6.4	1
Tianho (8/44)	2255	23.0	6.0	1

Notes：Controls：B＝C ＝47.6%；B ＝3.1%；C ＝3.4%；untreated Raji cells ＝0%. -, not test
[a] Local towns in Rauzhan County

REFERENCES

[1]　Ho JHC. An epidemiologic and clinical study of nasopharyngeal carcine Intl Radio Oncol Biol. Phys，1978，4：181.

[2]　Ito Y，Kawanishi M，Harayama T，Takabayashis. Combined effe of the extracts from Croton tiglum, Euphorbia lathyris or Euphorbia tirucalli ar n-butyrate on Epstein-Barr virus expression in human lymphoblastoid P3HR-1 al Raji cells. Cancer Letters，1981，12：175-180.

[3]　Ito Y Yanase，S Fujita J，Harayama T，Takashim M，Imanaka，H. A short-term in vtiro assay for promoter substances u-sing human lymphoblasoicl cell latently infected with Epstein-Barr virus. Cancer Letters，1981，13：29-37.

[4]　Ito Y，Yanase S，Tokuda H，Kishihita M，Ohi-gashi H，Hirota M，Koshi K. Epstein-Barr virus activation by tung oil, ex-tracts of Aleurites fordii a diterpene ester 12-O-hexadecanoyl-16-hydroxyphorbol-13-acetate. Cancer Let，1982,18：87-95.

[5]　Ito Y，Ohigashi H，Koshimizu K，Zeng Y. Epstein-Barr virus -acti principle in the ether extracts of soil collected from un-der plants which cont active diterpene esters. Cancer Letters，1983，19：113-117.

[6]　Mizuno F，Koizumi S，Osato T，Kokwaro JO，Ito，Y. Chinese African Euphorbiaceae plant extracts：markedly enhancing effect on Epstein virus- induced transformation. Cancer Letters，1983，19：199-205.

[7]　Zeng Y，Liu YX，Liu ZR，Zhen SW，Wei JN，Zhu JS，Zei，HS. Application of an immunoenzymatic method and an immu-noautoradiographic non for a mass survey of nasopharyngeal carcinoma. Intervirology，1980，13：162-168.

［In《Cancer Letters》1984，23：53-59］

Epstein-Barr Virus Activation by Human Semen Principle: Synergistic Effect of Culture Fluids of Bacteria Isolated from Patients with Carcinoma of Uterine Cervix

ZENG Y[1], GI ZW[1], ITO Y[2]

1. Institute of Virology, China National Centre for Preventive Medicine, Beijing (China)   2. Department of Microbiology, Faculty of Medicine, Kyoto University, Kyoto (Japan)

[SUMMARY] Rpsein -Barr virus early antigens (EBV EA) were induced in a Raji cell system in order to assay the activity of the EA inducer in human semen. In semen from 53 Chinese, 45.3% induced EBV EA in Raji cells. Such positive semen and EBV - inducing positive culture fluids of bacteria isolated from the uterine cervix of patients with cervical carcinoma had a synergistic effect on the induction of EBV EA. This synergistic effect as related to the cause of cervical carcinoma is discussed.

INTRODUCTION

EBV inducers have been detected in plants of Euphorbiaceae, Thymelaeaceae, Leguminosae, etc[1,2]. and 12-O-tetradecanoyl-phorbol-13-acetate (TPA) of croton oil, 12-O-hexadecanoyl-hydroxyphorbol-13-acetate(HHPA) of tung oil[5], Daphne genka and Wikstroemia Chamaedaphne extracts (Y. Zeng, unpublished data) proved to be potent tumor inducers. Some human semen also contains an EBV activating substance[6]. Here we report the detection of EBV inducer in human semen of Chinese and the synergistic effect of human semen and bacterial culture fluid on the induction of EBV EA.

MATERIALS AND METHODS

1. Cells

Human lymphoblastoid Raji cells derived from Burkitt lymphoma were cultivated in RPMI 1640 medium supplemented with 20% calf serum, penicillin (100 units/ml) and streptomycin(100μg/ml).

2. Semen sample

Samples were obtained from the fertility clinic of Beijing Friendship hospital and preserved at -20℃ until assay. After thawing, the samples were centrifuged at 18 000 r/min for 60 min and supernatant was used for EBV EA induction test.

3. Anaerobic bacterial culture fluid

Swabs were taken from the uterine cervix of patients with cervical carcinoma and were inoculated on the surface of plates of FM modified medium and cultured under anaerobic conditions(steel wool method, 10% CO_2/90% N_2)[3]. The pure culture of gram- negative bacteria and grampositive cocci were cultivated anaerobically in both medium. The culture fluid was passed through a Seitz bacterial filter. Positive and negative samples from such bacterial cultures were both used for EB vi- rus induction.

4. Experimental procedure

The synergistic assay method[4] was used. The cells were cultivated with 4mmol/L n -butyrate and varying concentrations of human semen were added. After cultivation at 37℃ for 48h, smears were made and the EBV EA expressing cells were identified using an immunoenzymatic test[7], The positive controls comprised of croton oil (500ng/ml) plus n - butyrate (4mmol/L) and a negative control using n - butyrate alone was included. In each assay, 500 cells were counted and the ratio of EA - positive cells recorded. For examination of the synergistic effect of semen and bacterial culture fluid, 2μl or 10μl of semen and 0. 05ml or 0. 1ml of bacterial culture fluid were added to 1ml of Raji cell culture.

RESULTS

1. Induction of EBV EA by human semen

Semen samples from 53 Chinese were assayed and the results are listed in Tab. 1. Twenty-four samples (45.3%) induced EBV EA in Raji cells, the positive rate of smen samples was 56%, and the positive rate of cells with EA ranged from 2.2% to 12.2%. Three samples (nos 9, 15, 20) showed a higher positive rate of cells with EA (9.8%-12.2%), such exceeding the 50% induced by croton oil and n-butyrate. The remaining samples showed a lower activity. There was no marked difference in the number of positive cells with EA between concentrations of semen varying from 0.4μl to 10μl in 1ml medium.

Tab. 1 Induction by human semen of EBV EA in Raji cells[a]

No. of semen specimens	Semen	Semen + n - butyrate（%）		
	10μl	10μl	2μl	0.4μl
15	1.2	10.8	12.2	9.0
9	1.2	9.4	10.4	8.0
20	1.2	9.2	9.8	8.2
36	0.6	7.6	6.0	8.2
41	0.6	7.4	6.2	6.0
33	0.6	7.2	6.0	6.2
12	0.6	6.8	6.0	5.2
17	1.2	6.2	5.4	6.6
18	1.2	5.8	6.4	5.4
23	1.0	5.8	6.2	4.8
45	0.6	5.4	4.2	3.4
13	0.8	4.2	5.4	3.4
40	0.4	5.2	4.2	5.8
48	0.4	5.0	4.0	3.4
2	0.4	4.6	3.4	4.0
3	1.0	4.0	4.4	3.0
1	0.8	4.2	3.6	3.4
14	0.8	4.0	2.6	3.4
31	0.4	3.2	3.8	2.6
27	0.4	3.2	3.8	3.8
22	0.8	3.4	3.0	2.8
25	0.4	2.8	3.2	2.2
50	0.4	5.2	4.2	3.4
58	0.4	4.2	3.8	3.0

Notes: [a] Controls: n - butyrate (4mmol/L) EA positive rate, 0.6%; croton oil (500ng/ml) EA positive rate, 1.4%; croton oil + n - butyrate EA positive rate, 17.6%

2. Synergistic effect of semen and bacte- rial culture fluid

The synergistic effect of semen and bacterial culture fluid was assayed in Raji cells and the results are listed in Tab. 2. A positive reaction was seen only in groups with a positive semen and a positive bacterial culture fluid. The positive rate of cells with EA was from 5.4% to 18.6%.

The potency of the sample (bacteria no. 13 plus semen no. 15, 18.6%) was comparable to that of the croton oil and n - butyrate (21.4%). Induction of EA was nil in negative semen and negative bacterial culture fluid, used alone or in combination.

Tab. 2 Synergistic effect of semen and bacterial culture fluid[a]

No. of bacterial culture fluid specimens	No. of semen specimens	Bacterial culture fluid (EA positive rate%)			
		0.1μl		0.05μl	
		10μl	2μl	10μl	2μl
13 (+)[b]	15 (+)	16.2	17.2	18.6	14.4
25 (+)	15 (+)	9.2	8.4	16.8	17.4
39 (+)	36 (+)	4.65	5.4	4.8	4.2
41 (+)	41 (+)	4.8	6.2	5.4	4.0
15 (+)	20 (+)	4.8	5.0	5.8	4.4
25 (+)	57 (−)	1.2	1.4	0.8	0.2
27 (+)	56 (−)	0	0	0	0
23 (−)	58 (+)	0	0	0	0
2 (−)	9 (+)	0	0	0	0
11 (−)	52 (−)	0	0	0	0
7 (−)	49 (−)	0	0	0	0

Notes:[a] Controls: n - butyrate (4mmol/L) EA positive rate, 0.6%; croton oil (500ng/ml) EA positive rate, 1.0%; croton oil + n - butyrate EA positive rate, 21.4%.

[b] Activity of samples when assayed alone

DISCUSSION

The present data confirmed our previous findings[6], that the semen from 45.3% of Japanese males induced EBV EA in Raji cells. Thus, we extended the study to determine whether the EBV EA inducer in semen possesses the activity of a tumor promoter. The EBV EA inducing substance was also found in the culture fluid of bacteria isolated from the uterine cervix of Chinese patients with cervical carcinoma. This substance was identified by gas chromatography to be butyric acid (Y. Zeng, unpublished data). For elucidating the etiology of cervical carcinoma, the possible synergistic effect of the semen and bacterial culture fluid on the induction of EBV EA was investigated. We found that these 2 natural components do have a synergistic effect, similar to the case of croton oil and n - butyrate[1]. Thus, further study on the synergistic effect of these 2 natural products in animal systems in warranted to determine if this effect plays a role as tumor promoter in the neoplastic processes of uterine carcinogenesis.

ACKNOWLEDGEMENTS

We thank M. Ohara for expert editing of the manuscript.

REFERENCES

[1] Ito Y, Kawanishi M, Harayama T, Takahayashi S. Combined effect of the extracts from Croton tigli- um, Euphorbia lathyris or Euphorbia tirucalli and n-butyrate on Epstein Barr virus expression in Raji cells. Cancer Letters, 1981, 12: 175-180.

[2] Zeng Y, Zhong JM, Mo YK, Miao MC. Epstein-Barr virus early antigen induction in Raji cells by Chinese medicinal herbs. Intervirology, 1983, 19: 201-204.

[3] Ito Y, Yanase S. Induction of Epstein-Barr virus antigens in human lymphoblastoid p3HR - 1 cells with culture fluid of Fusobacterium nucleatum. Cancer Res, 1980, 40: 4329-4330.

[4] Ito Y, Yanase S, Fujita J, Harayama T, Kashi- ma M, Imanka H. A short - term in vitro assay for promoter substances using human lymphoblastoid cells latently, with Epstein - Barr virus. Cancer Letters, 1981, 13: 29-37.

[5] Ito Y, Tokuda H, Ohigashi H, Koshimizu K. Distribution and characterization of environmental promoter sustances as assayed by synergistic Epstein - Barr - activating system. In: Cellular Interactions by Environmental Tumor Promoters, 1984, 125 - 127. Editors: Fujiki et al. Japan Sci Press Tokyo.

[6] Ito Y, Tokuda H, Morigaki T, Shimizu K, Kawana T, Sanada S, Yoshida O. Epstein - Barr virus- activating principle in human semen. Cetters, 1984, 23: 129-134.

[7] Zeng Y, Liu YX, Liu ZY, Zhen SW, Wei JN, Shu JS, Zai HJ. Application of immunoanti- radiographic method for the mass survey of nasopharyngeal carcinoma. J Clin Oncol, 1980, 1: 2-8.

[In《Cancer Letters》1985, 28: 311-315]

Prospective Studies on Nasopharyngeal Carcinoma in Epstein-Barr Virus IgA/VCA Antibody-Positive Persons in Wuzhou City, China

ZENG Y[1], ZHANG L G[2], WU Y C[2], HUANG Y S[2], HUANG N Q[2], LI J Y[2], WANG Y B[2] JIANG M K[1], FANG Z[1], MENG N N[2]

1. Institute of Virology, China National Center for Preventive Medicine, Beijing   2. Wuzhou Cancer Unit Wuzhou City, Guangxi Autonomous Region, People's Republic of China

[SUMMARY] A serological mass survey was carried out in Wuzhou City in 1980, 1136 IgA/VCA-positive persons being followed up for 4 years. Altogether 35 NPC cases were detected, of which 15(43%) were in stage I and 17(48.5%) in stage II, early cases(I + II) thus amounting to 91.5%. The detection rate of early cases was 2.9 times higher than in our outpatient clinic. IgA/VCA antibody could be detected 16-41 months prior to clinical diagnosis of NPC. We conclude that, if IgA/ VCA- positive individuals are examined routinely once a year, NPC can be detected in the early stages of evolution. The annual detection rate of NPC in IgA/VCA antibody-positive individuals was 31.7 times higher than that of the annual incidence of NPC in the general population in the same age group, while during the 4-year follow-up period the incidence was 7.5 times higher than in the general population for the same age group. These results further indicate that EB virus plays an important role in the development of NPC, and that serological screening and follow-up studies are valuable for the early detection of NPC.

INTRODUCTION

Serological mass surveys of NPC and folio-up studies on EB virus IgA/VCA antibody-positive individuals were carried out in the Zanwu County of Guangxi Autonomous Region using an immunoenzymatic test(Zeng et al., 1979, 1980, 1983). NPC patients could be detected in an early stage, but it was rather difficult to carry out follow-up studies because many of the IgA/VCA antibody-positive cases came from remote areas, and clinical examination was not carried out periodically for some patients, while in others the diagnosis was not established at an early stage. Therefore, another serological mass survey was carried out in Wuzhou City, starting in 1980(Zeng et al., 1982). Altogether 20 726 individuals aged 40 years and more were examined and the antibody-positive cases were followed up for 4 years. The results of the follow-up studies are reported here.

MATERIAL AND METHODS

1. Sera

Sera obtained from venous blood were stored at-20℃ in Wuzhou City and forwarded by air to the Institute of Virology, China National Center for Preventive Medicine, in Beijing.

2. Immunoenzymatic test

This was described previously(Zeng et al., 1980). B95-8 and horseradish-conjugated anti-human IgA/VCA antibody were used for the detectionof IgA/VCA antibody.

3. Clinical and histological examination

EB virus IgA/VCA antibody-positive cases were examined clinically once a year for 4 years. Biopsies were taken from the suspect NPC cases and individuals with high IgA/VCA antibody titers.

RESULTS

1. NPC patients detected by serological screening and follow-up studies

Among 20 726 persons examined 1136 presented an IgA/VCA antibody, the positivity rate thus being 5.5%. From this number, 18 NPC patients were diagnosed clinically and histologically. Ten were in stage I, 6 in stage II and 2 in stage III. Fourteen patients(77.8%) had IgA/VCA antibody titers of 1∶40 and over, with a geometric mean titer(GMT) of 1∶93.3(Tab. 1).

The IgA/VCA antibody-positive cases were clinically and histologically reexamined once a year for 4 years. During this time, 17 additional NPC cases were diagnosed, 5 in stage I, 11 in stage II and one in stage III. Sixteen cases(94.1%) were thus in early stages with a GMT of 1∶62.6. The unique stage III case had an antibody titer of 1：40 during the first bleeding episode. Some suspect lesions in nasopharyngeal mucosa were found，but the patient refused biopsy. The NPC developed into stage Ⅲ 2 years and 8 months later.

Tab. 1　Antibody titer of NPC patients detected during screening and follow-up studies

	Total	Titer							GMT
		10	20	40	80	160	320	640	
NPC found at									
Screening	18	4		3		7		4	1：93.3
Follow-up	17	2	1	7		6		1	1：62.6
Total	35	6	1	10		13		5	1：76.9

Altogether 35 NPC cases were detected by serological screening and follow-up studies within the 4-year period. Of these，32 cases(91.5%) were in an early stage. As a comparison，1036 NPC patients were diagnosed during this period in our outpatient clinic，most of them(68.1%) being in advanced stages(Ⅲ ＋ Ⅳ)，while only 330 cases(31.9%) were in an early stage. The percentage of outpatients with NPC in stage Ⅰ was 1.7%，but it increased to 43% when serological screening and follow-up studies were applied(Tab. 2). As shown in Fig. 1，IgA/VCA anti bodies were detected 16-41 months(average，30 months) prior to the diagnosis of NPC for stage Ⅰ，and 16-40 months(average，27 months) prior to diagnosis for stage Ⅱ.

Tab. 2　Clinical stage of NPC diagnosed at screening and in outpatient clinic

	Clinical stages				Total
	Ⅰ	Ⅱ	Ⅲ	Ⅳ	
Screening					
Number of cases	15	17	3	0	35
%	43.0	48.5	8.5		100.0
Outpatient clinic					
Number of eases	18	312	526	180	1036
%	1.7	30.1	50.8	17.4	100.0

There was no difference in GMT of IgA/VCA antibody in sera of patients with a first bleeding and of those bleeding when diagnosis was confirmed at stage Ⅰ. The GMT of IgA/VCA antibody in patients at stage Ⅱ was 1：96.1，while it was twice as high in patients bleeding for the first time(Fig. 2). No NPC patients were found among 19 590 individuals without detectable levels of IgA/VCA antibodies，during a period of 4 years.

2. Detection rate of NPC

Eighteen NPC patients were detected among 1136 IgA/VCA antibody-positive individuals by serological screening，the NPC detection rate being 86.8/100 000 for 20 726 persons examined and 1584/100 000 for 1136 IgA/VCA antibody-positive persons. These rates are respectively 1.7 and 31.7 times higher than the annual incidence of NPC(50/100 000) in the general population at a similar age. Twenty-two IgA/ VCA antibody-positive cases were found among 216 persons examined within one chemical factory. From these，3 NPC cases(2 in stage Ⅰ and 1 in stage Ⅱ) were diagnosed histologically. The NPC detection rate for individuals examined and IgA/VCA antibody-positive cases are 1380/100 000 and 13636/100 000 respectively，and these are 27.6 and 272.7 times higher respectively than the annual incidence in the general population of similar age. Seventeen cases were detected during the 4-year follow-up studies，the incidence rate of NPC being 374/100 000/year. This is 7.5 times the annual incidence in the general population of similar age(Tab. 3).

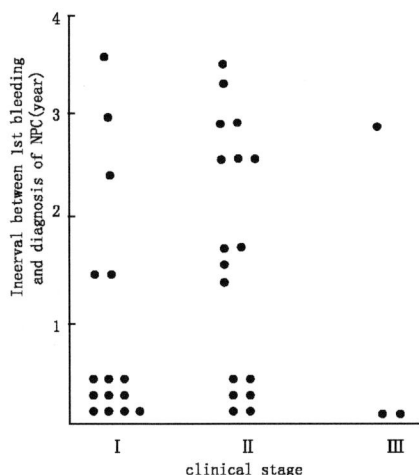

Fig. 1　Follow-up studies on IgA/VCA antibody positive individuals

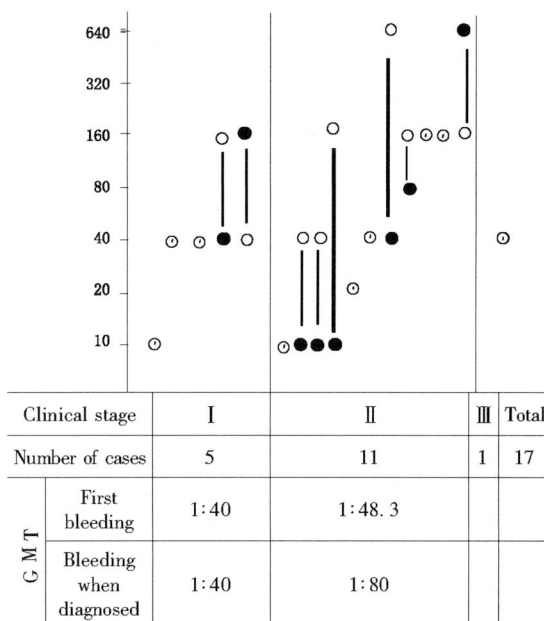

Clinical stage		I	II	III	Total
Number of cases		5	11	1	17
G M T	First bleeding	1:40	1:48. 3		
	Bleeding when diagnosed	1:40	1:80		

● first bleeding；○ bleeding when diagnosis was confirmed；⊙ two bleedings had same IgA/VCA titer

Fig. 2　Change in IgA/VCA titer and GMT from first bleeding to diagnosis of NPC.

Tab. 3　Comparison of detection rate and incidence rate of NPC

	Number of persons examined	IgA/VCA positive persons	Number of NPC cases	NPC detection rate (1/100 000) Persons examined	NPC detection rate (1/100 000) IgA/VCA positive person	Incidence rate by follow-up studies (1/100 000 per year)	Incidence rate in general population per year	Reference
Zangwu county	148029	3533	55	37. 0(1. 2)[1]	1566. 8(57. 9)[1]		30	Zeng et al. 1983 (screening)
Boat people in Zangwu	518	18	2	386. 0(12. 8)	11111. 0(370)		30	Zhu et al. 1983 (screening)
Wuzhou City	12932	680	13	100. 5(2)	1911. 8(38)		50	Zeng et al. 1982 (screening)
Wuzhou City	20726	1136	17	86. 8(1. 7)	1584. 5(31. 7)		50	(Screening)
	20726	1136	17			374(7. 5)[2]		(follow-up studies)
A chemical factory in Wuzhou	216	22	3	1380(27. 6)	13636. 0(272. 7)		50	(screening)

[1] Detection rate/incidence rate；[2] Incidence rate(follow-up studies)/incidence rate

DISCUSSION

Thirty-five NPC cases were detected among 20 726 individuals by serological screening and follow-up studies during a period of 4 years，91. 5% of them being at an early stage. This was 2. 9 times that(31. 8%) found in our outpatient clinic. Seventeen NPC patients except one, detected by follow-up studies, were in an early stage and IgA/VCA antibodies could be detected in their serum 16—41 months prior to diagnosis of NPC. These data support the notion that serological screening and follow-up studies are valuable for early detection of NPC.

The NPC detection rate for individuals examined and for the IgA/VCA antibody-positive cases detected by serological screening were 1. 7 and 31. 7 times higher respectively than the annual incidence in the general population of similar age. The annual incidence rate NPC among IgA/VCA antibody-positive individuals, follow-up was 7. 5 times higher than the annual incidence of NPC in the general population. These date similar to those concerning Zangwu county(Zo et al., 1983) and indicate that EB virus plays an important role in the development of NPC.

The NPC detection rates for the individuals examined and for the IgA/VCA antibody-positive cases one chemical factory were respectively 27. 6 and 272 times higher than the annual incidence in the generat population of similar age. This may indicate a relationship between environmental factors, activation of virus and development of NPC.

No NPC patients were recorded within the IgA/VCA antibody-negative group during a period of years. This fact should be useful in making decision concerning serological reexamination of IgA/ VCA antibody-negative individuals.

REFERENCES

[1] Zeng Y, Liu YX, Liu CR, Chen SW, Wei JN, Zhu JS, Zai HJ. Application of immuno autoradiographic method for the mass survey of nasopharyngeal carcinoma, Intervirology, 1980, 13:162-168.

[2] Zeng Y, Liu YX, Wei JN, Zhu JS, Cai SL, Wang PZ, Zhong JM, Li RC, Pan WJ, Li EJ, Tan BF. Serological screening of nasopharyngeal carcinoma. Acta Acad med Sin, 1979, 1: 123-126.

[3] Zeng Y, Zhang LG, Li HY, Jan MG, Zhang Q, Wu YC, Wang YS, Su GR. Serological mass survey for early detection of nasopharyngeal carcinoma in Wuzhou City, China. Int J Cancer,1982, 29:139-141.

[4] Zeng Y, Zhong JM, Li LY, Wang PZ, Tang H. Ma YR, Zhu JS, Pan WJ, Liu YX, Wei ZN, Chen JY, Mo YK, Li EJ, Tan BF. Follow-up studies on Epstein-Barr virus IgA/VCA antibody-positive persons in Zangwu county China. Intervirology, 1983, 20:190-194.

[5] Zhu JS, Pan WJ, Li LY, Zeng Y, Jan MK, Fang Z. Serological suvey of nasopharyngeal cancer of boat people in Zangwu county. Study on preven- tion and treatment of cancer(in Chinese), 1983,10:189-190.

[In 《Int J Cancer》 1985, 36:545-547]

Seroepidemiological studies on Nasopharyngeal Carcinoma in China

ZENG Y

Department of Tumor Viruses, Institute of Virologyc, China National Centre for Reventive Medicing, Beijing China

INTRODUCTION

There is great variation in the incidence of nasopharyngeal carcinoma(NPC)[1] in different ethnic groups. It is very common in Southern China and Southeast Asia(Atlas of Cancer Mortality, Editorial Committee, 1979). The serological relationship between Epstein-Barr(EB) virus and NPC was first demonstrated by Old et al.(1966)by means of immunodiffusion. It was subsequently shown by indirect immunofluorescence that NPC patients had various antibodies to EB virus(De Schryver et al., 1969; Henle et al., 1970), and by anticomplement immunofluorescence(Klein et al., 1974; Huang et al., 1974)and nucleic acid hybridization(Zur Hausen et al., 1970; Wolf et al., 1973)that EB virus markers(EBNA and DNA)are also regularly found in NPC cells. Henle and Henle(1976)first reported the presence of IgA antibody to EB virus as an outstanding feature of NPC. Other authors(Ho et al., 1976; Desgranges and de The. 1978)further confirmed that NPC patients from various geographic areas regularly exhibited IgA/VCA antibody and that detection of IgA/VCA antibody is useful for the diagnosis of NPC. The purpose of our studies is first to find simple and sensitive techniques that can be conveniently applied in the high-NPC risk field for the early detection of NPC, as early treatment gives a good diagnosis; and second to find the roles of EB virus, environmental factors, and genetic factors in the development of NPC. Here we summarize our serological studies on NPC.

DISTRIBUTION AND SPECTRA OF EB VIRUS ANTIBODIES IN NPC PATIENTS AND NOMAL INDIVIDUALS

EB virus infection is prevalent all over the world, but the specific incidence of primary infection varies with different social and economic groups. In order to study the prevalence of EB virus infection in China and its relation to NPC, complement-fixing antibody to EB virus was tested in sera from different age groups of normal individuals in high NPC risk areas(Guangzhou City and Zhangshan County of Guangdong Province)as well as in low NPC risk areas(Beijing City, Lufeng and Wuhua Counties of Guangdong Province). Of a total of 2300 normal sera from different age groups, 2080 were positive(≥1︰10). The positive rate was 90. 4% with a geometric mean titer(GMT) of 1︰52. 8. Seropositivity was relatively common in both the high and low NPC risk areas of the above groups, varying from 87% to 94%, and showing no great difference. The positive rate reached 90%-100% in the 3-5 year age group from different areas. These results indicated that EB virus spreads widely in China and people are infected with EB virus in early life. The age of primary infection in high and low NPC risk areas was similar(Tumor Control Team of Zhangshan County et al.,1978).

As NPC occurs more frequently in persons above 20 years of age in China it can be seen in Fig. 1 that the mean antibody titers of a healthy population over 20 in the high NPC risk areas were significantly higher than those in the low NPC risk areas(Tumor Control Team of Zhangshan County et al., 1978). This variation may indicate that the EB virus is more active in people living in high NPC risk areas and that this might be related to the development of NPC. The activation of EB virus may be due to internal or external factors. Recent data(Ito et al., 1980; Zeng et al., unpublished data) showed that the culture fluid of G-anerobic bacteria from the nasopharynx of patients with NPC or with ear-nose-throat disease could induce EB virus, EA, or VCA in Raji and P3HR-1 cells. Our data(Hu and Zeng, unpublished)also showed that n-butyrate and other extracts from the Euphorbiaceae and Thymeleaceae families could enhance the transformation of lymphocytes by EB virus. Therefore, it is necessary to study the possible role of butyric acid or these indigenous microbial products, which might activate the EB virus in vivo in the development of NPC. Ito et al(1983) reported that the ether extracts of soil samples from the ground under the plants of the Euphorbiaceae and Thymeleaceae families in Japan known to possess EB virusactivating diterpene esters induced EB virus EA in Raji cells. Our previous data(Ito et al.,1983; Zeng et al.,1983b)also reported that the extract from tung oil and the leaves and flowers of tung oil trees(Aleurites fordii)are strong inducers. There are plenty of such trees along the roads and rivers in NPC high-risk areas. In Wuzhou City and Zangwu County, the dust containing EB virus inducer from tung oil trees and other plants may be inhaled by the nasopharyngeal mucosa and thus acts as a promotor to the EB virus. Its genome is present in the normal epithelial cells, eventually leading to the malignant transformation of epithelial cells in the nasopharynx. The role of these environmental factors in the development of NPC needs to be further studied.

Various EB virus-specific antigens, including EA, VCA, membrane antigen(MA), and nuclear antigen(EBNA), are present in cells infected with EB virus; the corresponding antibody to these antigens are found in sera from persons after EB virus infection. IgA and IgG antibodies to EBV, VCA, or EA in sera from normal individuals were studied by immunoenzymatic test(no IgA/EA detected)(Fig. 2)(Zeng et al., 1983c). The positive rate of IgG/VCA antibody reached 90%-100% in the 3-5 year age group and maintained a high level for many years. The positive rate of IgG/EA antibody reached the peak(37%)at 3-5 years of age, then gradually declined to 17% at 20-29 years of age. It slightly increased at 50-59 years of age. The positive rate of IgA/VCA antibody also reached the peak(20%)at 3-5 years of age, and gradually declined. It rose slightly after 30-39 years of age. No IgA/EA antibody was found in any age group, even with the use of a very sensitive test: immunoantoradiography. This indicates that no such antibody, is produced or only very few people have such antibody after primary EB virus infection.

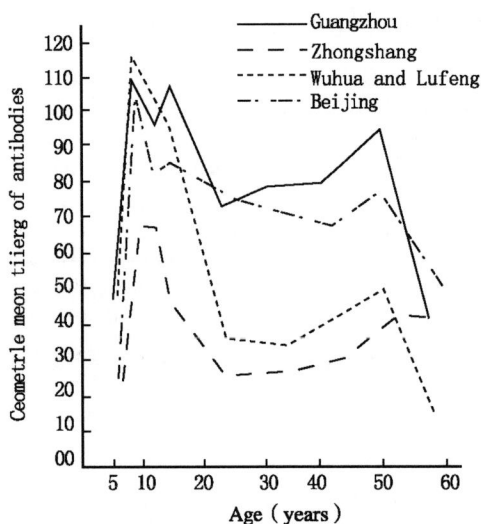

Fig. 1 Geometric mean titers of antibodies to EBV
tested by complement fixation method in the
population in high-and low-risk areas of NPC

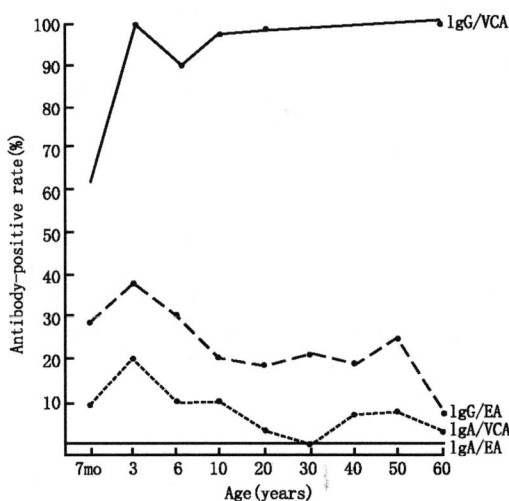

Fig. 2 Age-specific incidence of antibodies to EBV

The IgG/MA and IgA/MA antibodies in sera from NPC patients and from normal individuals were detected by immunofluorescence(Zhao and Zeng, unpublished). The positive rate and GMT of IgG/MA and IgA/MA from NPC patients was 97% and 1 : 210, 51% and 1 : 16, respectively, and those from normal individuals was 85% and 1 : 50.0% and 1 : 5, respectively. The positive rate of IgA/MA in sera from NPC patients and normal individuals is similar to that of IgA/EA from both these groups.

IgG/EA, IgA/VCA, and IgA/EA antibodies in sera from patients with NPC, with malignant tumors in head and neck other than NPC, with other malignan tumors and normal individuals were detected by immunofluorescence(Laboratory of Tumor Virus, Cancer Inst, et al., 1978, S J. Li et al., 1980; Zeng et al., 1979c). Totals of 96% and 81.5% of NPC patients had IgG/EA and IgA/VCA antibody with high GMT, respectively, whereas the positive rate of these two antibodies in three other groups was less than 6%. Of NPC patients, 50% had IgA/EA antibody, but no such antibody was found in other groups. These data indicate that IgG/EA and IgA/VCA antibodies are specific, with a high positive rate for NPC patients, and can be used for the diagnosis of NPC. But further studies showed that the positive rate of IgG/EA antibody in normal individuals was higher than that of IgA/VCA antibody, so the IgG/EA antibody was not as specific as IgA/VCA antibody for the diagnosis of NPC. The immunofluorescence test needs a fluorescence microscope and is not convenient for NPC detection in counties. An immunoenzymatic test was established in our laboratory for detection of IgA/VCA antibody(Liu et al., 1979a). As compared to immunofluorescence, the immunoenzymatic test is simpler and more sensitive. This test has been widely used in China for the diagnosis of NPC(Y. X. Liu et al., 1979；Wei et al., 1980；Jian et al., 1981；WJ. Li et al.,1982). As shown in Tab. 1, the positive arte of IgA/VCA antibody(≥1∶5) from NPC patients, patients with malignant tumors other than NPC, and normal persons was 92.5%-98.1%, 0-5.7% and 0-6%, respectively, and the GMT was 1∶35.7 to 1∶78.5, 1∶1.25 to 1∶2.7, and 1∶1.25 to 1∶5.4, respectively. The positive rate and GMT of IgA/VCA antibody was much higher than that in other control groups. Therefore, the detection of IgA/VCA antibody is valuable for the diagnosis of NPC, especially when there was no evidence of tumor in the nasopharynx, but when it had already invaded beneath the mucosa or metastasized to the lymph node of the neck rgeion.

Tab. 1 Detection of IgA/VCA Antibody to EB Virus in Sera from NPC patients and control groups

NPC patients			Patients with tumors other than NPC			Normal individuals			Reference
No. of cases	Positive rate(%)	GMT	No.of cases	Positive rate(%)	GMT	No. of Persons	Positive rate(%)	GMT	
80	92.5	1∶35.7	107	0	1∶1.25	91	0	1∶1.25	Liu et al.(1979)
628	98.1	1∶38.7	92	5.4	1∶1.25	210	0.5	1∶1.27	Wei et al.(1980)
78	92.3	1∶78.5				166	6	1∶5.40	Jian et al.(1981)
1006	93.8	1∶76.0	768	5.7	1∶2.70	756	1.9	1∶2.80	Li et al.(1982)

SEROLOGICAL MASS SURVEYS AND PROSPECTIVE STUDIES ON NPC

Detection of IgA/VCA antibody is helpful for the diagnosis of NPC, especially in its early stage. It is very important to apply the serological test in high NPC risk areas for the detection of early NPC cases. Therefore, serological mass surveys and follow-up studies were carried out in Zangwu County, Wuzhou City, and Laucheng County of the Guangxi Autonomous Region.

1. Zangwu County

A total of 148 029 persons aged 30 and over were screened by the immunoenzymatic test in1978-1980 in Zangwu County(Zeng et al., 1979a, b, 1980a, 1983c). The incidence of NPC in this county was 11/100 000, but in some communes it was up to 17/100 000. Of total NPC,91.4% occurs at age 30 and over. Sera were collected in plastic capillary tues by pricking the ear lobe, and 3533 persons were found to have EBV IgA/VCA antibody(≥1∶5). The positive rate was 2.4%. The antibody titer of the positive persons ranged from 1∶5 to 1∶2560, with a GMT of 1∶16, and 87% had antibody titers of 1∶5 to 1∶40. Only 13% had antibody with higher titer(≥1∶80). The positive rate of IgA/VCA antibody was shown to increase with age, and the age-specific prevalence curve of IgA/VCA antibody paralleled that of the NPC age-specific incidence.

All IgA/VCA antibody-positive persons were examined clinically and histologically. Biopsies were taken from suspected patients or persons with high antibody titer(≥1∶80). Among them, 55 cases were diagnosed histoologically as NPC. One was carcinoma in situ, 12 in stage Ⅰ, 19 in stageⅡ, 17 in stage Ⅲ, 6 in stage Ⅳ, and 31 cases(57%) were in early stages(Ⅰ and Ⅱ)(Tab. 2). The range of IgA/VCA antibody titer for these NPC patients was from 1∶10 to 1∶2560, with a GMT of 1∶99, and 34 cases(62%) had antibody titers of ≥1∶80.

The IgA/VCA antibody-positive cases were reexamined clinically and serologically, and biopsies were taken from the suspected patients once a year；32 new NPC patients were detected after follow-up studies for 1-3 years. All their tumors were diagnosed histologically as poorly differentiated squamous cell carcinoma or undifferentiated carcinoma. There were 10 cases in stage Ⅰ, 9 in stage Ⅱ, 11 in stage Ⅲ, and 2 in stage Ⅳ(Tab. 2)；21 cases(66%)had IgA/VCA antibody titer of ≥1∶80.. The GMT of antibody was 1∶85(Tab. 2).

There was no marked difference in GMT of IgA/VCA antibody in sera of patients in stage Ⅰ between the period before the onset of NPC and the diagnosis made at stage Ⅰ, but antibody titer was higher in stages Ⅱ-Ⅳ；e. g. when the carcinoma cells metastasized to the cervical lymph nodes, the antibody titer increased. The percentage (25.3%) of NPC at stage I detected by serological mass surveys was much higher than that(3%) diagnosed in an outpatient clinic. Of NPC patients diagnosed, 59% on follow-up studies were at stage Ⅰ and Ⅱ, with favorable outcome with radiotherapy. A total of 41% of NPC cases were diagnosed at advanced stages(Ⅲ and Ⅳ) because many IgA/VCA antibody-positive persons live in the countryside far from town, and clinical reexaminations were not carried out periodically of diagnosis was missed in the early stages. In some, carcinomas developed more rapidly. The detection rate of NPC from IgA/VCA antibody-positive persons was 82 times higher than the incidence rate of NPC in the general population of the same age group(Tab. 3).

Tab. 2   Detection of NPC cases in Zangwu County during 1978—1980 by serological mass surveys and follow-up study

	Number of NPC cases					Total
	Carcinoma in situ	Stage I	Stage II	Stage III	Stage IV	
1978-1980						
serological mass survey	1	12	19	17	6	55
Follow. up study	0	10	9	11	2	32
Total	1	22	28	28	8	87

Tab. 3   Comparison of NPC detection rates and incidence rates

Location	No. of persons examined	No. of IgA/VCA antibody- positive persons (5%)[a]	No. of NPC	NPC detection rate (1/100 000) among all persons examined (relative incidence rate)	NPC detection rate (1/100 000) among IgA/VCA antibody-positive persons (relative incidence rate)	NPC incidence rate per annum	Reference
Zangwu							
County(1978~1980)	148 029	3533(2. 4)	87	59(1. 96)[b]	2462(82)[b]	30	Zeng et al.(1983a)
Wuzhou City	12 930	680(5. 3)	13	100. 5(2)[b]	1900(38)[b]	50	Zeng et al.(1982a)
Chemical factory	216	22(10. 2)	3	1380(27. 6)[b]	13 636(272. 7)[b]	50	Zeng et al.
Zangwu							
County boat people	518	18(3. 5)	12	386(12. 8)[c]	11111(370)[c]		Zhu et al.(1983)
Laucheng							
County(Molaos)	15 324	151(0. 96)	7	45. 7(1. 5)	4636(154. 4)[c]		Wei et al.
							(unpublished data)

[a] No. of IgA/VCA-positive persons/no. of persons examined×100; [b] NPC detection rate/NPC incidence rate per annum; [c] NPC detection rate/ NPC incidence rate per annum in Zangwu Conunty

How long before clinical onset does IgA antibody develop? The IgA/VCA antibody was detected 8-30 months (average 13 months)prior to the clinical diagnosis of NPC in stage I cases, 10-18 months(average 14. 4 months) prior in stage II , 9-34 months(average 17. 3 months)prior in stage III , and 12-24 months(average 18 months)prior stage IV(Zeng et al., 1983c). These results are similar to those reported by Ho et al.(1978)and Lanier et al. (1980)in their retrospective studies. They found that IgA/VCA antibody was detectable 22-72 months before the clinical diagnosis was made in the advanced stages.

How long does IgA/VCA antibody persist? In follow-up studies of sera from normal individuals, 10% converted from IgA antibody positive to negative within 1-3 years.

2. Boat people

Ho(1978)reported that the marine population living in boats in Hong Kong has a much Higher incidence rate than the land dwellers living in congested apartments. Zangwu County is a high NPC risk area and there are still some people living and working on the boats. The incidence rate of NPC for boat people from four communes of Zangwu County was 20. 91/100 000 in 1978 and is higher than that(15. 3100 000)for people living on the land in the same communes. A serological mass survey was carried out in poeple aged 30 and over living on the boats(Zhu et al, 1983). A total of 518 sera were taken for examination of IgA/VCA and IgA/EA antibodies, of which 18 had IgA/VCA antibody(3. 47%), 5 had IgA/EA antibody(0. 97%), and 2 NPC patients(stage I and II)had both antibodies. The detection rate of NPC from persons examined from IgA/VCA antibody-positive boat people was 386/100 000 and 11 111/100 000, respectively; they were 12. 8 and 370-fold higher than the NPC incidence rate (30/100 000)of the general population of the same age groups in Zangwu County(Tab. 3). These data further confirmed that the boat people have a higher incidence rate of NPC than the people living on the land. There are many tung oil trees along the roads and rivers in Zangwu County and much rain in Southern China; thus, the soil particles with EB virus inducer easily reach the river after rain(Ito et al., 1983, Zeng et al., unpublished data). The boat people drink river water throughout their lives; therefore, the high incidence of NPC in boat people might be related to the drinking water containing EBV inducer from tung oil trees or from other sources. This needs to be confirmed.

3. Wuzhou city

In order to carry out a follow-up study on the EBV IgA/VCA antibody-positive persons and to reduce the mortality rate of NPC through early diagnosis and early treatment, another mass serological survey was carried out in Wuzhou City located in the center of Zangwu County. Wuzhou City(population 170 000)was a high risk for NPC; the mean annual incidence was 17/100 000. In the first atage, sera from 12 932 persons of the 40-59 age group were examined(Zeng et al.,1982a). IgA/VCA antibody($\geqslant 1 : 10$)was found in 680 persons with a GMT of 1 : 39, the positive rate being 5. 3%. About 70% of the people had VCA/IgA antibody titers from 1 : 10 to 1 : 40. There is a tendency for an increase with increasing age in the antibody-positive rate and in GMT. The frequency of VCA/IgA antibody for males and females was similar, and the rate was1. 2 : 1. Clinical, cytological, and histological examinations and the EBNA test were carried out in combination to detect NPC patients from IgA antibody-positive persons. Thirteen NPC cases were finally confirmed histologically. The frequency of NPC among 680 IgA/VCA antibody-positive persons was 1. 9%; 9 out of 13 NPC cases also had IgA/EA antibody. The frequency among IgA/EA antibody positive was 30%. The detection rate of NPC was 1900/100 000 for 680 IgA/VCA-positive persons. This is 38 times the NPC annual incidence(50/100 000)in the general population of the same age group(Tab. 3). The early diagnosis of NPC means a favorable outcome of radiotherapy(Chang et al., 1980). Of 13 NPC patients, 9 were in stage 1(70%)and 4 in stage Ⅱ(30%). According to the data obtained from Zangwu County and Wuzhou City, the NPC prevalence among individuals having IgA/VCA antibody was found to be related to the antibody titers:0. 9% for invididuals with IgA/VCA antibody titers between 1 : 10 to 1 : 20, 2. 3% for individuals with IgA/VCA antibody titers between 1 : 10 to1 : 20, 2. 3% for individuals with IgA/VCA antibody titers between 1 : 40 to 1 : 80, 5. 6% for individuals with IgA/VCA antibody titers between 1 : 160 and 1 : 320, and 18. 6% when IgA/VCA antibody titers reached 1 : 640 to 1 : 2560(Tab. 4).

Tab. 4　Prevalence of NPC by distribution of IgA/VCA antibody titers

	Reciprocal IgA/VCA titers				Total
	10—20	40—80	160—320	640—2560	
No. IgA/VCA +	850	520	178	59	1607
No. NPC	8	12	10	11	41
Prevalence (%)	0. 9	2. 3	5. 6	18. 6	2. 6

To date, 20 726 persons over 40 years of age have been examined, and 1136 persons were found to have IgA/VCA antibody. Among them 31 NPC cases were detected, 13 in stage Ⅰ(41. 9%), 15 in stage Ⅱ(48. 4%), and 3 in stage Ⅲ(9. 7%). The frequency of early cases(stage Ⅰ and Ⅱ)was up to 90. 3%. It was much higher than that in the outpatient clinic(3% NPC in stage Ⅰ, 39. 3% of NPC in stage Ⅱ). Therefore, it is possible to reduce the mortality rate of NPC in Wuzhou City through early detection and early treatment.

A serological survey was carried out in a chemical factory(Zeng et al. unpublished data). Samples of 216 sera from persons of age over 40 were tested, and 22 had IgA/VCA antibody. The positive rate was 10. 2%, which was higher than that(5. 3%)in Wuzhou City. Among them, 3 NPC cases in early stages(2 in stage Ⅰ, 1 in stage Ⅱ) were detected. The detection rate of NPC from persons examined and from IgA/VCA-positive persons was 1380/100 000 and 13 636/100 000, respectively. It was 27. 6 and 272. 7 times the incidence rate of NPC(50/100 000)in the general population of the same age group(Tab. 3). The retrospective study showed that 6 NPC cases were found in this factory from 1973 to 1982, and all of them were working or had worked in the oil-refining workshop. The IgA/VCA antibody-positive and detection rate of NPC was higher than that in Wuzhou City(Tab. 3), which possibly could be related to some chemicals found in the workshops that could activate the EB virus. These data further indicate that the EB virus plays an important role in the development of NPC and that relationships between the activation of EB virus and the environmental factors should be studied. A prospective follow-up study of the whole population over 30 years of age is being carried out in Wuzhou City to detect NPC patients in the early stages and to study the causative role of EB virus in the development of NPC.

4. Laucheng county

In order to determine the prevalence of IgA antibody and the NPC detection rate in the Molaos minority, sera frol 15 324 persons age 30 and over were tested for EB virus IgA/VCA and IgA/EA antibodies by means of the imunoenzymatic test(Wei et al. unpublished data). A total of 151 persons had IgA/VCA antibody and 10 from IgA/VCA antibody-positive persons had IgA/EA antibody. The positive rate of IgA/VCA antibody was 0.98% which was lower than that in Zangwu County and Wuzhou City. The positive rate of IgA/EA from IgA/VCA-positive persons was 6.6%. We detected7 NPC(2 in stage Ⅱ, 2 in stage Ⅲ, and 3 in stage Ⅳ)in IgA/VCA antibody-positive persons;4 of these in stage Ⅲ and Ⅳ also had IgA/EA antibody. The detection rate of NPC from IgA/VCA and IgA/EA antibody-positive persons was 4636/100 000 and 40 000/100 000, respectively, which was similar to that in Wuzhou City(Tab. 3). The detection rate of NPC from IgA/VCA antibody-positive persons was 154.4 times higher than the incidence rate of NPC in the general population of the same age group in high-risk areas in Zangwu County. It seems that a few more NPC patients in the early stages(stages Ⅰ and Ⅱ)should have been detected, since only 2 in stage Ⅱ out of 7 NPC patients were found. They might have been missed clinically or histologically and should be followed up. More sera from other national minorities are being studied.

IGA/EA ANTIBODY AS A SPECIFIC MARKER FOR NPC

The detection of EB virus IgA/EA antibody cannot be used alone for the routine diagnosis of NPC because other immunofluorescence test or immunoenzymatic test only reveals this antibody in 50%—75% of NPC patients (Henle and Henle, 1976; Lab. of Cancer Institute et al., 1978). IgA/EA antibody can only be detected in IgA/VCA antibody-positive but not in antibody-negative individuals. The detection rate of NPC among IgA/VCA antibody-positive individuals is 1.9% and that among IgA/EA antibody-positive individuals is 30%. The difference between these two groups is 15.8% fold. These data indicate that only a few IgA/VCA antibody-positive individuals eventually become IgA/EA antibody positive, and that IgA/EA antibody is more specific, but not so sensitive for the detection of NPC as IgA/VCA antibody. It is therefore necessary to improve the sensitivity of this test for the detection of IgA/EA antibody. An immunoautoradiographic method was established in our laboratory using ^{125}I-labeled anti-human IgA antibody for the detection of EB virus IgA/VCA antibody in sera and saliva(Liu et al., 1979a, b). This test is much more sensitive than the immunoenzymatic test, but it is too sensitive for detection of IgA/VCA antibody, so the positive percentage of IgA/VCA antibody in normal individuals in too high however, this test is useful for the detection of IgA/EA antibody(Zeng et al., 1982a). Sera from different groups were tested by immunoflrorescence, immunoenzymatic, and immunoautoradiographic methods. The positive rate and GMT of IgA/EA antibody by immunoautoradiography in sera from NPC patients were96% and 1:97, respectively. Those patients with clinically suspected NPC and who had been diagnosed histologically as having a chronic inflammation of the nasopharynx had a positive rate of 22% and a GMT of 1:9. Of 170 patients, 7 with malignant tumors other than NPC were positive(4%) to low titer 1:5.2. All normal individuals were negative. The positive rate and GMT detected by the immunoenzymatic test in these four groups were 80% and 1:25.6, 18% and 1:7.3, 0.6% and1:5, and 0% and 1:5, respectively. In the suspected NPC group(chronic inflammation)biopsies were taken again from 11 IgA/EA antibody-positive individuals, and histological examination showed poorly differentiated squamous cell carcinoma in 6 of them. Fourteen NPC patients had no IgA/VCA and IgA/EA antibodies detected by immunofluorescence and immunoenzymatic tests: however, among these 14 patients, 11 had IgA/VCA and 6 had IgA/EA antibody decected by immunoactoradiography. These data indicate that immunoautoradiography is more sensitive than either the immunofluorescence of the immunoenzymatic test in the dectection of IgA/EA antibody, and that IgA/EA antibody can serve as a specific marker for the detection of NPC. Therefore, for seroepidemiological study, it is better to proceed first using the immunoenzymatic or immunofluorescence test for the detection of IgA/VCA antibody. If this antibody is positive, the detection of IgA/EA antibody in the same serum by immunoautoradiography should then be carried out, and more NPC patients in the early stage will be detected. Recently, the immunoautoradiographic method was further simplitied by using X-ray film instead of nuclear emulsion in our laboratory(Pi et al. 1981). Similar resuits were obtained with these two methods, but the use of X-ray film is more convenient for large-scale screening in the NPC Held.

RELATIONSHIP BETWEEN IGA/VCA ANTIBODY AND EB VIRUS MARKERS(DNA AND EBNA)

In order to determine whether the presence of serum EBV/IgA antibody corresponded to the EB virus activity in the nasopharyngeal mucosa, 56 individuals having serum IgA/VCA antibody for15-18 months were clinically examined and biopsied(de The et al., 1981). A total of 4 NPC cases were found and 14 additional individuals, for whom no histopathological or clinical evidence of NPC was noted, were found to have detectable EBV/DNA sequences and/or EBNA in their nasopharyngeal mucosa(Desgranges et al., 1982). It seems therefore that the presence of EB virus markers in the nasopharyngeal mucosa could be another critical marker for the immediate risk of NPC. But it is important to know whether the EB virus DNA is also present in the nasopharyngeal mucosa from IgA/VCA antibody-negative individuals. As it was not posible to biopsy nasopharyngeal mucosa of normal and IgA/VCA antibody-negative individuals, a negative-pressure apparatus was used to collect the exfoliated cells from the nasopharynx of 62 IgA/VCA antibody-positive and39 IgA/VCA antibody-negative individuals from Wuzhou City. The exfoliated nasopharyngeal cells were tested for the presence of EBV/DNA sequences by spot followed by blot hybridization tests(Desgranges et al., 1983). Of 62 specimens, 13(21%)from IgA/VCA antibody-positive and 6 of 39 specimens(15.4%)from IgA/VCA antibody-negative individuals were found to contain EBV/DNA sequences(Tab. 5). We followed 46 persons(20 IgA/VCA antibody positive and 26 IgA/VCA antibody negative)for a year. Half of the individuals having EBV/DNA sequences in their exfoliated nasopharyngeal ceils in 1981 did not have detectable EBV sequences a year later, and 2 of the 15 negative individuals became EBV/DNA positive. These results suggest that the presence of EBV/DNA sequences and IgA/VCA antibody in the serum are not directly related.

EBNA is regularly found in nasopharyngeal carcinoma cells by means of the anticomplement technique(Klein et al., 1974; Huang et al., 1974). We have established an anticomplement immunoenzymatic method(ACIE)for the detection of EBNA(Zeng et al., 1980b, 1981; Pi et al., 1981)which thus proved to be a sensitive test. The exfoliated cells from the nasopharynx obtained by negative pressure were examined by ACIE for the detection of EBNA, for the diagnosis of NPC, and for the study of the relationship of EB virus and NPC. EBNA was found not only in NPC cells, but also in normal epithelial and hyperplastic cells(Zeng et al., 1981, 1982b). Further study of EBNA in the exfoliated cells of the nasopharynx of persons with nasopharyngeal chronic inflammation showed that 34.6% of IgA/VCA antibody-positive persons and 19.6% of IgA/VCA antibody-negative persons had EBNA in their epithelial cells(Tab. 5)(Shen et al., 1983). These data were similar to that of EBV DNA, but there was no obvious correlation between EB virus markers(DNA and EBNA) and EB virus serology.

Tab. 5 Detection of EBV markers in nasopharyngeal mucosa from IgA/VCA-positive and negative Individuals

EBV markers	IgA/VCA antibody positive	IgA/VCA antibody negative	Reference
DNA +	13/62(21%)	6/39(15.4%)	Desgranges et al(1983)
DNA−	49/62(79%)	33/39(84.6%)	
EBNA+	9/26(34.6%)[a]	9/46(19.6%0)[a]	Shen et al(1983)
EBNA−	7/26(65.4%)[a]	37/46(80.4%)[a]	

Notes:[a]Chronic inflammation of nasopharynx

RELATIONSHIP BETWEEN EB VIRUS IGA/VCA ANTIBODY AND CLINICAL CHANGES IN NASOPHARYNX

The correlation between mucosal hyperplastic lesion and the level of antibody to EB virus was studied by complement fixtion(Dept. of Microbiology, Zhangsham Medical College et al, 1980). It was interesting to note that the GMT(1:90)of anticomplement-fixing antibody to EB virus in persons with hyperplastic lesions was significantly higher than that(1:66)in normal individuals.

A serological mass survey was carried out in Wuzhou City in persons 40 to 59 years of age(Zeng et al., 1983a; Zhang et al., unpublished data). Among 20 726 sera, 867 persons having IgA/VCA antibody were examined with indirect nasopharyngoscopy. The GMT of IgA/ VCA antibody in persons with normal mucosa, polyps, residual adenoid, chronic inflammation, asymmetry of nasopharyngeal cavity, atropic changes of nasopharynx, and hypertrophic nodule or tumor-like nodule was 1:32.6, 1:20, 1:28.7, 1:28.7, 1:40, 1:47,1:52.2, and 1:78.6, respectively. According to their severity or clinical changes these seven types of conditions were classified into group 1(normal mucosa, polyps, and residual adenoid), group 2(chronic inflammation, asymmetry of nasopharyngeal cavity, and atrophic change of nasopharynx), and group 3(hypertrophic nodule or tumor-like nodule). There was a marked difference in GMT between these three groups. Among 38 cases with hypertropic nodules in group3, 24 NPC(63.2%)were detected. A group of 248 IgA/VCA antibody-negative persons was also examined for lesions in the nasopharynx as a control. Most(74.6%)belonged to group 1, and only a few were in group 2 (25.4%). NPC was not found in the antibody-negative persons. These data indicate that the clinical changes in the nasopharynx and the development of NPC were closely related to the presence of IgA/VCA antibody.

RELATIONSHIP BETWEEN EB VIRUS IGA/VCA ANTIBODY AND HISTOLOGICAL CHANGES IN NASOPHARYNX

From 1978 to 1981 serological mass surveys for NPC were carried out in Zangwu County; the antibody-positive persons were examined by nasopharyngoscope. Biopsies were taken from the following atibody-positive persons:(1)those diagnosed clinically as NPC patients or suspected of having NPC;(2)those having some lesions in the nasopharynx, such as hyperplasia or a residue of adenoidal tissue, rough mucosa, local congestion, or inflammation; and;(3)those without lesions, in the nasopharynx but with high antibody titer(E. J. Li et al., 1983). The GMT of IgA/ VCA antibody from group 1(persons with normal mucosa, simple hyperplasia, and simple metaplasia)and group 2(atypical hyperplasia and atypical metaplasia)was 1 : 25.2, 1 : 30.4, 1 : 22.4;1 : 105.4, and 1 : 80, respectively. There was a marked difference in GMT of IgA/VCA antibody between these two groups(1 : 25.3 and 1 : 86.7).

A group of 45 IgA/VCA antibody-positive persons persons without carcinoma were fwollowed for 8-33 months with serological and histological examinations. Nasopharynx changes were of the following three types:(1) simple hyperplasia and simple metaplasia evolved into atypical hyperplasia, atypical met aplasia, or into carcinoma;(2)atypical hyperplasia and atypical metaplasia evolved into carcinoma or remained the same form of lesion;(3)carcinoma in situ with little invasion found in the first and final biopsies. When the pathological changes were more advanced, their antibody levels were elevated. The difference was significant. In 32 persons without any lesions in the nasopharynx, there was no remarkable alteration shown in the initial and final clinical examinations; their antibody levels did not show any obvious difference. When antibody levels were found to be elevated in some persons, it may be assumed that the pathological changes in the nasopharynx were more severe. Therefore, IgA/ VCA antibody may be regarded as a reference index of the development of the pathological lesions in the nasopharynx. Among 45 IgA/VCA antibody-positive persons, 5 of17 with atypical hyperplasia or atypical metaplasia developed NPC(29.4%), whereas in 38 persons with simple hyperplasia, simple metaplasia, or normal mueosa, only 1 developed NPC(2.6%). The difference in the development of NPC in these two groups was significant(Li,1985). The frequency of atypical lesions in the antibody-positive cancerous group was highest, but it was lower in those in the antibody-positive noncancerous group, and least in the antibody-negative noneanerous group. All these results suggest that EB virus plays an important role in the development of NPG.

CONCLUSION

Serological studies showed that the GMT of complement-fixing antibody to EB virus in healthy individuals over 20 years of age in the high NPC risk areas was significantly higher than that in the low NPC risk areas; that the positive rate of IgA/VCA antibody in sera from the general population of 30 years of age and over in high NPC risk areas increased with increasing age; that the presence of IgA/VCA antibody was closely related to clinical and pathological changes in the nasopharynx; that IgA/VCA antibody to EB virus is specific for NPC; that the detection rate of NPC from[gA/VCA antibody-positive persons was much higher than that from the general population of the same age group; and that the IgA/VCA antibody can be detected 8-30 months prior to the clinical and histological diagnosis of NPC in stage I. The detection rate of NPC from IgA/EA-positive persons was up to 30%-40%. These data suggested that EB virus plays an important role in the development of NPC and that the mortality rate of NPC can be reduced through early detection and treatment. But EB virus is not the unique factor. Others, such as environmental and genetic factors and their synergistie effects with EB vires, might also play an important role. This needs further study.

REFERENCES

[1] Atlas of Cancer Mortality in the People's Republic of China, Editorial Committee. China Map Press. 1979.

[2] Chang CP, Liu TF. Chang YW, Cao SL. Acta Radiol. Oncol, 1980, 19;433-438.

[3] Dept of Microbiology and Cancer, Hospital of Zhongshan Medical College, Dept. of Virology, Cancer Institute; Dept. of Tumor Viruses, Institute of Virology; Cancer Inst. of Zhongshan County Chin. Med J, 1980, 93;359-364.

[4] De Schryver A, Friberg S Jr, Klein G, Henle G, Henle W, de-The G, Clifford. P Ho H C. Clin. Exp. Immunol, 1969, 5: 443-459.

[5] Desgranges, de The G(1978). IARC Sci. Publ 1978, 24;883-891.

[6] Desgranges C, Bornkamm GW, Zeng Y, Wang PC, Zhu JS, Shang M, med de The G.. Int J Cancer, 1982, 29;87-91.

[7] Desgranges C, Pi GH, Bornkamm GW, Lagrand. C Zeng Y. and de The G. Int J. Cancer,1983, 32: 543-545.

[8] De The G, Desgranges C, Zeng Y, Wang PC, Bornkamm GW, Zhu JS, Shang M. Int Syrup Nasopharyngeal Carcinoma, 11 th, Duesseldorf,1981, 5;111-118.

[9] Henle G, Henle W. Int J Cancer,(1976), 17:1-7.

［10］Henle W, Henle G, Ho HC, Burtin P, Cachin Y, Clifford P De, Schryyver A, de The G, Diehl V, Klein G. Cancer Inst, 1970, 44:225-231.

［11］Ho JHC, Int J Radiol Oncol Biol. Phys, 1978,4:181.

［12］Ho JHE, Ng MH, Kwan HC, Chan JCW, Br J Cancer, 1976, 34:655-660.

［13］Ho JHC, Kwan HC, Ng MH, de The G, Lancet, 1978, 1:436-437.

［14］Huang DP, Ho JHC, Henle W, Henle G. Int J Cancer, 1974, 14:580-588.

［15］Ito Y, Kishishita M, Yanase S. Cancer Res,1980, 40:4329-4330.

［16］Ito Y, Ohigashi H, Koshimizu K, Zeng Y. Cancer Lett, 1983, 19:113-117.

［17］Jian SW, Li ZW, Luo WL, Li MS, Pan WZ, Zhang XH. Cancer Res Rep Cancer Inst. Zhongshan Med College, 1981, 2: 23-25.

［18］Klein G, Giovanella BC, Lindahl T, Fialkow PJ, Singh S, Stehlin J. Proc Natl Acad Sci USA, 1974, 71:4737-4741.

［19］Lab of Tumor Viruses, Cancer Inst: Lab of Tumor Viruses, Inst. of Epidemiology; Dept. of Radiotherapy, Cancer Inst: Dept. of Otolaryngology. Beijing Worker-Peasant-Soldier Hospital. Acta Microbiol Sin, 1978, 18:253-258.

［20］Lanier AP, Henle W, Bender TR, Henle G, Talbot ML. Int J Cancer, 1980, 26:133-137.

［21］LiE J, Tan BF, Zeng Y, Wang PC, Zhong JM, Tang H, Zhu JS, Wei JN, Pan WT. Chin J Pathol, 1983, 12:9-11.

［22］Li EJ, Tan BF, Zeng YI, Wang PZ, Zhong JM, Tang H, Zhu JS, Liu YX, Wei JN, Pan WJ. Chin Med J In Press. 1985.

［23］LiS J, Zhon YB, Hu XT, Zeng Yi, Chin J ENT, 1980, 15:71-74.

［24］Li WJ, Li CC, Liang YR, Chen AM, Zhang F, Ho PY. Cancer(Chinese), 1982, 1:43-48.

［25］Liu YX, Zeng Y, Dong WP, Gao GR. Chin J Oncol, 1979, 1:8-12.

［26］Liu ZR, Shan M, Zeng Y, Han ZS, Dai HJ, Hu YL, Cao GR, Dong WP. Kexne Tongbao,1979a, 24:715-720.

［27］Liu ZR, Shan M, Zeng YD, Ai HJ, Du RS. Chin J Med Exam, 1979b. 2:197-198.

［28］Old LJ, Boyes EA, Oettgen HF, De Harven E, Geering G, Williamson B, Clifford, P. Proc, Natl Acad Sci USA, 1966, 56:1699-1704.

［29］Pi GH, Zeng Y, Zhao WP, Zhang Q. J Immunol Methods, 1981, 4473-78.

［30］Shen SJ, Chen CP, Ma. JL, Zhong W, and Zeng Y, Acta Zhanjiang Med, College, 1983,1:34-37.

［31］Tumor Control Team, Zhongshan County, Dept. Microbiology, Zhongshan Med. College; Lab of Tumor Viruses. Cancer Inst and Inst of Epidemiology, Chinese Academy of Medical Sciences. Chin J Ear Nose, Throat, 1978, 1:23-25.

［32］Wei JN, Zhang S, Tung SZ, Huang ZL. Guangxi Yi Xue, 1980, 6:5-6.

［33］Wolf H, Zur Hansen H, Becket V. Nature(London). New Biol, 1973, 244:245-247.

［34］Zeng Y, Liu YX, Liu CR, Chen SW, Wei JN, Zhu JS, Zai HG. Chin J Oncol, 1979A, 1:2-7.

［35］Zeng Y, Liu YX, Wei JN, Zhu JS, Cai SL, Wang PZ, Zhong JM, LiRC, Pan WJ, LiE J, Tan BF. Acta Acad. Med. Sin, 1979b, 1:123-126.

［36］Zeng Y, Zhang M, Liu ZR, Zheng YH, Du RS, Li XH, Gan BW, Hu MG, Zhen M, He SA, Mu GP, Chin J Oncol, 1979c, 1:81-83.

［37］Zeng Y, Liu YX, Liu ZR, Zhen SW, Wei JN, Zhu JS, Zei HS. Itercirology, 1980a,13:162-168.

［38］Zeng Y, Pi CH, Zho WP. Acta Acad. Med. Sin,1980b, 2:134-135.

［39］Zeng Y, Pi GH, Zhang Q, Shen SJ, Zhao ML, Ma JL, Dong HJ. Int Symp Nasopharyngeal Carcinoma, 11 th Duesseldorf, 1981, 5: 237-244.

［40］Zeng Y, Zhang LG, Li HY, Jan MC, Zhang Q, Wu YC, Wang YS, SuGR. Int J Cancer,1982a, 29:139-141.

［41］Zeng Y, Zhen SJ, Dan H, Ma TL, Zhang Q, Zhu JS, Zheng TR, Tan BF. Acta Acad Med Sin, 1982b, 4:254-255.

［42］Zeng Y, Cong CH, Jan MG, Fan C, Zhong LK. Int J Cancer, 1983a, 31:599-601.

［43］Zeng Y, Zhong JM, Mo YK, Miao XC, Intercirology, 1983b, 19:201-204.

［44］Zeng Y, Zhong JM, Li LY, Wang PZ, Tang H, Ma YR, Zhu TS, Pan WJ, Liu YX, Wei JN, Chen JY, Mo YK, Li. EJ, Tan. BF. Interoirology, 1983, 20:190-194.

［45］Zhu ZS, Pan WJ, Zhong JM, Li LY, Zeng Y, Jan MG, Fan C. J Tumor Precent Treat Study, 1983, 10:189-190.

［46］Zur Hausen H, Schulte Holthausen H, Klein G, Henle W, Henle G, Clifford P, Santessoni L. Nature(London). 1970. 228:1056-1058.

［In《Advance in Cancer Research》1985，44:121-139］

Nasopharyngeal Carcinoma: Early Detection and IgA-Related pre-NPC Condition, Achievements and Prospectives

ZENG Yi, de The Guy

Institute of virology-Beijing PRC and CNRS laboratory, FAC of med a carrel, lyon france

INTRODUCTION

Undifferentiated carcinomas of the nasopharynx(or NPC)represent a major cancer killer for more than 200 million people in South China, as well as in large areas of the southeast Asia, North and East Africa and in Eskimo populations. This cancer is closely associated with the ubiquitous Epstein Barr herpes virus. In contrast with the situation observed in Burkitt's Lymphoma, the association between EBV and NPC is constant in every part of the world where NPC is observed, and unrelated to its level of incidence. Such an association, most probably causative in nature, has recently been reviewed(de-The, 1982, 1984).

Following the observation of Wara, W. M. et al. in 1975, that NPC patients had high level of IgA antibodies, Henle and Henle(1976)and Desgranges and de-The(1978)showed that such IgA were directed against VCA and EA and were regularly observed in NPC patients from Chinese, Arabic and Caucasian origins, but absent in Patients with other ENT tumor. These data urged us to use the IgA/VCA test for early detection of this tumor in the endemic areas of South China(Zeng et al., 1979, 1980, 1982). We shall review first these population surveys, then discuss the pre- NPC conditions associated with rising titers of IgA.

The interplay between an ubiquitous EB Virus and nasopharyngeal carcinoma stresses the need for other environmental factors, possibly related to life-style, and to the reactivation of EBV.

1. Early detection of NPC in high risk populations of south china

(1)1978—1980: Survey in Zang-Wu County

A major survey was implemented in 1978, in a rural area of the Eastern part of the Guang-Xi autonomous region(Zeng et al, 1979, 1980). The County of Zeng-Wu. comprises 15 communes with a total population of 450 000. Starting in 1978, individuals aged 30 and above, were registered and a small amount of blood was collected. The sera were tested for IgA/VCA antibodies by the immunoenzymatic test(Zeng et al, 1980). As seen in Tab. 1, a total of 148 029 persons were thus screened and 3533 were found to have IgA/VCA antibodies. The positive sera were then titered and 13% showed titer superior or equal to 80, representing 460 individuals. All the 3533 IgA/VCA positive persons, were then clinically examined, and 55 NPC patients uncovered. The clinical stages at which the patients were recognized are given in Tab. 1. where it can be seen that the majority were at stage Ⅱ and Ⅲ of the disease.

The clinical follow-up of the IgA positive individuals for 1 to 3 years led to the diagnosis of an- other 32 cases. The distribution of these cases according to stages, was not dramatically different from that of the main survey although there was a shift to early ages of detection(Tab. 1).

Tab. 1　Detection of NPC Cases in Zang-Wu County during 1978-1980 by IgA/VCA Test and during 1 to 3 years follow-up

	No of surveyed person	Ca insitute	Stages of NPC detected								Total NPC detected
			Ⅰ	%	Ⅱ	%	Ⅲ	%	Ⅳ	%	
1978-1980 Serological mass survey	148 029	1	12	22	19	34	17	31	6	11	55
Follow-up	3478	0	10	31	9	28	11	34	2	6	32
for 1-3 years of IgA/VCA+Total		1	22		28		28		8		87

(2)Wu-Zhou City

The City of Wu-Zhou, located in the centre of the Zang-Wu County, with a population of 170 000, was an i-deal place to try and implement an early detection of NPC with a systematic survey and follow-up of the town dwellers.

Previous cancer registration in the town of Wu-Zhou, showed that the mean annual incidence of NPC was around 17 to 20 per 100 000. As seen in Tab. 2, survey of nearly 21 000 individuals aged 40 and above in Wu-Zhou, showed that 1136(5.5%)persons had IgA/VCA antibodies. Clinical examination of this later group allowed the detection of 31 cases of NPC, the clinical stages being given in Tab. 2. It is remarkable to see that in this survey of the Wu-Zhou City, the proportion of stage Ⅰ and Ⅱ represented 90% of the tumor detected. This was due to the fact that clinical detection of the tumor had been efficient since a few years in this town. The prevalence rate of NPC in the surveyed population thus reached 150/100 000, a very high figure if one considers tuat patients at stage Ⅲ and Ⅳ of the disease present in hopitals were not included.

Tab. 2　Survey in Wu-Zhou City

| | No persons examined | No IgA/VCA positive | % | No NPC | Stages of NPC | | | | | | | PC prey. rate in survey | NPC prev in IgA/VCA + indiv. |
					Ⅰ	%	Ⅱ	%	Ⅲ	%	Ⅳ		
General Popular	20 726	1136	5.5	35	15	43	17	48.5	3	8.5	0	1.5	27
Chemical Factory	216	22	10	3								14	136

A serological survey, carried out in a chemical factory, detected more NPC than expected. As seen in Tab. 2. 216 individuals were tested in this factory and 22 or(10%)were found IgA/VCA positive. Among those, 3 were discovered having NPC, Although this may be due to chance an experimental investigation of the chemicals handled in this factory has been implemented.

(3)Laucheng County

Situated in a Northern part of the Guang-Xi autonomous region, Laucheng County is inhabited by two sub-language groups, namely the Molaos and the Hans. As seen in Tab. 3, the survey of 15 324 individuals from the Molaos minority gave a prevalence of 1% IgA/VCA positive(151 persons)and 7 cases of NPC were detected. In the Han majority, 0.6% of the surveyed population had IgA/VCA antibodies and 6 cases of NPC were detected (Tao et al., in press).

Tab. 3　Survey of Laucheng County

Sub-language groups	No. persons examined	No. IgA/VCA positive	%	NPC detected	NPC prev-rate in survey	NPC prey. in IgA/VCA+indiv
Molaos	15 324	151	1	7	45/100 000	4.6%
Han	11 117	76	0.6	6	54/100 000	7.9%

(4)IgA/EA antibodies represent a better test for early detection of NPC

Whereas immunoflorescent(Desgranges and de The, 1978)and immunoenzymatic tests(Laboratory of Cancer Institute, 1978)detected IgA/EA antibodies in about 70% to 75% of NPC patients, the immuno-autoradiographic test developed by Zeng et al, 1983(using ^{125}I-labelled antihuman IgA ant ibodies)detected IgA/EA antibodies in 96% of NPC patients with a GMT titer of 1∶97. Using this later test, patients with chronic inflammation of the nasopharynx, had IgA/EA antibodies in 22% of the cases with a GMT titer of 1∶9. Patients with malignant tumors other than NPC were positive in 4% of the cases with a GMT titer of 1∶5. All normal individuals were found negative.

Tab. 4. gives the comparative results of both the IgA/VCA and IgA/EA tests in detecting NPC in Wu-Zhou City and Launcheng County. It can be seen that 30% to 43% of individuals with IgA EA antibodies have a detectable NPC.

Such test, sensitive and specific, could replase the IgA/VCA test for the early detection of NPC, since the background noise of IgA/EA in non NPC individuals is very low. Furthermor, IgA/ EA test Will be most instrumental for detecting and investigating pre-NPC conditions(see below).

Tab. 4　Comparison of IgA/VCA and IgA/EA in detecting NPC*

	No. persons surveyed	IgA VCA+	IgA/EA+	NPC detected	% of NPC among IgA+
Wu-Zhou	12 930	68013		2	
City			30	9	30
Laucheng	26 441	227		13	5.7
County			14	6	43
Total NPC detected					28

* by immunoenzymatic test

(5)an elisa test using monoclonal antibodies has been recently developed(Pi et al. submitted for publication)

Such a test, which has nearly the same sensibility and a better specificity for IgA/VCA and IgA/EA than the immunoenzymatic and immunoautoradiographical tests and which is best adapted to field conditions, should ease the implementation of population ser-oepidemiological surveys, in large areas of Souty-East Asia, where this cancer is a main killer.

2. IgA related pre-NPC conditions

It appears as if the presence of IgA antibody to VCA and to EA represents pre NPC conditions(de-The, Zeng et al., 1983). In order to see whether the presence of IgA antibodies corresponded to a specific viral activity in nasopharyngeal mucosa, 56 individuals with IgA/VCA antibodies for more than 18 months, were clinically examined, and biopsied. Four NPC cases were found(two at early stages of the disease)and further 14 individuals had detectable EBV/DNA sequences and/or EBNA antigen in their nasopharynegal mucosa without histopathological nor clinical evidence of NPC(Desgranges et al., 1982). As it was not possible to take nasopharyngeal biopsies from normal ivdividuals lacking IgA/VCA antibodies, exfoliated cells collected from the nasopharynx(using a negative pressure apparatus developed by Zhangjiang Medical College in 1976) in 62 IgA/ VCA antibody positive and 39 IgA/VCA antibody negative individuals were tested for the presence of EBV/DNA sequences by spot followed by blot-hybridization(Desgranges et al., 1983). As seen in Tab. 5, 13 of the 62 IgA/VCA positive specimen(21%), and 6 out of the 39 IgA negative specimen(15.4%), were found to contain EBV/DNA sequences. Among those, 20 IgA/VCA antibody positive and 26 IgA/VCA antibody negative individuals were followed a year later. Their exfoliated cells from the nasopharynx were again collected, and tested for the presence of EBV/DNA sequences. Three out of seven individuals who showed a year previously EBV/DNA sequence in exfoli- ated nasopharyngeal cells, failed to do so a year later. In parallel, 2 out of 15 EBV/DNA negative exfoliated cells became EBV/DNA positive a year later. Such results suggest that the presence of EBV/DNA sequences in the nasopharynx, and the presence of IgA/VCA or IgA/EA antibodies in the serum, are not directly related. Unfortunatly, the cell type harbouring the EBV/DNA could not be characterized in these studies. In situ, hybridizations made by A. Wolf et al. (unpublished)on a few samples from IgA/VCA positive individuals suggested that the EBV/DNA positive cells were of epithelial nature.

Tab. 5　Comparative detection of EBV/DNA and EBNA in IgA/VCA positive and negative individuals

	No. tested	EBV/DNA* positive		No. tested	EBNA** positive	
IgA/VCA positive individuals	62	13	21%	26	9	34%
IgA/VCA negative individuals	39	6	15%	46	9	20%

Notes: * Desgranges et al, 1983; ** Shen et al, 1983

Using an anticomplement immunoenzymatic method(ACIE), for the detection of EBNA(Shen et al., 1983), exfoliated cells from the nasopharynx obtained from positive and negative IgA/VCA individuals were tested by this anticomplement immunoenzymatic test. As seen in Tab. 5, 34% of IgA/VCA positive and 20% of IgA/VCA negative individuals has detectable EBNA in cells which were considered as epithelial. Thus the virus seems to be present in normal conditions in nasopharyngeal mucosa. The development of IgA/VCA antibodies must reflect a critical difference in the local immune response against the EB viral infection. In fact, IgA/EA antibodies are usually present in IgA/VCA positive individuals, thus reflecting a reactivation of the virus. That such reactivation takes place in the nasopharynx in highly probable, but not yet established, nor the fact that it precedes and not succeeds sub-clinical development of NPC.

In the Couny of Zang Wu 1138 individuals with IgA/VCA antibodies were followed for 3 years from both the serological and clinical view-points. Tab. 6 shows that 40% of them(455 individuals)exhibited stable IgA/VCA titers. Among those, 6 developed NPC within 3 years of follow-up(1.3%). 398 individuals(35%)lost their IgA/VCA antibodies within this period and no NPC was discovered among them. IgA/VCA antibodies increased by 4 dilutions of more in 81 individuals and 15 of them developed NPC(18.5%). These results(Zeng et al., in preparation)strongly support the hypothesis that EBV reactivation, reflected by a specific serological profile(increasing titers of IgG EA, IgA VCA, IgA EA)represents a pre-NPC condition. Whether or not such conditions reflect our inablility to detect sub-clinical tumorous growth in the submucosa of the naso- pharynx remains to be determined.

Tab. 6　Stability and fluctuations of IgA/VCA antibody over 3 years in relation to risk of NPC

Item	Perons IgA/VCA+	stability (no change in IgA/VCA Ab)	Loss of IgA/VCA Ab (retroversion)	Fluctuation in IgA/VCA Antibodies		
				Increase[a]	Decline[b]	Variations of IgA/VCA Ab[a,b]
n	1138	455	398	81	162	42
%	100%	40%	35%	7.1%	14.2%	3.9%
NPC patients detected		6		15		

Notes: a, b: 4 fold increase(a)or decrease(b)

3. Perspective and priorities

Early detection of NPC by the IgA/VCA or probably better by the IgA/EA test is feasible today, and should therefore be applied for the benefit of large populations at risk for this tumour which represent approximately 230 millions persons around the world. Tab. 7 gives the difference in the clinical stages of NPC patients diagnosed in out-patients clinicas, and of the patients detected during the above described early detection schemes. The shift towards early stages is obvious(43% versus 1.7% detected at stage Ⅰ). Such a shift should have a critical impact on mortality by NPC, if one considers the 5 year survival rates after radiotherapy according to clinical stages. In Shanghai, for example(Zeng personal communication), more than 90% of NPC patients treated at stage Ⅰ of the disease exhibited a 5 year disease free survival. In contrast, NPC patients diagnosed at stage Ⅳ and Ⅴ, which represent the majority in out-patients clinics of endemic areas, have less than one year survival in 70% of the cases.

It is therefore of great interest to see that EBV serology has such a critical and practical impact for patients' care before the nature of the relationship between the virus and this cancer was uncovered. It is a clear example where important applications for public health can be implemented prior to the understanding of the mechanism involved. If the final proof that EBV is cansually related to NPC is not yet at hand, the results shown in Tab. 1, 4, 6 and 7 strongly favour an etiolgical role of the virus in the development of undifferentiated carcinomas of the nasopharynx.

Tab. 7　Comparison of NPC stage from outpatient clinic and from serological screening

		No of cases	Stages			
			Ⅰ	Ⅱ	Ⅲ	Ⅳ
Outpatient Clinic	N	1066	18	312	556	180
Clinic	%	100%	1.7%	31.3%	51.3%	17.2%
Serological+	N	35	15	17	3	
screening	%	100%	43%	48.5%	8.5%	

The priorities in Prevention Research concerning NPC should focus on the understanding of the virological, molecular and immunological events taking place in the nasopharyngeal mucosa during the pre-NPC events. Such an understanding will in turn permit the implementation of primary prevention, either by anti EBV interventions or by eliminating co-factors. Such co-factors may be present in the immediate environment of individuals at risk(Ito et al., 1983, Zeng et al.,1983). or possibly accociated with bacterial flora in the nasopharynx(Zeng et al., in press).

ACKNOWLEDGMENTS

Some aspects of these studiees were supported by the CNRS, and the Fondation pour la Recherche Medicale, Paris.

REFERENCES

[1] Desgranges C, de The G. IgA and nasopharyngeal carcinoma, in: Oncogenesis and Herpesviruses Ⅲ (G. de The, Y. Ito, and F. Rapp eds). pp. 883-891, IARC Scientific Publications No,1978, 25, Lyon.

[2] Desgranges C, Born kamm GW, Zeng Y, Wang PC, Zhu JS, Shang H, de The G. Detection of Epstein-Barr viral DNA in the nasopharyngeal mucosa of Chinese with IgA/EBV-specific antibodies, Int J Cancer, 1982, 29:187-191.

[3] Desgranges C, Pi GH, Bornkamm GH. Legrand C, Zeng Y, de The G. Presence of EBV-DNA sequences in nasopharyngeal cells of individuals without IgA/VCA antibodies. Int J Cancer, 1983,32: 543-545.

[4] De The G, Epidemiology of Epstein-Barr Virus and Associated Diseases in Man. in Man. in: The Herpesviruses, vol 1. Roizman, B(ed). pp 25-103, Plenum Publishing Corporation, New York, 1982.

[5] De The G, The role of the Epstein-Barr Virus(EBV)in the etiology and control of nasopharyn- geal carcinma(NPC). In: Cancer of the Head and Neck, Williams and Wilkins Publishers,1984.

[6] De The G, Zeng Y. Desgranges C, Pi GH. The Existence of Pre-Nasopharyngeal Carcinoma Conditions Should Allow Preventive Interventions. In: Nasopharyngeal Carcinoma: Gurrent Concepts, Prasad et al,(eds). University ot Malaya, Kuala Lumpur, 1983, 365-374.

[7] Ito Y, Ohigashi H. Koshimizu K, Zeng Y. Epstein-Barr Virus-activating principle in the ether extracts of soils collected from under plants which contain active diterpene esters. Cancer Letters, 19, pp. 113-117, Elsevier Scientific Publishers Ireland Ltd, 1983.

[8] Hene G, Henle W. Epstein-Barr virus-specific IgA serum antibodies as an outstanding feature of nasopharyngeal carcinoma, Int J Cancer, 1976,17:1-7.

[9] Laboratory of Tumor Viruses of Cancer Institute, Laboratory of Tumor Viruses of Institute of Epidemiology, Department of Radiotherapy of Cancer Institute, Department of Otolaryngology of Beijing Worker-Peasant-Soldier Hospital, Detection of EB virus-specific serum IgG and IgA antibodies from patients with nasopharyngeal carcinoma, Acta Microbiol Sin, 1978, 18:253-258.

[10] Pi GH, Zeng Y, de The G. Enzyme-linked immunosorbent Assay for the detection of Epstein- Barr Virus IgA/EA antibody (submitted for publication).

[11] Shen SJ, Chen CP, Ma JL, Zhong W, Zeng Y. Further study on detection of EBNA from nasopharyngeal exfoliated cells of patients with nasopharyngeal carcinoma. Acta Zhanjiang Medical College, 1983, 1:34-37.

[12] Tao EG, Wang PC, Wei JN, Li EJ, Wei RF, Too CM, Gu ST, Tan SM, Tang H, Zeng Y, Pi GH. Serological Mass Survey of Nasopharyngeal Carcinoma in Laucheng County,(submitted for publication).

[13] Wara WM, Wara DW, Phillips TL, Ammahh A. Elevated IgA in Carcinoma of the Nasopharynx Cancer, 1975, 35: 1313-1315.

[14] Zeng Y, Liu YX, Wei JN, Zhu JS, Cai SL, Wang PZ, Zhong JM, Li RC, Pan WJ, Li EJ, Tan BF. Serological mass survey of nasopharyngeal carcinoma. Acta Acad Med Sin, 1979, 1: 123-126.

[15] Zeng Y, Liu YX, Liu ZR, Zhen SW, Wei JN, Zhu JS, Zei HS. Application of an immunoenzymatic method and an immunoautoradiographic method for a mass survey of nasopharyngeal carcinoma, Interviology, 1980, 13:162-168.

[16] Zeng Y, Zhang LG, Li HY, Jan MC, Zhang Q, Wu YC, Wang YS, Su GR, Serological mass survey for early detection of nasopharyngeal carcinoma in Wuzhou City, China. Int J Cancer,1982, 29:139-141.

[17] Zeng Y, Zhong JM, Li LY, Wang PZ, Tang H, Ma YR, Zhu TS, Pan WJ, Liu YX, Wei JN, Chen JY, MYK, Li EJ, Tan BF. Follow-up studies on Epstein-Barr, virus IgA/VCA Antibody Positive Persons in Zangwu County, China. Intervirology, 1983, 20:190-194.

[18] Zeng Y, Gi ZW, Wang PC, Tan HZ, Ito Y. Induction of Epstein-Barr Virus Antigen in Raji cells and P3HR-1 cells by culture fluids of anaerobes from nasopharynx of patients with nasopharyngeal carcinoma and with other ear-nosethroat diseases.(submitted for publication).

[19] Zeng Y, Miao XC, Jaio B, Li HY, Ni HY, Ito Y. Epstein-Barr Virus activation in Raji cells with ether extracts of soil from different areas in China. Cancer Letters, in press.

[20] Zeng Y, Gong MG, Jan MG, Zeng LG, Li HY. Detection of Epstein-Barr Virus IgA/EA antibody for diagnosis of nasopharyngeal carcinoma by immunoautoradiolgraphy. Int J Cancer, 1983,31:599-601.

[21] Zeng Y, Zhong JM, Mo YK, Miao XC. Epstein-Barr virus early antigen induction in Raji cells by Chinese medical herbs, Intervirology,1983, 19:201-205.

[22] Zhangjiang Medical College, Diagnosis of nasopharyngeal carcinoma by cytological examination of exfoliated cells taken by negative pressure suction. Chin Med J, 1976, 1:45-47.

[In《Epstein-Barr Virus and Associated Disease》1985, 151-163]

Nasopharyngeal Mucosal Changes in EB Virus VCA-IgA Antibody Positive Persons

LI Er-koe[1] , TAN Bi-fang[2] , ZENG Yi[3] , WANG Pei-zhong[1] , ZHONG Jian-ming[2] ,
DENG Hoog[2] , ZHU Chi-song, WEI Ji-neng[1] , PAN Wen-Jun[2]

1. People's Hospital, Guangxi Zhuang Autonomous Region; 2. Antitumor Office, Zangwu County, Guangxi;
3. Institute of Virology, Chinese Academy of Medical Sciences

[SUMMARY] The immuno-enzymatic method was used and serum VCA-IgA antibody was detected in mass surveys. The relationship between the antibody level and nasopharyngeal carcinoma (NPC) and non- NPC lesions were studied. The results showed that in the NPC or non-NPC antibody positive group, the occurrence of atypical hypereplasis or metaplasia was higher than in the antibody negative group of non-NPC patients and the antibody level in NPC atypical hyperplasia or methaplasia was higher than in simple hyperplasia or metaplasia, the increase being related to the mucous lesion stage.

Thus we presume that NPC is closely related to atypical hyperplasia or metaplasia and that EB virus may play an important role in nasopharyngeal mucosal transformation or the development of malignancy.

INTRODUCTION

In Zangwu County of Guangxi Province, a NPC high incidence district, we found that positive serum titer of VCA-IgA antibodies are characteristic in diagnosing the disease. However, the nasopharyngeal changes have not been reported so far. Our preliminary investigation of this is presented.

MATERIALS AND METHODS

In July 1978, January 1979 and January 1980, we went to Zangwu County to detect VCA-IgA antibody in people over 30 years old using immunoenzymatic method. The antibody titer over 1 : 2.5 was considered to be positive. Persons showing positive VCA-IgA antibody continuously were examined by specialists and had biopsies taken to determine whether they had NPC or were NPC suspects. It was discovered that they had some nasopharyngeal lesions such as adenoid gland hyperplasia or nondevolution, asymmetrical lymphoid tissue in both recesses or some congestion and inflammatory changes. Biopsy was perfouned in 201 cases; it was repeated in a few cases. Specimens were routinely made into paraffin scetions and HE stained, and some were arhynophil stained. 75 cases in whom NPC was excluded by antibody test and biopsy served as controls.

RESULTS

1. Distribution of antibody titer in NPC patients and non-NPC patients: This is shown in Tab. 1.

Tab. 1　The EB virus VCA-IgA antibody titer distribution of NPC patients and noncancerous antibody positive persons

		Antibody titer											GMT
		2.5	5	10	20	40	80	160	320	640	1280	Total	
NPC	Cases	0	1	3	15	14	20	9	4	3	4	2	75	1 : 76.4
patients	%	0	1.3	4.0	20	18.7	26.7	12.0	5.3	4.0	5.3	2.7	100.0	
Antibody positive	Cases	4	18	24	60	34	37	14	9	5	1	0	206	1 : 32.6
noncancer persons	%	1.9	8.8	11.7	29.1	16.5	18.0	6.8	4.4	2.4	0.5	0	100.0	

The geometric mean titer (GMT) in NPC patients was 1 : 76.4 and antibody titer was over 1 : 40 in 57 (74.7%). The GMT in non-NPC was 1 : 32.6 with antibody titer over 1 : 40 in 100(49%). The difference is obvious, the former being twice that of the latter.

There were 75 NPC cases in the series. According to the NPC clinical stage classification adopted by the National Conference on Tumors in 1965, there were 27 Stage Ⅰ cases (36.0%), 27 Stage Ⅱ. (36.0%), 14 Stage Ⅲ (22.7%) and 4 Stage Ⅳ (5.3%). Of these patients 21 showed no clinical signs at examination, of whom were Stage Ⅰ ($T_1 N_0 M_0$) and 2 Stage Ⅱ ($T_2 N_0 M_0$).

2. Comparison of antibody titer in different nasopharyngeal lesions: In most cases of NPC, atypical hyperplasia and atypical metaplasia, the antibody titer was over 1:20, being 94.7%, 93.8% and 100%. Frequent titer was over 1:80, being 56.0%, 62.5% and 66.7% in each category. The antibody titer in simple hyperplasia, simple mataplasia and normal mucosa was rarely over 1:20, being 69.6%, 82.1 and 55.6%, and titers over 1:80 were fewer, being 17.9%, 29.5% and 33.3% respectively. The difference in antibody distribution curves was statistically significant(Fig. 1).

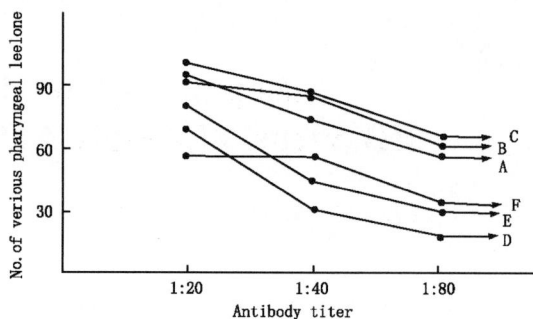

A. NPC; B. Atypical metaplasia; C. Atypical hyperplasia; D. Simple metaplasia; E. Simple hyperplasia; F. Normal mucosa

Fig. 1   Antibody titer distribution curves of NPC patients and those with various NP mucosal lesions.

3. The relation between pharyngeal lesions and VCA-IgA antibody titer in 206 non-NPC patients: No lesion was found in 9 cases(4.4%). 206 cases and the geometric mean titer was 1:25.20.

Simple hyperplasia was seen in 78(37%), the GMT was 1:30.4. This included hyperplasia of the columnal, basal or goblet epithelial cells(Figs. 2-4).

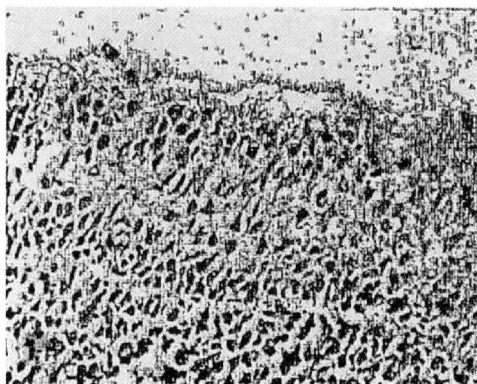

Fig. 2   Simple hyperplasia of columnar epithelium and basal cells. HE 10×20

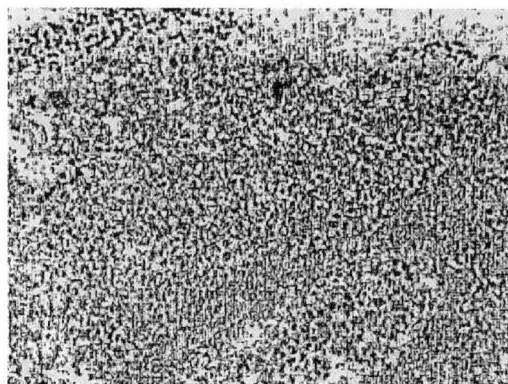

Fig. 3   Simple hyperplasia of columnar epithelium. HE 10×20

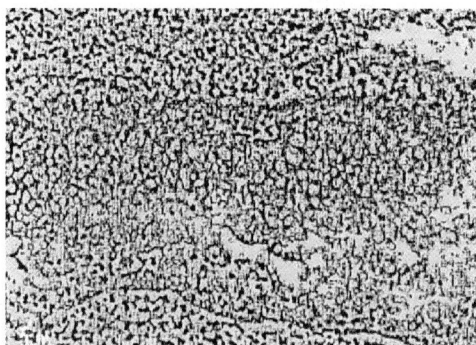

Fig. 4   Simple hyperplasia of Globic cell. HE 10×20

Simple metaplasia was seen in 112(50.4%)and the GMT was 1:22.3. At the beginning of metaplasia, some columnal cells transformed into layers of squamous cells. When mature, keratinization appeared on the superficial platiform epithelium(Figs. 5,6).

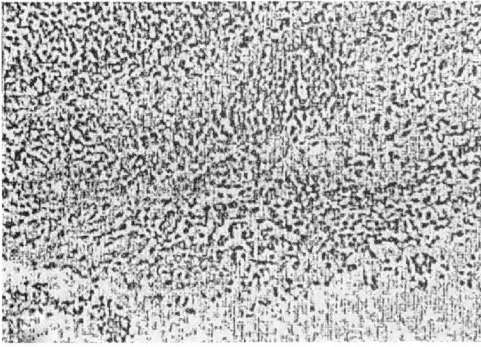

Fig. 5　Simple metaplasia of columnar epithelium. HE
10×20

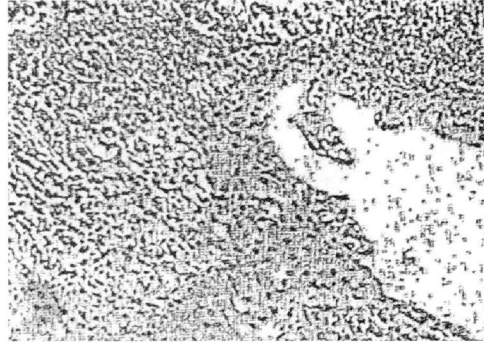

Fig. 6　Simple metaplasia of columnar epithelium. HE
10×20

Atypical hyperplasia was seen in 15(7.3%) and the GMT was 1∶105.40. There were atypical hyperplasia of the columnal cells or squamous cells(Figs. 7,8).

Atypical mucosal hyperplasia and metaplasia. Atypical hyperplasia was seen in 15(7.3%) and the GMT was 1∶105.40. There were atypical hyperplasia of the columnal cells or squamous cells(Figs. 8,9).

Atypical metaplasia was seen in 48(23.2%) and the GMT was 1∶80. When the columnal cells transformed into squamous cells, atypical hyperplasia also appeared(Fig. 9).

In normal mucosal simple hyperplasia or simple metaplasia the GMT was lower(under 1∶30.4). But the GMT of atypical hyperplasia or atypical metaplasia in NPC elevated markedly(over 1∶76.4) as shown in Fig. 10.

Fig. 7　Atypical hyperplasia of columnar epithelium.
HE 10×40

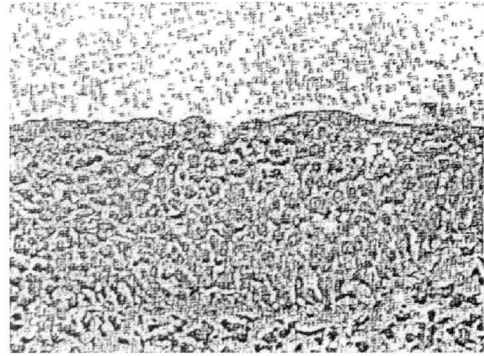

Fig. 8　Atypical hyperplasia squamous epithelium. HE
10×40

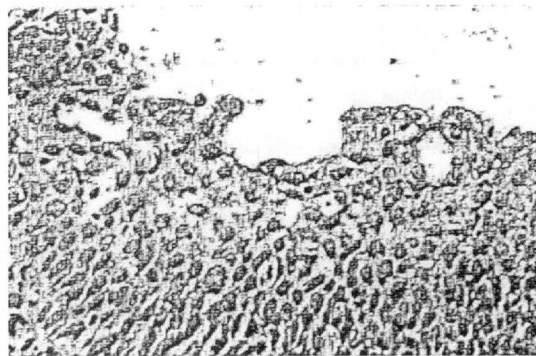

Fig. 9　Atypical metaplasia of columnar epithelium. HE
10×40

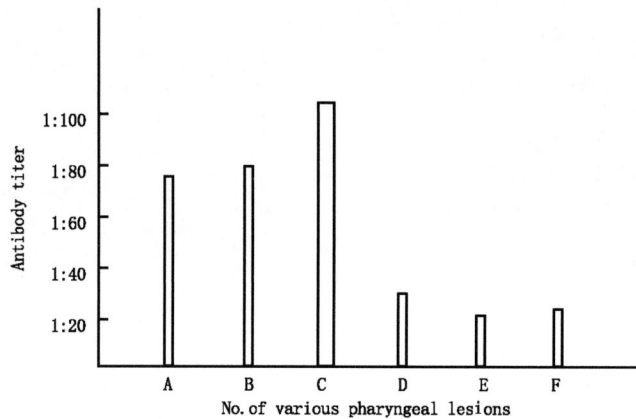

A. NPC; B. Atypical metaplasia; C. Atypical hyperplasia; D. Slimple metaplasia; E. Simple hyperplasia; F. Normal mucosa

Fig. 10　Antibody GMT distribution of NPC patients and other non- NPC lesions

Comparisons of pathologic changes of nasopharyngeal mucosa in VCA-IgA antibody positive and negative persons are shown in Tab. 2.

In tissue surrounding the cancer in75 patients, we found simple hyperplasia in 3(4%), simple metaplasia in 14(18.5%), atypical hyperplasia in 8(12%)and atypical metaplasia in 29(38.7%).

Some patients with antibody were followed up after the first biopsy. The interval between the 2 biopsies was 8-33 months. The pathologic examination results follow.

In 17 cases who had been initially diagnosed as having atypical hyperplasia or atypical metaplasia, 5 had NPC (29.4%), while in 38 with simple hyperplasia, simple metaplasia or normal mucosa, only in 1(2.6%), was NPC found(Tab.3). One case with atypical hyperplasia of some columnar cells was found on biopsy to have NPC 33 months later. This suggests that atypical hyperplasia and atypical metaplasia are closely related with NPC.

Tab. 2　Comparison of pathological changes of nasopharyngeal mucosa in VCA-IgA antibody-positive and negative persons

Groups (NP leslon)	Antibody-positive NPC patients		Antibody-positive non-NPC patients		Antibody-negative non-cancer persons	
	Cases	%	Cases	%	Cases	%
Atypical metaplasla	29	38.7	48	32.2	11	14.5
Atypical hyperplasla	8	12.0	15	7.3	3	4.0
Simple metaplasla	14	18.5	112	50.4	44	58.7
Simple hyperplasia	3	4.0	76	37.0	24	32.0

Tab. 3　Follow-up observations of various NP region lesions

Initial biopsy	Follow—up biopsy			% of NPC proved later
	Cases	Noneaneer	NPC	
Atypical hyperplasia } Atypicla metaplasia	17	12	5*	29.4
Simple hyperplasia } Simple metaplasia } Normal mucosa	38	37	1**	2.6
Total	55	49	6	12.2

Notes: * One case developed NPC(Stage 1) after 33 months. Two had NPC(Stage Ⅱ)after 12 months.

** One case developed NPC(Stage Ⅰ)after 8months

DISCUSSION

In 75 NPC patients with positive EB virus VCA-IgA antibody titration, there were 8(12%)cases of atypical hyperplasia of the surrounding tissue and 29(36.7%)cases of atypical metaplasia. In 75 non-NPC cases without antibody, 3(4%)had atypical hyperplasia of the surrounding tissue and 11(14.5%) had atypical metaplasia. There was a statistically significant difference between the 2 conditions, i. e. the frequency of atypical hyperplasia or metaplasia in the NPC and non-NPC group with antibody was higher than that in the non-NPC group without antibody. This shows that these changes are correlated with the VCA-IgA antibody level.

In the antibody positive group the GMT was higher(1 : 76.4)in NPC patients and lower(1 : 32.6)in non-NPC patients. It was also found that the level of patibody in simple hyperplasia and metaplasia was lower, while the level in atypical hyperplasia and metaplsia was higher.

Follow-up study showed that in some cases if the antibody level was elevated, the lesions increased 80 VCA-IgA titrations were closely related to the pathologic mucosal changes and may be taken as a reference index of epithelial lesion development. The level of VCA-IgA antibody titration was higher in NPC, atypical hyperplasia and metaplasia, the GMT being 1 : 76.4, 1 : 105 and 1 : 80 respectively.

Some authors reported that there was a close relationship between atypical hyperplasia or atypical metaplasia and NPC. The observed the presence of some transitory morphologic changes in simple hyperplasia and metaplasia, atypical hyperplasia and metaplasia, cancer in situ and tiny infiltrative cancers.

During follow-ups of 8-33 months, 5 NPC cases were disovered in 17 diagnosed as having atypical hyperplasia or metapiasia. Only 1 NPC case was found in 38 patients with biopsy proved simple hyperplasia, simple metapiasia or normal mucosa. Evidently, regardless of the morphologic changes or disease stage, there is a close relationship between atypical hyperplasia or metaplasia and NPC. Therefore, we may assume that they are not only related closely to VCA-IgA antibody level, but also to NPC occurrence. Therefore EB virus activation and existence of VCA-IgA antibody are intimately concerned with NPC. This suggests that EB virus may be one of the NPC causative agents.

VCA-IgA antibody titer in patients with atypical hyperplasia is higher than in NPC patients, but the difference is not statistically significant.

Acknowledgement: We thank Prof Zong Yong-sheng for his guidance.

REFERENCES

[1] Zeng Yi, et al. Application of an immunoenzymetic method and an immunoautoradiographic method for a mass survey of nasopharyngeal carcinoma. Inter- virology, 1980, 13:162.

[2] Immunopathological Department, Institute of Tumor, Zhongshand Medical College, Morphological observation on the process of carcinogencsis of nasopharyngeal epithelial cells. Selected paper, 1978, 1:44.

[In《Chinese Medical Journal》1985, 98:25-30]

ELISA for the Detection of Nasopharyngeal Carcinoma Using IgA Antibodies to EBV Early Antigen

Pi GH[1], Zeng Y[1], de-The G[2]

1. Institute of Virology, China National Center for Preventive Medicine, Beijing(People's Republic of China);
2. Laboratoire d Epidemiologie et d. Immunovirologie des Tumeurs du CNRS, Faculte de Medecine Alexis Carrel, 69372 Lyon Cedex 08(France)

[SUMMARY]　An enzyme-linked immunosorbent assay(ELISA)was established for the detection of IgA antibodies to Epstein-Barr virus early antigens. Crude extracts from P3HRI cells treated with phorbolesters, n-butyrate and Ara-C or from Raji cells treated with phorbolesters and n-butyrate were used as antigens. The ELISA assay consisted in three steps involving test serum, mouse monoclonal antiserum to human IgA and rabbit antimouse IgG. A good correlation was obtained between this simple ELISA and the previously described immunoenzymatic test[5], but ELISA was found to be 8 times more sensitive. This ELISA is a sensitive and rapid test which has been applied to field studies for early detection of nasopharyngeal carcinoma.

[Keywords]　EBV; Nasopharyngeal carcinoma; IgA; ELISA; Early antigen; Detection

INTRODUCTION

In our previous studies, we showed that the detection of IgA antibodies to Epstein-Barr virus(EBV)virion capsid antigen(VCA)by an immunoenzymatic test was useful for the early diagnosis of nasopharyngeal carcinoma (NPC)in high-risk populations[4,5]. We later showed that IgA antibodies against the EBV early antigen(EA)which were detected by the immunoenzymatic test were more specific than, but not as sensitive as, the IgA antibodies to VCA for the detection of NPC[6]. A very sensitive immunoautoradiographic test was then established to detect EA-IgA antibodies[7]. With such a test, 96% of NPC patients were positive for EA-IgA antibodies, but it was complicated and inconvenient for the screening of NPC in large populations. As described here, a sensitive, specific and rapid ELISA for detectionof EBV-IgA antibody was developed and tested in field conditions.

MATERIALS AND METHODS

1. Cells

The Burkitt's-lymphoma-derived and EBV-producing P3HR-1 and nonproducing Raji cell lines grown at 37℃ in RPMI-1640 medium supplemented with 20% newborn calf serum were used to prepare the antigens.

2. Preparation of EBV EA

To prepare crude EBV EA not containing late structural antigens(VCA), two techniques were used. The first consisted in using P3HRI cells cultured at a concentration of 5×10^5 cells per ml in RPMI tissue culture medium supplemented with 20% newborn calf serum, containing croton oil(500ng/ml), n-butyrate(4mmoL/L)and cytosine arabinosied(Ara-C)(0.25μg/ml). After 48h, the cells were studied for the proportion of EA-positive cells (from 20% to 45%)and for the lack of VCA-positive cells. Only batches with a proportion of 30% EA-positive cells with no VCA were selected. After two washings with PBS, cells were stored at -70℃.

The second technique used was to cultivate Raji cells at a concentration of 10^6 cells per ml for 72h in the presence of TPA(5ng/ml)and of BA(0.4ml 2M/200ml). After checking the proportion of EA-positive cells and the lack of VCA, batches with at least 30% EA-positive cells were washed and stored at-70℃ as above. The proportion of EA-positive cells was determined as usual by indirect immunofluorescence(IF) or by immunoenzymatic(IE) metod[5] comparing the results of two different sera containing IgG antibodies to VCA and VCA + EA, respectively. These two sera were used at dilutions giving the same final VCA antibody titres. As stated above, only batches of cells with 30% EA-positive cells were kept for preparing crude EA batches.

Ara-C=cytosine arabinoside	IF=immunofluorescence
BA=butyric acid	IgA=immunoglobulin A
BSA=bovine serum albumin	NPC=nasopharyngeal carcinoma
EA=early antigen	OD(A)=optical density
EB=Epstein-Barr	OPD=orthophenylenediamine
EBNA=EB nuclear an tigen	PBS=phosphate-buffer saline
EBV=EB virus	PMSF=phenylmethylsulphonyl
ELISA=enzyme-linked immunosorbent assay	TPA=12-O-tetradecenoyl-phorbol-13-acetate(croton oil phorbolester)
GMT=geometric mean titre	VCA=virion capsid antigen
IE=immunoenzymatic test	

The panel of sera used for evaluation of antigenic batches consised of three normal Chinese individuals possessing anti-VCA IgG at a titre of 1/320 and anti-EBNA antibodies at 1/160, and lacking EA-IgG antibodies, as tested IF. They were used at two dilutions of 1/5 and 1/20. Three Chinese sera from NPC patients were used with the following titres: VCA-IgG at 1/1 280, VCA-IgA at 1/160, EA/IgG at 1/320, EA-IgA at 1/40 and anti-EBNA antibodies at 1/1280, as tested by IF. These sera were used at two dilutions of 1/20 and 1/80.

To prepare crude antigenic batches, frozen pellets of 10^8 cells were suspended in 1ml of 150 mmol/L NaCl, 20mmol/L Tris buffer, pH 7.5, 1mmol/L EDTA and 0.5mmol/L phenylmethyl-sulphonyl fluoried(PMSF). They were sonicated 8 times for 10 seach on ice and then centrifuged at 18 000 r/min for 45 min. The supernates to be used as crude antigen were tested for protein concentration and then stored at-70℃ until use.

3. Sera

Sera were obtained from patients with NPC, from patients with tumours other than NPC and from normal individuals, and were stored at-20℃ until use.

4. Mouse monoclonal antibody to human IgA

A mouse monoclonal anti-human IgA antibody cell line was established in Beijing(Xia and Zeng, sFubmitted for publication). The original titre of the IgA antibody in ascitic fluid for mouse was 1/30 000.

5. Horseradish-peroxidase-conjugated rabbit anti-mouse IgG antibody

The appropriate dilrtion of this conjuagate was 1/30 000.

6. Preparation of ELISA plates

The antigen preparation was diluted in 0.05mol/L sodium carbonate buffer at pH 9.6, and 10μg/100ml of protein were added to each well of polystyrene microtitre plates. The plaes were incubated overnight at 4℃, then washed twice with 0.05mol/L sodium carbonate buffer at pH 9.6, supplemented with 0.1% bovine serum albumin(BSA)and dried for 20 min at room temperature. Unattached sites were saturated with 0.05mol/L sodium carbonate buffer at pH 9.6, supplemented with 1% BSA for 3h in a humid chamber at room temperature. The plates were then washed twice in PBS containing 0.05% Tween-20, dried for 1h at room temperature and stored at 4℃ until use.

7. ELISA method

A three-step technique was used. One-hundred microlitres of each test serum diluted 1/40 in washing buffer were added in duplicate wells, and the plates were incubated in a humid chamber at room temperature for 1h. The plates were then washed 5 times in washing buffer. One-hundred microlitres of mouse monoclonal antibody against human IgA(Xia and Zeng, submitted for publication), diluted 1/500 in washing buffer, were added to each well, and the plates were again put in a humid chamber at room temperature for 1h. After 5 washings with buffer, 100μl of horseradish-peroxidase-conjugated anti-mouse IgG antibody, diluted 1/30 000 in washing buffer was added and the plates put in a humid chamber at room temperature for 1h. After five washing with buffer, 100μl of the substrate solution(prepared by adding 40mg of orthophenylenediamine(OPD)and 30μl of 30% H_2O_2 in 100ml of phosphoric acid/citric acid buffer at pH 5.0 in 0.2mol/L Na_2HPO_4 and 0.1mol/L citric acid)were added to each microtitre well and the reaction was allowed to take place for 20 min at room temperature before it was stopped by addition of 50μg of 4mol/L H_2SO_4 The intensity of the colour reaction at 492 nm was recorded with a《Titertek Multiskan》.

8. Determination of results

P/N value was calculated according to the following formula:

$$P/N \text{ value} = \frac{\text{serum sample A figure-PBS control A value}}{\text{reference negative serum A figure-PBS control A value}}$$

P/N value≥2 was condidered as positive, and P/N value<2 as negative.

9. IE and IF tests

VCA-IgA and EA-IgA antibodies of the same sera were also detected by the IE test[5]. in Beijing, and by indirect IF in Lyon.

RESULTS

1. Titration of antigen

In order to determine the optimal concentration of antigen for ELISA, microtitre plates were coated with serial 2-fold dilution of cell extracts containing protein from 0.09μg to 100μg per well, whereas the known positive serum was also diluted from 1/40 to 1/2560. Tab. 1 gives the P/N values of a positive reference serum corresponding to the different concentrations of antigen and serum dilutions. Similar P/N value(2.4-3.0)and the same antibody titre were obtained when the concentration of antigen used varied from 6.25 to 100μg per well. Thus, 10μg of antigen per well was used as routine.

Tab. 1　Titration of EBV-EA antigen using IgA

Serum dilutions	P/N value Crude preparation of EA(μg) from P3HR1 cells											
	100	50	25	12.5	6.25	3.125	1.563	0.781	0.391	0.195	0.098	0.049
1/40	7.9	6.7	6.7	5.4	4.4	3.3	2.4	2.2	2.1	2.0	1.9	2.0
1/80	7.7	7.6	7.5	5.3	4.3	2.6	1.7	1.7	1.7	1.6	2.0	2.0
1/160	5.1	7.3	6.2	4.2	3.9	2.1	1.5	1.5	1.3	1.4	1.1	1.6
1/320	5.1	4.7	5.6	4.5	3.0	2.1	1.7	1.2	1.0	1.1	1.2	1.6
1/640	3.1	3.2	3.7	2.8	2.4	1.5	1.2	0.9	1.1	1.1	0.9	1.1
1/1280	2.9	2.4	3.0	2.6	2.4	1.1	0.7	0.8	2.0	0.8	1.0	1.5
1/2560	1.3	1.1	1.3	0.9	1.0	0.9	0.9	1.1	1.5	0.8	0.6	0.7

2. Titration of the monoclonal anti-human IgA antibody

To determine the optimal dilution of the mouse monoclonal anti-human IgA for the ELISA, a serial dilution from 1/125 to 1/4000 of anti-human IgA antibody was tested. As shown in Fig. 1, the P/N value of sera from NPC patients decreased with the dilution of anti-human IgA antibody. The highest dilution of anti-human IgA antibody giving positive results(P/N value≥2)for serum A and B was 1/500 and 1/2000 respectively, so 1/500 dilution of anti-human IgA antibody for ELISA was used as routine.

3. Specificity and sensitivity of the ELISA

Two known human positive sera and one negative serum with serial 2-fold dilution were tested with an optimal concentration of EA(10μg/ well). As seen in Fig. 2, the curves of the A data and P/N values of the positive and negative sera were markedly different. Then 19 known positive and 24 known negative sera were simltanously tested with this ELISA assay and the IE test. As seen in Fig. 3, a good correlation between antibody titres detected by the ELISA and the IE test was obtained using 19 sera from Chinese NPC patients and 24

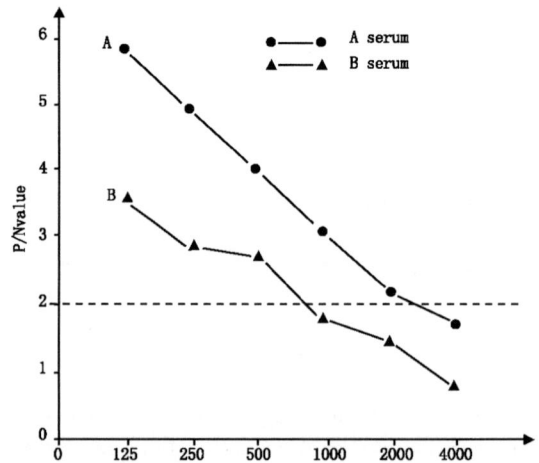

Fig. 1　Titration of the mouse monoclonal anti- human IgA antibody with two NPC sera having EA-IgA titers, as tested by IE, of 640 and320, respectively, using a P3HRI EA prepara- tion. IgA/ EA＝EA-IgA(see text)

controis lacking IgA antibodies to VCA and EA. The geo- metric mean titre(GMT)of the positive sera detected by ELISA was 1/710，or 8 times higher than the GMT(1/88. 8)obtained with IE titres.

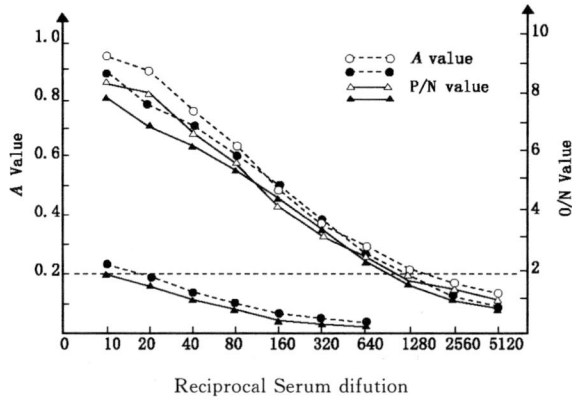

Fig. 2 Detection of EA-IgA antibodies by ELISA using 2 NPC Chinese sera with EA-IgA titres of 1/320 as tested by IE, and 1 EBV-negative serum. The antigen batch was used P3HRI-derived

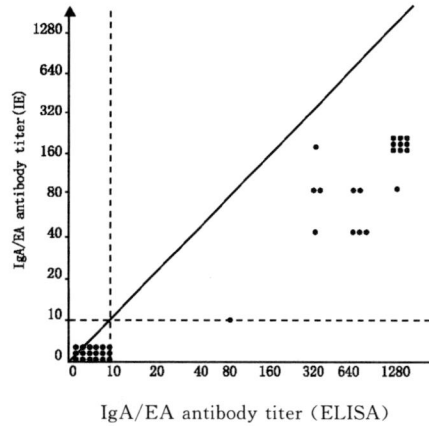

Fig. 3 Comparative EA-IgA antibody titres determined by ELISA and by IE[4]，of19 NPC sera and 24 controls lacking EA-IgA and VCA-IgA antibodies by the IE test. The antigenic batch was the same as that of Figs. 1 and 2

The use of《control》antigen(s)in the ELISA test using crude antigen extracts from an EBV-negative cell line such as BJAB or Ramos was considered. This was discarded for the following reasons：sera from patients with NPC are notoriously known to contain antinuclear factors，auto and iso-antibodies[3]，and to easily give false-positive ELISA results with non-EBV-related antigen preparations. In view of this difficulty，we preferred to assess the above ELISA in a pragmatic way by comparing the results of the present ELISA technique with the reproducible results as obtained by IE in Beijing or by indirect IF in Lyon. Experiments in Lyon comparing ELISA with IF tests gave a similar correlation to those comparing ELISA and the IE test，but with titres lower in IF than in IE.

4. Reproducibility of the ELISA

In order to determine the reproducibility of the ELISA，10 sera from NPC patients and 8 sera from normal individuals were tested in two separate experiments. The results seen in Tab. 2. were very similar，with a variation in P/N value of each serum within a 0. 1-0. 4 range(except for 2 positive sera). The shows that the ELISA assay is reproducible.

Tab. 2　Reproducibility of the ELISA assay

Serum	P/N value of IgA/EA antibody		Difference
	Exp. 1	Exp. 2	
1)357	5. 0	4. 7	0. 3
397	4. 6	4. 4	0. 2
359	4. 3	5. 5	1. 2
361	4. 2	5. 0	0. 8
376	3. 0	2. 9	0. 1
360	2. 7	2. 4	0. 3
375	2. 4	3. 6	1. 2
365	2. 4	2. 2	0. 2
353	2. 2	2. 4	0. 2
366	1. 2	1. 5	0. 3
2)120	1. 4	1. 1	0. 3

（续　表）

Serum	P/N value of IgA/EA antibody		Difference
	Exp. 1	Exp. 2	
109	1. 3	1. 3	0
106	1. 3	0. 9	0. 4
098	1. 3	1. 6	0. 3
118	1. 2	0. 9	0. 3
111	1. 2	1. 3	0. 1
107	1. 1	0. 9	0. 2
112	0. 4	0. 4	0

1＝NPC；2＝normal individuals

5. Detection of EA-IgA antibody from NPC patients, patients with tumours other than NPC and normal individuals by ELISA and IE(immunoenzymatic)test

Ninety-one sera from NPC patients, 59 sera from patients with tumours other than NPC and ninety normal individuals sera were tested by both the ELISA assay and by the IE test. As shown in Tab. 3, the percentage of EA-IgA antibody detected by the IE test was 60%, 0% and 0%, respectively and that tested by ELISA using the monoclonal anti-IgA antibody was 97%, 3.4% and 2.2%, respectively. The marked difference in the sensitivity of the ELISA as compared to the IE test should hepl to better differentiate the NPC sera from the two other groups.

Tab. 3　Comparison of ELISA and immunoenzymatic test(*)for detection of IgA/EA antibody

Sera	No. of cases	IgA/VCA		IgA/EA			
		IE		IE		ELISA	
		+	%	+	%	+	%
NPC	91	91	100	55	60	88	97
Tumour other than NPC	59	2	3. 4	0	0	2	3. 4
Normal individuals	90	2	2. 2	0	0	2	2. 2

IE＝immunoenzymatic test.

(*)Using P3HRI-derived EA.

DISCUSSION

The present results indicate that crude antigen preparations from P3HR-1 cells treated with croton oil, n-butyrate and Ara-C, or from Raji treated with TPA and BA can be used in ELISA for the detection of EA-IgA antibody by a simple three-step technique. This was made possible through the use of a monoclonal antibody prepared from a mouse immunized against the IgA prepared from an NPC patient(Xia and Zeng, in preparation). The fact that the results were not good when using commercially availabe anti-human IgA monoclonal antibodies suggests that our monoclonal antibody was directed against some idiotypic structure borne by IgA molecules with specificity for some epitope of EA. The use of mouse monoclonal anti-human IgA antibody probably enhances the sensitivity as well as the specificity of the ELISA assay, since EA/IgA antibodies were detected by ELISA in 97% of the NPC sera versus 60% by the IE test, while at the same time, the other two groups of sera showed only 0～3.4% of positivity. The sensitivity of the ELISA was found to be similar to that of the immunoautoradigraphy[7]. But immunoautoradiography is more complicated than the ELISA, which, being sensitive, specific and rapid was successfully applied to field studies. In the city of Wuzhou, a rate of EA-IgA antibody, as detected by IE test and by ELISA on 12 154 normal individuals was found to be 0.3% and1.2%, respectively(Zeng, unpublished). Low-cost, standardized, industrially prepared EBV-EA-IgA ELISA kits would be of great help for promoting early detection of NPC in Southeast Asia, where this tumour represents the number one cancer killer in very large populations of approximately 250 millions inhabitants[1]. When one realizes that NPC at an early stage of the disease is a highly curable tumour, one feels the urgency from a public health viewpoint to stress the use of such a simple test.

REFERENCES

[1] De-The G, Ho JHC, Muir CS. Nasopharyngeal carcinoma, in《Viral infections of humans, epidemiology and control》,(A S Evans),(pp, 621-652). John Wiley and Sons, Chichester, 1982.

[2] De-The G, Zeng Y, Desgranges, C, Pi GH. The existence of prenasopharyngeal carcinoma conditions should allow preventive interventions, in《Nasopharyngeal carcinoma: Current concepts》,(Prased et al).(p, 365-374). University of Malaya, Kuala Lumpur, 1983.

[3] Lamelis JP, De-The G, Revillard JP, Gabbiani G. Autoantibodies(cold lymphocytotxins and anti-actin and antinuclear factors) in nasopharyngeal carcinoma patients, in《Nasopharyngeal carcinoma: Etiology and control》,CIRC Publication Scientifique N 20,(G, De-The & Y. Ito),(pp, 523-436). Centre International de Recherches sur le Cancer, Lyon, 1978.

[4] Zeng Y, Liu YX, Wei JN, Zhu JS, Cai SL, Wang PH, Zhong, JM, Li RG, Pan WJ, Li EJ, Tan B F. Serological mass survey of nasophryngeal carcinoma. Acta Acad. Med. Sin, 1979, 1:123-126.

[5] Zeng Y, Liu YX, Lin CR, Chen SW, Wei JN, Zhu JS. Application of immunoenzymatic method for the mass survey of nasopharyngeal carcinoma. Intervirology, 1980, 13:162-168.

[6] Zeng Y, Zhang LG, Li HY, Jang MG, Zhang Q, Wu YC, Wang YS, Su GR. Serological mass survey for early detection of nasopharyngeal carcinoma in Wuzhou city, China Int J Cancer,1982, 29:139-141.

[7] Zeng Y, Gong CH, Jang MG, Fun Z, Zhang LG, Li HY. Detection of Epstein-Barr virus IgA/ EA antibody for diagnosis of nasophyaryngeal carcinoma by immunoautoradiography. Int J Cancer, 1983, 31:599-601.

[In《Ann Inst Pasteur Virol》1985. 136E: 131-140]

Detection of IgG and IgA Antibodies to Epstein-Barr Virus Membrane Antigen in Sera from Patients with Nasopharyngeal Carcinoma and from Normal Individuals

ZHU X X[1], ZENG Yi[1], Wolf H[2]

1. Institute of Virology, China National Centre for Preventive Medicine, 100 Ying Xing Jie, Beijing. People's Republic of China   2. Max von Pettenkofer-Institute, University of Munich, Pettenkofer Str. 9a, D-8000 Munich 2, Fed. Rep. of Germany

[SUMMARY] IgG and IgA antibodies to Epstein-Barr virus(EBV)membrane antigen(MA)were detected in sera from 96 NPC patients and normal individuals by the indirect immunofluorescence test. For MA/IgG antibody, 100% of NPC patients were positive with a GMT of 1 : 439. 7 and 97. 9% of normal individuals were positive with a GMT of 1 : 94. 7. In contrast, for MA/IgA antibody, 58. 3% of NPC patients were positive with a GMT of 1 : 7. 3 and none of the normal individuals were positive. There was no difference in the detection of antibodies to EBV MA when other P3HR-1 or B95-8 cell lines, differing in their major membrane antigen, were used.

Klein et al.(1966)first demonstrated EBV MA in cells from Burkitt lymphoma by the indirect immunofluorescence test, and then proved that the MA was specific to EBV by a direct blocking test(Klein et al. 1969). Other studies have shown that EBV MA exists on both the EBV envelope and the membrane of cells which carry EBV genomes and produce intact EBV particles(Sugawara and Osato, 1970; Silvestre et al. 1971). These data indicate that the antibody titer to MA correlates well with that of neutralizing antibody to EBV(Pearson et al. 1970). There are no published reports concerning IgA antibody to EBV MA. A hypothesis links blocking of ADCC with the appearance of IgA antibodies mainly directed to VCA or EA(Mathew et al. 1981). However, no data have been presented on the reactivity of IgG and particularly IgA antibodies in sera from NPC patients and normal individuals to the membrane antigen by indirect immunofluorescence tests.

MATERIAL AND METHODS

1. Sera
Sera were obtained from 48 NPC patients and 48 normal individuals, and stored at-20℃.

2. Indirect immunofluorescence test
The target cells used for detection of MA/IgG and MA/IgA antibodies were P3HR-1 or B95-8 cells. They were cultured in RPMI 1640 medium with 20% newborn calf serum.

P3HR-1 or B95-8 cells were activated for 48 hr by 4mmol/L n-butyrate and 500ng/m of croton oil. The activated cells were washed 3 times with Hanks' solution and adjusted to 1×10^6 cells/ml. Then 1×10^5 cells in 100μl were added to each well of 96-well U-shaped hemagglutination plates. The sera were diluted from 1 : 10 to 1 : 640 in 2-fold dilution and then placed in a humidified chamber at 37℃ for 45 min. Mter 3 washes with Hanks' solution, cell smears were prepared on slides, air-dried and fixed with cold acetone. FITC-conjugated sheep antibodies diluted 1 : 10 and directed to human IgG or IgA were added and the slides were kept at 37℃ for 30 min. The smears were again washed3 times with 0. 01mol/L PBS, pH7. 6 Mter counter-staining with 0. 006% Evansblue for 10 min, they were examined under an Olympus fluorescence microscope. Cell membranes stained with a specific green color were considered to be positive. The number of cells positive for MA was measured with the test described above, a mixture of several sera being used as first antibody.

3. Immunoenzymatic test
The test was performed as described by Zeng et al(1979).

RESULTS

1. Comparison of the EBV-MA-positivity in P3HR-1 and B95-8 cell lines
The positivity of the EBV MA in untreated P3HR-1 and B95-8 cells was 9. 1% and 11. 2% respectively. The numbers increased to 62. 1% and 63. 4% respectively after activation with croton oil and n-butyrate for 48hr. There was no further increase in MA positivity after activation for 72hr and more frgmnted cells were found(Fig. 1).

2. Comparison of the prevalence rate of EBV MA/IgG, MA/IgA, VCA/IgA and EA/ IgA antibodies in sera from NPC patients and normal individuals.
Sera from 48 NPC patients and from 48 normal individuals were tested for EBV MA/IgG and MA/IgA antibodies by the immunofluorescence test, and for VCA/IgA and EA/IgA antibodies by the immunoenzymatic test.

The positivity of the above 4 antibodies was 100％, 58.3％, 100％ and64.6％ respectively, in NPC patients, and 97.9％, 0％ and 0％ respectively, in normal individuals(Tab. 1).

Tab. 1 Comparison of positivity rate of IgA and IgG antibodies to VCA and MA from NPC patients and normal individuals

	Cases	MA/IgG[1]		MA/IgA[1]		VCA/IgA[2]		EA/IgA[2]	
		Number	％ positivity	Number	％ positivity	Number	％ positivity	Number	％ positivity
NPC patients	48	48	100	28	58.3	48	100	31	64.6
Normal individuals	48	47	97.9	0	0	0	0	0	0

[1] MA/IgG and MA/IgA detected by immunofluorescence test; [2] VCA/IgA and EA/IgA detected by immunoenzymatic test

3. Comparison of the distribution of EBV MA/IgG and MA/IgA antibody titers in NPC patients and normal individuals

As shown in Fig. 2, the range of the MA/IgG antibody titers for NPC patients was from 1：40 to1：1280 with a GMT of 1：439.7, and the range for normal individuals was from 1：10 to 1：640 with a GMT of 1：94.7. The range of MA/IgA antibody titers for NPC patients was from 1：10 to 1：160 with a GMT of 1：7.3; only 52％ of the patients had antibody titers higher than 1：20, but to such antibodies could be found in normal individuals. In most NPC cases the VCA/IgA antibody titer was higher than that of MA/IgA antibodies(Fig. 3). This difference was less significant in a comparison with EA/IgA antibodies(Fig. 4).

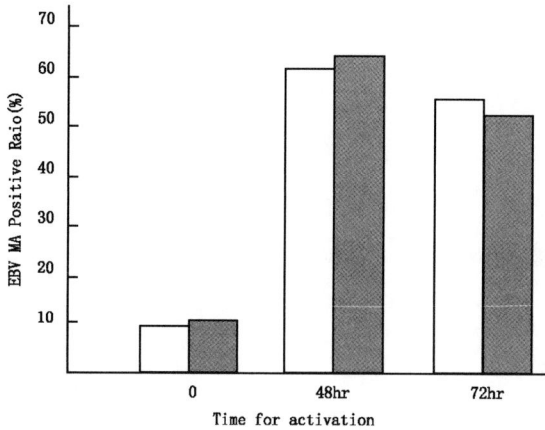

Fig. 1 Comparison of the EBV-MA positive rate in P₃ HR-1 (□)and B95-8(▨)cells.

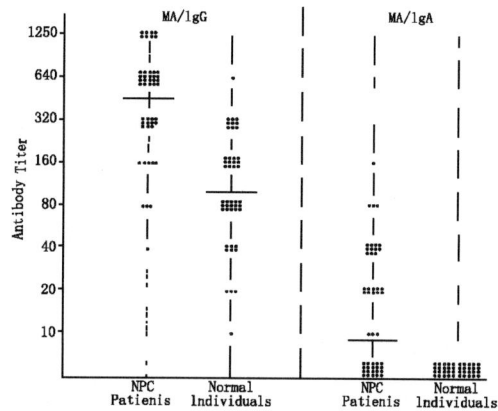

Fig. 2 Comparison of MA/IgG and MA/IgA antibodies from NPC patients and normal individuals

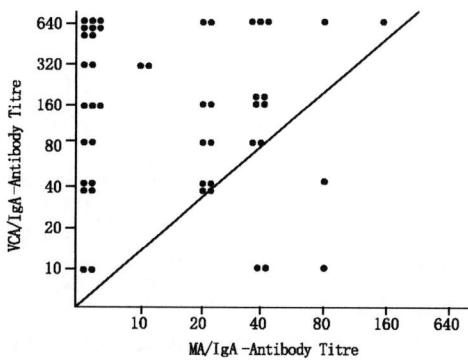

Fig. 3 Relationship between MA/IgA and VCA/ IgA antibodies in sera from NPC patients.

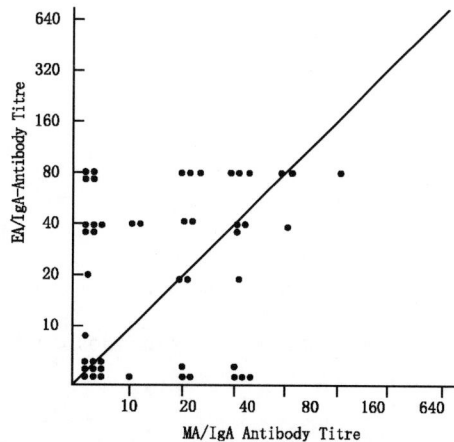

Fig. 4 Relationship between MA/IgA and EA/IgA antibodies in sera from NPC patients

DISCUSSION

It has been shown that the detection of IgA antibody to VCA and EA of EBV is of value for the diagnosis of NPC(Henal and Henle, 1976; Zeng et al, 1979a, b; 1980, 1983b). The positivity of MA/IgG antibody was very high both in NPC patients and in normal individuals. Although the GMT of MA/IgG antibody is much higher in NPC patients than in normal individuals, this test is of no value for the diagnosis of individuals cases. Of NPC patients, 58.3% had MA/IgA antibody, while all normal individuals lacked IgA antibodies to this antigen. The situation is similar to seen with EA/IgA antibodies in NPC patients and in normal individuals(Zeng et al, 1983b), hence detection of MA/IgA antibody can be used as a marker for the diagnosis of NPC.

The positivity of MA in P3HR-1 and B95-8 cells was similar, although the major membrane glycoprotein differs in both cell lines(Edson and Thorley-Lawon, 1983). suggesting that both lines can be used as targets for the detection of EBV MA/IgA antibodies. For a higher expression of MA, cells could be activated with croton oil and n-butyrate for 48hr before use.

Detection of EBV MA/IgA antibody is more specific, but not as sensitive for the diagnosis of NPC as detection of VCA-IgA antibodies. However, a more sensitive technique for the detection of EBV MA/IgA antibodies should considerably reduce the false negatives and give an even better diagnostic value(Jilg and Wolf, 1985).

The predictive value of MA/IgA antibodies for the prognosis of patients is under investigation. An economical production of MA, using genetic engineering technology, should prove helpful for the development of simpler tests which would allow screening of large quantities of serum.

ACKNOWLEDGEMENT

Part of this work was supported by Stiftung Volkswagenwerk.

REFERENCES

[1] Edsdn P, Thorley-Lawson D. Synthesis and processing of the three major enaelope glycoproteins of Epstein-Barr virus. J Virol, 1983, 46:547-556.

[2] Henle G, Henle W. Serum IgA antibodies to Epstein-Barr virus(EBV)-related antigens, a new feature for nasopharyngeal carcinoma. Bibl Haemat, 1976, 43:322-325.

[3] Jilg W, Wolf H. Diagnostic significance of antibodies to the Epstein-Barr virus-specific membrane antigen gp 250. J infect. Dis, 1985, 152:222-225.

[4] Klein G, Clifford P, Klen E, Stjernsward J. Search for tumor-specific immune reaction in Burkitt lymphoma patients by the membrane immunofluorescence reaction. Proc, nat, Acad, Sci.(Wash), 1966, 55:1628-1635.

[5] Klein G, Pearson G, Henle G, Henle W, Goldtein G, Clifford P. Relation between Ep- stein-Barr viral and cell membrane immunofluorescence in Burkitt tumor cells. J exp Med, 1969, 129:679-705.

[6] Mathew GD, Qualtiere LF, Nell HB Ⅲ, Pearson GR. IgA antibody, antibody-dependent cellular cytotoxicity and prognosis in patients with nasophryngeal carcinoma, Int J Cancer, 1981, 27:175-180.

[7] Pearson G, Dewey F, Klein G, Henle G, Henle, W. Relation between neutralization of Epstein-Barr virus and antibodies to cell-membrane antigens induced by the virus. J. nat. Cancer Inst, 1970,45:989.

[8] Silvestre D, Kourilsky FM, Klein G, Yata Y, Neauport Sautes C, levy J P. Relationship between the EBV-associated membrane antigen on Burkitt lymphoma cells and the viral envelope, demonstrated by immunoferritin labelling, Int J. Cancer, 1971,8:222-233.

[9] Sugawara K, Osato T. An immunoferritin study of a Burkitt lymphoma cell line harboring EB virus particles. Gann, 1970, 61:279-281.

[10] Zeng Y, Gong C, Jan M, Fun Z, Zhang LG, Li HY. Detection of Epstein-Barr virus IgA/EA antibody for diagnosis of nasopharyngeal carcino- ma by immunoautoradiography. Int J Cancer, 1983a, 31:599-601.

[11] Zeng Y, Liu Y, Liu C, Chen S, Wei J, Zhu J, Zai H. Application of an immunoenzymatic method and an immunoautoradiographic method for a mass survey of nasopharyngeal carcinoma. Intervirology, 1980, 13:162-168.

[12] Zeng Y, Liu YX, Wei JN, Zhu JS, Cai SL, Wang PZ, Zhong JM, Li RC, Pan WC, Li EJ, Tan BF. Serological mass survey of nasopharyngeal carcinoma. Acta Acad Med Sin,1979a, 1:123-126.

[13] Zeng Y, Yuxi L, Chunren L, Sanwen C, Jineng W, Jisong Z, Hunong Z. Application of an immunoenzymatic method and an immunoautoradiographic method for a mass survey of nasopharyngeal carcinoma. Chin J Cncol, 1979b, 1:2.

[14] Zeng Y, Zhong L, Li P, Wang P, Tang YR, Ma YR, Zhu JS, Pan WJ, Liu YX, WeiZ N, Chen J Y, Mo YK, Li EJ, Tan BF. Follow-up studies on Epstein-Barr virus IgA/VCA antibody-positive persnons in Zangwu county, China. Intervirology, 1983b, 20:190-194.

[In《Int J Cancer》1986, 37:689-691]

Epstein-Barr Virus Activation in Raji Cells by Extracts of Preserved Food from High Risk Areas for Nasopharyngeal Carcinoma

Shao YM[1,2,3], Poirier S[1,2], Ohshima H[2], Malaveille C[2], Zeng Y[3], de The G[1,4], Bartsch H[2,4]

1. CNRS Laboratory of Epideniology and Immunology of Tumours, Faculty of Medicine A. Carrel, 69373 Lyon Cedex 08; 2. International Agency for Research on Cancer, Unit of Environmental Carcinogens and Host Factors, 150 cours Albert Thomas, 69372 Lyon Cedex 08. France; 3. Institute of Virology, Chinese Academy of Preventive Medicine, Beijing 100052, China

[SUMMARY]　Epstein-Barr virus(EBV)activation of latent infection and traditional life styles, especially food habits, have been strongly associated with an increased risk of nasopharyngeal carcinoma(NPC)in humans. On the basis of anthropological studies in Tunisia, southern China and Greenland, extracts of representative preserved food items consumed frequently by the high-risk populations for NPC were assayed for the presence of EBV activators in Raji cells. A strong EBV activation activity was observed in aqueous extracts of some Cantonese salted dried fish from China, harissa (a spice mixture)and to a lesser extent qaddid(dry mutton preserved in olive oil)from Tunisia. These new data may support epidemiological evidence for the importance of Cantonese salted and dried fish and other food items in the etiology of NPC.

INTRODUCTION

Epstein-Barr virus(EBV*)DNA is regularly present in undifferentiated carcinoma of the nasopharynx(NPC) in humans[1]. IgA antibodies against EBV viral capsid antigens and early antigens(EA), reflecting EBV activation in vivo, have been reported in patients prior to turnout development[2-6]. In view of the restricted geographical distribution of NPC and the ubiquity of EBV, however, other cofactors must be considered in the etiology of NPC. Traditional life styles, especially consumption of Cantonese-style salted fish, has been found to be associated with the development of NPC with an increased relative risk of 37. 2 when exposure occurs in early age[7]. Further, an anthropological study on diet in southern China. Tunisia and Greenland suggested that preserved foods could be a risk factor for this tumour[8]. In a previous study, we analysed preserved foods frequently consumed in these three high-risk areas for NPC for their contents of volatile N-nitrosamines(VNA). We observed relatively high levels in some preserved food samples daily consumed[9]. such as salted and dried fish, fermented vegetables and qaddid (dried mutton preserved in olive oil). The aim of the present study was to examine extracts of the same food samples for the presence of substances that could activate EBV in EBV latently infected Raji cells.

MATERIALS AND METHODS

On the basis of consumption frequency and method of preservation used, 28 representative food specimens were selected from among those analysed previously for VNA[9]. Aqueous, hexane and ethyl acetate extracts of these specimens were prepared as follows: 10g of each food sample were homogenized with 20-50ml of deionized water in a Polytron homogenizer for 3 min. After incubation in a shaking water-bath for 30 min at 4℃, the homogenate was centrifuged at 15 000g for 20 min, and the pellet was re-extracted with the same amount of water. The combined supernatants were filtered through a 0. 45μmol/L Millipore filter and lyophilized. The lyophilate was then dissolved in 6ml of water. The residual material after aqueous extraction was further extracted in a Soxhlet apparatus, first with 100ml n-hexane, then with 100ml ethyl acetate(25 passages each). The solvent was evaporated using a rotary evaporator, and the residue was dissolved in 1. 6 ml dimethyl sulphoxide. All these aqueous and dimethyl sulphoxide extracts were stored at-80℃ prior to the analysis.

The method used for assaying EBV activation was that described by Ito et al[10]. with a minor modification, i. e. treatment of foetal calf serum by pH shock[11]. In brief, human lymphoblastoid Raji cells, bearing latent EBV genomes, were cultured in RPMI 1640 medium supplemented with 10% fetal calf serum in a humidified atmosphere of 5% CO_2 at 37℃. The test for indnotion of EBV(EA)was performed by incubating Raji cells at a density of 5×10⁵ cells/ml for 48h at 37℃ in the presence of the food extracts, supplemented with 4mmol/L sodium n-butyrate and 15% foetal calf serum. After incubation for 48h, aliquots of sedimented cells were transfered onto glass slides, air dried and fixed with acetone for 20 min at 4℃. Cells that expressed EBV-EA were detected by an immunoenzymic test[12] instead of the usual immunofluorescence method(as in[10]). This assay was performed with IgG antibodies against EA(as contained in 2-fold diluted, pooled NPC sera) and peroxidase-labelled protein A. In each assay, 500 cells were scored, and the percentage of EBV-EA-positive cells was recorded. The mean background value in the presence of 4mmol/L sodium n-butyrate was 3.05%±0.51 SD;(n=11). Positive controls treated with 12-O-tetra- decanoylphorbol-13-acetate(TPA)(20ng/ml) and 4mmol/L sodium n-butyrate gave a mean of 43.5%±8.96 SD;(n=11). The mean values listed in Tab. 1. were calculated from two series of duplicate experiments. Under these assay conditions, the samples were considered to be positive when the percentage of EA-positive cells after treatment of 4mmol/L sodium n-butyrate and test sample was >10%(i.e. three times background value in the presence of 4mmol/L sodium n-butyrate only)showing a dose-dependent increase(Tab. 1).

Tab. 1　EBV-EA activators in aqueous extracts of preserved food samples from southern China, Tunisia and Greenland

Country/food item	EBV-EA-positive cells(%)Concentration of food extract(mg wet weight equivalent of food/ml medium)			
	0.005-0.13	0.66	3.32	16.6
Southern China				
Cantonese salted, dried fish and shellfish:				
Japanese mackerel*	<5	8.4	10.2	17.8
Squid sample 1	<4.0	5.0	13.6	8.6
Squid sample 2	<3.2	3.4	8.8	16
Eight other Cantonese salted, dried fish and shellfish	<4.0	<5.1	<6.0	<5.2
Fermented shrimp/fish paste	<4.1	3.0	3.2	4.8
Fermented soya bean paste	<2.6	3.0	3.1	5.1
Cabbage fermented in brine	<3.5	3.3	4.2	4.1
Tunisia				
Harissa(spice mixture):				
Sample 1	<3.9	7.7	13.9	22.6
Sample 2	<4.9	10.0	14.9	19.9
Sample 3	<4.7	10.9	12.6	3.2
Sample 4(preserved in can)	<3.1	2.6	3.0	3.3
Qaddid(dried mutton preserved in oil)	<2.6	4.2	7.8	9.6
Touklia(stewing base)	<5.2	7.2	6.1	1.8
Turnips fermented in brine	<4.1	5.0	5.5	6.4
Salted anchovies	<3.0	2.4	2.8	2.2
Louben(sap from the mastic tree)	<3.1	3.2	4.0	4.1
Greenland				
Mikialak(dried Atlantic cod)	<2.4	3.0	3.2	2.8
Uuvag(dried polar cod)	<2.5	2.2	2.4	6.1
Amassat(dried capelin)	<2.4	2.0	2.1	4.8
Panerteq(dried fjord seal meat)	<2.8	4.2	6.1	7.2
Berries preserved in seal oil	<4.4	4.3	4.2	4.4

RESULTS AND DISCUSSION

The results on aqueous extracts are shown in Tab. 1. Of the preserved food samples from southern China, three out of 11 Cantonese salted dried fish and shellfish were found to contain substance(s) that activate EBV latency in Raji cells. Three out of four samples of harissa(a spice mixture) and, to a lesser extent, one sample of qaddid from Tunisia showed EBV activation activity. The activity found in these food extracts was comparable to those reported for extracts of Chinese vegetables, plants and medicinal herbs, some of which are known to contain phorbol ester-type com- pounds[13-15]. For most of the positive samples, a dose-response relationship between the amount of food extract tested and EBV activation in Raji cells was observed. Aqueous extracts of other selected preserved food samples from southern China. Tunisia and Greenland gave negative results; however, because of the wide variation in EBV activation by the same type of food(Tab. 1), further samples of each food are now being assayed. The variation may be due to different modes of preparation or even to individual differences in the mode of preparation. All n-hexane and ethyl acetate extracts up to 62.5mg wet weight equivalent of food/ml medium produced 1.2% to 6.1% EBV-EA- positive cells and thus were considered negative(data not shown).

Preliminary experiments were carried out to isolate and characterize the EBV-activating agents present in aqueous extracts of harissa. The substance(s)appears to be relatively stable, since no apparent loss of activity was observed when the harissa sample was heated at 100℃ for 10 min or incubated in 0.1mol/L NaOH solution at 37℃ for 30 min. However, about 50% of the activity was lost after incubation in 0.1mol/L HCl solution at 37℃ for 30 min. Preliminary partition experiments suggest that at least two different compounds are present in the harissa extract, including one extractable by ethyl acetate under neutral conditions and another soluble onyl in water.

In conclusion, the results reported here represent, to our knowledge, the first demonstration that Cantonese salted fish, karissa and qaddid-preserved foods consumed very frequently in high-risk areas for NPC-contain substance(s)capable of strongly activating EBV in Raji cells. Recent case-control studies conducted in Hong Kong show that consumption of Cantonesestyle salted fish is significantly associated with an increased risk of NPC[7], Similarly, an anthropological study conducted in the same three high-risk areas[8] also suggested that NPC could be associated with eating habits, especially consumption of preserved foods, including harissa, qaddid and salt-dried fish. Further studies should be underaken to isolate and identify the active substances in order to better understand the role of these foods in the etiology of NPC. A case-control study is now underway in the three high-risk areas for NPC, to study the correlation between NPC and consumption of food items containing VNA, EBV-activating substance(s)and other genotoxic substance(s). Results of experiments to detect mutagens present in the same food extracts used in this study will be reported separately elsewhere.

ACKNOWLEDGEMENTS

The authors would like to thank G. Lenoir for his valuble comments on this manuscript. We also thank N. Roche for technical assistance, A. Hubert for collecting the food specimens, E. Heseltine and M. B. D'Arcy for editorial and secretarial help, respectively. This study was supported by the CNRS(GGS17), the Association pour Recherche sur le Cancer(ARC)(Contract 6071)ant the Association for Virus Cancer Prevention.

REFERENCES

[1] De The G, Ho JHC, Muir CS. Nasopharyngeal carcinoma. In Evans, A S.(ed). Viral Infections of Humans Epidemiology and Control. John Wiley New York, 1982;621-622.

[2] Henle G, Henle W. Epstein-Barr virus-specific IgA serum antibodies as an outstanding feature of nasopharyngeal carcinoma. Int J Cancer, 1976,17;1-7.

[3] Desgranges C, De The G.(1978). IgA and nasopharyngeal carcinoma. In De The, G. Ito Y. and Rapp, F(eds), Oncogenesis and Herpesviruses Ⅲ. International Agency for Research on Cancer, Lyon, 1978, 24;883-891.

[4] Wara WM, Wara DW, Phillips TL, Ammahh, A. Elevated Ig A in carcinoma of the nasopharynx. Cancer, 1975, 35; 1313-1315.

[5] De The G, Zeng Y. Population screening for EBV markers toward improvement of nasopharyngeal carcinoma control. In Epstein, M. A. and Achong B. G(eds), The Epstein Barr Virus. Recent Advances. Willam, 1986.

[In《Carcinogenesis》1988，9；1455-1457]

Wikstroemia Indica Promotes Development of Nasopharyngeal Carcinoma in Rats Initiated by Dinitrosopiperazine

Tang WP[1], Huang P G[1], Zhao ML[1], Liao SL[1], Zeng Y[2]

1. Zhangjiang Medical College, Guangdong, China　2. Institute of Virology, Chinese Academy of Preventive Medicine, Beijing, China

[SUMMARY]　Nasopharyngeal carcinoma was induced in an initiation/promotion model in rats by s. c. injection of dinitrosopiperazine in the nasopharyngeal cavity. This was followed by repeated 10-cal administration of an extract of roots of the Chinese medicinal herb WI(botanical family: Thymelaeaceae). Three groups of rats were used: group-1 received DNP followed by repeated WI; group-2 received DNP once; group-3 received WI repeatedly. At 180-205 days after DNP+WI administration 26% of the rats in that group exhibited NPC(two were carcinomas in situ and four were early infiltrating carcinomas). In the other two groups no carcinomas were found. In the group which received DNP followed by WI, other pathological changes, such as hyperplasia of nasopharyngeal epithelium, squamous metaplasia, and papillary hyperplasia, were also more frequent than that in the other two groups.

INTRODUCTION

Using a combination of viral and environmental factors, in what may De considered an initiation/promotion protocol in Raji cells vitro(Hecker 1979; zur Hausen et al, 1979), many extracts from plants and herbs of Euphorbiaceae, Thymelaeaceae, and other plant families have been tested for promoting activity(Ito 1981; Zeng et al. 1983, 1984; Zhong et al. 1986; Zi et al. 1985). It was found that many of the extracts induced an early antigen of EBV in the Raji cells. Also, in lymphocytes transformation by EBV was enhanced by such extracts(Hu and Zeng 1985). Furthermore, some of the extracts enhanced the development of Rous sarcoma, papilloma, and cervical carcinoma in vivo(Hu et al. 1986; Zeng 1987; Sun et al. 1987.) Whether or not the same extracts would have an effect on inducing NPC in an initiation/promotion model in vivo requires investigation. It is well-documented that the plant WI of the family of Thymelaeaceae is found in high-risk areas of NPC such as Guangdong, Guangxi, and other provinces of China; it is used as a Chinese medicinal herb. On the other hand it has been shown in various laboratories that in rats and mice NPC may be induced by certain chemical carcinogens(Druckrey et al. 1964, 1967; Wang1965; Pan and Yao 1978; Yao et al. 1981; Tang and Juang 1978; Huang et al. 1977, 1978). For example, by a combination of nickel sulfate and DNP, Ou induced NPC in rats(Ou 1982). Here we report that NPC may be induced in rats by combined use of DNP and WI in an initiation/ promotion protocol.

MATERIALS AND METHODS

1. Initiator: DNP was synthesized in our laboratory, m.p. 157-158℃(Fan and Wen1985). It was mixed with a small amount of Tween 80 and distilled water to give a solution containing 9mg DNP/ml suit able for injection.

2. Promoter: An ether extract of roots of WI was prepared by repeated digestion of the plant material at room temperature with ether for 1 week. The dry residue of the extract was dissolved in ethanol to make up a solution containing 10mg WI/ml.

3. Animals: A total of 72 hybrid rats of unspecified strain, two months old, male: female were used 1 : 1. They were divided into 3 groups and the initiation/promotion protocol was as rollows:

（1）DNP followed by WI: 32 rats were each given 1ml DNP solution s.c. After 10 days 0. 1 ml of WI solution was dropped into the nasopharyngeal cavity twice a week, for 7 weeks.

（2）DNP once: 20 rats were given 1ml DNP s. c. only.

（3）WI alone: 20 rats were given 0.1ml WI solution twice a week by dropping it into the nasopharyngeal cavity.

After 7 weeks, the administration of WI was stopped, and all rats were observed continously for 180-205 days, then they were sacrified. The entire nasopharygeal cavity was removed and fixed in Bouin's solution, using Jenkin solution to eliminate calcium. It was embedded in paraffin and sectioned following routine staining with H&E for investigation under a light microscope.

RESULTS

Both of the control groups 2 and had no tumors with the exception of one case of an atypical dysplasia and one of papilloma of the nasopharyngeal epithelium in thi WI group. The main pathological change was squamous metaplasia and papillary hyperplasia (Tab. 1).

In the group which received DNP followed by WI six rats developed NPC, a tumor incidence of 26%. The other pathological changes, such as hyperplasia of the nasopharyngeal epithelium, squamous metaplasia, and papillary hyperplasia, were more frequent than in the control groups. The

Tab. 1　Survey of pathological changes of nasopharyngeal epithelium in rats

Survivors/tumors	Group		
	DNP followed by WI	DNP alone	WI alone
Survivors of 180-205 days	23/32	14/20	15/20
Squamous metaplasia	19	10	10
Papillary hyperplasia	18	8	8
Papilloma	0	0	1
Dysplasia	4	0	1
Carcinoma in situ	2	0	0
Early infiltrating carcinoma	4		0
Rate of carcinoma(%)	26. 1	0	0

tumor cells in the six cases grew towards the cavity as papilliform, gyrusform, or fungiform and even obstructed the cavity. Two of the NPC in the group were carcinomas in situ(Tab. 1), and four early infiltrating carcinomas. Among the four cases of early infiltrating carcinomas, three were poorly differentiated squamous cell carcinomas and showed no keratinization, another was cylindrical, and a few of them displayed an adenoid structure filled with mucin staining light blue. The cells of all four cases penetrated the basal membrane and infiltrated the masenchyme. Of the two carcinomas in situ, one was a carcinomatous change of cylindroepithelial cells, and the other was a carcinomatous change of squamous epithelial cells. Three cases of poorly differentiated squamous cell carcinomas were papilliform, gyrusform, and fungiform. The poorly differentiated cylindrocellular carcinoma was papilliform.

DISCUSSION

Poirier et al.(1987)found nitrosamines in common foods in high-risk areas for NPC in Tunisia, South China, and Greenland. Huang et al.(1977, 1978)reported that extracts from salted fish containing nitrosamines could induce NPC in rats. Experimentally it was found that DNP is a solitary carcinogen with relative organotropy for the nasopharyngeal epithelium(Le et al. 1982). As known for other nitroso compounds large dose or many small doses, repeat dely administered for a long time, may elicit NPC. For example, Pan and Yao(1978)induced NPC in rats by giving 1. 5 mg DNP s. c. twice a week, with a minimum cumulative dose of 99mg. Within 6 months after stopping the administration of DNP 64% of the rats had developed squamous carcinoma of the nasopharynx.

The plant WI is frequently used as a Chinese medicinal herb for treating infection. It is the main ingredient of the patent medicine "Jiedu-Yiaoyan Pian" made in Guangdong. Zeng et al. found(Zeng et al. 1983, 1984; Zhong et al. 1986; Ni et al. 1985)that the ether extract of the roots activated EBV in Raji cells and enhanced the EBV-induced transformation of lymphocytes.

With the background of the now classical initiation/promotion protocol with DMBA/diterpene ester in the mouse skin model(Hecker 1984; Hecker et al. 1984)and in view of the findings on systemic administration of the initiatior DMBA(Pyerin and Hecker 1980)our experiments show: (1) the rats in the DNP group were given a subcarcinogenic dose by injection of 9mg DNP s. c.(about 1/10 of the minimum cumulative dose for inducing cancer), as confirmed independantly by Lu(1983),(2) the WI group, which was given 14 doses of WI also received subcarcinogenic exposure, and(3) giving the same dose of DNP once, followed by the same dose of WI 14 times may truly be considered an initiation/promotion protocol: the experiments showed that in nasopharyngeal epithelium of ratd DNP may play the role of a tumor initiator and WI the role of a tumor promoter. Since the experiments lasted only 180-205 days, the observation of metaplasia, hyperplasia, and one papilloma after administration of WI alone was remarkable. This effect appeared to indicate that WI may act as a complete carcinogen when applied over longer periods. It will be important to carry out further experimental studies on the effects of nitrosamines and EBV in conjunction with environmental tumor promoters detected in high-risk areas of NPC.

REFERENCES

[1]　Druckrey H, lvankovic S, Mennel H, Preussmann R Selektive Erzeugung yon Carcinogen der Nasnhohle bei Ratten durch N-Di-Nitrosopiperazin, Nitrosopiperidin, Nitrosomorohol in Methyl-allyl-, Dimethylund Methyl-vinyl- Nitrosamin. Z

Krebsforsch, 1964, 66:138-150.

[2] Druckrey H, Preussmann R, Ivankovic S, Schmahl D Organotrope carcinogen Wirkungen bei 65 verschiedenen Nitroso-Verbindungen an BD-Ratten. Z Krebsforsch, 1967, 69:103.

[3] Fan JY, Wen HJ Chemical synthesis of several carcinogenic agents. Bull Hunan Med Coll,1985, 10(4):317-319, 3332.

[4] Hecker E. Diterpene ester type modulators of carcinogenesisnew findings in the mechanism of chemical carcinogenesis and in the etiology of human tumors. In: EC Miller et al.(eds)Naturally occurring carcinogens-mutagens and modulators of carcinogenesis. Japan Sci Soc Press, Tokyo/UNIV Park Press, Baltimore, 1979, 263-266.

[5] Hecker E. In: Kang et al.(translated)Scientific base of cancer. Academic Press, New York,1984, 385-394.

[6] Hecker E. Cocarcinogens of the diterpene ester type as principal risk factors of cancer in Curacao and possibly in South China: identiication of second order risk factors of cancer in multifactorial carcinogenesis. In: Wagner G, Thang YH(eds) Cancer of the liver, esophagus, and nasopharynx. Berlin Heidelberg New York, Springer, 1987, 101-113.

[7] Hecker E, Adolf W, Hergenhahn M, Schmidt R, Sorg B Irritant diterpene ester promoters of mouse skin: contributions to etiologies of environmental cancer and to biochemical mechanisms of carcinogenesis. In: Fujiki H et al.(eds) Cellular interactions by environmental tumor pro- moters. Japan Sci, Soc Press, Tokyo, VNU Science Press, Utrecht, 1984, 3-36.

[8] Hu YL, Zeng YThe extracts from some Chinese herbs enhanced the transformation of human lymphocytes by EBV. Chin J Oncol, 1985, 8:417-418.

[9] Hu YL, Zeng Y, Ito Y Croton oil, Wikstroemia chamaedaphne and Wikstroemia indica enhanced rabbit papilloma induced by papilloma virus. Chin J Virol, 1986, 2:81-82.

[10] Huang DP, Ho JHC, Gough TA, Webb KS Volatile nitrosamines in some traditional Chinese food products. J Food Saf, 1977, 1:1-6.

[11] Huang DP, Ho JHC, Saw D, Theoh TB Carcinoma of the nasal and paranasal regions in rats fed Cantonese salted marine fish. In: de The G, Ito G, Davis W(eds). Nasopharyngeal carcinoma: etiology and control. IARC Scientific Publications No. 20, Lyon, 1978, 315-328.

[12] Ito Y Induction and intervention of Epstein-Barr virus expression in human lymphoblastoid cell line. Cancer campaign, vol 5, New York, Nasopharyngeal carcinoma, Fischer, Stuttgart, 1981.

[13] Le JY, Pan SC, Yao KT The mechanism of organ specific carcinogenicity of N, N-Dinitrosopiperazine in rats. Bull Hum Med Coil, 1982,7(2):129-135.

[14] Lu YF The role of nickel sulfate in the induction of nasopharyngeal carcinoma in rats. Cancer,1983, 2:100-102.

[15] Ni HY, Zeng Y, Zhong JM Distribution of plants and herbs containing EBV inducer. J Ninbo Univ,1985, 1:86-88.

[16] Ou BX Trace elements and nasopharyngeal carcinoma. Cancer, 1982, 1:86-89.

[17] Pan SC, Yao KT Induction of nasopharyngeal carcinoma in rats by nitroso compounds. KEXUE TONGBAO, 1978, 12: 756-760.

[18] Poirier S, Ohshima H, Bourgade MC, de The G, Bartsch H Volatile nitrosamine levels in common foods from Tunisia, South Cina and Greenland high risk areas for nasopharyngeal carcinoma. Int J Cancer, 1987, 39:293-296.

[19] Pyerin WG, Hecker E Tumor initation in mouse skin by 7, 12-dimethyl-benz(a)anthracene: irrelevance of systemic activation. Cancer Lett, 1980, 8:317-321.

[20] Shen SZ Preliminary report on interstisural reaction of nasopharyngeal carcinoma in situ in rats by methylcholanthrene, J Zhangjiang Medical College, 1978:10-15.

[21] Sun Y, Chen MH, Zeng Y Tumor promoting effect of the extracts of Wikstroemia chamaedaphne and HHPA on cervical cancer induced by Heroes simplex virus type 2 in mice. Chin J Virol, 1987, 3:131-133.

[22] Tang WP, Huang SW Preliminary report on interstitial reaction of nasopharyngeal carcinoma in situ in rats by methylcholanthrene. J Zhangiang Medical College, 1978, 10-15.

[23] Wang HW Study on inducing nasopharyngeal carcinoma in mice. J Exp Biol, 1965, 10:190-199.

[24] Yao KT, Pan SC, Huang JI, Wen DS Further investigation of experimental induction of nasopharyngeal carcinoma in rats by dinitrosopiperazine. Bull Hunan Med Coll, 1981, 6(1):1-6.

[25] Zeng Y Prospective studies on nasopharyngeal carcinoma and Epstein-Barr virus inducers. In: Wagner G, Zhang YH(eds) Cancer of the liver, esophagus, and nasopharynx. Berlin Heidelberg New York, Springer, 1987, 164-169.

[26] Zeng Y, Zhong JM, Mo YK, Miao XC Epstein-Barr virus early antigen induction in Raji cell by Chinese medicinal herbs. Intervirology, 1983,19:201-204.

[27] Zeng Y, Miao XC, Jiao BO, Ito Y Epstein- Barr virus activation in Raji cells, with ether extracts of soil from different areas in China. Cancer, Lett, 1984, 23:53-59.

[28] Zhong JM, Mo YK, Ni HY, Huang CC, Zhin CZ, Tam ZT, Zeng Y Studies on EBV inducer from plants, herbs and foods. J Guangxi Med,1986, 8: 145-146.

[29] Zur Hausen H, Bomkamm GW, Schmidt R, Hecker E Tumor initiators and promoters in the induction of Epstein-Barrvirus. Proc Natl Acad Sci USA, 1979, 76:782-785.

[In《J Cancer Res Chin Oncol》1988, 114:429-431]

Linkage of a Nasopharyngeal Carcinoma Susceptibility Locus to the HLA Region

LU Sheng-jing[1], DAY Nicholas E[2], DEGOS Laurent[3], LEPAGE Virginia[4], WANG Pei-Chung[1], CHAN So-Ha[6], IMONS Maicolm[7], MCKNIGHT Barbara[6], EASTON Easton[9], Zeng YI[9], de-The G[8]

1. People's Regional Hospital, Nanning, Guangxi Autonomous Region, People's Republic of China　2. Medical Research Council Biostatistics Unit, 5 Shaftesbury Road, Cambridge CB2 2BW, UK　3. INSERM U 93, Hayem Research Center, Saint Louis Hospital, Paris, France　4. Microbiology Department, National University, Singapore　5. Immunogene Typing Laboratories, Immunoresearch, Melbourne, Australia　6. Department of Biostatistios, University of Washington, Seattle, Washington 98196, USA　7. Section of Epidemiology, Institute for Cancer Research, Sutton, Surrey SM2 5NG, UK　8. CNRS Laboratory of Epidemiology and Immunovirology of Tumors, Faculty of Medicine Alexis Carrel, 69372 Lyon Cedes 8, France　9. Institute of Virology, Chinese Academy of Preventive Medicine, Beijing, People's Republic of China

The frequency of nasopharyngeal carcinoma is nearly 100-fold higher in southern Chinese than in most European populations[1]. Earlier studies have suggested that an inceased risk of nasopharyngeal carcinoma is associated with specific haplotypes in the HLA region: relative risks slightly over twofold were found for haplotypes A2, Bw46 and the antigen B17(refs 2-4). We now report a linkage study based on affected sib pairs which suggests that a gene closely linked to the HLA locus confers a greatly increased risk of nasopharyngeal carcinoma. The maximum Likelihood estimate is of a relative risk of approximately 21. The relationship between this suspected disease susceptibility gene(or genes)and known viral and environmental aetiological factors remains to be elucidated.

Our approach was to identify sibships that had more than one individual affected with nasopharyngeal carcinoma(NPC), and for which sufficient individuals could be typed to permit unambiguous assignment of haplotypes[5]. The study began in Singapore and Hong Kong in 1976 and extanded in 1983 to Nanning in the Guangxi Autonomous region of the People's Republic of China, where more sib pairs were accessible(see Tab. 1 legend). In each area, the members of each sibship, their parents and children were visited and blood samples taken. Thirty-four sibships with more than one case of NPC were identified, 31 with two cases and the remainder with three cases (Tab. 1). Of the sib-pair families, four had to be excluded, one because the pair were twins of unknown zygosity (but HLA identical)and three because an excess of haplotypes was seen in the family and parentage was ambiguous.

Tab. 1　Sib-pair analysis

	Number of shared haplotypes											
	2 Expected under				1 Expected under				0 Expected under			
		No				No				No			
	Observed	linkage	Dominant	recessive	Observed	linkage	Dominant	recessive	Observed	linkage	Dominant	recessive
Sib pairs[1]	16	6.75	10.83	13.96	8	13.5	13.18	10.40	3	6.75	2.99	2.64
Triplestz	2[2]	2.25	3.30	4.01	4	4.50	4.39	3.91	3	2.25	1.31	1.08
Total	18	9.00	14.13	17.97	12	18.00	17.57	14.31	6	9.00	4.30	3.72

Notes: Number of sib pairs sharing two, one or zero HLA haplotypes identical by descent, together with the expected number under the null hypothesis of no linkage, and under the best fitting dominant and recessive models. For the sib trios, all possible sib pairs are considered.

Goodness of fit[11]of the hypothesis of no linkage, X^2(2d. f.)for sib pairs only$=17.0$, $P<0.001$; for all pairs(both sib paris and triples)$=12.0$, $P<0.005$. Goodness-of-fit tels of the recessive and dominant models are each given by a 1 d. f. Likelihood ratio test against a three-parameter model, with relative risk r_2 for the DS heterozygote, and r_2 for the DS homozy- gote. x_1^2 for recessive, model$=0.32$; x_1^2 for dominant model$=2.95.(P=0.08)$.

(1) 18 from China, 3 from Hong Kong, 5 from Singapore and 1 from Malaysia.

(2) from China and 1 from Hong Kong.

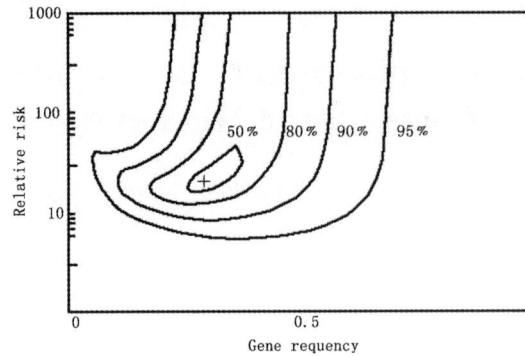

Fig. 1 For the model fitting, inference was based on the log-Likelihood difference conditional on the disease phenotypes, or lod score. The use of this conditional Likelihood allows inferences to be made free from ascertainment bial[6,8]. Likelihood calculations were performed using the program LINKAGE[7] for single-gene dominant and recessive models, varying the gene frequency relative risk associated with the disease susceptibility gene, and the recombination fraction θ between the susceptibility gene and the HLA region. In particular, the lower 95% confidence limit for the relative risk associated with the susceptibility gene, r_o, is given by:

$$2[\max_{r,p,\theta}I(r,p,\theta) - \max_{p,\theta}I(r_o,f,\theta)] = 3.84$$

where $I(r,f,\theta)$ denotes the log-Likelihood function and 3.84 is the upper 95% point for a x^2 distribution on 1 degree of freedom. The contours shown define confidence regions for r and f, at the 95%, 90%, 80% and 50% level with $\theta = 0$. The absolute maximum of the Likelihood occurs when $\theta = 0$, with values of $f = 0.29$, $r = 0.29$, and is marked by a cross (+).

HLA typing on the samples from Hong Kong and Singapore was performed in Singapore and restricted to locus A and B antigens, using a panel of over 200 antisera of Chinese, Malay, Janpanese, Filippino and Caucasian origin. HLA typing in Nanning used a panel of 143 allelic typing antisera(from Saint Louis Hospital, Paris)corresponding to HLA A, B, C and in most cases DR loci. Of the 38 NPC cases tested, the most common DR antigens were DR2(18/38)and DR4(16/38). No other DR antigen was present on more than seven individual cases.

The haplotype similarity of affected sibs and triplets is shown in Tab. 1, together with the expected numbers if no linkage were present. The total data show a clear divergence between observed and expected($P < 0.005$). Among the sib pairs, comparing observed with expected gives a χ^2 value of 17.0(2d. f.). This highly significant divergence demonstrates the existence of NPC disease susceptibility gene(s)linked to the HLA region.

For linkage analysis, single-gene models were explored[6-8], and as models assuming dominant inheritance fitted poorly(Tab. 1), the subsequent analyses were based on recessive models. Fig. 1 shows the Likelihood of the observed results(lod score)for varying values of the relative risk(r)and the gene frequency(f)of the putative disease susceptibility gene when the recombination fraction(θ)is zero. The maximum lod score under the recessive model is $+2.39$, and under the dominant model $+1.68$, with P values of 0.004, and 0.024 respectively.

The maximum Likelihood estimate occurs when $\theta = 0$, $r = 20.9$ and $f = 0.29$. Infinite values of r are only slightly less likely for a range of values of f; the minimum value of r consistent with the data is 5.1 at the 95% level, and 9.8 at the 90% level. With values of θ greater than zero, all the Likelihood contours are further removed from the axis given by $r = 1$.

These results show the existence of an NPC disease susceptibility gene(s)conferring an increased risk for NPC soime tenfold larger than that associated with Bw46 or B17, with the upper 90% comfidence bound being infinite. The results thus provide strong support for the original hypotyesis[5] that much of the high risk for NPC among the southern Chinese is due to HLA-associated genes. The lifetime risk of NPC among Cantonese males in Singapore[1] is 1.6%, indicating that the frequency of a recessive disease susceptibility gene should be at least 0.13.

The mechanism by which an HLA-linked disease susceptibility gene might act is unknown. Two proposed environmental aetiological agents for NPC are the Epstein-Barr virus(EBV)and some constituents of preserved foods, including salted fish[8-10]. Insight into the mechanism of action of NPC disease susceptibility gene(s)should help to clarify the respective role of EBV, environmental cofactors and genetic susceptibility in the development of NPC.

REFERENCES

[1] Shanmugaratnam K, Lee HP, Day NE. Cancer incidence in Singapore, 1968-1977, IARC Scientific Publication no. 47

(IARC, Lyon, 1983).

[2] Simons MJ, et al. Int J Cancer, 1974, 18:122-134.

[3] Simons MJ, et al. Lancet, 1975, 1:142-143.

[4] Chan SH, Day NE, Kunaratnam N, Chia K B, Simons M J. Cancerm, 1982, 32:171-176.

[5] Day NE, Simons MJ. Tissue Antigens, 1976,8:106-119.

[6] Rish N. Am J hum, Genet, 1984, 38:363-386.

[7] Lathrop GM, Laloual JM, Julies C, Ott. J Proc natn Acad Scl U S A, 1984, 81:3443-3446.

[8] Ewens WJ, Clarke CP. Am J hum Genet,1984, 83:853-372.

[9] Shanmugaratnam K. in Cancer Epidemiology and Prevention, 536-553 (eds Schottenfeid, D. & Fraumenl. J. F.) 536-553 (Sanders, London, 1982).

[10] Yu MC, Ho JHC, Lai SH, Henderson B E. Cancer Res, 1986, 46:956-961.

[11] Stsckweider WC, Elston RC. Genet. Epid, 1985,2:85-97.

[In《Nature》1990，346:470-471]

Diagnosis of Nasopharyngeal Carcinoma by Means of Recombinant Epstein-Barr Virus Proteins

LITTLER Edward[1,3], BAYLIS Sally A[1], ZENG Yi[2], CONWAY Margaret J[1],
MACKETT Michael[3], ARRAND John R[1]

1. Cancer Resesrch Campaign Laboratories, Paterson Institute for Cancer Research, Christie Hospital and Holt Radium Institute, Manchester, UK   2. Institute of Virology, Chinese Academy of Medical Sciences, Beijing, People's Republic of China   3. Correspondence to Dr E. Litter, Department of Moleculer Sciences, Wellcome Research Laboratories, Langley Court, Beckenham, Kent BR3 3BS, UK.

[SUMMARY]   The immune response of patients with nasopharyngeal carcinoma to Epstein-Barr virus(EBV) antigens is diagnostic of the tumour. Existing tests use EBV antigens produced in EBV-infected lymphoblastoid cells, but the virus replicates poorly in these cells. Serum samples from 18 patients diagnosed as having nasopharyngeal carcinoma were screened by western blot analysis, enzyme liked immunosorbent assay(ELISA), and immunofluorescence tests for antibodies to the EBV-coded alkaline deoxyribonuclease(DNase), thymidine kinase, and membrane antigen(gp340/220) produced in recombinant baculovirus of bovine papillomavirus systems. Each protein was a useful diagnostic marker for nasopharyngeal carcinoma, although in the gp340/220 ELISAs there was substantial overlap for both IgG and IgA antibodies between serum samples from nasopharyngeal carcinoma patients and those from healthy donors seropositiver for EBV. The EBV thymidine kinase was the most sensitive predictor of nasopharyngeal carcinoma; all such samples showed both IgG and IgA antibody responses to this protein and all gave clearly distinct titres from those of the EBV-seropositive donors in the IgA test. Each of the recombinant systems described is suitable for use in large-scale screening programmes for the early diagnosis of nasopharyngeal carcinoma.

INTRODUCTION

Nasopharyngcal carcinoma, a tumour of epithelial origin, is the commonest from of nasopharyngeal cancer.[1,2] Most nasopharyngeal carcinomas are radiosensitive, with survival rates of 33% after 3 years and 25% after 5 years for all cases(71% and 59%, respectively, for those confined to the nasopharynx).[2] In most countries cancer of the nasopharynx is rare, with rates of less than 1 per100 000 per year. However, in several Chinese populations(Southern provinces of China, Hong Kong, Taiwan, Singapore, and Malaysia)the incidence is 15-30 per 100 000 per year,[3,4] In these Chinese populations it is the commonest turnout among men and the second most common among women. The incidence of nasopharyngel carcinoma is also high in Inuit populations, and there is evidence of high mortality associated with the disorder among black American men aged 60-80.[5,6]

There is much evidence to support an association between infection with Epstein-Barr virus(EBV) and nasopharyngeal carcinoma. EBV infection occurs in the vast majority of all human populations. Infection in childhood occurs without clinical symptoms, but if infection does not occur until adolescence the symptoms of infectious mononucleosis develop in about 50% of cases. It is possible to detect EBV DNA, RNA, and protein in the majority of biopsy samples from nasopharyngeal carcinomas,[7-10] but the immune response fo nasopharyngeal carcinoma patients to EBV antigens is unusual. Seroepidemiological surveys have shown that the titre of antibodies against the EBV capsid antigen(VCA)is about ten times higher in patients with nasopharyngeal carcinoma than in those with other tumours of the head and neck region.[11] These patients also have high concentration of antibodies to the EBV early antigen(EA), particularly to the diffuse component. EA antibody titres in nasopharyngeal carcinoma patients increase with the progression of the disease from stage I to stage IV.[12] The high VCA and EA antibody titres are reflected in the presence in both serum and saliva of IgA antibody to the same antigens.[13,14] The presence of IgA antibody to EBV-coded antigens is a diagnostic characteristic of serum from patients with naopharyngeal carcinoma.

EBV EA consists of several proteins including some virus-coded enzymes. The EBV-coded enzymes alkaline deoxyribonucease(DNase), DNA polymerase, and thymidine kinase are specifically neutralised serum from nasopharyngeal carcinoma patients.[15-17] The best characterised immune response is to the EBV-coded alkaline DNase, which is a good diagnostic and prognostic marker for nasopharyngeal carcinoma.[18,19]

An improtant obstacle to the use of EBV-coded proteins for diagnosis of nasopharyngeal carcinoma is that there is no fully permissive cell culture system for the replication of EBV. We have reported the expression of several EBV-coded proteins in recombinant systems and preliminary evidence of their value for the diagnosis of nasopharyngeal carcinoma.[20-22] We describe here the use of the EBV-coded alkaline DNase, gp340/220, and thymidine kinase in western blot, immunofluorescent tests, and enzyme-linked immunosorbent assays(ELISAs)to detect the presence of reactive IgG and IgA antibody in serum from patients with naspharyngeal carcinoma.

METHODS

The construction of recombinant baculovirus expressing the EBV-coded alkaline DNase and thymidine kinase and bovinepapillomavirus-transformed cell lines expressing the EBV-coded membrane antigen have been described previously.[23,24] Cells producing the EBV recombinant proteins were resuspended in sodium dodecyl sulphate disruption buffer for polyactylamide gel electrophoresis; 0. 1% 'NP40' and 0. 1% sodium deoxycholate for ELISAs; or phosphate-buffered saline form immunofluotescence tests. For immunofluorescence cells were allowed to adhere to glass slides and then fixed in acetone for 10 min.

Conditions for polyactylamide gel electrophoresis and western blotting have been described previously.[21] Each strip contained about 10^5 cells infected with recombinant baculovirus. Serum samples were used at 1/50 dilution.

ELISA plates were sensitised with cells infected with recombinant baculovirus, resuspended as above and diluted in 0.01moL/L ammonium bicarbonate buffer at a concentration of 10^5 cells/ml, or with purified gp340/220 at 50-80mg/ml. Serum samples diluted 1/10 were added and the reaction was detected by means of phosphatase-conjugated sheep antibody to human IgG or IgA.

The antisera used consisted of samples from 30 normal, healthy EBV seropositive(VCA +) subjects from the Manchester ares; 7 clinically normal EBV seronegative(VCA-) subjects(L. Young, University of Birmingham); and 17 patients with nasopharyngeal carcinoma from Wuzhou, Guangxi, China. The clinical stage of the tumour was define by Chinese criterria.[25] Serum samples were also examined for the presence of IgA antibody to EBV VCA and EA[11]

RESULTS

The serum samples from nasopharyngeal carcinoma patients showed several patterns of reactions with the recombinant EBV proteins(Fig 1, Tab. 1). 3 serum samples(5, 6, and 14; Tab. 1)had IgA and IgG antibody to all three proteins, although the concentration of IgG against gp340/220 was low(Fig 1A). 2 samples (12 and 15) had only IgG and IgA antibody against EBV thymidine kinase(fig 1B); sample 12 had a low antibody titre to the EBV VCA and sample15 had no detectable IgA antibody to EBV EA. The remaining samples showed variable patterns of response to the three EBV proteins. Fig 1C shows the result for sample 18; it had IgG antibody to both DNase and thymidine kinase but IgA antibody only against thymidine kinase; this serum also had a low VCA titre. The remaining serum samples gave a variable reaction with both the EBV-coded alkaline DNase and gp340/220. For example, fig 1D shows the result for sample 10; it had IgG against DNase and thymidine kinase, but not gp340/20, and IgA against thymidine kinase and gp340/220, but not DNase.

Thus, on western hot analysis all serum samples from patients with nasopharyngeal carcinoma had IgG

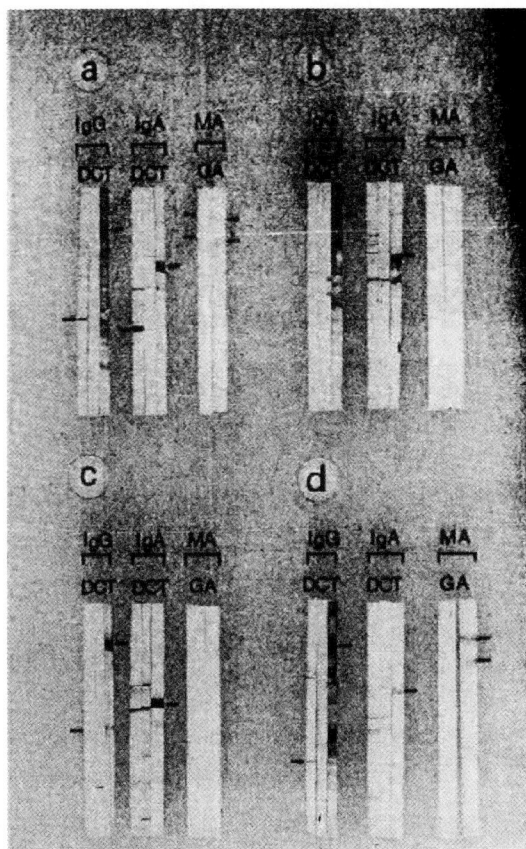

D= baculovirus-infected cells expressing EBV alkaline DNase; T= same cells expressing thymidine kinase; C= extract from control wild-type baculovirus-infected cells; MA = purified gp340/220(G = IgG, A = IgA). Location of unique reactive bands shown ty bars. Panel a= patient 5; b= patient 12; c= patient 18; and d= patient 10. Since the strips used for western blots were obtained from different experiments, there is some variation in the absltute mobility

Fig. 1 Western blot analysis of immunological reactivity with EBV proteins four samples from patients with nasopharyngeal carcinoma.

曾毅院士集

and IgA antibody against EBV thymidine kinase, including 2(samples 3 and 15)which had no detectable IgA anti-EA and low titres of IgA anti-VCA. 9 samples had IgG and 11 IgA antibodies against gp340/200. 11 samples had IgG and 7 IgA to the EBV DNase. These seemed to be no correlation with the histological findings on the tumour, but the reactivity of the serum samples to the three EBV proteins seemed to correlate broadly with the EBV serology based on VCA and EA. No substantial readtions were seen in serum samples from VCA+ or VCA-donors with any of the EBV-coded proteins, except for IgG anti-gp340/220.

Tab. 1   Immunoreactivity of nasopharyngeal carcinoma patients' serum samples to EBV proteins

| Patient | Extent of reactivity on western blot | | | | | | ELISA titre[1] | | | IF with TK | VCA IgA[2] | EA IgA | Clinical stage |
| | IgG | | | IgA | | | | | | | | | |
	DNase	TK	MA	DNase	TK	MA	IgA TK	IgG MA	IgA MA				
1	−	++	ND	−	++	ND	ND	ND	ND	ND	80	+	II
2	−	++	++	++	++	++	1.077	2.125	1.547	+	320	+	II
3	++	++	+	−	++	+	1.646	2.042	0.239	+	10	−	III
4	−	++	−	+	++	−	2.923	1.206	0.782	+	320	+	III
5	++	++	+	++	++	++	ND	1.885	1.508	+	320	+	III
6	++	++	+	+	++	++	0.981	1.890	1.115	+	80	+	III
7	−	++	−	−	++	++	2.098	1.209	0.443	W	80	+	I
8	++	+	+	−	++	−	1.727	1.808	0.361	+	20	+	I
9	++	++	−	++	++	+	1.160	1.526	0.514	+	80	+	III
10	++	++	−	−	+	++	1.085	2.045	0.673	+	80	+	III
11	++	++	+	−	++	++	2.007	2.168	0.533	++	640	+	III
12	−	++	−	−	++	−	0.992	0.251	0.169	+	10	+	III
13	−	+	+	++	++	++	2.780	1.300	1.997	+	160	+	II
14	++	++	+	+	++	+	2.065	1.192	0.662	+	320	+	III
15	−	+	−	−	+	−	ND	ND	ND	W	80	−	II
16	++	++	ND	−	++	ND	ND	ND	ND	ND	320	+	III
17	++	++	++	−	++	+	2.083	1.899	0.681	+	320	ND	III
18	++	++	−	−	++	−	1.978	2.109	0.828	+	320	ND	III

Notes: IF=immunofluorescence; TK=thymidine kinase; MA=gp340/220; ND=not done; W=week.
1. Absorbance at 450 nm
2. Reciprocal titre of IgA reaction with EBV VCA

Western blot analysis is not suitable for screening purposes. To provide a more quantitative and rapid immunological assay for antibody against EBV thymidine kinase and gp340/220 we developed ELISAs. In the ELISA for thymidine binase we could not determine an IgG titre, since it used a crude lysate of baculovirus-infected cells and the baculovirus and host cell proteins are themselves targets for the human immune response. However, human serum does not seem to have large amounts of IgA antibody to these proteins. Fig 2 shows titres of IgA antibody to thymidine kinase in the three groups of subjects. The mean titre was higher in the nasopharyngeal carcinoma patients(1.757[SD 0.639])than in the VCA+(0.510[0.136])and VCA-(0.366[0.045]) subjects. The lowest value for any nasopharyngeal carcinoma serum was 0.981(Tab. 1)and the highest for any VCA+ serum was 0.715.

Since purified gp340/220 was available, we could study the presence of both IgG and IgA antibody. The titres for IgG and IgA antibody against gp340/220 corresponded well to the presence of such antibody as determined by western blot analysis. There was also a good correlation with IgA antibody titres to the EBV VCA and EA. The titre of IgG anti-gp340/220 was not a good predictor of nasopharyngeal carcinoma(Fig. 2)-6 of 30 VCA+ samples had titres within the range of most of the nasopharyngeal carcinoma samples. The titre of IgA anti-gp340/220 was, however, a good indicator of nasopharyngeal carcinoma(mean[SD]titre 0.806[0.523]vs 0.162[0.080]for

VCA＋ and 0.141［0.050］for VCA-). Only 2 of the nasopharyngeal carcinoma samples had IgA anti-gp340/ 220 titres below the cutoff of 0.4 and would be falsely considered negative. In addition 1 VCA＋ sample consistently had a very high titre.

One of the traditional techniques in southeast Asia for the diagnosis of nasopharyngeal carcinoma uses EBV-infected cell lines as a target to detect antibody（IgA）to EBV VCA and EA by indirect immunofluorescence tests. Although we believe that our ELISA system is a more quantitative, reliable, and efficient diagnostic test, we studied whether our recombinant systems would be useful as reagents in immunofluorescence tests. SF9 cells infected with a recombinant baculovirus expressing the EBV TK were used as targets for immunofluorescent analysis（Fig. 3）. Although a good reaction was seen between serum from nasopharyngeal carcinoma patients and the target cells, only a low grade weak reaction was seen in the VCA ＋serum. All nasopharyngeal carcinoma patients' serum samples tested gave an immune response to the EBV thymidine kinase by immunofluorescence; 2 gave a weak response, 1 of which had no deteta- ble IgA anti-EA.

DISCUSSION

One requirement for improved treatment of nasopharyngeal carcinoma is a method of screening large, at-risk populations for the presence of tumour. The method should be able to detect tumours at an early stage of devel-

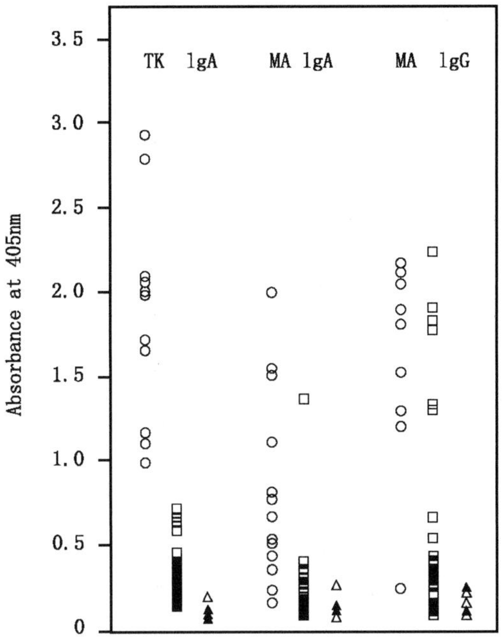

○＝basopharyngeal carcinoma（n＝17）；□＝VCA＋ （n＝30）；△＝VCA-(n＝7）；TK＝ thymidine kinase; MA＝gp340/220

Fig. 2　**Reactivity of serum samples with EBV-coded proteins in ELISAs.**

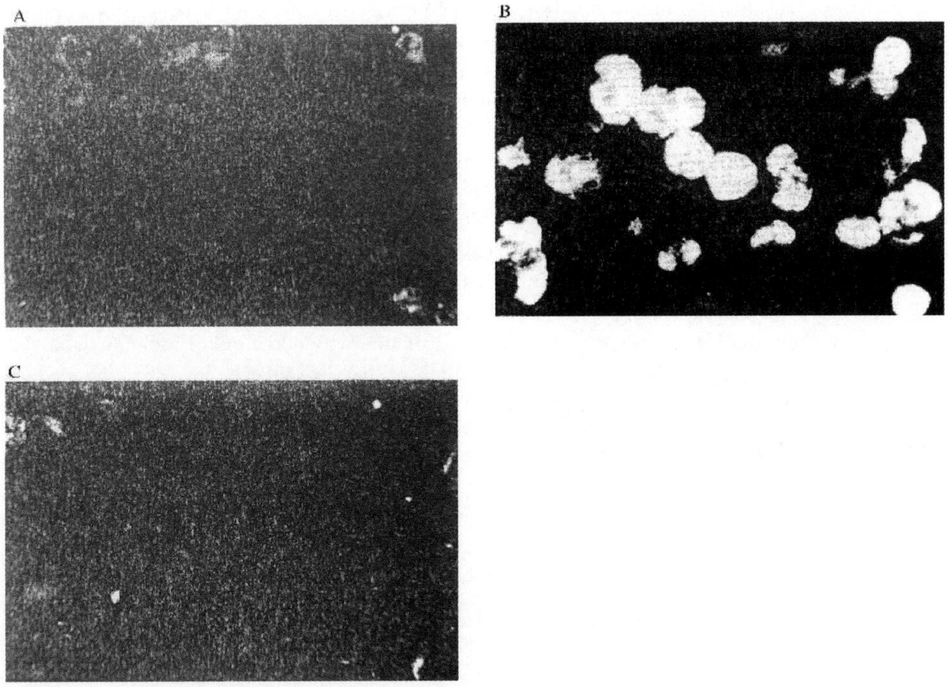

Fig. 3　Immunofluorescent analysis of cells expressing EBV thymidine kinase with serum samples from VCA＋ subjects（A）and patients with nasopharyngeal carcinoma（B）, C＝SF9 cells infected with non-recombinant baculovirus reacted with serum from nasopharyngeal carcinoma patient.×50

opment, have low rates of false-positive and false negative results, and be rapid and economically viable. The association of EBV with nasopharyngeal carcinoma results in an unusual immunoloical response to a range of EBV proteins. Patients have high IgA tires to the EBV VCA and EA and can neutralise the activity of some EBV enzymes.[13,16-18] Already these responses are being used for the diagnosis and prognosis of nasopharyngeal carcinoma in the People's Republic of China and(including Taiwan)[15,18,19]. However, EBV replicates poorly in the lymphablastoid cells used as the source of the diagnostic antigen, the cells are expensive to maintain, and the amount of EBV antigen present is variable. A consequence of the use of EBV-infected lymphoblastoid cells is that tests such as indirect immunofluorescence and enzyme neutralisation have to be used; these are difficult to apply in mass screening and give variable results owing to their subjective interpretation.

The three EBV-coded proteins used in our recombinant expression systems represent different classes of EBV protein: the EBV thymidine kinase and DNase are components of the restricted EA complex and gp340/220 is a late of VCA protein(unpublished). Each of the systems can produce milligram amounts of its respective protein in culture volumes of only one litre. Western blot analysis with the three proteins showed that each has a useful diagnostic capability, and the ELISA assays with thymidine kinase and gp340/220 as targets showed that a rapid diagnostic test is possible. Because some countries have already invested substantial resources in immunofluorescent and enzyme neutralisation tests, we have shown here and previously that the EBV thymidine kinase expressed in baculovirus and the gp340/220 expressed in bovine-papillomavirus transformed cells[20] may be used as sensitive replacements for immunfluorescent tests; the EBV alkaline DNase expressed in recombinant bculovirus can be used as a source of enzyme for neutralisation tests with the added bonus of ease of production and stability of the enzyme(unpublished).

Although all three proteins are useful as diagnostic targets, the EBV-coded thymidine kinase may be a particularly sensitive antigen. All of the serum samples from patients with nasopharyngeal carcinoma examined here(and a further 20 from other sources)show IgG and IgA antibodies to thymidine kinase; samples from VCA+ and VCA-donors and patients with infectious mononucleosis do not show any such reactivity. We have previously shown that about 50% of patients with Burkitt's lymphoma have IgG antibody to the EBV thymidine kinase but do not have any IgA antibody[22]. A single sample from a patient with chronic infectious mononucleosis had IgG and IgA antibody against EBV thymidine kinase but at lower titres than in nasopharyngeal carcinoma(unpublished). We have previously suggested that the sensitivity of the EBV thymidine kinase is due to an unusual, hydrophilic streak of 290 aminoacids at the amino terminus[22]. The role of this region in the biochemistry of the EBV thymidine kinase is not known, but it does seem to be unique to the thymidine kinase of EBV and herpesvirus saimiri. The region may be necessary for replication in a lymphoid environment, or it may be simply that there is high evoltionary conservation in this protein between EBV and herpesvirus saimiri.

Only a proportion of the serum samples from patients with nasopharyngeal carcinoma showed a good reaction with EBV DNase in western blots; we believe this result is due to the lower expression of the EBV protein in the recombinant baculovirus(probably caused by the toxicity of the protein). This low level expression also precludes the use of crude lysates in ELISA tests, as is done for thymidine kinase. It will be necessary to produce purified EBV DNase from the recombinant baculovirus-infected cells before such tests can be developed. EBV-coded gp340/220 seems to be a good diagnostic reagent for nasopharyngeal carcinoma and the expression systems and purification procedures should be suitable for the establishment of diagnostic tests[25].

In its 1982 report on the biology of nasopharyngeal carcinoma the International Union against Cancer recommended that"screening programmes and reliable test systems for the early detection of individuals at risk by immunological and biochemical surveys should be extended as a high priority"[3]. We believe that the systems described here may from the basis of such screening programmes.

ACKNOWLEDGEMENTS

This work was supported by the Cancer Research Campaign(UK). S. B. was supported by the Science and Engineering Research Council and the Wellcome Research Laboratories.

REFERENCES

[1] Shanmugaratnam K. The pathology of nasopharyngeal carcinoma. In: Biggs PM, de The G, Payne LN, eds. Oncogenesis and herpes viruses. Lyon: IARC Scientific Publications no 2, 1972, 239.

[2] Shanmugaratnam K, Chan SH, de The G, et al. Histopathology of nasopharyngeal carcinoma: correlations with epidemiology, survival rates and other biological characteristics. Cancer, 1979,44:1029-1044.

[3] Simons M J, Shanmugaratnam K, eds. The biology of nasopharyngeal carcinoma. Geneva: UICC Technical Report, 1982, 71.

[4] Waterhouse J, Muir CS, Shanmugaratnam K, Powell J, Caner incidence in five continents, vol IV. Lyon: IARC Scientific

Publication no 42,1982.

[5]　Neilsen NH, Mikkelsen F, Hansen JPM. Nasopharyngeal cancer in Greenland: the incidence in an arctic Eskimo popula-tion. Acta Pathol Microbiol Scand 1977, 85A:850-858.

[6]　Cancer mortality in the US(1950-1977). Bethesda: National Cancer Institute, Monograph 59.

[7]　Zur Hausen H, Schuhe-Holthauzen H, Klein G, et al. EBV DNA in bioposies of Burkitt tumours and anaplastic carcinomas of the nasopharynx. Nature, 1970, 228:1956-1958.

[8]　Tugwood JD, Lau W-H, O S-K, et al. Epstein-Barr virus-specific transcription in normal and malignant nasopharyngeal bniopsies and in lymphocytes from healthy donors and infectious mononucleosis patients, Gen Virol, 1987,68:1081-1091.

[9]　Young LS, Dawson CW, Clark D, et al. Epstein-Barr virus gene expression in nasopharyngeal carcinoma. Gen Virol, 1988, 69:1051-1065.

[10]　Raab-Traub N, Hood R, Yang C-S, Henry B, Pagano JS. Epstein-Barr virus transcription in nasopharyngeal carinoma. Virol, 1983, 48:580-590.

[11]　Henle W, Henle G, Ho HC, et al. Antibodies to Epstein-Barr virus in nasopharyngeal carcinoma, other head and neck neo-plasms and control groups. Natl Inst, 1970, 44:225-231.

[12]　Henle W, Ho H-C, Henle G, Kwan HC. Antibodies to Epstein-Barr virus-related antigens in nasopharyngeal carcinoma. Comparison of active cases with long-term survivors. Natl Cancer Inst, 1973, 51:361-369.

[13]　Zeng Y, Gong CH, Jan MG, Fun Z, Zhang LG, Li HY. Detection of Epstein-Barr virus IgA/EA antibody for diagnosis of nasopharyngeal carcinoma by immunoautoradiography. Int Cancer,1983, 31:599-601.

[14]　Zeng Y, Zhong JM, Li LY, et al. Follow-up studies of Epstein-Barr virus lgA/VCA antibody positive persons in Zangwu Couny, China. Intervirology, 1983, 20:190-194.

[15]　Cheng Y-C, Chen J-Y, Glaser R, Henle W. Frequency and levels of antibodies to Epstein- Barr virus-specific DN ase are el-evated in patients with nasopharyngeal carcinoma. Proc Natl Acad Sci USA, 1980, 77:6162-6165.

[16]　LiuM-Y, CouW-M, Nutter L, Hsu M-M, Chen J-Y. Antibody against Epstein-Barr virus DNA polymerase activity in sera of patients with nasopharyngeal carcinoma. Med Virol, 1989,28:101-105.

[17]　Turenne-Tessier M, Ooka T, Calander A, de The G, Daille J. Relationship between nasopharyngeal carrinoma and high antibody titres to Epstein-Barr virus-specific thymidine kinase, Int Cancer, 1989, 43:45-48.

[18]　Chen J-Y, Chen C-J, Liu M-Y, et al. Antibody to Epstein-Barr virus-specific DNase as a marker for field survey of patients with nasopharyngeal carcinoma in Taiwanl. Med Virol, 1989,27:269-273.

[19]　Tan RS, Cheng YC, Naegele RF, Henle W, Glaser R, Champion J. Antibody responses to Epstein-Barr virus-specific DNase in relation to the prognosis of juvenile patients with nasopharyngeal carcinoma, Int Cancer, 1982, 30:561-565.

[20]　Zeng Y, Du B, Miao X, Mackett M, Arrand JR. Detection of IgA/MA antibody in sera using PO_4 cells. Chin Virol, 1987, 3:396-397.

[21]　Baylis SA, Purifoy DJM, Littler E. The characterization of the EBV alkaline deoxyribonuclease cloned and expressed in E coli. Nucl Acids Res,1989, 17:7609-7622.

[22]　Littler E, Newman W, Arrand JR. Immunological response of nasopharyngeal carcinoma patients to the Epstein-Barr Vi-rus-coded thymidine kinase expressed in Escherichia coli. Int Cancer1990, 45:1028-1032.

[23]　Baylis S, Purifoy DJ, Littler E. High level expression of the Epstein-Barr Virus alkaline deoxyribonuclease using a recombi-nant baculovirus: application to the diagnosis of nasopharyngeal carcinoma. Virology, 1991, 181:390-394.

[24]　Conway M, Morgan A, Mackett M. Expression of Epstein-Barr virus membrane antigen gp340/220 in mouse fibroblasts u-sing a bovine papillomavirus vector. Gen Virol, 1989, 70:729-734.

[25]　Li S-L. Classfication of nasopharyngeal carcinoma by 5th National Nasopharyngeal Carcinoma Symposium, 1979. In: Tumours of the head and neck. Tianjin: Tianjin Science and Technology Publishing House, 1982, 251.

[In《The Lancet》1991, 337(874): 685-688]

Salivary and Serum IgA Antibodies to the Epstein-Barr Virus Glycoprotein gp340: Incidence and Potential for Virus Neutralization

YAO Q Y[1], ROWE M[1], MORGAN A J[2], SAM C K[3],
PRASAD U[3], DANG H[4], ZENG Y[5], RICKINSON A B[1,6]

1. Department of Cancer Studies, University of Birmingham; 2. Department of Pathology, University of Bristol, UK; 3. Institute for Advanced Studies, University of Malaya, Kualay Lumpur, Malaysia; 4. Cancer Institute, Wuzhou; 5. Institute of Virology, Beijing, China; 6. To whom correspondence and reprint requests should be sent, at the Department of Cancer Studies, University of Birmingham, Birmingham, B15 2TJ, UK.

[SUMMARY] Human antibody responses to the Epstein-Barr virus(EBV) glycoprotein gp340 have been measured using purified preparations of the native molecule as the substrate in ELISAs. This glycoprotein is the dominant component of the EBV envelope and a major target for the virus-neutralizing antibody response. Healthy virus carriers(both Caucasian and Chinese) regularly show detectable anti-gp340 IgG in serum and, unexpectedly, 21%-30% of these individuals are also serum anti gp340 IgA positive. Chinese patients with the EBV genome-positive malignancy nasopharyngeal carcinoma(NPC) show elevated serum IgA antibodies to gp340 but, given the background of responses among healthy virus carriers, anti-gp340 IgA titres are a poorer diagnostic indicator of NPC than serum IgA antibodies detectable by immunofluorescence against the multicomponent EBV early antigen(EA). Salivary IgA antibody responses to gp340 are potentially important as a means of neutralizing orally-transmitted virus. We detected salivary IgA(but not IgG) to gp340 in a minority(12%-19%) of healthy virus carriers and in a higher proportion(49%) of NPC patients. Even saliva samples chosen for their relatively high anti-gp340 IgA titres showed only weak neutralizing activity against transforming EBV preparations whether or from B98.5 cell culture supernatant or from the throat washing of an infectious mononucleosis patient. We conclude that in healthy virus carriers, salivary IgA responses to gp340 are unlikely to provide effective local immunity against re-infection with a second EBV strain.

INTRODUCTION

Epstein-Barr virus(EBV) infection is widepread in human populations and its incidence is usually monitored by immunofluorescence assays for serum antibodies to 1 of 3 multicomponent viral antigens. These are(i) the nuclear antigen EBNA which is expressed in latently-infected growthtransformed B lymphoblastoid cell lines and which is now known to be composed of 6 different gene products, EBNAs 1, 2, 3a, 3b, 3c and-LP, all of which are antigenically distinct(Kieff and Liebowitz, 1990); (ii) early antigen(EA) which is a composite of multiple viral proteins of the early lytic cycle, whose locations can be nuclear and/or cytoplasmic(Pearson et al., 1983, 1987), and(iii) virus capsid antigen(VCA) which is a composite of several viral structural proteins and glacoproteins present within infected cells late in the lytic cycle(Kishishita et al., 1984; Vroman et al., 1985). Despite the complex nature of the antigens being detected, these immunofluorescence assays have played an important role in the identification and monitoring of EBV-related disease states(Henle and Henle, 1982), perhaps the best example being the virus-genomepositive malignancy nasopharygeal carcinoma(NPC) in which the prevalence and titre of serum IgA antibodies to EA and VCA have significant diagnostic and prognostic value(Henle and Henle, 1976; Zeng, 1985).

Methods for measuring antibody responses to a 4th multicomponent EBV antigen, the membrane antigen(MA) which is expressed on the surface of lytically-infected cells late in the cycle, have also been available for many years(Klein et al., 1976). However, technical difficulties, not least the requirement for viable cells as the antigen-positive substrate, have greatly restricted anti-MA testing in large serological assays. Nevertheless, the MA complex, now known to be a composite of at least 3 virus-coded glycoproteins gp340/220(Beisel et al., 1985), gp85(Heineman et al., 1988) and gp78/55(Mackett et al., 1990), is of considerable scientific interest because it includes the dominant target antigens for virus-neutralizing antibody responses(Thorley-Lawson et al., 1982). There is clearly a need to re-analyse the whole question of antibody responses to the individual virus envelope glycoproteins using either purified or recombinant antigen as the substrate and assay methods which are more quantitative and more sensitive than the original MA test.

An important step forward came with the development, in 2 independent laboratories(Luka et al., 1984; Randile and Epstein, 1984; Uen, et al., 1988), of ELISAs for antibodies to the EBV glycoprotein gp340. This glycoprotein is the most abundant component of the viral envelope, mediates virion binding to the EBV receptor on B cells, and is a major target for virus-neutralizing antibodies(Dolyniuk et al., 1976; Nemerow et al., 1987; Thorley-Lawson and Poodry,1982). Despite the availability of these assays, there is still very, little published information on serological responses to gp340, particularly in EBV-related disease states, and no information on the potentially important question of salivary antibody responses to the glycoprotein. In the present work we have used fast protein liquid chromatography(FPLC)-purified gp340(David and Morgan, 1988)as the substrate in ELISA assays(i) of serum IgA(and IgG) antibodies to the antigen in control conors and in NPC patients, to determine whether elevated IgA anti-gp340 reactivity is a better diagnostic indicator of the tumour-bearer state than IgA anti-EA or anti-VCA, and(ii)of salivary IgA antibodies to gp340, to determine the frequency of local antibody responses which have the potential to neutralize orallytransmitted virions and to identify suitable saliva samples for direct testing of virus-neutralizing activity.

MATERIAL AND METHODS

1. Serum and saliva samples

Serum and saliva samples were taken from the same groups of donors. These groups were(i)20 healthy abult Caucasian donors from Birmingham, UK, known to be seronegative for anti-VCA IgG antibodies,(ii)50 healthy adult Caucasian donors from Birmingham, known to be seropositire for anti-VCA IgG antibodies,(iii)122 healthy adult Chinese donors from Wuzhou, China or from Kuala Lumpur, Malaysia, all of whom proved to be anti-VCA IgG seropositive,(iv)87 NPC patients at primary presentation, again from Wuzhou, and(v)20 NPC patients in remission from Kuala Lumpur. Saliva samples(from unstimulated saliva)were taken into salivettes(Sarstedt, Numbercht, Germany)and clarified by centrifugation, then(for Wuzhou and Kuala Lumpur donors)air-freighted on ice to Birmingham together with the serum samples. The salivary antibody assays were conducted within 3 days of receipt of the air-freighted material; preliminary work had shown that titres of anti-gp340 IgA in saliva samples were not altered by storage for up to a month at 4℃. Serum samples were also kept at 4℃ and titrated within 1 week of receipt.

2. ELISA for anti-gp340 antibodies

The method was adapted from an earlier protocol(Randle and Epstein, 1984)but now using as a substrate a purified preparation of the naturally glycosylated gp340 isolated by FPLC from the membranes of virus-producing B95.8 cells(David and Morgan, 1988). Briefly, purified gp340 in bicarbonate buffer pH 9.6 was coated on to ELISA plates by incubation overnight at 4℃. For the anti-gp340 IgG assay, each well on the ELISA plate received 50μl of buffer containing 1.5 units of gp340, whereas for the IgA assay each well received 6.5 units of gp340 (Northe et al., 1982, for definition of the arbitrary units). Following blocking with PBS containing 1% BSA and 5% normal rabbit serum for 2hr at room temperature, triplicate wells were incubated with one of a series of doubling dilutions of serum or saliva in blocking solution for 1hr at 4℃. The plates were washed 3 times with PBS containing 0.05% Tween 20 and then specifically bound antibody was detected by incubation with peroxidase-conjugated rabbit antihuman IgG or IgA(Dakopatts, Glostrup, Denmark; 1：500 dilution)for 30 min at 4℃. Conventional development with orthophenylene diamine(OPD)was followed by measurement of absorbance at 492 nm in an ELISA reader. Serum samples were assayed at serial doubling dilutions starting at 1：20, and saliva samples at serial doubing dilutions starting at 1：2.

3. Immunofluorescence assays for anti-EA and anti-VCA antibodies

All sera were also assayed by serial doubling dilution starting at 1：10 for IgG and IgA antibodies to EA and VCA by conventional indirect immunofluorescence, using acetonefixed slide preparations of P3HR1 virus-infected Raji cells and B95.8 cells respectively as the antigen-positive indicator cells(Henle and Henle, 1976).

4. Neutralization assays

Ten-fold dilutions of virus preparations, either B95.8 cell culture supernatant or throat washings from an infectious mononucleosis(IM)patient, were pre-incubated with an equal volume of the test saliva sample(or with medium as a control)for 1hr at 37℃, then added to cord-blood indicator lymphocytes for a further 1-hr incubation. The cells were then cultured in microtest plate wells as 6-8 replicates per test sample and observed over the next 6 weeks for the incidence of EBV-induced outgrowth of transformed cells.

RESULTS

1. Serum IgG antibodies to gp340

In the anti-gp340 IgG ELISA, all 20 negative control sera(i.e., sera already shown to be anti-VCA negative by conventional immunofluorescence assay)gave absorbance readings below 0.5 units at the lowest dilution tested. Representative readings form 10 such control sera are shown in Fig. 1A. Parallel assays regularly showed significant anti-gp340 IgG antibodies in sera from both Caucasian and Chinese seropositive(i.e., anti-VCA IgG-positive) donors, albeit sometimes at relatively low titres, representative results being shown in Fig. 1B. Chinese NPC patients'sera assayed in the same way were also anti-gp340 IgG-positive, the tendency towards elevated tires being apparent from representative results(Fig. 1C). A summary of the incidence and mean titre of anti-gp340 IgG antibodies in sera from the various groups of donros is presented in Tab. 1 alongside corresponding data for anti-EA and anti-VCA IgG antibodies detected by conventional immunofluorescence testing of the same sera. All the anti-VCA-positive sera from healthy donors showed anti-gp340 IgG detectable by ELISA, though not all were antiEA-positive. The elevation of anti-gp340 IgG titres in NPC patients versus healthy controls was not as marked as that observed when anti-VCA and particularly anti-EA IgG titres were compared between the same groups of sera.

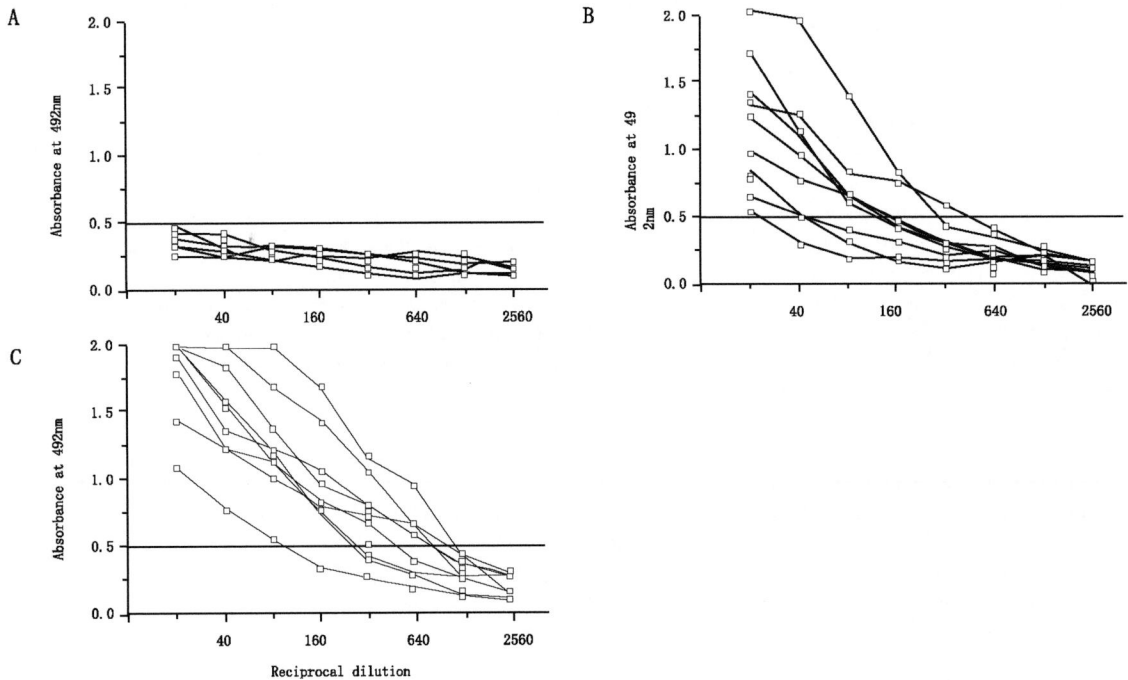

Fig. 1 Serum anti-gp340 IgG ELISA readings for doubling dilutions of 10 representative sera from: (a) healthy Caucasian anti VCA IgG seronegative donors, (b) healthy Caucasian anti-VCA IgG seropositive donors, and(c)Chinese NPC patients at primary presentation. On this basis an absorbance value of 0.5 at 492 nm was set as background and ELISA titres were defined as the highest doubling dilution of sermn which gave a reading above backround.

Tab. 1 Summary of serum antibody titres to gp340. EA and VCA[1]

Antibody	Assay[2]	Caucasian seropositive			Caucasian seropositive			Caucasian seropositive		
		Incidence	%	Mean titre[3]	Incidence	%	Mean titre[3]	Incidence	%	Mean titre[3]
Serum IgG	Anti-gp340	50/50	100	1∶283	122/122	100	1∶179	87/87	100	1∶745
	Anti-EA	34/50	68	1∶50	79/122	65	1∶54	87/87	100	1∶1221
	Anti-VCA	50/50	100	1∶428	122/122	100	1∶375	87/87	100	1∶5023
Serum IgA	Anti-gp340	15/50	30	1∶66	25/122	21	1∶42	82/87	94	1∶446
	Anti-gpEA	0/50	0	—	1/122	0.8	1∶10	85/87	98	1∶246
	Anti-VCA	5/50	10	1∶20	5/122	4	1∶10	84/87	97	1∶608

Notes: [1] Sera from 20 Caucasian EAV-negative donors were included as controls in the same assay and gave uniformly negative results(data not shown). [2] Anti-gp340 titres determined by ELISA assay: anti-EA and anti-VCA titres determined by conventional immunofluorescence using Ig class-specific second-step conjugated antibodies. [3] Mean titre of positive samples.

2. Serum IgA antibodies to gp340

Representative results obtained on testing the same groups of sera in the anti-gp340 IgA ELISA are presented in Fig. 2 for seronegative controls(a), seropositive donors(b)and NPC patients(c). Clearly, only a minority of EBV-seropositive donors have detectable anti-gp340 IgA antibodies in serum, and these are at much lower titres than anti-gp340 IgA antibodies in the serum of NPC patients. Overall results for the various groups of donors are summarized in Tab. 1, again with corresponding data for IgA antibodies to EA and VCA detected in the same sera by immunofluorescence tests. Interestingly, anti-gp340 IgA was more prevalent among Caucasian and Chinese ser-positive donors(21%-30%)than were anti-EA or anti-VCA IgA antibodies. All 3 types of IgA reactivity showed a much higher prevalence among NPC patients, but the increase was most marked for anti-EA IgA since this was almost absent from healthy seropositive donor sera.

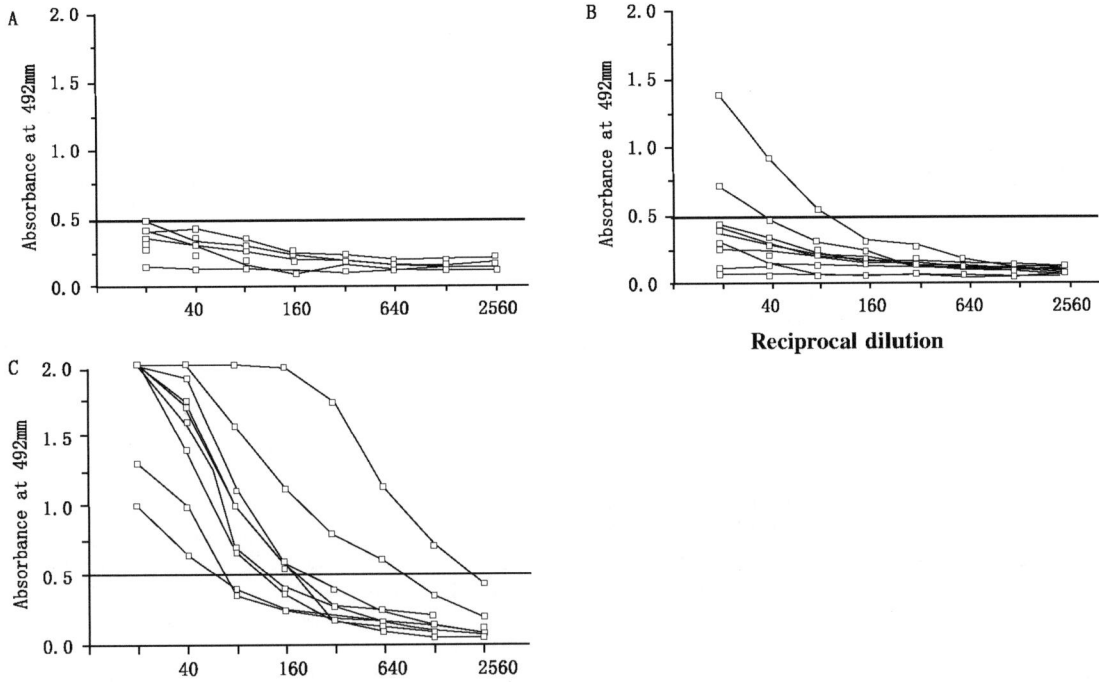

Fig. 2 Serum anti-gp340 IgA EKUSA reading for doubing dilutions of 10 representative sera from:(a)healthy Caucasian anti VCA IgG-seronegative donors,(b)healthy Caucasian anti-VCA IgGseropositive donors, and(c)Chinese NPC patients at primary presentation. Titres were defined as in Fig. 1

3. Salivary IgA antibodies to gp340

Saliva samples were collected, without salivary stimulation, from the same groups of donors and tested by ELISA for salivary IgA antibodies to gp340. Again, representative results from 10 seronegative control donors, 10 seropostive donors and 10 NPC patients are shown in Fig. 3 to illustrate the specificity and sensitivity of the assay. Significant anti-gp340 IgA reactivity could be detected in saliva from a minority of serpositive donors and from a higher proportion of NPC patients. The overall results are summarized in Tab. 2.

Tab. 2 Summary of salivary antibody titres to gp340[1]

Antibody	Assay	Caucasian seropositive			Chinese seropositive			Chinese NPC patients		
		Incidence	%	Mean titre[2]	Incidence	%	Mean titre	Incidence	%	Mean titre
Salivary IgG	Anti-gp340	0/50	0	—	0/122	0	—	0/87	0	—
Salivary IgA	Anti-gp340	6/50	12	1:3.7	23/122	19	1:3.0	43/87	49	1:7.6

Notes: [1] Saliva from 20 Caucasian EBV-negative donors were included as controls in the same assays and gave uniformly negative results(data not shown). [2] Mean titre of positive samples

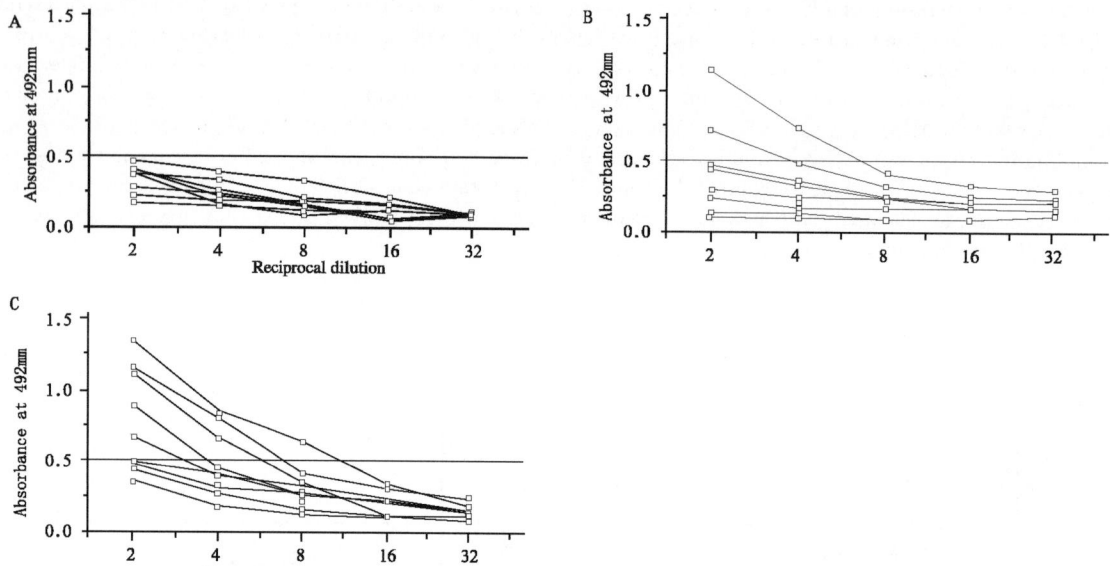

Fig. 3 Salivary anti-gp340 IgA ELISA reading for doubling dilutions of 10 representative saliva samples from: (a) healthy Caucasian anti-VCA IgG-seronegative donors, (b) healthy Caucasian anti-VCA IgG-seropositive donors, and (c) Chinese NPC patients at primary presentation. Titres were defined as in Fig. 1

In parallel tests, no saliva sample ever gave significant anti-gp340 reactivity in the IgG ELISA(Tab. 2). These IgG assays were conducted as an additional control to check whether any saliva samples were contained with serum antibodies coming from serous secretions.

4. Anti-gp340 antibody status of newly diagnosed versus remission NPC patients

Earlier studies have emphasized the correlation between anti-EA and anti-VCA IgA serum antibody status and tumour burden in NPC patients(Henle and Henle, 1976; Zeng, 1985). In the present study we have extended the analysis to anti-gp340 antibody responses in serum and saliva samples taken at one referral centre(Kuala Lumpur) from 20 newly-diagbised patients and from 20 patients whose NPC was in remission following treatment. The complete analysis of relevant IgG and IgA antibodies in these patients is summarized in Tab. 3. While there was no significant change in the incidence of serum IgA antibodies to gp340, EA and VCA, there was some reduction in all 3 antibody titres following treatment. Changes in the corresponding serum IgA antibodies were more marked, with remission patients showing a reduced incidence of detectable responses and a lower mean titre for IgA antibody-positive sera in all 3 assays; salivary IgA responses to gp340 also showed a reduced incidence in remission patients.

Tab. 3 Antibody status in newly diagnosed vs. remission NPC patients

Antibody	Assay[1]	Newly diagnosed NPC patients			Remission NPC patients		
		Incidence	%	Mean titre[2]	Incidence	%	Mean titre
Sernm IgG	Anti-gp340	20/20	100	1 : 794	20/20	100	1 : 425
	Anti-EA	20/20	100	1 : 1137	19/20	95	1 : 570
	Anti-VCA	20/20	100	1 : 4000	20/20	100	1 : 2268
Serum IgA	Anti-gp340	20/20	100	1 : 428	13/20	65	1 : 85
	Anti-EA	19/20	95	1 : 269	10/20	50	1 : 142
	Anti-VCA	19/20	95	1 : 1012	15/20	75	1 : 356
Salivary IgA	Anti-gp340	16/20	80	1 : 8	9/20	45	1 : 8

Notes: [1] Anti-gp340 titres determined by ELISA assay, anti-EA and anti-VCA titres by conventional immunofluorescence assay. [2] Mean titre of positive samples

5. Virus neutralization by anti-gp340 IgA-positive saliva

The final series of experiments was designed to look for EBV neutralization mediated by salivary antibodies to the virus, and thus to assess the possible functional significance of local IgA antibody responses. For this work, saliva specimens from 3 NPC patients, each with an anti-gp340 IgA titre of at least 1 : 20 by ELISA assay, were pooled, as were 3 control saliva samples again from NPC patients but lacking detectable anti-gp340 IgA activity. Ten-fold dilutions of B95. 8 culture supernatants and of throat washings from an IM patient were used as sources of transfroming virus; these preparations were pre-exposed to medium alone or to the pooled saliva samples before being added to cord-blood indicator cells. Tab. 4 shows the results of the subsequent transformation assay from which it is clear that the pooled anti-gp340 IgA-positive saliva samples mediated a significant, but incomplete, neutralization of EBV-transforming activity. This same partial nevtralization, both of B95. 8 virus and of IM throat washing virus, was observed at a second testing(data not shown).

Tab. 4 Nevtralzation of EBV by an anti-gp340 IgA positive saliva preparation

Virus dilutions pre-exposed to:	Incidence of transformation of cord cells exposed to:					
	B95. 8 virus dilutions			IM throat washing dilutions		
	10^{-3}	10^{-4}	10^{-5}	Neat	10^{-1}	10^{2}
Medium alone[1]	6/6	6/6	5/6	6/6	6/6	6/6
Anti-gp340 IgA negative salive[1]	6/6	6/6	4/6	6/6	6/6	6/6
Anti-gp340 IgA positive saliva[2]	6/6	5/6	0/6	6/6	6/6	1/6

Notes: [1] Pool of 3 NPC patient saliva samples lacking detectable anti-gp340 IgA. [2] Pool of 3 NPC patient saliva samples with anti-gp340 IgA titre of >1 : 20

DISCUSSION

The ELISA upon which the present work is based uses as a source of antigen a fully glycosylated gp340 preparation of proven immunogenicity which has been FPLC purified from the membranes of lyrically-infected cells(David and Morgan, 1988; Morgan et al., 1989). There is a distinct advantage in using the native glycoprotein rather than the product of the gp340 coding sequence expressed from a recombinant vector in bacterial, yeast or even mammalian cells(Beisel et al.,1985; Schuhz et al., 1987; Whang et al., 1987; Emini et al., 1988). It is likely that many anti-gp340 antibody reactivities in human serum are directed against conformational epitopes on the molecule and recombinant proteins may not faithfully reproduce all of these epitopes, particularly since the overall tertiary structure of native gp340 must be influenced by its pattern of glycosylation within infected cells(Whang et al., 1987; Emini et al., 1988). In this context, we were encouraged to find from our initial set of assays that all 172 healthy seropositive donors tested(i. e., all individuals with detectable anti-VCA IgG, the usual criterion for prior EBV infection)showed detectable serum IgG responses to gp340, whereas all 20 seronegative control donors were also antigp340 IgG-negative by ELISA(Fig. 1, Tab. 1). This bears witness to both the specificity and the sensitivity of the assay and strongly suggests that anti-gp340 IgG antibodies are maintained for life in the serum of virus-carrying individuals in a manner similar to anti-VCA IgA antibodies; by contrast, only a subpopulation of such individuals are detectably anti-EA IgG-positive.

By increasing approximately 4-fold the amount of purified gp340 substrate used in the ELISA, we were able to adapt the basic 2-step ELISA protocol used for analysing IgG responses to the measurement of gp340-specific IgA antibodies in both serum and saliva; other workers have reported the development of a 3-step ELISA to achieve the necessary sensitivity for anti-gp340 IgA antibody detection(Uen et al., 1988). On beginning the serological screening for IgA antibody responses, we were surprised to find that a significant minority of healthy seropositive donors(30% Caucasian donors, 21% Chinese donors)were anti-gp340 IgA-positive by ELISA(Fig. 2, Tab. 1). These numbers were significantly higher than the incidence of anti-VCA IgA positivity($<10\%$)and of anti-EA IgA positivity(1%)in the same group of sera. The anti-gp340 IgA-positive status of these healthy donor sera was reproducible on repeated testing and was unrelated to the titre of co-resident anti-gp340 IgG(data not shown). Indeed, in additional experiments(data not shown), we were able to completely remove anti-gp340 IgG reactivity from selected sera by adsorption on protein A Sepharose without significantly affecting the anti-gp340 IgA titre measurable by ELISA. We are therefore confident that the serum IgA results are not artefactual.

One consequence of the relatively high incidence of serum anti-gp340 IgA antibodies among healthy virus carriers is to reduce the usefulness of this response as a diagnostic marker for NPC. Thus, although the incidence and mean titre of serum anti-gp340 IgA responses are significantly raised in NPC patients, the increase is less marked than noted for IgA antibodies to VCA and in particular to EA. We conclude therefore that serum IgA responses to EA(Henle and Henle, 1976; Zeng, 1985)remain the best single marker distinguishing NPC patients from healthy controls(Tab. 1). Furthermore, our some what limited data on newly-diagnosed versus remission NPC patients (Tab. 3)again suggest that serum anti-EA IgA levels are the most sensitive to a change in tumour load. Accordingly, the search for the best possible serological marker of early NPC diagnosis should perhaps now focus on the individual viral proteins which together constitute the EA complex recognized in conventional immunofluorescence testing(Pearson et al., 1983, 1987).

Using the same anti-gp340 IgA ELISA protocol as used in the serological assays, we were able to detect salivary IgA to gp340 in only 12%-19% healthy seropositive donors, and then almost always at titres which were much lower than positive serum IgA titres(Fig. 3, Tab. 2). This is perhaps to be expected since total IgA levels in saliva are an order of magnitude lower than IgA levels in serum(Delacroix et al., 1982). It is nevertheless formally possible that EBV particles produced endogenously from sites of chronic virus replication in the oropharynx(Yao et al., 1985)could be engaging gp340-specific IgA and reducing the levels of free antibody detectable by ELISA. We are confident that the positive results which were obtained do reflect the existence of a local immune response and are not due to minor contamination of saliva samples by antibodies from serous secretions. Thus there was no correlation between the salivary IgA and serum IgA results for individual donors in the anti-gp340 ELISA(data not shown); furthermore there was never any detectable antigp340 IgG in saliva samples(Tab. 2)despite the fact that these same donors consistently displayed high titres of such antibodies in serum. Salivary IgA responses to gp340 were more frequent in NPC patients but generally the increases both in incidence and in mean titre were less marked than for serum IgA responses(compare Tab. 1 and Tab. 2). We provisionally conclude that in NPC patients EBV lytic antigen expression, eithe focally within the tumour itself of in adjacent normal epithelium, induces a strong systemic IgA response but a less marked secretory IgA response. A different picture appears to be emerging with respect to the EBV latent protein EBNA 1, one of the few viral gene products consistently expressed in NPC cells(Young et al., 1988; Fahraeus et al., 1988); a recent study measuring that subset of anti-EBNA 1 antibodies recognizing the immunodominant glyala repeat domain of the molecule found striking elevations of both serum and salivary IgA titres in NPC patients(Foong et al., 1990).

One of our main objectives in this work was to assess the potentially protective function of EBVspecific IgA responses. In preliminary experiments using protein A adsorption to completely deplete the IgG antibodies from selected human sera, we found that sera with detectable anti-gp340 IgA antibodies retained weak EBV-neutralizing activity whereas anti-gp340 IgA-negative sera did not(data not shown). A more important question concerned the neutralizing capacity of salivary IgA antibodies since these might provide a means of neutralizing virus transmitted by the natural oral route. It is clear from the data in Tab. 4 that even pooled NPC saliva with a relatively high titre of anti-gp340 IgA antibodies possessed only weak neutralizing activity, being active for instance against a 1 : 100 dilution but not against a 1 : 10 dilution of an EBV-containing throat washing from an IM patient.

The overall conclusion from this part of the work is that healthy virus carriers either have no detectable salivary IgA to gp340 or have such weak reactivity as to offer little practical protection against orally-transmitted virus. This is interesting when set against our recent finding that healthy virus carriers appear to carry just one isolate of EBV in the circulating B-cell pool(Yao et al., submitted for publication); at the B-cell level, therefore, such individuals seem to bc innune to reinfection with a second virus strain. It becomes very important to know whether such immunity to re-infection also extends to the virus' other target tissue, oropharyngeal epithelium(Sixbey et al.,1984, 1989). If this is indeed the case, then such immunity is unlikely to be conferred by salivary antibody responses and must have some other, as yet unidentificd, basis.

ACKNOWLEDGEMENTS

This work was supported by the Caner Research campaign, London, UK. M. R. is a Wcllcome Senior Research Fellow in Basic Biomedical Sciences. We thank Ms. D. Williams for excellent secretarial support.

REFERENCES

[1] Beisel C, Tanner J, Matsuo T, Thokley-lawson D, Kezdy F, Kieff E, Two major outer envelope glycoproteins of Epstein-Ban virus are encoded by the same gene. J Virol, 1985, 54:665-674.

[2] David EM, Morgan AJ. Efficient purification of Epstein-Barrvirus membrane antigen gp340 by fast protein liquid chromatography. J immunol Meth,1988, 108:231-236.

[3] Delacroix DL, Dive C, Rambaud JC, Vaerman JP. lgA subclasses in various secretions and is serum. Immunology, 1982, 47:282-285.

[4] Doi Yniuk M, Wolff E, Kieff E. Proteins of Epstein-Barr virus. Ⅱ. Electrophoretic analysis of the polypeptides of the nu-

cleocapsid and the glucosamine-and polysaccharide-containing components of enveloped virus. J Virol, 1976, 18:289-297.

[5] Emini EA, Schlief WA, Armstrong MC, Silberklang N, Schultz LD, Lehman D, Maigetter RZ, Qual Tiere L. F, Pearson GR, Ellis R W. Antigenic analysis of the Epstein-Barrvirus major membrane antigen(gp350/220)expressed in veast and mammalian cells: implications for the development of a sub-unit vaccine. Virology, 1988, 166:387-393.

[6] Fahraeus R, Fu HL, Ernberg I, Finke J, Rowe M, Klein G, Falk K, Nilsson E, Yadav M, Busson P, Tursz T, Kalln B. Expression of Epstein-Barr virus-encoded proteins in nasopharyngeal carcinoma. Int J Cancer, 1988, 42:329-338.

[7] Foong YT, ChengH M, Sam C K, Dillner J, Hingerer W, Prasad U. Serum and salivary IgA antibodies against a definedepitope of the Epstein-Barr virus, nuclear antigen(EBNA)are elevated in nasopharyngeal carcioma, Int J Cancer,1990, 45: 1061-1064.

[8] Heineman T, Gong M, Sample J, Kieff E. Identification of the Epstein-Barr virus gp85 gene. J Virol, 1988, 62:1101-1107.

[9] Henle G, Henle W. Epstein-Barr virus-specific IgA serum antibodies as an outstanding feature of nasopharyngeal carcinoma. Int J Cancer, 1976,171:1-7.

[10] Henle W, Henle G. Immunology of Epstein-Barr virus. In: B. Roizman(ed), The Herpesviruses, Vol. 1, pp. 2009-252. Plenum Press, New York, 1982.

[11] Kieff E, Liebowitz D. Epstein-Barr virus and its replication. In: B.N. Fields, D.M. Knipe, R. M. Sharock, M.S. Hirsch, J. L. Melnick, T. P. Morath and B. Roizman(eds.), Virology, pp. 1889-1920, Raven Press, New York, 1990.

[12] Kishishita M, Luka J, Vroman B, Poduslo J E, OPearson G R. Production of monoclonal antibody to a late intracellular Epstein-Barr virus-induced antigen. Virology, 1984, 133:363-375.

[13] Klein G, Cclfford P, Klein E, South R T, Minowada J, Kourilsky F, Burchenal J H. Membrane immunofluorescence reactions of Burkitt lymphoma cells from biopsy specimens and tissue cultures J nat Cancer Inst, 1967, 39:1027-1044.

[14] Luka J, CHASE RC, Pearson GR. AAsensitive enzyme-linked immunosorbent assay(Elisa)against the major EBV-associated antigens. I . Correlation between Elisa and immunofluorescence titers using purified antigens. J immunol Meth, 1984, 67:145-156.

[15] Mackett M, Conway MJ, Arrand JR, Haddad RS, Huttfletcher L M. Characterisation and expression of a glycoprotein encoded by the Epstein-Barr virus BamHI I fragment. J Virol, 1990, 64:2545-2552.

[16] Morgan AJ, Allison AC, Finerty S, Scullion FT, Byers NE, Epstein MA. Validation of a first generation Epstein-Barr virus vaccine preparation suitable for human use. J med Virol, 1989, 29:74-78.

[17] Nemfrow GR, Mold C, Schwend VK, Toliefson V, COOPER N R. Identification of gp350 as the viral glycoprotein mediating attachment of Epstein-Barr virus(EBV)to the EBV/C3d receptor of B cells: sequence homology of gp350 and C3 complement fragment C3d. J Virol, 1987,61:1416-1420.

[18] North JR, Morgan AJ, Thompson JL, Epstein MA. Quantification of an Epstein-Barr virus-Barr virus-associated membrane antigen(MA)component. J virol Meth, 1982, 5:55-65.

[19] Pearson G R, Luka J, Petti L, Sample J, Birkenbach M, Braun D, Kieff E. Identification of an Epstein-Barr virus early gene encoding a second component of the restricted early antigen complex. Virology, 1987, 160:151-161.

[20] Pearson GR, Vroman B, Chase B Scullfy, T Hummel M, Kieff E. Identification of polypeptide components of the Epstein-Barr virus early antigen complex using monoclonal antibodies. J Virol,1983, 47:193-201.

[21] Randle BJ, Epstein MA. A highly sensitive enzyme. linked immunosorbent assay to quantitate antibodies to Epstein-Barr virus membrane antigen gp340. J virol Meth, 1984, 9:201-208.

[22] Schultz LD, Tanner J, Hofmann KJ, Emini ea., Condra J H, Jones R E, Kieff E, Ellis R W. Expression and secretion in yeast of a 400 kD envelope glycoprotein derived from epstein-Barr virus. Gene, 1987, 54:113-123.

[23] Sixbey JW, Nedrud JG, Raab-Traub N, Hanes RA, Pagano J S. Epstein-barr virus replication in oropharyngeal epithelial cells. New Engl. J. Med, 1984, 310, 1225-1230.

[24] Sixbey JW, Shirley P, Chesney PJ, Buntin DM, Resnick L. Detection of a second widespread strain of Epstein-Barr virus. Lancet, 1989, 11,761-765.

[25] Thorley-Lawson DA, Edson CM, Geilinger K. Epstein-Barr virus antigens-a challenge to modem biochemistry Advanc. Cancer Res, 1982,36, 295-348.

[26] Thodey-Lawson DA, Poodry CA, Identification and isolation of the main component(gp350-gp220)of Epstein-Barr virus responsible for generating neutralising antibodies in vivo. J Virol,1982, 43, 730-736.

[27] Uen W-C, Luka J, Pearson G R. Development of and enzyme-linked immunosorbent assay(Elisa) for detecting IgA antibodies to the Epstein-Barr virus, Int J Cancer, 1988, 41:479-482.

[28] Vroman B, Luka J, Rodriguez M, Pearson GR. Character-isation of a maior protein with a molecular weight of 160,000 associated with the viral capsid of Epstein-Barr virus. J Virol, 1985,52, 107-113.

[29] Whang Y, Silberklang M, Morgan A, Munshi S, Lenny A B, Ellis, R.W. and Kieff, E., Expression of the Epstein-Barr virusgp350/220 gene in rodent and primate cells. J Virol, 1987,61:1796-1807.

[30] Yao QY, Rickinson AB, Epstein, MA. A reexamination of the Epstein-Barr virus carrier state in healthy seropositive individuals, lnt J Cancer,1985, 35:35-42.

[31] Young LS, Dawson CW, CLlarkD, Rupani H, Busson P, Tursz T. Johnson, A. and Rickinson, A. B., Epstein-Barr virus gene expression in nasopharyngeal carcinoma. J gen Virol, 1988, 69:1051-1065.

[32] ZENG Y. Seroepidemiological studies on nasopharyngeal carcinoma in China. Advanc. Cancer Res,1985, 44:121-138.

[In《Int J Cancer》1991. 48:45-50]

Detection of Anti-Epstein-Barr-Virus Transactivator(Zebra)Antibodies in Sera from Patients with Nasopharyngeal Carcinoma

JOAB Irène[1,6] , NICOLAS Jean-Claude[2] , SCHWAAB Guy[1] , de-The G[1] ,
CLAUSSE Bernard[4] , PERRICAUDET Michel[1] , ZENG Yi[5]

1. Institute Gustave Roussy, CNRS, URA1301, 39 rue Camille Desmoulins 94800 Villejuif; 2. Hpital Roths-child, Boulevard de Picpus 75012 Paris; 3. Institute Pasteur, 25 rue du Docteur Roux 75015 Paris; 4. Institute Gustave Rouss, CNRS URA 1156, 39 rue Camille Desmoulins 94800 Villejuif France;5. Chinese Academy of Preventive Medicine, 100 Ying Xin Jie, Beijing, China.

[SUMMARY] The Epsteln-Barr virus(EBV)is a ubiquitous Herpes virus which causes infectious mononucleosis and is associated with such different neoplasms as Burkitt's lymphoma and nasopharyngeal carcinoma. EBV latently infects its target cells; nevertheless, evidence of viral relication in NPC tumours has been uncovered. Among the EBV transactiva-tors, the ZEBRA protein plays a crucial role in switching the virus from a latent to a productive mode. ZEBRA protein was produced using a eukaryotic expression vector; the open reading frame containing the BZFLI cDNA has revlously been inserted down-stream from the adenovirus major late promoter leading to expression of a 38×10^3 nuclear protein. We performed sero-logical studies by employing ZEBRA protein expressed in human cells for immunofluorescence and Western-blot assays. We were able to detect IgG anti-ZEBRA antibodies(IgG/ZEBRA)in 87% of NPC patients. These antibodies were absent in control sera; IgG/ ZEBRA antibodies can be proposed as a useful marker for diagnosis of NPC tumors.

INTRODUCTION

The Epstein-Barr virus(EBV)is a ubiquitous human Herpes virus. It causes infectious mononucleosis and is closely associated with 2 neoplasms: Burkitt's lymphoma(BL)and naso-pharyngeal carcinoma(NPC)(de-Thé, 1982). In NPC epithelial cells the viral genome has been detected both in tumor biopsies by hybridization tech-niques and in tumors transplanted in nude mice(which are free of infiltrating B lymphocytes). EBV can latently in-fect its target cells, but different observations favor the hypothesis that viral replicaton occurs in the tumor: analy-sis of the structure of viral DNA termini has demonstrated the presence of linear viral DNA, specifically indicating that the viral productive cycle may occur in these tumors(Raab-Traub and Flynn, 1986); in NPC tumor biopsies different RNAs from the replicative phase of the EBV life cycle have been detected. InNPC patients, elevated IgG and IgA antibodies directed against EA and VCA viral protein may suggest that EBV reactivation occurs. The mo-lecular mechanism leading to EBV activation is beginning to be understood and transactivators encoded by the EBV genome have been identified and have been shown to be involved in the activation of the lytic cycle(Chevalier-Greco et al., 1986; Countryman and Miller, 1985; Countryman et al., 1987; Hardwick et al., 1988; Lieberman et al., 1986; Wong and Levine, 1986). ZEBRA(BamHI Z EBV Replication Activator), also called Z or EBI, is encoded by BZLFI(BamHI Z left frame l); it switches the EB virus from the latent to the productive cycle. In NPC tumors where the EB virus seems to be partially reactivated, it is thus likely that viral transactivators are being produced; we describe here the detection of antiZEBRA antibodies in the sera of most NPC patients. EBV-specific IgA anti-bodies are characteristic of NPC patients: IgA/VCA, IgA/EA, IgA anti-thymidine kinase antibodies(IgA/TK), have been detected in serological analysis and have been proposed as useful markers for the early diagnosis of NPC tumors. The specific use of the detection IgG/ZEBRA antibodies is discussed.

SUBJECTS AND METHODS

1. Plasmid
The plasmid pMLP BZLF1 has been previously described(Ronney et al., 1986).

2. Cell line
Line 293, a human embryonic kidney fibroblast cell line transformed by adenovirus 5(Harrison et al., 1977), was transfeted with recombinant DNA by the calcium phosphate precipitation method(Graham and Van der Erb, 1973). Westernblot experiments have been described elsewhere(Joab et al., 1987).

3. Serological tests

The sera were tested for specific IgG anti-VCA and anti-EBNA antibodies to EBV by an indirect immunofluorescence assay. The sera were tested for specific IgG anti-EA antibodies by an indirect immunoperoxidase assay. Anti-ZEBRA antibodies were assayed by indirect immunofluorescence experiments performed as described(Joabet al., 1991).

4. Sera

Sera from 41 NPC patients were studied. The controls used for serological test consisted of 50 healthy French and 48 healthy Chinese individuals.

RESULTS

The humoral immunological response to ZEBRA transactivator was studied in different EBV-related disorders. Tab. 1 shows the comparison of different antibodies to EB virus in sera of NPC patients;87% of these patients contain anti-ZEBRA antibodies in their sera. This proportion is similar to that observed in NPC patients for IgA/VCA antibodies which represent the marker used for early diagnosis of NPC tumors in high-risk areas (Zeng et al., 1983b). The anti-ZEBRA antibodies found in sera of NPC patients are mostly of IgG type and only 13% of NPC patients exhibit IgA/ZEBRA antibodies. The frequency of NPC patients with IgG/ZEBRA is higher than that of patients with IgA/EA antibodies. The same serological tests were performed with sera from healthy control individuals. Ninety-eight control individuals(50 French and 48 Chinese)were tested for the presence of anti-ZEBRA antibodies in their sera;these groups may have differd in their ages of primary EBV infection. The results are shown in Tab. 2;only one individual was positive for anti-ZEBRA antibodies although these subjects were positive for other anti-EBV antibodies to VCA and EA. The presence of anti-ZEBRA antibody-positivity could be related to an activation of the EBV lytic cycle. We tested sera from IM patients for the presence of different antibodies to EB virus;the results(Tab. 3) show that the percentage of IgG/ZEBRA antibody-positive patients is high (79%), although the GMT is lower in sera from IM than from NPC patients. Replication of the EB virus and the presence of IgG/ZEBRA in the sera of patients could be linked.

Tab. 1 comparison of different antibodies to EB virus in sera from NPC patients

	Number positive/number tested(%)	GMT
IgG/ZEBRA	36/41(87)	1/85
IgG/VCA	28/28(100)	1/409
IgG/EA	26/28(92.8)	1/25
IgG/EBNA	25/28(89)	1/44
IgA/VCA	23/28(82)	1/27
IgA/EA	12/28(42)	1/4

Tab. 2 comparison of different antibodies to EBV in sera of control individuals

	Nnmber positive/number tested (%)	GMT
IgG/ZEBRA	1/98(1)	1/5
IgG/VCA	45/50(90)	1/162
IgG/EA	0/11(0)	>1/5
IgG/EBNA	40/50(90)	1/63

Tab. 3 comparison of defferent antibodies to EB virus in sera from IM patients

	Number positive/number tested(%)	GMT
IgG/ZEBRA	15/19(79)	1/31
IgG/VCA	18/19(94)	1/96
IgG/EA	18/19(94)	1/3
IgG/EBNA	7/19(36)	1/2.7
IgA/VCA	10/19(52)	1/4.2

Tab. 4 detection of anti-EB virus transactivator (ZEBRA) antibodies in sera from patients with different pathologies

Pathologies	Number positive/ number tested(%)
Hepatocarcinoma	0/50(0)
Chronic hepatitis	0/30(0)
Acute lymphoblastoid leukemia	0/50(0)
Berger's disease	1/43(2)
Graft rejection	2/20(10)
Multiple sclerosis	0/15(0)
Sjögren's syndrome	0/15(0)
Head and neck tumors	11/81(13)
NPC	36/41(87)
IM	26/31(83)
BL(EBV$^+$)	11/22(50)
Asymptomatic HIV$^+$	75/229(32)
AIDS	12/49(24)
French controls	1/50(2)
Chinese controls	0/48(0)

In order to check the specificity of anti-ZEBRA antibodies for EBV-related diseases, we performed serological tests on samples from a variety of different diseases(Tab. 4): we tested more than 700 subjects and only found anti-ZEBRA antibodies in sera of patients with EBV-related disorders: 50% of BL patients were IgG/ZEBRA-positive(GMT of 1/10). The highest titers were found in NPC sera. It is seen(Tab. 4) that in HIV-positive subjects and in AIDS patients in whom active EBV infection may occur, anti-ZEBRA antibodies are present in more than 30% of the sera tested(Joab et al., 1991). We were surprised to observe that 13% of the patients with a head and/ or neck tumor displayed anti-ZEBRA antibodies in their sera. This may suggest that EBV replication has occurred in those patients; this phenomenon may be unrelated to the presence of the tumor.

DISCUSSION

Among EBV-associated antibodies, IgA/VCA has been considered to be a prominent feature of NPC (Henle and Henle, 1976). Serological surveys and follow-up studies of NPC in China have been used to show that IgA/VCA and IgA/EA are valuable markers for early detection of the disease(Zeng et al., 1983a, b, 1985). In the present study we found a significantly high prevalence of EBV anti-ZEBRA transactivator antibodies in patients with NPC. In NPC patients the increase in anti-ZEBRA antibody production may be due to an over-production of ZEBRA protein either in epithelial cells of the tumor or in the(circulating or infiltrating) lymphocytes. IgG/ZEBRA antibodies were found in 87% of NPC patients, while only 1 healthy individual out of 100 displayed antibodies to this antigen; this result shows that the presence of IgG/ZEBRA in sera can be used to help in the diagnosis of NPC tumors. IgG/ZEBR has also been found in 85% of infectious mononucleosis(IM) patients and in 32 of the HIV-seropositive patients(Joab et al., 1991). In IM patients, anti-ZEBRA antibodies may appear following intensive primary multiplication of the EB virus, before establishment of the latent infection. Only 50% of BL patients were positive for IgG/ZEBRA antibodies. The presence of anti-ZEBRA antibodies in the sera of HIV seropositive patients could be one of the consequences of EBV reactivation occurring in those subjects. High frequency and high level of antibodies to EBV DNase(Cheng et al., 1980), to EBV DNA polymerase(Tan et al., 1986) and to EBV thymidine kinase(de Turenne-Tessier et al., 1989) are found in NPC sera. Other methods for detecting anti-ZEBRA antibodies in sera are now being studied in our laboratory to enable us to scale up the number of tests which can be performed. The use of anti-ZEBRA antibody detection for early diagnosis and postherapeutic surveillance is under current investigation.

ACKNOWLEDGEMENTS

The authors are grateful to Drs. G. Lenoir, J. Gozlan, J. Leverger, J. D. Sraer, P. Lebon, L. Edelman, J. L. Lefrere and C. André for providing different sera.

REFERENCES

[1] Gheng YC, Chen JY, Glaser R, Henle W. Frequency and levels of antibodies to Epstein Barr virus specific DNase are elevated in patients with nasopharyngeal carcinoma. Proc nat Acad Sci,(Wash.), 1980, 77:6161-6165.

[2] Chevallier-Greco A, Manet E, Chavrier P, Mosnier C, Daillie J, Sergeant A. Both Epstein-Barr virus(EBV)-encoded transacting factors, EB1 and EB2, are required to activate transcription from an EBV early promoter. EMBO J, 1986, 5: 3243-3249.

[3] Countryman J, Jenson H, Seibl R, Wolf H, Miller G. Polymorphic proteins encoded within Bzkfi of defective and standard Epstein-Barr viruses disrupt latency. Virology, 1987, 61:3672-3679.

[4] Gountryman J, MILLER G. Activation of expression of latent Epstein-barr herpes virus after gene transfer with a small cloned subfragment of heterogeneous viral DNA. Proc nat Acad Sci,(Wash.), 1985, 82:4085-4089.

［5］ De-the G. Epidemiology of Epstein-Barr virus and associated diseases, In：B. Roizman(ed.), The herpesviruses, 1A, pp. 25-103, Plenum, New York, 1983.

［6］ Deturenne-Tessier M, OOKA T, CALENDER A, DE-THE G, Daillie J. Relationship between nasopharyngeal carcinoma and high antibody titers to Epstein-Barr virus specific thymidine kinase. Int J Cancer, 1989, 43：45-48.

［7］ Graham PL, Van Der Erb, AJ. Anew technique for the assay of infectivity of human adenovirus 5 DNA. Virology, 1972, 52：456-467.

［8］ Hardwick JM, Lieberman PM, Hayward SD. A new Epstein-Barr virus transactivator, R, induces expression of a cytoplasmic early antigen. J Virol, 1988, 62：2274-2284.

［9］ Harrison T, Graham F L, Williams J. Host range mutant of Adenovirus type 5 defective for growth in HeLa cells. Virlolgy, 1977, 77：319-329.

［10］ Henle G, Henle W. Epstein-Barr virus specific IgA serum antibody as an outstanding feature of nasopharyngeal carcinoma. Int J Cancer, 1976,17：1-7.

［11］ Joab I, Rowe DT, Bodescot M, Nicolas JC, Farrell PJ, Perricaudet M. Mapping of the gene coding for Epstein-barr virus determined nuclear antigen Ebna3 and its transient overexpression in a human cell line by using an adenovirus expression vector. J Virol, 1987, 61：3340-3344.

［12］ Joab I, Triki H, De Saint Martin J, Perricaudet M, Nicolass JC. Detection of anti-Epstein-Bar virus transactivator(Zebra) antibodies in sera from HIV patients. J infect Dis, 1991, 63：53-56.

［13］ Liberman PM, O'hare P, Hayward GS, Hayward SD. Promiscuous transactivation of gene expression by an Epstein-barr virus encoded early nuclear protein. J Virol, 1986, 60：140-148.

［14］ Raab-tranb N, Flynn K. The structure of the termini of the Epstein barr virus as a marker of clonal proliferation. Cell, 1986, 47：883-889.

［15］ Ronney CM, Rowe DT, Ragot T, Farrell PJ. The spliced BZLF1 gene of Epstein-Barr virus(EBV) transactivates an early EBV promoter and induces the virus productive cycle. J Virol,1986, 63：3109-3116.

［16］ Tan RS, Li JS, Grill SP, Nutter LM, Cheng YC. Demonstration of Epstein-Barr virus specific DNA polymerase in chemically induced Raji cells and its antibody in serum from patients with nasopharyngeal carcinoma. Cancer Res, 1986, 46：5024-5028.

［17］ Wong KM, Levine AJ. Identification and mapping of Epstein Barr virus early antigens and demonstration of a viral gene activator that functions in trans J Virol, 1986, 60：149-156.

［18］ Zeng Y, Gong CH. Jan MG, Fun Z, Zhang LG, LI HY. Detection of Epstein-Barr virus lgA EA antibodies for diagnosis of nasopharyngeal carcinoma by immunoautoradiography, Int J Cancer,1983, 31：599-601.

［19］ Zeng Y, Zhang LG, Li HY, Jan MG, Zhang Q, WU YC, Wang YS, SU GR. Serological mass survey for early detection of nasopharyngeal carcinoma in Wuzhou City, China. Int J Cancer,1985, 29, 139-141.

［20］ Zeng Y, Zhong JM, Li HY, Wang PS, Tang H, Ma YR, Zhu JS, Pan WJ, Liu YX, Wei ZN, Chen JY, Mo YK, Li EJ, Tan BF. Follow-up studies on Epstein-Barr virus IgA VCA antibody-positive persons in Zangwu county, China. Intervirology, 1983, 20：190-194.

［In《Int J Cancer》1991, 48：641-649］

A Research for the Relationship between Human Papillomavirus and Human Uterine Cervical Carcinoma

I. The identification of viral genome and subgenomic sequences in biopsies of Chinese patients

SI Jing-yi[1], IEE Kun[1], HAN Ri-cai[1], ZHANG Wei[1], TAN Bing-bing[1], SONG Guo-xing[1], HU Shi-de[1], CHEN Lian-fong[1], ZHAO Wei-ning[1], JIA Li-ping[1], MAI Yong-yan[2], ZENG Yi[3], ZHOU Yi-nan[4], WANG Yue-zhu[4], LING Jian[4], SUN Yu[5], MENG Xiang-jin[5], YU Zhang-fong[6], PU Li-ning[6]

1. Department of Biophysics, Instiute of Basic Medical Sciences, Chinese Academy of Mdedical Sciences and the Peking Union Medical College, 5 Dong Dan San Tiao, Beijing 100005, China; 2. Department of Gynecology and Obstetrics, The First Teaching Hospital, Beijing Medical University, Beijing 100034, China; 3. Department of Tumor Viruses, Institute of Virology, Chinese Academy of Preventive Medicine, 100 Yin Xin Jie, Beijing 100052, China; 4. Department of pathology, Gynecology and Obstetrics, The First Teaching Hospital, Xinjiang Medical College, Urumchi 830054, Xinjiang Uighur Autonomous Region, China; 5. Institute of Virology, Hubei Medical College, Wuuhan 430071, Hubei Province, China; 6. Department of Epidemiology, Faculty of Public Health, Harbin Medical University, Harbin 150001, Heilongjiang Province, China

[SUMMARY] Biopsies from 318 cases with squamous cell carcinoma of the uterine cervix, 48 with cervical and vulvar condylomata, 14 with cervical intraepithelial neoplasia(CIN), 34 with chronic cervicitis and 24 with normal cervical epithelium were collected from different geographic regions with different cervical cancer mortalities. The NDA. DNA dot-blot and Southern blot hypridization results show that there is a close relationship between HPV-16 and the uterine cervical squamous cell carcinoma in China. One very interesting observation is that the finding of HPV-16-homologous DNA differs significantly among five geographic regions, and corresponds with the mortalities from cervical cancer of these five regions. HPV-11 was found mainly in benign lesions. The rate of detection of HPV-16 in Chinese women increased from 8.3% in normal cervical epthelium to 20% in chronic cervicitis, 28% in cervical condyloma. 50% in CIN and 60.4% in cervical cancer. It is suggested that HPV-16 infection may be an etiological factor in the development of human cervical carcinoma. From the results of Southern blot hybridization, it appeared that HPV-16 DNA had been integrated into the genome of the host cell in cervical cancer. Whereas the HPV-16 DNA sequence was only present as an episome in normal cervical epithelium and cervical benign lesions. The rate of occurence of E6-E7 genes is the highest (88.9%)compared with that of other subgenomic fragments of HPV-16 in specimens of human cervical cancer in China. This implies that E6 and E7 may be the oncogenic genes of HPV-16 and play an important role in the carcinogenesis of human cervical epithelial cells. The amplification and rear-rangement of the c-myc protooncogene are closely associated with the occurrence of cervical cancer. The results presented here revealed that the activated cmyc oncogene may cooperate with HPV-16 in the carcinogenic processes.

[Keywords] Uterine cervical carcinoma; Human papillomavirus; Moleculat epidemilolgy; Carcinogenesis; Viral oncogene

INTRODUCTION

Many authors have shown that the risk of cervical carcinoma in women is strongly associated with hygiene (Beral 1974). This suggests that a sexually transmitted infectious agent may be involved. For over 20 years, much attention has been focused on herpes simplex virus type2(HSV-2)(McDougall et al. 1984; Vonka et al. 1984; Frenkel et al. 1972; Aurelian et al 1981), but its role in cervical carcinoma has not been confirmed(Eglin et al. 1981). In recent years, there has been more support for the view that papillomavirus(HPV)infection might be an etiological factor in the development of human cervical cancer(Howley 1989; Lee et al. 1988; Orth et al. 1977; zur Hausen 1989a). HPV is a subgroup of the papovaviruses and is a species-specific small DNA virus containing about 7.9×10^3 bases(7.9kb)of double-stranded DNA in its genome. To date, more than 60 genotypes of HPV have been isolated and characterized, of which HPV-6, 11, 16, and 18 appear in a high percentage of cervical, vulvar and penial cancer tissues, whereas HPV-6 and HPV-11 are found mainly in benign lesions of the female genital tract(Pecoraro et al. 1989; zur Hausen 1989b).

The squamous cell carcinoma of the uterine cervix is one of the most common cancers in Chinese women(Lee et al. 1958). As there are few reports concerning the relationship between Chinese patients and HPV, the present study is designed to detect the viral DNA sequences in the proliferative lesions of the female genital tract and in cervical cancer, using HPV-11, 16 and 18 probes, and nucleic acid hybridization methods in order to ascertain whether the development of cervical cancer is associated with HPV infection in China.

MATERIALS AND METHODS

Biopsics from 318 cases with squamous cell carcinoma of the uterine cervix, 48 with cervical and vulvar condylomata, 14 with cervical intracpithelial ncoplasia(CIN), 34 with chronic cervicitis and 24 subjects with normal cervical cpithclium werc diagnosced by the Department of Pathology, and were collected from different geographic regions of China Xinjiang Uighur Autonomous Region(western China), Beijing(northern China), Heilongjiang Province(northeastern China), Hubei Province(central China)and Guizhou Province(southwestern China).

All specimens were prepared for DNA · DNA dot-blot hyridization assay by using HPV-11. 16, 18 whole genomic DNA labelled with[^{32}p] dNTP as probes to detect viral homologous sequences in samples. Among those casses with positive results on dot-blot hybridization(with HPV-16 DNA as probe), 30 were randomly chosen for Southern blot hybridization with HPV-16 whole genomic DNA and its subgenomic sequences, E6, E7, E1, E4; as well as E5, L1 and L2 as separate probes.

1. Nucleic acid hybridization DNA preparation(Davis et al. 186; Cai1987)

Tissues were homogenizcd in an ice bath and resuspended in TRIS/EDTA buffer. After adding proteinase K to a final concentration of $100\mu g/ml$ and sodium dodecyl sulphate(SDS)to a final concentration of 0.5%, the samples were incubated at 55℃ for 5h and phenol/chloroform was added for cxtracting DNA followed by ethanol for DNA precipitation. Finally, DNA was disolved in TRIS/EDTA buffer and stored at-20℃.

2. DNA · DNA dot-blot hybridization(Denhardt 1966)

To prepare the blot DNA, $2\mu g$ DNA of each sample, $2\mu g$ salmon sperm DNA for the negative control and $1\mu g$ HPV plasmid DNA from each type for positive control were transfered to a nitroccllulose filter; they were then denatured with 0.5mol/L NaOH and the filter was dried in air for hybridization. To prepare the probes, HPV-11, 16, 18 rccombinant DNA in pBR-322 plasmids was radiolabelled with[^{32}p] dTTP or dCTP by the nick-translation method[specific activity,$(1-3)\times10^{8}$ cpm/μg DNA](Rigby et al. 1977), For the hybridization, filtcrs were incubated in 0.25% low-fat milk and 6×standard salinc citrate(SSC; Sambrook et al, 1989)for 2h at 60℃. ^{32}p-labelled HPV DNA probes were then added to the solution and incubated for 16h at 68℃.

The filter was washed three times with a mixture of $2\times$SSC, 0.1% SDS and 0.2% low-fat milk for 30min. Filters were then dried, placed in a plastic mount and exposed to X-ray film with an intensifying screen for 12-72h at -70℃.

3. Soutern blot hybridization(Southern 1975)

DNAs extracted from samples were digested with *Pst* 1, and separated on a 0.8% agarose gel(10μg DNA/sample)for electrophoresis for 12-24h at room temperature with low voltage(1-2 V/cm length of gel). After denaturation with 0.15mol/L NaOH for 1h, the neutralized gcl was transferred onto a nitrocellulose filter by the modificd method of Southern(Guo at al. 1987).

HPV-16 total DNA as well as its subgenomic fragments, such as the 1.3-kb fragment(containing the E6-E7 open reading frame) and the 1.0-kb (E2, E4) and 2.6-kb(E5, L1 and 1.2 open reading frames) fragments recovered from the digestion of EcoRI, *Pst*1 and *Ava*11 after electrophoresis, were radiolabelled with[^{32}p]-CTP $(10\mu Ci/\mu l)$by the nick-translation method to a specific activity of$(1-3)\times10^{8}$ cpm/μg DNA to become the probes.

Hybridization was carried out by a modification of the procedure of Denhardt(Denhardt1966). The filter was put into a sealed plastic bag containing prehybridization solution($100\mu g/ml$ salmon sperm DNA, 0.25% low-fat milk, 6×SSC)for prehybridization at 68% 6-18h. Then, hybridization was performed in the solution of prehybridization plus the ^{32}P-radiolabelled probes at68℃ for 16-24h. The filter was then washed three times in $2\times$SSC plus 0.1% SDS(15 min/ time) at room temperature, and three times in $0.1\times$ SSC solution plus 0.5% SDS at 62℃ for15min.

The filter was exposed to X-ray film in a plastic mount with an intensifying screen for autoradiography at -70℃.

RESULTS AND DISCUSSION

1. Identification of HPV DNA sequences from lesions of the epithelial tissues of the female genital tract

The results of dot-blot hybridization of 318 cases of ccrvical carcinoma collected from five geographic regions of China, using ^{32}P-labelled HPV-11, 16 and 18 DNA as probes, is shown in Figs. 1 and 2, and summarised in Tab. 1.

Fig. 1 Part of the results of dot-bolt hybridization of DNA from cervical cancer specimens using HPV-16 DNA as probe. HPV-16 DNA serves as the positive control($\Rightarrow$), and salmon sperm DNA, as the negative control($\Rightarrow$)

Fig. 2 Part of the results of dot-blot hybridization of DNA of cervical cancer specimens from Guizhou Province showing less hybridization with HPV-16 DNA as probe. HPV-16 DNA serves as the positive control($\Rightarrow$), and salmon sperm DNA, as the negative control($\Rightarrow$)

Tab. 1 The homologous sequences of human papillomavirus(HPV)DNA in human uterine cervical carcinoma tissue

Geographic regions	No. of patients	No.(percentage positive)		
		HPV-11	HPV-16	HPV-18
Xinjiang	99	4(4%)	77(77%)	7(7%)
Beijing	49	1(2%)	32(65.3%)	3(6.1%)
Heilongjiang	50	0	28(56%)	2(4%)
Guizhou	21	0	10(47.6%)	0
Hubei	99	1(1%)	45(45%)	2(2%)
Total	318	6(1.9%)	192(60.4%)	14(4.4%)

Of the 318 cases analysed, 60.4% had detectable HPV-16 DNA. This result shows that there is a close relationship between HPV-16 and human cervical carcinoma in China. The high detection rate of HPV-16-homologous DNA in cervical cancer in China coincides with some recent reports from different countries(Durst et al. 1983; Crum et al. 1984; Gissmann 1984; Coleman et al. 1986). Our findings also revealed that HPV-16 infection was more prevalent than that with PV-11 and 18 in the Chinese cancer cases. However, the frequency of HPV-16-homologous DNA was significantly different among five geographic regions. Biopsies from Xinjiang Uighur Autonomous Region showed the highest positive rate(77%). Further analysis revealed that there were significant variations in the rate between rural areas and Urumchi city in Xinjiang-a much higher percentage(88%)occurring in the former compared with only 66% in the latter. The positive rates were lowest in biopsies collected from Guizhou and Hubei. It is interesting that the occurrence of HPV-16-homologous DNA corresponds with the mortality rate of cervical cancer in the five different regions, as illustrated in Fig. 3. Up to now, there has been no report on the above resuit. The reasons why different areas show different homlolgies with the viral genome, and why these correspond to the mortality rates of the areas are still unknown, and demand further study.

2. HPV DNA sequences in other lesions of the female genital tract

The results with other lesions of the female genital tract, including CIN, Condyloma and chronic cervicitis, are summarised in Tab. 2.

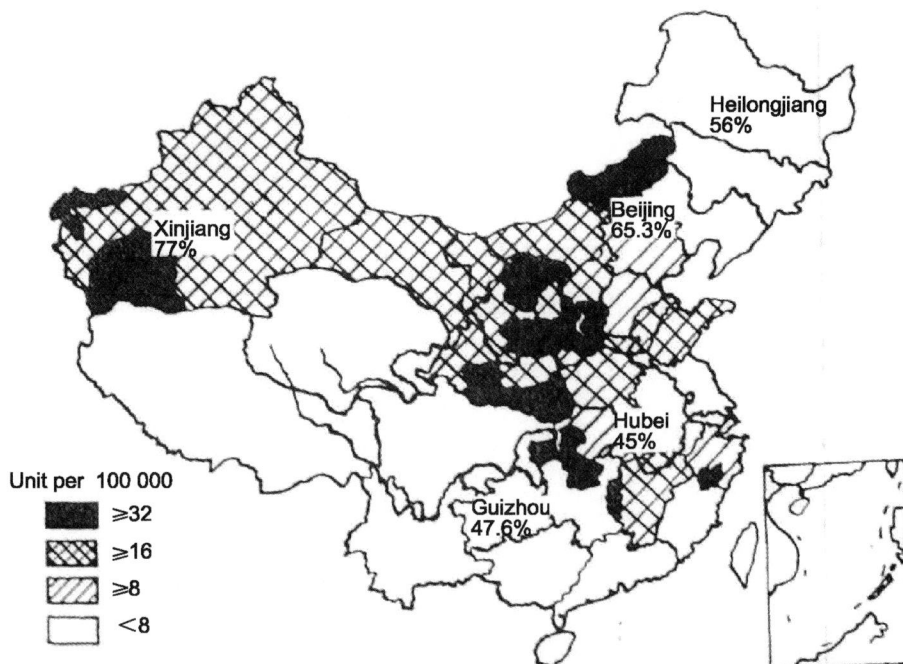

Fig. 3 The geographic distribution of mortality from uterine cervical carcinoma in China. The percentages in this figure indicate the extent to which cervical carcinoma tissue from different geographic regions is homologous to HPV-16 DNA

Tab. 2 The homologous sequences of HPV DNA in cervical intraepithelial neoplasia(CIN), condyloma, chronic cervicitis and cervical carcinoma compared with normal cervical tissue

Pathological diagnosis	No. of cases	No.(percentage positive)		
		HPV-11	HPV-16	HPV-18
Cervical carcinoma	318	6(1.9%)	192(60.4%)	14(4.4%)
CIN	14	0	7(50%)	0
Cervical condyloma	25	8(32.0%)	7(28.0%)	0
Vulvar condyloma	23	10(43.5%)	2(8.7%)	0
Chronic cervicitis	34	0	7(20.6)	0
Normal cervical epithelium	24	0	2(8.3%)	0

The percentage of HPV-16 DNA detected in cancer cases was much higher than that in patients with other lesions of the female genital tract, whereas the rate of detection of HPV-11 DNA in biopsies from other lesions was higher than that in carcinoma cases. These results showed that HPV-11 existed mainly in benign lesions such as condyloma. The patients with CIN revealed as association with HPV-16 in fection the positive rate of HPV-16-homologous DNA being 50% in the CIN cases.

The rate of detection of HPV-16 in Chinese women has increased from 8.3% in normal cervical epithelium, 20.0% in cervicitis, 28.0% in cervical condyloma and 50.0% in CIN to 60.4% in cervical cancer. The findings in our study support the widely accepted views that there is a close relationship between HPV infection, CIN and cervical carcinoma.

Sequences homologous to HPV-16 have been detected in 8.3% of normal cases. It is possible that normal women with no clinical evidence of cervical HPV infection could harbour HPV DNA in their cervical epithelium. The risk of cancer in these normal cases is not yet understood, and this can only be resolved by olngterm prospective studies.

The rate of HPV-18 infection was decidedly lower than that of HPV-16 in China, whereas a cervical cell line derived from a Chinese patient with cervical squamous epithelial cell carcinoma, CC801, was proved to be positive for HPV-18 DNA by Southern blotting in our laboratory. This finding coincides with results for several other cervical cancer cell lines, including Hela cells(Han et al. 1989). Its meaning and significance deserve further study.

3. Detection of HPV-16-DNA-homlolgous sequences from biopsies of cervical lesions by the Southern blot hybridization method

In order to analyse the physical state of HPV DNA in cervical benign lesions including condyloma, chronic cervicitis, CIN and cervical carcinoma as well as in normal cervical epithelium, Southern blot hybridization was employed.

A random selection of 32 cases among those that were positive on dot-blot hybridization(with HPV-16 DNA as probe) was used for Southern blot analysis, including 8 cases of condyloma, 2 of CIN, 20 of cervical cancer and 2 of normal epithelium. All the samples were digested by different restriction endonucleases and subjected to electrophoresis on a 0.8% agarose gel; Southern blot hybridization was then carried out with ^{32}p-labelled HPV-16 DNA as the probe.

From the results it appeared that the HPV-16 DNA sequence ould only be detected as an episome in normal cervical epithelium and cervical benign lesions such as condyloma. On the other hand, HPV-16 DNA was found to have been integrated into the genome of host cell of cervical cancer. Several positive bands were shown in these cervical samples; that is, there was multisite integration of HPV-16 DNA sequences into the host cell genome (Fig. 4).

As for CIN, the situation differed between the benign lesions and cancerous tissue: in one case, the HPV-16 DNA sequence existed in the form of an episome, and in another case these was integration(Fig. 5).

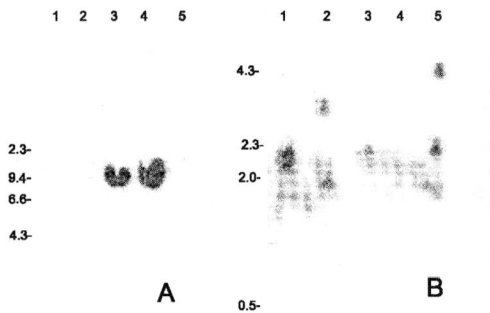

Fig. 4 a, b. Part of the results of Southern blot hybridization of the DNAs from cervical cancer specimens with HPV-16 DNA as probe. Cervical cancer DNAs were digested with(a)BamHI and(b)with PstI and subjected to electrophoresis on a 0.8% agarose gel. The specimen of lane I(a) serves as negative control and is from a case of normal cervical epithelium showing no dot-blot hybridization with HPV-16 DNA. The numbers at the left of each panel represent the sizes(kb)of the fragments of λ phage DNA digested with HindIII

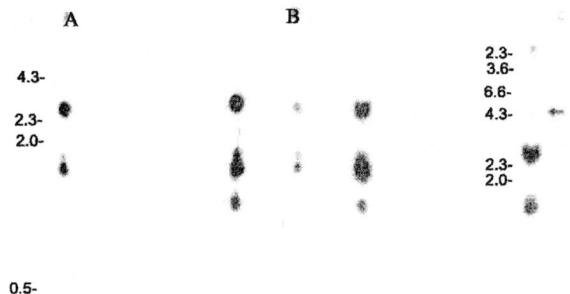

Fig. 5 A-C. Southern blot hybridization analysis of the DNA from different cervical lesions with HPV-16 DNA as probe. DNAs(10μg/sample)extracted from normal cervical epithelia (A), cervical condyloma (B), and cervical intraepithelial neoplasia (CIN) (C) were digested with PstI, separated on a 0.8% agarose gel and then subjected to Southern blot analysis. Arrowhead indicates the additional fragment in *Pst* I-digested DNA from CIN. In one case of CIN(C lane h), HPV-16 DNA sequences were integrated, and in another case(*C lane* u) they were present as an episome. The numbers at the left of each panel represent the sizes(kb)of the fragments of λ phage DNA digested with HindIII

4. Determination of HPV-16 oncogenic genes

Inorder to determine which fragments of the HPV-16 genome are responsible for the carcinogenicity, three fragments of HPV-16 DNA, E6-E7, E2-E4 and E5-L1-L2, were collected(Fig. 6) and labelled with[^{32}p]dTTP as probes after digestion of HPV-16 DNA by restriction endonucleases, PstI, EcoRI and AvaII.

A group of 29 specimens were chosen from those cases found to be positive by dot-blot hybridization using the whole HPV-16 genome as a probe. The highest rate of positivity was found with E6-E7 as the probe(88.9%).

This means that E6-E7 openreading frames were always retained completely in the cancer cell genome, and that other fragments may be defetive in the carcinogenic process(as shown in Tab. 3). Schwarz et al. (1985) and Smotkin and Wettstein(1986)indicated that the E6 and E7 early genes of papillomavirus were implicated in the induction and maintenance of ncoplasias. In vitro, E6 and E7 of HPV-16 were shown to induce anchorage independence in rodent fibroblasts(Kanda et al. 1988; Zhang et al. 1991). In our laboratory, NIH3T3 cells were transformed successfully by recombinant retrovirus containing E6 and E7 of HPV-16, and the specific mRNA of E6 and E7 was detected in transformed cell(Si et al. 1991).

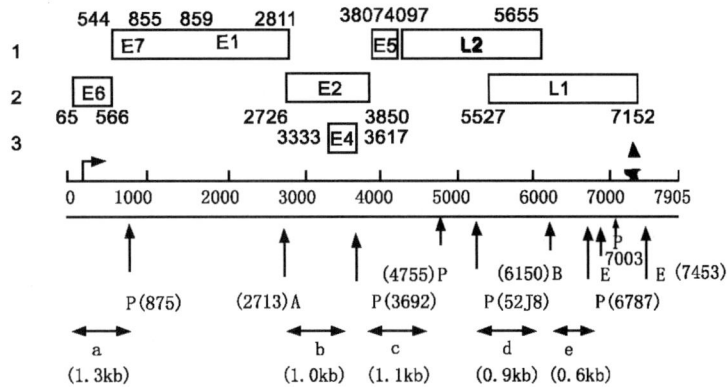

Fig. 6 Genomic organization of HPV-16 and subgenomic probes. Restriction sites of *Ava* II *Bam* HI, Eco RI are indicatcd by *A. B. E* and *P*. respectively. Below the line, subgenomic probes are indicated by *a*, *b*, *c*, *d* and *c*

Tab. 3 The result of southern blot hybridization of HPV-16 subgenomic fragments from 27 cascs of cervical canccr specimens that were proved to be positive for HPV-16 whole genome

HPV-16 subgenomic probes	No.of patients	No. positive	Percentage positive
E6, E7	27	24	88. 9
E2, E4	27	3	11. 1
L1, L2, E5	27	15	55. 6

Our studies reported here imply that the E6 and E7 genes of HPV-16 are required for establishment and maintenance of the transformed phenotype. Therefore, E6 and E7 may be the oncogenic genes of HPV-16, and play a key role in the transformation processes.

5. Analysis of protooncogenes in the genomes of cervical cancer specimens

The DNA of 15 cases of cervical cancer that hybridized with HPV-16 DNA, and DNA of 2 normal cases were digested by E. cor:or Hind III and run on an 0. 8% agarose gel. Mter denaturing, the DNA was transferred from the gel to a nitroccllulose membrane, and finally hybridized with the radiolabelled probes c-mye, c-Ha-ras and c-fosby Southern blotting.

It was found that the protooncogenc c-myc was either amplified or rearranged, and that both alterations were present in 10 cervical carcinoma specimens, which contained integrated HPV-16 DNA in their genomes(Fig. 7). There were no similar alterations to be found in normal specimens. Only one sample from a cancer case appeared to have the c-Ha-ras protooncogene rearrangcment and none appeared to have amplification of rearrangement of c-fos protooncogenc.

This finding suggests that amplification and rearrangement of the c-myc protooncogene arc closely associated with the occurrence of cervical cancer. The data presented here revealed that the activated c-myc oncogene could cooperate with HPV-16 in the carcinogenesis of human cervical cancer. Some other agents, such as HSV-2, smoking and so on, may also be needed and cooperate in the oncogenic processes. The mechanism by which HPV, oncogenes and other agents exert their cooperative actions remains to be studied.

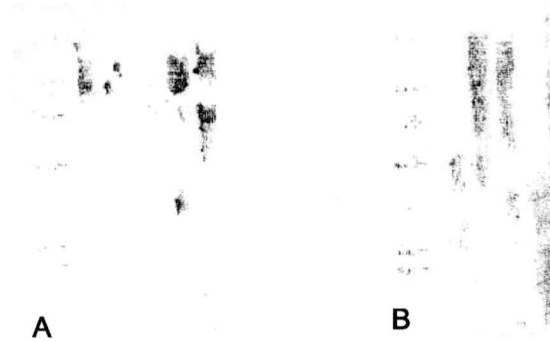

Fig. 7 A，B. Simultaneous amplification and rearrangement of c-myc protooncogcne in invasive cervical carcinoma. Tumour DNA(lanes C1-C5, 10 pg/sample)were digested with EcoRI (A). or HindIII(B), subjected to elcctrophoresis on a 0.8% agarose gcl. Blotted onto nitrocellulose membrane, and hybridized with the radiolabelcd probe. Normal cervical epithelium DNA(lane N. 10 μg/sample)was used as a control The numbers at the *left* of each panel represent the sizes(kb)of the fragments of λ phagc DNA digested with HindIII

6. Conclusions

From the DNA • DNA dot-blot and Southern blot hybridization results，it shows that there is a close relationship between HPV-16 and uterinc cervical squamous cell carcinoma in China. One very interesting finding is that the occurrcnce of HPV-16-homologous DNA differs significantly among the five geographic regions，and corresponds with the cervical cancer mortalitics of those regions.

HPV-11 existed mainly in benign lcsions. The rate of detection of HPV-16 in Chinese women increased from 8.3% in normal cervical epithelium to 20.0% in chroruc cervicitis，28.0% in cervical conodyloma，50.0% in CIN and 60.4% in cervical cancer. It is suggested that HPV-16 infection may be an etiological factor in the development of human cervical carcinoma.

From the results of Southern blot hybridization，it appears that HPV-16 DNA was integrated into the genome of the host cell in cases of cervical cancer，whereas the HPV-16 DNA scquence was only present as an episome in normal cervical epithelium and cervical benign lesions.

The occurrence of E6-E7 genes is highest(88.9%)compared with other subgenomic fragments of HPV-16 in the specimens of human cervical cancer in China. This implies that E6 and E7 genes may be the oncogenic genes of HPV-16 and play an important role in the carcinogenesis of the human cervical epithelial cell.

The amplification and rearrangement of c-myc protooncogene are closely associated with the occurrence of cervical cancer. The results presented here reveal that the activated c-myc oncogene may cooperate with HPV-16 in the carcinogenic processes.

ACKNOWLEDGEMENTS

This project was supported by the National Natural Science Foundation of China，the Science Foundation of the Ministry of Public Health and the Science Foundation of the National Seventh Five-Year Plan of China.

REFERENCES

[1] Aurelian L，Dessler II，Roscnshein NB，Barbour G. Viruses and gynecologic cancers:herpesvirus protein(ICP10/AG-4)，a cervical tumor antigen that fulfills the criteria for a marker of carcinogenecity. Cancer，1981，48:455-471.

[2] Bcral V. Cancer of the cervix: a scxual transmitted infeetion. Lancct，1974: 11073.

[3] Cai L. In: Cai L(ed). The techniqucs in research for nuclcic acid. Science Press，Beijing，1987.

[4] Coleman DV，Wickenden C，Malcolm ADB Association of human papillomavirus with squamous carcimoma of the uterine cervix. Ciba Founda Symp，1986，120:175 186.

[5] Crum CP，lkenberg H，Richart RM，Gissmann L. Human papillomavirus type 16 and early cervical neoplasia. N Engl J Med，1984，310:880-883.

[6] Davis LG，Dibner M，Battey JF. Guanidine isothiocyanate preparation of total RNA. In: Basic methods in molecular biology. Elscvier. Amsterdam，1986: 130-135.

[7] Denhardt D. TA membrane-filter technique for the detection of complementary DNA. Biochem Biophys Res Commun，1966，23:641-646.

[8] Durst M，Gissmann L，Ikenberg H，zur Hausen H. A papil-lomavirus DNA from a cervical carcinoma and its prevalence in

canccr biopsy samples from different geographic regions. Proc Natl Acad Sci USA, 1983, 80:3812-3815.

[9] Eglin RP, Sharp F, Maclean AB, Macnab JCM, Clements JB, Wilkie NM. Detection of RNA complementary to herpes simplex virus DNA in human cervical squamous cell neoplasms. Cancer Rcsm, 1981, 41:3597-3603.

[10] Frenkel N, Roizman B, Cassai E, Nahmias A. A DNA fragcervical cancer tissue. Proc Natl Aead Sci USA, 1972, 69:3784-3789.

[11] Gissmann L. Papillomaviruss and their association with cancer in animal and man. Cancer Surv,1984, 3:161-181.

[12] Guo Xiaojun, Wang Shcnwu Low fat milk used for nucleic acid hybridization. Adv Biochcm Biophys, 1987, 2:7.

[13] Han R, Si J, Zhang W, Lce K. The detection of the human papillomaviruses type 18 and 11 homologous DNA sequences and their transcription in human cervical cancer and its cell line(CC-801). Chin J Cancer, 1989, 8:383-384.

[14] Hauscn H zur. Papillomaviruses as carcinoma viruses. In: Klein G(ed)Advances in viral oncology, vol8. Raven, New York, 1989a: 1-26.

[15] Hausen H zur. Papillomaviruses in anogenital cancer as a model to understand the role of viruses in human cancer. Cancer Res, 1989b, 49:4677-4681.

[16] Howley PM. The role of papillomaviruses in human cancer. In: Devita VT, Hellan S, Rosenberg SA(eds)Important advance in oncology. Lippincott, Philadelhia, 1989: 55-73.

[17] Kanda T, Furuno A, Yoshiike K. Human papillomavirus type 16 open reading frame E7 encodes an transforming gene for rat 3Y1 cells. J Virol,1988, 62:610-613.

[18] Lee K, Hu S, Chen M, Ding L, Liu T, Hu Z. A statistical analysis of 27149 biopsy cases of cancer in China. Chin J Pathol, 1958, 4:258-260.

[19] Lee K, Si J, Han R, Wang S, Zhang W, Song G, Liu S, Chen L, Y, Sun Y, Meng X. An ultrastructural research for the relationship between human uterine cervical carcinoma and human papillomavirus: II. A combined gene molecular and ultrastructural study. In: Hashimoto H, Kuo KH, Lee K, Ogawa K(eds). Recent devclopment of electron microscopy. Nakanishi, Kyoto, 1988: 305-312.

[20] McDougall JK, Smith P, Tamimi Hk, Tolentino E, Galloway DA. Molecular biology of the relationship between Herpcs simplex virus-2 and cervical cancer. In: Giraldo G, Beth E(eds)The role of viruses in human cancer. Elscvier, Amsterdam, 1984: 59-71.

[21] Orth G, Brettburd F, Favre, Croissant O. Papillo-maviruses: possible role in human cancer. In: Hiatt HH, Watson JK, Winsten JA(eds)Origins of human cancer. Gold Spring Harbor Laboratories, New York, 1977: 1043-1068.

[22] Pecoraro G, Morgan D, Defendi V. Differential cffects of human papillomavirus type 6, 16 and 18 DNAs on immortalization and transformation of human cervical epithelial cells. Proc NatlAcad Sci USA, 1989, 86:563-567.

[23] Rigby PWJ, Dieckmann M, Rhodes C, Berg P. Labelling deoxyribonucleic acid to high specific activity in vitro by nick translation with DNA polymcrase I.J Mol Biol, 1977, 113:237-251.

[24] Sambrook J, Fritsch EF, Maniatis T. In: Sambrook J, Fritsch EF, Maniatis T(eds)Molecular cloning, a laborolory manual. 2nd edn, vol3, B. 13, Preparation of reagents and buffers used in molecular cloning. Cold Spring Harbor Laboratory, New York, 1989.

[25] Schwarz E, Freese UK, Gissmann L, Mayer W, Roggenbuck B, Strcmalav A, Hauscn II zur. Structure and transcription of human papillomavirus sequences in cervical carcinoma cells. Nature, 1985, 314:111-114.

[26] Si J, Lec K, Zhang W, Han R, Song G, Chen L, Zhao W, Jia L, Liu S, Mai Y, Zeng Y. A research for the relationship between human papillomavirus and human utcrine cervical carcinoma: II. Molecular genetic and ultrastructural study on the transforming activity of recombinant retrovirus containing human papillomavirus type16 subgenomic scquences. J Cancer Res Clin Oncol, 1991, 117:460-472.

[27] Smotkin D, Wettstein FO. Transcrption of human papillomavirus type 16 carly genes in a cervical cancer and a cancer-derived cell line and identification of the E7 protein. Proc Natl Acad Sci USA, 1986, 83:4680-4684.

[28] Southern EM. Detection of specifie sequences among DNA fragments separated by gel clectrophoresis. J Mol Biol, 1975, 98:503.

[29] Vonka V, Kanka J, Jelinck J, Subrt l, Zuchanek A, Havranbova A, Vachal M, Hirsch I, Domorazbova E, Zavadova H, Richterova V, Naprstkova J, Dvorakova V, Svoboda B Prospective study on the rclationship between cervical neoplasia and Herpes simplex type-2 virus: I. Epidemiological characteristics. Int J Cancer, 1984, 33:49-60.

[30] Zhang W, Si J, Lee K, Chen L, Zhao W, Han R. Cytological study on transforming activity of human papillomavirus type 16 subgenomic DNA in vitro. Chin J Med, 1991.

[In《J Cancer Res Clin Oncol》1991, 117:454-459]

A Research for the Relationship between Human Papillomavirus and Human Uterine Cervical Carcinoma

II. Molecular genetic and ultrastructural study on the transforming activity of recombinant retrovirus containing human papillomavirus type 16 subgenomic sequences

SI Jing-yi[1], LEE Kun[1], ZHANG Wei[1], HAN Ri-cai[1], SONG Guo-xing[1], CHEN Lian-fong[1], ZHAO Wei-ming[1], JIA Li-ping[1], LIU Shi-de[1], MAI Yong-yan[2], ZENG Yi[3]

1. Department of Biophysics, Institute of Basic Medical Sciences, Chinese Academy of Medical Sciences and the Peking Union Medical College, 5 Dong Dan Sam Tiao, Beijing 100005, China; 2. Department of Gynecology and Obstetircs, The First Taching Hospital, Beijing Medical University, Beijing 100034, China; 3. Department of Tumor Viruses, Instiue of Virology, Chinese Academy of Preventive Medicine, 100 Yin Xin Jie, Beijing 100052, China

[SUMMARY] In order to elucidate the role of HPV-16 in the development of genital cancer, NIH3T3 cells were transfected by HPV-16 whole genome and its two early genes, E6-E7. Besides ordinary calcium phosphate/DNA coprecipitation technique, a newly designed recombinant retrovirus containing the HPV-16 genome or subgenomes was used to infect cells for transfer of the target genes. The transforming activities have been demonstrated to be most efficient when a bioengineering technique of this kind is used. HBV-16 DNA was proved to have transforming potential for NIH3T3 cells, and the DNA of HPV-16 was proved to undergo muhisite integration into transformed cells and nude mice tumour cells. The E6-E7 open reading frames are sufficient for transforming NIH3T3 cells independently in vitro, which implies that E6-E7 open reading frames are transforming genes or even viral oncogenes of HPV-16. The RNA transcribed by the E6-E7 of HPV-16 was expressed in transformed cells and in tumour cells of nude mice. The use of a recombinant retrovirus for gene transfer in this study is much more efficient than of calcium phosphate/DNA coprecipitation. The lack of a tissueculture system suitable for HPV replication in vitro makes HPV gene recombination into a specially engineered retrovirus for viral-mediated gene transfer of particular significance for the possible application of viral carcinogenesis, both in vitro and in vivo, for basic and clinical research.

[Keywords] HPV; Transforming activity; Recombinant retrovirus; Viral oncogene

INTRODUCTION

In recent years, there has been increasing evidence that human papillomaviruses(HPV) are emerging as the major agents for the etiology of human cervical carcinoma through clinical, epidemiological, molecular biological and tumour virological studies(Stanbridge et al, 1981; Fukushima et al. 1985; Howley 1989; zur Hausen 1985; Gao et al, 1988). More than 60 HPV genotypes have been isolated and characterized, and the heterogeneity of HPV types is considered to reflect the adaptation of these viruses in specific differentiated tissues(zur Hausen 1989). HPV-6, 11, 16, and 18 have been found in neoplastic lesions of the genital tract(Pecoraro et al. 1989).

In our laboratory, a molecular hybridization study showed that 60.4% of biopsies obtained from Chinese patients with cerviral cancer contained a sequence homologous to HPV-16 DNA; it is therefore the most prevalent viral type in Chinese women(Si et al. 1987). Our earlier work also showed that the early-region E6 and E7 genes of HPV-16 might play a key role in the carcinogenesis of cervical cancer(Si et al, 1990).

Clinical observations and recent experimental results have suggested that the development of cervical cancer, like other cancers, involves multistage processes and multiple etiological agents(Weinstein 1988). In order to elucidate the role of HPV-16 in the development of gential cancer, the present study was designed to transfect cultured NIH3T3 cells with HPV-16 whole genome and its two subhenomic genes, E6 and E7, separately. In addition to the ordinary calcium phosphate/DNA coprecipitation technique, the method of a newly designed recombinant retrovirus containing the HPV-16 genome or subgenomes was used to infect cells for transferring the target genes. The transforming activities have been demonstrated to be more efficient when this kind of bioengineering technique is used compared with the results of ordinary methods.

The transforming activity of HPV-16 was first observed in mouse NIH3T3 cells(Yasumoto et al, 1986; Noda et al. 1988; Bedell et al. 1987). Several laboratories have shown that much more recalcitrant cells, both of fibroblast and epithelial origin, are efficiently transformed by HPV DNA singly or cooperatively with other agents such as oncogene EJ-ras, etc.(Tsunokawa et al. 1986; Matlashewski et al. 1988). Up to now, no report has been found on the use of a recombinant retrovirus as a vector for HPV gene transfection.

MATERIALS AND METHODS

1. Plasmid preparation

A plasmid pSV2-neo/HPV16, containing the whole HPV-16 genome, cloned into the BanHI site of pSV2-neo, and plasmids HZIP-16 and HZIP-16K, containing the total early genes(6.6kb) as well as the E6-E7(1kb) subgenomic sequence in plasmid pZIP-NeoSV(X)1, were kindly provided by McCance(Matladhewski et al. 1987) (Fig. 1 and 2)

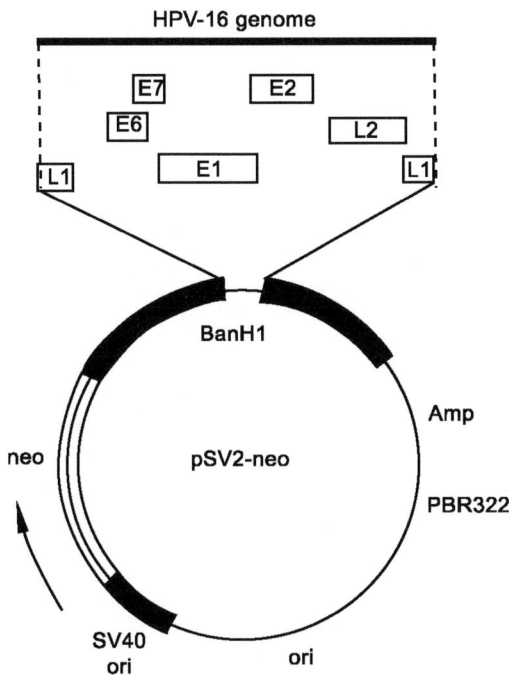

Fig. 1　Structure of recombinant plasmid pSV2-neo/HPV16. The HPV-16 DNA was linearized at the unique BamHI site and doned into the BamHI site of pSV2-neo. Amp, ampicillin; SV40, simian virus 40; ori, origin

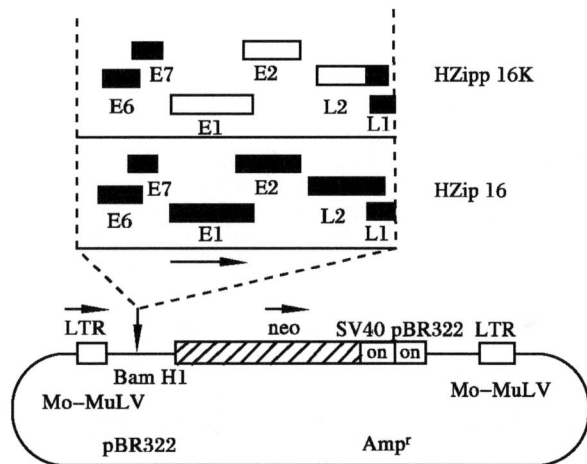

Fig. 2　Structure of recombinant plasmid HZip16, the HPV-16 6.6-kb fragment including nucleotides0-6150 and 7454-7904. HZip16K is the HZip16 deletion mutant lacking the Kpnl fragment from nucleotides 880-5377

Recombinant plasmids pSV2-neo/HPV16, HZip16, HZip16K and pZI P-NeoSV(X)1 were transfected into E. coli by a modified method of Mandel(Mandel and Higa 1970).

2. Preparation of pSV2-neo, pZIP-NeoSV(X)1 vector plasmids

The pZIP-NeoSV(X)1 vector consists of the Moloney murine leukemia virus(M-MuLV) transcriptional unit, derived from an integrated M-MuLV provirus, and PBR322 seqences necessary for the propagation of the vector DNA in E. coil. HZip16K was hydrolysed into two parts[pZIP-NeoSV(X)1 and E6-E7]by BamHI after electrophoresis. The pZIP-NeoSV(X)1 part was collected and ligated into a circular plasmid by T4 ligase, pSV2-neo was collected after pSV2-neo/HPV16 had been digested by BamHT.

The amplification and purification of plasmids were performed as described by Mandel and Cai(Cai 1987).

NIH3T3 and ψ-2 cells culture. NIH3T3 cells were maintained in Dulbecco modified eagle medium(DMEM) supplemented with 10% calf serum, 0.2mmol/L glutamine, 100units/ml penicillin and 100μg/ml streptomycin. Cells were grown in a humidified 5% CO_2 incubator at 37℃ and fed every 3 days.

ψ-2 cells were cultured in the same conditions as NIH3T3 cells.

3. Transfections

pSV2-neo/HPV16 plasmid transfection into NIH3T3 cells was performed by the calcium phosphate/DNA co-precipitation technique as described by Wigher(Wigher et al. 1978)and Davis(Davis et al. 1986). After transfection for 72h, NIH3T3 cells were digested by trypsin and cultured in DMEM with G418(400μg/ml)until anti-G418 clone formation.

HZIP-16, HZIP-16K and pZIP-NeoSV(X)I were transfected into ψ2 cell by calcium phosphate/DNA coprecipitation. The ψ2 cell line contains integrated copies of the M-MuLV proviurs genome, which provides all the trans functions necessary for the encapsidation of a recombinant genome, whereas it is unable to encapsidate its own RNA. ψ2 cells were digested by trypsin 72h after infection and cultured in DMEM medium containing G418 (400μg/ml), until the formation of an anti-G418 cell clone that could produce defective retrovirus(pZIP-ψ2, HZ-IP16-ψ2 and HZIP16K-ψ2cells). After culture for 18h, the culture fluid of cloned ψ2 cells(PZIP-ψ2, PZIP16-ψ, HZIP16K-ψ cells) containing a large number of virions(viral fluid)was harvested, filtered through a0.45-μm microporefilter, then added into NIH3T3 cell culture medium at 37℃ in a 5% CO₂ incubator. After 2h, some fresh medium was added to the NIH3T3 cell culture flask. The transformed NIH3T3 cells(HZIP16-3T3 and HZIP-16K-3T3 cells)could be formed by infection with recombinant retrovirus after culture in G418-containing(400μg/ml) DMEM medium for selection of transformed cells.

The experimental design is illustrated in the schematic diagram shown in Fig. 3.

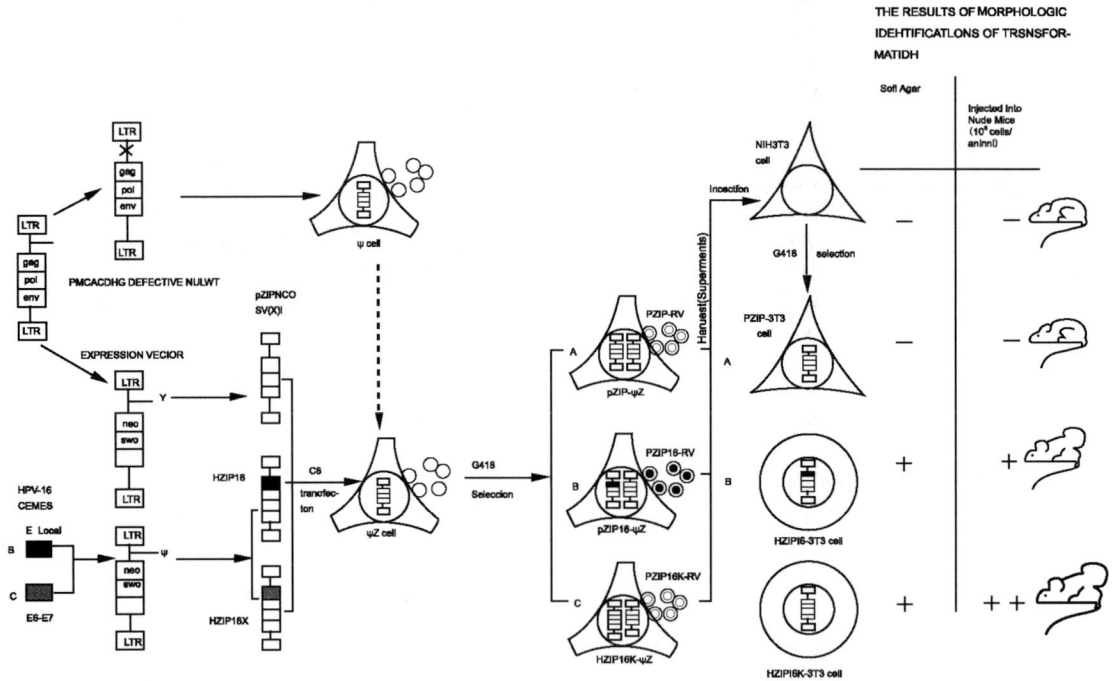

Fig. 3　A schematic diagram of the mechanism and results of the transformation of NIH3T3 cell by the recombinant retroviruses containing HPV-16 subgenomes

4. Transforming activity

Soft agar assay. Samples of 5×10^5 transformed cells were suspended in serum-free DMEM containing 0.3% agar(Difco Lab), and the suspending mixture was plated onto the 0.5% agar medium layer in culture dishes. After 15 min at room temperature, the dishes were removed into a CO₂ incubator at 37℃.

Tumorigenicity assay: HZIP16-3T3, HZIP16K-3T3, pZIP-3T3 and NIH3T3 cells were injected separately into nude mice subcutaneously at 1×10^6 cells/animal, pZIP-3T3 and NIH3T3 cells were used for negative controlls. Five mice were injected with each kind of cell.

5. DNA·DNA hybridization

DNA extracted from the cells mentioned above was digested by restriction endonuclease BamHI, then run on an 0.8% agarose gel in buffer containing 0.04mol/L Tris-acetic acid,0.002mol/L EDTA. In addition to the above buffer, 0. 2μg/ml ethidium bromide was added. After UV transilluminator photograping, the gel was placed in a denaturing solution(0. 25moL/L NaOH and 1. 5moL/L NaCl)with shaking for 30 min(repeated twice)and, after neutralization, was subjected to Southern blotting. The DNA was transferred to a nitrocellulose filter from the gel by the method of Southern(Southern 1975).

The HPV-16 DNA was radiolabelled with[^{32}p]dCTP by nicktranslation(Rigby et al. 1977)[specific activity (0. 5-2)×10^8 cpm/μg"]as a probe. Hybridization was performed by a modified method of Cai(Cai 1990)under stringent conditions(42℃ for 16-24h). The filter was washed twice in 2×SSC(150mmol/L NaCl plus 15mmol/L sodium citrate, pH7. 0)containing 0. 5% sodium dodecyl sulphate(SDS)for 30 min at room temperature and twice in 0. 1×SSC containing 0. 1% SDS at 65℃ for 20 min, and then exposed to X-ray film in a plastic mount with an intensifying screen for 7-12 days at-70℃.

6. DNA・RNA hybridization

Cell hybridization in situ(Paeratakul et al. 1988). NIH3T3 cells transformed by HZIP-16 and HZIP-16K(HZ-IP16-3T3 and HZIP16K-3T3)were plated onto nitrocellulose filters in graded concentrations of 2×10^5, 1×10^5 and 5×10^4, then fixed with 1% glutaraldeyhde at 4℃ for 1h, washed with buffer(100mmol/L TRIS, pH 8. 0; 50mmol/L EDTA)three times and digested with 20μg proteinase K/ml buffer at 37℃ for 30 min. Instead of proteinase K, 1mg RNase/ml buffer was used for the control filter. The filter was suspended in 3×SSC solution(containing 35% formamide, 3×SSC, 1×Denhard's solution, 0. 5% SDS and 100μg salmon sperm DNA/ml) and subjected to prehybridization at 65℃ for 12h and then to hybridization(prehybridization solution plus ^{32}p-labelled HPV-16 DNA probes and 10mmol/L EDTA/L at 65℃ for 12h). The filter was washed in 2×SSC, 0. 5% SDS at room temperature for 15 min, 1×SSC, 0. 5% SDS at55℃ for 15 min and 0. 1×SSC, 0. 5% SDS until there was no evident background, and finally exposed to X-ray film for 7-15 days at-70℃.

DNA・RNA Northern blot hybridization. Total cellular RNA was extracted with guanidine hydrochloride and by the hot phenol method. Samples of 20μg RNA were electrophoresed throughagarose gel containing 2. 2mol/L formaldehyde. The gel was washed twice in 10×SSC for 20 min. The procedures of gel transfer, hybridization and autoradiography were the same as those for Southern blot hybridization described above.

7. Preparation of specimens for light and electron microscopy

Light microscopy. Tumour tissues obtained from nude mice were prepared for light microscopy by routine procedures.

Electron microscopy. The cells(pZIP-ψ2, HZIP16K-ψ2, the transformed HZIP16-3T3 and HZIP16K-3T3 as well as the control NIH3T3 and pZIP-3T3 cells)and tumour tissues from nude mice were fixed in 3. 8% glutaraldehyde in phosphate-buffered saline, postfixed in 1% osmium tetroxide for 2h, dehydrated in graded ethanol (50%, 70%, 90%and 100%)and embedded in Epon812. The ultrathin sections were stained with uranyl acetatc and lead citrate and observed under a JEM-2000EX electron microscope.

RESULTS

1. Estimation of the transforming activity of pSV2-neo/HPV16

Transformed foci were detected morphologically 4-6 weeks after the transfection of pSV2neo/HPV16 plasmid by the calcium phosphate/DNA coprecipitation method. The transfectants were selected with G418. Some cells survived and a number of colonies were found to be G418resistant. The transformed cells appeared more reflective and were larger and round-shaped with rapid growth. The mitotic figures could easily be seen throughout the culture. The transformed cells also showed loss of contact inhibition and a decrease in serum dependence(Fig. 4). Five monoclones were selected randomly from the transformed cell colonies and expended to become cell lines, namely, Z102, C202, Z303, Y16, and Q16.

Total cellular DNAs from five monoclones were extracted and subjected to Southern blot analysis by using ^{32}P-labelled HPV-16 DNA(7. 9kb)as probe. When non-digested cellular DNA was analysed, DNA sequences homologous to HPV-16 were found in all of the transformed cell lines(Fig. 5). No HPV-16-homologous sequence could be deteced in nontransfected NIH3T3 ceils. The number of copies of HPV-16 DNA per cell line was different among the five cell lines. Viral genes appeared with obvious amplification in both Q16 and YI6. All the detectable HPV-16 DNA

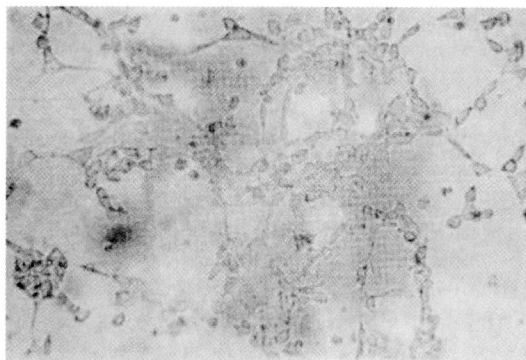

Fig. 4　Morphologically transformed cells induced by pSV2Nco/HPV16 transfectional DNA. ×845

sequences comigrated with high-molecular-mass cellular DNA. The migration of the HPV-16-related sequences was not characteristic of pSV2-neo/HPV16 form 1 (close supercoiled circular), form 2(open circular)or form 3(linear), and might represent the integration of HPV-16 DNA into hostcell chromosomal DNA.

To analyse further whether or not HPV-16 DNA had been integrated into the host-cell genome, DNA of five transformed cell linecs was digested by BamHI. Because the HPV-16 DNA catenated into the BamHI site of the pSV2-neo vector, after the BamHI digestion the unit length of the HPV-16 DNA(7.9 kb) was excised from the pSV2-neo sequence. The results of Southern blot hybridization revealed that in addition there was positive reaction at the 7.9-kb site; additional hybridized bands were also observed(Fig. 5). The fragments larger than 7.9kb may represent the integration of HPV-16 sequences into host chromosomal DNA, the integrated HPV-16 segments being linked with the host sequence. The fragments less than 7.9kb, on the other

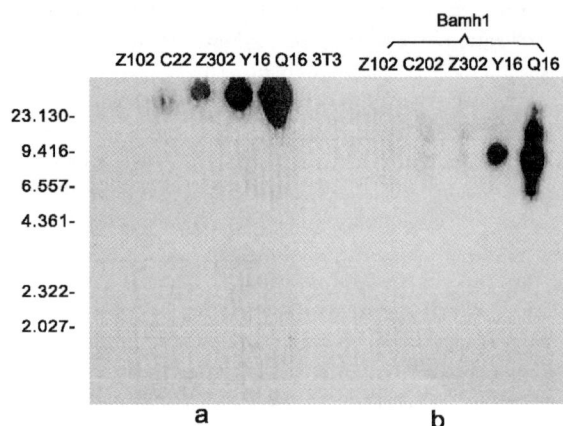

Fig. 5 A, B. Southern blot analysis of HPV-16 DNA sequences in transformed cells(Z102, C202, Z302, Y16 and Q16) that had been transfected with pSV2Neo/HPV16. A Nondigested DNAs; B DNA digested by BamHI.

hand, may indicate that there was a partial gene junction between the host-cell and virus DNA, or rearrangements and deletions within HPV-16 dNA sequences.

The presence of multiple hy bridized bands meant that there was muhisite integration of HPV-16 DNA into the host chromosome and that the integrated sites were different from each other.

2. Estimation of the transforming activity of the whole HPV-16 early gene and E6-E7

①Growth properties of transformed-cells

Plasmids of HZIP16 and HIP16K(containing the whole early gene and E6-E7 respectively) were transfected into NIH3T3 cells by infection of recombinant retrovirus(HZIP16-RV, HZIP16KRV). The recombinant viruses are termed viral vectors, and are derived from retroviruses(Fig. 3).

Retroviruses are small viruses with a genome comprising RNA, and they consist of a peptide and a capsule surrounding the RNA genome. When a cell is infected by a retrovirus, the RNA genome is imjected into the cell and copied into DNA by an enzyme, reverse transcriptase. This DNA passes into the nucleus of the infected cell and becomes integrated into the host chromosomal DNA. This process is highly efficient and can yield stable integration of the viral gene into nearly all cells in culture.

Plasmid pZIPNeoSV(X)I was transfected into ψ-2 cells to form a kind of recombinant retrovirus containing no HPV-16 genome, and this virus was used to transfect NIH3T3 cells as a negative control by the same method as described above. One week after the infection of HZIP16-RV and HZIP16K-RV as well as the control recombinant retrovirus(pZIP-RV), there were three kinds of cells surviving the selection with G418, and these were termed HZIP16-3T3, HZIP16K-3T3 and pZIP-3T3 respectively(Fig. 3). Among them, HZIP16K-3T3 and HZIP16-3T3 showed evident signs of transformation. Under the light microscope, The HZIPI6-3T3 and HZIP16K-3T3 cells became large and round-shaped, being strongly reflective and, in an unpolarized manner, grew into criss-cross multilayers. Mitotic figures could easily be seen throughout the culture. In addition, HZIP16K-3T3 were much larger and grew faster than HZIP16-3T3 cells, whereas the pZIP-3T3 cells retained the same morphology as the normal NIH3T3 cells, having a spindle shape, monolayer growth and being less reflective(Figs. 6-8).

②Analysis of anchorage dependence

Samples of 5×10^5 cells of each kin(HZIP16-3T3, HZIPI6K-3T3, pZIP-3T3 and NIH3T3 cells)were suspended in 0.3% soft agar containing serum-free DMEM. After 2 weeks incubation, Many colonies of various sizes were seen in the HZIP16-3T3 and HZIP16-3T3 cell groups. This meant that the cells transformed by HPV-16 subgenomic fragments showed the characteristics of anchorage-independent growth. By contrast, pZIP-3T3 and NIH3T3 cells grew slowly in soft agar and no colonies were discovered(Fig. 9). These results suggest that the cells receiving HPV-16 DNA are stimulated to grow in soft agar and this stimulation must be due to the direct effect of an HPV-16 genomic function. It is possible that HZIP16-3T3 and HZIP16K-3T3 show a malignant phenotype because of HPV-16 subgenomes integrating into NIH3T3 cells.

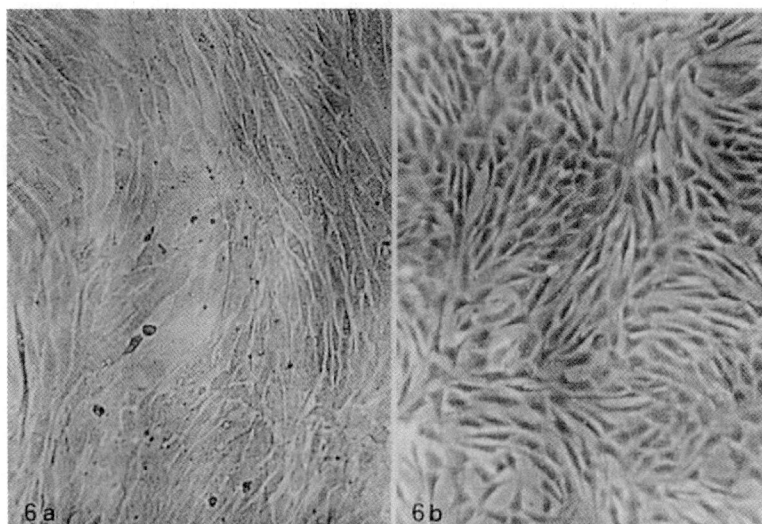

Fig. 6 Light micrographs of control groups: a. morphology of NIH 3T3 cells; b. morphology of pZIP 3T3 cells; the morphology and pattern of arrangement are similar to those of NIH3T3 cells. ×590

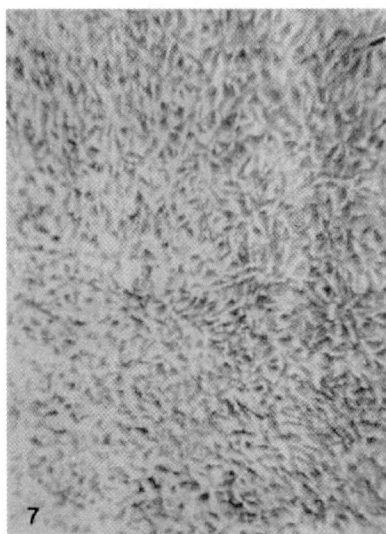

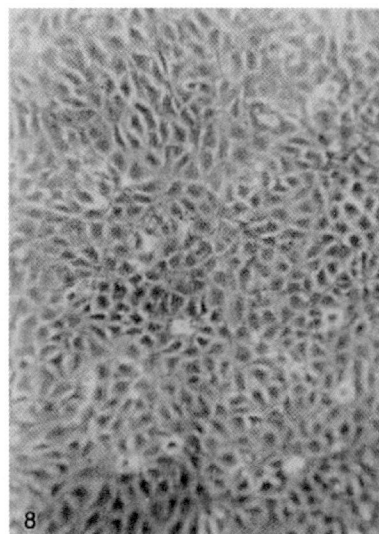

Fig. 7 Micrograph of the morphology of HZIP16-3T3 cells showing that the NIH3T3 cell was transformed by recombinant tetrovirus(HZIP16RV) containing HPV-16 whole early genes, and prominant alterations both in cell morphology and the pattern of arrangement. ×590

Fig. 8 The morphology of HZIP16K-3T3 cells showing that the NIH3T3 cell was evidently transformed by the recombinant retrovirus(HZIP16KRV)containing HPV-16 E6-E7 early genes, and remarkable alterations both in cell morphology and the pattern of arrangement. ×590

③Tumorigenicity of the transformed cells

HZIP-3T3, HZIP16K-3T3 and controlled NIH3T3, pZIP-3T3 cells were injected into athymic nude mice(1×10⁶ cells/animal), five mice per group, in order to assay for tumorigenicity. In the HZIP16-3T3 and HZIP16K-3T3 groups, tumours were formed in all mice within15 days after inoculation, reaching more than 15mm in diameter, adn all the tumours transplanted with HZIP16K-3T3 were considerably larger than those with HZIP16-3T3. However, no tumour was observed in any of the ten animals of the control groups(inoculated with pZIP-3T3 and

NIH3T3 cels)as long as 50 days after injection(Fig. 10). Although both HzIP16-3T3 and HZIP16K-3T3 appeared highly tumorigenic within nude mice, the latent trmorigenic ability of HPV-16 E6-E7 early genes was stronger than that of HPV-16 total early genes.

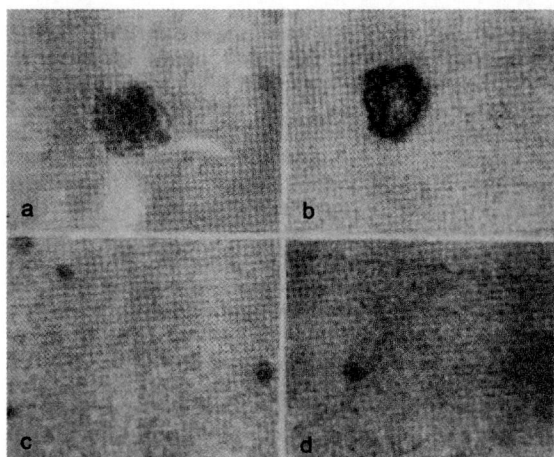

Fig. 9 a-d. Micrographs of the test for anchorage dependence. Cells were suspended in 0.3% soft agar, and incubated for 2 weeks, colonies were formed in a (HZIP16-3T3 cells) and b (HZIP16K-3T3). No colony was found in c(pZIP-3T3)and d(NIH3T3)

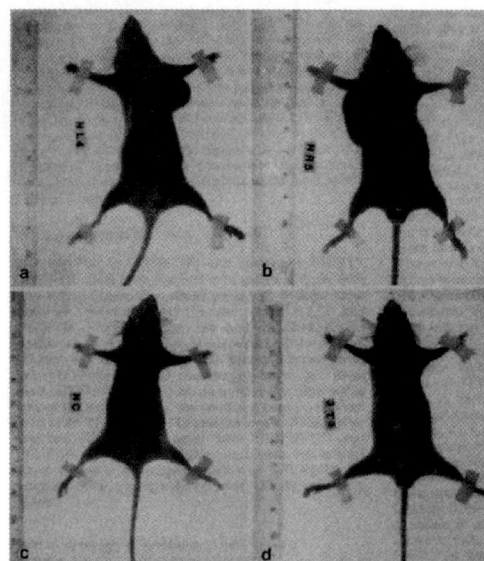

Fig. 10 Tumours formed in nude mice on the 14th day after injection of 1×10^6 cells of(a)HZIP16-3T3 and(b)HZIP16K-3T3. No tumour had formed in nude mice by the 49th day after injection of 1×10^6 cells of(c)pzIP-3T3 and(d)NIH3T3

④The morphology of transformed cells in vitro and tumour tissues formed in nude mice

Electron microscopic observation of recombinant-retrovivus-producing cells. HZIP16-ψ2 and HZIP16K-ψ2 cells, harbouring and producing recombinant retroviruses with HPV-16 whole early genes and its E6-E7 subgenomes, revealed oval or spindle shapes. Some nuclei were remarkably swollen with large amounts of euchromatin. Interchromatin granules and perichromatin granules, often seen in other vivus-infected cells(Lee et al. 1987), were easily observed in this kind or nucleus. There were some dense particles(45-50 nm in diameter)dispersed singly or in clusters beneath the thickened endoplasmic reticulum or plasma membranes from which the mature retroviruses were budding, with the processes of encapsidation of the dense viral core. These dense particles were, therefore, proposed to be the precursors of the RNA core of the recombinant retrovirus. Fig. 11 shows that the viruses were budding from the plasma membrane and Fig. 12 shows some virus particles in the cavity of the endoplasmic reticulum.

The morphology and morphogenesis of the recombinant retrovirus is very similar to that of other retroviruses described in previous reports (Fraenkel-Conrat et al. 1988).

The morphlogy of tumour tissues induced in nude mice. The whole tumours were round, oval or nodular in shape with a clear margin. The crosssection of the tumour appeared pink in shape with a clear margin. The cross-section of the tumour appeared pink in colour and homogeneous. Under a

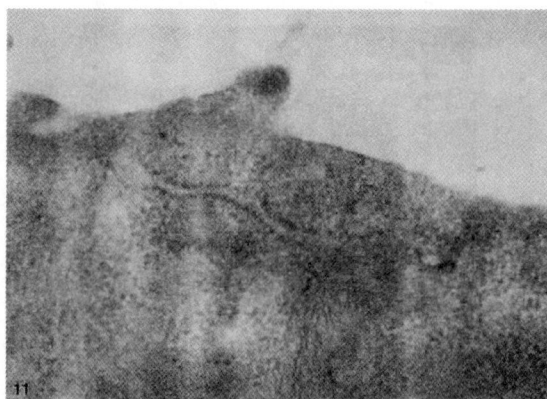

Fig. 11 Recombinant retrovirus budding from the thickened plasma membrane of virus-producing cell(HZIP16-ψ2). Dense precursor core can be seen beneath the membrane. $\times 80\ 000$

light microscope, a large number of spindle cells with different sizes were compacted in a disorderly manner. The nuclei of tumour cells appeared to be of different size and shape; some were very large with a lot of mitotic figure. The pathology of the pictures gave rise to the diagnosis of a typical fibrosarcoma(Fig. 13).

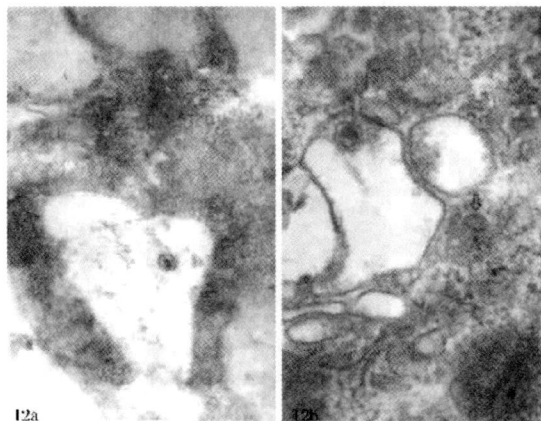

Fig. 12 Electron micrographs of mature recombinant retrovirus in dilated endoplasmic reticulum of virus-producing cell: a HZIP16-ψ2, ×30 000; b HZIP16K-ψ2, ×40 000. Precursor viral core(⇒) can be seen in the cytoplasm of HZIP16K-ψ2 cell

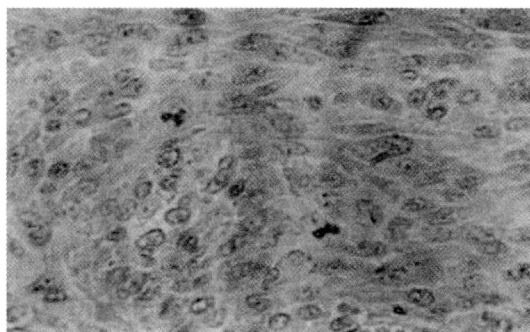

Fig. 13 Micrograph of the morphology of tumour tissue induced in nude mice(H&E stain). A large number of spindle cells of different size were compacted. The nuclei of tumour cells appeared to be of different sizes and shapes with a lot of mitotic figure.×600

Under the electron microscope, the cell nuclei were very large with several large nucleoli and abundant euchromatin. Interchromatin granules, perichromatin granules and nuclear bodies were frequently seen in some nuclei. As well as a few variousley sized, vacuous mito-chondria and endoplasmic reticulum, a great number of free ribosomes were scattered through out the cytoplasm of the tumour cells. Some collagen fibers were seen in the intercellular space of the tumour tissue. The mitotic figures were easily found(Fig. 14 and 15). All the evidence given by light and electron microscopy demonstrated that the tumour cells were of a malignant character with poor differentiation.

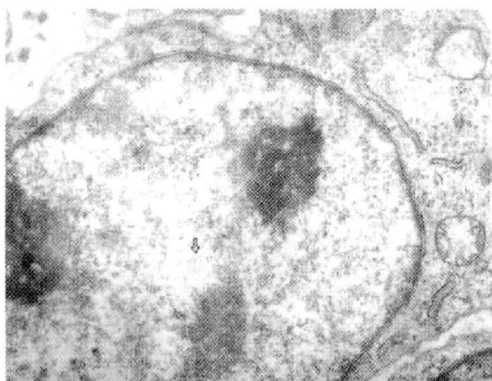

Fig. 14 Electron micrograph of tumour tissue in nude mice. A noticeably large nucleus with abundant euchroma-tin, two large nucleoli, interchromatin granules and a nuclear body(⇒) were seen. A great number of free ribosomes, scattered throughout the cytoplasm, and swollen mitochondria were observed

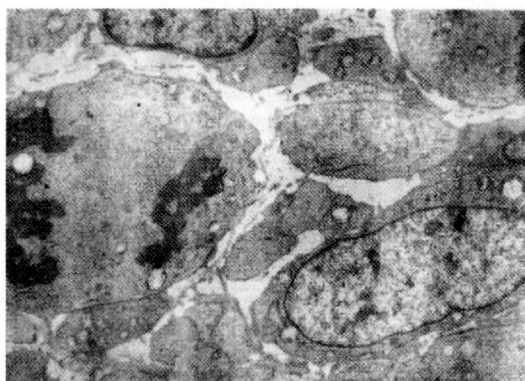

Fig. 15 Electron micrograph of tumour tissue in nude mice. Malignant cells with large nuclei and two cells in mitotic division stage were seen. Collagen fibers present in the intercellular space between tumour cells showed the fibrous cell origin of this malignant tumour

The ultrastructure of transformed cells. HZIP16-3T3 and HZIP16K-3T3 cells showed characteristics of low differentiation, like the tumour cells described above, such as an increased nuclear/cytoplasm ratio, abundant euchromatin in the nuclei and a large number of free ribosomes in the cytoplasm, etc.

No retrovirus particles could be observed in any of the malignant tumour cells and transformed cells although there were related homologous sequences of HPV-16 DNA or its E6-E7 subgenomes in the DNA of these cells, as shown in our DNA • DNA hybridization. This again shows the fact, described in our previous paper(Lee et al. 1988), that once the carcinogenic viral genome or subgenomes are integrated into the cellular genome and have caused the cell to transform into a malignant state, the virus itself as a whole is no longer detectable.

3. The detection of HPV-16 subgenomes in transformed cells

The nondigested DNA obtained from HZIP16-3T3, HZIP16K-3T3 and tumour cells of nude mice were subjected to Southern blot hybridization with ^{32}P-labelled E6-E7 subgenomes of HPV-16 as the probe, showing that the fragment in the position of high-molecular-weight DNA (23kb) presented a clear hybridization signal. This means that HPV-16 DNA has been integrated into the host cell genome. The DNAs of these transformed cells, digested by BamHI, gave rise to several hybridized bands in addition to the 23-kb fragment (Fig. 16). This again means that multisite integrations of the HPV-16 sequence into transformed cellular DNA have tave taken place. Considering these data, it is unlikely that the HPV-16 sequences are present in the episomal form in the transformants. It is suggested that the integration of the HPV-16 DNA is needed for the maintenance of the malignant phenotype of transformed cells.

4. The detection of transcriptional activity of HPV-16 subgenomes in transformed cells

DNA • RNA hybridization in situ was used for detecting the transcriptional activities of HPV-16 subgenomes in HZIP16-3T3 and HZIP16K-3T3 cells. This method is more sensitive and fast than that of Northern blot hybridization. All three concentrations of HZIP16-3T3 and HZIP16K-3T3 cells(2×10^5, 1×10^5 and 5×10^4) revealed positive hybridization to the ^{32}p-labelled HPV-16 E6-E7 DNA probes, whereas the hybridization signals became much weaker after RNase digestion of transformed cells

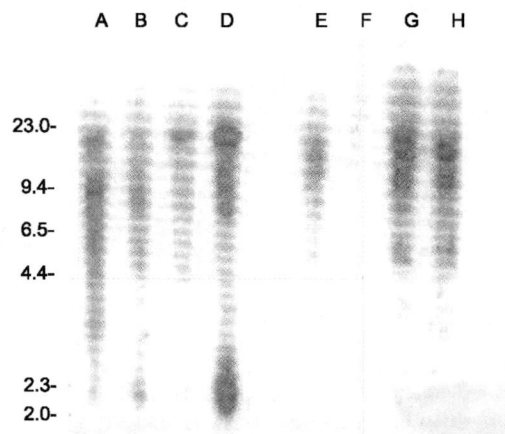

Fig. 16　Southern blot analysis of HPV-16 sequence in transformants and their tumours. Each DNA was digested with BamHL Lanes A and B were from tumour produced by HZIP16K-3T3; C was from transformed cells, HZIP16K-3T3, and D was from HZIP16K-ψ2 cells. Lanes E abd F were from tumour produced by HZIP16-3T3. G was from transformed cells of HZIP16-3T3 and H was from HZIP16-ψ2 cells. All of them showed positive hybridization with HPV-16 E6-E7 DNA as the probe and high-molecular-weight DNA (23kb) gave dearly positive signals

(Fig. 17). It is suggested that this result indeed represents DNA • RNA hybridization, and demonstrates that HPV-16 E6-E7 early genes are expressed in transformed cells.

5. The comparison of gene-transfer effects between the methods using recombinant retrovirus and calcium phosphate/DNA coprecipitation

Hundreds of cell colonies appeared with NIH3T3 cells infected by recombinant retrovirus after G418-selected culture for 1 week(Fig. 18). However, no clone formed in transformed cells when the calcium phosphate/DNA coprecipitation method was used, after the same time of selective culture mentioned above. There were only a few cell colonies formed after selective culturing for 3 weeks. The formation of cell colonies after the same recombinant plasmid had been used to transfer genes into NIH3T3 cells by different methods was quite different in time and number. From the results of our experiment, the retrovirus vector produced by the genetic engineering method is a more efficient method for gene transfer than others at present.

DISCUSSION

The results presented here have indicated that the plasmids containing the HPV-16 genome were efficient for the transformation of NIH3T3 cells, and that the transformed cells have clearly undergone changes that alter morphology, growth characteristics and tumorigenicity in vivo. The transformation is indeed due to the effect of HPV-16 DNA, as the recombinant retrovirus pZIP-RV, containing no HPV-16 genes, is unable to transform HIH3T3.

The data from this study showed that the E6-E7 open reading frames of HPV-16 were sufficient for the trans-

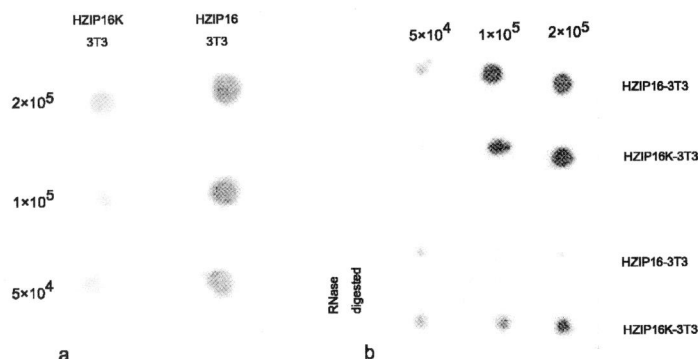

Fig. 17 a. The result of DNA · RNA hybridization in situ for detecting the transcriptional activity of HPV-16 subgenomes in HZIP16-3T3 and HZIP16K-3T3 cells revealed positive hybridization with HPV-16 E6-E7 DNA as probe, b A comparison of RNA · DNA hybridization in situ between cells(HZIP16-3T3 and HZIP16K-3T3)digested and not digested by RNase. The hybridization signals become much weaker after RNase digestion

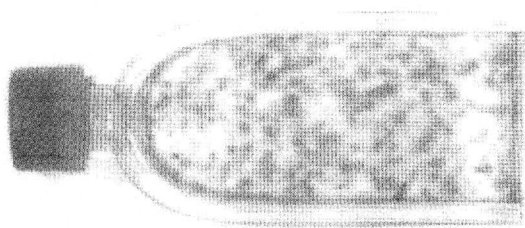

Fig. 18 Hundreds of cell colonies appeared with NIH3T3 cells in fected by recombinant retrovirus after G418-selective culture for 1 week

formation of NIH3T3 cells. The efficiency of transformation by the E6-E7 construct was higher than that observed with the entire early genes of HPV-16. The reason for this is still to be studied.

In our other paper(Si et al. 1990), the HPV-16 DNA was digested by Pst I to produce several pieces and these were labelled with ^{32}p to create probes to detect viral DNA sequences in biopsies of cervical cancer, which showed a positive reaction with a HPV-16 total DNA probe by dot-blot hybridization. The results showed that 89% of samples gave a positive reaction with the E6-E7 subgenome probe. The results of our transforming experiment coincide with the earlier report. We conclude, therefore, that a major transforming function of HPV-16 is localized in the E6-E7 genes, and that the E6-E7 open reading frames encodes a transforming gene, which plays a pivotal role in the careinogenic processes.

The transformation experiments in this study have shown that, in nude mice, not only transformed cells, induced by either HPV-16 whole genome or its subgenomic fragments(total early genes and E6-E7 genes), but also tumour cells all contain integrated HPV-16 DNA. It has been proved in our laboratory that HPV-16 DNA is ususally integrated into cellular DNA in biopsy tissues of cervical cancer, but that in cervical benign lesions such as chronic cervicitis and condyloma it is in an episomal form. The evidence from our study suggests that the integration of HPV-16 genes into cellular DNA may play an important role in the processes of malignant conversion of cervical epithelial cells.

Some reports of transforming experiments with HPV-16 DNA in vitro were describe the use of routine methods involving calcium phosphate/DNA coprecipitation, electrophoration, protoplast fusion and microinjection etc. Transfection by these methods is rather inefficient. The DNA will be stably integrated into the chromosomes of only 1 in 100 000 cells by calcium phosphate/DNA coprecipitation, and the other techniques of gene transfer have generally similar results(Ledley 1987).

In our method forcing genes are packaged into a specially engineered virus, and introduced into cells by infection with the recombinant viruses. This process is called viral-mediated gene transfer, and the recombinant viruses are termed viral vectors. The recombinant retrovirus vector for HPV-16 gene transfer was employed in this study to investigate the transforming effect of HPV-16. This method or retroviral-mediated gene transfer has proved to be highly efficient and can yield stable integration of genes into virtually all cells in culture, as shown by our experiments, up to now, no report of a recombinant retrovirus being used for the study of HPV-16 DNA transformation in vitro has been found.

A typical retroviral sequence includes the sequences necessary for encoding the gag, pol and env polypeptides, the long terminal repeats(LTRs)necessary for the initiation of viral transcription and polyadenylation of viral transcripts and for integration, and a descrete sequence(ψsite) near the LTR, required for packaging the RNA genome in the viral capsule, called the package signal sequence(Fig. 3).

By means of recombinant DNA techniques, two kinds of viral mutant have been obtained. One is capable of directing synthesis of retroviral core protains and assembly of a retroviral capsule, which, however, lacks the packaging sequence(ψ). The mutant can then be introduced into cultured cells to produce a packaging-defective cell line($\psi2$)that secretes cmpty virus capsules. The second mutant is an expression vector called pZIPNeoSV(X)I containing a recombinant foreign gene in place of the viral genes but retaining the packaging sequence(ψ). If HPV-16 genes are recombined into this expression vector and introduced into cells that also contain the packaging-defective mutant($\psi2$ cells), defective retrovirus-producing cells(HZIP16-$\psi2$, HZIP16K-$\psi2$)are formed. In these cells, the expression vector containing recombinant HPV-16 genes is packaged into empty virus capsules, producing defective retroviruses(HZIP16-RV and HZIP16K-RV), which retain the ability to infect cells efficiently and integrate the foreign genes into the host chromosome. These virus particles can be used to infect NIH3T3 cells and transform them to detect the transformation potential of HPV-16 genes. Since the defective retroviruses do not contain genes for any viral protains, a cell infected with this kind of defective retrovirus is incapable of inducing viral proliferation or viral disease.

Because of the lack of a tissue-culture system suitable for HPV replication in vitro, a method that uses recombination of HPV genes into a specially engineered virus is of significance for studying the biological behavior of HPV. Furthermore, a number of retroviruses carrying the HPV gene are obtained by this method, and these viruses will be available for universal studies both in vitro and vivo. This gene-transfer method may make it possible to infect live animals with viral vectors leading to transformation of cells in vivo. As a model for introducing recombinant genes into live animals, allowing experiments to develop from those from in vitro to ones vivo and from cell model to animal model, it is certainly of particular significance for basic medical research and clinical application.

ACKNOWLEDGEMENTS

This project was supported by the National Natural Science foundation of China, the Science foundation of the Ministry of Public Health and the Science Foundation of the National Seventh Five-Year Plan of China.

REFERENCES

[1] Bedell MA, Jones KH, Laimins LA. The E6E7 region of human papillomavirus type 18 is sufficient for transformation of NIH3T3 and Rat-1 cells. J Virol, 1987, 61:3635-3640.

[2] Cai L. In: Cai L(ed). The techniques in rescatch for nucleic acid. Science Press, Beijing,1987: 32.

[3] Cai L The application of detection for HBV DNA in the liver cell. In: Cai L(ed). The application of genomic engineering techniques in basic and clinic medicine. People's Health Press, Beijing, 1990: 191-192.

[4] Davis LG, Dibner MP, Battey JF. Calcium phosphate transfection of nonadherent and adherent cells with purified plasmid. In Basic methods in molecular biology. Elsevier, 1986: 286-289.

[5] Fraenkel-Conrat H, Kimball PC, Levy JA. Retroviridae. In: Fraenkel-Conrat H, Kimball PC, Levy JA(eds) Virology, 2nd edn. Prentice Hall, Englewood Cliffs, New Jersey, 1988;108-125.

[6] Fukushima M, Okagaki T, Twiggs LB, Clark BA, Zachow KR, Ostrow RS, Faras AJ. Histological types of carcinoma of the uterine cervix and the detectability of human papilloma virus DNA. Cancer Res, 1985, 45;3252-3255.

[7] GaoH, Si J, Lee K, Han R, Wang S, Gu S, Zeng Y, Zhou Y, Wang Y. Detection of human papillomavirus DNA in cervical carcinoma cells in Chinese patients. Acta Acad Med Sin, 1988,10:276-278.

[8] Hausen H zur. Genital papillomavirus infection. In: Rigby PWJ, Wilkie NM * eds(Viruses and cancer. Cambridge University Press, 1985: 83-90.

[9] Hausen H zur. Papillomaviruses in anogenital cancer as a model to undersand the role of viruses in human cancer. Cancer Res, 1989, 49:4677-4681.

[10] Howley PM. The role of papillomaviruses in human cancer. In: Devita VT, Hellan S, Rosenberg SA(eds)Important advance in oncology. Lippincott, Philadelphia, 1989: 55-73.

[11] Ledley FD. Somatic gene therapy for human diseaseLBack-ground and prospects. Part 1. J Pediatr,1987, 110;1-8.

[12] Lee K, Bao J, Wang J, Zhao W, Liu S, Si J, Wang Y, Zhang W, Jiang J. Ultrastructural study of the morphogenesis of herpes simplex virus type 2 in organ cultured human uterine cervix and the interactions between virus and host cell. J Elec-

tron Microsc Tech, 1987, 7:73-84.

[13] Lee K, Si J, Han R, Wang S, Zhang W, Song G, Liu S, Chen L, Zhao W, Jia L, Sheng Q, Mai Y, Zeng Y, Gu S, Sun Y, Meng X, Zhou Y, Wang Y. An ultrastructural research for the relationship between human uterine cervical carcinoma and human papillomavirus: I. An electron microscopic observation on human genital condyloma and the morphogenesis of human papillomavirus in host cells: II. A combined gene molecular and ultrastructural study. In: Hashimoto H, Kuo KH, Lee K, Ogawa K(eds)Recent development of electron microscopy 1987. Nakanishi, Kyoto, Japan, 1988: 293-312.

[14] Mandel M, Higa A. Calcium dependent bacteriophage DNA infection. J MOl Biol, 1970, 53:154.

[15] Matlashewski G, Schneider J, Banks L, Jones N, Murray A Crawford L. Human papillomavirus type 16 DNA cooperates with activated ras in transforming primary cells. EMBO J, 1987, 6:1741-1746.

[16] Madashewski G, Osborn K, Banks L, Stanley M, Crawford L. Transformation of primary human fibroblast cells with human papillomavirus type 16 DNA and EJ-ras. lnt J Cancer, 1988, 42:232-238.

[17] McCance DJ, Kopan R, Fuchs E, Laimisus L. Human papil-lomavirus type 16 alters human epithelial cell differentiation in vitro. Proc Natl Acad Sci USA, 1988, 85:7169-7173.

[18] Noda T, Yajima H, Ito Y. Progression of the phenotype of transformed cells after growth stimulation of cells by a human papillomavirus type 16 gene function. J Viol, 1988, 62:313-324.

[19] Paeratakul U, DeStasio PR, Taylor MW. A fast and senitive method for detecting specific viral RNA in mammalian cells. J Virol, 1988, 62:1132-1135.

[20] Pecoraro G, Morgan D, Defendi V. Differential effects of human papillomavirus type 6, 16 and18 DNAs on immortalization and transformation of human cervical epithelial cells. Proc Natl Acad Sci USA, 1989, 86:563-567.

[21] Rigby PD, Rhodes MD, Berg P. Labelling deoxyribonucleic acid to high specific activity in vitro by nick translation with DNA polymerase I. J Mol Biol, 1977, 113:237-351.

[22] Si J, Lee K, Han R, Wang S, Zhang W, Song G, Liu S, Chen L, Zhao W, Sheng Q, Jia L, Mai Y, Gu S, Zeng Y. Gene molecular and ultrastructural studies on relationship between human squamous epithelial carcinoma of uterine cervix and human papillomavirus. Acta Acad Med Sin, 1987, 9:264-270.

[23] Si J, Luo W, Lee K, Han R, Tan B, Ling J, Zhang W, Zhao W, Liu S, Chen L, Jia L. Detection of human papill omavirus subgenomic fragments in the biopsies of Chinese cervical cancer cases. Acta Academic Medicine sinicae,1990, 12:136.

[24] Si J, Lee K, Han R, Zhang W, Tan B, Song G, Liu S, Chen L The identification of viral genome and subgenomic sequences in biopsies of Chinese patients. Acta Acad Med Sin(in press),1991.

[25] Southern E. Detection of specific sequence among DNA fragment separated by gel electrophoresis. J Mol Biol, 1975, 98:503.

[26] Standbridge CM, Mather J, Curry A, Buder EB. Demonstration of papillomavirus particles in cervical and vaginal scrape material: a report of 10 cases. J Clin Pathol, 1981, 34:524-531.

[27] Tsunokawa Y, Takebe N, Kasamatsu T, Terada M, Sugimura T. Transforming actvity of human papillomavirus type 16 DNA sequence in a cervical cancer. Proc Natl Acad Sci USA, 1986, 83:2200-2203.

[28] Weinstein IB. The origins of human cancer: molecular mechanisms of carcinogenesis and their implications for cancer prevention and treatment. Twenty-seventh G H A Clowes Memorial Award Lecture. Cancer Res, 1988, 48:4135-4143.

[29] Wigher M, Pellicer S, Silverstein S, Axel R. Biochemical transfer of single-copy eukaryotic genes using total cellular DNA as donor. Cell,1978, 14:725-731.

[30] Yasumoto S, Burkhardt AL, Doniger J, Dipaolo JA. Human papillomavirus type 16DNA induced malignant transformation of NIH3T3 cells. J Virol, 1986, 57:572-577.

[In《Cancer Res Clin》1991, 117:460-472]

Suppression of Human Nasopharyngeal Carcinoma Cell Growth in Nude Mice by the Wild-Type p53 Gene

CHEN Wei-ping[1], LEE Yang[1], WANG Hui[1], YU Geng-geng[1], JIAO Wei[2], ZHOU Wei-ya[2], ZENG Yi[1]

1. Department of tumor Virus and HIV, Institute of Virology, Chinese Academy of Preventive Medicine, Beijing 100052, People's Republic of China; 2. Guangxi Regional Hospital, Nanning, Guangxi, People's Republic of China

[SUMMARY] Wild-type and mutant human p53 genes were transfected into the nasopharyngeal carcinoma(NPC)cell line CNE-3. Tumorigenicity in nude mice showed that the tumor resulting from the cells transfected with the wild-type p53 gene grew more slowly and was smaller that from control CNE-3 cells. In contrast, the tumor from the cells transfected with the mutant p53 gene grew faster than that produced by cells transfected with the wild-type p53 gene and that produced by control CNE-3 cells. The results demonstrate that the wild-type p53 gene could inhibit the NPC cell growth in nude mice and the mutant p53 gene could enhance the NPC cell growth in nude mice. The p53 gene may also play an important role in the pathogenesis of NPC.

[Keywords] Nasopharyngeal carcinoma; Suppressor gene; Nude mice; Tumorigenicity

INTRODUCTION

The p53 gene is a nuclear protein. Because it is often overexpressed in transfected cells and can transform the primary rodent cells with oncogene ras, p53 has been suspected to be an oncoprotein for many years(Rogel et al. 1985). Recent studies showed that the wild-type p53 gene did not have a transforming function and, on the contrary, could inhibit the tumor cell growth. If the wild-type p53 gene mutated it would have transforming potential (Hinds et al. 1989; Finlay et al. 1989). Mutations of the p53 gene occur in many types of human tumors(Nigro et al. 1989). Baker et al.(1990) transfected the colorectal carcinoma cell lines with wild-type and mutant p53 gene. The results demonstrated that the wild-type p53 gene could inhibit cell growth in nude mice, but until now there has been no report on the p53 gene and its function in nasopharyngeal carcinoma(NPC) cells. In this work NPC cell line CNE-3 was transfected with wild-type and mutant p53 genes, and the tumorigenicity in nude mice was compared.

MATERIALS AND METHODS

Plasmids pC53-SN3(wild-type) and pC53-SCX3(mutant) were obtained from Professor Bert Vogelstein, John Hopkins University, USA; PAB 1801 mAb against p53 protein was obtained from Professor Lionel Crawford, Cambridge, UK; G418 and polybrene are the products of Sigma.

1. Cell line and DNA transfection: CNE-3 is the cell line established from a patient with metastatic nasopharyngeal carcinoma in the liver(W. Jiao, W. Y. Zhou, P. Z. wang, and Y. Zeng, unpublished data). The cells were cultivated in RPMI-1640 medium, 10% fetal bovine serum, 2 mmol/L 1-glutamine, 100U/ml penicillin, 100μg/ml streptomycin, at 37℃ in 5% CO_2. Plasmids pC53-SN3 and pC53-SCX3 were transfected into the cells by polybrene-induced DNA-mediated transfer previously described by Rhim et al.(1989), and then selected with G418 (500μg/ml) for 12 days until the control CNE-3 cell died completely. Cultivation of the cells was then continued with 100μg/ml G418. Cell colonies formed were counted.

2. Colony formation in soft agar: A 5-ml sample of cell suspension(2×10^5 cells/ml)in 0.35% agar was overlayed on a 60-mm dish containing a 0.6% agar base. The dish was incubated at 37℃ in 5% CO_2. Viable colonies were scored after 21 days.

3. Tumorigenicity in nude mice: Balb/c nude mice, 4 weeks old, were inoculated subcutaneously with 1×10^7 freshly trypsinized cells in order to determine tumorigenicity. Tumors were observed for 5 weeks. The speed and size of tumor growth were recorded.

RESULTS

1. DNA transfection and screening

Colony formation after transfection with wild-type and mutant p53 genes and selection of geneticin were compared(Tab. 1). The cells transfected with pC53-SN3 formed twofold fewer colonies than those transfected with pC53- SCX3. The number of colonies in soft agar were similar for the two plasmids and no significant difference was found. But the CNE-3-p53-wt colonies appeared 1 week later than those of CNE-3-p53-mt and the CNE-3 control.

Cell size and speed of growth in vitro were also compared and no difference was found between the cell samples. In order to identify p53 protein expression in both transfected and non-transfected cells, an indirect immunofluorescent assay(IFA) with PAB 1801 mAb against p53 protein was carried out. Fluorescent intensity showed that both wild-type-and mutant-p53-transfected cells could express detectable p53 protein. In contrast, p53 protein could not be detected in control CNE-3 cells with IFA(data not shown).

Tab. 1　Colony formation of CNE-3 cells

Cells	Colonies
G418 screening	
CNE-3	0
CNE-3-p53-wt	55
CNE-3-p53-mt	108
Growth in soft agar	
CNE-3	70
CNE-3-p53-wt	65
CNE-3-p53-mt	87

2. Tumorigenicity in nude mice

Samples of 1×10^7 cells were inoculated subcutaneously into the back of nude mice. Tumorigenicity was determined and compared. Tumor from the control cells and tumor from the cells transfected with the mutant type p53 gene appeared 1 week later, but the tumor from cells transfected with the wild-type p53 gene appeared 3 weeks later. Tumor growth speed showed significant difference among them(Fig. 1).

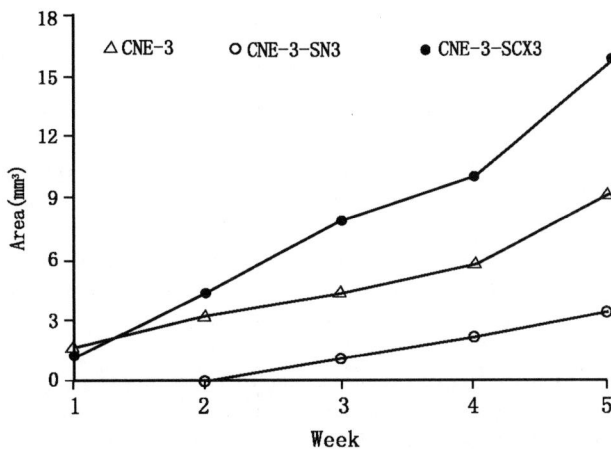

Fig. 1　Comparison of tumor growth speeds in nude mice. CNE-3, control cells; CNE-3-SCX3, CNE-3 cells transfected with mutant p53 gene. CNE-3-SN3, CNE-3 cells transfected with wild-type p53 gene. Initially the tumor resulting from the control cells grew a little faster than that of the cells transfected with mutant p53 gene, but 2 weeks later, the control cells tumor was growing significantly more slowly than that resulting from cells lransfeeted with the mutant p53 gene($P < 0.001$). In contrast, tumor from the cells transfected with the wildtype p53 gene grew more slowly than that of the control cells and that of the cells transfected with mutant p53 gene($P < 0.001$). The volume and weight of tumor at the 5th week are shown in Tab. 2 and Fig. 2. An approximately threefold difference was found among them

Tab. 2　Comparison of tumors in nude mice at the 5th week

Parameter	Origin of tumors		
	CIN-3-p53-mt	CNE-3	CNE-3-p53-wt
Volume of tumors(mm³)	15.7	9.33	3.50
Weight of tumors(g)	1.27	0.42	0.12

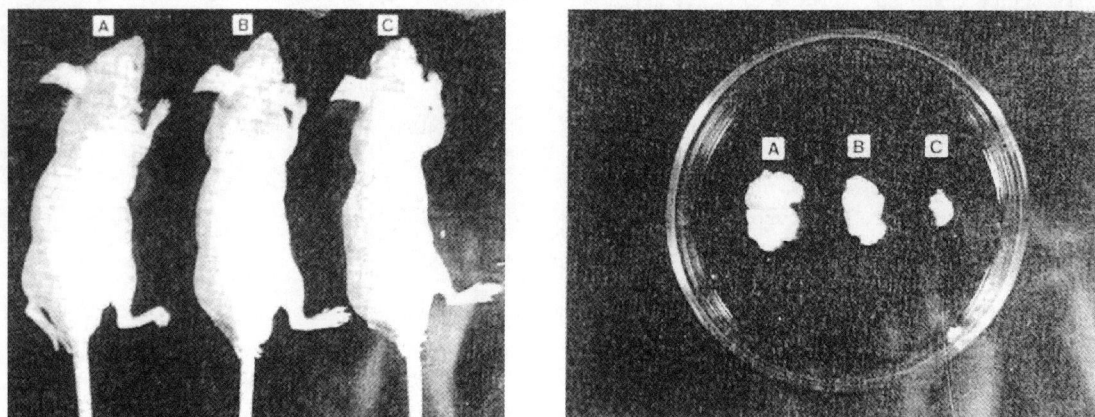

Fig. 2 Tumors in nude mice. A, CNE-3 cells transfected with mutant p53 gene; B CNE-3 control cells; C, CNE-3 cells transfected with wild-type p53 gene

DISCUSSION

In this work the nasopharyngeal carcinoma cell line CNE-3 was transfected both with mutant and wild-type p53 genes. The results of tumorigenicity assays in nude mice demonstrated that the wild-type p53 gene could inhibit cell growth in nude mice. This is the first report that the p53 gene can act as a suppressor gene in NPC cells.

Baker et al.(1990) transfected colorectal carcinoma cell lines with both mutant and wildtype p53 genes. The results suggest that the wild type p53 gene can specially suppress cell growth in nude mice and may act as a suppressor of growth of colorectal carcinoma cells; however, until now there has been no report of the p53 gene in nasopharyngeal carcinoma cells.

Mutations of the p53 gene occur commonly in many kinds of tumor such as haptocellular carcinoma(Hsu et al. 1991; Bressas et al. 1991), and colorectal carcinoma(Nigro et al. 1989). Whether or not hte p53 gene is mutated in NPC cells, deserves further study.

In cells transformed by simian virus(SV)40, adenovirus and human papilloma virus, p53 protein could form a complex with SV40 large T antigen, EIB 55×10^3 protein, and HPV E6 protein respectively(Lane and Crawford 1979; Linzer and Levine 1979; Sarnow et al. 1982; Werness et al. 1990). It may be a mechanism for the functional inactivation of the p53 gene.

Cang Wu County and Wu Zhou city of Guang Xi Autonomous Region in south China are highrisk areas for NPC. Seroepidemiological studies have shown that NPC development is related to Epstein-Barr virus (EBV) infection(Zeng 1985). The EBNA and LMP genes were found in NPC tissues. But the relation between p53 and EBNA or LMP is not yet clear. Further studies on this subject will be very helpful in the study of the EBV transforming function and in research into the molecular mechanism of NPC pathogenesis.

ACKNOWLEDGEMENTS

We thank Prof. B. Vogelstein at John Hopkins University, USA, for providing plasmids PC53-SV3 and PC53-SCX3, and Prof. L. Crawford Cambridge, UK, for monoclonal antibody against p53 protein.

REFERENCES

[1] Baker SJ, Markowitz S, Fearon ER, Willson JKV, Vogestein B. Suppression of human colorectal carcinoma cell growth by wild type p53. Science, 1990,249:912-919.

[2] Bressac B, Key M, Wands J, Ozturk M. Selective G to T mutations of p53 gene in hepatocellular carcinoma from southern Africa. Nature, 1991,350:429-431.

[3] Finlay CA, Hinds PM, Levine AJ. The p53 protooncogene can act as a suppressor of transformation. Cell, 1989, 57: 1083-1093.

[4] Hinds P, Finlay C, Levine AJ. Mutation is required to activate p53 gene for cooperations with the ras oncogene and transformation. J Virol,1989, 63:739-736.

[5] Hsu IC, Metcalf RA, Sun T, Welsh JA, Wang NJ, Harris CC. Mutational hotspot in the p53 gene in human hepatocellular carcinomas. Nature,1991, 350:427-428.

［6］　Lane DP，Crawford LV. T antigen is found to host protein in SV40-transformed cells. Nature，1979，278:261-263.

［7］　Linzer DIH，Levine AJ. Characterzation of a 54 kdalton cellular SV40 tumour antigen present in SV40-tranformed cells and uninspected embryonal carcinoma cells. Cell，1979，17:43-52.

［8］　Nigro JM，Baker SJ，Preisinger AC，Jessuo JM et al. Mutations in the p53 gene occur in diverse human tumors types. Nature，1989，342:705-708.

［9］　Rhim JS，Park JB，Jay G. Neoplastic transformation of human keratinocytes by polybrene-induced DNA mediated transfer of an activated oncogene. Oncogene，1989，4:1403-1409.

［10］　Rogel A，Popliker M，Webb CG，Oren M. p53 cellular tumour antigen: analysis of mRNA levels in normal abult tissuse, embryos and tumours. Mol Cell Biol，1985，5:2851-2855.

［11］　Sarnow P，Ho YS，Williams J，Levine AJ. Adenovirus Elb-58 kdtumour antigen and SV40 large tumour antigen are physically associated with the same 54 kd cellular protein in transformed cells. Cell，1982，28:387-394.

［12］　Werness BA，Levine AJ，Howley PM. Association of human papillomavirus 16 and 18 E6 proteins with p53. Science，1990，284:76-79.

［13］　Zeng Y. Seroepidemiological studies on nasopharyngeal carcinoma in China. Adv Cancer Res，1985，44:121-138.

［In《J Cancer Res Clin Oncol》1992，119:46-48］

A 10-Year Prospective Study on Nasopharyngeal Carcinoma in Wuzhou City and Zangwu County, Guangxi, China

ZENG Yi[1], DENG Hong[2], ZHONG Jian-ming[2], HUANG Nai-qin[2] LI Ping-jun[3],
HUANG Yu-ying[2], LI Yue[2], WANG Pei-zhong[4], de-The Guy[5]

1. Institute of Virology, Chinese Academy of Preventive Medicine, People's Republic of China; 2. Wuzhou Cancer Institute, Wuzhou City, Guangxi, People's Republic of China; 3. Zangwu Cancer Institute, Zangwu County, Guangxi, People's Republic of China; 4. Guangxi Autonomous Reginal Hospital, Nanning, Guangxi, People's Republic of China; 5. Institute Pasteur, 25, rue du Docteur Roux, 75015 Paris, France

[SUMMARY] Population ser-epidemiological surveys in Wuzhou City and Zangwu Cunty on South China established the value of the IgA/VCA and IgA/EA immunoenzymatic tests for an early detection of NPC at early clinical stages(I and II)in 87% of the cases, where radiotherapy ensures high survival rate(60% at 10 years, all clinical stages included). Furthermore such tests permitted to characterize the high risk group(IgA/VCA positive individuals) who are at more than 200 fold higher risk for later development of the tumor, than IgA negative persons. These data strongly support an etiological role of EBV in NPC pathogenesis.

INTRODUCTION

Serologic screening was implemented using an immunoenzymatic test in Zangwu County and Wuzhou city in 1978 and 1980 respectively, permitting an increase in detecting early clinical stages I and II nasopharyngeal carcinoma(NPC) from 18.6%-31.5% to 61%-88.8% respectively(Zeng et al 1980, 1982). Then a 4-year follow-up observation of EBV IgA/VCA antibody-positive persons was conducted in both Zangwu county and Wuzhou city (Zeng et al, 1983, 1988)leading to the detection of thirty-two new early cases of NPC increasing the early diagnosis rate to 91.5%. These results indicate that serologic examination of the anti-EBV/IgA/VCA antibody does greatly increase the early diagnosis rate of NPC. However, there were some remaining problems to be clarifed, since the EBV IgA/VCA antibody persists for long time. In such conditions, can the EBV IgA/VCA antibody test be used as an index for predicting the occurrence of NPC? To answer this question, continuous clinical and histologic follow-up observations on the EBV IgA/VCA antibody positive persons were carried out. Results of a 10 year follow-up observation are reported herewith.

1. Ten year follow-up studies of NPC in Wuzhou City

As shown in Tab. 1 and Tab. 2 1136 out of 20 726 orginally screened in 1980(aged over 40 years) were found positive for the an anti-EBV/IgA/VCA antibody immunoenzymatic test. Furthermore eighteen cases of NPC were originally found clinically and histologically confirmed, of which 16(88.9%) were at an early stage (I and II). Additional 29 cases were detected during a 10 year regular follow-up observation(1980-1990) among the IgA positive individuals regularly follows up, of whom 25(86.2%) were detected at an early stage of the tumor. Altogether, 47 patients were thus detected by serologic screening and follow-up observation, of which 41(87.2%) were at the early stage. In contrast, among 3374 cases of NPC which were detected in the outpatient clinics during the 1980-1989 period, without serological screening, only 873(25.8%) were at an early stage.

Tab. 1   NPC early diagnostic rate from serological screening and follow-up studies in Wuzhou City(1980-1990)

		Clinical Stage				Total	Early diagnostic rate
		I	II	III	IV		
Original screening,	No.	10	6	2	0	18	
(1980)	(%)	(55.5)	(33.3)	(11.2)		(100)	(88.8)
10 year Follow-up,	No.	5	20	4	0	29*	
(1980-1990)	(%)	17.2	(69.0)	(13.8)		(100)	(86.2)

（续　表）

| | | Clinical Stage | | | | Total | Early diagnostic rate |
		I	II	III	IV		
Screening, and	No.	15	26	6	0	47	
Follow-up	(%)	(31.9)	(55.3)	(12.8)		(100)	(87.2)
Patients out clinic							
without screening,	No.	27	846	2043	458	3374	
(1980-1989)	(%)	(0.8)	(25)	(60)	(13.6)	(100)	(25.8)

Notes：* Among those, 23(79.3%)were detected within five years after serologic screening and 6(21.7%)between the 6th and 10th year(one case). Furthermore 14(48.3%)showed a 4 fold increase of anti-Ebv/IgA/VCA antibody titer at time of diagnosis as compared to initial screening. The remaining cases showed no change or a fluctuation of only 2-fold in the antibody titer

Tab. 2　NPC patients from EBV IgA/VCA antibody positive and negative persons without follow-up

Serum No.	Sex	IgA/VCA titer at screening	IgA/VCA titer at diagnosis	Clinical stage	Time interval between screening & diagnosis
427	M	40	40	III	3　year
8797	M	10	<50	III	3
5839	M	80	40	III	3
1338	F	10	160	IV	3
9453	M	80	320	III	4
462	F	10	320	III	6
1280	M	<5	80	II	4
8483	F	<5	160	IV	5
11921	M	<5	20	III	6
13522	M	<5	<5	III	7

As seen in Tab. 2, there were 6 persons diagnosed as NPC and originally found to have EBV IgA/VCA antibody at serologic screening, but who lacked yearly follow-up. They were at an advanced stage when examined in hospital 3-6 years after original serologic screening. Among them, five were at stage III and one at stage IV. Three cases showed a 2 to 5 fold rise in the antibody titer. 2 cases showed no significant rise, and 1 case who had a titer of 1 : 10 at the time of serologic screening showed no detectable antibody when the diagnosis was established.

Beside, as seen in Tab. 3, four cases of NPC were diagnosed among the original EBV IgA/ VCA antibody-negative individuals group, who were not followed up. When the diagnosis was established, three cases had an antibody titer of 1 : 20-1 : 160 and one case had no detectabe antibody. They were diagnosed as NPC between 4 and 7 years after original serologic screening.

Tab. 3　Detection rate and incidence of NPC in IgA/VCA positive and negative persons

	Total	IgA/VCA positive	IgA/VCA negative
Persons	20726	1136	19590
NPC cases, No.	57	53(93%)	4(7%)
10 y detection rate (per 100 000)	275	4665.5	20.4
Yearly incidence (per 100 000)	27.5	466.5	2.0

To sum up, and as seen in Tab. 3, 57 cases of NPC were detected among 20 726 persons during a 10 years period, giving an NPC detection rate of 275/100 000, with an average annual incidence of 27. 5/100 000. Among them, 53 cases(93%) were detected among the EBV IgA/VCA antibody-positive individuals and only 4 in the IgA/VCA negative group, giving a NPC detection rate of 20/100 000 and a yearly incidence of 2. 0/100 000 in such a group. The difference in NPC risk between IgA/VCA positive and negative was 233 fold.

2. Survival rate of NPC after radiotherapy

A post-radiotherapy follow-up observation was conducted on NPC patients in Wuzhou City. Results are presented in Tab. 4. The 5 years and the 10 years survival rate of patients detected by serologic screening were 68. 7% and 59. 8% respectively, whereas, those patients undeted by serologic screening exhibited significantly lower survival rates(50. 9% and 32. 0% respectively at 5 and 10 years).

Tab. 4 Survival rate of NPC after radiotherapy(all stages)

Year	Survival Rate %		
	Original screened individuals	Non screened	Total
1	96. 49	88. 09	89. 68
2	87. 30	73. 79	76. 43
3	75. 54	59. 19	62. 45
4	71. 28	54. 85	58. 16
5	68. 69	50. 99	54. 62
6	68. 69	48. 02	52. 36
7	59. 83	44. 87	48. 00
8	59. 83	44. 87	48. 00
9	59. 83	44. 87	48. 00
10	59. 83	32. 05	39. 27

3. Ten-year prospective studies in Zangwu County

In the rural Zangwu county, serological screening was implemented in 1979 and 931 individuals with IgA/VCA antibody were also followed up for10 years, As seen in Tab. 5, the early detection rate of NPC markedly increased from 18. 6% to 66. 7% due to the serologicalcal screening and kept high(80. 9%)during the 10 years follow-up.

Tab. 5 Serological screening and follow- up studies on NPC Zangwu County(1979-1989)

		Clinical Stages				Total	Early diagnostic rate
		I	II	III	IV		
Before screening	No.	0	11	24	24	59	
	%	(0)	(18. 6)	(40. 7)	(40. 7)	(100)	(18. 6)
At time of	No.	5	5	3	2	15	
screening(1979)	%	(33. 3)	(33. 3)	(20)	(13. 3)	(100)	(66. 7)
During follow-up	No.	5	12	4	0	21	
(1979-1989)	%	(23. 8)	(57. 1)	(19. 1)	(0)	(100)	(80. 9)

As seen in Tab. 6, NPC could be detected 7 years after initial serologycal calscreening especially in individuals where IgA/VCA antibody titer increased, with development of IgA/EA antibodies up to 3 years to dignosis.

Tab. 6　EBV IgA/VCA and IgA/EA antibody changes and detection of NPC during follow-up in Zangwu

Name	Sex	Age	IgA Ab. titers	0	1	2	3	4	5	6	7	NPC stage at diagnosis
				(year of follow up)								
Pan	M	60	VAC	20	20	20	20	20	40	80		I
			EA									
Liu	F	40	VAC	20	20	20	20	10	160	160		I
			EA									
Li	F	52	VAC	20	20	20		20	40	40	80	I
			EA									
Pan	F	50	VAC	20	20	10	10	10	10	10	10	II
			EA									
Wu	M	48	VAC	20	20	20	20	20	80	160	160	II
			EA					10	10	20	40	

As seen in Tab. 7, when mean variations in IgA/VCA antibody titers were considered in the original IgA/VCA positive group of 931 individuals, the percentage of IgA/VCA antibo dy-positive persons either losing or showing fluctuating or having constantly low or stable titer or those increasing or declining their titer were 32.7%, 7.3%, 39.4%, 7.1% and 13.6% respectively. It is of interest that only two sub-groups were at high risk for developing NPC: (a) individuals who increased their IgA/VCA antibody titer by fourfold or more and who exhibited a22.7% chance of developing NPC; and (b) individuals who had stable IgA/VCA antibody titers with a chance of 1.6% of developing NPC.

As seen in Tab. 8, reexamination of 2300 EBV IgA/VCA antibody negative individuals at the 10th year after initial serologic screening showed that only 4.1% became positive.

Tab. 7　Relationship between increasing EBV/VCA antibody titers and development of NPC in Zangwu County

No. of Persons foll—owup(10 years)	Negative Seroc—onversion	Fluctuation	No Change	4X increase	4X Decline
931	304	67	367	66	127
(100%)	(32.7%)	(7.3%)	(39.4%)	(7.1%)	(13.6%)
No. of NPC	0	0	6	15	0
NPC detection rate			(1.6%)	(22.7%)	

Tab. 8　Positive seroconversion rate(from IgA/VCA antibody negative to antibody positive)10 year after initial screening

IgA/VCA Negative persons at original screening	IgA/VCA seroconversionant titers				Total
	1 : 5	1 : 10	1 : 20	1 : 40	
2300	47	40	4	3	94
Positive rate(%)	(2.0)	(1.74)	(0.17)	(0.13)	(4.1)

CONCLUSION

EBV IgA/VCA and IgA/EA antibodies were found to be very valuable markers for early diagnosis of NPC. More than 90% of NPC could be detected in the IgA antibody-positive individuals, especially when the IgA/VCA antibody titer increased and IgA/EA antibody developed. The clinical stage of NPC at diagnosis can be reversed and the 5 years survival rate was found significantly better in these early detected cases. According to both IgA/VCA and IgA/EA antibodies markers the risk of developing NPC can be predicted 5-10 years before clinical diagnosis of NPC. These data strongly support EBV virus playing an etiological role in the development of NPC.

REFERENCES

[1] Zeng Y, Liu Yuxi, Chun ren, Chen Sanwen, Wei Jineng, Zhu, Jisong, Zai Huijong. Application of immunoenzymatic method and immunoautoradiographic method for the mass survey of nasopharymgeal carcinoma, Intervirology, 1980,13: 162-168.

[2] Zeng Y, Zhang IG, Li HY, Tan MG, Zhang Q, Wu YC, Wang YS, Su GR. Serological mass survey for early detection of nasopharyngeal carcinoma in Wuzhou City, China Int J Cancer,1982, 29: 139-141.

[3] Zeng Y, Zhang JM Li, LY Yang PZ, Tang H, Ma TR Zh, JS, Pan WJ, Liu YX, Wei, ZN, Chen JY, Mo YS Li, EJ, Tan BF. Follow-up studies on Epstein-Barr IgA/VCA antibody positive persons in Zangwu county, China Intervirology, 1983, 20: 190-194.

[4] Zeng Y, Zhang LG, Wu YC, Huang NQ, Li JY, Wang YB, Jian MK, Meng NN. Prospective strdies on nasopharyngeal carcinoma in EpsteinBarr virus IgA/VCA antibody positive persons, Wuzhou city, China Int J Cancer, 1986, 36: 545-547.

[In《The Epstein-Barr virus and associated Diseases》1993, 225:735-741]

Urinary Excretion of Nitrosamino Acids and Nitrate by Inhabitants of High and Low Risk Areas for Nasopharyngeal Carcinoma in Southern China

ZENG Yi[1] , OHSHIMA Hiroshi[2] , BOUVIER Guy[2] , ROY Pascal[2] , ZHONG Jian-ming[3] LI Binjun[2] , BROUET lsabelle[2] , de The Guy[4] , BARTSCH Helmut[2]

1. Institute of Virology, Chinese Academy of Preventive Medicine, Beijing, People's Republic of China; 2. International Agency for Research on Cancer, 69372 Lyon Cedex 08, France; 3. Zangwu Cancer Institute, Zangwu, People's Republic of China; Unite d' Epidemologie des Oncogenes Institute Pasteur, 75724 Parts, France

[SUMMARY] The hypothesis that endogenous synthesis of nitrosamines from dietary precursors is a risk factor for nasopharyngeal carcinoma(NPC) in China was tested by applying the nitrosoprolint(NPRO) test to subjects living in high-and low-risk districts for NPC in Zangwu County, Guangxi region, in southern China. Samples of 12-h urine were collected from 77 subjects:(a) before any treatment;(b) after ingestion of proline; and(c) after ingestion of proline together with vitamin C. NPRO, other nitrosamino acids, and nitrate were measured as indices of exposure to preformed and endogenouely formed nitrosamines of their precursors. The NPRO level after proline intake was significantly increased in subjects from the low-risk area($P=0.012$)and markedly reduced after ingestion of ascorbic acid($P=0.007$), but such an effect was not seen in subjects from the low-risk area. Levels of N-nitrosothiazolidine-4-carboxylic acid and the sum of nitrosamino acids in subjects in the high- risk area were significantly reduced by ascorbic acid($P<0.01$)but were not reduced in subjects from the low-risk area. The urinary nitrate level was about twice as high in subjects from the high-risk area. In subjects from high-and low-risk area combined, NPRO levels in any of the three dose groups were highly correlated with nitrate levels($P=0.0001$). These results demonstrate a higher potential for endogenous nitrosation in subjects living in the high-risk area of NPC and suggest the occurrence of nitrosation inhibitors in the diet consumed in the low-risk area. Thus, in addition to infection by Epstein-Barr virus and genetic predisposing factors, dietary habits that may entail higher nitrosamine exposure appear to play a role in NPC etiology.

INTRODUCTION

NPC exhibits wide variations in incidence throughout the world; it is most common in China and southeast Asia, and among Magrebian Arabs in north Africa and Eskimos in the Arctic[1]. Risk factors for NPC that have been identified include genetic predisposition(HLA haplotypes)[2,3], infection by EBV, and environmental factors, especially food consumption habits[4-7]. Earlier studies have shown that some samples of Cantonese-style salted fish contain relatively high levels of volatile nitrosamines[8,9], some of which induce tumors in the nasal cavities of experimental animals[10,11] Recent studies in high-risk area for NPC in Tunisia, southern China, and Greenland revealed that these widely different populations all commonly consume preserved foods[12]. A study in GuangXi in southern China has shown that consumption before the age of 2 years of a number of presered foods, such as Cantonese-style salted fish, is strongly associated with an increased risk for NPC[6]. However, similar Japanese dried fish and vegetables were also reported to contain relatively high concentrations of volatile nitrosamines, but the incidence of NPC in Japan is very low.

We have searched, therefore, for additional hitherto unkown environmental risk factor for NPC and analyzed food extracts from high-risk areas for the presence of substances that activate EBV. Catonese-style soft salted dried fish and harissa, a Tunisian spice mixture, were found to contain agents with EBV-inducing activity[13]. Furthermore, our previous studies revealed that certain preserved food items contained high levels of precursors that, upon nitrosation in vitro, yielded volatile nitrosamines and direat-acting mutagens[14], suggesting that in vitro nitrosation could occur after ingestion of precursors and nitrosating agents in the diet. In the present study, we applied the NPRO test to inhabitants of high-and low-risk area for NPC in southern China to compare their endogenous nitrosation potential. The excretion of urinary mitrosamino acids and of nitrate was used as an index of individual exposure to nitrso compounds or their precursors, ingested in food or formed endogenously[15]

MATERIALS AND METHODS

1. Subjects and Sample Collection: Samples of 12-h urine were collected in the spring of 1990 from 77 healthy

subjects living in two villages in Zangwu county in the Guangxi region of southern China with contrasting incidence rates for NPC. The high-risk district had an incidence of NPC of 28/100 000/year, while for the low-risk district the corresponding figure was 2.9/100 000/ year[16]. These figures are taken from the local cancer registry, which was established in 1976. Characterisics of the study subjects who were selected at random are shown in Tab. 1. Three urine specimens were collected(for 12-h overnight starting 1 h after the evening meal)on three consecutive days from each subject according to the following protocols: (a) urine samples(groups H1, L1) were collected before dosing in order to determine the background levels of nitrosamino acids and nitrate; (b)proline specimens (groups H2, L2)were collected after subjects had ingested 300 mg L-proline 1 h after the evening meal; (c)proline plus vitamin C specimens(groups H3, L3) were collected after subjects had ingested 300mg L-proline together with 300 mg ascorbic acid 1h after the evening meal. Analyses of nitrosamino acids and nitrate were performed as reported by Lu et al.[17]. Study subjects were asked to complete a questionnaire to obtain information on demography, food items, beverages consumed, and number of cigarettes smoked during the urine collection period.

Tab. 1　Characteristics of study subjects

	n	Median age (SE)(years)	No. of	
			Smokers	Nonsmokers
High-risk district				
Male(M)	18	40.5(1.2)	12	6
Females(F)	19	39.0(1.4)	0	19
Low-risk district				
Males	20	48.0(2.9)	15	5
Females	20	44.0(3.5)	1	19
Comparison between low- and high-risk areas				
High-risk(M+F)	37	40.0(0.9)	12	25
Low-risk(M+F)	40	47.0(2.9)	16	24
P value of comparison		0.004	Nonsignificant	

2. Statistical Analyses: Because the distribution of the variables was skewed, nonparametric tests were used. Descriptive analysis included mecian and its standard error(SE in Tab. 1-3) as proposed in the BMDP software[18]. To compare the distribution of the concentration of nitrosamino acids and of nitrate excreted by inhabitants from high-and low-risk ares, a Wilcoxon rank-sum statistical test was used. In each area the differences between samples 1, 2, and 3 were compared using the Wilcoxon signedrank test for comparison of matched samples. Correlation between continuous variables was calculated using natural logarithmic transformation(to normalize the variables)or Box-Cox transformation[19] when the log transformed variables were still not normal. All the tests were two-sided, and the level of significance chosen was 5%.

Tab. 2　Median(SE of median)for volume of 12-h urine and for amounts of N-nitrosamino acids, and creatinine detected in urine

Urine sample from	Excretion of N-nitrosamino acids(μ-g/12h)			Urine volume (ml/12h)	Creatinine (mmol/12h)	Nitrate (mmol/12h)
	NPRO	NTCA	Sum[a]			
High-risk district[b]						
H1	3.90(0.87)	21.30(4.30)	33.30(5.25)	350(40.41)	3.18(0.40)	0.87(0.14)
H2	7.60(2.86)	39.30(10.71)	68.50(13.42)	300(28.87)	4.14(0.35)	2.01(0.31)
H3	3.40(0.84)	18.70(3.78)	28.40(4.50)	350(28.87)	3.65(0.40)	1.13(0.24)
P(H1 vs. H2)[c]	0.012	0.073	0.067	0.530	0.006	0.004
P(H2 vs. H3)	0.007	0.004	0.007	0.812	0.105	0.030
Low-risk district[a]						

（续　表）

Urine sample from	Excretion of N-nitrosamino acids(μ-g/12h)			Urine volume (ml/12h)	Creatinine (mmol/12h)	Nitrate (mmol/12h)
	NPRO	NTCA	Sum[a]			
L1	3.30(0.80)	23.26(4.11)	31.30(7.79)	300(28.87)	2.94(0.37)	0.62(0.10)
L2	3.17(1.24)	13.78(2.26)	20.10(4.59)	300(37.53)	2.82(0.30)	0.39(0.08)
L3	2.44(0.80)	13.33(3.00)	18.70(4.62)	250(28.87)	2.68(0.33)	0.45(0.07)
P(H1 vs. H2)	0.485	0.008	0.035	0.458	0.553	0.526
P(H2 vs. H3)	0.936	0.687	0.545	0.662	0.936	0.643
Comparison between areas						
P(H1 vs. L1)	0.930	0.839	0.819	0.751	0.693	0.027
P(H2 vs. L2)	0.090	<0.001	0.002	0.437	0.018	<0.001
P(H3 vs. L3)	0.495	0.737	0.340	0.078	0.210	<0.001

Notes: [a] Sum also includes N-nitrososarcosine and N-nitroso-2-methyl-thiazolidine 4-carboxylic acid(values not shown)

[b] Samples from undosed subjects(1). proline-dosed subjects(2). and proline-and vatamin C-dosed subjects(3)

[c] p values of comparison are also listed, with significant values underlined

Tab. 3　Medians(SE of mdeian) for volume of 12-h urine and amounts of N-nitrososomino acids and nitrate detected in urine(expressed per mmol creatinine levels)

Urine sample from	n	Excretion of N-nitrosamino scids(μg/mmol creatinine)			Nitrate(mmol/ mmol creatinine)
		NPRO	NTCA	Sum[a]	
High-risk district[b]					
H1	37	1.40(0.30)	7.79(1.72)	11.00(2.17)	0.41(0.07)
H2	37	1.83(0.47)	9.85(1.65)	15.30(3.35)	0.46(0.13)
H3	37	0.94(0.21)	4.51(0.62)	7.20(0.69)	0.41(0.09)
P(H1 vs. H2)[c]		0.225	0.531	0.656	0.307
P(H2 vs. H3)		0.018	0.018	0.032	0.422
Low-risk district[b]					
L1	39	1.09(0.16)	8.44(1.54)	10.60(1.36)	0.16(0.02)
L2	40	1.25(0.45)	4.23(1.69)	8.25(2.28)	0.15(0.04)
L3	40	1.21(0.18)	5.78(0.87)	8.15(1.96)	0.21(0.03)
P(L1 vs. L2)		0.413	0.046	0.120	0.597
P(L2 vs. L3)		0.872	0.619	0.773	0.350
Comparison between areas					
P(H1 vs. L1)		0.835	0.759	0.666	0.002
P(H2 vs. L2)		0.335	0.019	0.040	<0.001
P(H3 vs. 13)		0.771	0.318	0.714	0.005

Notes: [a] See Footnote a in Tab. 2.

[b] Urine form(1)undosed.(2)proline-dosed，and(3)proline plus vitamin C-dosed subjects.

[c] P values of comparison are also listed, with significant values underlined

RESULTS

The nitrosamino acids analyzed were NPRO, NTCA, N-nitrososarcosine, and N-nitroso-2-methylthiazolidin-4-carboxylic acid. The latter two are not individually listed but are inclued in the sum levels of all four nitrosamino acids. Tab. 2 summarizes urine volume, levels of nitrosaamino acids(μg/12h/person), nitrates(mmol/12 h/person), and creatinine(mmol/12 h/person) that were detected in the sixsets of urine samples. The volumes of the 12-h urine samples showed no difference between the two areas. Median urinary levels of NPRO, NTCA, and the sum of nitrosamino acids in the samples from undosed subjects did not differ between subjects from the high-and low-risk areas. Intake of proline(300 mg)increased urinary NPRO excretion by the subjects in the high-risk area from 3. 9 to 7. 6μg/day($P=0.012$)but did not significantly change NPRO levels among subjects in the low-risk area. Intake of ascorbic acid together with proline(300mg)by the high-risk subjects significantly decreased the urinary level of NPRO, NTCA, and the sum of nitrosamino acids($P<0.01$). This inhibiting effect was not significant in subjects from the low-risk area. The marked reduction of urinary excretion of nitrosamino acids after intake of ascorbic acid indicates that endogenous formation of these compounds was inhibited by ascorbic acid; this decrease provides an indication of an individual's nitrosation potential in vivo, which was found to be higher in subjects living in the high-risk area.

Since, for logisitic reasons, no 24-h urines could be collected, we determined the creatinine concentration in the urine and expressed the levels of nitrosamino acids per mmol of creatinine(Tab. 3). However, as shown before, endogenously formed NPRO is almost totally excreted within 12h[20]. Creatinine concentrations in the urine did not show any consistent difference between subjects from the two areas(Tab. 2). Comparisons of urinary nitrosamino acid levels, expressed per mmol of creatinine levels, led to essentially the same conclusions as for the uncorred values in Tab. 2, although some comparisons were not statistically different. For example, NPRO levels after proline intake did not increase when expressed per creatinine(H1：H2 in Tab. 2 versus Tab. 3). A correlation between creatinine and NPRO excretion has been observed earlier and could be attributable to an increased meat or protein intake[21]. However, the major findings presented in Tab. 2 are confirmed in Tab. 3; after proline intake, NTCA levels and the sum of nitrosamino acids were significantly higher in subjects from the high-risk area(by roughly a factor of 2). After ascorbic acid intake, the urinary levels of NPRO, NTCA, and the sum of nitrosamino acids were significantly re- duced in subjects living in the high-risk area, while no such reduction was seen in the subjects in the low-risk area.

The effect of smoking on urinary excretion of nitrosamino acids was examined. In the group 1 samples(undosed subjects), the amounts of either NPRO($P<0.01$), NTCA($P<0.01$), and the sum of nitrosamino acids($P<0.001$)were higher in smoker than in nonsmokers. In group 2(proline specimens)and group 3(proline plus vitamin C specimens), there were no statistical differences between smokers and nonsmokers. The proportions of smokers in high-and low-risk ares were similar(Tab. 1).

The urinary levels of nitrate per 12h or those corrected for creatinine are listed in Tab. 2 and 3. The nitrate levels excreted in subjects from the high-risk area in all three dose groups were significantly higher than those from the low-risk area. This approximately 2-fold difference remacined significant when nitrate levels were expressed per mmol of creatinine(Tab. 3). After Box-Cox trans- formation of data on urinary volumes from undosed subjects and those receiving proline, the urinary volume was positively correlated with log NPRO($P<0.01$); this positive correlation, however, became nonsignificant when the proline values were corrected for creatinine. The Pearson correlation coefficients(each at $P=0.0001$)between urinary levels of NPRO and of nitrate(both log transformed)were 0. 47 in undosed specimens(combined groups H1 and L1; 0. 67 in proline specimens[combined groups H2 and L2 (Fig. 1)], and 0. 42 in proline plus vitamin C specimens(combined groups H3 and L3). Similarly, in undosed specimens(groups H1 and L1 combined), log[sum of nitrosamino acids]versus log nitrate were correlated(r=0. 33 and $P<0.01$; Fig. 2). The linear regression lines(shown in Fig. 1 and 2)had slopes of 0. 75 and 0. 38, respectively. Recorded food items consumed by subjects during the day of urine collection included meat, salted and fresh fish, vegetables, and fruits. Each type of nutrient was poorly represented, and the relationship between the levels of nitrosamino acids and the amount of any type of food item could not be adequately analyzed.

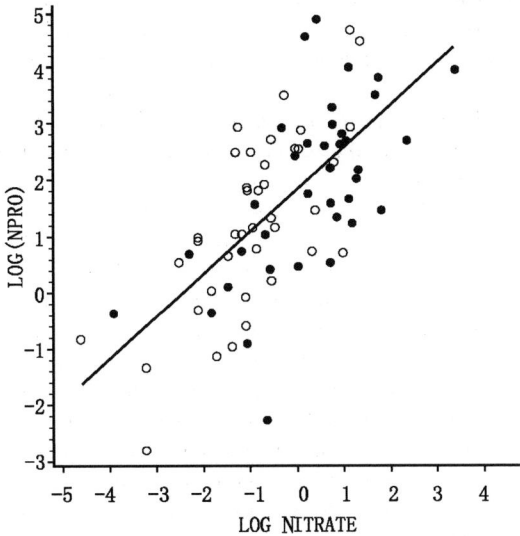

Fig. 1 A plot of log(NPRO) versus log(nitrate) concentration in the urine in subjects dosets with proline from high-risk(●) and low-risk(○) districts for NPC in southern China($r = 0.67$, $P < 0.001$). The corresponding linear regression line is shown

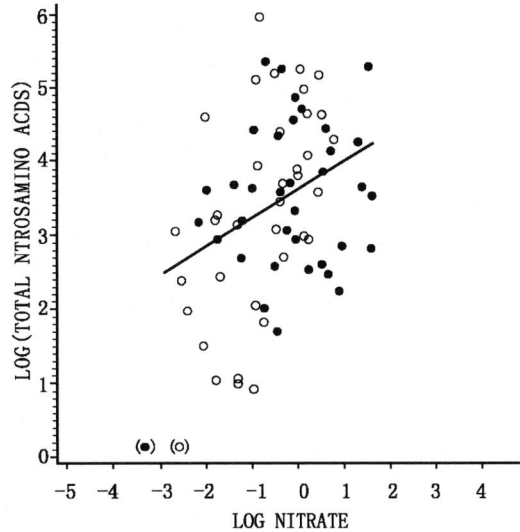

Fig. 2 A plot of log(sum of nitrosamino acids) versus log (nitratel concentration in the urine of undosed subjects from high-risk(●) and low-risk(○) districts for NPC in southern China ($r = 0.33$, $P < 0.001$). The corresponding linear regression line is shown. Two outliving points(in parentheses) with very low levels of mtrosamine acids were exduded for this analysis.

DISCUSSION

The NPRO test has previously been applied to subjects living in high-and low-risk ares for stomach cancer in Japan, Poland, and Costa Rica and for esophageal cancer in northern China[22]. In general, the nitrate exposure and potential for endogenous nitrosation, measured by the increased levels of urinary NPRO after intake of proline, were much higher in the high-risk populations. Furthermore, low-risk subjects may ingest sufficient amounts of protective agents to suppress endogenous nitrosation. Results from this study provide for the first time an indication that intragastrically formed N-nitroso compounds(or other nitrite-derived mutagens/carcino-gens) may be risk factors for NPC in southern China. The roughly 2-fold higher nitrosation potential that we have observed in the high-risk subjects appears attributable to their higher nitrate intake and lack of nitro- satin inhibitors that are probably present in the diet of subjects living in the low-risk area. Our study was not designed to enable us to pinpoint a particular food item that could inhibit nitrosation. Vegetables and fruits contain not only nitrate but other constituents as well, such as vitamin C and phenolic compounds which generally inhibit N-nitrosation. The subjects from the high-risk area, after intake of vitamin C, had a drastically lowered level of nitrosamino acids, and no such decrease was observed in subjects from the low-risk area. These results strongly suggest that nitrosation of dietary precursor compounds ingested by high-risk subjects may generate mutagens or carcinogens that play a role in the etiology of NPC. This hypothesis fits with the ealier suggestion by Ho[23], who proposed that risk factors for NPC involve an interaction between genetically determined susceptibility, early infection by the Epstein-Barr virus, and exposure to chemical carcinogens through the consumption of traditional preserved food, especially salted fish in southern China, from the weaning period onward. Since then, several case-control studies(4-7) have been conducted in southern Chinese living in different locations, and all of the results support Ho's hypothesis, that diet play a role in NPC etiology.

We have previously screened preserved food items that are frequently consumed in areas endemic for NPC in southern China, Tunisia, and Greenland for the presence of mutagens and volatile nitrosamines, before and after nitrosation[9,14]. The levels of preformed volatile nitrosamines(N-nitrosodimethylamine, N-nitrosopiperidine, and N-nitrosopyrrolidine)ranged from nondetectable up to $500\mu g/kg$ wet weight and was highest in hard salted and dried fish from China. After chemical nitrosation, 9 of 15 samples(aqueous food extracts)showed increased mutagenicity, and the levels of volatile nitrosamines were elevated in 12 of 15 samples; the highest level of N-nitrosodimethylamine was found in nitrosated extracts of hsrd salted and dried fish from China (1200μg/kg wet weight) and the highest N-nitrosopyrrolidine level in a nitrosated harissa sample (about 3800μg/kg wet weight). These two food item are among those that recent studies in high-risk areas have implicated as NPC risk factors. Some volatile nitrosamines induce tumors in the nasal cavity of experimental animals[10,11] and are therefore candidates for involvement in NPC etiology.

Our observation that nitrosation potential is increased in subjects living in a high-risk area for NPC implies that volatile nitrosamines could be formed in vivo at high exposure levels in subjects who ingest dietary nitrosamine precursors from early childhood onward. In fact, Yu et al[5].have shown in a case-control study on young NPC patients that consumption of Cantonese-style salted fish during childhood, especially between 1 and 10 years of age, is associated with NPC; the relative risk for weekly as compared to rare consumption, at the age of 10, was 37.7. It was estimated that over90% of NPC cases in Hong Kong Chinese under the age of 37 could be linked to consumption of salted fish during childhood. The nature and levels of nitrosamines and nitrite-derived mutagens formed after nitrosation of high-risk food items such as salted fish have not been characterized, apart from the three volatile nitrosamines mentioned above. Two animal bioassays have demonstrated the carcino-genic effects of Cantonese-style salted fish: Huang and Ho[24] reported that 4 of 10 female Wistar albino rats which consumed steamed Cantonese-style salted fish developed carcinoma (both adenocarcinoma and squamous cell carcinoma) of the nasal and paranasal regions, and Yu et al.[25] found nasal cavity tumors (squamous cell carcinoma, undifferentiated and spindle-cell carcinomas) in 3 of 74 Wistar-Kyoto rate fed powdered diet containing salted fish.

In order to identify additional risk factors for NPC, we have further analyzed food iterms consumed by inhabitants from areas of high NPC risk for the presence of substants that activate EBVin vitro[13]. We found that aqueous extracts of Cantonese-style salted and dried fish, and harissa, a Tunisian spice mixture, can induce EBV early antigen in latently infected Raji cells[13,26]. This activity may be important, since it is known that lgA antibodies against EBV viral and capsid antigen and early antigens reflect in vivo EBV activation; these are regularly present in NPC patients and appear in subjects before tumor development[27]. However, since EBV-inducing activity did not parallel either mutagenicity of the level of volatile nitrosamines in the food extracts investigated[13], we are now undertaking the isolation and characterization of EBV-inducing substances in food item that have been associated with NPC risk.

In conclusion, our results support the hypothesis that diet plays a role in NPC etiology, as indicated by case-control studies[28]; the latter consistently demonstrated that consumption of Chinese-style salted fish is strongly related to risk for nasopharyngeal cancer. Nitrite-derived carcinogens (fromed from dietary precursors) and EBV-inducing substance are also implicated as risk factors.

ACKNOWLEDGMENTS

We thank Dr. J. Cheney for editorial help and Mrs. Wrisez for typing the manuscript.

REFERENCES

[1] de Thé G. Epidemiology of the Epstein-Barr virus and associated diseases. In: B. Roizman(ed). The Herpes Viruses, New York: Plenum Press,1982, 1 A: 25-103.

[2] Simons MJ, Chan SH, Wee GB. Shanmugaratnam K, Goh EH, Ho JHC, Chau JCW, Darmalingham S, Prasad U, Betual H, Day NE, de Thé. Nasopharyngeal carcinoma and histocompat-ibility antigens. In: G. de Thé and Y. lto(eds.) Nasopharyngeal Carcinoma: Etiology and Control, IARC Scientific Publication. Lyon: International Agency for Research on Cancer,1978, 20:271-282.

[3] Lu SJ, Day NE, Degos L, Lepage V, Wang PC, Chan SH, Simons M, McKnight B, Esaton D, Zeng Y, de Thé G. Linkage of a nasopharyngeal carcinoma susceptibility locus to the HLA region. Nature(Lond.), 1990, 346:470-471.

[4] Geser A, Charnay N, Day NE, Ho H C, de Thé, G. Environmental factors in the etiology of nasopharyngeal carcinoma: Linkage of a casecontrol study in Hong Kong. In: G. de The and Y. lto(eds.), Nasopharyngeal Carcinoma: Etiology and Control, IARC Scientific Publication. Lyon. International Agency for Research on Cancer, 1978, 20:213-229.

[5] Yu C, Ho JHC, Lai SH, Henderson BE. Cantonesestyle salted fish as a cause of nasopharyngeal carcinoma: report of a case-control study in Hong Kong. Cancer Res, 1986, 46:956-961.

[6] Yu MC, Mo CC, Chong WX, Yeh FS, Henderson BE. Preserved foods and nasopharyngeal carcinoma: a case-control study in Guangxi, China. Cancer Res, 1988, 48:1954-1959.

[7] Yu MC, Huang TB, Henderson BE. Diet and nasopharyngeal carcinoma: a case-control study in Guangzhou, China Int J Caner, 1989, 43:121-138.

[8] Fong YY, Walsh WC. Carcinogenic nitrosamines in cantones salted-dried fish. Lancet,1971, 2:1032.

[9] Poirier S, Ohshina H, de Thé G, Hubert A, Bourgade MC, Bartsch H. Volatile nitrosamine levels in common foods from Tunisia, South Chia and Greenland, high risk areas for nasopharyngeal carcinoma(NPC). Int J Cancer, 1987,39:293-296.

[10] Druckrey H, Preussmann R, lvankovic S, Schmahl D. Organotropic carcinogenicity of 65 different N-nitroso compounds in BD rats. Z. Krebsforsch, 1967,69:103-210.

[11] Magee P N, Montesano R, Preussmann R. N-Nitroso compounds and related carcinogens, ln: C.E. Searle(ed.), Chemical Carcinogens, ACS Symposium Series. Washington, DC: American Chemical Society, 1976, 173:491-625.

[12] Jeannel D, Hubert A, De-Vathaire F, EllouzE, Camoun M, Ben Salem M, Sancho-Gamier H, de Thé, G. Diet, living conditions and nasopharyngeal carcinoma in Tunisia-a case-control study, lnt J Cancer, 1990, 46:421-425.

[13] Shao YM, Poirier S, Ohshima H, Malaveille C, Zeng Y, de Thé G, Bartsh H. Epstein-Barr virus activation in Raji cells by extracts of preserved food from high risk areas for nasopharyngeal carcinoma. Carcinoma(Lond), 1988, 9:1455-1457.

[14] Poirier S, Bouvier G, Malaveille C, Ohshima H, Shao YM, Hubert A, Zeng Y, de ThéG, Bartsh H. Volatile nitrosamine levels and genotoxicity of food samples from high-risk areas for nasopharyngeal carcinoma before and after nitrosation. Int J Cancer, 1986, 44:1088-1094.

[15] Ohshima H, Bartsh H. Quantitative estimation of endogenous nitrosation in humans by monitoring N-nitrosoproline excreted in the urine. Cancer Res, 1981, 41:3658-3662.

[16] Pan W, Wu C, Li L, Liao J. Analysis of the epideminologicaltrend of nasopharyngeal carcinoma: Cangwu county, Guangxi (in Chinese). Cancer(Phila), 1988, 7:345-348.

[17] Lu S-H, Ohshima H, Fu H-M, Tian Y, Li FM, Blettner M, Wahrendorf J, Bartsh H. Urinary excretion of N-nitrosamino acids and nitrate by inhabitants of high-and low-risk areas for esophageal cancer in northern China: endogenous formation of nitrosoproline and its inhibition by citamin C. Canner Res, 1986, 46:1485-1491.

[18] BMDP Statistical Software. B MDP, 1990 Re- lease. Los Angeles: BMDP Statistical Software, lnc, 1990.

[19] Box GEP, Cox DR. An analysis of transformations. J. R. Star. Soc., Ser. B(Methodol.),1964, 26:211-243.

[20] Stich HF, Ohshima H, Pignatelli B, Michelon J, Bartscn H. Inhibitory effect of betel nut extracts on endogenous nitrosation in humans. J Nat Cancer lnst, 1983, 70:1047-1050.

[21] Mirvish SS, Grandjean AC, Moiler H, Fike S, Maynard T, Jones L, Rosinsky S, Rosinsky S, Nie G. N-Nitrosoproline excretion by rural Nebraskans drinking water of varied nitrate content. Cancer Epidemiol., Biomarkers & Prey,1992, 1: 455-461.

[22] Bartsch H, Ohshima H, Pignatelli B, Calmels S. Human exposure to endogenous N-nitroso compounds: quantitative estimates in subjects at high risk for cancer of the oral cavity, oesophagus, stomach and urinary bladder. Cancer Surv, 1989,8: 335-362.

[23] Ho J H C Genetic, environmental factors in nasopharyngeal carcinoma, ln: W. Nakahara, K. Nishioka, T. Hirayama, and Y. lto(eds.), Recent Advances in Human Tummunology. Tokyo: University of Tokyo Press, 1971:275-295.

[24] Huang DP, Ho JH. Carcinoma of the nasal and paranasal regions in rats fed Cantonese salted marine fish. In G. de Théand Y. lto(eds.), Nasopharyngeal Carcinoma: Etiology and Control, IARC Scientific Publication no. 20, Lyon: International Agency for Research on Cancer, 1978, 315-318.

[25] Yu MC, Nichols PW, Zou XN, Estes J, Henderson B E. Induction of malkgnant nasal cavity tumors in Wistar rats fed Chinese salted fish. Br J Cancer, 1989, 60:198-201.

[26] Bouvier G, Poitier G, Poirier S, Shao Y M, Malaveille C, Ohshima H, Polack A, Bornkam G W, Zeng Y, de Thé G, Bartsch H. EpsteinBarr virus activators, mutages and volatile nitrosamines in preserved food samples from high-risk areas for nasopharyngeal carcinoma, ln: L. K. O'Neill, J. Chen, and H. Bartsch(eds.), Relevance to Human Cancer of N-Nitroso Compounds, Tobacco Smoke and Mycotoxins, IARC Scientific Publication. Lyon. International Agency for Research on Cancer, 1991, 105:204-209.

[27] de Vathaire F, Sancho-Garnter H, de Thé H, Pieddeloup C, Schwaab G, Ho J H C, Ellouz R, Micheau C, Cammoun Y, Cachin Y, de Thé G. Prognostic value of EBV markers in the clinical management of nasopharyngeal carcinoma(NPC): a multicenter follow-up study, lnt J Cancer, 1988, 42:176-181.

[28] International Agency for Research on Cancer. Some naturally occurring substances, some food items and constituents, heterocyclic aromatic amines and mycotoxins. lARC Monogr. Eval. Carting. Risks Hum., 56: in press, 1993.

[In《Cancer Epidemiology Biomarkers and prevention》1993, 2:195-200]

Environmental and Dietary Risk Factors for Nasopharyngeal Carcinoma: A Case-Control Study in Zangwu County, Guangxi, China

ZHENG Y M[1], TUPPIN P[2], HUBERT A[2] JEANNEL D[2], PAN Y J[3], ZENG Y[4], de The G[2]

1. Cancer Institute of Wuzhou 543002, Guangxi Autonomous Region, People's Republic of China; 2. Unit on Epidemiology of Oncoviruses, Pasteur Institute, 28 rue du Dr Roux,75724 Paris Cedex 15, France; 3. Nasopharyngeal Carcinoma Institrte, Zangwu, Guangxi Autonomous Region, People's Repubic of China; 4. Institute of Virology, Chinese Academy of Preventive Medicine, Beijing 100052, People's Republic of China.

[SUMMARY]　A case-control study was conducted on 88 incident cases of histologically confirmed undifferentiated nasopharyngeal carcinoma(NPC) in Zangwu County, China, and 176 age-sex-and neighbourhood-matched controls. The design of this study was defined after an anthropological survey on living habits in regions of high NPC incidence and the evidence of carcinogenic substances in some commonly consumed preserved foods. Subjects were interviewed regarding living conditions and diet in the year preceding the diagnosis of NPC and, with the help of their families, during childhood and weaning. After adjustment for a living conditions score to eliminate a confounding effect, an increased risk associated with consumption of salted fish during weaning and childhood was confirmed, especially for salted fish in rice porridge. The consumption of leafy vegetables was associated with a reduced risk for NPC, and consumption of melon seeds between 2 and 10 years of age with an increased risk. After multivariate analysis and adjustment according to the living conditions score, the consumption of salted fish in rice porridge before age 2($OR=3.8$, $P=0.005$), exposure to domestic woodfire($OR=5.4$, $P=0.01$) and consumption of herbal tea($OR=4.2$, $P=0.02$) were found to be independently related to the risk of NPC. The excess risk associated with the use of domestic wood fire increased if there were no windows in the house and with poor ventilation and cooking outside the house in a shack. As well as confirming the importance of the consumption of salted fish in childhood, this study has been the first to provide unequivocal evidence for two other factors implicated in increasing the risk of NPC in China, the adult consumption of traditional medicines(herbal tea) and exposure to domestic wood fumes.

INTRODUCTION

Nasopharyngeal carcioma(NPC) is common among Chinese(especially the Cantonese), with an age-standardised annual incidence rate of $30/10^5$ for males and $13/10^5$ for females(Muir et al.,1987); among the Maghrebian Arabs in North Africa(Parkin, 1986)($3.4/10^5$ for males and$1.1/10^5$ for females in Algeria); and among the Eskimos in the Arctic(Lanier et al., 1976)($10/10^5$ for males and $4/10^5$ for females). Elsewhere the incidence is low with an age-standardised annual incidence of less than $1/10^5$ reported in Europe and North America(Waterhouse et al.,1982).

The undifferentiated type of nasopharyngeal carcinoma(UCNT)seems to be associated with three aetiological factors: firstly, the Epstein-Barr virus(EBV), which is regularly present in the carcinomatous cells(Andersson-Anvret et al., 1978; see review by de Thé, 1982); secondly, a disease susceptibility gene, close to, but different from, an HLA gene, evidence for which was obtained in Chinese families with multiple NPC cases among sibs(Lu et al., 1990); thirdly, environmental factors associated with traditional preserved food(Ho, 1971; Geser et al., 1978). Several case-control studies conducted among southern Chinese have indicated an association between the consumptin of salted fish, especially during weaning, and the risk of developing NPC(Armstrong et al., 1983; Yu et al., 1986, 1989; Ning et al., 1990). More recent studies in China and Tunisia have suggested that the consumption in early youth of salted and preserved foods other than salted fish is also associated with an increased risk of NPC(Yu et al., 1988, 1989; Jeannel et al., 1990). ln addition, NPC has been found to be associated with low socioeconomic level and a traditional lifestyle, and some potential risk factors associated with a traditional lifestyle, including the use of domestic wood fires, have been proposed(Armstrong *et al.*, 1978; Geser *et al.*, 1978; Jeannel et al., 1990).

The present epidemiological study was part of a multidisciplinary NPC project(Hubert *et al.*,1993). The first step was to conduct an anthropological study in the three high-risk groups for NPC(Cantonese Chinese, Mahrebian Arabs and Eskimos) with the aim of identifying common or commparable factors which could be linked to this tumour. This approach provided detailed background data on food habits and lifestyle, and after a comparative analysis the conclusion was that traditional preserved food preparations could represent the common factors(Hubert *et al.*, 1993). Food samples were then collected in South China, Macao, Tunisia and Greenland, and laboratory analysis revealed the presence of volatile nitrosamines and reactivants of EBV(Poirier *et al.*, 1987; Shaoet al., 1988). Case-control studies were carried out in Tunisia(Jeannel *et al.*, 1990), in Macao(Hubert *et al.*, 1993), and in Wuzhou City and Zangwu County(China), presented here. The aim was to investigate simultaneously a broad range of socioeconomic and environmental factors as well as dietary history, with details of consumption frequencies and types of traditional food preparation which may increase the risk of NPC.

POPULATION AND METHODS

1. Area: The population of Wuzhou City is 170 000 and that of Zangwu County, a rural area, is 550 000, predominantly Cantonese Chinese belonging to the Han ethnic group. This area belongs to the Guangxi Autonomous Region, which had the second highest mortality rates of NPC among all the Chinese provinces(8.5/10^5 age-standardised male mortality rates). These areas were selected because of the facilities offered by the cancer register in Wuzhou and clinical units specialising in the treatment of NPC in wuzhou and the county of Zangwu.

2. Subjects: This study included all incident cases of undifferentiated NPC diagnosed and histologically confirmed from the starting date of 1 January 1986, until 90 cases were accumulated. Wuzhou cases were recruited at the Wuzhou Cancer Institute, providing the patients were residents in Wuzhou at the time of diagnosis. Zangwu cases were identified from the Nasopharyngeal Carcinoma Institute of Zangwu, which specialises in NPC detection. No other institution in Wuzhou or Zangwu could diagnose or treat NPC. Eighty-eight patients(29 in Wuzhou and 59 in Zangwu) were included in the case-control study. In each case, the area of residence was ascertained and two controis who agreed to participate were selected by the interviewers in the immediate neighbourhood. Matching criteria were sex, age(plus or minus 4 years)and place of residence. These controis were interviewed within the same week as the patients and in the same conditions.

3. Data collection: Interviews were conducted at home using the local dialect in the presence of the family members and particularly parents, as far as when ever possible. In China many family members often live under the same roof as an extended family, so it was relative easy to collect data on childhood diet and weaning from subjects' mothers whenever possible, or from the female relative who took care of the subject during infancy. For 60% of cases and 60% of controls one or both parents were household members. For the other 40%, anther relative who cared for the subject during youth was present. Only one case and four controls had to older relatives at home and data comcerning their youth were noted as missing. The six interviewers were physicians at the Wuzhou Cancer Institute and Nasopharyngeal Carcinoma Institute of Zangwu, and they participated in several clinical and epidemiological studies carried out by those institutes. These interviewers had been trained by our team's nutritional anthropologist(A. H.)especially for this study.

4. Lifestyle questionnaire: This questionnaire was prepared by the anthropologist in our team(A. H.) and was submitted to preliminary field testing; it requested information on past and present socioeconomic conditions, housing and diets. Data on lifestyle, including educational levels, marital status, place of birth, residential history, personal or family income, housing, types of fuel used, kitchen and toilet equipment and sleeping conditions, were checked for two periods: childhood and the year preceding the diagnosis of NPC. This second period was chosen to investigate adult habits immediately before the onset of disease and deterioration of health(for the NPC cases)while limiting recally bias. Data on diet covered fourperiods: weaning, childhood and adolescence, and the year prior to diagnosis of NPC reflecting adult diet, with the same periods for matched controls. For all food categories, except some spices and condiments, subjects were asked to choose between six frequency categories(1-2 times a day, 3-4 times a week, 1-2 times a week, 1-2 times a month, 1-2 times ayear or never). Food groups covered all dietary intake including drinks as well as methods of preparation and preservation and evolution of consumption over the past 20 years.

5. Statistical analysis: We used matched pairs and conditional logisitic regression to obtain for each study variable odds ratios(ORs) (estimates of the relative risk)and their P-value and95% confidence intervals. In order to adjust for socioeconomic variables, we estimated aliving condition score using variables from the lifestyle questionnaire indicating poor socioeconomic conditions found to be linked with NPC. The selection of such variables was monitored using a conditional logistic regression procedure. The score was established by weighting each selected variable by coefficients obtained in this way. For each food item, the OR was adjusted on this score. In each conditional logistic regression we inc2ued all variables associated with NPC with a P-value less than or equal to 0.2.

RESULTS

The 88 NPC cases were poorly differentiated or undifferentiated carcinomas. Four were stage Ⅰ according to

Ho's classification(Ho. 1971), 27 were stage Ⅱ, 44 stage Ⅲ and two stage Ⅳ; one subclassifiable case was unknown. Sixty-four(73%)of the patients were males, with a mean age of 41. 6 years(95% CI 31. 9-51. 3)for cases, and 41. 5 years(95% CI 31. 9-51. 3)for controis. The age distribution among cases was:15. 9% less than or equal to 30 years old, 32. 9% between 31 and 40 years, 34. 2% between 41 and 50 years, and 17% more than 50 years.

Two cases(2%)and ten controls(6%)were born outside the Guangxi Region, but all the cases and controls belonged to the Han ethnic community. There was no significant difference between cases and controls in their marital status or their level of education. Tab. 1 presents the sociodemographic variables linked with NPC and used to establish the living conditions score. The risk of NPC was higher for a monthly income between 101 and 200 yuan per month($OR = 3. 2$, $P = 0. 02$) and greater still for an income less than 101 yuan per month($OR = 5. 5$, $P = 0. 001$)as compared with income of more than 200 yuan per month(trend test. $P = 0. 001$). We included two further variables in the score: type of housing in childhood and lack of house windows during the preceding year, both variables having a weak association with NPC. There are clearly more NPC cases than controls with high score reflecting a low economic level($P = 0. 006$).

Tab. 1　Odds ratio(OR)for sociodemographic factors used to create a sociodemogrphic score

	Cases (88)	Controls (176)	Matched odds ratio(OR)			
			Crude analysis		Logisic model	
			OR	p	OR[a]	p
In childhood						
Type of houseing						
Apartment or single-storey house	28	66	1		1	
Rural dwelling	60	110	2. 5	0. 09	2. 3	0. 1
In year before diagnosis						
House windows						
Yes	80	169	1		1	
No	8	7	2. 8	0. 1	3. 1	0. 04
Monthly income(yuans per month)						
>200	10	43			1	
101-200	39	79	3. 2	0. 02	3. 5	0. 01
<101	39	54	5. 5	0. 001	6. 5	<0. 001
The sociodemographic score[b]						
0	5	29	1			
1-5	21	35	3. 5			
>5-8	24	69	2. 0			
>8	38	43	5. 1	trend test $P = 0. 006$		

Notes:[a]OR adjusted for the other factors, [b]This score was established by the sum of the three variables above weighting by coefficients obtained with a conditional logistic model

As shown in Tab. 2, concering the consumption of salted fish during the three studied periods of life, significant associations with salted fish in rice porridge were observed with monthly and weekly consumption duing the three periods, when adjusted for the living conditions score: weaning($OR = 2. 4$, $P = 0. 01$), before the age of 2 ($OR = 3. 5$, $P = 3. 5$, $P = 0. 006$)and between the ages of 2 and 10($OR = 3. 2$, $P = 0. 003$). Consumption of salted fish during the year preceding NPC was very low for both cases(2. 3%)and controls(0. 6%)and decreased significantly for both over the pasr 20 years.

Tab. 2 Odds ratio(*OR*) for nasopharyngeal carcinoma in relation to consumption of salted fish

| | Cases (88) | Controls (176) | Matched odds ratio (OR) | | | |
| | | | Crude analysis | | Adjustment for the score | |
			OR	*p*	OR[a]	*p*
During weaning						
Salted fish						
No	65	148	1		1	
Yes	22	23	2	0.03	2.4	0.01
Before the age of 2						
Salted fish(steamed of fried)						
Rarely	52	115	1		1	
Monthly and weekly	35	57	1.3	0.3	1.4	0.3
Salt fish soup						
Rarely	76	150	1		1	
Monthly and weekly	11	12	1.9	0.2	1.8	0.2
Salt fish in rice porridge						
Rarely	71	158	1		1	
Monthly and weekly	16	14	2.5	0.02	3.5	0.006
Between the ages of 2 and 10						
Salted fish(steamed or fried)						
Rarely	33	77	1		1	
Monthly and weekly	55	99	1.3	0.3	1.4	0.2
Salt fish soup						
Rarely	73	159	1		1	
Monthly and weekly	15	17	2.0	0.8	2.3	0.05
Salt fish in rice porridge						
Rarely	66	156	1		1	
Monthly and weekly	22	20	2.6	0.006	3.2	0.003

[a]*OR* adjusted for the sociodemographic score

Among the studies food items, consumption of the following foods and condiments during the preceding year was shown to be significantly associated with a reduced crude risk for NPC(Tab. 3): leafy vegetables, beef, monosodium glutamate(MSG). But after adjustment for the living conditions score, only the consumption of leafy vegetables remained associated with a reduced risk for NPC. Consumption of salted, dried or tinned foods such as meat, eggs or vegetables in brine was not found to be significantly linked with risk for NPC except for consumption of melon seeds during childhood before and alcoholic drinks were not found to be significantly associated with NPC risk. Furthermore, the use of wood as domestic fuel during the preceding year was shown to be associated with increased risk for NPC($OR=3.7$, $P=0.02$)(Tab. 3). After adjustment for the living conditions score, the risk associated with use of woodfire increased($OR=6.4$, $P=0.003$). Herbal tea drinking was associated with an increased risk for NPC before and after adjustment for score. In a multivariate matched logistic regression analysis taking into account the living conditions score, three variables remained significantly associated with NPC: use of wood as fuel, consumption of salted fish in rice porridge before the age of 2 and herbal tea drinking the year preceding diagnosis(Tab. 4). When considering separately urban and rural areas(Wuzhou City and Zangwu County), the independent risk factors in Zangwu County were consumption of salted fish in rice porridge before the age of 2 and herbal tea drinking in the year preceding diagnosis, whereas in Wuzhou City consumption of salted fish during weaning andmelon seeds between the age of 2 and 10 emerged as risk factors.

Tab. 3 Odds ratio(*OR*)for nasopharyngeal carcinoma by diet and environmental factors

| | Cases (88) | Controls (176) | Matched odds ratio(OR) | | | |
| | | | Crude analysis | | Adjustment for the score | |
			OR	*p*	OR[a]	*p*
In year before diagnosis						
Wood fuel						
No	8	31	1		1	
Yes	80	145	3.7	0.02	6.4	0.003
In childhood(2-10 year)						
Melon seeds						
No	74	163	1		1	
Yes	14	11	2.6	0.02	2.8	0.02
In year before diagnosis						
Beef						
Rarely	55	97	1		1	
Monthly	21	40	0.7	0.3	0.8	0.6
Weekly	12	38	0.3	0.03	0.6	0.3
Leafy vegetables						
Monthly	10	4	1		1	
Weekly	40	88	0.2	0.007	0.2	0.014
Daily	38	84	0.2	0.006	0.1	0.008
Monosodium glutamate(MSG)						
No	42	65	1		1	
Yes	46	111	0.6	0.05	0.7	0.3
Herbal tea						
No	55	130	1		1	
Yes	33	46	3.7	0.007	4.5	0.006

[a]*OR* adjusted for the sociodemographic score

Tab. 4 Odds ratio (*OR*) for nasopharyngeal carcinoma, 95% confidence intervals (*CI*), in a multiple conditional logistic regression model

	OR[a]	95% *CI*	*P*-value
Before the age of 2			
Salted fish in rice porridge (monthly and weekly)	3.8	(1.5-9.8)	0.005
In year before diagnosis			
Use of wood fuel	5.4	(1.5-19.8)	0.01
Consumption of herbal tea	4.2	(1.3-13.0)	0.02
Sociodemographic score	1.4	(1.2-1.7)	<0.001

Note: [a]*OR* adjusted for the other factors and the score

In Tab. 5, the risk for NPC of the use of wood fire was studied in conjunction with environmental factors which may modify the level of fumes. Absence of windows, poor ventilation and cooking outside the house in a shack increased the excess of risk for NPC associated with domestic woodfires with statistically significant trends.

Tab. 5　Odds ratio(OR) for nasopharyngeal carcinoma by use of wood fire associated with factors which may modify the level of fumes

Factor	n	No woodfire %	n	Woodfire%	n	Woodfire%	Trend test P
Windows in house				present		absent	
Cases	8	(21)	73	(34)	7	(54)	
Controls	31	(79)	139	(66)	6	(46)	0.008
Total(264)	39		212		13		
Crude OR(P)	1		3.6	(0.03)	7.8	(0.009)	
Ventilation				good		poor	
Cases	8	(21)	24	(32)	56	(34)	
Controls	31	(79)	50	(68)	95	(66)	0.01
Total(264)	39		74		151		
Crude OR(P)	1		3.1	(0.07)	4.7	(0.01)	
Kitchen				inside house		outside in a shack	
Cases	8	(21)	66	(34)	14	(45)	
Controls	31	(79)	128	(66)	17	(55)	0.01
Total(264)	39		194		31		
Crude OR(P)	1		3.4	(0.04)	5.9	(0.01)	
Window in the kitchen				present		absent	
Cases	6	(19)	59	(33)	7	(41)	
Controls	26	(81)	118	(67)	10	(59)	0.07
Total(264)	32		177		17		
Crude OR(P)	1		3.4	(0.008)	5.4	(0.06)	

Nosebleeds and buzzing in the ears, considered to represent early symptoms of NPC, were most frequent among cases(Tab. 6). Consumption of herbal tea in the year before diagnosis was more frequent for cases than for controls, but this association was not related to stage of NPC and it persistent when subjects with nosebleeds and buzzing(possible early symptoms of NPC) were excluded(Tab. 6). This indicates that the consumption of herbal tea was not a response to the onset of NPC. Moreover, consumption of herbal tea was not significantly associated with nosebleeds($P=0.3$) and buzzing ($P=0.5$). Consumption of herbal mixtures during weaning and childhood was associated with a relative risk of 1.8 after adjustment for the living conditions score, but the excess risk was not significant($P=0.07$).

Tab. 6　Relationship between consumption of herbal tea and non-specific symptoms of NPC and stage

	Cases		Controls		P	OR	P
	n	%	n	%			
For all cases and controls							
Herbal tea							
Yes	33	(37)	46	(26)		4.1[a]	0.01
No	55	(63)	130	(74)	<0.01		

（续　表）

	Cases		Controls		P	OR	P
	n	%	n	%			
Bleeding from the nose							
Yes	10	(11)	4	(2)		2.7[a]	0.2
No	78	(89)	172	(98)	<0.01		
Buzzing in the ears							
Yes	15	(17)	7	(4)		2.4[a]	0.1
No	73	(83)	169	(96)	<0.001		
For cases without nasebleeds and buzzing and their controls only							
Herbal tea							
Yes	22	(37)	35	(29)		3.6[a]	0.06
No	38	(63)	85	(71)	<0.01		
For cases in stage Ⅰ and Ⅱ their controls only							
Herbal tea							
Yes	14	(45)	16	(26)		6.01[b]	0.03
No	17	(65)	46	(74)			
For cases in stage Ⅰ and Ⅱ their controls only							
Herbal tea							
Yes	19	(33)	30	(26)		3.9[b]	0.07
No	38	(67)	84	(74)			

Note: [a] OR adjusted for the two other factors. [b] OR only adjusted for the score.

DISCUSSION

This study confirmed the role of consumption of salted fish as a risk facter for NPC and identified a specific risk associated with salted fish in rice porridge during weaning. Moreover, it established associations between the consumption of herbal tea, the use of domestic wood fire and an increased risk of NPC, and these were still significant after adjusting for a living conditions score and so were independent of socioeconomic status. These three risk factors were independently linked to an increased risk of NPC after selection by a stepwise logistic regression.

This study may be affected by some bias inherent in case-control studies, especially as data on diet taken almost 30 years ago were collected. To minimise recall bias, only close relatives who took care of the subject during youth were interviewed together with the subject. Recall bias due to cognition of disease status and risk factors should be minimal because no specific preventive campaign about risk factors had been conducted prior to the study in the area. This is also supported by the fact that among all the types of salted fish preparation investigated only salted fish in rice porridge emerged as a risk factor. The data on the frequency intake inevitably include a certain percentage of misclassification, particularly with older subjects recalling the past. If these errors can be assumed to be random and similar for cases and controls, they lead to an observed odds ratio closer to the unity than the true relative risk.

In previous studies, indicators of lower socioeconomic status and poor housing conditions were found to be positively associated with NPC in South-East Asia and Tunisia(Greser et al., 1978; Armstrong et al., 1983; Jeannel et al., 1990). Few studies have analysed the risks associated with traditional dietary risk factors while adjusting for socioeconmic factors(Geer et al., 1978; Jeannel et al., 1990).

Our results highlighted in Zangwu Region the importance of salted fish in rice porridge eaten during weaning and childhood as a risk factor for NPC, and the relative risk was even higher when adjusted for living conditions score. The salted fish is usually steamed prior to mixing with rice porridge, Similarly, a study performed in a low-risk region for NPC, Tianjin(China), showed that the consumption of steamed salted fish at the age of 10 years carried a higher relative risk than consumption of fried, grilled or boiled salted fish at the same age(Ning et al., 1990). Methods of cooking(duration, temperature, associated food)could have an effect on the amount and/or the activity of carcinogenic substances present in salted fish. Interestingly, the excess risk acquired during infancy persisted, although exposure to this risk factor dramatically decreased, with only 2% of cases and 0.6% of controls continuing to eat salted fish, whatever the type of preparation, as compared with respectively 43% and 33% in childhood. The apparent evolution of diet in the Zangwu Region, characterised by a large decrease in consumption of preserved food, fish as well as vegetables or meat, and its replacement by fresh products has not yet affected the risk in the generations concerned by this change, as shown by the persistence of a high rate of NPC incidence in Zangwu Region, but an effect may be observed in future decades. Regular consumption of leafy vegetables was associated with a reduction of the risk for NPC, as reported in other studies for other vegetables(Yu et al., 1989; Ning et al., 1990).

An increased risk was found for melon seed consumption between the ages of 2 and 10(especially in Wuzhou City, where this snack is sold on the streets). It would be interesting to investigate the presence of carcinogenic substances in this dried salted snack, and it should be mentioned that several reports on animal models for NPC have suggested aflatoxins as potential co-carcinogens(Levine et al., 1990).

Two factors, not well established before, were independently linked to the risk of NPC: using wood fuel during adulthood and drinking herbal tea. A positive association with occupational exposure to smoke and fumes or working in poorly ventilated places has also been reported(Lin et al.,1973; Henderson et al., 1976; Jeannel et al., 1990; Yu et al., 1990). In two previous casecontrol studies, patients with NPC used firewood for cooking more frequently than controls, but this association was not studied together with diet and not adjusted for socioeconomic level(Djojapranata & Soesilowati, 1967; Shanmugaratnam et al., 1978). In the present study, the risk associated with the use of wood fuel during adulthood was higher after adjustment for the living conditions score, and increased with lack of windows, poor ventilation or cooking outside in a shack. The lack of association during childhood is probably because everyone used firewood 40 years ago, as shown by our data. Thus, our observation might suggest the role of certain fumes in NPC deveplopment; this has been under discussion since a high incidence of NPC has been observed in Hong Kong boat people who cooked in the open air, and so were supposed to be little exposed to fumes(Ho, 1967). Thus, it would be interesting to investigate which type of wood and dried plants are for woodfire in the Guangxi Region. Besides, the amounts of 3, 4-benzpyrene(3, 4-BP) in smoke samples collected from a high-risk area were higher than those from a low-risk area(Kai-Tai et al.,1987).

Medicinal herbal preparations, such as herbal tea, are frequently used to prevent or to treat many diseases in China, and they have been postulated to be a risk factor for NPC(Zeng et al,1983). One could object that a more frequent use of herbal tea among cases could have been a consequence of the appearance of symptoms of NPC. This is not supported by the present data: there was no significant difference between cases and controls with respect to the evolution of consumption1 year before diagnosis compared with 20 years before. Furthermore, there was no association between the use of herbal tes and the presence of nasal discharge, nosebleed or buzzing in the ears during the year preceding diagnosis of NPC. Having no details on the types of preparation used by cases and controls, this point cannot be further evaluted. lt is interesting to note that several species of plants of the Euphorbiance family used in common Chinese herbal mixtures contain diterpene, an EBV reactivator and tumor promoter(Hirayama & lto, 1981; Zeng et al., 1983). But in Guangzhou, two members of the Euphorbiacese family(P. emblicaand C. crassifolius)used as herbal ingredients were not found to present a risk of NPC(Yu et al., 1990). ln Tunisia the use of traditional remedies in youth such as poultices of castor plant leaves(Ricinus communisL, Euphorbiaceae) was found to be associated with an increased risk of NPC(Jeannel et al., 1990). A study conducted by Hildesheim et al.(1992)in the Philippines suggested that if herbal medicines interact with EBV in the development of NPC, it is rather through a direct proliferative effect on EBV-transformed cells than through reactivation of EBV infection.

Furthermore, if we compare our results in Zangwu Region in China with that of a case-control study on 29 Chinese incident cases in Macau conducted by our laboratory using the same design and questionnaire, similar risk factors emerged: salted fish consumption before age of 2 years($OR=15.5$, $P=0.02$)($OR=15.5$, $P=0.02$)and fireplace in kitchen during childhood($OR=5.9$, $P<0.01$). Besides, it was interesting to note a protective effect associated with the use of powdered milk before the age of 2($OR=0.04$, $P<0.01$)(Hubert et al., 1993).

In summary, the data presented here confirm the role of environmental and dietary factors in NPC carcinogenesis. In addition to the known increased risk associated with early consumption of salted fish, this study pointed out that the type of salted fish preparation might be of importance. Moreover, the fact that herbal tea and use of woodfire appear to be risk factors opens a new area of research concerning the role of carcinogens and EBV reactivants of plant origin. When one considers the environmental risk factors associated with NPC in different parts of the world, one is left with the view that, besides EBV and genetic factors ethnic differences in lifestyle, particularly food preparation or consumption, remain the best aetiological hypothesis for explaining the geographical distribution of the disease.

We are grateful to the medical teams of the Cancer Registy of Wuzhou and the Cancer Unit of Zangwu Hospital for their active collaboration in the field study and Dr H. Sancho-Gamier and F. de Vathaire, Institu Gustave Roussy, Villejuif, France, for their methodological help in statistical analysis. We wish to thank Dr R. Bomford for his helpful review of the manuscript. This study was supported by the Chinese National Sciences and Technology Committee, the CNRS(SDI 5660, URA 1157), ARC contract 6071 and Virus Cancer Prevention.

REFERENCES

[1] Andersson-anvrest M, Forsby N, Klein G, Henle W. The association between undifferentiated nasopharyngeal carcinoma and Epstein-Barr virus shown by correlated nucleic acid hybridization and histo-pathological studies. In Nasopharyngeal Carcinvma: Etiology and Control. de Thé G, lto Y.(eds). IARC: Lyon. 1978, 20:347-357.

[2] Armstrong RW, Kannan Kuty M, Armstrong MJ. Self-specific environments associated with nasopharyngeal carcinoma in Selangor, Malaysia Soc Sci Med, 1978, 12D: 149-156.

[3] Armstrong RW, Armstrong MJ, Yu MC, Henderon B E. Salted fish and inhalants as risk factors, for nasopharyngeal carcinoma in Malaysian Chinese. Cancer Res, 1983, 43: 2967-2970.

[4] De The G. Epidemiology of Epstein-Barr virus and associated diseases. In The Herpes Viruses, Vol. lA. B. Roizman(ed.). Plenum Press: New York, 1982: 25-103.

[5] Djqjapranata M, Soesilowati S. Nasopharyngeal cancer in East Java(Indonesia). In Cancer of the Nasopharynx, Vol. 1, UICC Mongraph Series, Muir, C.S. & Shanmugaratnam, K.S.(eds). Munksgaard: Copenhagen, 1967: 43-46.

[6] Geser A, Charnay N, Day NE, HO HC, De The G. Environmental factors in the etiology of nasopharyngeal carcinoma: report of a case control study in Hong Kong. In Nasopharyngeal Carcinoma: Etiology and Control, Vol. 20, de Thé, G. &lto, Y.(eds). IARC. Lyon. 1978: 213-229.

[7] Henderson B E, Louie E, J1NG J S, Buell P, Garoner M B. Risk factors associated with nasopharyngeal carcinoma. N Engl J Med, 1976,295:1101-1106.

[8] Hildesheim A, West S, De Veyra E, De Guzman M, Jurado A, Jones C, lmai J, Hinuma, Y. Herbal medicine use, Epstein-Barr virus, and risk of nasopharyngeal carcinoma. Cancer Res,1992, 52:3048-3051.

[9] Hirayama T, Ito Y. A new view of the etiology of nasopharyngeal carcinoma. Prev. Med, 1981,10: 614-622.

[10] Ho H C. Nasopharyngeal carcinoma in Hong-Kong. In Cancer of the Nasopharynx, Vol. 1, UICC Monograph Series, Muir, C.S. & Shanmugaratnam, K.S.(eds). Munksgaard: Copenhagen, 1967: 58-63.

[11] Ho, H. C. Genetic and environmental factors in nasopharyngeal carcinoma. In Recent Advance in Human Tumor Virology and Immunology Nakahara, W., Nishioka, K., Hirayama. T. & lto, T.(eds) Proceedings of the First lnternational Cancer Symposium of the Princess Takamatsu Cancer Research Fund, University of Tokyo,1971: 275-295.

[12] Ho, H.C. Stage classification of nasopharyngeal carcinoma: a review. In Nasopharyngeal carcinoma: etiology and control, Vol. 20, de Thé, G. & lto, Y.(eds). IARC: Lyon, 1978: 99-113.

[13] Hubert A, Jeannel D, Tuppin P, De The G. Anthropology and epidemiology: a pluridisplinary approach of environmental factors of nasopharyngeal carcinoma. In: The Associated Epstein-Barr Virus and Diseases, Vol. 225, Colloque Inserm, Tursz, T., Pagano, J.S., Ablashi, G., de Thé, G. Lenoir, G. & Pearson, G.R.(eds). John Libbey Furotexi Ltd, 1993: 777-790.

[14] Jeannel D, Hubert A, De Vathaire F, Ellouz R, Camoun M, Ben Salen M, Sancho-garnier, H, De The, G. Diet, living conditions and nasopharyngeal carcinoma in Tunisia: a case-control study, Int J Cancer, 1990, 46:421-425.

[15] Lanier AP, Bender TR, Blot WJF, Hurlbert WB. Cancer incidence in Alaska natives, Int J Cancer, 1976, 18:409-412.

[16] Kai-Tai Y, Peng-nian W, Ji-Wen J.. The role of promotion in the carcinogensis of nasopharyngeal carcinoma. In Cancer of the Liver, Esophaus and Nasopharynx, Wagner, G. & Zhang, Y.H.(eds). Spring: Berlin, 1987: 187-193.

[17] Levine PH, Huang AT, Weiland L, Hildesheim A, Brizel D, Boyce cole T, Fisher S R, Panells T J, Jian J. Nasopharyngeal carcinoma: 1990. In Epstein-Barr Virus and Human Disease, Ablashi, D., Huang, A., Pagano, J., Pearson, G. & Yang, C.(eds). Humana Press: Clifton, NJ, 1990: 313-330.

[18] Lin TM, Chen KP, Lin CC, Hsu MM, Chiang TC, Jung PF, Hirayama T. Retrospective study on nasopharyngeal carcinoma. J Natl Cancer lnst, 1973, 51:1403-1408.

[19] Lu SJ, Day NE, Degos L, Lepage V, Wang PC, Chan SH, Simons M, Mcknight B, Easton D, Zeng Y, De The G. Linkage of a nasopharyngeal carcinoma susceptibility locus to the HLA region Nature, 1990, 346:470-471.

[20] Muir C, Waterhouse J, Mack T, Powell J, Whellen S. (eds). Cancerlncidence in Five Continents, Vol. 88. IARC: Lyon, 1987.

[21] Ning JP, Yu MC, Wang QS, Henderson BE. Conaumption of salted fish and other risk factors for nasopharyngeal carcinoma(NPC)in Tianjin, a low-risk region for NPC in the People's Republic of China. J. Natl. Cancer lnst, 1990,82:291-296.

[22] Parkin D M.(ed.)Cancer Occurrence in Developing Countries. Vol. 75, IARC: Lyon, 1986.

[23] Poirier S, Oshima H, De The G, Hubert A, Bourgade MC, Bartsch H. Volatile nitrosamine levels in common foods from Tunisia, South China and Greenland, high risk areas for nasopharyngeal carcinoma, Int. J. Cancer, 1987, 39:293.

[24] Shanmugaratnam K, Tyk CY, goh EH, Chia KB. Etiological factors in nasopharyngeal carcinoma: a hospital based, retrospective, casecontrol, questionnaire study. InNasopharyngeal Carcinoma: Etiology and Control, Vol. 20, de Thé, G. & lto, Y.(eds). IARC. Lyon, 1978:199-212.

[25] Shao YM, Poirier S, Oshima H, Malavielle C, Zeng Y, De The G., Bartsch, H. Epstein-Barr Virus activation on Raji cells

by extracts of preserved foods from high risk areas for nasopharyngeal carcinoma. Carcinogenesis，1988，9：1455-1457.

[26] Waterhouse J A H，Muri C，Shanmugaratnam K，3 others. Cancer Incidence in Five Continents，Vol. 42. IARC. Lyon，1982.

[27] Yu MC，Ho JHC，Lai SH，Henderson BE. Cantonese-style salted fish as a cause of nasopharyngeal carcinoma：report of a case-control study in Hong Kong. Cancer Res，1986，46：956-961.

[28] Yu MC，Mi CC，Chong WX，Yeh FS，Henderson B E. Preserved foods and nasopharyngeal carcinoma：a case-control study in Guangxi China. Cancer Res，1988，48：1954-1949.

[29] Yu MC，Huang TB，Henderson BE. Diet and nasopharyngeal carcinoma：a case-control study in Guangzhou China. lnt. J Cancer，1989，43：1077-1082.

[30] Yu MC，Garabrant DH，Huang TB，Henderson BE. Occupational and other non-dietary risk factors for nasopharyngeal carcinoma：a casecontrol study in Guangzhou China. Int. J Cancer，1990，45：1033-1039.

[31] Zeng Y，Zhong JM，MIAO XC. Epstein-Barr Virus early antigen induction in Raji cells by Chinese medicinal herbs，Inter-virology，1983，19：201-204.

［In《Br J Cancer》1994，69：508-514］

Establishment of a Human Malignant T Lymphoma Cell Line Carrying a Retrovirus-like Particle with RT Activity

LAN Xiang-ying[1] , ZENG Yi[1] , ZHANG Dong[1] , HONG Ming-li[2] , WHANG De-xin[2]
ZHANG Yong-li[1] , FENG Zi-jing[2] , TANG Mei-hua[3] , FENG Bao-zhang[3]

1. Institute of Virology, Chinese Academy of Preventive Medicine, Beijing; 2. Friendship Hospital, Beijing;
3. Institute of Hematology, Chinese Academy of Medical Sciences, Tianjin

[SUMMARY] We have established an IL-2 independent malignant lymphoma line(CM-1)from peripheral T lympho-cytes donated by a female patient with nervous system disease, the biological characteristics of CM-1 cells was studied in this paper, Another T lymphocytes, such as peripheral T lymphocytes donated by a male patient with multiple sclero-sis, could be transformed into a malignant lymphoma line by using filtered supernatant of the CM-1 cultured medium, thus the CM-2 cell line was established. The CM-1 and CM-2 cells were transplanted by subcutaneous inoculation into nude mice, and could cause the occurrence of typical malignant lymphoma. The observation of electron micrographs sug-gested the existence of virions in the CM-1 and CM-2 cells, and these virions were similar to retrovirus in the ultra-structure characteristice. It was found that this virus possesses reverse transcriptase activity. Results obtained from se-rological assay, molecular hybridization and PCR excluded the existence of other human viruses, which were commonly used in our laboralory. The unknown virus possesses strong transformation activity, and probably is a new retrovirus. Meanwhile, the work on the clone and sequence analysis of this virus are being carried out.

INTRODUCTION

Profound studies on human retroviruses led to the discovery that HTLV-I is the cause of adult T cell leukemi-as-lyphomas(Hinuma et al., 1981)and also related to some nervous system diseases(Gessain et al., 1985; Osame et al., 1987; Bartholomew et al., 1986). We had established the CL- 8 cell line from the blood cells of a Chinese patient with leukemia and demonstrated that is was the CL-8 cells harbour HTLV-I by immunological and molecu-lar biological methods(Lan et al., in press). We had also found the antibody against HTLV-I from five patients with nervous system diseases(Lan et al., 1993). So we attempted to determine if there are other retroviruses which are related to nervous system diseases and leukemias in China. Through ten years' hard working, we have established a human malignant T lymphoma cell line carrying a retrovirus from peripheral blood lymphocytes do-nated by a patient with nervous system disease(Lan et al., 1992; Hong et al., 1992). This unknown retrovirus is able to transform normal human T lymphocyte. Results are reported as follows.

MATERIALS AND METHODS

1. Establishment of the CM-1 cell line

The CM-1 cell line was derived from peripheral blood lymphocytes of a 36-yearold woman. She was admitted to the Beijing Friendship Hospital on 2nd February 1990 on account of limb paralysis for more than one month and coma for 4 days. On the next day, her body temperature went up to 39-40℃ and she was complicated with pneu-monia. After two weeks, the body temperature returned to normal, but she was still in a state of semicoma. At that time, 5ml venous blood was collected and the lymphocytes were separated by Ficoll-Conray gradient centrifu-gation, and cultured with RPMI-1640 medium and supplemented with 20% fetal calf serum(FCS)containing 1% penieillin, 1% streptomycin and 1% glutamine. The culture was incubated at 37℃ in 5% CO_2 atmosphere. No growth factor was used. The cell line thus established was designated as CM-1(Chinese malignant T lymphoma cel line-1).

2. Biological characteristics of the CM-1 cell

The growth and morphological characteristics of the CM-1 cells were directly observed under an inverted optic microscope,

The determination of CM-1 cell growth curve: The suspension of new passaged CM-1 cells with 5×10^4 cell/ml concentration was distributed into 42 small culture bottles with 3ml per bottle. The culture was incubated at 37℃ in 5% CO_2 atmosphere. Three bottles were taken out every 24 hours and the supernatant was aspirated out. The cells growing on the wall of bottles dropped after treatment with trypsin solution. The number of cells was counted. The procedure was carried out for 14 days without change of the medium. The growth curve was plotted.

3. Studies on the CM-1 cell surface marker

The CM-1 cell surface marker was studied by indirect immunofluorescence technique with 5 systems and 28 kinds of anti-leukocyte monoclonal antibodies.

（1）Target cell：the CM-1 ceils and the CM-1 clones.

（2）Monoclonal antibodies against the leucocyte：

a. Monoclonal antibodies against T lymphocyte CD1，DC2，CD3，CD4，CD5，CD6，CD7，CD8，CD27.

b. Monoclonal antibodies against the activated lymphocyte，CD25，CD71，HLA-DR.

c. Monoclonal antibodies against myelocyte CD11(B)，CD13，CD15，CD33，CD15(H198).

d. Monoclonal antibodies against B lymphocyte CD9，CD19，CD20，CD21，CD22，CD10(CALLA)，Smig.

e. Monoclonal antibodies against other leukocyte CD38，CD45，CD45R，HLA-1.

4. Establishment of the CM-2 cell line

The suspension of new passaged CM-1 cells was frozen and thawed three times, and then was centrifugalized at 3000r/min for 10 min. The supernatant was passed through a 0.45μm filter. The peripheral blood from a 67-year-old woman with multiple sclerosis was treated by the same process as mentioned above. T lymphocyte was cultured at 37℃ in 5% CO_2 atmosphere with RPMI-1640 medium supplemented with 20% FCS(1% penicillin G, 1% streptomycin and 1% glutamine), the filtered supernatant of 1/10 volume, 5μg PHA and 20 U/ml IL-2 was added into the medium. The cell line thus established was designated as CM-2(Chinese malignant T lymphocyte cell line-2).

5. Studies on tumorigenesis in nude mice

The suspensions of new passaged CM-1 and CM-2 cells were separately collected and centrifugalizad at 2000r/min for 10 min. The pellet was resuspended in a small volume. The 2×10^7 cells of CM-1 and of CM-2 cells were separately transplanted into nude mice by subcutaneous inoculation, the mice were reared and preserved.

The tumors were taken out of the mice and cut into the size of $1 \times 1 \times 1$mm, and were transplanted into new nude mice again, thus the tumor was subcultured as such.

6. Electron microscopy

The subcultured CM-1 and CM-2 cells and the cells of CM-1 and CM-2 that were separately induced by 5μg/ml PHA and 25ng/ml TPA for 48-72 hours, were separately collected and centrifugalized at 1000r/min for 10 min. The pellets were fixed with 4% glutaraldehyde and 1% OsO_4, and were embedded in cpoxyresin(Epon 618). Ultrathin sections were nade by using an ultramicrotome(LKB NOVE), then were stained with uranyl acetate and lead citrate. Electron micrographs were tahen with a JEM 1200EX electron microscope.

7. Viral identification and assay

A. Serological Assay

a. CM-1 cells acted as target cells, and were tested for antibodies against some known viruses by indirect immunofluorescence technique with standard antisera against these viruses.

b. 0.1ml cells(CM-2 cells, MT-2 cells carrying HTLV-I, MT-4 cells infected by HIV-1 and B9-58 cells carrying EBV)were separately placed on the microscope slide, and fixed by cold acetone at -20℃ for 15 min, and dried in air. 0.1 ml of diluted serum or cerbrospinal fluid(CSF)of CM-1 donor was added on the slide, incubated at 37℃ for 45 min, washed three times in the washing solution(10 mmol/L pH7.4 PBS, 0.01% Triton X-100). 0.05ml fluorescein-labelled mouse anti-human IgG diluted in 0.01% Even's blue was added, incubated at 37℃ for 30 min, washed three times, observed under the Olympus fluorescence microscope.

c. The serum and cerebrospinal fluid were tested for HIV-1 antibody by Western blot method with the standard kit(Bio-Rad).

B. Test for the Viral Genes in the CM-1 Cells

The suspension of subcultured CM-1 cells and the whole blood cells of the CM-1 cell donor in convalescent phase were collected and centrifugalized. The cell DNA was extracted by phenolchloroform.

a. Probe Hybridization

The cell DNA was digested and cleaved by Hing Ⅲ and tested for genes of some known viruses with Southern-blot method. The probes include W-fragment, LMP gene and EBNA-1 gene of EBV DNA, and labelled by ^{32}p-dCTP with nick-translation method.

b. Test for HIV-1 and HTLV-I Genes with PCR

The concentration of CM-1 cell DNA was 0.1μg/ml, the primer for HIV-1 was gag-pol, and the primer for HTLV-I was gag-env.

After an initial 5-min denaturation ai 49℃, 30 cycles ao 95℃ for 1 min, 50℃ for 1 min, 72℃ for 1 min were performed(Perking, Automated Thermal Cycler), a final 7-min extension at 72℃ followed. The PCR products were analyzed by electrophoresis on a 4% agarose gel and the bands were visualised by ethidium bromide staining.

8. Purification of the virus and test for RT activity

A. Purification of the virus：The subcultured CM-2 ceils activated yb PHA and TPA for 48-72 hours were collected and centrifugalized at 3000r/min and 4℃ for 20 min. The supernatant was placed in a dialyzer and was concentrated by PEG(22 000) at 4℃, then was centrifugalized at 10 000r/min for 30 min to remove cell debris. The pellets of cells were suspended with a small amount of TNE buffer, the suspension was frozen and thawed three times, and then was centrifugalized at 10 000r/min for 30 min. This supernatant was combined with the concentrated supernatant and passed through a 0.45μm fiter. The filtered solution was centrifugalized ai 35 000r/min and 4℃ for 2 hours, in TFT70.38 rotor of the Kontron T-2080 ultracentrifuge. The pellets were suspended in TNE buffer to about 1/200 of the volume at beginning. 0.4ml of the concentrated prepatations were layered on the top of a 20%-60% sucrose gradients and centrifugalized at 50000r/mol and 4℃ for 16 hours in the Kontron TST 60.4 rotor. The gradients were collected dropwise(0.5ml per fraction) and the density of fractions were determined.

B. Test for reverse transcriptase activity: 50μl of each fraction was added into round bottom wells of 12-well plate. 50μl of disruption buffer was added into each well with the sample. The mixtures were incubated at 37℃ for 15 min. The components of disruption buffer are 100mmol/L Tris-HCl(pH 8.0), 300mmol/L KCl, 10mmol/L DTT and 0.1% Triton X-100. Twenty-five μl of reaction mixture was added into each well. The mixtures were incubated at 37℃ for 20 hours. The components of the reaction mixture are 50mmol/L Tris-HCl (pH 8.0), 150mmol/L KCl, 12mmol/L $MgCl_2$, 5mol/L DTT, 0.05% Triton X-100, 50μg/ml Poly(rA):oligo(dT)$_{15}$ and 10μCi/ml ^{3}H-TTP. The reaction was stopped by adding 0.1ml of ice-cold 10% TCA and the reactants were placed at 4℃ for 20 min. The products of the reaction were collected with glass-fibre filters, and washed by 2ml of ice-cold 10% TCA twice and 2ml of ice-cold 95% ethanol once. The incorporated radioactivtity of the filters in the solution of liquid scintillation was ceasured with a liquid scintillation counter(Beckman LS-5000 TA).

RESULT

1. Establishment and biological characterization of the CM-1 cell line

On the second day, the cells grew very actively. On the third day, they could be subcultured. Since then, they were subcultured twice a week, and up to now they have been subcuhured in vitro for more than two years and their growth is still vigorous. CM-1 cells were preserved in liquid N_2, the rate of resuscitation was more than 90%.

CM-1 cells can adhere and grow on the wall of wares and dissociate continuously into the suspension. The adhered cells are polymeric and aggregate to form clumps.

After the CM-1 cell line was established, the blood of the patient in convalescent phase was collected. T lymphocytes were separated and cultured under the same condition as that in establishing the CM-1 cell line, but it was failed.

The growth of CM-1 cells in culture follows the patten depicted in Fig. 1. A lag following seeding is followed by a period of exponential growh(log phase, from the 2nd day to the 7th day). The amount of cells reached 2.5×10^6 cells per ml of medium which is 50 times more than at the start. The plateau phasc began from the 11th day. The CM-1 cells could survive on the 14th day. They could be subcultured by changing new medium.

Fig. 1 The CM-1 cells growth curve

2. Surface marker of CM-1 cells

The results of assay by indirect immunofluorescence technique with 28 kinds of anti-leucocyte monoclonal antibodies showed that characteristic marker of T lymphocyte was present on the membrane of all CM-1 cells, and 20%-30% of which also showed myclocyte marker.

All results are showed in Tab. 1.

3. Establishment of CM-2 cell line

After three weeks, clones of the cells were visible to the naked eyes(Fig. 2). The cells could be subcultured and a continuous cell line was established designated as CM-2. The characteristics and morphology were the same as those of the CM-1 cells. The control lymphocytes without the filtered supernatant of the cultured CM-1 cells were all broken and dead three weeks later.

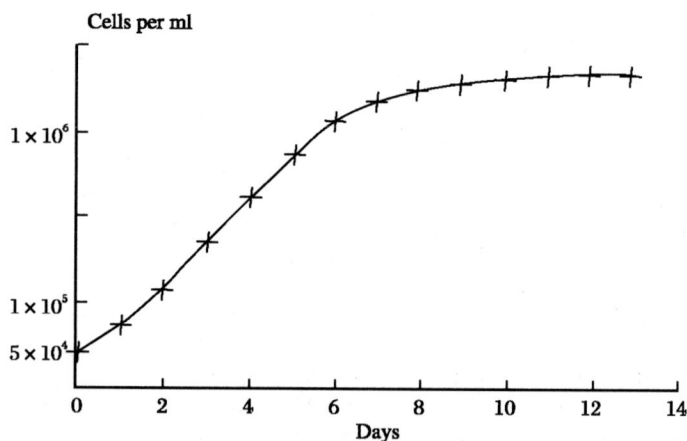

Tab. 1 Analysis of the surface markers of CM-1 cells and clonal cell lines by antileukocyte monoclonal antibodies(McAbs)

McAbs	Kinds of cells				
	CM-1	Colony5	Colony9	Colony A-30	Suspended Colony 3
CD1	0	NT	NT	NT	NT
CD2	59	NT	NT	NT	NT
CD3	25	90	<5	46	90
CD4	>90	>90	NT	90	>90
CD5	>90	>90	>90	>90	>90
CD6	0	NT	NT	NT	NT
CD7	>90	>90	>90	>90	>90
CD8	0	NT	NT	NT	NT
CD27	95	NT	NT	NT	NT
CD25	0	NT	NT	NT	NT
CD71	95	>90	NT	>90	>90
HLA-DR	0	0	0	0	0
CD11(B)	0	NT	NT	NT	NT
CD13	<5	NT	NT	NT	NT
CD14	0	NT	NT	NT	NT
CD33	0	<10	<5	<12	0
CD15(H198)	34	4	16	17	10
CD10(CALLA)	>95	>90	>90	>90	>90
CD9	>95	NT	NT	NT	NT
CD19	0	0	0	0	<5
CD20	0	NT	NT	NT	NT
CD21	0	NT	NT	NT	NT
CD22	0	NT	NT	NT	NT
Smig	0	NT	NT	NT	NT
CD38	100	NT	NT	NT	NT
CD45	100	NT	NT	NT	NT
CD45R	<10	NT	NT	NT	NT
HLA-1	>95	NT	NT	NT	NT

NT: no test

4. Tumorigenic result

After the CM-1 cells were transplanted into nude mice by subcutaneous inoculation, the tumors grew in the size of $5 \times 7 \times 3$ mm about 10 weeks later. The histopathological section showed that the tumor was a typical malignant T lymphoma.

The cultured cells of CM-2 were transplanted into nude mice by subcutaneous inoculation. The tumors appeared in 75% of the mice 4-5 weeks later, and grew in size to $5 \times 6 \times 4$ mm about 10 weeks later(Fig. 3). The histopathological section showed that the tumor caused by CM-2 cells was also a typical malignant lymphocytoma.

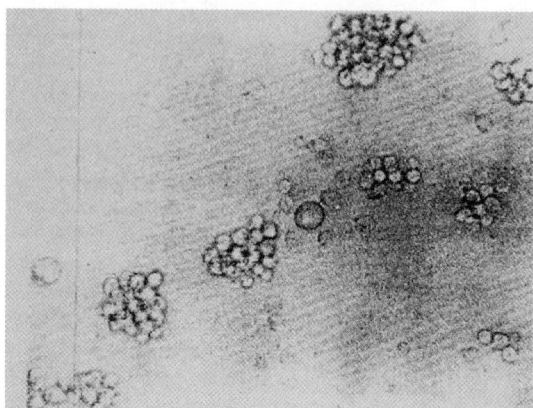

Fig. 2   The picture of clones of the CM-2 cells

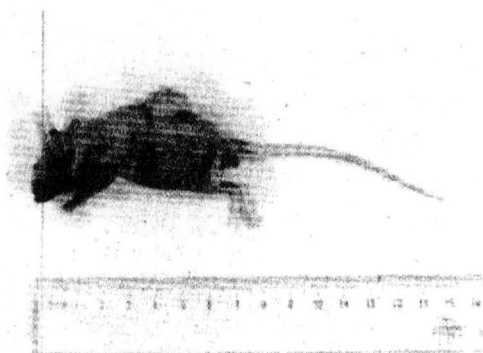

Fig. 3   The picture 0f the nude mouse with T malignant lymphoma caused by the CM-2 cells

The tumors were subcutaneously transplanted into the new nude mice again, the tumors grew in all of the mice 7-8 weeks later. The growth period of the tumor was shortened. Up to now a tumor of nude mouse has been subcultured for six generations (more than one year).

5.Electron micrograph

The clectron micrograph of the ultrathin section of the CM-1 cells showed the following facts.

The CM-1 cell was poorly difierentiated, and Was polynuclear. The endoplasma reticulurn was found thickened. Some globular virus particles of 80-120nm in diameter were found in the cytoplasm, with big and loose nucleoid substance in the center. The diameter was similar to that of human retrovirus. The electron micrograph(Fig. 4)shows that a mature virus particle Was releasing by means of budding.

The size of CM-2 cells was 9-15μm in diameter, and the diameter of a few cells was more than 20μm.

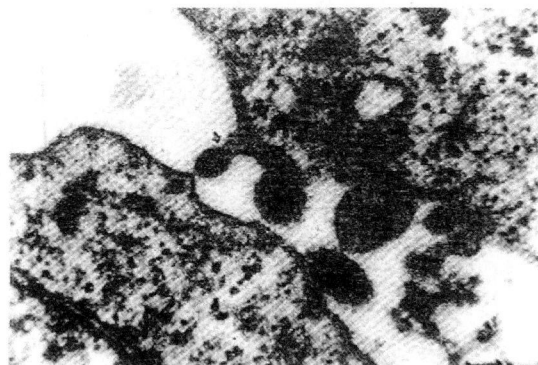

Fig. 4   The micrograph of ultrathin section of the CM-1 cell Arrow shows a virus particle budding from cytomembrane.(Bai:100 nm)

The nucleus of CM-2 cells appeared polymorphic. The main part of endoplasma was incarnation. Abundant nucleoprotein was found in the cytoplasm. Growth annulate lemmas were found in some of the CM-2 cells, and this phenomenon usually appears in malignant cells of tumor.

The vesicles of rough-surfaced endoplasmic reticulum(RER)enlarged, and most of them enclosed viral particles(Fig. 5-A). This is a characteristic feature of the CM-2 cells. Not only globular viral particles, but also some coalescence of two or more viral particles were found(Fig. 5-B). This virus released by means of budding out from cytomembrane or budding from RER membrane into the cistern of RER. There were some clumps of electronic dense granular substance, which usually located next to RER, in the cytoplasm. Viral particles budded from these clumps into the cisterns of RER(Fig. 6). These clumps possibly were viral matrixes created when viruses grew in cytoplasm.

The quantity of viruses was more in the induced cells than in the non-induced cells. The quantity of virus in the CM-2 was obviously more than in CM-1.

The particles looked like type C virus. The globular particle had two layers of membranous structure(like capsule and nucleocapsid)enclosing a electronic dense nucleus near the center(Fig. 7), there were also many viruses without dense nucleus. But in the cistern a lot of particles without dense nucleus were found, and only in a few particles the dotted dense nucleus was found. The size of the viral particle is 68. 3-94. 3nm in diameter, with an average about 81. 2nm.

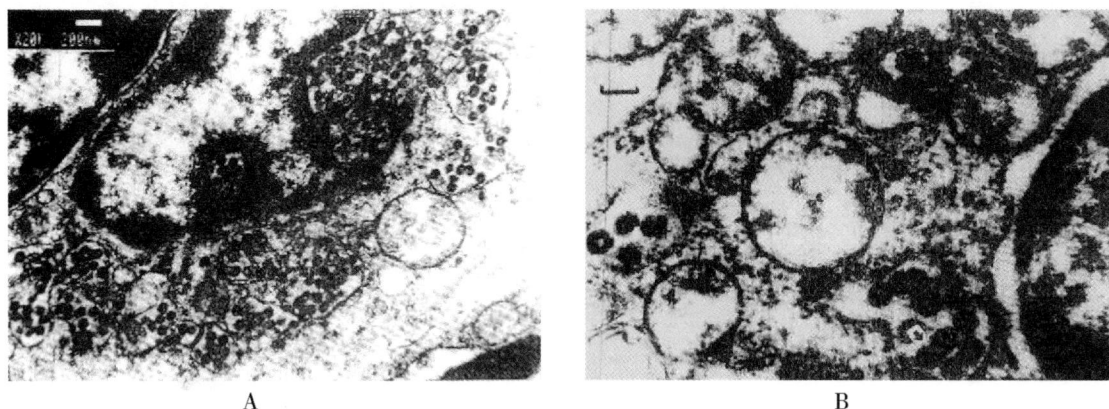

A. The vesicles of rough-surfaced endoplasmic reticulum enclose many virus particles(Bar:200nm) 1;

B. Globular virus particles and some coalescences of viruses are found(Bar:100nm)

Fig. 5　The micrograph of ultrathin section of the CM-2 cell

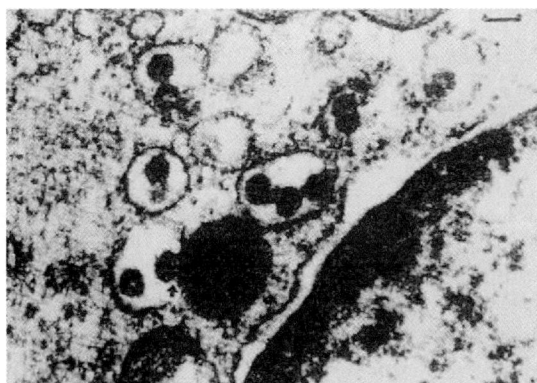

Fig. 6　The micrograph of ultrathin section of the CM-2 cell Arrow shows that a virus partide is budding from the membrane of rough-surfaced endoplasmic reticulum into the cisterns(Bar:100nm)

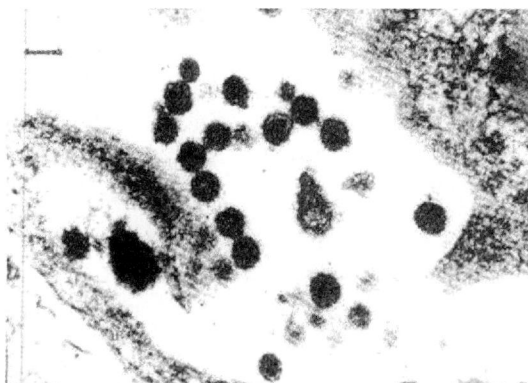

Fig. 7　The micrograph of ultrathin section of the CM-2 cell showing ultra-structure characteristics of the virus(Bar:100nm)

6. Viral identification and assay

A. Serological assays

（a）The immunological reactions between the serum of cerebrospinal fluid of CM-1 donor and the antigens of the above-mentioned viruses tested by Western Blot or immunofluorescence assay were all negative. This showed that the patient was not infected by the above-mentioned viruses.

（b）The assay for the virus antigens in the CM-1 cclls by immunofluorescence assay showed that the virus in the CM-1 cells did not possess the antigenicity of HTLV-I, HIV-1 and EBV, which were often used in our laboratory.

（c）There was no immunological reaction between the CM-2 cells and the serum of its donor. The CM-2 ceils acted as target cells, but the CM-2 cells could react with the serum of the CM-1 donor. It seems that the antigen in CM-2 cells(transformed cells)came from the filtered supernatant of the cultured CM-1 cells.

B. Tests for viral gene in CM-1 cell

（a） Molecular hybridization test: The results obtained from molecular hybridization test showed that the W-fragment, LMP and EBNA-1 gene were all negative, this excludes the existence of EBV genes in the CM-1 cells.

（b）The results of PCR confirmed that the viral gene and antiviral gene have no relationship with the certain human retrovirus, such as HIV-1 and HTLV-I.

7. Reverse transcriptase(RT) activity.

All fractions obtained by ultracentrifugation in sucrose density gradient were assayed for RT activity with poly (A): oligo(dT)$_{15}$ as template-primers. The results showed that RT activity appeared in the tube 5, its density was 1. 16g/ml(Fig. 8).

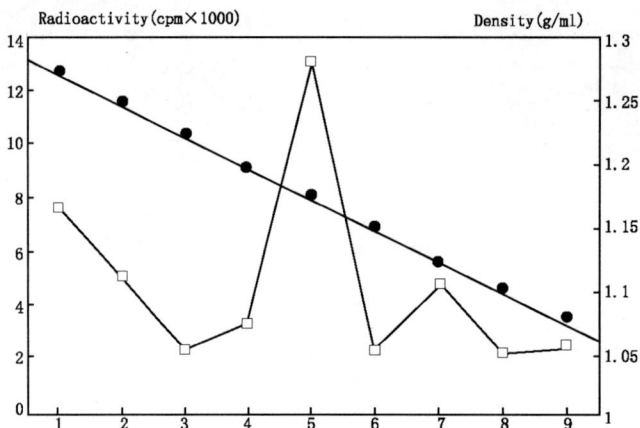

Fig. 8   RT-activity distribution according to density after eentrifugation in sucrose density gradient

DISCUSSION

No breakthrough had been made in the long-term culture of T lymphocyte in vitro, untill the time between the late 1970s and the early 1980s. Since then, two methods for the long-term culture of T lymphocyte in vitro became available. First, the IL-2 dependent T lymphocyte lines can be established by adding the growth factors such as IL-2 into the culture medium(Steven and James,1981); second, to immortalize the T lymphocytes by certain retroviruses infection(Miyoshi et al.,1981). The malignant T lymphoma cell line that we had established from the peripheral blood lymphocytes donated by a female patient with limb paralysis and coma, proliferated rapidly and actively. The number of cells could increase by 50 times in 10 days. Further more, they were able to grow spontaneously in vitro without addition of growth factors such as IL-2. The above features showed that there were many growth factors produced by cells themselves. This is really a rare phonomenon.

The CM-1 and CM-2 cells were transplanted into nude mice by subcutaneous inoculation, and coule developed tumors that were typical malignant T lymphoma proved by the histopathological section. The electron micrographs suggested the existence of 80 nm diametered viral particles, which had two layers of membranous structure enclosing a electron dense nucleus near the center and released by budding out from cytomembrane, all these are similar to the ultra-structural characteristics of retrovirus. This virus has reverse transcriptase activities and is capable of transforming normal T lymphocytes in vitro. The results of serological assay, probe hybridization and PCR showed that the viruses in the CM-1 and CM-2 cells had no relation with the human viruses often used in our laboratory, these excluded the possibility of contamination from other human viruses. The conclusion drawn from these data is that a possible new kind of retrovirus existed in the CM-1 and CM-2 cells.

The observation of electron microscope showed that the CM-2 cells carried more virions than the CM-1 cell, and more antigen to the serum of the CM-1 cell donor was found in the serological detection. The CM-2 cells are more suitable to be used as the antigen to the virus in the immouno-fluorescence assay.

At present, the patient who donated the CM-1 ceils is still alive, no signs of concerned tumor, but degradation of intelligance and motion difficulties can be found. Whether the virus has any relation with diseases of the CM-1 cells donor is not clear yet, more work is needed on this question. We are trying to screen more sera from patients with varions diseases by immounofuorescence assay, in order to make research on which disease relates to this virus. Meanwhile, the work on further purification, clone and sequence analysis are being carried out. The classification and name of this virus still need more intensive work.

REFERENCES

[1] Bartholomew C, Cleghorn F, Charles W, Ratan P, Roberts L Maharaji K, Jankey N, Daisley H, Hanchard B, Blattner W. HTLV-I and tropical spastic paraparesis. Lancet, 1986, 2:99-100.

[2] Gessain A, Barin F, Vernant JC, Gout O, Maurs JC, Gout O, Maurs L, Calender A, de The G. Antibodies to HTLV-I in patients with tropical spastic paraparesis. Lancet, 1985, 2:407-410.

[3] Hinuma Y, Nagata K, Hanaoka M, Matsumoto T, Kinoshita K, Shirakakawa S, Miyoshi L. Adult T-cell leukemia: antigen in an ATL cell line and detection of antibodies to the antigen in human sera. Proc. Acad. Sci. USA, 1981, 78: 6476-6480.

[4] Hong ML, Lan XY, Zhang DF, Feng ZJ, Wang DX, Zeng Y. Morphology of type C retrovirus-like particles from a patient with cerebritis. Journal of Electron Microscopy Society, 1992, 11:375-376.(in Chinese).

[5] Lan XY, Zeng Y, WANG DX, Feng ZJ, Tang MH, Ji Y, Yu G, Li K. Establishment of a human malignant T lymphocytic cell line releasing retrovirus-like particles. Chinese Journal of Virology, 1992, 8:187-190.(in Chinese).

[6] Lan XY, Zeng Y, Wang DX, Chen Z, He SQ, Guo SS, Ouyang MQ, Du B. HTLV-I and the neuromyelopthics in Chinese, Chinese Journal of Virology, 1993, 9:382-385.(in Chinese).

[7] Lan XY, Zeng Y(In press). Establishment of a cell line carrying HTLV-I from the blood donated by a patient with lcukemia. Chinese Journal of Virology.(in Chinese).

[8] Miyoshi I, Kubonishi I, Yoshimoto S, Akagi T, Ohtsuke Y, Shiraishi Y, Nagata K, Hinuma Y. Typc C virus particles in a cord T-cell line derived by co-cultivating normal human cord T-cell line derived by co-cultivating normal human cord lcukoeytes and human leukaemic T ceils. Nature, 1981, 294:770-771.

[9] Osame M, Matsumoto M, Usuku K, Izumo S, Ijichi N, Amitani H, Tara M, lgata A. Chronic progressive myclopathy with elevated antibodies to HTLV-I and ATL cells. Ann. Neurol, 1987, 21:117.

[10] Steven G, James W. Lnterleukin-2 dependent culture of cytolytic T cell times, lmmunolog-ical Rev, 1981, 54:81-109.

[In《Biomedical and enviromental Sciences》1994, 7:1-12]

Screening of Epstein-Barr Virus Early Antigen Expression Inducers from Chinese Medicinal Herbs and Plants

ZENG Yi[1] , ZHONG Jian-ming[2] , YE Shu-qing[1] , NI Zhi-yu[1] MIAO Xue-qian[1] , MO Yong-kun[2] , LI Zi-lin[3]

1. Institute of Virology, Chinese Academy of Preventive Medicine, Beijing; 2. Nasopharyngeal Control and Treatment Institute of Cangwu, Guangxi, Guangxi Herbs Botany Garden, Naning; 3. Institute of Chinese Materia Medica, China Academy of Traditional Chinese Medicine, Beijing

[SUMMARY] Ether extracts of 1693 Chinese medicinal herbs and plants from 268 families were studied for the induction of Epstein-Barr viral(EBV) early antigen(EA) expression in the Raji cell line, Fifty-two from 18 families were found to have inducing activity Twenty-five and seven of them were from Euphorbiaceae and Thymelaeaceae, respectively. Some of them, such as Croton tiglium, Euphorbia kansui, Daphne genkwa. Wikstroemia chamaedaphen, Wikstroemia indica, Prunus mandshuricd Koehne and Achyramhes bidemdid are commonly used drugs. The significance of these herbs in the activation of EBV in vivo and their relation to the development of nasopharyngeal carcinoma were discussed.

INTRODUCTION

EB virus is closely related to the development of nasopharyngeal carcinoma, while environmental carcinogens and tumor promotor may also play a role in the development of nasopharyngeal carcinoma. The known tumor promotor TPA extuaeted from croton oil can be an EB viral inducer for B lymphocyte transformation, and an enhancer of cancer growth caused by viral or chemical carcinogens. We used the method of induction for EB viral early antigen(EA)expression in Raji cell to detect the EB viral EA expression inducer in 495 species of Chinese medicinal herbs. Some medicinal herbs were found acting as EB viral EA indueers(Zeng et al., 1984; Zeng et al., 1985), and as a inducer of lymphocyte transformation by EB virus and rat embryonic cell transformation by adenovirus(Hu and Zeng, 1985), as well sa a tumor promotor(Hu et al., 1986; Sun et al., 1987a; Sun et al., 1987b). It was also found that Chinese patent medicines such as croton cream formulation sold from drug stores in Beijing also contained tumor promotor(Zeng et al., 1986). Application of Chinese medicinal herbs to treat various diseases are widespread, hence it is very necessary to continue screening tests for EB viral EA inducers. Among pharmacetitical plants and other plants, 1693 plant species have been screened, of them 52 species have the function in inducing EB viral EA expression.

MATERIALS AND METHODS

1. Cell line
Raji cell carrying EB virus genome in RPMI 1640 culture medium containing 10% calf serum.

2. Plant origin
Plants were collected from the Guangxi Herbs Botany Garden; Cangwu County, Wuzhou City and Nanning City of Guangxi; and the Beijing Chinese Drug Store. All the plants had passed the evaluation by the Guangxi Herbs Botany Garden.

3. Method of extraction
The Ito method was taken. Plant extracts, after the plants were immersed in 100ml egher for 72 h, were filtrated with filter paper and evaporated with ether. The extracts were dissolved in dehydrated alcohol to reach a concentration of 10mg/ml. Then the alcoholic solution was kept in refrigerator at 4℃ for further dilution when in use.

4. Experimental steps
(1)Different concentrations of sample extracts were added into Raji cell culture containing 10^5 cells per ml reaching the final concentrations of 12. 5μg cell/ml.

(2)The Raji cell culture contained 4mmol · L^{-1} sodium butyrate. Another sample extract was added into a sodium butyrate-free culture as the control.

(3)Croton oil positive controls were also ser up.

(4)Incubation at 37℃ for 48h.

(5)Cell smear preparations for the detection of EB viral EA using immunoenzymatic test.

（6）If the percentage of EA positive cells in the experimental group was 3 times higher than that in the sodium butyrate group, the result of the experiment was considered as positive for EA activation.

RESULTS

Tab. 1 lists 52 species of EA induction positive plants, of which most belong to the family Euphorbiaceae. Strong positives（induced Raji Cells contain EA positives above 20%）include 34 species（Euphorbiaceae 21, Thymelaeaceae 7, Verbenaceae 2, Rubiaceae 1, Solanaceae 1, Amaranthaceae 1, Iridaceae 1）. Moderate positives （EA positives between 10% and 19%）include 6 species（Euphorbiaceae 3, Sinopteridaceae 1, Spargoniaceae 1, Iridaceae 1）. Weak positives（EA positives below 10%）include 11 species. Among 52 species some are in common use （such as Croton tiglium, Euphorbia kansui, Daphne genkwa, Wikstroemia chamaedaphne, Wikstroemia indica, Belamcanda chinensis, Prunus mandshuria Koehne and Achyranthes bidentata, etc.）.

Tab. 1　List of Positive Herbs and Plants

No.	Family	Herbs and plants	EA positive cell rate	
			12. 5g/ml	2. 5g/ml
1	Euphorbiaceae	Aleurites moluecana	6. 4	2. 8
2		Codiaeum veriegatum	50	26
3		Codiaeum veriegatum forma taeniosum	37	26
4		Codiaeum veriegatum CV	19. 2	26. 4
5		Croton calcarsus	16. 2	14. 2
6		Croton lachnocarpus	9. 6	22. 4
7		Croton tiglium	42. 8	26. 0
8		Euphorbia antiqnorura CV "cristata"	28	36
9		Euphorbia tumdata	17. 2	9. 8
10		Euphorbia helioseopia	36. 4	34. 8
11		Euphorbia kansui	18. 0	38. 0
12		Euphorbia lathvris	20. 0	10. 0
13		Euphorbia marginata	7. 2	20. 8
14		Euphorbia milli	25. 8	20. 4
15		Euphorbia thymifolia	40	32
16		Excoecaria cochinchinensis	36. 8	52. 8
17		Excoecaria venenata	13	42. 4
18		Jatropha multifida	21. 6	35. 8
19		Pedilanthus tithvmaloides	11. 6	22. 4
20		Sapium discolor	35	30. 2
21		Sapium sebiferum	5. 4	24. 8
22		Sapium rotundifolium	21. 4	1. 5
23		Vernicia fordii	17. 0	15. 8
24		Vernicia montana	49. 6	43. 2
25		Euphorbia antiquorum	20. 8	7. 4
26	Thvmelaeaceae	Daphne genkwa	46	45

（续　表）

No.	Family	Herbs and plants	EA positive cell rate	
			12. 5g/ml	2. 5g/ml
27		Edgeworthia ehrysantha	43	28
28		Stellera chamaejasme	36	46
29		Wikstroemia chamaedaphne	32	53
30		Wikstroemia indicd	42	50
31		Aquilaria sinensis	25. 6	22
32		Wikstroemia nutans	28. 6	17. 2
33	Leguminasae	Caesalpinia sappan	8	4
34		Desmodium stvrqcifolium	6	4
35	Rubiaceae	Knoxia valerianoides	3. 2	0. 8
36		Galium aparina var tenrum	36	10
37	Verbenaceae	Prenna fulva	52	42
38		Duranta repens	24. 6	36
39	Iridaceae	Belamcanda chinensis	0. 8	36. 4
40		Iris tectorum	16	6
41	Sinopteridaceae	Aleuritopteris argentea	6	17
42	Ranunculaceae	Clematis intricata	3	2
43	Menispermaeeae	Tinospora sagittata	7	3
44	Solanaceae	Datura atramonium	0	25
45	Spargoniaceae	Spargonium stoloniferum	16	2
46	Balsaminaceae	Impatiens balsamina	8. 6	7
47	Compositae	Ixeris debilis	6. 8	9
48	Caprifoloaceae	Viburnum sempervirens	8. 6	8
49	Actinidiaceae	Actinidia latifolia	3. 6	0
50	Piperaceae	Piper hainaense	7. 2	4
51	Rosaeeae	Prunus mandshurica Koehne	18. 4	14
52	Amaranthaceae	Achyranthes bidentata	23. 9	10

Notes：Control：Sodium butyrate＋croton oil EA cell positive rate 42. 8％-45. 7％；sodium butyrate EA positive cell rate 0. 4％-1％；croton oil EA positive cell rate 0. 8％-1. 6％

DISCUSSION

One-thousand six-hundred and ninety-three species of Chinese medicinal herbs and plants were screened for EB viral EA inducer with Raji cell line, and 52 species of 18 families were found having the function of inducing expression of EB viral EA. Among them some are in common use, such as Croton tiglium, Euphorbia kansui, Daphne genkwa, Wikseroemia chamaedaphne, Wikstroemia indica, Belamcanda chinensis, Prunus mandshurica Koehne and Achyranthes bidentata. EB viral EA inducers and even tumor promotors(Zeng et al., 1986)were also found in 9 Chinese patent medicines. It was proved that some of them, such as W. indica used in Guangdong, could stimulate lymphocyte transformation induced by EB virus, and D. genkwa which was widely used in inducing labor could enhance rat nasopharyngeal carcinoma induced by chemical carcinogens(Tang et al., 1988a；Tang et al., 1988b；Zhong et al., 1987). Among 50 more species screened as EA activation positive plants, 39-40 are distributed in nasopharyngeal carcinoma highly prevalent areas in Guangdong and Guangxi provinces. In the areas abundant in these plants, EB viral inducers ortumor promotors may exist in soil, vegetables and bees, and this may further explain the linkage of environmental factors with human life. The nasopharyngeal carcinoma is high in incidence along the banks of the Xijiang Valley, and the incidence in boat dwellers is also 2-3 times higher than in land rewidents(Zhu et al., 1983). Whether EB viral inducer and tumor promotors exist in the Xijiang River is a problem to be solved, because the river water is turbid and muddy. Imai et al.(1988)reported that Burkit Lymphoma and nasopharyngeal carcinoma occurred in Kenya, Uganda and Eastern African countries, where many EB viral inducers and tumor promotors existed, even in pond water. Hence, the high incidence of nasopharyngeal carcinoma in the Xijiang Valley, especially in boat dwellers may be related to drinking of water containing EB viral inducers and tumor promotors. This conjecture should be further confirmed and studied. Tomei and Glaser(1988)reported that TPA and EB virus could stimulate SV40 virus inducing human epithelium multiplication. Thus, the in vitro synergistic action of EB viral inducer and tumor promotors in connection with EB virus occurred in the epithelial cells should be studied. It was also found in our laboratory that some plants or foods contained both EB viral inducers and tumor promoters, and also mutagens(Shao et al., 1988). Faggioni et al.(1983)reported that N-methyl-N-nitroguanidine could activate lymphocyte transformation induced by EB virus. Hence, the possibility of the occurrence of synergism between EB viral inducers, tumor promotors carcinogens and EB virus, causing the transformation of epithelium of nasopharynx into cacer cells, is worthwhile for further exploration. Serological surveys and 10-year follow-up observations in Wuzhou City and Cangwu County were carried out. Early diagnosis rate of nasopharyngeal carcinoma can be greatly raised by using EB viral IgA/VCA antibody and EA antibody markers; and the occurrence of nasopharyngeal cancer can be predicted 5-10-year in advance. It indicated that EB virus played an important role in the development of nasopharyngeal carcinoma(Deng et al., 1992). Our study(Lu et al., 1990)on genetic factors of nasopharyngeal carcinoma was suggesting the existence of nasopharyngeal carcinoma susceptibility gene linked with HLA. From the above, we put forwar the idea on the etiology of nasopharyngeal carcinoma, i. e. gene factor is the basis of the disease occurrence, EB virus plays an important role in the development of the disease; EB viral inducers, tumor promotors and carcinogens in environments act as synergists in the development of nasopharyngeal carcinoma. Further researches are undergoing.

REFERENCES

[1]　Deng H, Zeng Y, Huang N, Huang Y, Li Y, Su LM, Zhong HX, Lian YX, Wang PZ, G. de The. Prospective studies of nasopharyngeal carcinoma for 10 years in Wuzhou City, Guangxi Chinese J Viology, 1992, 8:32.(in Chinese).

[2]　Faggioni A, Ablashi DV, Armstrong G, Dahl-berg J, Sundar S K, Rice JM, Donovan PJ. Enhancing effect of N-Metgtl-N-Nitrosoguanidine(MNNG) on Epstein-Barr Virus Replication and comparison of continuous and discontinuous TRA treatment of ESV nonproducer and producer cells for antigen induction and/or stimulaiton. In Nasopharyngeal Carcinoma: Current Concepts(W. Prasad, D. V. Ablashi, P.H. Levinc, and G. R. Pearson, Eds.), University of Malaya,1983: 333.

[3]　Hu YL, Zeng Y. Enhanced transformation of human lymphocytes by Chinese herbs. Chinese Journal Oncology, 1985, 7: 417.(in Chinese).

[4]　Hu YL, Zeng Y, Lto Y. Croton oil, Wikstroemia chamaedaphne and Wikstroemia india cnhanced the rabbit papilloma induced by papilloma induced by papilloma virus. Chinese J Virology,1986, 2:81.(in Chinese).

[5]　Imai S, Kinoshita T, Koizumi, Aya T, Matsunra A, Sugiura M, Bray Kyi Mizuno F, Osato T, Yamaka T, Chiba S, Ohigashi H, Koshimizu K, Miyazaki T, Agishi Y. An environmental plant factor enhancing EBV-specific event in East Africa: Redution of killer T-cell function and its protection by hot spring water. In Epstein Barr and Human Disease (D. V. Ablashi, A. Faggioni, G. R. F. Krueer, J. S. Pagano, and G. R. Pearson Eds.), Hamana Press, 1988: 48.

[6]　Lu SJ, Day NE, Degos L, Lepage V, Wang PC, Chan SB, Simons M, McKnight B, Easton D, Zeng Y. Linkage of a nasopharyngeal carcinoma susceptibility locus to the HLA region. Nature, 1990, 346:470-471.

[7]　Shao YM, Poiricr S, Ohshima H, Malaveile C, Zeng Y, G de The, Bartsch, H. Epstein-Barr virus activation in Raji cells by extracts of preserved food from high risk areas for nasopharyngeal carcinoma. Carcinogenesis, 1988, 9:1445-1447.

[8]　Sun Y, Chen MH, Xiao H, Liu HY, Chen X, Zeng Y. Ito, Y. Tumor promoting effect of diterpene ester HHPA and extract of Wikstroemia chamaedaphne of HSV-2 induced carcinoma in mice. Chinese J Virology, 1987, 3: 131.(in Chinese).

[9]　Sun Y, Chen Mh, Zang YX, Xiao H, Liu HY, Chen X. Promoting effects of the Chinese medical herb. Wikstroemia chamaedaphne and the tung of extracts on carcinoma of uterine cervix induced by HSV-2 or methylcholanthrene(MCA)in mice. Chiese J Oncology, 1987b, 9, 345.(in Chiese).

[10]　Tang WP, Huang PG, Zhao ML, Cai QZ, Liao SL, Zeng Y. The role of Wikstroemia chamaedaphne Meise in promoting experimental nasopharyngeal carcinoma(NPC)in rats. Cancer, 1988a, 7:171-172.(in Chinese).

[11]　Tang WP, Huang PG, Zhao ML, Liao SL, Zeng Y. Wikstroemia indica promotes development of nasopharyngeal carcinoma in rats initiated by dinitrosopiperazine. J. Cancer Res, Clin Oncol, 1988b, 114:429-431.

[12]　Tomei LD, Glaser R. Enhanced SV40 immortalization of primary human epidermal cells following phorbol Ester Dependent EBV Transformation. In Epstein-Barr and Human Disease(D.V. Ablashi, G Armstrong, J. Dahlberg, S.K. Sundar, J. M. Rice, and P. J. Donovan, Eds.). Hamana Press, 1988: 495.

[13]　Zeng Y, Miao XQ, Jiao W, Hu YL. EpsteinBarr Virus early antigen expression induction and enhancement of lymphocyte

transformation by Yuauhuadine Ⅱ and Wikstroemia chamaedaphne. Chinese J Virology，1985，1：229.(in Chinese).

[14] Zeng Y，Wan Y，Ye SQ，Miao XQ，Zhong JM. Induction of Epstein-Barr Virus early antigen in Raji cell by some Chinese patent medicine. Chinese J Virology，1986，2：306.(in Chinese).

[15] Zeng Y，Zong JM，Mo YK，Miao XQ. EpstemBarr Virus early antigen expression induction in Raji cell by Chinese medicinal herbs. Acta Academiae Medicinae Sinicae，1984，6：84.(in Chinese).

[16] Zhong JM，Cheng JY，Mo YK，Tang CT，Zeng Y. Study on the Epstein-Barr Virus Inducers in the ether extracts of soil and vegetables in Zangwu County. Cancer，1987，6：35-37.(in Chinese).

[17] Zhu JS，Pan WJ，Zhong JM，Li LY，Zeng Y，Jiang MK，Fang Z. A serological survey on nasopharyngeal cancer in boat dwellers of Cangwu County. Cancer Research on Prevention and Treatment，1983，10：189-190.(in Chinese).

［In《Biomedical and Environmental Sciences》1994，7：50-55］

Serological Survey of Nasopharyngeal Carcinoma in 21 Cities of South China

DENG Hong[1], ZENG Yi[2], LEI Yi-ming[3], ZHAO Zheng-bao[3], WANG Pei-zhong[4], LI Bing-jun[5], PI Zhi-ming[1], TAN Bi-fang[1], ZHENG Yu-ming[1], PAN Wen-jun[5], ZHONG Zheng-yi[6], Wu Jue-yan[7]

1. Wuzhou Institute for Cancer Research. Wuzhou City 543002, Guangxi; 2. The Academy of Preventive Medical Sciences of China, Beijing; 3. Guangxi Public Health Department, Nanning, Guangxi; 4. Guangxi People's Hospital. Nanning, Guangxi; 5. Cangwu Institute for Prevention and Treatment of Nasopharyngeal Carcionma, Cangwu, Guangxy; 6. Wangning Public Health Bureau, Wanning, Hainan; 7. Fengkai Public Health Bureau, Fengkai, Guangdong

[SUMMARY] This pater reports the results of serological survey of 318912 persons for nasopharyngeal carcinoma (NPC)in 21 cities and counties of south China. There were 8441 persons with positive VCA-IgA antibody(sinle item positive)of EB virus(EBV), with a rate of 2. 65%. In these VCA-IgA positive persons, 287 persons also had positive EA-IgA(double items positive)of EBV. The over- all positive rate was 0. 09%. 100 cases of NPC were found and 87 of them(87. 0%)were in early stage. NPC found in the group with single item positive accounts for 1. 19%, but the rate in the group with double items positive was 19. 16%(55 cases). In NPC patients with double items positive, 49 cases were in early stage(89. 1%). In 100 cases of NPC found, 45 cases appeared with negative EA-IgA, only with positive VCA-IgA, which indicated that for diagnosis of NPC, sensitivity of EA-IgA was lower than that of VCA-IgA, but its specificity was higher. Therefore, both can increase the detecting rate and early diagnosis rate of NPC. The age of people checked varied with different antibody positive rate and NPC detecting rate. The three items showed a positive correlation. The results are compatible sith those of the prospective study for NPC in Wuzhou City, Guangxi, China. The method for NPC serological diagnosis can be extended and applied to raise the NPC detecting rate and early diagnosis rate at secondary prevention, And, it is further proved theat there is a close relationship between NPC and EBV.

INTRODUCTION

We used the method for nasopharyngeal carcinoma(NPC) serological diagnosis to detect VCA- IgA antibody of EBV in the prospective study in Wuzhou City, Guangxi, China. NPC early diagnosis rate has increased from 20% to 49. 4% at outpatient service and 94. 74% in the mass survey. The 5-year survival rate of NPC in population of the urban district has risen to 54. 62% and the 10-year survival rate 39. 27%. In other words, we have attained the aim of secondary prevention for NPC.[1,2] In order to understand whether the results of the prospective study can be applied and promoted in other areas, we made an NPC serological mass survey of 318912 persons in 21 cities and counties of Guangxi Province, Fengkai County of Guangdong Province, and Wanning County of Hainan Province, from January 1991 to July 1993. The data are reported below.

MATERIAL AND METHODS

1. **Areas of the mass survey**: There were altogether 5 cities: Guigang, Qinzhou, Yulin, Liuzhou and Beihai; and 16 counties: He, Rong, Teng, Lingshan, Cenxi, Hepu, Lipu, Luchuan, Bobai, Luzhai, Guiping, Mengshan, Zhongshan, and Fuchuan in Guangxi Province, Wanning in Hainan Province and Fengkai in Guangdong Province.

2. **Subjects**: Cadres and workers of offices, farms, forestry centres, factories, mines and other enterprises and institutions from above cities and counties.

3. **Population**: Altogether 318 912 persons were surveyed, including 194 118 men and 124 794 women. Proportion of male to female was 1. 6 : 1. Age groups are shown in Tab. 1.

Tab. 1 The relationship among age, VCA-IgA and NPC

Item	Age(years)										Total
	<30	30-	35-	40-	45-	50-	55-	60-	65-	>70	
Population	89433	46089	46874	46013	30488	28271	18356	8314	3068	1992	318912
VCA-IgA positive	1800	916	1163	1223	964	938	776	400	159	102	8441
VCA-IgA positive rate(%)	2.01	1.99	2.48	2.66	3.16	3.32	4.23	4.81	5.18	5.11	
NPC cases	6	2	13	29	21	14	9	4	2	0	
NPC detecting rate(%)	6.7	4.3	27.73	63.0	68.9	49.5	48.03	48.1	65.2	0	

4. **Sera**: One to two drops of blood were collected with a plastic tube of 1.5mm in diameter and sent to the laboratories of Wuzhou Institute of Cancer Research, Guangxi People's Hospital, and Cangwu Insitute of Prevention and Treatment of NPC. Sera were obtained there.

5. **Immunoenzymatic method[3,4]**: B95-8 cells were used for the detection of VCA-IgA antibody, and Raji cells were used for the detection of EA-IgA antibody. Sera diluted at 1 : 5 and 1 : 10 were added to cells in separate wells of slides. The slides were incubated at 37℃ for 30 min at a humid atmosphere and washed 3 times with PBS. Horseradish peroxidase labelled antihuman IgA antibody in appropriate dilution was added to the slides. The slides were incubated for 30 min, washed 3 times with PBS and flooded with diaminobenzene solution and H_2O_2 for 10 min. Positive and negative controls were included in each experiment. A serum dilution of 1 : 10 for VCA-IgA or 1 : 5 for EA-IgA showing a characteristic brown colour of this test was considered positive and tested with further 6 dilutions. Tests were completed in 5-10 days after the collection of blood specimens.

6. **Clinical examination**: Persons being serologically positive received clinical examination at nasopharynx within 5-15 days after the collection of blood specimens. Biopsies were taken from suspected NPC cases.

7. **Histological examination**: Biopsies were sent to Wuzhou Cancer Research Insitute and Guangxi People's Hospital for histological examination.

RESULTS AND DISCUSSION

Among the 318 912 subjects, 8441 had positive VCA-IgA antibody(single item positive)of EBV, the positive rate being 2.65%, and geomatric mean titre(GMT)of the antibody was 1 : 33.84. There were 287 persons being both VCA-IgA and EA-IgA(double items positive)of EBV positive. The positive rate of EA-IgA was 0.09% and GMT of EA-IgA was 1 : 10.52. A total of 100 cases of NPC were found in the group with single item positive(not including the patients diagnosed of treated before the survey). NPC detecting rate in the positive VCA-IgA cases was 1.18%, In persons with double items positive, 55 cases of NPC were found(19.16%), which was 16.2 times as many patients as in the single item positive group. In 100 NPC cases in the group with single item positive, there were 87 cases in early stage(according to the TNM staging standard of Chinese Hunan Conference in 1979, stages Ⅰ-Ⅱ as early stage; T: primary tumor at nasopharynx; N: transferred to neck lymphaden; M: transferred to lymphaden in other parts; stage Ⅰ: T<0.5cm, N=0, M=0; stage Ⅱ: T>0.5cm, but not over cavum nasopharyngeum, N=0 or N<3×3cm, M=0; one or two of following is stage Ⅲ or stage Ⅳ: T over cavum, N>3×3cm, M=1, basion destroyed, cranial nerve damaged), and early diagnosis rate was 87.0%. On the other hand, in55 NPC cases of the group with double items positive, there were 49 cases in early stage(89.1%), In the above 100 NPC cases, 45 cases had negative EA-IgA, only with positive VCA-IgA. It shows that in diagnosis of NPC, sensitivity of EA-IgA is lower than that of VCA-IgA, but its specificity is higher. Therefore, both can increase the detecting rate and early diagnosis rate of NPC(Tabs. 2, 3).

Tab. 2 Antibody titre distribution and NPC cases in 8441 persons

Item	Titre							Toal	Positive rate(%)
	1 : 5	1 : 10	1 : 20	1 : 40	1 : 80	1 : 160	1 : 320		
VCA-IgA positive	0	6837	1161	327	89	25	2	8441	2.65
NPC cases	0	25	19	24	24	8	0	100	
NPC detecting rate(%)	0	0.37	1.64	7.34	26.97	32.0	0		

（续　表）

Item	Titre							Toal	Positive rate(%)
	1 : 5	1 : 10	1 : 20	1 : 40	1 : 80	1 : 160	1 : 320		
EA-IgA positive	110	131	36	10	0	0		287	0. 09
NPC cases	15	25	12	3	0	0		55	
NPC detecting rate(%)	13. 64	19. 68	33. 33	30. 0	0	0			

Tab. 3　Positive antibodies and NPC clinical stages and histological classification

Item	Clinical stages					Detecting rate (%)	Early diagnosis rate(%)	Poorly diff ca.	Histological classification		
	I	II	III	IV	Total				Rate (%)	Vesicular nuc. ca.	Rate (%)
VCA-IgA cases	34	53	10	3	100	1. 19	87. 0	75	75. 0	25	25. 0
Rate(%)	34. 0	53. 0	10. 0	3. 0	100						
EA-IgA cases	14	35	4	2	55	19. 16	89. 1	42	76. 4	13	23. 6
Rate(%)	25. 5	63. 6	7. 3	3. 6	100						

In the group with VCA-IgA titre of 1 : 10 there were 25 NPC cases(0. 37%). When VCA-IgA titre was 1 : 20, 1 : 40, 1 : 80 and 1 : 160, NPC finding rate was 1. 64%, 7. 34%, 26. 97% and 30. 0% respectively. This shows that there is a positive correlation between VCA-IgA titre and NPC detecting rate. When EA-IgA titre was 1 : 5, 1 : 10 and 1 : 20, NPC detecting rate was 13. 64%, 19. 08%, and 33. 33% respectively. Both standards showed positive relationship. But when EA-IgA was 1 : 40, NPC detecting rate dropped to 30. 0%, and when EA-IgA$\geqslant$1 : 80 the rate was zero. The result may be related with the lower sensitivity of EA-IgA in the NPC diagnosis. In 100 NPC cases with single item positive, 75(75%)were poorly differentiated carcinoma and 25(25%)were vesicular nucleus cell carcinoma. No highly differentiated carcinoma was found. In 55 NPC cases with positive EA-IgA, 42(76. 4%)were pooly differentiated carcinoma and 13(23. 6%)were vesicular nucleus cell carcinoma. Proportion of NPC histological classification was similar in the two groups(Tabs. 1, 2).

In the 318 912 persons, there were 89 433 aged <30 year(28%). 14. 5%, 14. 7%, and14. 4% aged 30-34, 35-39, and 40-44 years respectively. The rate dropped gradually after 45 years of age. Age, VCA-IgA positive rate and NPC detecting rate showed a positive correlation. In the group aged <30 years, VCA-IgA positive rate was 2. 01%; in the group aged 30-65 years the rate increased with age; in the groups aged 65-69 years and over 70 years, the rate was 5. 18% and 5. 11% respectively. In other words, there is a positive relationship between age and VCA-IgA positive rate. NPC detecting rate in the group aged below 30 years was 6. 7/10^5 and in the group aged65-69 years was 65. 2/10^5. Between the age 30 and 64 years, the rate increased with age. There were two peaks of NPC detecting rate between the age 30 and 69 years. The first occurred in the group aged 45-49 years (68. 9/10^5)and the second in the group aged 65-69 years(65. 2/10^5). In groups with 50-54, 55-59, and 60-64 years of age NPC detecting rate was 49. 5/10^5, 49. 03/10^5, and 48. 1/10^5 respectively(Tab. 3).

The results of this survey coincide with one of the prospective studies on NPC in Wuzhou City Guangxi, as well as with the study in high incidence areas of NPC. This indicates that NPC serological diagnosis for mass survey can find NPC or early stage NPC for secondary prevention. [5,6] The method can be extended and applied to mass survey of NPC in other areas and people. And, it is further proved that there is a close relationship between NPC and EBV.

REFERENCES

[1]　Zeng Y, Liu YX, Wei JN, et al. Serological mass survey of nasopharyngeal carcinoma. Acta Academiae Medicinae Sinicae Sinicae 1979, 1(2):123.

[2]　Deng H, Zeng Y, Wang NQ, et al. Follow-up studies on serological screening of NPC for 10 years in Wuzhou City in Guangxi Province. Proceedings of The 10th Asia Pacific Cancer Conference, Beijing, 1991:86.

[3]　Zeng Y, Liu YX, Liu CR, et al. Application of immunoenzymic method and immunoautoradiographic method for the mass survey of nasophayngeal carcinoma. Chin J Oncol, 1979, 1(2):81.

[4]　Zeng Y, Zhang LG, Li JY, et al. Serological mass survey for early detection of nasopharyngeal carcinoma in Wuzhou city,

China Int J Cancer，1982，29：139.

［5］ Zeng Y，Zhang LG，Wu YC，et al. Follow-up studies on NPC in Epstein-Barr virus IgA/VCA antibody positive persons in Wuzhou city，China，ChinJ Virol，1985，1(1)：7.

［6］ Deng H，Zeng Y，Wang NQ，et al. Prospective study of NPC scene in Wuzhou city，Guangxi，Chinese Medical Abstracts. Internal Medicine Supplement，1993：318.

［In《Chinese Medical Journal》1995，108(4)：300-303］

Detection of Epstein-Barr Virus DNA in well and Poorly Differentiated Nasopharyngeal Carcinoma Cell Lines

ZHI Ping-teng[1], OOKA Tadamasa[2], HUANG Doll P[3], ZENG Yi[1]

1. Institute of Virology, Chinese Academy of Preventive Medicine, 100 Yin Xin Jie, Beijing, 100050, China;
2. Laboratoire de Virologie Moleculaire, IVMC, UMR30, Faculte de Medecine Alexis Carrel, 69372, Lyou, France; 3. Department of Anatomical and Cellular Pathology, Faculty of Medicine, Chinese University of Hong-Kong, Hong-Kong

[SUMMARY] Undifferentiated and poorly differentiated nasopharyngeal carcinoma(NPC) were known to be tightly associated with Epstein-Barr Virus(EBV). Its association with well differentiated NPC was also reported. In the present study, the presence of EBV was investigated by nucleic acid hybridization, Polymerase Chain Reaction(PCR), Immunoblot and in situ hybridization in two well differentiated NPC cell lines(CNE-1 and HK-1)and two other poorly differentiated NPC cell line(CNE-2 and CNE-3), Contrary to previous report indicating the absence of EBV in these cell lines, EBA DNA and proteins were present in all cell lines. The detection of EBV became more easily when the investigation was carried out on the nude mice tumor induced by transplantation of each NPC epithelial cell line. The EBV latent membrane protein(LMPI)was found by in situ hybridization to be intergrated partly in the chromosomal DNA of these cell lines. The observations indicate that EBV could persist for a long time in the carcinoma cells established directly from well and poorly differentiated tumor biopsies and from transplantable NPC tumor in nude mice.

[Keywords] Epstein-Barr Virus; Nasopharyngeal Carcinoma(NPC)

INTRODUCTION

Nasopharyngeal carcinoma(NPC)is one of the most prevalent malignant tumors in Southern China and South Asia. The presence of EBV genomes not only in poorly and undifferentiated, but also well differentiated NPC carcinoma biopsies and the serological evidence of EBV in NPC patients indicate that the virus plays an important role in the development of NPC[1,2,4-6]. There carcinoma cell lines were established directly from NPC biopsies in our laboratory, CNE-2 from poorly differentiated NPC, CNE-1 and HK-1 from well differentiated NPC, and another one CNE-3 cell line was established from transplantable poorly differentiated NPC tumor in nude mice. Among them, the presence of EBV genome in CNE-1, CNE-2 and HK-1 was not evident, since nucleic acid hybridization and anticomplement immunoenzymatic test done in these cell lines were revealed negative[7,9-11] CNE-1 and CNE-2 were generally used as EBV negative epithelials cells so far[3]. A possible explanation was the loss of EBV during a long culture in vitro or the absence of tight of association of EBV with well differentiated NPC.

We asked whether these cell lines are really negative to EBV. Four methods such as PCR, immunoblot, in situ hybridation and Southern blot were used to search for the presence of EBV. The data reported here showed that some of established cell lines contained both EBNA-1 and LMP-1 genes and expressed their proteins. Moreover EBV DNA or protein became easily detectable in the tumors induced by these cell lines in nude mice. Not only well differentiated, but also poorly differentiated cell lines contained EBV DNA. These data confirmed earlier report an association of EBV in both well and poorly differentiated NPC biopsies[6]. The NPC cell lines established since 15-18 years and considered as EBV negative cells contained EBV DNA sequence and expressed two EBNA-1 and LMP-1 latent proteins.

MATERIALS AND METHODS

1. Cell Lines and Culture

Poorly differentiated human NPC cell line; CNE-2[7] and two well differentiated NPC cell lines, CNE-1 and HK-1[9,11] were established directly from NPC biopsies in our laboratory. Another poorly differentiated NPC cell line(CNE-3)was established from transplantable poorly differentiated NP tumor in nude mice[8]. They were maintained in RPMI-1640 medium supplemented with 20% foetal calf serum(FCS)at 37℃ in 5% CO_2. The RHEK-1 cell line, an immortalized human epithelial cell line kindly provided by Dr. Rhim(NIH, Washington), was grown in Dulbecco's Modified Eagle's Medium with 10% FCS and antibodies.

2. Transplantation of NPC Cell Lines in Nude Mice

The cells growing exponentially were harvested and washed three times with fresh RPMI-1640 medium. The cell suspension(2×10^6) was transplanted nuder the dorsal skin of the nude mice. The tumors with masses of 2-3cm³ were obtained in about 30 days and they were frozen imediately at -160℃.

3. Southern Blot Hybridization

For Southern blot, the DNAs were extracted by standard methods; briefly, tumor tissues from nude mice were weighed, washed with phosphate saline buffered(PBS) and ground in a little basin with liquid nitrogen. 10 ml of TEN buffer(15mmol/L Tris-HCl, pH 8.0, 15mmol/L EDTA,15mmol/L NaCl)was added per gram of tissue or 10^8 cultured cells. 50 μg/ml of proteinase K(Boehringer Mannheim)and 1/20(v/v)of 20% sodium dodecyl sulfate(SDS)were then added in samples and incubated for 4-5 hrs at 55℃ followed by phenol-chloroform(V/V)extraction. 10μg of the DNA precipitated by ethanol were suspended in TE buffer(10mmol/L Tris-HCl, pH 7.5, 0.1mmol/L EDAT), digested with Xho-1 restriction enzyme(Sino-American Biotech. Co.)for 7 hrs at 37℃, electrophoresed through 0.8% agarose and tranerred onto nitrocellulose membranes(Bio-Rad). Menbranes were baked for 2 hrs at 80℃. The hybridization was dons in 50mmol/L sodium phosphate(pH 7.2), 7% SDS, 1% BSA and 100μg/ml denatured salmon sperm DNA, with about 10^6cpm/ml of probe at 65℃ overnight. Membranes were then washed in $1 \times$ SSC containing 0.1% SDS, and exposed to X-ray film at -70℃. Radiolabelled DNA probes were prepared with ^{32}p-dCTP(Amersham, England)by nick translation(specific activity=$>5 \times 10^7$ cpm/μg DNA), using 3.1×10^3 EBNA-1 and 2.9×10^3 full length LMP-1 sequences prepared respectively from pBR322-W plasmid(a girl from Dr. H. Wolf, Germany)and pUC-ly plasmid(a gift from Dr. E. Kieff, Harvard Medical School, Boston)after BamH1 digestion.

4. Immunoblotting

Pelleted cells were suspended in protein extraction buffer(1% SDS, 1% β-mercaptoethanol,1mmol/L PMSF, 20mmol/L Tris-HCl, pH 7.0)and sonicated twice for 3 min at 5Hz. Guanidine-HCl was then added to 5mmol/L and samples were centrifuged for 10 min at 5000g. The supernanrants were electrophorsed on a 12.5% polyacrylamide gel containing SDS and the proteins were transferred onto nitrocellulose filter. Then the filter was incubated overnight at 4℃ with monoclonal anti-EBNA-1 and anti-LMP-1 antibodies(with 1 : 50 000 dilution)as well as with sera from NPC patients, After washing, the filters were incubated for 1 hr at room temperature with peroxidase labelled anti-rabbit antibodies. A monoclonal antibody S12 directed against LMP-1 was from Dr. E. Kieff(Harvard Medical School, Boston). A monoclonal antibody against EBNA-1 was obtained in our laboratory.

5. Polymerase Chain Reaction(PCR)Assay

PCR was carried out using PCR kit(Hua Mei Biotech Company)on Perkin Elmer thermal cycler(Perkin-Elmer). The reaction mixture was in total 25μl containing 1μg of DNA, 0.2mmol/L dNTP, 3mmol/L $MgCl_2$, 1U Taq polymerase(Amplitaq, Perkin-Elmer)and 2.5μmol of each primers.

The sequence for BamH1-W fragment: 5′primer: W1, 5′CCA GAG GTA AGA GGA CTT3′; 3′primer: W2. 5′GAC CGG TGC CTT CTT AGG 3′, respectively at position 1399 and 1520 on Bam H1-W giving 121 bp of amplified fragment. Amplification condition was denaturation at 94℃ for 35 sec, annealing at 50℃ for 40 sec, extension at 72℃ for 45 sec and 30 cycles.

The sequence for BARFI open reading frame: BAI: 5′-CCAGAGCAATGGCCAGGTTC -3′, BA4: 5′-CAAGGTGAAATAGGCAAGTGCG-3′, respectively at positions 165 496 and 166 192on BARF1 sequence, giving 697 bp of amplified fragment. After 10 min incubation at 95℃,1 unit of Taq polymerase(Perkin Elmer)was added. The samples were subjected to 35 cycles of:1 min at 95℃, 1 min at 55℃ and 2 min at 72℃; after the last cycle, they were held at 72℃ for7 min. Specificity of PCR product was tested by dotblot or Southern blot hybridization. For dot blot, 5μl of the above PCR products was deposited onto the membrane of nitrocellulose and dried. 200μl of denaturing buffer(0.5mol/L NaOH, 1mol/L NaCl)were then added to each well and ater 15 min, 200μl of neutralizing buffer(0.5mol/L TrisHCl, pH 7.4, 2mol/L NaCl)was added. The membrane was baked for one hour at 80℃ and the hybridization was carried out in the abovementioned condition with BamH1 -W sequence as probe.

For Southern blot, 10μl of the above PCR products was electrophoresed on 2% standard agarose gel and transferred onto Hybond nylon filter. The hybridization was carried out using BARF1 sequence as probe as previously described(see Southern blot hybridization).

6. Nonisotopic In Situ Hybridization

The cells recovered on the slide were pretreated for 15 min with proteinase K (0.9 U/ml) at room temperature. The slides were denatured for 5 min in70% formamide, $2 \times$SSC and then dehydrated by ethanol series. LMP-1 probe labelled with Bio-11-dUTP by random priming DNA labelling kit(Beijing Medical Universith, Hematology Institute) were denatured for 10 min at70℃ in the following hybridization mixture; 50% formamide, $2 \times$SSC and 10% dextran sulfate. Hybridization was carried out at 42℃ overnight. The slides were washed by $2 \times$ SSC containing 50% formamide for 30 min at 42℃, then in $2 \times$SSC with avidin fluorescein for 30 min, After washing in PBS for 30 min, the slides were incubated with biotin labelled antiavidin antibody for 30 min. Cell nuclei were stained with PI and observed in an inverted fluorescence microscope.

RESULTS

1. Detection of EBV DNA in Cells Lines by In Situ Hybridization

The detection of EBV DNA was carried out by in situ hybridization using LMP-1 probe. The positive signal was obtained as pale yellow points in cell nuclei under an inverted fluorescence microscope(Fig. 1). A hybridization ratio of 95% was obtained with B95-8 cells. CNE-3 as a poorly differentiated NPC, and CNE-1 and HK-1 as a well differentiated NPC had hybridiaztion ratio of 20% and 5%-10% respectively.

2. Detection of EBV Genes Products by Immunoblot

The detection of both EBNA-1 and LMP-1 proteins was carried out by immunoblot on CNE-2 cell line, TPA-SB-treated CNE-1 cell line or the tumors biopsies induced by CNE-1 and CNE-2 cell lines, named as CNE-1 and CNE-T2 respectively using a monoclonal antibody against EBNA-1 or sera from NPC patients(containing a high titer of anti-EBNA-1). A band of approximately 60×10^3 was detected in CNE-2, CNE-T1, CNE-T2 and in NPC-T5(extracted from NPC tumor in nude mice, used as positive control)by a monoclonal anti-EBNA-1 antibody (Figs. 2A; 1-5). The same size of protein was identified when the immunoblots were tested by polyclonal human sera from NPC patients(Fig. 2B; 6-9). EBNA-1 expression in CNE-1 cells was only found by the same antibody when the cells were activated with TPA-SB(Fig. 3).

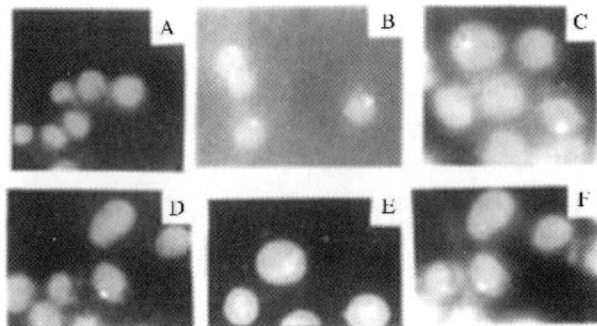

A: EBV negative CEM cell. B: EBV positive positive B95-8 cell. C: CNE-2 cell. D: CNE-1 cell. E: CNE-3 cell. F: HK-1 cell

Fig. 1 Detection of EBV DNA in cell lines by in situ hybridization. Nonisotopic in situ hybridization was carried out using LMP1 probe labelled with Bio-11-dUTP. The cells were stained with PI, then observed by microscopy at 10×40

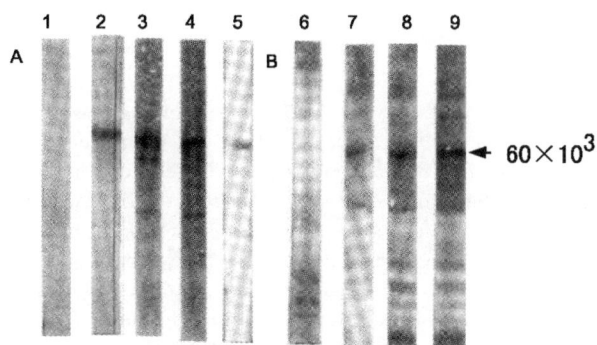

A. monoclonal anti-EBNA1 antibody
1. Colon cancer(as negative control)   2. CNE-2   3. CNE-T2
4. CNE-T1   5. NPC-T5(as positive control)
B. Sera from NPC patients
6. CNE-1   7. CNE-2   8. CNE-T1   9. CNE-T2

Fig. 2 Detection of EBNAI protein by immunoblot. The cellular extracts from cell lines and tumors were electrophoresed on 12% SDS-polyacrylamide. The proteins were transferred onto nitrocellulose filter and the filters were incubated with monoclonal adti-EBNA antibody or sera from NPC patients

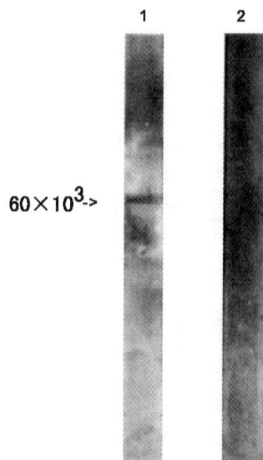

1. CNE-1 treated with TPA plus sodium butyrate
2. RHEK-1 cell(as EBV negative control)

Fig. 3 Detection of EBNA1 protein NPC cell line treated with TPA-SB. The immunoblot was incubated with sera from NPC patients

A monoclonal S12 antibody directed against LMP-1 protein was then tested on these sampies. Two bands of 63×10^3-66×10^3 were found in all CNE-2, CNE-T1, CNE-T2, TPA-SB-treated CNE-1 and NPC-T5(Fig. 4, A to D), while CNE-1 and CNE-3 as well as the biopsy from colon cancer(Fig. 4. E)were negative to this antibody.

3. Detection of EBV DNA by southern blot hybridization

The investigation of LMP-1 nucleotide sequence appeared negative when NPC cell lines were examined on Southern blot hybridization. We therefore searched for the LMP-1 sequence in Xho-1 digested DNA from tumor biopsies CNE-T1, CNE-T2 and CNE-T3(Fig. 5). A typical LMP-1 band around 6.1kb became detectable in all tumors as well as in B95-8(used as positive control), but negative in CNE-2 cell line(lane 4)and in a biopsy from colon cancer(lane 5).

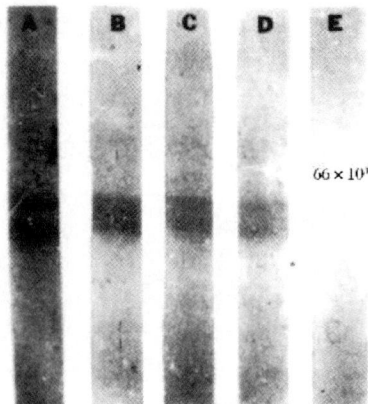

A: CNE-T1   B: CNE-T2   C: NPC-T5
D: CNE-2   E: Colon cancer(as negative control)

Fig. 4   Detection of LMP1 antigen by immunoblot. The cellular extracts from cell fines and tumors were electrophoresed on 12% SDS-polyacrylamide. The proteins were transferred onto nitrocellulose filter and the filters were incubated with S12 monoclonal antibody directed against LMP1 protein

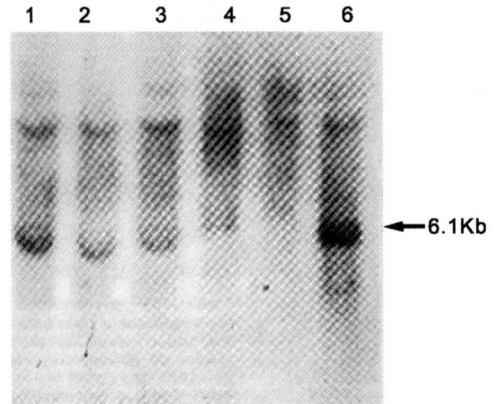

Fig. 5   Detection of LMP1 sequence in CNE-2, CNE-T1, CNE-T2 and CNE-T3 by Southern blot hybridization. DNAs extracted from three tumors, CNE -T1(1), CNE-T2(2)and CNE- T3(3), NPC cell line CNE-2 (4), Colon cancer(5) and B95-8 cell line(6)were digested by Xho-1 restriction enzyme, electrophoresed, transfered onto nitrocellulose filter and hybridized with radiolabelled LMP1 sequence used probe

4. Detection of EBV DNA by PCR

In order to further confirm the presence of EBV DNA in NPC cells, a sensitive PCR assay was carriy out on the tumor DNAs extracted from CNE-T1, CNE-T2, and CNE-T3. A viral sequence, Bam H1-W fragment was subjected to investigation by PCR. Amplified products were examined on 6% polyacrylamide gel electrophoresis (PAGE). The 121 bp(Fig. 6. B and D-F) sequence amplified by the primers directed to Bam H1-W fragment was identified in B95-8, CNE-T1, CNE-T2 and CNE-T3 DNA, whereas no such sequence was present in EBV negative RHEK-1 epithelial cell DNA(Fig. 6, lane C). In order to verify whether the amplified products from CNE-T1, CNE-T2, CNE-T3 and B95-8 DNA is specific, the dot-blot assay was carried out with the amplofied sequences. The probes of Bam H1-W hybridized specifically with the amplified products(data not shown). The BARF1(one of EBV oncogenes[11], was also examined by PCR on NPC cell lines(Fig. 7). A major 679 bp BARF1 sequence was present in all CNE cell lines as well as the positive controls(BamHIA and P3HR1 DNA)(lanes 1 to 3), while DNAs from Raji(deleted by BARF1)and RHEK-1 cells(an EBV negative epithelial cell line) failed to show any positive signal(lane 4 and 5). Among the NPC cell lines, CNE3 showed a high hybridization signal(lane 3), whereas a slight signal was obtained with CNE2 DNA(lane 2).

DISCUSSION

The data presented here showed and four NPC cell lines established from well and poorly differentiated NPC contained EBV DNA. This was demonstrated by different methods and summarized in Tab. 1. Particular attention should be taken concerning the identification of viral DNA in two cell lines established from well differentiated NPC, because these cell lines were cultured over 15-18 years in the laboratories and considered most of cases as EBV negative cell lines. This result could reinforce the previous observations not only on a tight relationship between EBV and undifferentiated NPC, but also its association with well differentiated NPC[1,6]. The diverse methods used here for the detection of EBV DNA or protein did not give a constant positive signal in in vitro-cultured cell lines. It however is worth to notice that LMP-1 gene was already cloned from CNE-1 and CNE-3 cell lines[10] and moreover EBV EBERs molecules have been detected in more than 90% of cells of all cell lines by in situ hybridization[14]. In taking together the observations, EBV DNA is present in these cell lines.

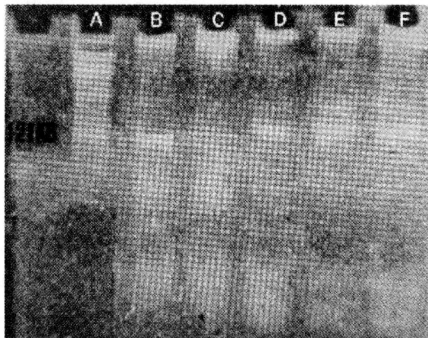

A: Marker; B: B95-8 DNA; C: EBV negative RHEK-1 DNA K-1 DNA; D: CNE-T1; E: CNE-T2; F: CNE-T3

Fig. 6 Detection of EBV BamH1-W fragment by PCR. PCR reaction was carried out as described in Materials and Methods. A 121 bp of amplified fragment correspond to the position between 1399 and1520 on BamH1-W fragment

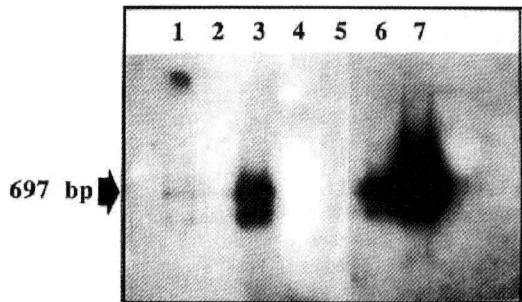

1: CNE-1 cell line; 2: CNE-2 cell line; 3: CNE-3 cell line; 4: Raji DNA(BARF1 negative control); 5: RHEK-1 cell line(EBV negative control); 6: Namalwa cell line (EBV positive control); 7: B95-8(EBV positive control)

Fig. 7 Detection of BARFI sequence by PCR in NPC cell lines. A 697 bp of amplified fragment correspond to the position between 165 496 and 166 192 on EBV genome

Tab. 1 Detection of EBV DNA and proteins in NPC cell lines and in nude mouse tumors -derived from NPC cell lies

	CNE-1	CNE-1-TS*	CNE-2	CNE-3	CNE-T1	CNE-T2	CNE-T3	HK-1	B95-8
In situ hybrid.									
LMP1(%)	5—10	ND	5—10	20	ND	ND	ND	5—10	95
Immunoblot									
EBNA-1	−	+	+	−	+	+	ND	ND	+
LMP-1	−	+	+	−	+	+	ND	ND	+
Southern blot									
LMP-1	−	−	−	−	+	+	+	ND	+
PCR									
BamH-W	+	ND	ND	ND	+	+	+	+	+
BARF1	+	ND	+	+	ND	ND	ND	ND	+

Note: * NPC cell line was treated with TPA and sodium butyrate for three days

Interestingly the 60×10^3 LMP-1 protein became detectable with CNE-1 cells were treated with TPA-SB. These activators may act on the transcriptional regulation of the LMP-1 gene to trigger expression, so that a productive EB virus cycle is activated in vitro.

In comparison with the results from NPC cell lines, relatively constant EBV positive signal was obtained in nude mice tumors. This may come from EBV DNA replication which could occur more easily in tumor in nude mice than in cell lines in vitro[15,16]. Whereas our and previous[6] reports showed a tight association of EBV with well differentiated NPC, there is no EBV IgA/VCA antibody in sera from many NPC patients with well differentiated carcinoma. This may be due to the restriction of the EBV DNA amplification and expression by cellular differentiation. It is suggested that our results stress the need to investigate another well differentiated head and neck cancer and other cancers in relation with EBV.

NPC cell lines with EB virus could consititute as a model for studying the molecular event in vitro and in vivo between EBV and tumor epithelial cells at different states of differentiation.

ACKNOWLEDGMENTS

We thank Prof. Sir A. M. Epstein and Dr. G. de The for revising this manuscript. This work was supported in part by research grants from the European Communities contract N°CI1CT930010 for T. O, Z. Yand the Chinese National Scientific Committee for Z.P.T, D.P.H, Z. Y.

REFERENCES

[1] Wolf H, Zur Hausen H, Becket Y, Nature, New Biol, 1973, 244:245-247.
[2] Desgranges C, de The G in de The G, Henle W, Rapp F.(eds). Oncogenesis and Herpesvirus Ⅲ. IARC Scientific Publications N° 25, Lyon, 1978:883-891.
[3] Lerman MI, Sakai A, Kai-Tai Y, Colburn NH. Carcinogenesis, 1987, 8:121-127.
[4] Desgranges C, Bornkamm G, Zeng Y, Wang P C, Zhu J S, Shang M, de The G. Int J Cancer,1982, 29:87-91.
[5] Zeng Y, Liu YX, Liu CR, Chen SW, Wei JN, Zai HJ. Intervirology, 1980, 13:162-168.
[6] Raab-Traub N, Flynn K, Pearson G, Huang A, Levine P, Lanier A, Pagano J. Int J Cancer, 1987, 39:25-29.
[7] Gu SY, Tan BG, Zeng Y, Zhou WP, Li K. Nasopharyngeal Carcinoma Current Concept(Prasad U. et al. eds)University of Malaya,1978:273-276.
[8] Jiao W, Zhou WY, Teng ZP, Wang PC, Zeng Y, Chinese J Virology in press.
[9] Huang DP, Ho JHC, Pooh YF, Chew EC, Saw D, Lui M, Li CL, Mak LS, Lai SH, Lan WH. Int J Cancer, 1980, 26: 127-132.
[10] Su L, Teng ZP, Zeng Y. Chinese J. Virology,1994, 11:114-118.
[11] Laboratory of Tumor Viruses of Cancer Institute, Laboratory of Tumor Viruses of Institute of Epidemiology Chinese Academy of Medical Sciences, Sci Sin. 21, 127-134, 1978.
[12] Wei M. X. and Ooka T., The EMBO. J, 1989,8:2897-2903.
[13] Yuan F, Zeng Y. Journal of Nanjin Medical College, 1986, 9:3-7.
[14] Liu CS, Teng ZP, Zeng Y. Chinese J. Virology in press.
[15] Trumpet PA, Epstein MA, Giovanelia BC, Finerty S, Int J Cancer, 1977, 20:655-662.
[16] Trumpet PA, Epstein MA, Giovanelia BC. Int J Cancer, 1976, 17:578-587.

[In《Virus Genes》1996, 13(1):53-60]

Epstein-Barr Virus Strain Variation in Nasopharyngeal Carcinoma from the Endemic and Non-Endemic Regions of China

SUNG Nancy S[1], EDWARDS Rachel H[1], SEILLIER-MOISEIWITSCH Francoise[2],
PERKINS Ashley G[1], ZENG Yi[3], RAAB-TRAUB Nancy[1]

1. Lineberger Comprehensive Cancer Center, University of North Carolina, Chapel Hill, NC, USA; 2. Department of Bisostatistics, School of Public Health, University of North Carolina. Chapel Hill, NC, USA; 3. Instivute of Virology, Chinese Academy of Preventive Medicine, Beijing, People's Republic of China

[**SUMMARY**] Nasopharyngeal carcinoma(NPC) occurs with a striking geographic incidence and is endemic in parts of southern China, where it is the major cause of cancer death. Epstein-Barr virus(EBV) is detected in all cells of the majority of NPC cases regardless of geographic origin. A small subset of EBV genes is expressed in NPC, including the latent membrane protein(LMP-1). LMP-1 is essential for transformation of B lymphocytes and is considered to be the EBV oncogene. This analysis of the DNA sequence variation within the LMP-1 gene reveals a consensus sequence for a strain, denoted China1, which predominates in East Asis where NPC is endemic. The China1 strain is characterized by nucleotide changes at 13 loci in the amino terminal portion of the LMP-1 gene when compard with the B95-8 prototype, including a point mutation resulting in the loss of an Xhol restriction site. This strain was present in 9 of 15 NPC biopsy specimens from the endemic region and in 7 of 13 from northern China, where NPC is non-endemic. A second strain, China2, was detected in 4 of 15 endemic isolates and in 2 of 13 nonendemic isolates; this strain was characterized by a cluster of 5 nucleotide changes in the amino terminal portion of LMP-1 in addition to those seen in China1. It was also marked by distinct changes in the carboxy terminal region of LMP-1 including the retention of amino acids 343-352. All China1 isolates were EBV type 1, whereas the China2 isolates did not correlate with EBV type. Phylogenetic relationships between these 2 strains were determined, as were signature amino acid alterations that discriminate between them.

INTRODUCTION

Nasopharyngeal carcinoma(NPC) occurs with a remarkable geographic pattern of incidence and is considered to be endemic in parts of southern China, where it is the major cause of cancer death. Mediterranean African and the Alaskan Inuit people also have elevated incidences of NPC(de The, 1982). An etiologically complex disease, NPC has been linked to several environmental, dietary, viral and genetic co-factors. Nitrosamines and other tumor-promoting agents have been identified as co-factors present in food products in the high-incidence areas(Armstrong et al., 1983). Perhaps the most compiling contributing factor is the Epstein-Barr virus(EBV), which is detected in all cells of undifferentiated NPC biopsy specimens regardless of geographic origin(reviewed in Raab-Traub, 1996). Although EBV is ubiquitous in the human population, it is possible that one contributing factor to the endemic incidence of NPC could be the presence of a particular viral variant predominating in the endemic region.

All EBV isolates can be classified as type 1 or type2(or types A and B)based on sequence divergence in the EBNA-2, 3A, 3B and 3C genes(Adldinger et al., 1985; Sample et al., 1990). Type1 EBV is more prevalent in Chinese NPC(Abdel-Hamid et al., 1992; Zimber et al., 1986), although none of the type -discriminating EBNA genes are expressed in NPC. Sorting independently of these 2 EBV types are several strains defined by DNA sequene polymorphisms in the LMP-1 gene(Miler et al., 1994). The LMP-1 protein, detected in at least 65% of NPC tumors(Young et al.,1988), is able to transform rodent fibroblasts in viro and is essential for EBV-mediated transformation of B lymphocytes(reviewed in Kieff, 1996). In addition to the induction of several B-cell activation antigens and adhesion molecules, LMP-1 protects infected cells from apoptosis by upregulaiton of the bel-2 and A-20 genes(reviewed Kieff, 1996). It also interacts with and engages the TRAF signal transduction pathway, resulting in the induction of EGFR expression and activation of NK-kB(Hammarskjold and Simurda, 1992; Miller et al., 1995; Mosialos et al., 1995).

The predominant EBV starin in China, designated here as China, is characterized by a cluster of 13 nucleotide changes with respect to the B95-8 prototype strain in the amino terminal region of LMP-1(Miller et al., 1994). These include a point mutation resulting in the loss of an Xho restriction site. The China 1 strain is also distinguished by changes in the carboxy terminal region of LMP-1, most notable the deletion of amino acids 343-352

(Abdel-Hamid et al., 1992; Chen et al., 1992; Hu et al., 1991; Miller et al., 1994). A related strain, previously found in Alaskan isolater, shares 14 of the 15 amino terminal changes with China 1, including the Xhol polymorphism, but at the carboxy terminus retains amino acids 343-352 and harbors 15 additional nucleotide changes not found in China 1(Miller et al., 1994).

Our present study was undertaken to determine the prevalence of EBV strains, based on sequence variation in the LMP-1 gene, in NPC tumors from patients from northern China, where the incidence of this malignancy is much lower than in southern China and where EBV typing has not been done. For comparison, tumors from patients from the NPC endemic area of southern China were also examined, and the relatedness of the various EBV strains found in China was determined by phylogenetic analysis.

MATERIAL AND METHODS

1. Patient tissue specimens

NPC tissue biopsies were obtained from patients at the Cancer Hospital in Beijing(specimens 108, 423, 509, 525, 614 and 615), the Bai Qiu En Medical Univerity Hospital in Changchun, Jilin Province(specimens 14-27 and 121-126)and the Guangxi Regional Hospital in Nanning, Guangxi Autonomous Region(specimens GX1-6, 127-129, 132-133, 136-145)in the People's Republic of China. Patients were interviewed to verify whether their ancestral home was within the endemic or non-endemicregion.

Tissues were Dounce-homogenized on ice in buffer containing 15mmol/L NaCl, 15mmol/L Tris-HCl(pH 8.0)and 1mmol/L EDTA, subjected to 4 rounds of freeze/thaw and digested with Proteinase K/SDS for 4 hr at 56℃. Following extracton in phenol/chloroform and ethanol precipitation, DNA was resuspended in 10mmol/L Tris-HCl(pH 8.0)/1mmol/L EDTA.

2. DNA sequencing

The DNA sequence corresponding to the amino terminal portion of LMP-1 was determined by first amplifying 0.3μg of tumor DNA with the polymerase chain reaction(PCR)using the primers LMPEXC and LMP9747(Tab. 1), followed by asymm etric amplification and dideoxy sequencing using the primers LMP9550 and LMP9233, as previously described(Miller et al., 1994). For sequencing of the carboxy terminus, 10 of the isolates(127, 133, 142, 145, 16, 26, GX1, 132, 614, 615 and 126) were subjected to PCR amplification using primers LMPFUE and LMP8808(Tab. 1). PCR products were subcloned into the pGem3Z vector. One clone from each isolate was selected for dideoxy sequencing using the LMPFUB primer, with the exception of isolate 145, for which 3 positive clones were sequenced.

Tab. 1　Primers used in PCR and Sequencing

Primer	EBV coordinates	Sequence
LMPEXC	168813—168832	5'CAACCAATAGAGTCCACCAG 3'
LMP9747	169747—169767	5'TTCTGTTGCACTTGGC 3'
LMP9550	169570—169550	5'GCCCTACATAAGCCTCTCAC 3'
LMP9233	169233—169250	5'TCCAGTGGACAGAGAAG 3'
LMPFUB	168736—168756	5'ACAACGACACAGTGATGAACACCACC 3'
LMPFUB2	168328—168348	5'GAAGAGGTTGAAAACAAAGGA 3'
LMPFUE	168163—168183	5'GTCATAGTAGCTTAGCTGAC 3'
LMP8808	168808—168830	5'GTGGACTCTATTGGTTGATCTC 3'
EBNA3C-5'	99938—99960	5'AGAAGGGGAGCGTGTGGTTGTGT 3'
EBNA3C-3'	100092—100071	5'GGCTCGTTTTTGACGTCGGC 3'
EBNA3C-type 1-Pr		5'GAAGATTCATCGTCAGTG 3'
EBNA3C-type 2 Pr		5'CCGTGATTTCTACCGGGAGT 3'

3. LMP-1 deletion analysis

Genomic DNA(100-200ng)from each isolate was subjected to PCR amplification for 30 cycles, at an annealing temperature of 55℃ and an extension time of 1 min, using the primers FUE and FUB2(Tab. 1)which flank the region of the deletion. In isolates that retain or delete amino acids 343-352, the PCR yielded 186 bp and 156 bp products, respectively. Products were resolved on 10% acrylamide/TBE gels and transferred to Hybond N+ membrane (Amersham, Arling-to Heights, IL) for 15 min using a gel dryer with no heat. Following denaturation in 0.4mol/L NaOH for 10 min, membranes were baked for 2hr at 80℃, pre-hybridized for 15 min at 65℃ in Rapid-Hyb solution(Amersham), hybridized for 2 hr to a riboprobe containing a 1.9 kb XhoI fragment from the LMP-1 gene and visualized by autoradiography.

4. EBNA typing

Genomic DNA from NPC isolates was amplified by PCR using the primers EBNA3C-5′ and EBNA3C-3′(Tab. 1)(Sample et al.,1990). For each reaction, 100-200 ng of DNA was amplified for 35 cycles with an annealing temperature of 55℃ and an extension time of 1 min. Products were resolved on agarose gels, blotted to Hybond N+ membrane, and hybridized at 40℃ as described above to each of 2 eng-labeled oligonucleotide probes, EBNA3C-type 1-Pr and EBNA3C-type2 Pr(Tab. 1)(Sample et al.,1990). These probes distinguish EBV types 1 and 2 based on size heterogeneity of the PCR products, yielding a 246 bp product in type 1 EBV and a 153 bp product in type 2 EBV.

5. Phylogenetic and statistical analyse

Using 12 Chinese isolates, a consensus sequence for the N-terminal region of LMP-1 was generated using the PRETTY program from the Wisconsin Package(Genetics Computer Group, Madison, WI). The 12 samples included the previously published Cao, 1510, C11 and C13 isolates(Chen et al., 1992; Hu et al., 1991; Miller et al., 1994)as well as 8 samples first reported here(GX1, 132, 126, 127,133, 142, 145, 16). Loci that diverge from the B95-8 prototype strain are reported in Tab. 2.

Tab. 2　Consensus definiton of EBV China strain based on Lmp-1 N-Terminal region[1]

EBV coordinate	LMP-1 codon	Change	Frequency(%)
169467	3	CAC/His>CGC/Arg	19/26(73.1)
169437	13	CGA/Arg>CCA/Pro	17/26(65.4)
169425	17	CGA/Arg>CTA/Leu	27/27(100)
169402	25	CTA/Leu>ATA/lle	27/27(100)
169379	32	C>G	26/27(96.3)
169361	38	T>C	26/27(96.3)
169352	41	C>T	20/27(74)
169339	46	GAC/Asp>AAC/Asn	24/27(88.9)
169322	51	C>G	22/26(84.6)
169286	63	A>T	22/24(91.6)
169280	65	A>C	19/22(86.4)
169276	67	T>C	17/20(85)
169274	67	G>C	17/20(85)

Notes:[1]China 1 strain consensus was compiled fron 5 previously published isolates(Chen et al., 1992; Hu et al., 1991; Miller et al., 1994)and from 22 isolates reported in Fig. la, b. A nucleotide change, relative to the B95-8 strain, at a particular locus was defined as characteristic of of the China 1 strain if it appeared in at least 65% of the isolates. Not included in the consensus are 5 Chinese isolates that were identical to B95-8

To determine the phylogenetic relationships within various EBV isolates from China, the LMP-1 sequence, including codons 1-70 and 192-386, was compiled from the 12 samples described above as well as from the previously pubished AL, pOT and B95-8 isolates(Miller et al., 1994). Sequences were aligned using the Wisconsin Package Version 9.0 sequence editor(Genetics Computer Group), and all constant positions were eliminated. Distance matrices were calculated with the PHYLIPI DNADIST program(Felsenstein, 1995), using both the Jukes and Cantor(1969)and Kimura(1983)two-parameter methods with a transition/transversion fixed at 2. Phylogentic trees were constucted from these distance matrices by both the neighbor-joining(Saitou and Nei, 1987)and UPGMA methods, using the NEIGHBOR and DRAWTREE programs from the PHYLIP package.

Classification and Regression Tree(CART) methodology(Wadsworth international Group, Belmont, CA)was used to construct regression trees to determine predictive amino acid positions for a particular strain, using sequence from the 15 isolates described above, A total of 34 amino acid positions were analyzed, which included only those loci at which an amino acid change had occurred in more than one isolate.

RESULTS

1. Analysis of the LMP-1 amino terminus: a consensus definition of the predominant Chinese strain, China 1

NPC biopsy specimens were collected from the Guangxi Autonomous Region of southern China, where NPC is endemic, as well as from the cities of Beijing and Changchun, regions of northern China where NPC incidence is much lower, Strain prevalence was first determined by DNA sequencing of the amino terminal portion of the LMP-1 gene. In this region, spaning from EBV genone coordinates 169474 to 169280, variations from the B95-8 prototype strain were noted at 28 loci, resulting in changes at 16 amino acid residues(Fig. 1).

Whereas 5 of 28 isolates(17.8%), including 1 from the endemic region and 4 from the nonendemic region, were identical to the B95-8 prototype strain, 22 of 28 isolates examined(78.5%)harbored a cluster of 13 nucleotide alterations resembling the predominat Chinese strain previously reported(Miller et al., 1994). A consensus definition of this strain, designated China1, was then derived from these data from 4 previously reported Chinese isolates(Chen et al.,1992; Hu et al., 1991; Miller et al., 1994). The DNA sequence variation defining this strain is reported in Tab. 2 and is also indicated by grey shading in Fig. 1c. This cluster of changes always includes the loss of an Xhol restriction enzyme site at nucleotide position 169425 and an amino acid substitution at codon 25. Other changes-including amino acid substitutions at codons 3, 13, 17 and 46 as well as silent changes within codons 32, 38, 41, 51, 63, 65 and 67-are detected in a majority but not all of the isolates. Two of the isolates, 129 from the endemic region and 125 from the non-endemic region, may have undergone recombination within this portion of the LMP-1 gene, as both are identical to the B95-8 genotype following codons 25 and 38, respectively.

2. Identification of a distinct strain of EBV, China 2

DNA sequence analysis of the LMP-1 amino terminus also revealed a distinct cluster of unique nucleotide changes, in addition to those found in the China 1 strain, in 6 of 28 isolates(21.4%). These included 4 from the endemic region and 2 from the non-endemic region(Fig. 1a, b, boxed). Of these 5 nucleotide changes, 3 have to been previously reported in NPC from any geographic location, including a change from CTA/Leu to ATG/Met at codon 25, CTC/Leu to ATC/Ile at amino acid 33 and a silent change(CTC→CTG)within codon 60. Interestingly, the 2 other changes, GTT/Val to ATT/Ile at codon 43 and a change from TCC/Ser to GCC/Ala at codon 57, have been previously observed only in EBV-associated tumor isolates from Alaska(dashed boxes in Fig. 1; Miller et al., 1994). All of the changes are conservative, with the exception of the substitution of the non-polar alanine residue within the transmembrane domain at position 57. This new strain is designated China 2.

Four of 6 NPC biopsy specimens harboring the China 2 strain originated in the endemic area of southern China, whereas the remaining 2 were from the non-endemic area in northeastern Chian. Surprisingly, the 2 China 2 isolates from northern China both lacked the Alaskan-associated change at amino acid 43. They were further distinguished by an additional change from GAA/Glu to GAC/Asp in codon 2. Taken together, isolates bearing either the China 1 or China 2 strains and having lost the Xho l restriction site account for 22 of 28 isolates(78.6%), and are distributed fairly evenly, being found in 13 of 15 isolates(86.7%)from the endemic area and in 9 of 13 isolates (69.2%)from the non-endemic area. One other sample from the endemic region(GX1) lacked the China 1 or China 2 changes but had 2 nucleotide changes, compared with B95-8, that were not detected in any of the other isolates. Both rexulted in non-conservative amino acid changes, from Gly to Ala at position 11; and Pro to Arg at position 12, and did not include loss of the Xhol restriction site(Fig. 1a).

Although previous studies reported the presence of the Xhol polymorphism in 88 of 89(98.9%) of Chinese NPCs(AbdelHamid et al., 1992; Chen et al., 1992; Hu et al., 1991; Miller et al., 1994), in the patient population analyzed here, the prevalence of this polymorphism is approx, 22% lower, weakening its correlation with NPC incidence, In this survey, the wild type or B95-8 strain of EBV is more prevalent in Asia than has been previously reported. Additionally whereas the Xhol polymorphism was foud in the majority of Asian NPCs, analysis of this polymorphism does not allow a distinction to be made between the China 1 and China 2 strains, and its use may obscure the genetic diversity existing within the LMP-1 gene.

3. Prevalence of the deletion of amino acids 343-352: China 2 isolates are uniformly undeleted

In addition to the nucleotide changes present in the amino terminal portion of LMP-1, Chinese NPCs are also characterized by the delection of amino acids 343-352 within the carboxy terminal cytoplasmic domain of LMP-1 (Chen et al., 1992; Hu et al., 1991; Miller et al., 1994). This deletion was also detected in a significant portion of EBV-positive Hodgkin's tumors from Europe(Knecht et al., 1993), with the suggestion that it is associated with a more aggressively transforming phenotype(Hu et al., 1993; Knecht et al., 1993; Li et al., 1996). The Alaskan

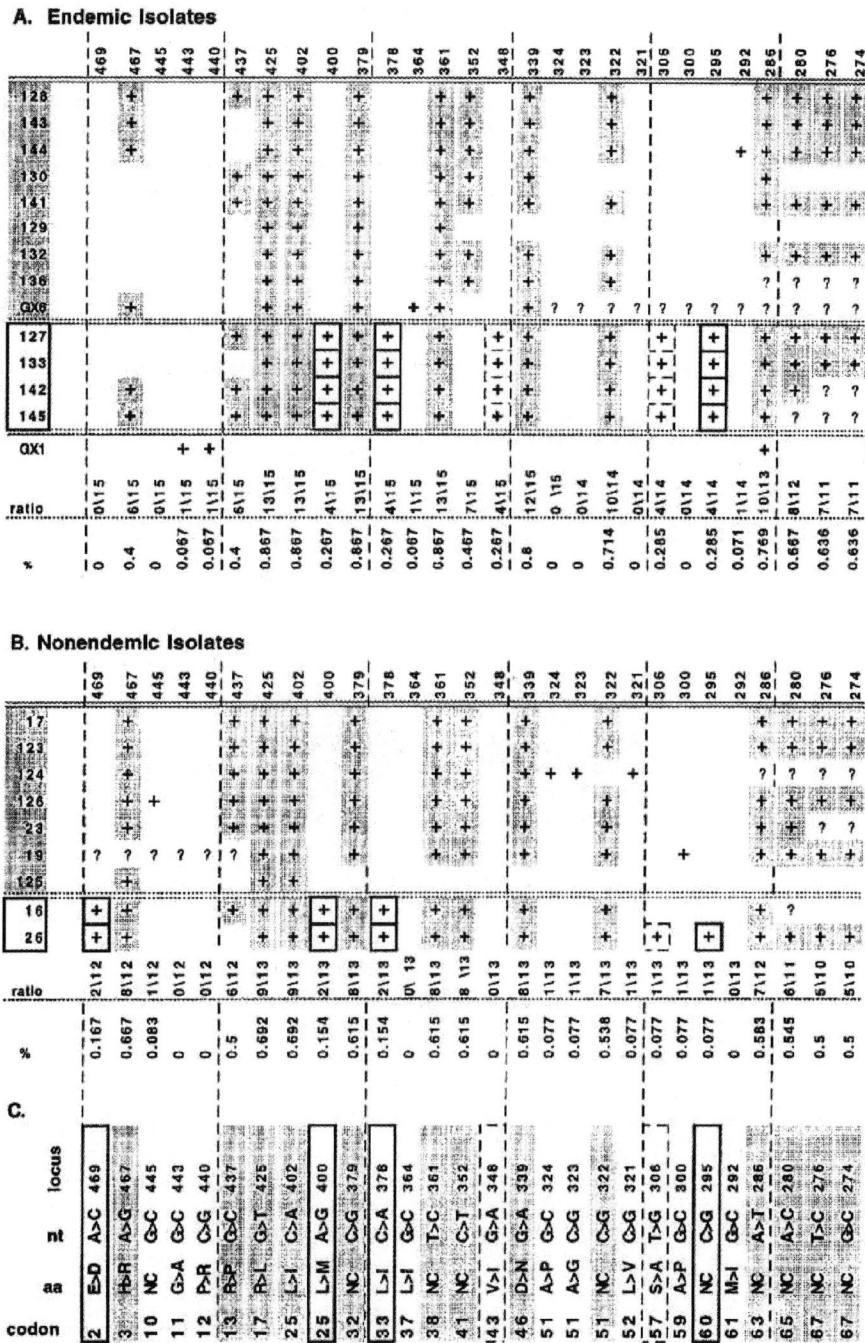

Fig. 1 Sequence variation in the amino terminal portion of LMP-1. Numbers actrss top tow correspond to EBV genome coordinates 169469 to 169274; numbers in left-hand colume refer to individual isolates. A plus sign indicates variaton from the B95-8 prototype strains at this locus; a question mark indicates sequence beyond this point is unknown. Cluster of base changes associated with the China1 strein is indicated by grey shading; base changes associated with the China2 strain are boxed; base changes associated with the Alaskan strain are marked with a dashed box. "Ratio" includes results from 1 endemic and 4 non-endemic isolates that were identical to the B95-8 prototype strain. (a) LMP-1 sequence variation in isolates from the NPC endemic region of southern China. (b) Sequence variation in isolates from the NPC non-endemic region of northern China. (c) Consensus profile of nucleotide(nt) and amino acid(aa) changes associated with the China1, China2 and Alaskan strains

strain is undeleted, as is the B95-8 prototype strain(Miller et al., 1994). To further define the relationshop between the China 2 and other strains, the prevalence of the deletion was determined in42 NPC isolates from China.

The deletion was detected in 16 of 21(76.2%) NPC biopsy specimens from the endemic area, in 14 of 21 (66.1%)from the non-endemic area(Tab. 3), but in none of the 6 China. 2 isolates analyzed. In isolate 145, PCR revealed the deleted form; however, analysis of individual clones revealed 2 distinct forms present in this 1 isolate (Fig. 2). Subsequent sequencing revealed that the undeleted China 2 form would not be readily amplified from genomic DNA due to base pair changes in the primer region and that the co-present deleted form was actually a distinct strain(discussed in the following section). The China 2 strain is therefore further distinguished from the China 1 strain by the uniform retention of amino acids 343-352. This deletion can also sort independently from the Xhol polymorphism in the amino terminus of LMP-1, found in both China 1 and China 2 isolates. Additionally, as evidenced by sample 145, it is clear that both deleted and undeltetd forms of the LMP-1 gene can co-exist in the same tumor.

Tab. 3   Prevalence of the Deletion of LMP-1 amino Acids 343-352 in Chinese NPC

	Endemic isolates	Non-endemic isolates	Total
aa343-352 deleted	16/21(76.2%)	14/21(66.1%)	30/42(71.4%)
aa343-352 undeleted	5/21(23.8%)	7/21(33.3%)	12/42(28.5%)

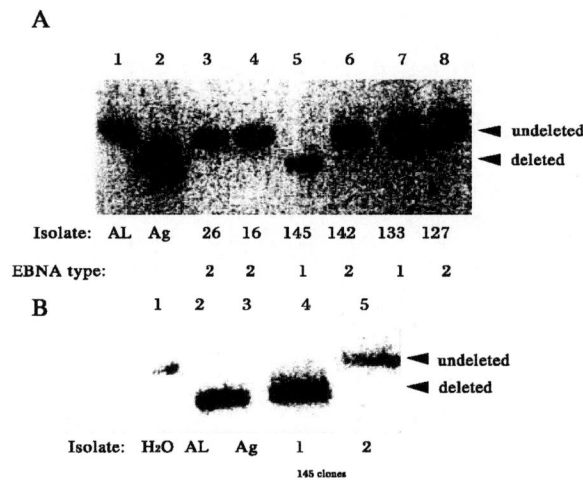

(A) Detection of deletion of LMP-1 amino acids 343-352 by PCR of genomic DNA extracted from tumor biopsy material. EBNA type for each isolate is also shown.(B) Detection of deletion of LMP-1 amino acids 343-352 in 2 separate clones of China 2 isolate 145.

Fig. 2   Deletion status of China 2 isolates. PCR products were resolved on polyacrylamide gels, blotted to nylon membrane and probed with an oligonucleotide specific for sequence flanking the deleted region. AL, Alaskan liver biopsy specimen containing undeleted LMP-1 sequence, and Ag, from he AG876 cell line carrying deleted LMP-1 sequence, were included as controls. Other isolates are as shown

4. The China 2 strain can also be distinguished by nucleotide changes at the carboxy terminus of the LMP-1 gene

To determine whether the China 2 isolates identified in Fig. 1 also have characteristic changes within the LMP-1 carboxy terminus, the DNA sequence of 5 of these isolates was determined and analyzed from nucleotides 168755 to 168163. Distinct, consistent nucleotide changes were detected at 9 nucleotide loci, resulting in 7 alterations at the amino acid level(Fig. 3). Analysis of 2 additional isolates from the non-endemic region(614 and 615), which were undeleted by the PCR assay, revealed the same pattern of changes and are therefore also classified as China 2. These changes, within codons 192, 229, 245, 252, 331, 344 and 355, were all found in at least 5 of the 7 China 2 isolates analyzed. Another change within codon 338(TTG/Leu→CCG/Pro), fond in all 7 samples, is identical to that detected in Alaskan isolates. The China 1 isolates also are altered at this locus, but the substituted amino acid is serine rather than proline.

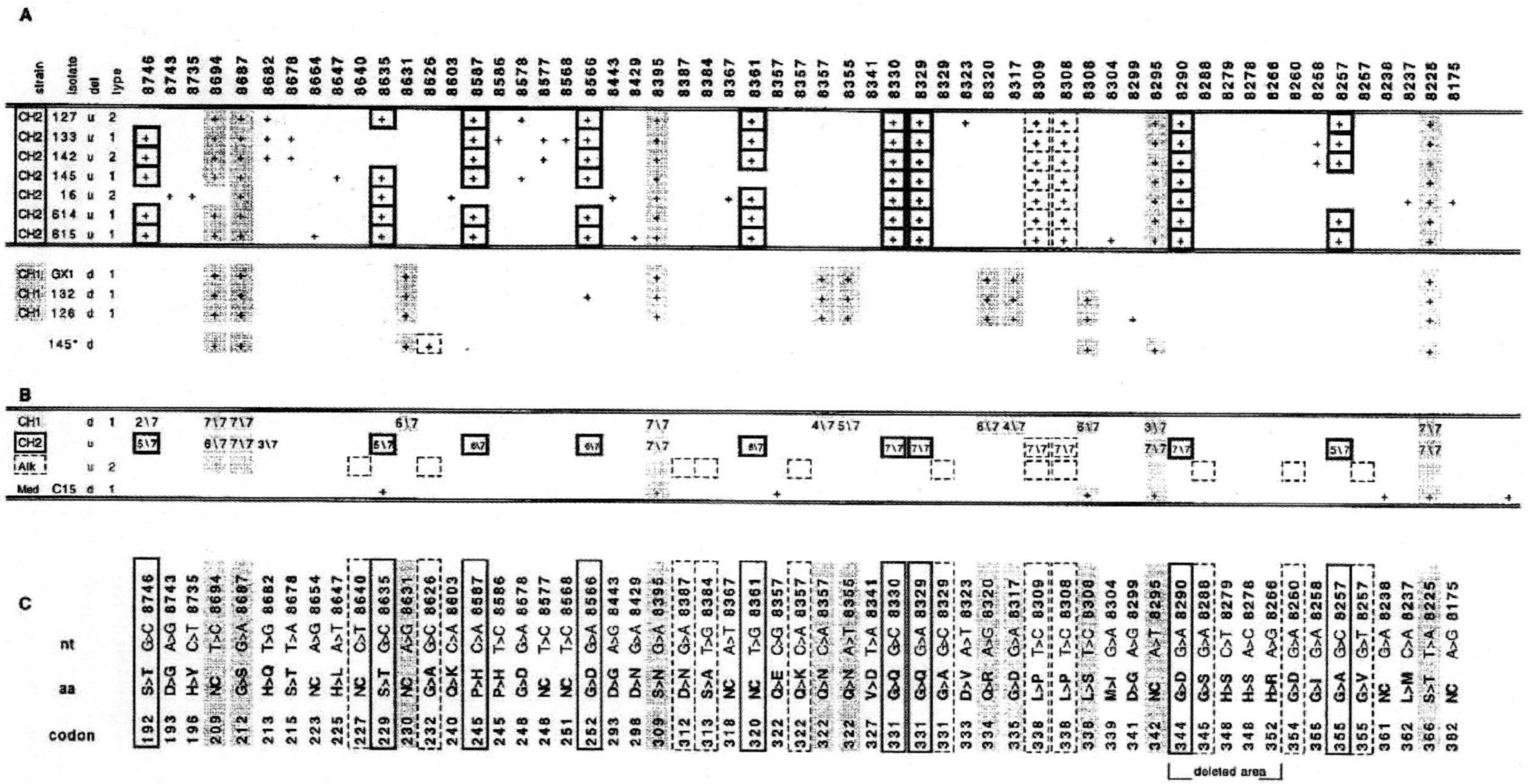

Fig. 3 LMP-1 sequence variation in the carboxy terminus. Numbers across top row correspond to EBV genome coordinates 168746 to 168175. Variation from the B95-8 prototype strain at the locus shown is indicated by a plus sign. Deletion of amino acids 343-352 is indicated by "d"in "del" column; "u"denotes undeleted. EBNA typing results are shown in "type"column. Base changes associated with the China1 strain are indicated by grey shading; variations associated with China2 strain are boxed; Alaskan changes are in dashed boxes. (a)Strain variation in the 7 China2 isolates, also 3 Chinaisolates, and 1 coinfectiong strain from isolate145(145*). (b)Consensus profile of nucleotide changes characteristic of the China1, China2 and Alaskan strina as well as a Mediterranean isolate. China1 consensus was compiled from 7 isolates, 4 of which were published elsewhere(Chen et al., 1992; Hu et al., 1991; Miller et al.,1994). A change is noted if it appeared in at least 4 of the 7. Alaskan consensus includes changes noted in 2 isolates from Alaska(Miller et al., 1994).(c)Nucleotide and amino acid coordinates of variations characteristic of China1, China2 and Alaskan strains indicated as described above

Of the 9 changes in China 2, 1(within codon 320; CCT→CCG)was silent, and 3(codon192, AGT/Ser to ACT/Thr; codon 229, AGT/Ser to ACT/Thr; and codon 331 GGA/Gly to CA/L/GLn)were conservative. The change at aa 192 was also detected in 2 previously reported sequences(Chen et al., 1992; Hu et al., 1991), and the change at aa 229 has been detected in only 1 other isolate, C15 from the Mediterranean region(Miller et al., 1994). Another conservative change at residue 213, found in only 3 of 7 isolates, lies within the TNF-receptor-associated factor(TRAF)-interacting domain of LMP-1 but is outside the core TRAF binding motif, PXQXT(Mosialos et al., 1995). Other non-conservative changes included CCT/Pro to CAT/His at codon 245, GGC/Gly to GAC/Asp at codon 252, GGC/Gly to GAC/Asp at codon 344 and GGT/ Gly to GCT/Ala at codon 355. Isolate 16, however, harbored changes at only 3 of he 7 codons.

For the purpose of comparison, a consensus profile of changs characteristic of the China l strain is shown in Fig. 3b. This consensus was derived from a total of 7 isolates; 4 previously reported(Chen et al., 1992; Hu et al., 1991; Miller et al., 1994) and 3 isolates(GX1, 126 and132) sequenced in this study(Fig. 3a). Also included for comparison are sequence changes derived from 2 previously analyzed Alaskan isolates and 1 Mediterranean NPC xenograft, C15(Miller et al., 1994). As was the case in the amino terminal portion of LMP-1, China 2 and China 1 share common nucleotide variation from B95-8 at several loci. Analysis of the carboxy terminal region, however, reveals a clearer divergence between these strains, as there ate consistent changes in China 1 that are not found in China 2(codons 322, 334, 335 and 338). China 2 shares the substitution of proline for leucine at codon 338 with the Alaskan isolates and the retention of codons343-352, but none of the other changes in the carboxy terminus are in common between the China 2 and Alaskan strains(Fig. 3b). The nucleotide and corresponding amino acid changes associated with the China 2, China 1 and Alaskan strains are shown in Fig. 3c.

Isolate GX1 had 2 unique changes but none of the China 1-associated changes in its amino terminus, yet had 8 of the 9 China 1-associated nucleotide changes in the carboxy terminus(Fig. 3a), suggesting that interstrain recombination had occurred within the transmembrane domain of LMP-1. Two other isolates, 125 and 129, may also be chimeras of the predominant China 1 strain and the prototype B95-8 strain, as they both appear to flip from one strain to the other following codons 25 and 38, respectively.

The sequence of hte co-infecting deleted strain in isolate 145 was also determined and is shown in Fig. 3a (145*). It did not contain any of the China 2-associated changes but did contain 1 Alaskan-associated change(in amino acid residue 232), indicating that it is a unique strain distinct from the China 2 found in the same tumor biopsy specimen. It also provides evidence of recombination within LMP-1, as it resembles China 1 from codons 192 to 230 and from codons 338 to 382, but in the intervening sequence is identical to B958. These results suggest that recombination within the LMP-1 gene may occur, but does so infrequently in NPC and, somewhat unexpectedly, does not necessarily occur across the internal repeat region(amino acids 250-298)within the carboxy terminus.

5. Phylogenetic analysis of viral nucleotide sequence differences

To determine the phylogenetic relationships among various EBV isolates from China, the LMP-1 DNA sequences from both the amino and carboxy terminal regions of 15 isolates were aligned and constant positions removed. Using he one-parameter model(Jukes and Cantor, 1969), in which the rate of substitution between all nucleotides is assumed to be equal, a distance matrix was constructed. A phylogenetic tree was then drawn using the neighborjoinjing method (Saitou and Nei, 1987). Shown in Fig. 4, the China 2 isolates form a clear cluster and were more closely related to the Alaskan isolates than to the other China 1 isolates, which was not unexpected because both groups retain amino acids 343-352 and share several other nucleotide changes. The China 1 isolates also form a cluster; however, it is not as well defined as that formed by the China 2 isolates. Using the Kimura (1983) two-parameter method, which assumes that transition-type changes are more likely to occur than transversion-gype changes, a tree with an identical branching pattern resulted(data not shown). A very similar result was obtained when the UPGMA method was used to construct the trees and when using sequence data from either the aminoor carboxy terminal portion of LMP-1(data not shown). Therefore, the China 2 cluster is robust to different methods of both calculating distances and constructing trees.

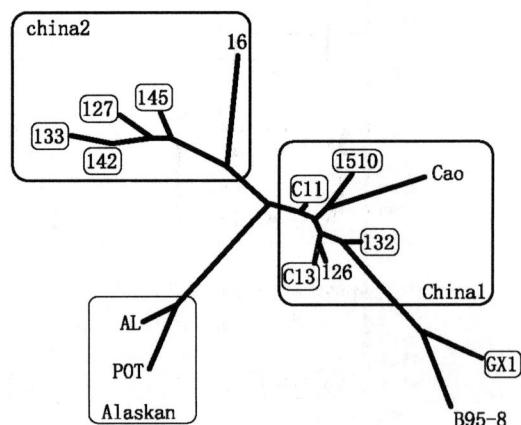

Fig. 4 Phylogenetic analysis of China 1, China 2 and Alaskan strains. Isolates from the endemic region of China are circled

None of the phylogenetic reconstructions indicated strain sorting based on geographic location within China, although the 2 Alaskan isolates included in the analysis were quite distinct. Whereas most Chinese isolates are clearly different from the B95-8 prototype, the EBV strains isolated from the NPC endemic area of southern China are not markedly different from those found in the non-endemic area of northern China.

6. Classification of strains based on amino acid signature patterns

Because the China 1, China 2 and Alaskan strains share much of their divergence from B95-8, particularly in the amino terminus, the CART methodology was applied to determine the amino acid positions that could categorize them. In 15 isolates for which sequence from both the amino and carboxy terminal portions of LMP-1 had been determined, 34 amino acid loci at which changes were found in more than 1 isolate were analyzed. Each of the 4 loci in Tab. 4 showed perfect discrimination between the China 2 strain and the others. These include 2 positions in the amino terminus and 2 in the carboxy terminus. Also, a combination of positions 245 and 229 rerfectly classify the China 2 strain. At position 245, 4 of 5 China 2 isolates had substituted histidine for proline, and the other China 2 isolate remained unchanged at this position. The substitution of threonine for serine at position 229 then classifies it as China 2. Positions capable of perfectly classifying the China 1 strain included the substitution of isoleucine at position 25, serine at position 338, and also the deletion of amino acids 343 -352. The Alaskan strain could be discriminated perfectly at 9 different loci(Tab. 4), mostly clustered in the carboxy terminus. Further definition of the Alaskan strainu awaits sequence information from more than the 2 isolates included here.

Tab. 4 Aminoacid positions within LMP-1 that discriminate among the China 2 and alaskan strains

Strain	Locus	Change
China 1	25	Leu to Ile
	338	Leu to Set
	343 -352	deleted
China 2	25	Leu to Met
	33	Leu to Ile
	331	Gly to Gin
	344	Gly to Asp
Alaskan	22	Set to Pro
	63	Ile to Val
	232	Gty to Ala
	312	Asp to Ash
	313	Ser to Ala
	331	Gly to Ala
	345	Gly to Ser
	354	Gly to Ser
	355	Gly to Val

7. LMP-1 sequence variation in the China 2 strain sorts independently of EBV EBNA type

All EBV isolates can be classified as type 1 or type 2(or types A and B) based on sequence divergence in the EBNA-2, 3A, 3B and 3C genes(Adldinger et al., 1985; Sample et al.,1990). China 1 isolates uniformly contained type 1 EBV, and both Alaskan isolates were type 2(Abdel-Hamid et al., 1992); however, the deletion within the LMP-1 gene has been shown to sort independently of EBNA type(Miller et al., 1994). Of the 8 China 2 isolates analyzed, 4 carried type 1 and 4 carried type 2(Fig. 3a). Furthermore, the EBNA types were equally distributed among the isolates from the endemic and non-endemic regions despite the closer geographic proximity of the non-endemic region(northeastern China) to Alaska, where only type 2 was previously described. This finding further substantiates the lack of correlation between EBNA type and LMP-1 genotype originally suggested by Miller et al. (1994).

DICUSSION

This study represents the first comparison of EBV strains in isolates from the NPC-endemic region of southern China with those from the NPC non-endemic region of northern China, and reports a new strain, China 2, based on DNA sequence variation in the LMP-1 gene.

Based on DNA sequence analysis of the amino-terminal 68 codons of LMP-1, the isolates could be divided into 3 strains, summarized in Tab. 5. Five of the 28(17. 8%) were indistinguishable from the B95-8 prototype strain. Sixteen of the 28(57. 1%) had the predominant China 1 strain, characterized by a cluster of 13 nucleotide changes in the amino terminal portion of LMP-1, including loss of an Xhol restriction enzyme site. Six of the 28(21. 4%), although sharing some common nucleotide changes with China 1 including the Xhol polymorphism, carry a previously unrecognized viral strain here designated China 2. The divergence between China 1 and China 2 was more apparent in the carboxy terminal portion of LMP-1, most notably in that amino acid residues343-352 were retained in all the China 2 isolates.

Characterized by 3 distinct amino acid changes in the amino terminus and 7 in the carboxy terminal portion of LMP-1, China 2 was found in 26. 6% of the primary tumor isolates from the endemic area of China and in 15. 4% from the non-endemic region. China 2 appears to be closely related to the "Minor strain 2", recently reported in 5 of 74(6. 8%)primary NPCs from Hong Kong, also carrying changes within LMP codons 331, 338, 344 and 355 (Cheung et al., 1996) A similar cluster of changes has also been reported in other EBV -associated diseases in Asia, including 1 infectious mononucleosis(IM)and 1 chronic EBV case in Japan(Itakura et al.,1996), as well as 4 cases of chronic tonsillitis, 1 lung carcinoma and 1 sinonasal carcinoma from Hong Kong(Leung et al., 1997). It is likely that these isolates are in fact China 2; however, it is not known if they also carry the distinct China 2 residues in the amino terminus of LMP-1. Because previous determinations of EBV strain prevalence in NPC were based primarily on the Xhol polymorphism that does not distinguish among the China 1, China 2 and Alaskan strains, it is likely that LMP-1 sequence is more divergent within Asian NPC and other EBV-associated diseases than has been reported previously. There was no marked difference in the distribution of EBV strains in the endemic and non-endemic regions(Tab. 5), with the exception of the B95-8-like isolates, which were more prevalent in northern China. Several previous studies have suggested that the strains detected in EBV-associated malignancies may reflect the prevalence of strains found in the general population(Cheng et al., 1996; Khanim et al.,1996). The detection of China 1, China 2 and a surprising number of B95-8-1ike isolates in primary NPC from the non-endemic region suggests that all strains of EBV can contribute to the etiology of NPC.

Tab. 5 Distribution of EBV strains Based on Variation in LMP-1N -Terminus

Strain	Endemic region	Non-endemic region	Total
China 1	9/15(60. 0%)	7/13(53. 8%)	16/28(57. 1%)
China 2	4/15(26. 6%)	2/13(15. 4%)	6/28(21. 4%)
B95-8	1/15(6. 7%)	4/13(30. 8%)	5/28(17. 9%)
Other	1/15(6. 7%)	0/13	1/28(3. 6%)

Functional analysis of the LMP-1 protein has focused on the carboxy terminal region. Notably, amino acids 204—208 contain a PXQXT motif, through which LMP-1 binds to the TNF receptorassociated factors(TRAF) (Mosialos et al., 1995). It is through activation of this TRAF signaling pathway that LMP-1 induces expression of the EGFR(Miller et al., 1997). This TRAF- binding motif, as well as a similar PXQXS motif at amino acids 379-383, are conserved in all of the isolates examined here(Fig. 3)and are also conserved within the LMP-1 homologue in simian EBV(Franken et al., 1996), underscoring the importance of TRAF signaling for LMP-1 funciton. On the other hand, an additional perfect PXQXT motif at amino acids 320—324 is disrupted in the China 1 and Alaskan strains but is conserved in China 2.

It is likely that some of the changes in cellualr gene expression induced by LMP-1 are a result of the activation of NF-kB through at least 2 independent activating regions on the LMP-1 C-terminus(Huen et al., 1995). The proximal region, extending from amino acids 157 to 231, is fairly conserved among the isolates examined here. The only non-conservative change found was CAT/His to CAG/GIu at codon 213 in 3 of the China 2 isolates. In the more distal NF-kB activating region, extending from amino acids 352 to 386, a conservative change from TCT/Ser to ACT/ Thr at codon 366 was found in all of the isolates, as well as in the Alaskan and Mediterranean isolates previously reported(Miller et al., 1994). A non-conservative change, from GGT/Gly to GCT/Ala at codon

355, was found in 5 of 7 China 2 isolates.

That EBV genomes can undergo interstrain recombination during productive replication is well established (Walling and Raab-Traub, 1994), and some areas of the genome that contain repetitive sequence ate highly susceptible to homologous recombination. In addition, inter-typic recombinants of EBV have been isolated(Burrows et al., 1996). Within the carboxy terminus of LMP-1 is an 11 amino-acid repeat region, extending from codons 250 to 308, which is present in varying numbers in different EBV isolates and is thought to be a site at which homologous recombination might occur between different strains(Miller et al., 1994). Four of the NPC isolates reported here(isolates 125, 129, 145* and GX1)appear to have undergone interstrain recombination within the LMP-1 gene, as does the previously reported C11 isolate(Miller et al., 1994). C11 carries all of the China 1-associated changes in the amino terminus of LMP and up to codon 309 of the carboxy terminus, is identical to the B95-8 strain between codons 309 and 338, then flips back to China 1 from codons 338 to 386, as does isoate 145*. Interestingly, in only one of these isolates(C11) has the apparent recombination occurred at the repeat region within the carboxy terminal portion of LMP-1.

It has been proposed that the region around and including amino acids 343-352 may constitute a deletional hot spot and that the 30 bp deletion occurs as a result of mispairing of the short repeats flanking the deleted region during replicaiton(Sandvej et al., 1994). This hypothesis would also explain why the 7 China 2 isolates examined remain undeleted, as they carry a change from G to A at nucleotide position 165290, and 5 of the 7 carry an additional change from G to C at position 168257. Both of these changes disrupt the 9-bp repeat unit and would presumably prevent any mispairing from occurring(Fig. 5). In the deleted China 1 isolates, not only are these point mutations not present, but also in 6 of the 7 isolates analyzed, a change from A to T at position 165295 extends the perfect repeat unit from 9 to 10 base pairs(Fig. 5). This hypothesis fails to explain, however, why the B95-8 strain has remained undeleted despite having 2 perfect repeat units. The identification of homologous elements flanking the site of deletion suggests that a deletion variant coule theoretically be produced from an undeleted form. In our study, a single sample(isolate 145) contained both deleted and undeleted form, and the sequence analysis revealed the presence of two distinct strains. This suggests that a rare NPC may harbor 2 strains of EBV. Although the clonality of this tumor was not determined, the detection of 2 strains may indicate that this is either a biclonal tumor or that the progenitor cell was simultaneously infected by 2 different strains. Alternatively, oneEBV strain may be present in the tumor cells and an additional strain in the infiltrating lymphocytes.

```
B95-8      aGGCGGCGGT   catagtcatgattccggcca tGGCGGCGGT    undeleted
China 1    TGGCGGCGGT   (catagtcatgattccggcca TGGCGGCGGT)   deleted
China 2    TGGCGACGGT   catagtcatgattccggcca TGGCGGCGCT    undeleted
           168295                                    168256
```

Fig. 5 DNA sequence flanking the 30 bp deletion in the C-terminus of LMP-1 DNA sequence from EBV genome coordinates 168 295 to 168 295 is shown. Perfect repeat units(Sandvej et al.,1994)are in uppercase; deleted portion of China 1 strain is in parentheses. Point mutations that either enhance or disrupt the repeat structure are underlined and bold

In conclusion, we report a new EBV strain, China 2, which is related to both China 1, the predominant strain in Asia, and the Alaskan strain; we furthermore identified specific amino acid positions that distinguish between them. The distribution of the China 1 and China 2 strains is not markedly different in the NPC non-endemic region of northern China compared with the NPC endemic region in southern China, with the exception that the B95-8 prototype strain that was found more often in NPC from the non-endemic region. This finding suggests that other risk factors for NPC, such as exposure to environmental carcinogens and genetic susceptibility, may be more likely than EBV strain variation to account for the high incidence of NPC in southern China.

ACKNOWLEDGEMENTS

We gratefully acknowledge the help of Dr. Cai Wei Ming of the Beijing Cancer Hopital, Dr. Du Bo of the Bai Qiu En Medical University Hospital in Changchun, Jilin Province, and the Guangxi Regional Hospital in Nanning, Guangxi Autonomous Region, People's Republic of China, for supplying patient tissues. We also thank Ms. Xiaomei Zhang, Ms. Ling Zhou and Mr. Zhiwu Ji of the Instiute of Virology in Beijing for helpful advice and discussions; Mr. B. Lesser for help running the Wisconsin Package Version 9. 0; Ms. M. DeLuca for assistance with the PHYLIP package; Mr. R. Budrevich and Mr. M. Jensen assistance with the CART package; and Dr. W. Miller for critical review of the manuscript. N. S. was supported by a postdoctoral fellowship from the WHO International Agency for Research on Cancer and by a National Research Service Award(5F32-CA68751-02)from the National

Cancer Institute, United States Public Health Service. These studies were also supported by NIH grants CA32979 and CA67384 to N. R. T.

REFERENCES

[1] Abdel-Hamid M, Chen JJ, CONSTANTNE N, MASSOUD M, RAAB-TRAUB N. EBV strain variation: geographical distribution and relation to disease state. Virology, 1992, 190:168-175.

[2] Adldinger HK, Delius H, Freese UK, Clarke J, Bornkamm GW. A putative transforming gene of Jijoye virus differs from that of Epstein-Barr virus prototypes. Virology, 1985, 141:221-234.

[3] Armstrong RW, Armstrong MJ, Yu MC, Henderson BE. Salted fish and inhalants as risk factors for nasopharyngeal carcinoma in Malaysian Chinese. Cancer Res, 1983, 43:2967-2970.

[4] Burrows JM, Khanna R, Sculley TB, Alpers MP, Moss DJ, BURROWS SR. Ientification of a naturally occurring recomv-binant EpsteinBarr virus isolate from New Guinea that encodes both type 1 and type 2 nuclear antigen sequences. J. Virol, 1996, 70:4829-4833.

[5] Chen ML, Tsal CN, Liang CL, Shu CH, Huang CR, Sulitzeanu D, Liu ST, Chang YS. Cloning and characterization of the latent membrane protein(LMP)of a specific Epstein-Barr virus variant derived fron the nasopharyngeal carcinoma in the Taiwanses population. Oncogene, 1992, 7:2131-2410.

[6] Cheung ST, Lo KW, Leung SF, Chan WY, Choi PH, Johnson PJ, Lee JC, Huang DP. Prevalence of LMP1 deletion variant of Epstein-Barr virus in nasopharyngeal carcinoma and gastric tumors in Hong Kong[letter]. Int J Cancer,1996, 66: 711-712.

[7] De The G. Epidemionlogy fo Epstein-Barr virus and associated diseases in man. In: B. Roizman(ed.), Herpesvirus, 25-87, Plenum Press, New York, 1982:25-87.

[8] Felsenstein J. PHYLIP(Phylogeny Inference Package), University of Washington, Seattle,1995.

[9] Franken M, Devergne O, Rosenzweig M, Annis B, Kieff E, Wang F. Comparative analysis identifies conserved tumor nec-rosis factor receptorassociated factor 3 hinging sites in the human and simian Epstein-Ban. virus oneogene LMP1, J Virol, 1996, 70:7819-7826.

[10] Hammarskjold ML, Simurda MC. Epstein-Ban. virus latent membrane protein transactivates the human immunodeficiency virus type 1 long terminal repeat through induction of NFkB activity. J Viral, 1992, 66:6496-6501.

[11] Hu LF, Chen F, Zheng X, Ernberg I, Cao SL, Christensson B, Klein G, Winberg G. Clonability and tumorigenicity of hu-man epithelial cells expressing the EBV encoded membrane protein LMP1. Oncogene, 1993, 8:1575-1583.

[12] Hu LF, Zabarovsky ER, Chen F, Cao SL, Ernberg I, Klein G, Winberg g. Isolation and sequencing of the Epstein-Ban. virus BNLF-1 gene(LMP1)from a Chnese nasopharynageal carcinoma. J gen Virol, 1991, 72:2399-2409.

[13] Huen DS, Henderson S, Croon-Carter S, Rowe M. The Epstein-Barr virus latent protein 1(LMP-1) mediates activation of NF-kB and cell-surface phenotype via two effector regions in its carboxy terminal cytoplasmic domain. Oncogene, 1995, 10:549-560.

[14] Itakura O, Yamada S, Narita M, Kikuta H. High prevalence of a 30-base pair deletion and single-base mutations within the carboxy terminal end of the LMP-1 oncogene of Epstein-Barr virus in the Japanese population. Oncogene, 1996, 13: 1549-1553.

[15] Jukes TH, Cantor CR. In: H.N. Munro(ed.), Mammalian protein metabolism Ⅲ, Academic Press, New York, 1969, 21.

[16] Khanim F, Yao QY, Niedobitek G, Sihota S, Rickinson A B, Young L S. Analysis of Epstein-Barr virus gene polymor-phisms in normal donors and in virus-associated tumors from different geographic locatlions. Bolld, 1996, 88:3491-3501.

[17] Kieff E. Epstein-Barr virus and its replication. In: B. Fields, D. Knipe and P. Howley(eds.), Fields virology. Lippincott-Raven, Philadelphia, 1996, 2:2343-2396.

[18] Kinura M. The neutral theory of molecular evolution, Cambridge University Press, New York,1983.

[19] Knecht H, Bachmann E, Brousset P, Sandvej K, Nadal D, Bachmann F, Odermatt BF, Delsol G, Pallesen G. Deletions within the LMP1 oncogene of Epstein-Barr virus are clustered in Hodgkin's disease and identical to those observed in naso-pharyngeal carcinoma. Blood, 1993, 82:2937-42.

[20] Leung SY, Yuen ST, Chung LP, Chan AS, Wong MP. Prevalence of mutations and 30-bp deletion in the C-terminal region of Epstein-Barr virus latent membrane protein-1 oncogene in reactive lymphoid tissue and non-nasopharyngeal EBV-associ-ated carcinomas in Hong Kong Chinese. Int J Cancer, 1997, 72:225-230.

[21] Li SN, Chang YS, Liu ST. Effect of a 10-amino acid deletion on the oncogenic activity of latent membrane protein 1 of Ep-stein-Barr virus. Oncogene, 1996, 12:2129-2135.

[22] Miller WE, Earr HS, Raab-Traub N. The Epstein-Barr virus latent membrane protein 1 induces expression of the epider-mal growth factor receptor. J Viroil, 1995, 69:4390-4398.

[23] Miller WE, Eowards RH, Walling DM, Raab-Traub N. Sequence variation in the Epstein-Barr virus latent membrane pro-tein 1[erratum in J gen Virol., 1995 May; 76:1305]. J gen Virol, 1994, 75:2729-2740.

[24] Miller W E, Mosialos G, Kieff E, Raab-Traub N. Epstein-Barr virus LMP1 induction of the epidermal growth factor recep-tor is mediated through a TRAF signaling pathway distinct from NF-kappa B activation. J Virol, 1997, 71:586-594.

[25] Mosialos G, Birkenbaeh M, Yalamanehili R, Van Arsdale T, Ware C, Kieff E. The Eptein- Barr virus transforming pro-tein LMP1 engages signaling proteins for the tumor neerosis factor receptor family. Cell, 1995, 80:389-399.

[26] Raab-Traub N. Pathogenesis of Epstein-Barr virus and its associated malignancies, Semin Virol, 1996, 7:315-323.

[27] Saitou N, Nei M. The neighbor-joining method: a new method for constructing phylogenetic trees, Mol biol Evol, 1987,

4：406-425.

[28] Sample J，Young L，Martin B，Chatman T，Kieff E，Rickinson A，Kieff E. Epstein-Barr virus types 1 and 2 differ in their EBVA-3A，EBNA-3B, and EBNA-3C genes. J Virol，1990，64：4084-4092.

[29] Sandvej K，Peh SC，Andresen BS，Pallesen G. Identification of potential hot spots in the carboxy-terminal part of the Epstein-Barr virus(EBV) BNLF-1 gene in both malignant and benign EBV-associated diseases：high frequency of a 30-bp deletion in Malaysian and Danish peripheral T-cell lymphomas，Blood,1994，84：4053-4060.

[30] Walling DM，Raab-Traub N. Epstein-Barr virus intrastrain recombination in oral hairy leukoplakia. J Virol，1994，68：7909-7917.

[31] Young LS，Dawson CW，Clark D，Rupani H，Busson P，Tursz T，Johnson A，Rickinseon A B. Epstein-Barr virus gene expression in nasopharyngeal carcinoma. J gen Virol，1988，69：1051-1065.

[32] Zimber U，Adldinger HK，Lenoir GM，Vuillauem M，Knebel-Doeberitz MB，Laux G，Desgranges C，Wrrtman P，Freese U K，Schneider U，Bomkamm G. Geographical prevalence of two types of Epstein-Barr virus. Virology，1986，154：56-66.

[In《Int J Cancer》1998，76：207-215]

Synergistic Effect of Epstein-Barr Virus and Tumor Promoters on Induction of Lymphoma and Carcinoma in Nude Mice

LIU Zhen-sheng，LIU Yan-fang，ZENG Yi

[SUMMARY] Balb/c nude mice were subcutaneously transplanted with fetal nasopharyngeal mucosa infected with B95-8 Epstein-Barr virus(EBV)，n-Butyrate and/or 12-O-tetradecanoylphorbol 13-acetate(TPA)were injected subcutanously on the third day and once a week thereafter. About 10 days later，tumor masses gradually grew in these mice. Histopathological examination was carried out15 weeks later. Three cases of lymphomas(two T cell lymphomas and one B cell lymphoma) were observed in the group receiving EBV and TPA，and one T cell lymphoma and three cases of undifferentiated carcinoma were found in the group receiving EBV，TPA and n-butyrate，but to case was found in the control groups that were transplanted with fetal nasopharyngeal tissue infected with EBV，or TPA and n-butyrate alone. Polymerase chain reaction amplification and in situ hybridization revealed that lymphoma and carcinoma cells contained the EBV LMP1 and EBERs genes. LMP1 protein was also found in the carcinoma. The T and B cell lymphomas and the nasopharyngeal carcinoma in nude mice were derived from human nasopharyngeal mucosa；this was proved by using human specific monoclonal antibodies to CD3 for T cells，to CD20 for B cells，and to epithelial membrane antigen for epithelial cells. Nucleotide sequence analysis indicated that the homologies of EBV LMP1 genes in the induced malignant lymphomas and undifferentiated carcinomas to the B95-8 cell gene were around 96％ and 99％ respectively. The results showed that EB virus can infect nasopharyngeal mucosa of the human fetus and consequently induce malignant transformation by the synergistic effect of the tumor promoters，and that EBV DNA can persist in the lymphomas and carcinomas.

[Keywords] EBV Tumor promoters；Lymphoma Carcinoma；Nude mice

INTRODUCTION

Epstein-Barr virus(EBV)is known to be the agent causing human infectious mononucleosis and to be closely related to nasopharyngeal carcinoma(Wof et al. 1973；Zeng 1985；Zeng et al. 1979，1980；Pi et al. 1981). Transfection of the EBV latent membrane protein 1(LMP1) gene into immortalized cells can induce tumors in nude mice (Wang et al. 1985；Fahnaeus et al. 1990；Christopher et al. 1990；Hu et al. 1993). Nevertheless，there is no direct evidence yet showing that EBV is the etiological cause of nasopharyngeal carcinoma. However，Ito et al.(1981) reported that the synthesis of EBV antigens in EBV-carrying cells was significantly increased when these cells were trested with a combination of 12-O-tetradecanoylphorbol 13-acetate (TPA) and n-butyrate. Zeng et al. also reported that some Chinese medoconal herbs contanining TPA-like sub- stances in combination with n-butyrate could induce the synthesis of EBV antigens enhance the transformation of EBV-infected lyphocytes and promote the development of nasopharyngeal carcinoma in rats by dinitrosopiperazing(Zeng et al. 1994；HU and Zeng 1985. 1986；Tang et al. 1988). Huang et al. found that cantonese salted fish contains nitrosamine and could induce carcinoma in the nasal and paranasal regions of rats(Huang et al. 1978). Shao et al.(1988) reported that salted fish also contains EBV inducers. Aya et al.(1991) showed that dual exposure of human lymphocytes to EBV and purified 4-deoxyphorbol ester could induce chromosome rearrangement and development of lymphoma. Ji et al.(1990) demonstrated that the metabolic products of anaerobic vacteria isolated from the nasopharyngeal cavity contain butyric acid which could markedly induce the expression of EBV antigens in Raji and P3HR-1 cells in synergy with TPA. Shao et al.(1995，1997) reported that there was an EBV receptor gene(CR2) in human fetal nasopharyngeal mucosa and nasopharyngeal carcinoma cells. Our previous work also showed that EBV nuclear antigen was present in the normal and hyperplastic epithelial cells of human nasopharyngeal mucosa(Zeng 1981). Therefore，attempts were made to induce lymphoma and carcinoma in nude mice by simultaneously administering EBV-infected human fetal nasopharyngeal mucosa and tumor promoters. When EBV-infected human fetal nasopharyngeal mucosa was transplanted subcutaneously into nude mice treated with TPA and n-butyrate，lymphomas and carcinomas were successfully induced. The experiments provided evidence for the etiological role of EBV in the development of nasopharyngeal carcinoma in man.

MATERIALS AND METHODS

1. Animals

A group of 26 Balb/c nude mice(4-6 weeks old), fed with food and water sterilized by autoclave, were obtained from the Animal Center, Chinese Academy of Medical Sciences.

2. Cell, plasmids, and reagents

B95-8 cells were obtained from the Institute of Virology, Chinese Academy of Preventive Medicine. pRV2-EBERs and pUC-LMP1 were provided by Dr. Irene Joab(Institute Gustave Roussy, Paris). A digoxigenin labelling and detection kit(Boehrnger Mannheim GmbH Mannheim Germany), Apal nuclease, the four nucloside triphosphates and Taq polymerase(Chinese-American Bioengi-neering Company)were purchased.

3. Preparation of EBV

B95-8 cells were cultivated in RPMI-1640 medium supplemented with 2mmol/L glutamine,100μg/ml streptomycin, 100 IU/ml penicillin and 15% fetal bovine serum. The cells were treated with 20ng/ml TPA and 4mmol/L n-butyrate for 48h. More than 90% of the cells were alive at a density of 10^6 cells/ml. After centrifugation at 1000 r/min for 20 min, the cell pellet was removed. The supernatant was collected and centrifuged at 20 000 r/min for 2h. The pellet was immediately resuspended in fresh medium. All procedures were carried out at 4℃. The B95-8 EBV solution was concentrated 150 times through a 0. 45-μm-pore-size filter(virus titer 10^1log/ml) and stored in liquid nitrogen.

4. Tumor formation

Under aseptic condition, nasopharyngeal mucosa from a human fetus(4-5 months old)was separated and cut into pieces of 0. 5-1. 0mm^3; 1. 5ml concentrated B95-8 EB viral suspension was then added to the tissue pieces and incubated at 37℃ for 2h. After virus adsorption, the viral suspension was removed by centrifugation at 1500 r/min for 10 min. The tissue pieces were subcutaneously transplanted into nude mice and 200μg n-butyrate and/or 50ng TPA were injected subcutaneously into each mouse on the 3rd day after transplantation and once a week thereafter. Nude mice were also transplanted with either nasopharyngeal mucosa alone, or nasopharyngeal mucosa infected with EBV, or nasopharyngeal mucosa plus TPA and n-butyrate as controls. All animals were observed for 15 weeks.

5. Extraction and amplification of tissue DNA

A piece of tumor tissue was frozen and ground, tissue DNA was obtained by sodium dodecyl sulfate lysis/proteinase K digestion and phenol extraction. The following primers were used for amplification, Primer sequences for exon 1, 2 and intron 1, 2 of the LMP1 gene were primer 1 : 5'- GCCAGAGCATCTCCAATAA-3', and primer 2 : 5'-GGTCGTGTTCCATCCTCAG-3'. The LMP1 geme was amplified in a 50-μl polymerase chain reaction (PCR) mixture for 30 cycles at 94℃ for 1 min, 55℃ for 1 min and 72℃ for 1 min, and was followed by an estension at 72℃ for10 min. A 10-μl sample from each PCR product was analyzed by electrophoresis through 2% agarose and stained with ethidium bromide.

6. Immunohistochemical studies

Tumor tissue sections were incubated with a 1 : 50 diution of CD3 momoclonal antibody, a1 : 100 dilution of CD20(Dako), or monoclonal antibodies to epithelial membrane antigen(EMA), cytokeratin AEI/EA3 and EBV LMP1(Zymed) at 37℃ for 30 min separately. The sections were washed with phosphate-buffered saline and incubated with horseradish-peroxidase-conjugated goat anti-(mouse IgG)at 37℃ for 30 min. After that, the substrate solution was applied for 5 min to yield a brown reaction product in tumor samples.

7. In situ hybridization

A 600-bp Accl restriction fragment was obtained from pRV-2 EBERs containing the EBV EBERI/and EBER2 genes and a 1800-bp LMP1 fragment was from pUC-LMP1. DNA fragments were labelled by random hexanucleotide priming with digoxigenin to create EBERs and LMP1 probes. Sections 5μm thick were cut from the blocks of formalin-fixed and paraffin-embedded tissue specimens, dewaxed in xylene, dehydrated in serially graded ethanol washes(100%, 95% and 75%), digested with proteinase K for 30 min at 37℃ and hybridized with the probes. After that, the hybridization procedure was completed by the use of sheep antidioxin antibody and the nitroldue tetrazolium 5-Bromo-4-Chloro-3-Indolyl-phosphate system.

8. Cloning and analyzing PCR products

The amplified products were ligated to the pGME-T vector and transformed into JM109 bacteria. The transformants were plated on 5-bromo-4-chloro-3-indolyl β-D-galactoside selective defined medium. The single white colony was picked out, and the insertion of PCR products into plasmids was verified with Apal restriction digestion. The positive clone was cultivated under shaking, and the plasmid DNA was extracted and purified by the polyethyleneglycol PEG 8000 precifptation method. PCR products were sequenced by a DNA sequencer 373a-18 system.

RESULTS

1. Tumor formation in nude mice

EBV-infected fetal nasopharyngeal mucosa were transplanted subcutaneously onto the backs of nude mice. On the third day after transplantation and subsequently once a week, 200μg n-butyrate and 50 ng TPA were injected subcutaneously into each mouse. After 10 days, transplanted tisues began to enlarge and, within a period of about 2 months, they reached $2.1 \pm 0.39 cm^3$, at which stage they were movable nodules. After 7-15 weeks, tumor tissues were removed from nude mice and examined histopathologically. Tumor from 1 mouse was diagnosed at T cell lymphoma and tumors from the other 3 mice were undifferentiated carcinomas (Figs. 1, 2). After EBV-infected fetal nasopharyngeal mucosa had been transplanted into nude mice and they had been treated with TPA only, 3 of the6 mice developed malignant lymphomas, with 2 T cell lymphomas and 1 B cell lymphoma. The nude mice that received either EBV-infected fetal nasopharyngeal mucosa or normal fetal nasopharyngeal mucosa alone did not develop tumor within 15 weeks. Also, no tumors were observed in any nude mice transplanted with tissues from fetal nasopharyngeal mucosa treated with TPA and n-butyrate within13-15 weeks. Human nasopharyngeal mucosa formed cysts in 2 of the 6 nude mice treated with EBV alone. The mucosa transplanted into other control groups was degraded (Tab. 1).

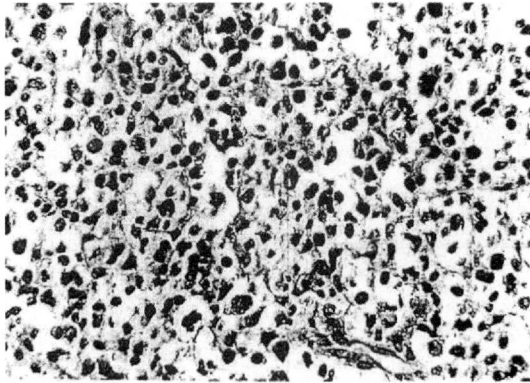

Fig. 1 Micrographs of paraffin section of lymphoma in nude mice formed by transplantation of Epstein-Barr virus (EBV)-infected fetal nasopharyngeal mucosa and treated with 12-O-tetradecanoylphorbol 13-ace-tate (TPA). Malignant lymphoma stained by hematoxylin eosin(H&E); ×200

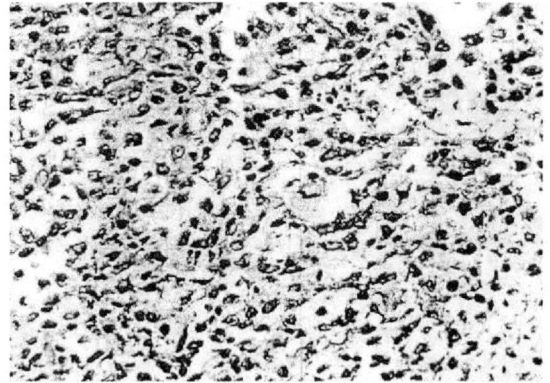

Fig. 2 Micrographs of paraffin section of carcinoma in nude mice formed by transplantation of EBV-infected fetal nasopharyngeal mucosa and treated with TPA and n-butyrate. Undifferentiated carcinoma with irregular nuclei and rich cytoplasm; mitosis can be seen. H&E; ×200

Tab. 1 Tumor formation from fetal nasopharyngeal mucosa infected with Epstein-Barr virus (EBV). NPT nasopharyngeal tissues. TAP 12-O-tetradecanoylphorbol 13/-acetate

Group	Numbers of nude mice	Time after transplantation(week)	Cyst formation	Mallignant T(B) lymphoma	Undifferentiated-carcinoma
NPT	4	15	0	0	0
NPT+EBV	6	15	2	0	0
NPT+TPA+n-butyrate	4	13-15	0	0	0
NPT+EBV+TPA	6	8-15	0	2(1)	0
NPT+EBV+TPA+n-butyrate	6	7-15	0	1	3

Determination of the human origin of undifferentiated carcinomas and lymphomas

Immunohistochemical staining of carcinoma tissues from nude mice with human specific monoclonal antibody to EMA on human epithelial cells showed a positive reaction in undifferentiated carcinoma(Fig. 3) but was negative in the control rat exophageal cancer cells. Both the undifferentiated carcinoma cell and the rat esophageal cancer cells showed a positive reaction to nonspecific monoclonal antibody cytokeratin AE1/AE3 to epithelial cells. Immunohistochemical staining of lymphona cells with human specific CD3 and CD20 monoclonal antibodies further demonstrated that three malignant lymphomas were originally from human T cells and one was from human B cells(Fig. 4a, b). However, there was no reaction of undifferentiated carcinoma cells with CD3 or CD20 monoclonal antibodies.

2. Detection of EBV LMP1 protein in undifferentiated carcinoma cells

Undifferentiated carcinoma cells, produced in nude mice from human fetal nasopharyngeal mucosa, were stained with monoclonal antibody to LMP1. A positive reaction was observed in these cells(Fig. 5).

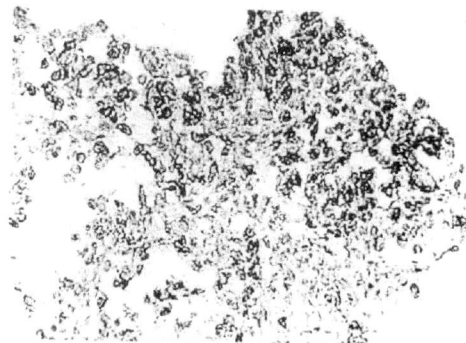

Fig. 3 Immunohistochemical staining of undifferentiated carcinoma from human fetal nasopharyngeal mucosa and esophageal carcinoma of rat. Routine peroxidase/antiperoxidase immunohistochemical staining. Immunohistochemical staining of undifferentiated carcinoma Epithelial membrane antigen positive. Peroxidase/antiperoxidase；×200

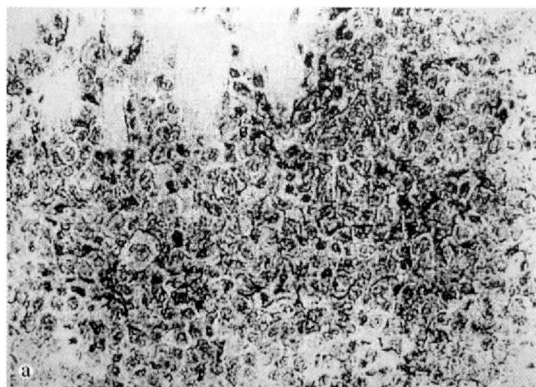

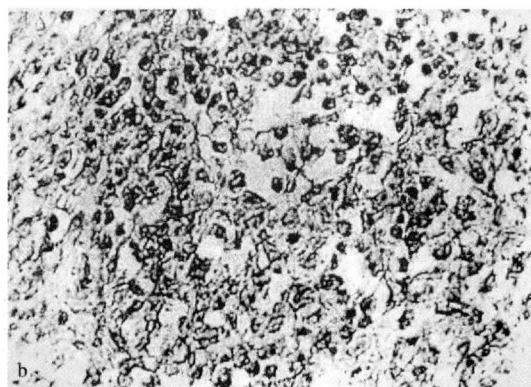

Fig. 4 a，b Immunohistochemical staining of malignant lymphoma. Routine peroxidase / antiperoxidase immunohistochemaical staining, a：Malignant T lymphoma. immunohistochemical stainin CD3 positive Peroxidase/antiperoxidase，×200. b：Malignant B lymphoma，immunohistochemical staining CD20 positive. Peroxidase / antiperoxidase，×200

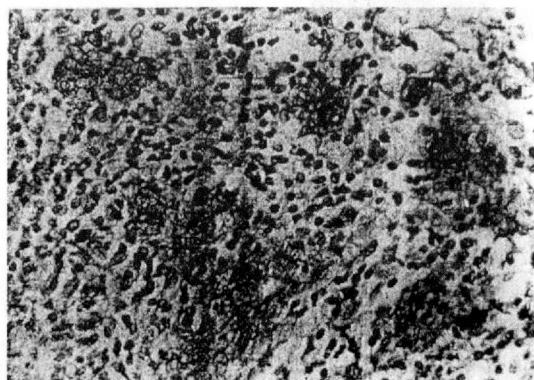

Fig. 5 Immunohistochemical staining of undifferentiated carcinoma. EBV LMPI positive. Peroxidase/antiperoxidase；×200

3. Determination of EBV genes by in situ hybridization

Digoxigenn-labelled LMP1 and EBERs gene probes were used for in situ hybridization. The results showed hte presence of the EBERs gene in the cellular nuclei of lymphoma tissues and of the LMP1 gene in undifferentiated carcinoma(Fig. 6a, b). There were no specific hybridization signals in the cellular nuclei of the controlled breast carcinoma. These indicated that EBV genes did exist in malignant lymphoma and undifferentiated carcinoma originating from EBV-infected human fetal nasopharyngeal mucosa.

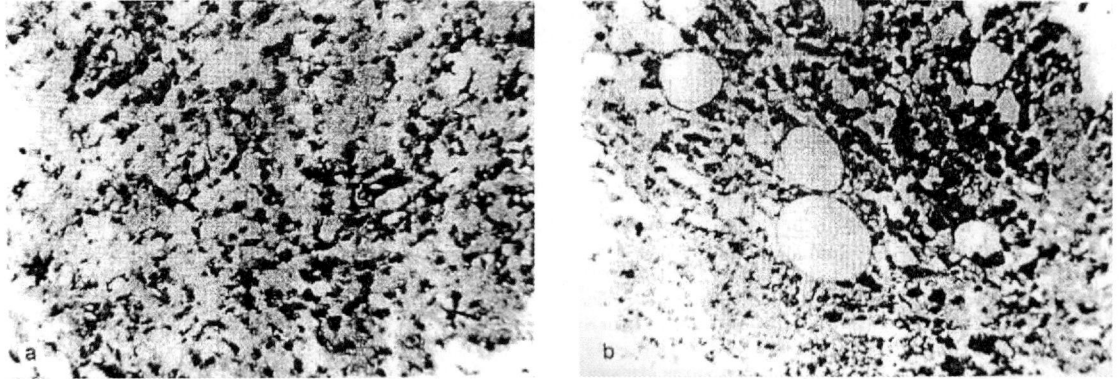

Fig. 6　a, b In situ hybridization of EBV genes in tumor tissues, a: In situ hybridization of EBERs gene in malignant lymphoma. Purpleblue minute granules, as positive signal, located in the cell nucleus. b: In situ hybridization of LMP1 gene in undifferentiated carcinoma. Purple-blue minute granules as positive signal, mainly located in the cell nucleus and cytoplasm

4. PCR amplification

Amplification of EBV DNA from lymphoma and undifferentiated carcinoma was performed with LMP1 primers, Electrophoresis of the PCR products in 1.0% agarose gels showed a 553-bp DNA fragment from lymphona and carcinoma(Fig. 7a. b), and then the PCR products were ligated to the pEGM-T vector, and Apal digestion showed that the PCR DNA fragment LMP-1 had been inserted into the vector.

5. DNA sequence analysis of the LMP-1 gene of B95-8 cells and tumor tissues

Analyses of EBV LMP1 exon 1, 2 and intron 1, 2, and DNA of B95-8 cells and tumor tissues showed the homologies of LMP1 sequences from malignant lymphoma and undifferentiated carcinoma to B95-8 EBV LMP1 to be about 96% and 99% respectively(Fig. 8). The results revealed that EBV in tumor tissues was concordant with B95-8 EBV.

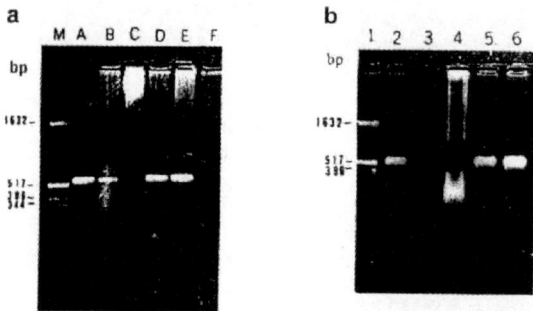

Fig. 7　a, b Result of the polymerase chain reaction(PCR) detection of tumor DNA, a: Result of the PCR detection of malignant lymphoma DNA. M: PBR322/hinf 1 DNA marker; A: B95-8 cell DNA; B, D, E: malignat lymphoma DNA; C: malignant lymphoma DNA(not amplified); F: 293 cell DNA. b: Result of the PCR detection of undifferentated carcinoma DNA. 1: PBR322/Hinf 1 DNA marker; 2: B95-8 cell DNA; 3, 5, 6: undifferentiated carcinoma DNA; 4: 293 cell DNA

Fig. 8　Comparison of the nucleotide sequences of EBV-LMP 1 gene(168927-168945)from(1) B95-8,(2) malignant lymphoma and(3)undifferentiated carcinoma

DISCUSSION

Our study revealed that EBV infection of nasopharyngeal mucosa alone can not induce lymphoma or undifferentiated carcinoma, but that these can be induced under the synrgetic effect of inducers and tumor promoters(TPA and/or n-butyrate). An interesting finding is that lymphomas are induced by the synergistic effect of TPA; T cell lymphoma is more active than B cell lymphoma and undifferentiated carcinoma induction needs another inducer, such as n-butyrate. In another study, we induced poorly differentiated carcinoma in nude mice by EBV-infected immortalized 293 cells(carrying CR2 receptors)together with TPA, showing that the process involved in EBV induction of lymphoma and carcinoma may be somewhat different(Li et al. 1997).

The origin of lymphoma and carcinoma induced in transplanted nude mice was identified by immunohistochemical staining with human specific monoclonal antibodies. Lymphomas of T and B cells reacted positively with monoclonal antibodies CD3 and CD20 respectively nd carcinoma reacted positively with EMA. The results clearly demonstrated that the tumors in transplanted nude mice are originally from the EBV-infeted human fetal nasopharyngeal mucosa.

Zeng(1981) found EBV nuclear antigen in normal and hyperplastic epithelial cells of nasopharyngeal mucosa. Shao et al.(1995, 1997) had detected the gene for the EBV receptor CR2 in nasopharyngeal mucosa. These data indicate that there are CR2 receptors located on the epighelial cells of human nasopharyngeal mucosa. The inability of EBN to infect in vitro culticated monolayer epithelial cells may be due to there beijing no of little expression of CR2, but more expression in vivo. EBV spreads widely in the human population and, in China, more than 95% of EBV infection occurs in childhood. In areas of southern China where there is a high risk of nasopharyngeal cancer there are a lot of Chinese herbs, plants and foods containing EBV inducers and tumor promoters(Zeng et al. 1983, 1994; Hu and Zeng 1985, 1986; Tang et al. 1988). Besides, the anaerobic bacteria producing butyric acid occur frequently in the human nasopharynx(Ji et al. 1990). These factors, together with EBV nay play an important role in the development of nasopharyngeal carcinoma. A previous study by us showed that a 21 times higher risk will occur when there is a HLA link- age to a nasopharyngeal carcinoma susceptibility gene(Lu et al. 1990). Our studies lead us to suggest that, for nasopharyngeal carcinoma development, EBV, genetic factors and host immunity play an etiological role, and tumor promoters and/or chemical carcinogens may have a synergistic effect.

In brief, our study describe the synergetic effect of EBV and tumor promoters on the induction of lymphomas and cad carcinomas in transplanted nude mice and also provides an important animal model for studing the etiology and mechanism of nasopharyngeal carcinoma development. The data further suggest that EBV plays an etiological role in the development of nasopharyngeal carcinoma.

ACKNOWLEDGEMENTS

We thank Professor Sir Athony Epstein and Professor G. Dethe for comments and revisisons on the manuscripts. This work was suppotred by grants from the Commission of the European Communittee and National Scientific Committee of China.

REFERENCES

[1]　Aya T, Kingoshita T, lmai S, Koizumi S, Mizuno F, Osato T, Satoh C, Oikawa T, Kuzumaki N, Ohigashi H, Koshimizu K. Chromosome translocation and c-myc activation by EpsteinBarr virus and Euphorbia tirucalli in B lymphocytes. The Lancet, 1991, 337:1190.

[2]　Christopher WD, Alan BR, Lawrence SY. EpsteinBarr virus latent membrane protein inhibits human epithelial cell differentiation. Nature, 1990, 344:777-780.

[3]　Fahraeus R, Rymo L, Rhim JS, Klein G. Morphological transformation of human keratinocytes expressing the LMP gene of Epstein-Barr virus, Nature, 1990, 345:447-449.

[4]　Hu YL, Zeng Y. Enhanced transformation of human lymphocytes by Chinese herbs. Chin J Oncol, 1985, 7:471-419.

[5]　Hu YL, Zeng Y. The enhancing effects of sodium butyrate on the transformation of human lymphocytes by EBV. Chin J Cancer, 1986, 5:243-246.

[6]　Hu LF, Chen F, Zheng X, Emberg 1, Cao SL, Christensson B, Klein G, Winberg G. Clonability and tumorigenicyty of human epithelial cells expresing the EBV encoded membrane protein LMP1. Oncogene, 1993, 8:1575-1583.

[7]　Huang DP, Ho JH, Saw D, Teo TB. Carcinoma of the nasal and paranasal region in rats fed Cantonese salted marinefish. Scientific publication20. ARC, Lyon, 1978:315.

[8]　Ito Y, Kawanishi M, Harayama T, Takabayashi S. Combined effect of the extracts from Croton tiglium, Euphorbia lathyris or Euphorbia tirucalli and n-butyrate on Epstein-Barr virus expression in human lymphoblastoid P3HR1 and Raji cells. Cancer Lettm, 1981, 12:175-180.

[9]　Ji ZW, Zeng Y, Wang PZ, Tan HZ. Induction of antigens in Raji ceils and P3HR-1 cells by anaerobiec bacterium isolated from nasopharynx of patients with nasopharyngeal carcinoma and other diseases. Chin J Cancer, 1990, 1:1-3.

[10]　Li BM, Ji ZW, Liu ZS, Zeng Y. Epstein-Barr virus in synergy with tumor-promoter-induced malignant transformation of

immortalized human epithelial cells, J Cancer Res Clin Oncol, 1997,123:441-446.

[11] Lu SL, Day NE, Degos L, Lepage Y, Hung PC, Chan SHM. Mcknight B, Easton D, Zeng Y, The G de. The genetic basis for nasopharyngeal carcinoma linkage to HLA region. Nature, 1990, 346:479-481.

[12] Pi GH, Zeng Y, Zhao WP, Zhao Q. Development of an anticomplement immunoenzyme test for detection of EB virus nuclear antigen(EBNA) and antibody to EBNA. J Immunol Methods, 1981, 44:73-78.

[13] Shao YM, Poiries S, Oshima H, Malaveille C, Zeng Y, The G de, Bartsch H. Epstein-Barr virus activation in Raji cells by extract of pre- served food from high risk areas for nasopharyngeal carcinoma. Carcinogenesis, 1988, 9:1455-1457.

[14] Shao XY, Chen ZC, Yao KT. DNA sequencing of the Epstein-Barr virus binding site fo EBVR/ CR2 gene in nasopharyngeal carcinoma, Chin J Viro, 1995, 11:15-20.

[15] Shao XY, He ZM, Chen ZC, Yao KT. Expresion of an Epstein-Barr virus receptor and Epstein-Barr virus dependent transrormation of human nasopharyngeal epithelial cells. Int J Cancer, 1997, 71:750-755.

[16] Tang WP, Huang PG, Zhao ML, Liao SL, Zeng Y. Wikstroemia indica promoters development of nasopharyngeal carcinoma in rats initiated by dinitrosopiperazine. J Cancer Res Clin Oncol, 1988, 114:429-431.

[17] Wang D, Laebowitz D, Kieff E. An EBV membrane protein expressed in immortalized lymphocytes transforms established rodent cells. Cell, 1985, 43:831-840.

[18] Wolf H, Zur Hansen H, Becker V. EB viral genomes in epithelial nasopharyngeal carcinoma cells. Nat New Biol, 1973, 244:245-247.

[19] Zeng Y, Shen JJ, Pi GH, Ma JL, Zhang Q, Zhao ML. Application of anticomplement immunoenzymatic method for the detection of EBNA in carcinoma cells and normal epithelial cells from the nasopharynx, 1lth International Symposium on Nasopharyngeal Carcinoma, Dusseldorf, West Germany, Grundman et al(eds). Fischer, Stuttgart, New York Cancer Campaign, 1981,5:237-245.

[20] Zeng Y. Seroepidemiological studies on nasopharyngeal carcinoma in China. Adv Cancer Res, 1985, 44:121-139.

[21] Zeng Y, Liu YX, Wei JN, Zhu JS, Cai SL, Wang PZ, Zhong JM, Li RC, Pan W J, Li EJ, Tan BF. Serological mass survey of nasopharyngeal carcinoma(in Chinese). Acta Acad Med Sin, 1979, 1:123-126.

[22] Zeng Y, LIU YX, Liu CR, Chen SW, Wei JN, Zhu JS, Zai HJ. Application of an immunoenzymatic method and an immunoautoradiographic method for a mass survey of nasopharyngeal carcinoma, Intervirology, 1980, 13:162-168.

[23] Zeng Y, Zhong JM, Miao XO. Epstein-Barr virus early antigen induction in Raji ceils by Chinese medicinal herbs, Intervirology, 1983, 19:201-204.

[24] Zeng Y, Zhong JM, Ye SQ, Ni ZY, Miao XQ, Mo YK, Li ZL. Screening of Epstein-Barr virus early antigen expression inducers from Chinese medicinal herbs and plants. Biomed Environ Sci,1994, 7:50-55.

[In《J Cancer Res Oncol》1998，124:541-548]

Study of Immortalization and Malignant Transformation of Human Embryonic Esophageal Epithelial Cells Induced by HPV18 E6E7

SHEN Zhong-ying[1] , CEN Shan[2] SHEN Jian, CAI Wei-jia[1] , XU Jin-jie[1] ,
TENG Zhi-ping[2] , HU Zhi[1] , ZENG Yi[2]

1. Department of Tumor Pathology, Medical College of Shantou University; 2. Institute of Virology, Chinese Academy of Preventive Medicine

【SUMMARY】 In order to study the effect of viruses and tumor promoters on the tumorigenicity of the esophagus, human embryonic esophageal epithelial cells were infected with human papilloma virus HPV18 E6E7-AAV in synergy with 12-O-tetradecanoylphorbol 13-acetate(TPA)to observe their malignant transformation. The cultured esophageal epithelial cells incubated with HPV18 E6E7-AAV were divided into two groups: the SHEEC1 group was exposed to TPA (5ng/ml) for 4 weeks at the5th passage of the cells; the SHEE group served as the control and was cultured in the same medium without TPA. The morphological phenotype, the DNA content during the cell cycle and the chromosomes were analyzed. The tumorigenicity was assessed by colony formation after cultivation in soft agar and transplanting the cells into nude mice. HPV18 E6E7 DNA was assayed by fluorescent in situ hybridization(FISH)and the polymerase chain reaction(PCR). The SHEE group, at its 20th passage, grew as a monolayer with the cells showing anchorage dependence and contact inhibition. The chromosome analysis showed diploidy, and soft-agar cultivation and injection into nude mice showed the cells to be non-tumorigenic. They were therefore immortalized cells. In contrast, the SHEEC1 group(TPA group)showed increased DNA synthesis and a proliferative index that was higher(45％)than that of the SHEE group (34％). The number of large colonies of dense multi- layer cells(positively transformed foci) in soft agar was high in SHEEC1 group(4.0％)but low in the SHEE group(0.1％). Tumors resulting from transplantation were observed in all six nude mice injected subcutaneously with cells of the SHEECI group but no tumor developed in mice receiving cells of the SHEE group. In both groups of cells, HPV18 E6E7 DNA was positively detected by FISH and PCR. The malignant transformation of human embryonic epithelial cells was induced in vitro by HPV18 E6E7 in synergy with TPA. This is a good evidence for the close relationship between HPV and the etiology and pathogenicity of esophageal carcinoma. It is also a reliable model for studying the cellular and molecular mechanisms of carcinogenesis of esophageal carcinoma.

【Keywords】 Human embryonic esophageal epithelium; HPV18 E6E7 genes; Immortalization; TPA; Malignant transformation

INTRODUCTION

Induction of malignant transformation in cells cultured in vitro is an important way to study carcinogenesis. It is used to study not only the etiology of carcinogenesis, but also the tumor-promoting factors, and it is more feasible than an animal model. We have previously successfully induced squamous cell carcinoma by subcutaneously transplanting human embryonic esophageal cells into nude mice in synergy with benzopyrene(Shen et al. 1997). Lu et al.(1989) also induced squamous cell carcinoma from human embryonic esophageal epithelium cultivated in vitro with N-methyl-N-benzylnitrosamine. These results demonstrated that strong chemical carcinogens may induce carcinogenesis in cultured cells. Liu et al.(1996) induced human nasopharyngeal carcinoma in nude mice by infecting fetal nasopharyngeal mucosa with Epstein Barr virus in combination with tumor promoters 12-O-tetradecanoylphorbol 13-acetate(TPA)and n-butyrate. On the basis of the theory that there are many factors and many stages in tumorgenesis, we used human papilloma virus HPV18 E6E7-AAV to infect human embryonic esophageal mucosa to establish an immortalized epithelial cell line SHEE(Shen et al. 1999). This experiment was then repeated with epithelial cells exposed to the tumor promoter(TPA)to induce malignant transformation, thus establishing a carcinogenic model of human embryonic esophageal epithelial cells. This work has both theoretical and practical significance in the study of viral etiology and mechanisms involved in the carcinogenesis of esophageal carcinoma.

MATERIALS AND METHODS

Construction and identification of HPV18

1. E6E7 PAAV3 vector

E6E7 genes were amplified by the polymerase chain reaction(PCR) from the template PGEM/ HPV18(provided by Prof. Zeng Yi)in which the E6E7 genes were ligated to the PGEM-T vector. The E6E7 genes were cleaved from the vector and inserted into the PAAV3 vector. The involvement of the E6E7 genes in the PAAV3 vector was demonstrated by Southern blot hybridization. PAAV- E6E7 and PAd8 were transfected into HEK 293 cells to obtain recombinant virus containing E6ET.

2. Cultivation of human embryonic esophageal mucosa

One esophagus, obtained from a 4-month-old embryo, which was proved to be normal, was cut into small pieces and cultivated in 199 medium(Gibco)with 10% calf serum and antibiotics(100 U/ml penicillin, 100 U/ml streptomycin).

3. HPV18 E6E7-AAV infection and TPA treatment

Pieces of human embryonic esophageal tissue were cultivated in serum-free medium for 2h, incubated with HPV18 E6E7-AAV for 2h after removal of the medium, and cultured again in 199 medium with calf serum. The growing human embryonic esophageal epithelium infected with HPV18 E6E7AAV was divided into two groups: cells of the SHEEC1 group were exposed to TPA at their 5th and 13th passages, for 2 weeks in each case; TPA was added to the culture medium at the dosage of 5ng/ml. The SHEE group served as the control without TPA. The assays for the two groups were the same. In the another group, the original cultured epithelium was exposed to TPA only, but it could not passaged continuously.

4. Morphological observation

The cultured epithelial cells were observed under a phase-contrast microscope, under a light microscope with Giemsa staining, and in the electron microscope(Hitachi 300).

5. Cell cycle and chromosome analyses

Cells of the 20th passage were digested, washed twice with phosphate-buffered saline PBS, fixed by 70% alcohol, prepared as a single-cell suspension and stored at 4℃. The cells were stained with propidium iodide(Sigma) and analyzed by flow cytometry(FACSort, B-D Co.). The Cells in the proliferative phase, the percentage of cells that were more than tetraploid and the proliferation index($S+G_2M/G_0G_1+S+G_2M$)were calculated. The mitotic index of the cells in the two groups at the 20th passage was calculated by counting the number of cells undergoing mitosis in their exponential phase. The cultured cells that showed more mitosis were chosen for colchicine treatment($10\mu g/ml$)and cultured for 2-3h. The cells were collected for routine Giemsa staining for chromosome analysis.

6. Cell colony formation in soft agar

The exponential-phase cells of the two groups were trypsinized and stained with trypan blue to count the number of living cells. The living single-cell suspension[10^3 cells/ml in 0.35% agar(Agarose, V312A, Promega)]was overlaid on 0.7% agar in petri dishes. Five dishes for each group were incubated in 5% CO_2 in a 37℃ incubator for 40 days and the cell colonies were then counted.

7. Tumorigenesis in nude mice

Six-week-old BALB/C nude mice(supplied by the Experimental Animal Center of Zhongshan Medical University)were bred in isolated conditions. Six nude mice were subcutaneously injected with SHEEC1 cells in the 20th passage(1×10^6 cells/mouse). Another six nude mice were injected with SHEE cells in the same manner. They were observed every 3 days for 2 months and then killed for histopathological examination.

8. Fluorescent in situ hybridization(FISH)

Cells grown on cover slides were fixed with 4% paraformaldehyde, pretreated, digested with proteinase K and hybridized with an HPV18 E6E7 probe overnight at 42℃. The hybridized cells were treated with formamide and ftuorescently labeled(fluoresceinisothiocyanate linked to Avidin-D). The cell nucleus was stained with propidium iodide($10\mu g/ml$)and observed under a fluorescence microscope.

9. HPV18 E6E7 detection by PCR

The PCR primers for HPV18 E6E7 were designed according to oligo software, synthesized by the Shanghai Bioengineering Company.

Upstream primer: 5'-GAC ACT AGT ACT ATG GCG CGC TIT GAG -3'

Downstream primer: 5'-AGT ACT AGT TTA CAA CCC GTG CCC TCC -3'

The SpeI sita is shown in bold type.

Template DNAs were extracted from SHEE cells, SHEECI cells and the tumors developing following transplantation in nude mice. The PCR kit was purchased from the Sai-Bai-Sheng Biocompany and the samples were amplified by PCR(GTC-2; Applied Res Co. USA). In 40 automated cycles, denaturing, annealing and extension time and temperature were as follows: 60s at 94℃; 30s at 50℃ and 120s at 72℃. The PCR products were analyzed by agarose gel electrophoresis.

RESULTS

1. Morphological observation

Under a light microscope, the cells in the SHEE group were uniform in size and shape(Fig. 1A), and grew as an even monolayer showing anchorage dependence and attachment inhibition. Cells in the SHEEC1 group crowded together and were of different sizes; many more cells with giant nuclei cells and several nucleoli(Fig. 1B) were seen. Under the electron microscope, cells with an ovoid nucleus and a small nucleolus were seen in the SHEE group and there were tonofilaments in the cytoplasm(Fig. 2A). In the SHEE1 group, however, the nucleus was full of folds and hollows with an enlarged nucleolus and a lack of tonofilaments(Fig. 2B). This show that the cells were over-proliferating and poorly differentiated.

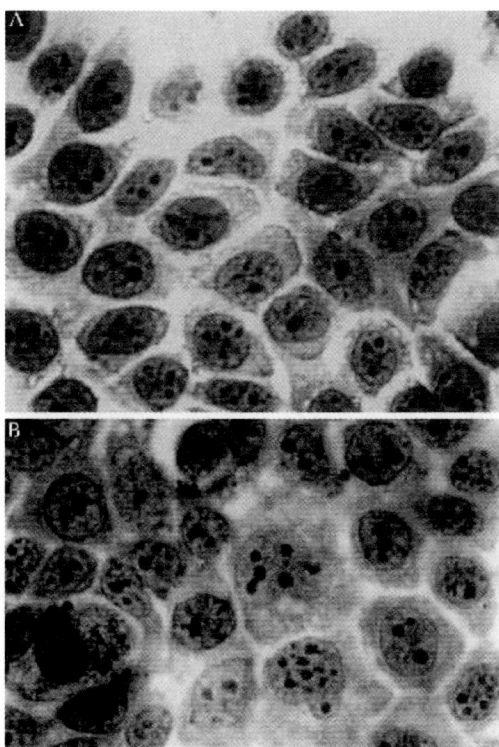

A. The immortalized cells of the SHEE group were grown in monolayers and had a uniform cell nucleus and small nucleolus(Giemsa; ×400). B. The malignantly transformed cells of the SHEEC1 group had enlarged nuclei of different sizes with several nucleoli(Giemsa; ×400)

Fig. 1 A, B Morphology of cultured cells

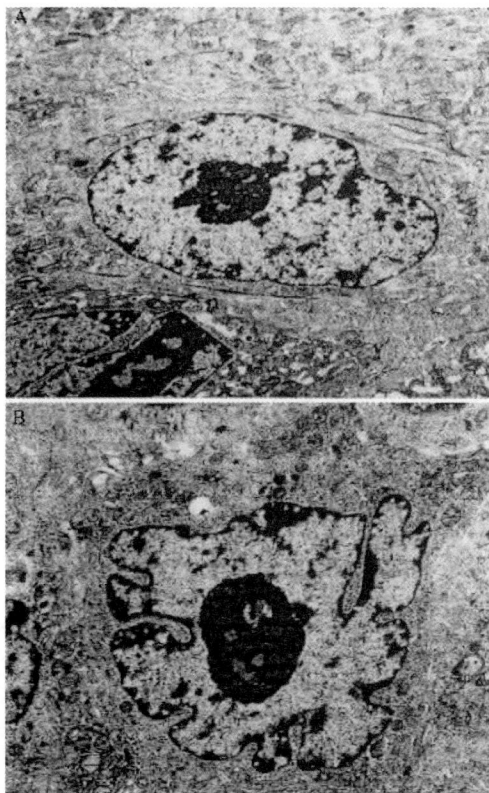

A. The immortalized cells of the SHEE group had an ovoid nucleus and tonofilaments in the cytoplasm(arrow)(electron microscope, EM; ×7000). B. The malignantly transformed cells of the SHEEC1 group had irregularly shaped nuclei with folds and hollows on the nuclear membrane; the nucleoli were enlarged and there were few tonofilaments. EM; ×7000

Fig. 2 A, B Micrographs of cultured cells

2. Chromosome analysis

The number of chromosomes in the SHEE group ranged from 45 to 54 per nucleus, nuclei containing more than 46 chromosomes accounting for 23.08%. The modal number of chromosomes was still diploid(Fig. 3A). In the SHEEC1 group, the number of chromosomes increased to 96 per nucleus(Fig. 3B), the proportion of nuclei containing more than 46 chromosomes rising to 55.56%(Tab. 1); the modal chromosome content hyperdiploid.

3. Kinetics of cell proliferation assayed by flow cytometry

The DNA histograms(Fig. 4A, B)show the proliferation index of the SHEEC1 group to be greater(45%)than that in the SHEE group(34%). A more than tetraploid cell content was found to be more frequent in the SHEEC1 group than in the SHEE group(5.70%, 1.53%).

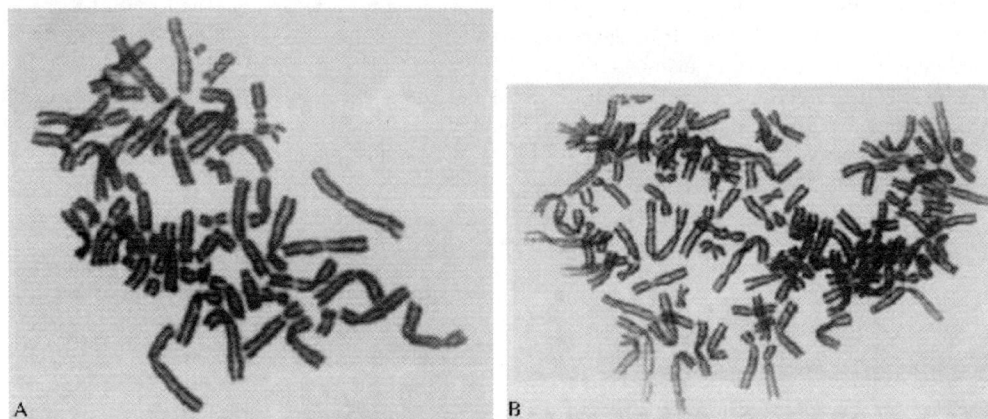

A. The chromosome number of cells in the SHEE group was in the diploid range. B. In the SHEEC1 group, the chromo some number was more than tetraploid. Giemsa; ×1000

Fig. 3　A, B Chromosome analysis

Tab. 1　Chromosome analysis of the SHEE and SHEEC1 groups

Cell group	Number of cells						Percentagegroup of cells with>46 chromosomes (%)
	Dividing	Having a chromosome number					
		<46	46	-52	-72	-96	
SHEE	26	6	14	6	0	0	23.08
SHEEC1	27	4	8	7	5	3	55.56

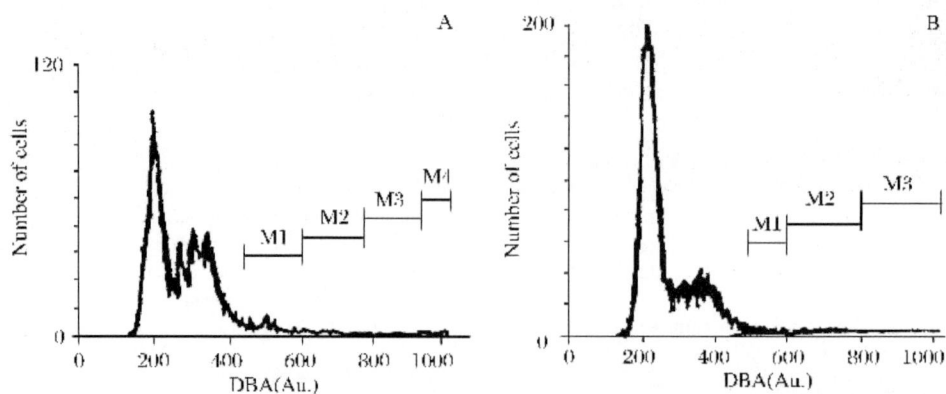

A. DNA histogram of the SHEEC1 group: M1-M4 DNA>4n. B. DNA histogram of the SHEE group: M1, M2, M3, DNA>4n

Fig. 4　A, B Flow-cytometric assay

4. Cell colony formation in soft agar

Cells were cultivated in soft agar and were observed once every 10 days. Small colonies(fewer than 10 cells) were found in the SHEE group and large colonies(more than 20 cells), which grew rapidly to form multilayer colonies, swelling in the center and protrusions at the margin(Fig. 5), were found in SHEEC1 group.

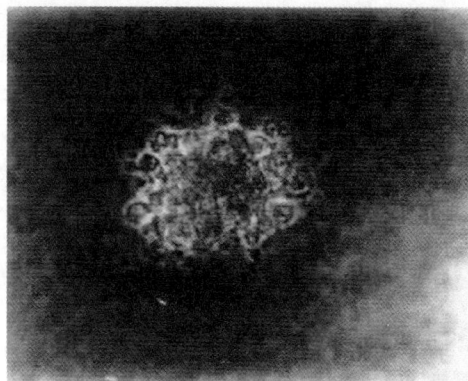

Fig. 5　A large colony formation in soft agar. Phase contrast; ×100

5. Tumor development in nude mice

When SHEEC 1 cells were injected into the axilla of nude mice, they grew rapidly to form tumor in 20 days (Fig. 6A). In histological examination on the 30th day, the cells showed a large nucleus, less cytoplasm, a large nucleolus, and infiltration and destruction of muscular fibers(Fig. 6B). The tumor could be passaged continuously in nude mice and a cell line was established that grew faster than the primary SHEEC1 cells. But when the cells of the SHEE group were injected into the nude mice, they gradually reduced and disappeared in 20 days.

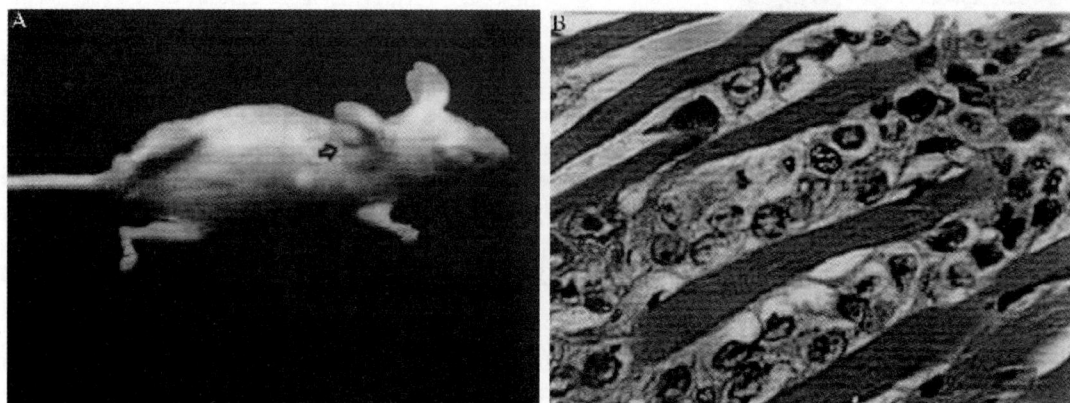

Fig. 6　A. Two tumor masses developing 20 days after 10^6 SHEEC1 cells were injected into the axilia of a nude mouse (arrow). B. Infiltration of tumor cells and the damaged muscular stratium seen microscopically. Hematoxylin/ eosin; ×400

6. HPV18 E6E7 detection by FISH

Scattered hybridized spots were seen under a fluorescent microscope in cells of both the SHEEC1(Fig. 7A) and SHEE groups(Fig. 7B), proving the existence of HPV18 E6E7 genes in the cell nucleus.

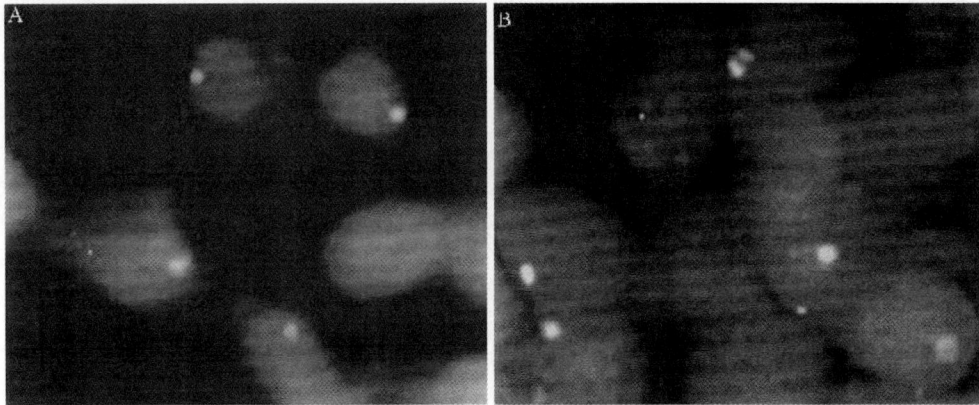

A. Cells of the SHEE group. B. Cells of the SHEEC1 group. FISH; ×1000

Fig. 7 A, B Detection of HPV18 E6E7 by fluorescent in situ hybridization(FISH)in two groups of cells, shown as light hybridized spots within the cell nucleus

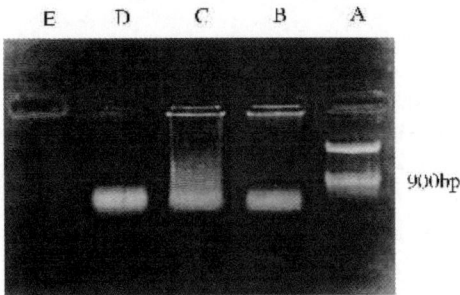

900bp

A. PBR322/BstNI, B. SHEE group, C. SHEEC1 group, D. tumors developing after transplantation into a nude mouse, E. negative control

Fig. 8 Agarose gel electrophoresis of polymerase chain reaction products

7. Detection of HPV18 E6E7 by PCR

Fig. 8 showed the bands of PCR DNA products of the SHEE group, the SHEEC1 group and of tumors growing following transplantation into nude mice, analyzed by agarose gel electrophoresis. A specific band fragment of 875 bp was found as a marker in each of them, proving the existence of an HPV18 E6E7 gene fragment in the cells of all three groups.

DISCUSSION

To assess the cell transformation, this experiment was based on four approaches: (a) the morphological changes of the cell;(b)analysis of the chromosome ploidy;(c)cell colony formation in soft agar;(d) tumorigenesis in nude mice. In the course of 20 passages, the SHEE group grew as a monolayer and still retained the characteristics of anchorage dependence and contact inhibition. In soft-agar cultivation and when transplanted into nude mice, SHEE proved to be nontumorigenic; they were therefore immortalized cells(Hopfer et al. 1996).

Under the transmission electron microscope, they showed tonofilaments in the cytoplasm indicating a certain degree of differentiation of the epithelial cells.

HPV16 E6E7 can induce cell immortalization in human oral epithelial cells(Oda et al. 1996), mammary epithelial cells(Wazer et al. 1995), bronchial epithelial cells(Viallet et al. 1994)and in epithelial cells of human pancreatic ducts(Furukawa et al. 1996). The induction of immortalization of epithelial cells by HPV18 E6E7 is considered to be caused by the action of products expressed by the HPV E6E7 genes on the antioncogenes, since the E6 protein may degrade the p53-encoded protein(Demers et al. 1994) and the E7 protein may act on retinoblastoma protein(Boyer et al. 1996). The degradation and inactivation of the products of the tumor-suppressor genes promote entry into the cell cycle, thus leading to cell proliferation.

TPA is a strong tumor-promoting compound. The dosage used may vary from 0. 1ng/ml(Bessi et al. 1995) to 300ng/ml(Sakai et al. 1995)and the time of induction may be from several hours to several weeks. In any event, TPA exerts a synergetic effect in the malignant transformation of cells. In this work, we have induced the malignant transformation of the SHEECI group of cells, using a low dosage(5ng/ml)and long-term cultivation. As reported previously, the synergetic effect of TPA is due to its action upon the cytokine signal system, specifically acting on protein kinase C through a diglyceride to promote protein synthesis and cell proliferation(Wolf 1985).

Carcinogenesis is a prolonged event with many etiologies and many stages, and our experiment was designed on the basis of two etiologies and two stages(IARC/NCI 1985). The HPV18 E6E7 infection, as the initiating factor, was the first stage and adding the tumor-promoting factor TPA was the second stage. Giving alow dosage of

TPA for 4 weeks induced the malignant trans-formation in 10 weeks. The delayed transformation, which involved a quantitative change and qualitative change of cellular characteristics and a small number of transformed cells becoming a large number of transformed cells, needs a definite period of time. So, given that people are usually exposed to frequent small doses of carcinogens and tumor promoters, carcinogenesis has to be experienced for a long time. Our in vitro experimental design, using a low dose and a long time for it to take effect, therefore corresponds to the actual conditions as far as possible.

The human embryonic epithelial cells used in this experiment were free from various external factors, were infected with HPVI$ E6E7 to induce immortalization and were infected with HPV18 E6E7 in synergy with TPA to induce malignant transformation. This provides direct evidence for the close relationship between HPV and the etiology and pathogenesis of esophageal carcinoma. It is also a reliable model for studying the viral etiology of e-sophageal carcinoma, environmental carcinogens, the molecular biological changes of cell carcinogenesis, and the biology of cell proliferation, differentiation and reversion. This work has both theoretical and practical value.

REFERENCES

[1] Bessi H, Rast C, Rether B, Nguyen Ba G, Vasseur P. Syn-ergistic effects of chlordane and TPA in multistage morpho-log-ical transformation of SHE cells. Carcinogenesis, 1995, 16:237-244.

[2] Boyer SN, Wazer DE, Band V. E7 protein of human pap-illoma virus-16 induces degradation of retinoblastoma protein through the ubiquitin-proteasome pathway. Cancer Res, 1996, 56:4620-4624.

[3] Demers GW, Halbert CL, Galloway DA. Elevated wild-type p53 protein levels in human epithelial cell lines immortalized by the human papilloma virus type 16 E7 gene. Virology, 1994, 198:169174.

[4] Furukawa T, Duguid WP, Rosenberg L, Viallet J, Galloway DA, Tsao MS, Long-term culture and immortalization of ep-ithelial cells from normal adult human pancreatic ducts transfected by E6E7 gene of human papilloma virus 16. Am J pathol, 1996,148:1763-1770.

[5] Hopfer U, Jacobberger JW, Gruenert DC, Ecker RE, Jar PS, Whitsett JA. Immortalization of epithelial ceils. Am J Physi-ol, 1996, 270:CI-11.

[6] IARC/NCI/EPA working group Cellular and molecular mechanisms of cell transformation and standardization of transfor-mation assays of established cell lines for the prediction of carcinogenic chemical. Overview and recommended protocols. Cancer Res, 1985, 45:2395-2399.

[7] Liu ZS, Li BM, Liu TF, Zeng Y. Studies on human nasopharyngeal malignant lymphoma and undifferentiated carcinoma induced the synergetic effect of EB virus and promotors(in Chinese). Chinese J Virol, 1996, 12:1-8.

[8] Lu SY, Cui XX, Xie JG. Esophageal carcinoma in human fetus induced by N-methyl-N-benzylnitrosamine(NMBZN). Chin J Oncol, 1989,11:401-403.

[9] Oda D, Bigler L, Lee P, Blanton R, HPV immortalization of human oral epithelial cells: a model for carcinogenesis. Exp Cell Res, 1996, 226:164-169.

[10] Sakai A, Miyata N, Takahashi A. Initiating activity of quinones in the two-stage transformation of BALB/3T3 cells. Carci-nogenesis, 1995, 16:477-484.

[11] Shen ZY, Cai WJ, Shen J, Xu JJ, Cen S, Ten ZP, Hu Z, Zeng Y. Immortalization of human fetal esophageal epithelial cells induced by E6 and E7 genes of human papilloma virus 18(in Chinese). Chin Exp Clin Virol, 1999, 13:121-123.

[12] Shen ZY, Xu JJ, Fang D, Shen J. A study or human fetal esophagus heterotransplantation and induced carcinoma in nude mice(in Chinese). In: Li CH(ed)Current advances in tumor biology. MMS, Beijing, 1997:185.

[13] Viallet J, Liu C, Emond J, Tsao M. Characterization of human bronchial epithelial cells immortalized by the E6 and E7 genes of human papilloma virus type 16. Exp Cell Res, 1994, 212:3641.

[14] Wazer DE, Liu XL, Chu Q, Gao Q, Band V. Immortalization of distinct human mammary epithelial cell types by human papilloma virus 16 E6 or E7. Proc Natl Acad Sci USA, 1995, 92:3687 3691.

[15] Wolf M. A model for intracellular translocation of protein kinase C involving synergism between calcium and phorbol ester. Nature, 1985, 315:546-549.

[In《J Cancer Res Clin Oncol》2000, 126:589-594]

Detection of Human Papillomavirus in Esophageal Carcinoma

SHEN Zhong-ying[1], HU Sheng-ping[1], LU Li-chun[1], TANG Chun-zhi[1],
KUANG Zhong-sheng[1], ZHONG Shu-ping[1], ZENG Yi[2]

1. Shantou University Medical College, Shantou, Guangdong; 2. The Virus Research Institute Chinese Academy of Preventive Medicine

[SUMMARY] The aim of the study was to assess the prevalence of human papillomavirus(HPV) in the esophagus in the coastal region of Eastern Guangdong, Southern China, an area with a high incidence of esophageal carcinoma. Fresh surgical resection esophageal specimens were obtained from 176 esophageal carcinoma patients admitted to the Tumor Hospital of Shantou University Medical College. The samples were subjected to polymerase chain reaction(PCR)to detect HPV infection using consensus and type-specific primers for HPV type 6, 11, 16, and 18. The incidence rate was 65.5%, 69.1%, and 60% in tissues of cancerous, paracancerous and normal mucosa, respectively. Further analysis of the distribution of HPV types in the three sections of tissues showed that the high-risk HPV types 16 and 18 were found mainly in the cancer cells(43.2%), whereas the low-risk HPV types 6 and 11 were seen mainly in the normal mucosa (52.3%). The total infection rate of the high-risk HPV types 16 and HPV 18 was the highest in cancerous tissues (54.5%), followed by paracancerous tissues(19.5%), and the lowest in normal mucosa(11.7%). There was high incidence of HPV infection in the esophageal epithelium in Eastern Guangdong, Southern China, where esophageal carcinoma is prevalent. HPV was seen in the normal, paracancerous and cancerous tissues, with the high-risk HPV type 16 and 18 more common in cancerous tissues. The results indicate that the high incidence of esophageal carcinoma in this area is associated with HPV infection.

[Keywords] Epidemiology; Esophageal squamous cell carcinoma; Human papillomavirus

INTRODUCTION

Esophageal squamous cell carcinoma is common in China as well as in some parts of the world, but is rare in the occidental countries, and the different distribution of esophageal carcinoma between high-and low-incidence areas can be as high as 300-fold(Day, 1984). Although most high-incidence areas of esophageal carcinoma are seen inland(He et al., 1997), the region of the Eastern Guangdong is, however, the only coastal area with high-incidence esophageal carcinoma with morbidity of $197.82/10^5$ world standardized population for males and $81.32/10^5$ world standardized population for females(Chen et al., 1996).

The etiology of esophageal carcinoma remains unclear. Studies of esophageal carcinoma have suggested that genetic predisposition(Tada et al., 2000), dietary(Ren and Han, 1991)or environmental factors(Ribeiro et al., 1996), such as nitrosamine(Siddiqi et al., 1991; Gurski et al., 1999), tobacco smoking(Zambon et al., 2000), alcohol consumption(Talamini et al.,2000), spicy food(Sharma, 1999), malnutrition(Franceschi et al., 2000), trace element deficiency(Newberne et al., 1997), and fungal toxin(Liu et al., 1992)could be important factors in the carcinogenesis of this tumor. Since the first report of human papillomavirus(HPV)in esophageal carcinoma in 1982, implicating a potential risk factor of HPV in the development of esophageal carcinoma(Syrjanen, 1982), the existence of HPV in esophageal carcinoma was confirmed further by methods of immunohistochemistry, serology, Southern hybridization, polymerase chain reaction (PCR), in situ hybridization(ISH)and others. Recent evidence has shown that esophageal infection with HPV, particularly high-risk types 16 and 18, increased esophageal carcinoma morbidity13-fold(Dillner et al., 1995), indicating that HPV may have pathogenic significance in esophageal carcinoma(Bjorge et al., 1997; Poljak et al., 1998; Takahashi et al., 1998). The detection rate of HPV in esophageal lesions is varied geographically(Sur and Cooper, 1998), however, ranging from 0%(Stairs et al., 1995; Kok et al., 1997)to 60%(Chen et al., 1994). The role of HPV in the pathogenesis of esophageal carcinoma remains to be determined.

The objective of the present study was to determine whether HPV infection in esophageal tissues was common in esophageal carcinoma patients residing in the coastal region of the Eastern Guangdong area. The study was also designed to explore the role of HPV infection, most notably HPV 16 and 15, in esophageal carcinogenesis.

MATERIALS AND METHODS

1. Specimens

During the period from 1994-1997, 176 fresh specimens of resected esophagus were obtained from patients, who were treated for esophageal cancer at the Affiliated Tumor Hospital, Shantou University Medical School, China, while living in the high-incidence area for esophageal carcinoma in the coastal region of the Eastern Guangdong. All specimens had esophageal squamous cell carcinoma confirmed histologically. Every specimen was cut into three parts: cancerous, paracancerous, and normal tissues, and each cut used a new microtome blade to avoid contamination of the samples.

The specimens were subjected to the following tests: 1)165 samples from 55 patients were tested by PCR using HPV consensus primers for general HPV infection; 2)132 samples from 44 patients were tested by PCR using type-specific primers to determine the infection rates of high-risk types16 and 18 and low-risk types 6 and 11, respectively; and 3)231 samples from 77 patients were tested by PCR using type-specific primers for infection with HPV types 16 and 18, respectively.

2. Cell Lines

Cell lines Ec/CUHK1 and Ec/CUHK2 were human esophageal carcinoma cell lines free of HPV infection (gifts from Prof. Y. Chew of Hong Kong Chinese University). Cells were cultured in a humidified incubator at 37℃ with 5% CO_2 in air in M199 medium(Gibco BRL, Gaithersburg, MD)supplemented by 10% calf serum, 100U/ml each of penicillin and streptomycin, pH 7.0. Cells were harvested at confluency by 0.25% trypsin. DNA extracted as described below was used as HPV negative control in the experiments.

3. DNA Extraction

Tissues were homogenized followed by proteinase K(200μg/ml; Promega, Madison, WI)digestion in thepresence of 0.5% SDS at 37℃ overnight. Samples were then subjected twice to phenol-chloroform-isoamyl alcohol extraction. DNA was precipitated with absolute ethanol followed by washing twice with 70% ethanol. After air drying at room temperature, DNA was dissolved in TE buffer(10mmol/L Tris HCl, 1mmol/L EDTA, pH 7.8)and stored at 4℃ until used.

Recombinant plasmid DNA HPV 16-pBR322 was obtained from Prof. S. Lu, the Cancer Research Institute, Chinese Academy of Medical Sciences and HPV 18-pBR322 was a gift from Prof. K. Yao, the Cancer Research Institute, Hunan Medical University. Plasmid DNA extracted as above was used as positive control and the plasmid DNA extracted from cell lines Ec/CUHK1 and Ec/CUHK2 was used as negative control in PCR.

4. PCR Analysis

Five different sets of primers(Tab. 1)were used in this study. The consensus primers L1C1 and L1C2, synthesized by the Cancer Research Institute(Chinese Academy of Medical Science, Beijing), were designed as described[Yoshikawa et al., 1991]to amplify HPV types 6, 11, 16, and 18 and targeted a segment of 144 bp in the highly conserved HPV L1 gene(90% homologous among the HPV types). The primer sets 2-4, synthesized by the Department of Biology, Fudan University, Shanghai, were type-specific primers for detection of HPV type 6, 11, 16, and 18, respectively(Kiyabu et al., 1989).

Tab. 1 Sequence of Primers Used

Set	Primers	Sequence[a]
1	L1C1	CGTAAACGTTTTCCCTATTTTTTT
	L1C2	GTTATGTCTCATAAATCCCAT
2	HPV 6	GCACGTCTAAGATGTCTTGTTTAG
		AGACCAGTTGTGCAAGACATTTAA
3	HPV 11	AGACCAGTTGTGCAAGACATTTAA
		AAGGGAAAGTTGTCTCGCCACACA
4	HPV 16	ATGAACTAGGGTGACATTT
		CCTCTTAGGCACATATTTT
5	HPV 18	GCTGGTTAGGCACATATTT
		ATGTATGCACAGCTTAGTC

Note: [a] All the sequences are shown from 5′ to 3′.

Samples of 10ng DNA were mixed with one set of primers flanking the DNA fragments to be amplified. Reactions were set in 25μl × PCR buffer containing 10mmol/L Tris HCl, pH 8.4, 50mmol/L KCl, 1.5mmol/L

MgCl2,4mmol/L dNTP and 1.5U Taq DNA polymerase(Promega). DNA was subjected to 40 cycles of amplification in PCR(GeneAmp PCR System 2400, Perkin-Elmer, Foster City, CA)with denaturing at 94℃ for 30 sec, annealing at 50℃ for 30 sec, and elongating at 72℃ for 1 min. In each experiment, 10ng plasmid DNA(HPV 16-pBR322 or HPV 18-pBR322), 20ng DNA from Ec/CUHKI or Ec/CUHK2, anti a no-DNA reaction were included as positive, negative and blank controls, respectively. The amplified product was resolved by electrophoresis on a 2% agarose gel (Promega) containing 0.5% μg/ml of ethidium bromide in 1 × TAE buffer. Samples were considered positive if bands of 263 bp(HPV 6),144 bp(HPV 11), 130 bp(HPV 18), and 100 bp(HPV 16)were observed under the UV light.

5. Statistical Analysis

The difference was tested by X^2 tests. The HPV infection rate was analyzed by X^2 analysis. Statistical significance is assumed if P-value$<$0.05.

RESULTS

1. Overall detection rate of HPV DNA: The overall detection rate in 165 samples from 55 patients by PCR using the consensus primers for all HPV types DNA was greater than 60%, with 60% for normal mucosa(33/55), 69.1% for paracancerous mucosa(38/55), and 65.5%(36/55)for cancerous tissues, respectively(Tab. 2). The results indicated that HPV infection was common in esophagus in the patients residing in the local region, and the infection was widely distributed all over the esophageal mucosa.

Tab. 2 Detection of HPV in 55 Specimens

Location	Number of positive specimens	Percent
Normal	33	60.0
Paracancerous	38	69.1
Cancerous	36	65.5

2. Different detection rates of high and low risk HPV types in tissues with different pathological states: HPV is classified broadly in terms of its carcinogenesis into two groups: high risk(HPV16 and 18)and low risk (HPV 6 and11). PCR amplification in 132 samples from 44 patients using type-specific primers was performed to determine the prevailing group. As shown in Tab. 3, the detection rates in both groups were similar. The distribution of the two groups differed in the tissues of various pathology. For the high risk group, the highest detection rate was seen in cancerous tissues(19/44, 43.2%), decreasing in paracancerous mucosa(17/44, 38.6c2), and the lowest in normal mucosa(6/44, 13.6%). The difference in detection rates between the cancerous tissues and the normal mucosa was highly significant($P<$0.01). In the low risk group, the order of the detection rates in tissues of different pathological states was contrasted to that of the high risk group: highest in normal mucosa(23/44, 53.3%), intermediate in paracancerous mucosa(17/44, 38.6%),and lowest in cancerous tissues(15/44, 34.1%). There was no significant difference between the cancerous tissues and the normal mucosa($P>$0.05). These results suggested that high-risk group HPV types 16 and 18 might have a closer association with the development of esophageal carcinoma. There were five patients with mixed HPV infection of high and low risk types(data not shown).

Tab. 3 Comparison of HPV High Risk and Low Risk Type Infection in 44 Specimens

HPV type	Number of positive specimens(%)		
	Normal	Paracancerous	Cancerous
HPV 6 and 11	23(52.3)*	17(38.6)	15(34.1)*
HPV 16 and 18	6(13.6)**	17(38.6)	19(43.2)**

Notes: * $\chi^2=$0.198, $P>$0.05.
       ** $\chi^2=$7.22, $P<$0.008

3. Detection rates of HPV 16 and 18: To determine further whether infection of one type in the high risk group was prevalent over the other, PCR was applied in 231 samples from 77 patients using type-specific primers for HPV16 and 18, respectively. The results showed(Tab. 4)that HPV 16 infection rate in all the tissues of vari-

ous pathological states was higher than that of HPV 18. There were eight patients with mixed HPV infection of types 16 and 18(data not shown).

Tab. 4　PCR for HPV 16 and 18 in 77 Specimens

Location	Number of positive specimens(%)		
	HPV 16(+)	HPV 18(+)	Total
Cancerous	30(39. 0)	17(22. 1)	42[a](54. 5)
Paracancerous	14(18. 2)	3(3. 9)	15[a](19. 5)
Normal	8(10. 4)	2(2. 6)	9[a](11. 7)

Note: a Mixed infection, total eight cases.

DISCUSSION

It is well known that HPV infection of squamous cells can lead to hyperplasia and papilloma [Sandvik et al., 1996]. Since its first identification of HPV as a causative factor of human warts in 1907, it has been recognized that HPV is an important human carcinogen for various cancers of the skin, oral cavity, pharynx, larynx, lung, cervix, and anogenital system(Zur Hausen, 1987). The role of HPV in the etiology of esopheal carcinoma is now attracting attention. There is a close relationship between papilloma and squamous cell carcinoma of the esophagus (Sandvik et al., 1996) considering that the multi and micropapillary lesion in the paracancerous mucosa displayed HPV DNA(Shen et al., 2000). We established recently an immortalized human fetal esophageal epithelial cell line by introducing the HPV 18 E6E7 genes into the cells(Shen et al., 1999a) and a transformed human fetal esophageal epithelial cell line by infecting the cells with the HPV 18 E6E7 genes in synergy with phorbol acetate (TPA)treatment(Shen et al., 1999b). These results strongly suggest an important carcinogenic role of HPV in the development of esophageal carcinoma. HPV detection rate in esophageal lesions varies geographically. An obvious phenomenon is that the HPV detection rate is absent(Morgan et al., 1997; Saegusa et al., 1997)or significantly lower in areas with moderate or low incidence of esophageal carcinoma(Lam et al., 1997), 4. 3% in Beijing and 4. 4% in Cincinnati, Ohio(Suzuk et al., 1996); in high incidence areas of the disease, however, the detection rate is much higher(43. 1% in Linxian, China(Chang et al., 1990) and 60% in Fuzhou, China(Zambon et al., 2000). It appears that the role of HPV in esophageal carcinogenesis might be more pronounced in areas of the world with a high prevalence of esophageal carcinoma(Chang et al., 2000). Our study patients all came from a high incidence area for esophageal carcinoma in the Eastern Guangdong, Southern China. The overall HPV detection rate in these specimens was up to 60% or higher, with the high risk HPV types16 and 18 being predo-minant in cancerous tissues(43%-54%). Our result was consistent with the findings reported indicating that HPV infection, particularly the high risk types, may be one, of the major risk factors in esophageal carcinogenesis in this high frequency area of esophageal carcinoma(Chang et al., 2000).

As shown in Tab. 2-4, HPV infection is not limited to cancerous and precancerous tissues. Normal epithelial tissues are also HPV positive. High risk types are predominant in cancerous tissues, whereas low risk types are more common in healthy tissues, indicating that high risk types may play a more important role in carcinogenesis. Mixed infections of high and low risk types are also seen(Chang et al., 2000). Because low risk types can cause proliferation of epithelium, mixed infections of high and low risk types 16, 18, 6, and 11 may have synergic effects in the enhancement of cell proliferation and transformation(deVilliers et al., 1999).

The Eastern Guangdong coastal region of Southern China is one of the 6 high incidence areas for esophageal carcinoma in China, and also of the few coastal regions with high frequency of esophageal carcinoma in the world. The morbidity and mortality of esophageal carcinoma is ranked as number one in the overall malignant tumors in this region. Our results suggest that the high incidence of esophageal carcinoma in this particular region may he associated with the high infection rate with HPV, and HPV may be one of the major risk factors in the development of this tumour. Multiple risk factors have been implicated in the development of esophageal carcinoma in this region, such as nitrosamine(Shen et al., 1987; Lin et al., 1985)and trace element deficiency(Shen et al., 1997).

ACKNOWLEDGEMENTS

This work was supported by Dr. R. Potter, PhD, Professor of Biology, California University. The authors would like to thank Prof. H. Lin of Sun Yi-shun Medical University; Prof. S. Lu uf the Cancer Research Institute, Chinese Academy of Medical Sciences; Prof. K. Yao of Hunan Medical University; and Prof. Y. Qiu of Hong Kong Chinese University who kindly dunated HPV plasmid DNA and cell lines.

REFERENCES

[1] Bjorge T, Hakulinen T, Engeland A, Jellum E, Koskela P, Lehtinen M, Luostarinen T, Paavonen J, Sapp M, Schiller J, Thoresen S, Wang Z, Youngman L, Dillner J. A prospective, seroepide miological study of the role of human papillomavirus in esophagea cancer in Norway. Cancer Res, 1997, 57:3989-3992.

[2] Chang F, Syrjanen S, Shen Q, Ji HX, Syrjanen K. Human papillomavirus(HPV)DNA in esophageal precancer lesions and squamous cell carcinomas from China. Int J Cancer, 1990, 45:21-25.

[3] Chang F, Syrjanen S, Shen Q, Cintorino M, Santopietro R, Tosi P Syrjanen K. Human papillomavirus involvement in esopha-geal carcinogenesis in the high incidence area of China: a study of 700 cases by screening and type-specific in situ hy-bridization. Scand J Gastroenterol, 2000,35:123-130.

[4] Chen B, Yin H, Dhurandhar N. Detection of human papilloma-virus DNA in esophageal squamous cell carcinomas by the polymerase chain reaction using general consensus primers Hum Pathol, 1994, 25:920-923.

[5] Chen WS, Cai SS, Qiu JW. Lin K, Yah H, Zhang C. Epidemiologic features of esophageal cancer in Nanao county Guang-dong Province from1987-92(in Chinese). Aizheng, 1996, 15:274-276.

[6] Day NE. The geographic pathology of cancer of the esophagus. Br Med Bull, 1984, 40:329-334.

[7] deVilliers EM, Lavergue D, Chang F, Syrjanen K, Tosi P, Cintorino M, Santopietro R, Syrjanen S. An interlahoratory study to determine the presence of human papillomavirus DNA in esophageal carcinoma from China. Int J Cancer, 1999, 81:225-228.

[8] Dillner J, Knekt P, Schiller JT, Hakulinen T. Prospective seroepidemiological evidence that human papillomavirus type 16 infection is a risk factor for oesophageal squamous cell carcinoma. Br Med J, 1995, 311:1346.

[9] Franceschi S, Bidoli E, Negri E, Zambon P. Talamini R, Ruol A, Parpinel M, Levi F, Simonato L, La Vecchia C. Role of macronutrients, vitamins and minerals in the aetiology Of squamouscell carcinoma of the oesophagus. Int J Cancer,2000, 86:626-631.

[10] Gurski RR, Schirmer CC, Kruel CR, Komlos F. Kruel CD, Edelweiss MI. Induction of esophageal carcinogenesis by diethy-lnitro-samine and assessment of the promoting effect of ethanol and N-nitrosonornicotine: experimental modcl in mice. Dis Esophagus, 1999, 12:99-105.

[11] He D, Zhang DK, Lam KY, Ma L, Ngan HY, Liu SS, Tsao SW. Prevalence of HPV infection in esophageal squamous cell carcinoma in Chinese patients and its relationship to the p53 gene mutation. Int J Cancer, 1997, 72:959-964.

[12] Kiyabu M, Shibata D, Arnheim N, Martin W J, Fitzgibbons PL. Detection of human papillomavirus in formalin fixed, in-vasive squamous carcinomas using the polymerase chain reaction. Am J Surg Pathol, 1989, 13:221-224.

[13] Kok TC, Nooter K, Tjong-A-Hung SP, Smits HL, Ter-Schegget JJ. No evidence of known types of human papillomavirus in squamous cell cancer of the oesophagus in a low-risk area. Eur J Cancer, 1997, 33:1865-1868.

[14] Lam KY, He D, Ma L, Zhang D, Ngan HY, Wan TS, Tsao SW. Presence of human papillomavirus in esophageal squa-mous cell carcinomas of Hong Kong Chinese and its relationship with p53 gene mutation. Hum Pathol, 1997, 28:657-663.

[15] Lin K, Shen ZY, Cai SS. The preliminary detection of nitrosamines in the fish juice pickle vegetable and dry pickle radish in the high incident area of the esophageal carcinoma(in Chinese). Chung-Hua Zhongliu Zazhi, 1985, 7:32-33.

[16] Liu GT, Qian YZ, Zhang P, Dong WH, Qi YM, Gun HT. Etiological role of Alternaria altemata in human esophageal cancer. Chin Med J(Engl),1992, 105:394-400.

[17] Morgan RJ, Perry AC, Newcomh PV, Hardwick RH, Ahterson D. Human papillomavirus and oesophageal squamous cell carcinoma in the UK. Eur J Surg Oncol, 1997, 23:513-517.

[18] Newberne PM, Schrager TF, Broitman S. Esophageal carcinogenesis in the rat: zinc deficiency and alcohol effects on tumor induction. Pathobiology, 1997, 65:39-45.

[19] Poljak M, Cerar A, Seine K. Human papillomavirus infection in esophageal carcinomas: a study of 121 lesions using multi-ple broad-spectrum po] ymerase chain reactions and literature review. Hum Pathol, 1998, 29:266-271.

[20] Ren A, Han X. Dietary factors and esophageal cancer: a case-control study. Chung Hua Liu Hsing Ping Hsueh Tsa Chih, 1991, 12:200-204.

[21] Ribeiro U Jr, Posner MC, Safatle Ribeiro AV, Reynolds JC. Risk factors for squamous cell carcinoma of the oesophagus. Br J Surg, 1996, 83:1174-1185.

[22] Saegusa M, Hashimura M, Takano Y, Ohbu M, Okayasu I. Absence of human papillomavirus genomic sequences detected by the polymerase chain reaction in oesophageal and gastric carcinomas in Japan. Mol Pathol, 1997, 50:101-104.

[23] Sandvik AK, Aase S, Kveberg KH, Dalen A, Folvik M, Naess O. Papillomatosis of the esophagus. J Clin Gastroenterol, 1996, 22:35-37.

[24] Sharma D. Carcinoma of oesophagus-aetiological factors and epidemiology: an overview. J Indian Med Assoc, 1999, 97: 360-364.

[25] Shen ZY, Chen ZP, Lu SX. Investigation on nitrosamines in the diets of the inhabitants of highrisk area for esophageal cancer in the southern China and analysis of the correlation factors(in Chinese). J Hygiene Res, 1987, 26:266-269.

[26] Shen WY, Shen ZY, Chen MH. A multivariable discriminant analysis on the trace elements content of hair in the districts of high, middle and low incidence of the esophageal cancer. World Elemental Med, 1997, 4:5-8.

[27] Shen ZY, Cen S, Cai WJ, Teng ZP, Shen J, Hu Z, Zeng Y. Immortalization of humann fetal esophageal epithelial cells in-duced by E6 and E7 genes of human papillomavirus 18. Chinese J Exp Clin Virol, 1999a, 13:121-123.

[28] Shen ZY, Cai WJ, Shen J, Xu JJ, Cen S, Ten ZP, Hu Z, Zeng Y. Human papilloma virus18E6E7 in synergy with TPA in-

duced malignant transformation of human embryonic esophageal epithe-lial cells. Chinese J Virol, 1999b, 15:1-6.

[29] Shen J, Shen ZY, Zheng RM, Li LC. Study on micropapilloma-tosis of the esophageal mucosa adjacent to the cancer. Shijie Huaren Xiaohua Zazhi, 2000, 8:1289-1290.

[30] Siddiqi MA, Tricker AR, Kumar R, Fazili Z, Preussmann R. Dietary sources of N-nitrosamines in a high-risk area for oesophageal cancer: Kashmir, India. LARC Sci Publ, 1991, 105:210-213.

[31] Smits HL, Tjong-A-Hung SP, ter-Schegget J, Nooter K, Kok T. Absence of human papillomavirus DNA from esophageal carcinoma as determined by multiple broad spectrum polymerase chain reactions. J Med Virol, 1995, 46:213-215.

[32] Sur M, Cooper K. The role of the human papilloma virus in esophageal cancer. Pathology, 1998, 30:348-354.

[33] Suzuk L, Noffsinger AE, Hui YZ, FenoglioPreiser CM. Detection of human papillomavirus in esophageal squamous cell carcinoma. Cancer, 1996, 78:704-710.

[34] Syrjanen KJ. Histological changes identical to those of condylomatous lesions found in esophageal squamous cell carcinomas. Arch Geschwulstforsch, 1982, 52:283-292.

[35] Tada K, Oka M, Hayashi H, Tangoku A, Oga A, Sasaki K. Cytogenetic analysis of esophageal squamous cell carcinoma cell lines by comparative genomic hybridization: relationship of cytogenetic aberration to in vitro cell growth. Cancer Genet Cytogenet, 2000, 117:108-112.

[36] Takahashi A, Ogoshi S, Ono H, Ishikawa T, Toki T, Ohmori N, Iwasa M, Iwasa Y, Furihata M, Ohtsuki Y. High-risk human papillomavirus infection and overexpression of p53 protein in squamous cell carcinoma of the esophagus from Japan. Dis Esophagus, 1998, 11:162-167.

[37] Talamini G, Capelli P, Zamboni G, Mastromauro M, Pasetto M, Castagnini A, Angelini G, Bassi C, Scarpa A. Alcohol, smoking and papillomavirus infection as risk factors for esophageal squamous-cell papilloma and esophageal squamouscell carcinoma in Italy. Int J Cancer, 2000, 86:874-878.

[38] Yoshikawa H, Kawana T, Kitagawa K, Mizuno M, Yoshikura H, Iwamoto A. Detection and typing of multiple genital human papillomaviruses by DNA amplification with consensus primers. Jpn J Cancer Res, 1991, 82:524-531.

[39] Zambon P, Talamini R, La Vecchia C, DalMaso L, Negri E, Tognazzo S, Simonato L. Smoking type of alcoholic beverage and squamous-cell oesophageal cancer in northern Italy. Int J Cancer, 2000, 86:144-149.

[40] Zur Hausen H. Papillomaviruses in human cancer. Cancer, 1987, 59:1692-1696.

[In《J Med Viral》2002, 68:412-416]

Progressive Transformation of Immortalized Esophageal Epithelial Cells

SHEN Zhong-ying[1], XU Li-yan[1], CHEN Min-hua[1], SHEN Jian[1], CAI Wei-jia[1], ZENG Yi[2],
SHEN Zhong-ying，XU Li-yan，CHEN Min-hua，SHEN Jian，CAI Wei-jia

1. Department of Tumor Pathology; Medical College of Shantou University; 2. Institute of Virology, Chinese Academy of Preventive Medicine

[SUMMARY] Objective: To investigate the progressive transformation of immortal cells of human fetal esophageal epithelium induced by human papillomavirus, and to examine biological criteria of sequential passage of cells, including cellular phenotype, proliferative rate, telomerase, chromosome and tumorigenicity. Methods: The SHEE cell series consisted of immortalized embryonic esophageal epithelium which was in malignant transformation when cultivated over sixty passages without co-carcinogens. Cells of the 10th, 31st, 60th and 85th passages were present in progressive development after being transfected with HPV. Cells were cultivated in a culture flask and 24-hole cultural plates. Progressive changes of morphology, cell growth, contact-inhibition, and anchorage-dependent growth characteristics were examined by phase contrast microscopy. The cell proliferation rate was assayed by flow cytometry. The modal number of chromosomes was analyzed. HPV18E6E7 was detected by Western blot methods and activities of telomerase were analyzed by TRAP. Tumorigenicity of cells was detected with soft agar plates cultivated and with tumor formation in SCID mice. Results: In morphological examination the 10th passage cells were in good differentiation, the 60th and 85th passages cells were in relatively poor differentiation, and the 31st passage cells had two distinct differentiations. The characteristics of the 85th and 60th passage cells were weakened at contact-inhibition and anchorage-dependent growth. Karyotypes of four stages of cells belonged to hyperdiploid or hypotriploid, and bimodal distribution of chromosomes appeared in the 31st and 60th passage cells. All of these characteristics combined with a increasing trend. The activities of telomerase were expressed in the latter three passages. Four fourths of SCID mice in the 85th passage cells and one fourth of SCID mice in the 60th passage cells developed tumors, but the cells in the 10th and 31st passage displayed no tumor formation. Conclusion: In continual cultivation of fetal esophageal epithelial cells with transduction of HPV18E6E7, cells from the 10th to the 85th passage were changed gradually from preimmortal, immortal, precancerous to malignantly transformed stages. All of these changes were in a dynamic progressive process. The establishment of a continuous line of esophageal epithelium may provide a in vitro model of carcinogenesis induced by HPV.

INTRODUCTION

The cell line SHEE was derived from immortalized embryonic esophageal epithelium induced by gene E6E7 of HPV 18 in our laboratory[1,2] being cultivated and propagated over 100 passages. The 31st generation(SHEE31) had begun to express partial cell differentiation into two directions with some nests of cells with good differentiation and some with poor differentiation[3]. The 61st generation cells(SHEE61) were premalignant cells[4], and displayed a fully malignant transformation with a strong invasive potency at the 85th passage(SHEE85)[5]. We believe that this established cell line(SHEE), continually affected by expression of HPV, would change its biological characters such as cell proliferation, differentiation, chromosome and telomerase, and that this might be controlled by cytogenesis(chromosomes)and molecular genetics(genes).

In general, the immortalized or transformed cells caused by carcinogens are always accompanied by chromosome abnormality and mutation of gene[6]. The chromosome's changes are manifested in structure and the number of chromosomes[7,8]. All of these changes appear in the procedure from quantitative to qualitative changes. The length of telomere in living cells was continually shortened after cellular mitosis[9]. Because the somatic cells have no or lower levels of telomerase activity, telomere would be shortened, so it limits the division and lifespan of cells[10,11]. Immortal or malignant cells manifest telomerase activities, which can maintain the telomere length[12,13], so they will be immortal. With exposure of the early passage of immortal cell line to viral oncogenes, HPV or SV40T, conversion of these telomerase from negative expression to high levels of telomerase activity resulted[4]. Telomerase would be present in benign lesions and activated during the late stage of carcinogenesis[15].

Changes occurred in SHEE cells from the 10th to the 85th passage, with emphasis on their phenotypes, cytogenetic changes, telomerase activity and tumorigenicity, were studied in this paper. Phenotype of cells included the morphological changes of proliferation and contact-inhibition growth, and the modal number of chromosomes and the tumorigenicity, especially soft-agar culture and tumor formation in severely combined immuno-deficient(SCID) mice.

MATERIALS AND METHODS

1. Cell culture

The SHEE cells were routinely cultivated in culture medium 199(GIBCO)with 10% bovine serum，100 units of penicillin and streptomycin in a humidified atmosphere of 5% CO_2. Selected generations at the 10th passage (SHEE 10), 31st passage(SHEE31 60th passage(SHEE60) and 85th passage(SHEE85) were inoculated in culture flask and 24-hole culture plate with glass slide inside.

2. Living cell examination

The cell shape，anchorage dependent and contact-inhibited growth were examined by phase-contrast microscopy.

3. Cell cycle analysis

Cultured cells of each passage were collected from suspended and digested cells, fixed by 70% alcohol, then filtered through nylon mesh, to generate single-cell suspension(1×10^6/ml). The cells were stained with propidium iodide (Sigma) and were analyzed using flow cytometry(FCM)(FACSorte Becton-Dickinsn). Data of DNA of cells were collected and analyzed with Lysis II software, then a histogram was drawn and the cell percentages of each proliferatot ion stage in the cell cycle and the number of cells more than 4n of DNA were calculated. The proliferation index formula: $S+G_2M/G_0G_1+S+G_2M$ and the cell amount at pre G_0G_1 stage, the apoptotic cells, were calculated.

4. Cytogenetic analysis

Metaphase spreads were obtained using standard cytogenetic methods. Briefly, the culturing cells of each passage were preserved at 3-4℃ for 3-4h to make cells on synchronous stage, then cultivated at 37℃ for 3-4 h, and added in 0.05ng/ml colchicine for 1h. Harvesting was by standard method and stained with Giemsa, 50-100 metaphases were scored for each line.

5. Telomerase activity assay[16]

Telomerase activity was measured using the telomeric repeat amplification protocol(TRAP). Frozen samples were homogenized in 10-50μl of ice-cold lyses buffer(10mmol $\cdot$ L^{-1} Tris-HCl, pH7.5, 1mmol $\cdot$ L^{-1} EGTA, 0.1mmol $\cdot$ L^{-1} Benzamidine, 5mmol $\cdot$ L^{-1} βmercaptothanol, 5g $\cdot$ L^{-1} CHAPS, 100ml $\cdot$ L^{-1} glycerol). After 30 min of incubation on ice, the lysate was centrifuged at 12000g for 20 min at 4℃. TRAP-eze Telomerase Detection Kit(Oncor Inc.)reaction was performed using 1μl lysate or 1/10 diluted lysate, 2.5μl 10×TRAP buffer(200mmol $\cdot$ L^{-1} Tris-HCl, pH8.3, 15mmol $\cdot$ L^{-1} $MgCl_2$, 630mmol $\cdot$ L^{-1} KCl, 0.5% Tween 20, 10mmol $\cdot$ L^{-1} EGTA, 1g $\cdot$ L^{-1} BSA), 0.5μl 2.5mmol $\cdot$ L^{-1} dNTP, 0.5μl Ts primer, 0.5μl TRAP primer mix, 19.5μl water, 0.5μl taq(2μ $\cdot$ L^{-1}). After incubation at 30℃ for 30 min, the reaction mixture was immediately transferred to 94℃ and performed PCR(GenAmp PCR System 2400, PE, USA)at 94℃ for 30s, 55℃ for 30s, for 35 cycles. PCR products were separated in a non-denaturing 125g $\cdot$ L^{-1} PAGE in 1×TBE at 5V $\cdot$ cm^{-1}. The gel was stained using $AgNO_3$ and was photographed.

6. Soft agar assays

Four passages of cells(1×10^4)were cultivated in each hole of the 6-hole plastic plate(Coming Co.)which was covered with two layers agarose(Agarose, V312A, Promega), the bottom, 1% and the upper. 0.5%. The cells were incubated in 5% CO_2 at 37℃ incubator for 40 d and the cell colony formations were scored every ten days. Each soft-agar cloning experiment was carried out at least in duplicate.

7. Tumorigenicity assays

In vivo tumor graft experiments were performed on the severely combined immunodeficient(SCID)mice(C. B-17/IcrJ-scid, Animal Lab of Chinese Academy of Medical Sciences). Cells of each passage were injected into the subaxillary skin of four mice with 1×10^6 cells for every one. Mice were observed weekly for two months and the tumor tissues were examined histopathologically.

8. HPV18E6E7 assays

The protein expression of HPV 18E6E7 was detected by Western blot method. The cells were washed three times with ice-cold PBS, then were lysed in buffer[50mmol/L Tris-HCl, pH8.0, 150mmol/L NaCl, 100μg/ml phenyl-methyl-sulfonyl fluoride(PMSF), 1% TritonX-100] for 30 min at ice. After removal of cell debris by centrifugation(12 000g, 5 min), the protein concentration of lysates was measured by Bradford method. 50μg proteins of different passage boiled for 5 min in sample huffer were separated by 10% SDS-PAGE, transferred onto nitrocellulose membrane(Bio-Rad). Nonspecific reactivity was blocked by incubation overnight at 4℃ in buffer (10 mmol/L Tris-HCl, pH7.5, 150mmol/L NaCl, 2% Tween-20, 4% bovine serum albumin). The membrane was then incubated with antibody of mouse anti HPV $18E_6$,(SC-264, Zhong Shan Biotech Co.), followed by reaction with anti-mouse IgG antibody. Reactive protein was detected by ECL chemiluminescence system(Amersham).

RESULTS

1. Proliferation and differentiation of SHEES

The cells of SHEE10 grew evenly on the flask. Cells appeared to have the characteristics of squamous epithelium(Fig. 1, A)with muhiangular outline and oval nucleus. SHEE31 were attached to the dish with partial differentiating into squamous epithelium and partial undifferentiated basal cells(Fig. 1, B). The cells of SHEE60 and SHEE85 were differently shaped and sized and cells were crowded and overlapped(Fig. 1C, D).

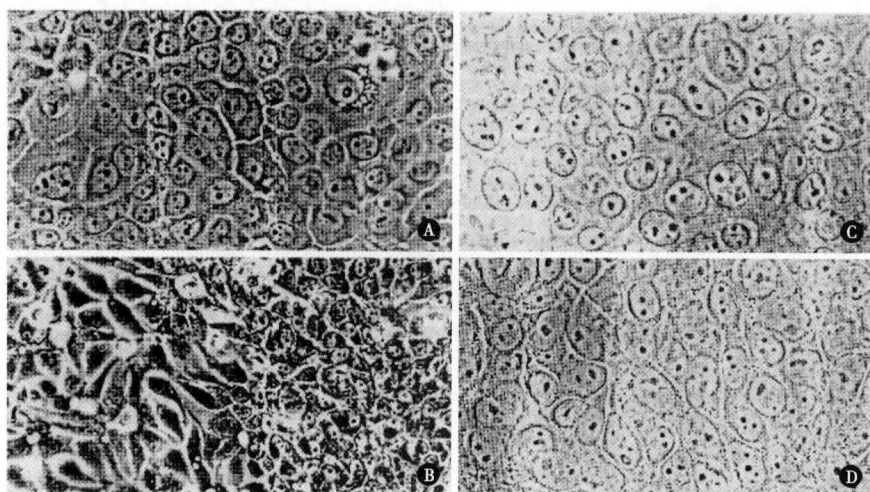

A, SHEE10, good differentiation (× 400); B, SHEE31, differentiated to two directions, well differentiated(left), and poorly differentiated(right)(×200); C, SHEE60, poor differentiation(×400); D, SHEE85 shows different shape and size with larger nucleolus(×400)

Fig. 1　Morphology of SHEE cell(photographs of phase contrast microscope)

2. FCM analyzed cell cycle

In the DNA histogram(Fig. 2), the distribution of DNA content of SHEE31 was similar to that of SHEE10, the proliferative indexes of SHEE 10 and SHEE 31 were at the same level(32.0%, 35.2%), but different from SHEE60(47.5%) and SHEE85(54.3%). Of all DNA>4n cells there were SHEE10, 2.5%; SHEE31, 4.7%; SHEE60, 6.1% and SHEE85, 7.2%. This showed that heteroploid and hyperploid tumor cells increased with progressive culture of SHEE.

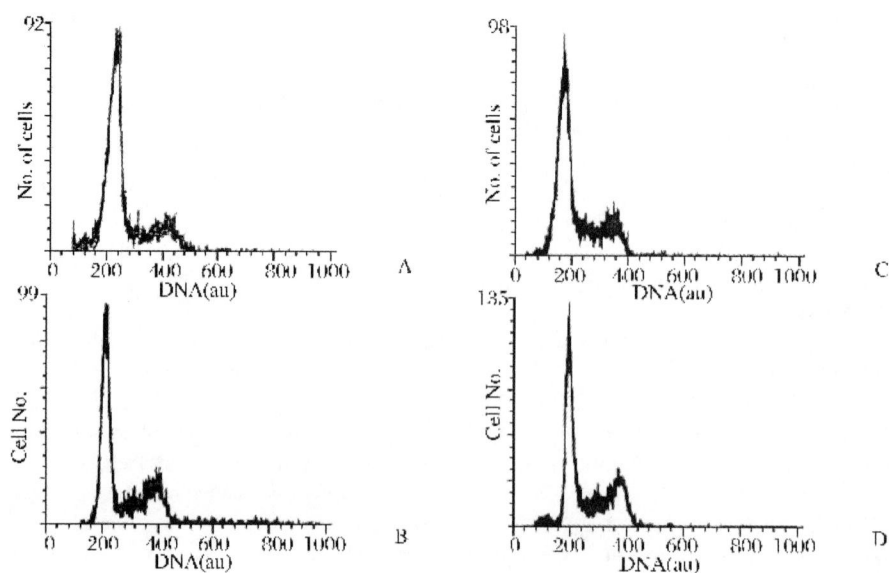

A, SHEE10; B, SHEE31; C, SHEE60; D, SHEE85; au, arbitrary unit

Fig. 2　DNA histograms of SHEE

3. The modal number of chromosome

The number of chromosomes in SHEE10, SHEE31, SHEE60 and SHEE85(Tab. 1)ranged between 32 and 196, and these chromosomes were mainly hyperdiploids and hypotriploids. Most cells of hypertriploids were found at SHEE60. Modal number of chromosomes at SHEE10 was 58-62, at SHEE31 and SHEE60 were bimodal distribution, 55-57, 61-63, and 58-60, 63-65 respectively, at SHEE85 was 59-65. The modal number from the 10th passage to the 85th passage increased slowly.

Tab. 1 Number of Chromosome in SHEE Series

Number of passage	Number of cell	≤46 (%)	47-57 (%)	58-68 (%)	≥69 (%)	modal number
SHEE10	91	17(18.7)	45(49.5)	22(27.7)	4(4.3)	58—62
SHEE31	100	12(12.0)	38(38.0)	46(46.0)	4(4.0)	55—57, 61—63
SHEE60	52	5(9.6)	13(25.0)	22(42.3)	12(23.1)	58—60, 63—65
SHEE85	85	4(4.7%)	16(18.8%)	54(63.5)	11(12.9)	59—65

4. Telomerase activity

Telomerase activation was absent in normal esophageal epithelium and SHEE10. The activity of telomerase appeared in the 31st passage, and it was strongly positive in SHEE60 and SHEE85 (Fig. 3).

5. Expression of HPV18E6E7

The expression of HPV18E6E7 was examined by Western blot method. The figure(Fig. 4) showed the expression of protein of HPVISE6E7 at cells of four stages of SHEE cell lines.

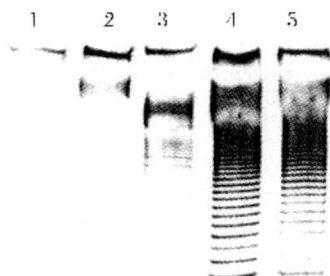

series 1, normal esophageal epithelium; 2, SHEE10;
3, SHEE31; 4, SHEE60;5, SHEE85
Fig. 3　Activity of telomerase SHEE

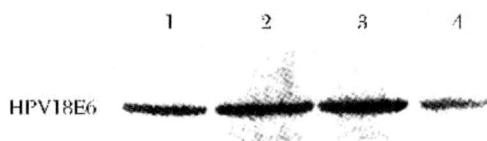

1, SHEE10; 2, SHEE31; 3, SHEE60; 4, SHEE85
Fig. 4　Western blot analysis of protein of HPV18E6 in SHEE

6. Tumorigenicity

SHEE 10 could not grow on soft agar, but SHEE31, SHEE60 and SHEE85 could. SHEE31 formed small colonies,(less than 20 cells in a colony)compared to SHEE60and SHEE85 in which large colonies(more than 50 cells in a colony)were formed. SCID mice inoculated with cells of SHEE10 and SHEE31 did not form tumors, but one quarter of SCID mice with inoculation of SHEE60 cells formed tumors with a latency period of over 2 months (data not shown). It was determined that a percentage of cells of SHEE60 manifested malignancy. All SCID mice inoculated with SHEE85 cells manifested tumor formation, which infiltrated into muscular layer histopathologieally(Fig. 5).

DISCUSSION

Cellular proliferation, differentiation and apoptosis are fundamental life activities, and are also the growth markers of immortal cells. According to the DNA content and proliferation index, the cells of SHEE10, SHEE31, SHEE60 and SHEE85 all show proliferative characteristics. The proliferation index and cell numbers of polyploid (DNA>4n) of each passage were compared as a result of SHEE10<SHEE31<SHEE60<SHEE85. SHEE31 cells

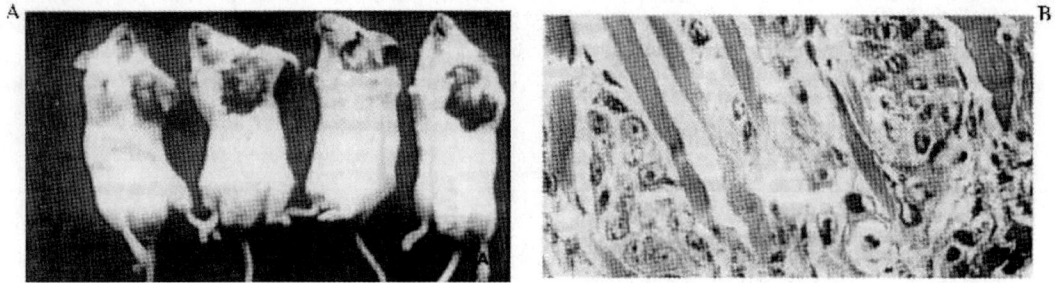

Fig. 5　Heterotransplanting SHEE85 cells into SCID mice Tumors in right axiua(arrow)of SCID mice are found(A). Invasion of tumor cells is found in muscular layer(B). HE，×400

showed differentiation in two directions: one displayed relatively large and multiangular cells with abundant cytoplasm and oval nucleus; the others displayed small cells with less cytoplasm and small round nucleus. SHEE60 cells overlapped to grow, which were differently shaped and poorly differentiated. SHEE85 cells were crowed in cultivation with cells of poor differentiation and received less contact-inhibition. Detecting anchorage growth and contact inhibition specificity by cultivation on the soft agar is of help to judge its malignant character[17,18]. The small colony formation of SHEE10 and SHEE31 cultivated in soft agar, and large colonies in SHEE85 and SHEE60 showed that the characteristics of anchoragedependent growth decreased but tumorigenicity increased. A few tumors are formed in SCID mice incubated with SHEE60. So we judged that they were not at a fully malignant stage but at a premalignant stage. SHEE85 cells, which were transplanted into 4 SCID mice and developed tumors in all mice, expressed malignant transformation.

There were more hyperdiploid and hypotriploid in the chromosomes of four stages of SHEE cell lines. The separate modal number of chromosomes first appeared in SHEE31 and continued to SHEE60. The number of chromosomal sets and the percentage of hyperploid in SHEE31 varied between SHEE10 and SHEE60, and SHEE85 has more hypotriploid cells than the others. All above showed that chromosomes of SHEE series cell lines were unstable and more susceptible to malignant transformation by promoters[19,20]. The changes of cytogenetics will control the proliferation and differentiation of cells[21].

In 1965, Hayrick reported that the culture life of human diploid fibroblast was limited to 50-100 generations, the same to epithelial cells. In 1985, Greider discovered the activity of telomerase. In 1994, Kim also identified a specific association between the telomerase activity and immortal cells or cancer cells. Telomerase activity was demonstrated in cancers of the digestive tractt[22-24], such as gastric[25-29], hepatic[30-32] colorectal[33-35] and esophageal cancer[36-38]. The telomerase activity is possibly both a prerequisite and a diagnostic criterion for immortal cells[39]. Weitzman and Hahn believed T-antigen of SV40 and ras gene induce transformation of normal epithelium cells which require expression of telomerase activity[40,41], so over-expression of telomerase related to proliferation is the early event of cancer[42]. In our data the telomere was 30kb in length in the normal fetal esophageal cell, shortened to 17kb in SHEE 10, then further shortened to 3.5kb in SHEE 31, and then maintained at this level continually[43]. The telomerase, first appeared in the 20th passage, could not prevent shortening of telomere, because it was in a low-or noncatalytic function, therefore cells had difficulty to survive in cultivation before the 20th passage. The cells grew stably alter the 31st passage. Our results indicated that immortalization of SHEE might require activation of telomerase.

Infection of HPV can cause karyotype confusion, such as breaking of chromosome, abnormal structure and number of chromosomes[44]. It also suggests that immortal esophageal cells induced by HPVI8 E6E7 may affect the changes of chromosomes, and cause instability of genetic characters[45]. Viruses can cause loss of contact inhibition, decrease of adhesion between cells, confusion of cellular skeletal structure, and loss requiring to growth factr[46]. The virus gcnome inserts and integrates with the chromosome of host, eausing the activation and expression of oneogenest[47]. HPV E6E7 protein is conjugated with anti-oncoprotein p53 and pRb[48], thus causing loss of control of cellular growth, and encouraging the phenotyping production of cellular transformation. Previous reports have shown that activation of telomerase can be achieved by the E_6 and E_7 proteins of HPV[49] It has been reported that E6 could promote malignant change, while E_7 may cause benign neoplasm[50]. It has been indicated elsewhere that virogene HPVI6 E6 alone can cause cellular malignant change[51]. In this experiment, we found that immortal cells contained HPV18 E6E7 and that, therefore, the SHEE series can gradually lead to the malignant transformation. It is also postulated that HPV is likely be a major risk factor for esophageal cancer[52].

In summary, of all these cells, some underwent aging, apoptosis and died, whereas others proceeded to malignant transformation. To search the direction of development of cells, we evaluated these changes by referring to the cytogenetic index. In these four series of immortal cells, the chromosomes presented characteristics of hyperdiploid and hypotriploid along with separation of modal number. The positive activity of telomerase can help determine the cells that are progressing from preimmortal toward immortal stages. The SHEE60 passage showed initial partial malignant change which could be regarded as premalignancy. The ceils of SHEE85 were in fully malignant transformation with tumor formation and invasive potential. In conclusion, it is possible to demonstrate multiple stages in the transformation process that are associated with different genetic and phenotypic characteristics.

REFERENCES

[1] Shen ZY, Cen S, Cai WJ, Ten ZP, Shen J, Hu Z, Zeng Y. Immor-talization of human fetal esophageal epithelial ceils induced by E6 and E7 genes of human papilloma virus. Zhonghua Shiyan He Linchuang Bingduxue Zazhi, 1999, 13:121-123.

[2] Shen ZY, Shen J, Cai WJ, Cen S, Zeng Y. Biological characteristics of human fetal esophageal epithelial cell line immortalized by the E6 and E7 gene of HPV type 18. Zhonghua Shiyan He Lin-chuang Bingduxue Zazhi, 1999, 13:209-212.

[3] Shen ZY, Xu LY, Chen MH, Cai WJ, Chen JY, Hon CQ, Shen J, Zeng Y. Biphasic differentiation of immortalized esophageal epitheliums induced by HPV 18E6E7. Bingdu Zuebao, 2001,17:210-214.

[4] Shen ZY, Chen XH, Shen J, Cai WH, Chen JY, Huang TH, Zeng Y. Malignant transformation of immortalized human embryonic esophageal epithelial cells induced by human papillomavirus. Bingdu Xuebao, 2000, 16:97-101.

[5] Shen ZY, Shen J, Cai WJ, Chen JY, Zeng Y. Malignant transformation of the immortalized esophageal epithelial cells. Zhonghua Zhongliuxue Zazhi, 2002, 24:107-109.

[6] Evan G, Littlewood T. A mattor of life and cell death. Science, 1998, 281:1317-1322.

[7] Shen ZY, Xu LY, Chen XH, Cai WJ, Shen J, Chen JY, Huang TH, Zeng Y. The genetic events of HPV-immortalized esophageal epithelium cells, Int J Mol Med, 2001, 8:537-542.

[8] Fusenig NE, Boukamp P. Multiple stages and genetic alterations in immortalization, malignant transformation and tumor progression of human skin keratinocytes. Mol Carcinog, 1998, 23:144-158.

[9] Shen ZY, Xu LY, Li EM, Cai WJ, Chen MH, Shen J, Zeng Y. Telomere and telomerase in the initial stage of immortalization of esophageal epithelial cell. World J Gastroenterol, 2002, 8:357-362.

[10] Tsao SW, Zhang DK, Cheng RY, Wan TYS. Telomerase activation in human cancer. Chin Med J, 1998, 111:745-750.

[11] Jones C J, Kipling D, Morris M, Hepburn P, Skinner J, Bounacer A, Wyllie FS, Ivan M, Bartek J, Wynford-Thomas D, Bond JA. Evidence for a telomere-independent "clock" limiting RAS oncogene-driven proliferation of human thyroid epithelial cells. Mol Cell Biol, 2000,20:5690-5699.

[12] Zhang DK, Ngan HY, Cheng RY, Cheang AN, Liu SS, Tsao SW. Clinical significance of telomerase activation and telomeric restriction fragment(TRF)in cervical cancer. Eur J Cancer, 1999,35:154-160.

[13] Hsieh HF, Ham HJ, Chiu SC, Liu YC, Lui WY, Ho LI. Telomerase activity correlates with cell cycle regulators in human hepatocel-lular carcinoma. Liver, 2000, 20:143-151.

[14] Mutirangura A, Sriuranpong V, Termrung graungleft W, Tresukosol D, Lertsaguansinchai P, Voravul N, Niruthisard S. Telomerase activity and human papillomavirus in malignant, premalrgnant and benign cervical lesions. Br J Cancer,1998, 78:933-939.

[15] Nowak JA. Telomerase, cervical cancer, and human papillomavirus. Clin Lab Med, 2000, 20:369-382.

[16] Hou M, Xu D, Bjorkholm M, Gruber A. Realtime quantitative telomeric repeat amplification protocol assay for the detection of telomerase ac- tivity. ClinChem, 2001, 47:519-524.

[17] Sakaguchi M, Miyazaki M, Inoue Y, Tsuji T, Kouchi H, Tanaka T, Yamada H, Namba M. Relationship between contact inhibition and intranuclear S100C of normal human fibroblasts. J Cell Biol, 2000, 149:1193-1206.

[18] Calaf G, Russo J, Tait L, Estrad S, Alvarado ME. Morphological phenotypes in neoplastic progression of human breast epithelial cells. J Submicrosc Cytol Pathol, 2000, 32:83-96.

[19] Shen ZY, Cai WJ, Shen J, Xu JJ, Cen S, Ten ZP, Hu Z, Zeng Y. Human papilloma virus18E6E7 in synergy with TPA induced malignant transformation of human embryonic esophageal epi-thelial cells. Bingdu Xuebao, 1999, 15:1-6.

[20] Shen ZY, Shen J, Cai WJ, Wu XY, Zheng RM, Zeng Y. The promtor effects of malignant transformation of sodium butyrate on the immortalized esophageal epithelium induced by human papillomavirus. Zhonghua Binglixue Zazhi, 2002, 31:39-41.

[21] Weitzman JB, Yaniv M. Rebuilding the road to cancer. Nature 1999, 400, 401-402.

[22] Yakoob J, Hu GL, Fan XG, Zhang Z. Telomere, telomerase and digestive cancer. World J Gastroenterol, 1999, 5:334-337.

[23] He XX, Wang JL. Activity of telomerase and oncogenesis. Huaren Xiaohua Zazhi, 1998, 6:1100-1101.

[24] Yang SM, Fang DC, Luo YH, Lu R, Lit, WW. Telomerase activity in gastroeintesind submucosal tumors and its clinical significance. Huaren Xiaohua Zazhi, 1998, 6:765-767.

[25] Zhan WH, Ma JP, Peng JS, Gao JS, Cai SR, Wang JP, Zheng ZQ, Wang L. Telomerase activity in gastric cancer and its clinical implications. World J Gastroenterol, 1999, 5:316-319.

[26] He XX, Wang JL, Wu JL, Yuan SY, Ai L. Telomerase expression, Hp infection and gastric mucosal carcinogenesis. Shijie Huaren XiaohuaZazhi, 2000, 8:505-508.

[27] He XX, Wang JL, Wu JL, Yuan SY, Ai L. Telomere, cellular DNA content and gastric mucosal carcinogenesis. Shijie

Huaren Xiaohua Zazhi,2000，8：509-512.

[28] Yao XX，Yin L，Zhang SY，Bai WY，Li YM，Sun ZC. hTERT expression and cellular immunity in gastric cancer and precancerosis. Shijie Huaren Xiaohua Zazhi，2001，9：508-512.

[29] Xia ZS，Zhu ZH，He SG. Effects of ATRA and 5 Fu on growth and telomerase activity of xenografts of gastric cancer in nude mice. Shijie Huaren Xiaohua Zazhi，2000，8：674-677.

[30] Meng ZQ，Yu EX，Song MZ. Inhibition of telomerase activity of human liver cancer cell SMMC7721 by chemotherapeutic drugs. Shijie Huaren Xiaohua Zazhi，1999，7：252-254.

[31] Fu JM，Yu XF，Shao YF. Telomerase and primary liver cancer. Shijie Huaren Xiaohua Zazhi,2000，8：461-463.

[32] Qu B，Li BJ，Lu ZW，Pan HL. Clinical significance of telomerase activity detected in finencedle aspiration speciments to liver cancer diagnosis. Shijie Huaren Xiaohua Zazhi，2001，9：538-541.

[33] Qiu SL，Huang JQ，Wang YF，Peng ZH. Analysis of telomerase activity in colorectal cancer，precancerous lesions and cancer washings. Shijie Huaren Xiaohua Zazhi，1998，6：992-993.

[34] Sobti RC，Kochar J，Singh K，Bhasin D，Capalash N. Telomerase activation and incidence of HPV in human gastrointestinal tumors in North Indian population. Mol Cell Biochem，2001,217：51-56.

[35] Jia L，Li YY. Telomerase activity of exfoliated cancer ceils in colonic luminal washings. Huaren Xiaohua Zazhi，1998，6：955-957.

[36] Koyanagi K，Ozawa S，Ando N，Takeuchi H，Ueda M. Kitajima M. Clinical significance of telomerase activity in the noncancerous epithelial region of oesophageal squamous cell carcinoma. Br J Surg，1999，86：674-679.

[37] Hiyama T，Yokozaki H，Kitadai Y，Haruma K，Yasui W，Kajiyama G，Takara E. Overexpression of human telomerase RNA is an early oesophagaeal carcinogenesis. Virchows Arch，1999，434：483-487.

[38] Kiyozuka Y，Asai A，Yamamoto D，Senzaki H，Yoshioka S，Takahashi H，Hioki K，Tsubura A. Establishment of novel human esophageal cancer cell relation to telomere dynamics and telomerase activity. Dig Dis Sci，2000，45：870-879.

[39] Koyanagi K，Ozawa S，Ando N，Mukai M，Kitagawa Y，Ueda M，Kilajima M. Telomerase activity as an indicator of malignant in iodinenonreactire lesions of the esophagus. Cancer，2000,88：1524-1529.

[40] Hahn WC，Counter CM，Lundberg AS，Beijersbergen RL，Brooks MW，Weinberg RA. Creation of human tumour cells with defined genetic elements. Nature，1999，400：464-468.

[41] Xu LY，Shen ZY，Li EM，Cai WJ，Shen J，Li C，Hong CQ，Chen JY，Zeng Y. Telomere length and telomerase activity in immortalized and malignantly transformed human embryonic esophageal epithelial cell lines by E6 and E7 genes of HPV18 type. Aibian Qibian Tubian，2001，13：137-140.

[42] Morales CP，Lee EL，Shay JW. In situ hybridization for the detection of telomerase RNA in the progression from Barrett's esophagus to esophageal adenocarcinoma. Cancer，1998，83：652-659.

[43] Shen ZY，Xu LY，Li C，Cai WJ，Shen J，Chen JY，Zeng Y. A comparative study of telomerase activity and malignant phenotype in multistage carcinogenesis of esophageal epithelial cells induced by human papillomavirus. Int J Mol Med,2001，8：633-639.

[44] Steenbergen RD，Hermsen MA，Walboomers JM，Meijer GA，Baak JP，Meijer CJ. Non-random allelic losses at 3p llp and 13p during HPV-mediated immortalization and concomitant loss of terminal differentiation of human keratinocytes. Int Jcancer，1998，76：412-417.

[45] Duensing S，Lee LY，Duensing A，Basile J，Piboonniyom S，Gonzalez S，Crum CP，Munger K. The human papillomavirus type 16E6 and E7 oncoproteins cooperate to induce mitotic defects and genomic instability by uncoupling centrosome duplication from the cell division cycle. Proc Natl Acad Sci USA，2000，29：10002-10007.

[46] Garbe J，Wong M，Wigington D，Yaswen P，Stampfer MR. Viral oncogenes accelerate conversion to immortality of cultured conditionally immortal human mammary epithelium cells. Oncogen，1999，18：2169-2180.

[47] Wang P，Peng ZL，Wang H，Liu SL. Study on the carcinogenic mechanism of human papilomaviurs type 16 E7 protein in cervical carcinoma. Zhonghua Shi Yah He Linchuang Bing Du Xue Zazhi，2000，14：117-120.

[48] Zur Hausen H. Papillomaviruses in human cancers. Proc Assoc Am Physicians，1999，111：581-587.

[49] Song S，Liem A，Miller JA，Lambert PF. Human papillomavirus types 16 E6 and E7 contribute differently to carcinogenesis. Virology，2000，26：141-150.

[50] Song S，Pitot He，Lambert PF. The human papillomavirus type 16 E6 gene alone is sufficient to induce carcinomas in transgenic animals. J Virol1999，73：5887-5893.

[51] Shen ZY，Cen S，Shen J，Cai WJ，Xu JJ，Teng ZP，Hu Z，Zeng Y. Study immortalization and malignant transformation of human embryonic esophageal epithelial cells induced by HPV18 E6E7. J Cancer Res Clin Oncol，2000，126：589-594.

[52] Shen ZY，Hu SP，Shen J，Lu LC，Tang CZ，Kuang ZS，Zhong SP，Zeng Y. Detection of human papillomavirus in esophageal carcinoma. J Med Virol. 2002. 68：412-416.

[In《World J Gastroenterol》2002，8(6)：976-981]

The Multistage Process of Carcinogenesis in Human Esophageal Epithelial Cells Induced by Human Papillomavirus

SHEN Zhong-ying[1], XU Li-yan[1], LIEn-min[2], CAI Wei-jia[1], SHEN Jlan[1], CHEN Ming-hua[1], CEN Shan[4], TSAO Sai-wah[3], ZENG Yi[4]

Departments of 1 Pathology; 2. Biochemistry, Medical College of Shantou University, 3. Department of Anatomy. The University of HongKong; 4. Institute of Virology, Chinese Academy of Preventive Medicine

〔SUMMARY〕 To investigate the multistage process of carcinogenesis, the progressive alteration of the morphology, telomerase, cytogenesis, oncogenes and tumorigenicity in the process of immortalization and malignant transformation of the human fetal esophageal epithelial cell(SHEE)was studied. The SHEE cells were immortalized by gene E6E7 of human papilloma virus(HPV)type 18 in our laboortory and continually cultivated over 100 passages, which had been malignantly transformed. Calls at the 11th, 35th, 65th and 100th passage were examined according to the following criteria; morphological changes of cell growth, contact-inhibition and anchorage-independent growth(AIG); the cell proliferative and apoptotic index; the modal number of chromosomes; c-myc, p53, bet-2, ras; telomere length and activities of telomerase and tumorigenicity in nude mice or severe combined immunodeficient(SCID)mice. The cells of the 11th passage were well differentiated and the cells of 100th passage were relatively poorly differentiated with polymorphism, while the cells of 35th and 65th had two distinct differentiations. The proliferative indexes were 21.1%, 32.5%, 33.2%, and 40.9% and the apoptotic indexes were 3.3%, 2.7%, 3.5%, 2.7% in the 11th, 35th, 65th and 100th passage respectively. Karyotypes of four cell passages belonged to hyperdiploidy and hypotriploidy. C-myc, ras, p53 genes were low in the 10th and 35th, and high in the 65th and 100th passage, hut bcl-2 was low in 4 passages. Telomere length sharply decreased from normal fetal esophagus cells until the 35th passage, but it was stably expressed in the 65th and 100th passage. The activities of telomerase were expressed in cells of the 35th, 65th and 100th passages. The efficiency of AIG varied in different passages of the SHEE ceil and was absent in the 11th passage, low efficiency in the 35th passage and 65th passage, and high efficiency in the 100th passage. Transplanted cells of the 65th and 100th passage into SCID mice resulted in tumor formation, but only the 100th passage calls could grow in nude mice. All of these characteristic changes were in dynamic progressive process. These data demonstrate that carcinogenesis of esophageal epithelial cells induced by HPV is the multistage process, which goes through the initial, immortal, premalignant and malignant transformation stages. The generation of esophageal carcinoma is caused by the accumulation of cellular, genetic and molecular changes.

〔Keywords〕 Esophagus; Carcinogenesis; Human papillomavirus; Immortalization; Malignant transformation

INTRODUTION

Tumorigenesis in humans is a multistep process, as reported in lung[1,2] gastric cancer[3,4], oral[5,6], bladder[7] and skin[8] cancers. Carcinogenesis is a multistep phenomenon, beginning with precancerous conditions through stages of cell hyperplasia and dysplasia and ending in fully maliguant transformation. Cell lines can provide powerful model systems for the study of human tumorigenesis[9,10]. The transformation of a normal into a malignant cell is a multistep mechanism, which involves various alterations at the cellular, molecular and genetic level[11,12]. For neoplstic transformation of normal human cells, they must be first immortalized and then be converted into neoplastic cells. It is well known that the immortalization is a critical step for the neoplastic transformation of cells.

It is well accepted that cancer arises in a multistep fashion in which exposure to environmental carcinogens is a major etiological factor. Human papillomaviruses(HPV), more than 120 genotypes have been identified, cause certain common human cancers, most notably carcinoma of the cervix. HPVs are also associated with a broad spectrum of cutaneous and mucosal lesions. In 1982 Syrjanen firstly reported the relationship of HPV and esophageal cancer in the light of pathomorphological data and suggested that HPV might be a cause of esophageal cancer[13]. Extensive investigation has provided insights into the relationship between HPV and esophageal cancer in last two decades[14-16]. In our previous study the positive rate of HPV in samples of esophageal cancers was as high as 60%-66% in areas with a high incident rate[17] and most researchers agree that HPV might play an important role in esophageal carcinogenesis[18,19].

BY HPV18E6E7 inducement, we have established an immortal esophageal epithelial cell line SHEE[20]. which keeps the characteristics of monolayer growth, contact inhibition, and the squamous epithelium origin[21,22]. The coatinually cultivated cells of SHEE developed into the malignant transformation[23,24]. The cell line offered a unique system for investigating the multistage process of carcinogenesis in human esophageal epithelial cells.

The mechanism underlying the process towards malignant conversion, usually covering a long latency period between primary infection of HPV and cancer emergence is presently not fully understood. The aim of this study was to investigate the cellular genetic and molecular biological characteristics in various passages of SHEE to explore the multistage process of carcinogenesis of esophageal epithelial cells induced by HPV18E6E7

MATERIALS AND METHODS

1. Cell culture: The SHEE cell line was a kind of immortal embryonic esophageal epithelium induced by genes E6E7 of human papilloma virus(HPV)type 18 in our laboratory and has been propagated over 100 passages. From the liquid nitrogen storage, different generation of cells, the 11th passage(SHEE11), 35th passage(SHEE35), 65th passage(SHEE65)and 100th passage(SHEE100), were revived and inoculated to culture flask. The cell line was routinely cultivate in culture medium 199(Giboo)with 10% bovine serum, 100 units, of penicillin and streptomycin in a humidified atmosphere of 5% CO_2 and 95% air. The cell shape and size, anchorage-dependent growth and contactinhibited growth were examined by phase-contrast microscopy.

2. Analysis of cell proliffereteive index and apoprotic index: Cells of SHEE11, SHEE35, SHEE65 and SHEE100 in the flask were trysinized, washed twice with PBS, fixed by 70% alcohol, prepared as single-cell suspension and stored at 4℃. Cells was stained with propidium iodide(Sigma)and analyzed with flow cytometry(FCM FACSort, B-D Co.). In DNA histogram, the percentage of cells in various stages of the call cycle, the apoptotic index(AI)and prcoliferation index(PIx=S+G_2M/$G_0$$G_2$+S+$G_2$M)were calculated.

3. Telomere length analysis: The DNA of samples containing fetal esophagus, SHEE11, SHEE35, SHEE65 and SHEE100 were extracted. Telomeric restriction fragment(TRF)was measured by Southern blot. Briefly, 20μg of genomic DNA was digested with Hinff and run on 0.7% agarose gel with marker DNA/Hind Ⅲ. After electrophoresis the gel was blotted to nylon membrane(Hybond™ N+ nylon membrane, Amersham Life Science)and hybridized to the Dig-labeled probes(CCCTAA)₃ at 50℃ in 5×SSC, 0.1% Sodium N-lauroylsarcosine(SLS), 0.02% SDS for 12-16h and washed twice at room temperature in 2×SSC, 0.1% SDS for 5 min, once at 50℃ in 1×SSC, 0.1% SDS for5 min twice, at 50℃ in 0.1×SSC, 0.1% SDS for 5 min, stained with NBI/BCIP and the middle points were measured to obtain the mean tetomere length.

4. Telomerase activity assay: Telomerase activity was measured using TRAP-eze Telomerase Detection Kit (Oncor Inc.). Cells were added 10-50μl of ice-cold lysis buffer(10mmol/L TrisHCl pH 7.3, 1mmol/L EGTA, 0.1mmol/L benzamidine, 5mmol/L β-mereaptoethanol, 0.5% CHAPS, 10% glycerol). After 30 min of incubation on ice the lysate was centrifuged at 12 000g for 20 min at 4℃. The telomeric repeat amplification protocol (TRAP)reaction was performed using 1μl lysate or 1/10 diluted lysate, 2.5μl 10×TRAP buffer(200mmol/L TrisHCl, pH 8.3, 15mmol/L $MgCl_2$, 630mmol/L KCl, 0.5% Tween 20, 10mmol/L EGTA), 0.5μl 2.5mmol/L dNTP, 0.5μl Ts primer, 0.5μl TRAPprimer mix, 19.5μl water, 0.5μl Taq(2 U/μl). After incubation at 30℃ for 30 min the reaction mix was immediately transferred to 94℃ and performed PCR at 94℃ for 30 sec, 59℃ for 30 sec, for 30 cycles. PCR products were separated in a non-denaturing 12% PAGE in 1×TBE at 5 V/cm. The gel was stained using $AgNO_3$.

5. Preparation of chromosome: The cells of SHEE11, SHEE35. SHEE65 and SHEE100 at their exponential phase of growth appeared as mitotic cells. These cultured cells were added with 0.05μg/ml colchicine(Fluka AG, CH-9470 Buchs.) for 1-1.5h before harvest, and then digested with 0.25% trypsin to obtain cell suspension. After centrifugating, harversted cells were added with 0.075mol/L KCl for a hypoosmotis treatment at 37℃ for 30 min. And then, 1ml of fixed solution(methyl alcohol: glacial acetic acid=3:1)was added to fix cells for 30 min and repeated twice. The cells were then dropped on slide and Giemsa stained. The chromosome number of metaphase of cells in four groups was scored.

6. C-myc, bcl-2, p53 and ras genes assay by multi-PCR(mPCR): mPCR was performed by Maxim mPCP Kit (APO-MO50G, Maxim Biotech Inc.)including the primers of c-myc, bcl-2, p53, ras and a house-keeping gene GAPDH. The isolation of undegraded and intact RNA of SHEE series without RNase contamination of buffers and containers was a prerequisite. PCR thermocycle profile: 96℃ 1 min and 57℃ 4 min for 2 cycles; 94℃ 1 min and 57℃ 25 min for 30 cycles; 70℃ 10 min and 25℃ soak. The ras mPCR Kit(RAS-MO50G, Maxim)contains ras positive contrast, K-ras, H-ras primer and DNA marker. The electrophoresis of PCR products was used in the visual inspection of an EB-stained agarose gel containing 0.5μg/ml ethidium bromide(Sigma).

7. Cell cultured in soft agar cultivation: The efficiency of anchorage-independent growth(AIG) was determined by two different approaches to assess the efficiency of colony formation. It is feasible in the case of two layers of soft agar conditions or in liquid medium over-agar, namely over agar condition[25]. The exponential growth cells of SHEE series were trypsinized, stained with trypan blue to count the number of living cells. The living single cell suspensions(10³ cells/

ml) were cultured in 0.35% agar(Agarose, V312A, Promega)overlaid on 0.7% agar in a 6-well plate(Coming), and in another plate of over-agar condition cells were cultured in liquid cultured medium over 0.7% agar and incubated in 5% CO_2 at 37℃ for 20 days. The cell colonies with more than 20 cells were then counted.

8. Tumorigenaais in nude mice and SCID mice: Six-week-old BALB/C nude mice(supplied by the Experimental Animal Center of Zhongshan Medical University)and severe combined immunodeficient mice(SCID, C. B-17/IcrJ-scid, supplied by Animal Center of Chinese Academy of Medical Science) were bred in isolated conditions respectively. Four groups of SCID mice and made mice were injected subcutaneously with SHEE series cells in $1×10^6$ cells/mouse respectively. They were observed every 10 days for 2 months and then sacrificed for histopathological examination.

9. Western blot analysis: Cells cultured in flasks were washed three times with ice-cold PBS, and then were lysed in buffer(50mmol/L Tris-HCl, pH 8.0, 150mmol/L NaCl, 100μg/ml PMSF, 1% Triton X-100)for 30 min on ice. After removal of cell debris by centrifugation(12 000g, 5 min), the protein concentration of lysates was measured by Bradford method. Proteins(50μg)of different groups were boiled for 5 min in sample buffer and were separated in 10% SDS-PAGE and transfered onto a nitrocellulose membrane(Bio-Rad). Nonspecific reactivity was blocked by incubation overnight at 4℃ in buffer(10mmol/L Tris-HCl, pH 7.5, 150 mmol/L NaCl, 2% Tween-20, 4% bovine serum albumin). The membrane was then incubated with primary antibody(mouse anti HPV18E$_6$, MAB-0308 Maixin Bio.). The secondary antibody was used to detect bound primary antibody. Reactive protein was detected by ECL Western blot analysis Amersham Pharmacia Biotech).

RESULTS

1. Cell morphology: In the initial passages, the cells in the SHEE11 group were uniform in size and shape, and grew as an even monolayer with characteristics of squamous epithelium(Fig. 1A). SHEE35 ceils proliferated and exhibited diphasic differentiation, some cells displayed the undifferentiated basal epithelium and others displayed differentiated squamous epithelium(Fig. 1B). Cells in SHEE65 crowded together with undifferentiated, and mere mitotic nuclei(Fig. 1C). SHEE100 ceils lost the pattern of maturation and cells displayed evidence of polymorphism with much more giant nucleus cells and multinucleoli(Fig. 1D).

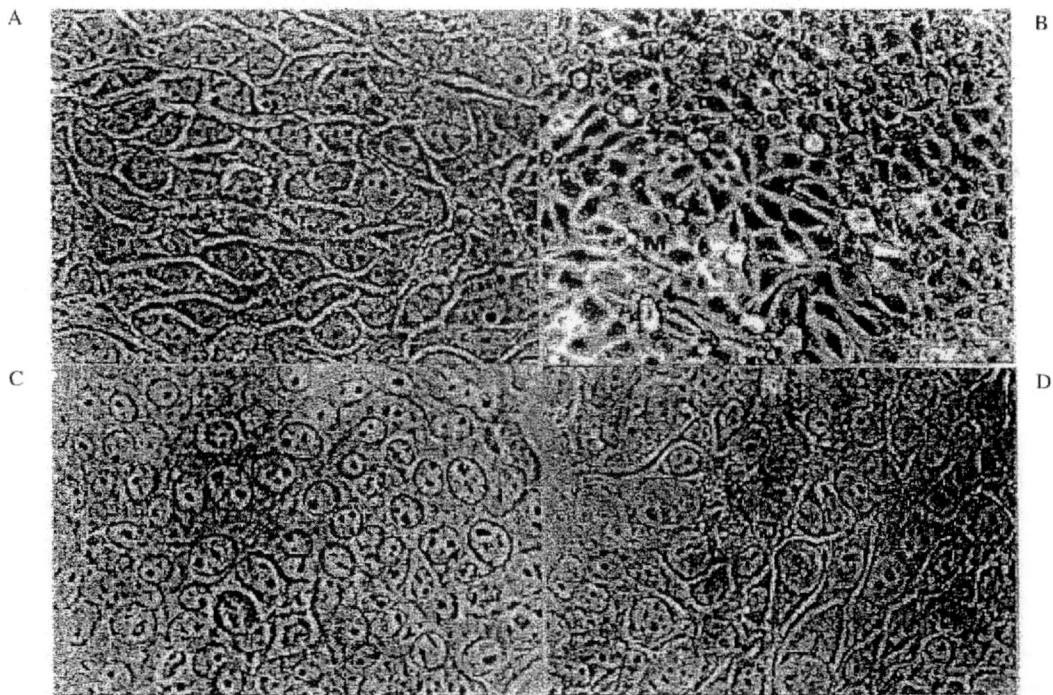

(A), Cells of SHEE11 displayed good differetiation and squamous epithelium in outlook(×400); (B), Cells of SHEE35 displayed two differentiated directions, partilly well differentiated(M)and partial poorly(N)(×200); (C), Cells of SHEE65 crowded together(×400); (D), Cells of SHEE100 displayed poor differentiation with polymorphism and meganuclei(×400)

Fig. 1　Morphology of living cells in the SHEE cell series was observed by phase contrast microscopy

2. Cell cycle analyzed by FCM: In the DNA histogram the distribution of DNA content of SHEE series cells is shown in Fig. 2. The proliferative indexes were 21.1%, 32.5%, 33.2% and 40.9% in SHEE11, SHEE35, SHEE65, and SHEE100 respectively. Accounting DNA < 2 cells, the apoptotic indexes were 3.3%, 2.7%, 3.5%, 2.7% in SHEE11, SHEE35, SHEE65, SHEE100 respectively.

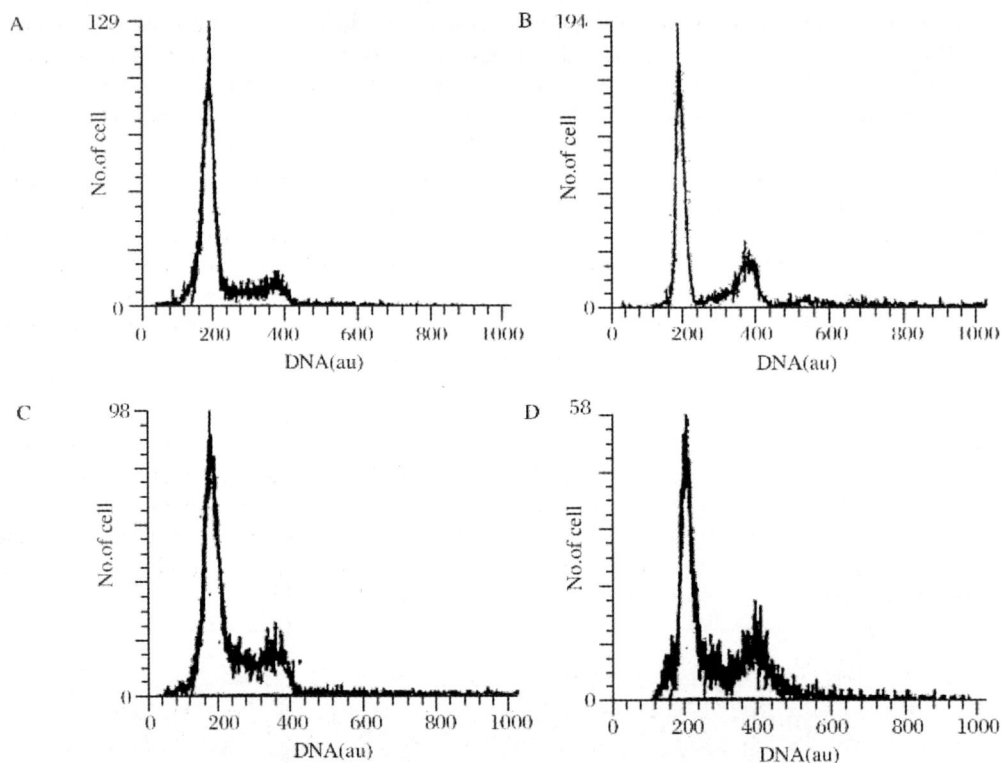

(A), SHEE11;(B), SHEE35;(C), SHEE65;(D), SHEE100; an, arbitraly unit

Fig. 2　DNA histograms of cell cyste

3. Cytogenesis abnormality: The number of chromosomes in SHEE11, SHEE35, SHEE65 and SHEE100 ranged between 30 and 178. These chromosomes were mainly hyperdiploids(Fig. 3A) and hypotriploids(Fig. 3B). More hypertriploid cells were found at SHEE65 and SHEE100. Modal number of chromosomes at SHEE11 was 51-54, at SHEE35 and SHEE65 were bimodal in distribution, 57-55, 62-64; and59-61, 63-65 respectively, at SHEE100 was60-67. The modal number from SHEE11 to SHEE100 increased slowly.

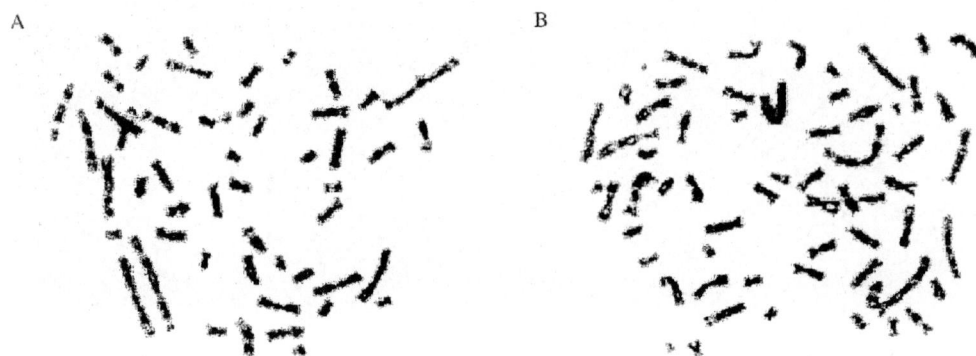

(A), Hyperdiploid of chromosome in SHEE11;(B), Hypotriptoid of chromosome in SHEE100

Fig. 3　Hyperploid karyotype of SHEE(Giemsa, ×1000)

4. Telomere length and telomerase activity: Telomeric restriction fragment(TRF)length of SHEE series cells and fetal esophageal tissue was measured by Southern blot analysis. The mean telomere length of fetal esophageal tissue was 30.0 kb; telomere length of SHEE11 shortened sharply to 17.0 kb; SHEE35 to 3.2 kb; SHEE65 and SHEE100, to 3.5 and 3.7 kb(Fig. 4A). Telomerase activation was absent in fetal esophageal tissue and SHEE11. Our results proved that the shortening telomere and absence of telomerase activity contributes to cellular senescence and cell death. The activity of telomerase first appeared in SHEE35, and appeared strongly positive in SHEE65 and SHEE100(Fig. 4B).

5. p53, bd-2, c-myc, ras and GAPDH: The p53 gene(mutant)appeared in all cells of four passages, but shifted-up in SHEE65 and SHEE100. The c-myc expressed in cells of SHEE11 and 35 in low level and expressed apparently in SHEE65 and SHEE100. Bel-2 expression in the 4 passages was low(Fig. 5A). The electrophoresis bands of ras mPCR products, including H-ras and K-ras were low in SHEE11 and SHEE35, intermediate in SHEE-65 and high in SHEE100(Fig. 5B). The housekeeping gene GAPDH was expressed at a similar level in the four groups.

6. HPV18E6: The expression of HPV18E6 was examined by Western blot analysis. The results showed the presence of HPV18E6 in the four groups of SHEE cells(Fig. 6).

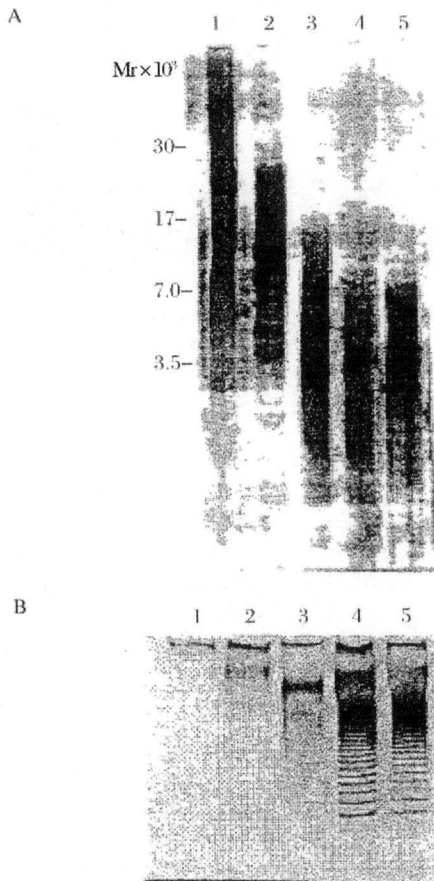

(A), Telemere length;(B), Telomerase activity,
Lanes: 1, normal esophagus; 2, SHEE11; 3, SHEE33; 4, SHEE65; 5, SHEE 100

Fig. 4 Telomere and telomerse of SHEE

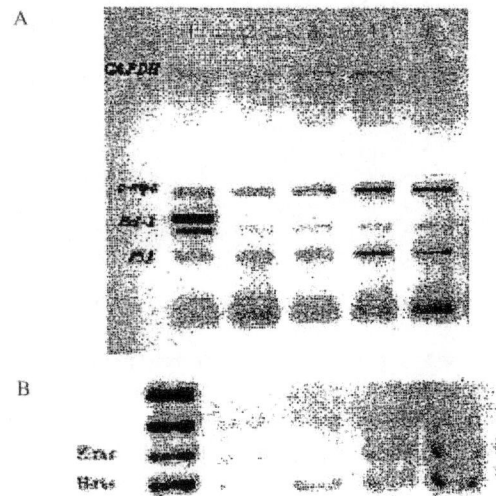

(A), p53, bel-2, c-myc GAPDH (B), H-rasand K-ras.
Lanes: 1, marker; 2, SHEE11; 3, SHEEE35; 4, SHEE65; 5, SHEE100

Fig. 5 The products of mPCR

Lanes: 1, marter; 2, SHEE11; 3, SHEE35; 4, SHEE65; 5, SHEE100

Fig. 6 Western blot analysis of protein of HPV18E

7. Colony formation on soft agar: The culture method of over-agar as an ancharage-independent growth(AIG) condition permitted more efficient recovery of cells compared with those in semisolid soft agar. The efficiency of AIG varied in different passages of SHEE ceils and was absent in SHEE11, low in SHEE35(0.05%-0.1%)and SHEE65(1.0%-3.0%); and high in SHEE100(8.0%-12.0%)(Fig. 7). The over-agar culture can be considered valid for the study of malignant transformation and to search for colonigenic cells.

8. Tumor formation: In order to observe the tumorigenicity, the ability of tumor formation and invasive potency were observed by means of cells in various passages transplanted into nude mice and SCID mice subcutaneously, Cells of SHEE11 and SHEE35 did not develop tumors in either group cells of SHEE65 developed a tumor in one of four SCID mice but not in nude mice. Cells of SHEE100 formed rumors in both trade and SCID mice(Fig. 8). In the tissue sections tumor cells invaded the adjacent tissues.

A   B

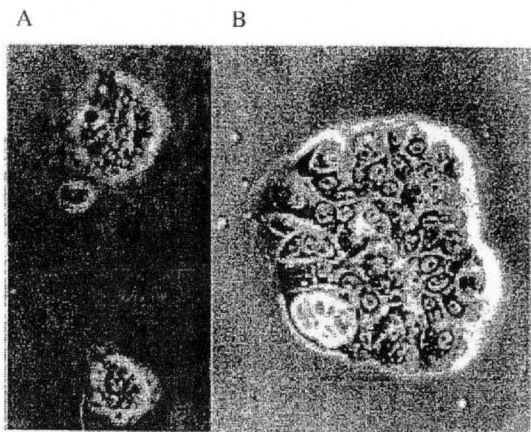

(A), A few cells grew on the soft agar in SHEE65;(B), A large colony grew on over-agar in SHEE100

Fig. 7   Colony formation on agar medium(phase contrast microscopy, ×200)

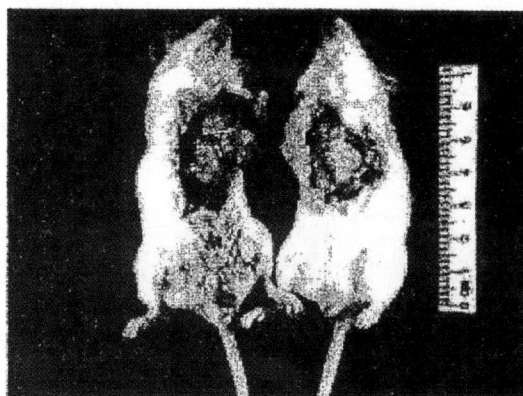

Fig. 8   Cells of SHEE100 transplanted into SCID mice and the tumor formed subcutaneously

9. Comparison of biological criteria in four stages of SHEE: The biological criteria in various passage of SHEE are shown in Tab. 1, SHEE11 cells revealed proliferative morphological phenotype with good differentiation and shortening of telomere length without telomerase activity and the modal number of chromosome increased from 51 to 54. It was designated as the initial stage. In middle stage, SHEE35 revealed cell proliferation and two differentiated phenotypes accompanying the telomerase activity and the telomere length was sustained, but the phenotype was non-tumorigenic. The changes of cytogenesis were bi-modal chromosomes 57-58, 62-64. It was designated as the immortal stage. Cells of SHEE65 displayed bipotenial differentiation, bi-modal chromosome, 59-61, 63-65 and telomerase activation. Cultured on soft agar, ceils of SHEE65 grew in different size of cooloies in which large, ones could develop into malignant tumorigenic clones. SHEE65 was judged in premalignant stage. In transformed stage, SHEE100 cells overlapped to grow with different shape and poor differentiation and less contact-inhibition with colony formation in soft agar. According to the invasive tumor formation in nude and SCID mice. SHEE100 cells revealed fully malignant tranformation.

Tab. 1   Comparison of biological criteria of variant passages of SHEE

Cell passages	SHEE11	SHEE35	SHEE65	SHEE100
Proliferative index(%)	21.1	32.5	33.2	40.9
Apoptotic index(%)	3.3	2.7	3.5	2.7
Differentiation	Good	Biphasic	Biphasic	Poor
Contact inhibition	+	+	±	−
Telomere length($\times 10^3$)	17	3.2	3.5	3.7

（续　表）

Cell passages	SHEE11	SHEE35	SHEE65	SHEE100
Telomerase activits	−	+	+ +	+ +
Modal no. of chromosomes	51−54	57−58, 62−64	59−61, 63−6.5	60−67
C-myc	+	+	+ +	+ +
p53	+	+	+ +	+ +
Ras	±	±	+	+
Bcl-2	±	±	+	+
Colong growing in soft agar	−	−	+	+ +
Tumor formation in SCID mice	0/4	0/4	1/4	4/4
HPV18E6	+	+	+	+

DISCUSSION

We first established an in vitro multistep esophageal carcinogenesis model by exposure of normal human fetal esophageal epithelium to HPV18E6E7 genes. The newly established esophageal epithelial cell line SHEE was cultured over 100 passages and went through a multistage process: the initial, immortal, premalignant and malignant stages. Upon introduction of the HPV genome, the cells bypassed the senescence checkpoint and commened proliferating, but without immortal life span during which telomcre DNA continued to shorten, called the initiate stage (SHEE11). In SHEE35 clones surviving beyond the crisis, the immortalization was formed while telomerase activity appeared and telomere length stabilized. Large colonies on soft agar in SHEE65 and SHEE100 showed that the characteristics of anchorage-dependent growth decreased but tumorigenicity increased. A few tumors formed in SCID mice incubated with SHEE65 cells but not in nude mice. So we judged that they were at a premalignant stage. SHEE100 cells, which were transplanted into nude and SCID mice and developed tumors in all mice with invasive pathern, expressed malignant transformation.

In 1994. Kim et al. also found specific association among the telomerse activity with immortal cells and cancer cells[26]. The telomerase may be a prerequisite and the diagnostic criteria to immortal cells[27]. In our data the telomere length of the normal fetal esophageal cell was 30 kb in length shortened to 17 kb in SHEE11, and 3.5kb in SHEE35, and then maintained this level continually to SHEE65 and SHEE100. The telemerase activity appeared im SHEE35, SHEE65 and SHEE100. The activation of telomerase to maintain telomere lengh was necessary for immortalization arid malignancy but was not sufficient for malignant transformation in the SHEE cell line. Our results indicated that immortalization and malignant transformation of SHEE cells might require activation of telomerase and other genes, which abrogated normal proliferation and differentiation of the cells.

Strong evidence in favor of the aberrant chromosome of cancer is early and essential events in tumor development. There was more aneuploidy(hyperdiploidy and hypotriploidy) in the chromosomes of the faur passages of SHEE. The separate modal number of chromosomes first appeared in SHEE35 and continued to SHEE65, SHEE65 and SHEE100 had more hypotriploid cells than the others. The above showed that chromosomes of the SHEE series were unstable, which would mean easier malignant transformation by promoters[28]. It was possible that in the initial stage progessive chromosomal changes induced by papillomavirus transfection might result in the genetic instability and phenotypic variability as described elsewhere[29,30]. Aneuploidy renders the chromosome structure and segregation error-prone, because it unbalances mitosis proteins and the many teams of enzymes that synthesize and maintain chromosomes. The resulting karyotype instability sets off a Chain reaction of aueuploidizations, which generate ever more abnormal and eventually cancer-specific rearrangements of chromosomes[31]. Thus carcinogenesis is initiated by a random aneuploidy and the drivimg force of carcinogenesis is the inherent instability of the aneuploid karyotype. This dynamic process might result in the acquisition of full transformation with the parade of sufficient time.

The changes of cytogenetics will control a lot of gents, which affect proliferation, differentiation, apoptosis and other phenotype of cells. Some genes, such as c-mye, ras, p53 and bel-2, are related to immortalization and malignant transformation of cells. In our data, c-myc, K-ras, H-ras and p53(mutant) were shifted-up in SHEE65 and SHEE100. In SHEE11 and SHEE35 c-myc, ras, bcl-2 and p53 were at a low level. In general, c-myc and p53 (mutant)promote proliferation of cells[32,33] and bcl-2 can prevent apoptosis[34]. Ras is a transforming growth signal causing rapid anenploid and malignant transformation of cells[35,36]. It has been reported that the cell transformation induced by virus ras was a required gene[37].

The alterations of telomere, chromosome and some genes mentioned above were closely related with HPV infection. Infection of HPV can cause karyotype confusion[38], such as break of chromosome, abnormal structure and number of chromosomes[39]. Out data also hints that the immortal esophageal cells induced by HPV18E6E7 may effect the changes of chromosomes. Abnormal chromosomes cause liability of genetic character[40,41]. The virus genome inserts anti integrates with chromosomes of the host[42], and causes the aetivation and expression of oncogenes[43]. HPV E6E7 protein is conjugation with anti-oncoprotein p53 and pRb[44,45], thus losing control of cellular growth and urging the phenotyping production of cellular transfomation[46]. Previous reports have shown that activation of telomerase can be achieved by the E6 and E7 proteins of HPV[47]. Therefore, E6 could promote malignant change, while E7 may cause benign neoplasm[48]. The virogene HPV16E6 alone can cause cellular malignant change[49]. It has also been suggested that the viral oncoproteins E6 and E7 are essential components in malignant conversion, although, they are not sufficient for the development of the malignant phenotype[50]. In this experiment, we find that SHEE series cells containing HPV18E6E7 can gradually be the way to malignant stage. It is also postulated that HPV will be a major risk factor for esophageal cancer.

In summary, we have developed a malignant transformed cell model to facilitate the study of carcinogenesis in esophageal carcinoma in vitro through immortalization of human fetal esophageal epilthelium induced with HPV18E6E7. The muttistep process of malignant transformation consists of initial(transduction of E6E7 genes), preimmortalized(by pass senescence), immortalized(activity of telomerase), premalignant(anchorage-independent growth)and malignant transformation(tumor formation in immunodeficient mice). Our data reveal that the viral oncogene of HPV type 18 is one of important causes in etiology of esophageal cancer and it can initiate cell immortalization and malignant transformation in vitro through molecular and genetic alterations.

ACKNOWLEDGEMENTS

Contract grant sponsor: National Natural Science Foundation of China(39830380, 39800069, 30170428); Research and Devetopment Foundation of Shantou University(L00012), and supported by the Chinese National Human Genome Cemer, Beijing.

REFERENCES

[1] Jeanmart M, Lantuejoul S, Fievet F, More D, Stum N, Brambilla C and Brambilla E. Value of immunohistochemical markers in preinvasive bronchial lesions in risk assessment of lung cancer. Cancer Res, 2003, 9:2195-2203.

[2] Chyczewski L, Niklinski J, Chyczewska E, Niklinska W and Naumnik W. Morphotogical aspects of carcinogenesis in the lung. Lung Cancer 34(Suppl2), 2001:517-525.

[3] Kang GH Lee S, Kim JS and Jung HY. Profile of aberrant CpG island methylation along muhistep gastric carcinogenesis. Lab Invest, 2003, 83: 519-526.

[4] Yasui W, Yokozaid H, Fujimoto J, Naka K, Kuniyasu H and Tahara E. Genetic and epigenetic alterations in multistep carcinogenesis of the stomach. J Gastroenterol, 2000, 12:111-115.

[5] Shintani S, Mihara M, Nakahara Y, Kiyota A, Ueyama Y, Matsumura T and Wong DT. Expression of cell cycle control proteins in normal epithelium, premnalignant and nalignant lesions of oral cavity. Oral Oncel, 2002, 38:235-243.

[6] Kang MK and Park NH. Conversion of normal to malignant pherotype, tehunere shotening, telomerase activation, and genomic instability during immortalization of human oral keratinocytes. Crit Rev Oral Biol Med, 2001, 12:38-54.

[7] Brandau S and Bohle A. Bladder cancer. 1. Molecular and genenc basia of carcinogenesis. Eur Urol, 2001, 39:491-497.

[8] Kub QY, Murao K, Matsumoto K and Arase. S Molecular carcinogenesis of squamous cell carcinomasof the skin J Med Invest, 2002, 49:111-117.

[9] Schwab TS, Stewart T, Lehr J, Pienta K J, Rhim JS and Macoska JA. Phenotypic characterization of immortalized normal and primary tumorderived human prostate epithelial cell cultures. Prostate, 2000, 44:164-171.

[10] Rajah N. Pruden DL. Kaznari H, Cao Q, Anderson BE, Duncan JL and Schaeffer AJ. Characterization of an immortalized human vaginal epithelial cell line. J Urol, 2000, 163: 616-622.

[11] Ming SC. Cellular and molecular pathology of gastric carcinoma and precursor lesions: a critical review. Gastric Cancer, 1998, 1:31-54.

[12] Fusenig NE and Boukmnp P. Multiple stages and genetic alterations in immnortalization, malignant transformation and tumor progression of human skin keratinocytes. Mol Carcinog, 1998, 23: 144-158.

[13] Syrjanen KJ. Histological changes identical to those of coudylomatous lesions found in esophageal squamous cell carcinomas. Arch Geschwulstforsch, 1982, 52:283-292.

[14] He D, Zhang DK. Lain KY, Ma L. Ngau HY, Liu SS and Tsao SW. Prevalence of HPV infection in esophageal squamous cell carcinoma in Chinese patients and its relationship to the p53 gene mutation. Int J Cancer, 1997, 72:959-964.

[15] Sur M and Cooper K. The rote of the human papilloma vires in esophgeal cancer. Pathology, 1998, 30:348-354.

[16] Poliak M Ceras A and Sent K. Human papillomavirus infection in esophageal carcinomas: a study of 121 fesions using multiple broad-spectrum polymerase chain reactions and literature review. Hum Pathol, 1998, 29:266-271.

［17］ Shear ZY, Hu SP, Shen J, Lu LC. Tang CZ, Kuang ZS and Zeng Y. Detection of human papillomavirus in esophageal carcinoma. J Med Virol, 2002, 68:412-416.

［18］ Chang F Svrianen S Shen Q Cintorino M, Santopietro R, Tosi P and Syrianen K. Human papillomavirus involvement in esophageal carcinogenesis in the high-incidence area of China. A study of 700 cases by sereerring and type-specific in situ hybridization. Scand J Gastroenterol, 2000, 35: 123-130.

［19］ Lavergne D and De-Villiers EM. Papillomavirus in esophageal papillomas and carcinomas. Int J Cancer, 1999, 80:651-684.

［20］ Shen ZY, Cen S, Xu LY, Cai WJ Chen MH, Shen J and Zeng Y. E6/E7 genes of human papilloma virus type 18 induced immortization of human fetal esophageal epithelium. Oncol, 2003, 10:1431-1436.

［21］ Shen ZY, Cen S, Cai WJ, Xu JJ, Ten ZP, Shen J, Hu Z and Zeng Y. Immortalization of human fetal esophageal epithelial cells induced by E6 and E7 genes of human papilloma vires 18. Chin J Exp Clin Virol, 1999, 13:121-123.

［22］ Shen ZY, Shen J, Cai W J, Cen S and Zeng Y. Biological characteristics of human fetatl esophageal epithelial cell line immortalized by the E6 and E7 gene of HPV type 18. Chin 1 Exp Clin Virol, 1999, 13:209-212.

［23］ Shen ZY, Xu LY, Chen MH, Shen J, Cai WJ and Zeng Y. Progressive transfomation of immortalized esophageal epithelial cells. World J Gastroenterol, 2002, 8:976-981.

［24］ Shen ZY, Shen J, Cai WJ, Chen JY and Zeng Y. Identification of malignant transformalion in the immortalized esophageal epithelial cells. Chin J Oncol, 2002, 24:107-109.

［25］ Donz Z, Cmaik JL. Wendel EJ and Colburn NH. Differential transtformation efficiency but not AP-1 induction under anchoragedependent and independent conditions. Carcinogenesis, 1994, 15:1001-1004.

［26］ Kim NW, Piatyszek MA, Prowse KR. Harley CB, West MD Ho PL Coviello GM Wright WE, Weinrich SL and Shay JW. Specific association of human telomerase activity with immortal cells and cancer. Science, 1994, 266:2011-2015.

［27］ Farwell DG, Shera KA, Koop JL, Bonnet GA, Matthews CP, Reuther GW, Coltrera MD, McDougall JK and Klingelhutz AJ. Genetic and epigenetic changes in human epithelial cells immortalized by telomerase. Aan J Pathol, 2000, 156: 1537-1547.

［28］ Shen ZY, Cen S, Shen J Cai WJ, Xu JJ, Teng ZP, Hu Z and Zeng Y. Study of immortalizaion and malignant tranformation of human embryonic esophageal epithelial cells induced by HPV18E6E7 J Cancer Res Clin Oncol, 2000, 126:589-594.

［29］ Shen ZY Xu LY, Chen MH, Cai WJ, Shen J, Ceng JY and Zeng Y. Cytogenetic and molecular genetic changes in malignant transformation of immortalized esophageal epithelial cells. Int J Mol Med, 2003, 12:219-224.

［30］ Shen ZY, Xu LY, Chen XH, Cai WJ Shen J, Chen JY, Huang TH and Zeng Y. The genetic events of HPV immnortalized esophageal epithelium cells. Int J Mol Med, 2001, 3:537-542.

［31］ Duesberg P and Li R. Multistep carcinogenesis, a chain reaction of aneuploidizations. Cell Cycle, 2003, 2:202-210.

［32］ De-Mighio MR, Simile MM, Muroni MR, Pussceddu S, Cahvisi D, Carru A, Seddaiu MA, Daino L, Deiana L, Pascale RM and Feo F. Correlation of c-myc oyerexpression and amplification with progression of preneoplastic liver lesions to malignancy in the poorly susceptible Wistar rat strain. Mol Carcinog, 1999, 25:21-29.

［33］ Tarapore P and Fukasawa K. p53 mutation and mitotic infidelity. Cancer Invest, 2000, 18: 148-155.

［34］ Adams JM and Cory S. The Bcl-2 protein family: arbiters of cell survival Science, 1998, 281: 1322-1326.

［35］ Mutter GL, Wada H, Faquin WC and Enomoto T. K-ras mutations appear in the premalignant plase of both microsatellite stabie and unstable endometrial carcinogenesis. Mot Pathol, 1999, 52:257-262.

［36］ Chin L. Tam A, Pomerantz J, Wong M, Holash J, Bandeesy N, oncogenic Ras in tumor maintenance. Nature, 1999, 400: 468-472.

［37］ Weitzman JB and Yaniv M. Rebuilding the road to cancer Nature, 1999, 400:401-402.

［38］ Duensing S, Lee LY, Duening A, Basile J, Piboonniyom S, Gonzalez S, Cmm CP and Munger K. The human papillomavirus type 16 E6 and E7 oncoproteins cooperate to induce mitotic defects and genomic instability by uncoupling centresome duplication from the call division cycle. Proc Nail Acad Sci USA, 2000, 97:10002-10007.

［39］ Villa LL. Human papillomaviruses and cervical cancer. Adv Cancer Res, 1997, 71:321-341.

［40］ Weijerman PC van Drunen E, Konig JJ Teubel W, Romijn JC, Schroder FH and Hagemeijer A. Specific cytogenetic aberrations in two novel human prosiatic cell lines immortalized by human papillomavirus type 18 DNA. Cancer Genet Cytogenet, 1997, 99:108-115.

［41］ Mullokandov MR, Kholodilov NG, Atkin NB, Burk RD, Johnson AB, Klinger HP. Genomic alterations in cervical carcinoma: losses of chromosome heterozygosity and human papilloma virus tumor status. Cancer Res, 1996, 56:197-205.

［42］ Pfeffer A, Schubbert R, Orend G, HilgerEversheim K and Doerfler W. Integrated viral genomes can be lost from adenovirus type 12-induced hamster tumor cells in a clone-specific, multistep process with retention of the oncogenic phenotype. Virus Res, 1999, 59:113-127.

［43］ Choo KB, Chen CM, Han CP, Cheng WT and Au LC. Molecular analysis of cellular loci disrupted hy papillomavirus 16 integration in cervical cancer: frequent viral integration in topologically destabilized anti transriptionally active chromosomal regions, J Med Virol, 1996, 49:15-22.

［44］ Demers GW, Halbert CL and Galloway DA. Elevated widtyge p53 protein levels in human epithelial cell lines immortalized by the human papillomavirus type 16 E7 gene. Virology, 1994, 198:169-174.

［45］ Bover SN, Wazer DE and Band V. E7 protein of human papilloma virus-16 induces degradation of retinblastoma protein through the ubiquitinproteasome pathway. Cancer Res, 1996, 56: 4620-4624.

［46］ Itakura M, Mori S, Park NH and Bonavida B. Both HPV and carcinogen contribute to the development of resistance to apoptosis during oral carcinogenesis. Int J Oneol, 2000, 16:591-597.

［47］ Shen ZY, Xu LY, Li C, Cai WJ Shen J, Chen JY anti Zeng Y. A comparative study of telomerase activity and malignant phenotype in multistage carcinogenesis of esophageal epithelial cells induced by human papilomavirus. Int J Mol Med, 2001, 8:633-639.

[48] Klingelhutz AJ, Foster SA and McDougall JK. Telomerase activation by the E6 gene product of human papillomavius type 16. Nature, 1996, 380:79-82.

[49] Song S, Pitot HC, and Lambert PF. The human papillomavirus type 16 E6 genc alone is sufficient to induce carcinomas in transgenic animals. J Virol, 1999, 73:5887-5893.

[50] Zur Hausen H. Immortalization of human cells and their malignant conversion by high risk human papillomavirus genotypes. SeminCancer Biol, 1999. 9:405-411.

[In《Oncol Rep》2004，11:647-654]

Malignant Transformation of Human Embryonic Liver Cells Induced by Hepatitis B Virus and Aflatoxin B_1

GUO Xc[1], LAN Xy[1], ZHOU L[1], ZHANG Yl[1], ZENG Y[1], TENG Zp[2], SHEN Zy[3]

1. Institute for Virus Disease Control and Prevention; 2. Molecular Biology Lab, Institute of Hematology; 3. Medical College of Shantou University

[SUMMARY]　In order to investigate the effect of hepatitis B virus(HBV) and aflatoxin B_1 (AFB_1)on hepatocarcinogenesis, the human embryonic liver cells infected with HBV were transplanted to nude mice Dy subcutaneous route and the transplanted mice were divided into 4 groups for study, in which the group A of mice was injected with HBV-infected human embryonic liver cells and followed by injections of AFB_1 once a week(HBV AFB_1); the group B was treated with HBV as group A, but no AFB_1 was given(HBV^+); the group C was injected with normal human embryonic liver cells and AFB_1 was used as group(AFB_1^+)and the group D or control group was injected with normal embryonic liver cells without addition of AFB_1. The experimental results showed that the incidences of tumor formation in different groups were 27.3%(6/22)in group A; 0%(0/13) in group B; 13.3%(2/15)in group C and 0%(0/14)in group D respectively. All the tumors formed were proved to De human hepatocellular carcinoma(HCC)by pathological examinations and the tumor tissues were anthrogenetic as demonstrated by EMA monoclonal antibody. The HBV-X and HBV-S genes could be detected in the tumor tissues by means of slot hybridization and PCR amplification, indicating that the HBV-DNA genes had integrated into DNA of host cells. Thus, we have successfully induced the human HCC through HBV infection and introduction of AFB_1 with a synergistic effect between HBV and AFB_1 in hepatocarcinogenesis.

[Keywords]　Human embryonic liver cells; HBV; Aflatoxin; Malignant; Transformation; Cell line

INTRODUCTION

Hepatocellular carcinoma(HCC)is a worldwide distributed disease accounting for 473000 newly developed cases of HCC annually in the world and 235000 cases in China[1]. Epidemiological and laboratory investigations have demonstrated that hepatitis B or C virus infection and afliatoxin exposure are the major and possibly synergistic risk factors for the development of HCC. Individuals with chronic hepatitis B virus(HBV)infection have a 200-fold of greater risk to develop HCC than the agematched uninfected controls[2]. Therefore, it is important to explore the role of HBV infection and the aflatoxin(AFB₁)exposure in hepatocareinogenesis. Ahhough more and more experiments support a direct effect of HBV on the hepatocarcinogenesis, but there is still no direct evidence in this regard. It has been shown that Epstein-Barr virus(EBV)can directly induced malignant transformation of the nasopharyngeal mucosa cells from human fetus through the synergistic effect of EBV and the tumor promoters[3]. The objective of the present investigation is to explore the synergistic effect HBV and AFB1 in hepatocarcinogenesis and to develop an experimental model for further studies.

MATERIAL AND METHODS

1. Mice

BALB/c nude mice(4-6 week old)were obtained from the Animal Center, Chinese Academy of Medical Science. Female and male were all used. They lived in SPF(specific pathogen free) clear room and was fed with food and water sterilized by autoclave.

2. Hepatitis B virus and reagents

Serum that contained 10^6-10^7 copies of HBV DNA was collected from hepatitis B patients. The serum was supplied by Beijing 2nd Infectious Disease Hospital. Aflatoxin B_1 came from Institute of Nutrition and Sanitation, Chinese Academy of Preventive Medicine.

3. Tumor formation

The liver specimens were obtained from a human fetus(3-4 months old)under aseptic condition. Liver cells suspensions were prepared by mincing specimens through steel mesh, and then subjecting the cells to a concentration of 2×10^7/ml with RPMI 1640. The experiment was divided into 4 groups. Group A(HBV＋AFB₁): The liver cells were infected with serum that contained HBV and incubated at 37℃ for 2h. After virus adsorption, cells were centrifugation for 5-10 min by 1500r/ rain. And then about 0.5×10^7-1×10^7 cells were xenografted subcutaneously to the back of nude mice. At the same time 400ng AFB₁ was injected subcutaneously into the other side of back and once a week thereafter. Group B(HBV⁺): The liver cells and nude mice were treated with HBV as group A, but no AFB₁ was used. Group C(AFB₁⁺): The liver cells without HBV were incubated at 37℃ for 2h too and then were transplanted subcutaneously into the back of nude mice. And AFB₁ was used as group A. Group D: Control group, the liver cells and nude mice were treated as group C and no AFB₁ was used. The whole experiment was finished by 3 times and 64 nude mice were used. All animals were observed for 3-4 months.

4. Histological procedures and HBV status

The tumor tissues obtained from group A and group C were fixed in 10% neutral formalin, embedded in paraffin, sectioned, and stained in hematoxylin and eosin.

To prepare tumor tissues DNA, the fresh tumor tissues obtained from group A were treated for 12h at 55℃ with 500 volumes(μl)of a solution containing 200μg/ml of proteinase K(Merck) dissolved in 10mmol/L Tris-HCl (pH8. 0), 2mmol/L EDTA, 40mmol/L NaCl and 0. 5% SDS, then followed phenol extraction. The samples were stored at -20℃ until used. Hepatitis B status was assessed by polymerase chain reaction(PCR)and by slot hybridization for the presence HBV S and X genes. Primers for HBV S gene were 5'-GGTATG 3TGCCGTTTGTCCTCT-3' and 5'GGTATGTTGCCCCGTTTGTCCTCT-3' and primers to amplify the X region were 5'-CCATGGCT-GCTCGGGTGTG-3' and 5'-GCTCTAGATGATFAGGCAGAGG-3'. The length of the expected amplified product is 228 bp for S gene, 465 bp for X gene. The PCR conditions were 1 cycle at 94℃ for 3 min; 35 cycles at 94℃ for 45s, 55℃ for 1 min, and 72℃ for 1 min; and 1 cycle at 72℃ for 10 min. Aliquots of each reaction were electrophoresis in 1. 5% agarose gels which was stained with ethidium bromide.

Using HepG2 DNA that contains HBV DNA as template, HBV S and X genes were amplified by PCR. The products were purified with DNA retrieved kit and then labeled with Digoxin. Dig-labeled gene probes were hybridized with tumor tissues DNA blotted in nylon membrane by slot hybridization. The method was followed by directions of DNA test kit(BOEHRINGER MANNHEIM).

5. Establishment of cell lines

Three tumor tissues from group A were immediately placed in a modified Eagle medium respectively and eliminated necrosis tissues and contaminating fibroblasts. About 0. 5cm³ of pieces were got by cutting specimens and separately transplanted to nude mice by subcutaneous again. When transplanted tumor developed about 1. 5cm³, the nude mice were put to death and the tumor tissues were treated as above. After 5 generations in nude mice the tumor tissues were taken out and washed twice by Hanks medium that contained double antibiotic, then were washed twice by RPMI 1640 medium. After that the tissues were sheared into tiny pieces and cultured in RPMI 1640 medium plus 15% fetal bovine in vitro. Cultures were maintained in a humidified incubator at 37℃ in an atmosphereof 5% CO₂. Cells were passaged when they grown at 90% confluence. Cells were passaged once a week at beginning and after 6 generation they were passaged once about 3-4 d. For cell line development, containating fibroblasts were initially removed by differential subcuhuring.

6. Morphology, immunochemistry, and growth kinetics of cell lines

For the morphological study of CBH-la, CBH-lb and CBH-2, cultured cells were observed by phase-contrast microscopy. The ultrastructure of cell was observed by transmission and scanning electron microscope. Cells were cultured in cover slice and fixed, then were stained for human early membrane antigen by indirect immunofluorescence assay(Genezene, USA)and Ki67 was detected by immunochemistry. Ki67 positive nuclei were counted in 500 cells and the percentage of proliferative nucleus was statistic. Alpha fetoprotein was determined in the supematant of the culture, using complete medium as a blank, by radioimmunoassy(Abbott Laboratories, USA).

For cell growth studies, 5000 cells were seeded in different columns across 96-well microtiter plates. Growth rate estimated by the measurement of absorbance following the MTT(Sigma Chemical Co.)assay in 3 cell lines[4]. All results represent the average of a minimum of 8 wells.

7. HBV status in cell lines

HBV S and X genes in 3 cell lines were detected by fluorescence in situ hybridization(FISH) and PCR. The cells were collected from 10 subculture cells. The method of PCR was described above. NBT/Bcip test kit and random biotin-labeled primer kit were purchased from Institute of Hematology, Beijing Medical University. Pd(N)6 primer was purchased from Promega Company. Avidin D and anti-avidin D-were purchased from Vector Company. The detail method of FISH was used as described previously[5].

8. Tumnorgenesis in nude mice

After the 60 passages, the cell lines of CBH-1a, CBH-1b and CBH-2 were harvested separately. About 10⁶/ 0. 2ml cells were transplanted subcutaneously to the back of nude mouse. Four nude mice were used in each cell line anti 12 nude mice were observed.

RESULTS

1. Tumor formation in nude mice

There was an about 0. 5-1. 0cm³ bulge in back of mouse after just injection of embryonic liver cells and it would be gradually disappeared during 3-5d. The tumors of group A occurred during 1-2 months and increased gradually. They reached 1. 5cm×1. 5cm×1. 0cm, the substance was hard and the surface was uneven. The tumors of group C occurred during 1. 5-2. 0 months and they grew slowly. The size of tumor was smaller than group A and there was necrosis in center of tumor. There were no tumors observed in the group B and D. The comparison of tumor formation in different groups was summarized in Tab. 1.

Tab. 1 Developing tumor induced by HBV and AFB₁ in different group

Groups (Times of experiment)	A (HBV+AFB₁)	B (HBV)	C (AFB₁)	D (Control)
1	2/6	0/4	1/5	0/4
2	3/9	0/5	1/6	0/6
3	1/7	0/4	0/4	0/4
Sum total(%)	6/22(27. 3)	0/13(0)	2/15(13. 3)	0/14(0)

The tumors of groups A and C were confirmed as hepatocellular carcinomas(HCC)by histopathological examination. The most cancer cells were square round and line up. The cell plasma was abundant and nuclear size was not slightly identical. There were some fibrocytes around the cancer nest(Fig. 1).

2. HBV status in tumor tissues

DNAs of the tumors from group A were amplified by 2 pairs of primers covering 2 different regions of the HBV genome: S and X genes. PCR results revealed that the strip in 228 bp was amplified in 5 tumors and positive control for S gene and the strip in 465 bp was in all samples for X gene, except for negative control(Figs. 2 and 3). For the further confirming the results above, Dig-labeled S and X genes probes were hybridized with tumor tissues DNA by slot hybridization. The findings were consistent with PCR results.

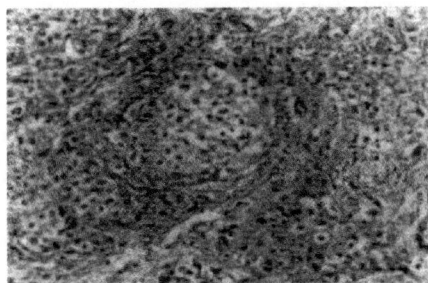

Fig. 1 Micrographs of paraffin section of hepatocellular carcinoma in nude mice H and E(×400)

M: DNA marker; 1: Positive control; 2-7: Tumor tissue DNA; 8 Negative control

Fig. 2 S gene result of PCR in tumnor tissues

3. CBH-1a, CBH-1b and CBH-2 Cell lines

The tumor tissues from group A were cultured and passaged in vitro in a long time and 3 cell lines were established. Three cell lines were named CBH-1a, CBH-1b and CBH-2. CBH-1a and CBH-1b were rooted in first time of experiment, and CBH-2 was from second time of experiment. The cell lines were subcuhured nearly 100 generations. The cell shape was typical epithelioid cell. The limit of cell was clear and cells were tightly arranged. The cell size was equal, plasma was plentiful and binucleate cells were easy to see under the phase contrast microscope(Fig. 4). The Cell surface had microvilli, nuclear was round and located in the middle by transmission electron microscope. There were many organelles, such as mitochondrion, endoplasmic reticulum, ribosome and glycogen in plasma(Fig. 5). The shape of cell displayed oval or fusiform during growth movement state. There were many microvilli and pseudopodia in cell surface under scanning electron microscope. The cell was boll in cell division(Fig. 6).

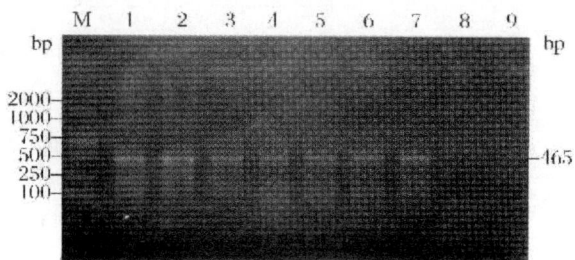

M: DNA marker; 1: Positive control; 2-7: Tumor tissue DNA; 8: Negative control; 9: Bland control

Fig. 3   X gene result of PCR in tumor tissues

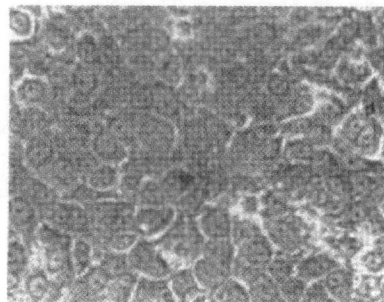

Fig. 4   Phase contrast microscope(×200)

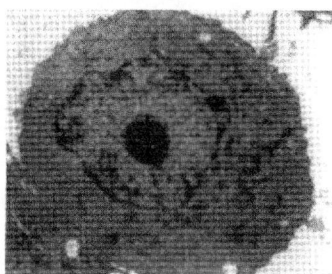

Fig. 5   TEM(×7000)

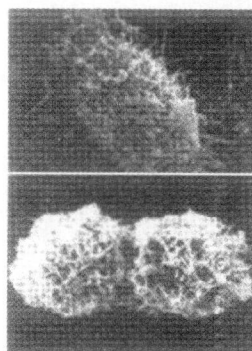

Fig. 6   SEM(×7000)

4. Biological characteristic of cell lines

The cell from 3 cell lines was anthropogenetic by test EMA monoclonal antibody. The positive cells showed that the cell membrane was yellow fluorescence(Fig. 7). Counting the cell proliferative nucleus revealed that Ki67 positive nuclear was 38.2%. The positive nuclear was stained by tawny(Fig. 8). Alpha fetoprotein in supernatant of culture medium was 0.8-1.0mmol/L and lower than normal level of serum. Growth curve of cell line indicated that cell growth rapidly and cell number went up straight line.

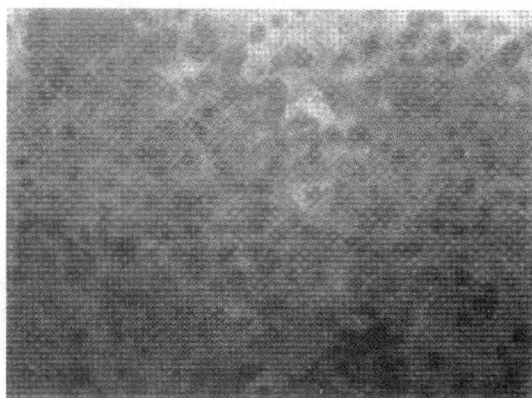

Fig. 7   Hmnan early membrane antigen is positive in tumor cell

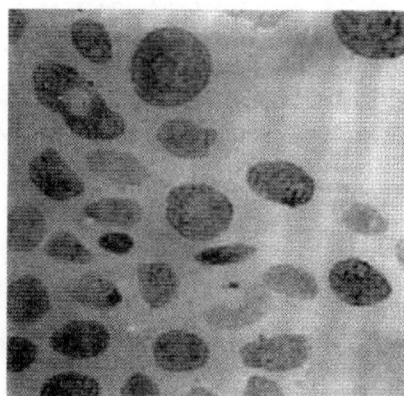

Fig. 8   Immunohistochemical staining of CBH-la ceil, the positive nuclei of Ki67 are tawny(×200)

5. HBV status in cell lines

HBV S and X genes could be detected in nuclei of cell lines by FISH. The positive signal was green yellow bright spot on red-apricot nucleus(Figs. 9 and 10). PCR amplification indicated that there was HBV X gene in cell lines(Fig. 11).

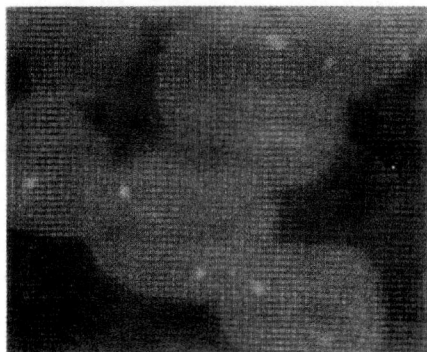

Fig. 9　The result of X gene by hybridization in situ(fluorescence microscope ×400)

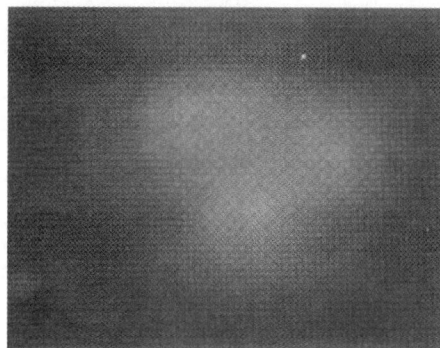

Fig. 10　The result of S gene by hybridization in situ(fluorescence microscope ×400)

6. Tumorgenesis of cell lines

The cells of CBH-la, CBH-lb and CBH-2 were respectively inoculated to nude mice. The lesser tubercle under skin in nude mice occurred after 2-3wk that cells of celllines were inoculated. Since then the tumors developed rapidly and reached 1.5cm×1.5cm×1.0 cm after 6wk. The rate of tumorgenesis was 100% and all the tumors were hepatocellular carcinomas(HCC)by histopathological examination.

DISCUSSION

Hepatitis B virus is an important etiological agent of hepatitis, cirrhosis and hepatocellular carcinoma (HCC) and it is suggested that HBV infection and the aflatoxin exposure are the major synergistic risk factors for the development of HCC[6-8]. In the present study, the development of malignant tumor formation in nude mice was observed in experiments with HBV-infected human embryonic liver cells plus the synergistic effect of aflatoxin B1(AFB$_1$).

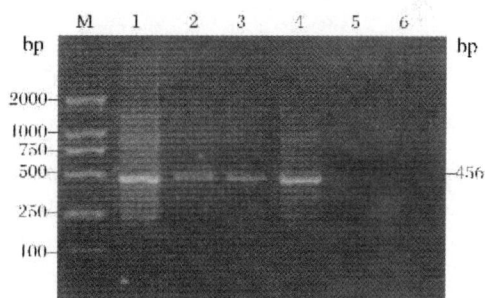

M: DNA marker; 1: Positive control; 2: CBH-1a; 3: CBH-1b; 4: CBH-2; 5: Negative control; 6: Bland control.

Fig. 11　The result of X gene by PCR amplification

It was found that the incidences of tumor formation were 27.3% in group of HBV-infected cells with addition of AFB$_1$; 13.3% in group with single AFB1 and 0% in group of single HBV or control group. These results indicate that there is synergism with HBV and AFB$_1$ and HBV infection can increase the incidence of tumorgenesis. Many factors are associated with tumorgenesis in which the tumor viruses play an important role. It is well known that tumor viruses cause transformation as a consequence of their ability to integrate their genetic information into DNA of host cells. Most often they also induce the chronic production of the oncoproteins that maintain the infected cells in a transformed state. Most oncproreins encoded by oncogenes in viral genomes are intracellular products. The X gene of HBV seems to play an important role in the HBV-associated hepatocarcinogenesis. Recent studies have shown that the promoter activity of the human p53 gene is strongly repressed by HBV X protein(HBV X)[9]. In the present study, the HBV X gene was detected in the tumor tissues of group of nude mice and it was illustrate that the HBV-DNA had reached to the fetus liver cells. These results were consistent with those reported by Li et al[10], in which HCCs were induced by HBV infection and dietary AFB in tree shrews with the incidence of 67% in group of HBV + AFB$_1$, 30% in group of AFB$_1$ and 0% in group of HBV respectively.

On the basis of tumor formation induced by HBV and AFB$_1$, we established 3 HCC cell lines with a clear inducement. By analyzing the biological characteristics of these 3 cell lines, we found that the cells grew rapidly and were anchorage-independent, and the Ki67 positive cell was 38.2% by counting the nucleus of the proliferative cells. The incidence of tumor formation was 100% when the cell lines were inoculated into nude mice. The HBV X and S genes were found to be positive by fluorescence in situ hybridization, and the PCR amplification, revealed the X gene in early subcultures. These results suggest that the viral DNA had been integrated into DNA of host cells.

Qidong area of Jiangsu province is one of the highly prevalent regions of HCC in China the annual incidence rate HCC in this area is 910.89/100000 in population with chronic carriers of HBV, and this figure is significantly higher than that of 24.24/100 000 in the control group. It had been reported that the aflatoxin exposure could increase the danger for developing HCC in those people who had infected with HBV[11]. The present experiment supports the previous survey on the cellular and molecular levels.

So far, it is still uncertain how HBV and AFB$_1$ interact within liver cells in the course of hepatocarcinogenesis. More studies show that X gene is an important oncogene in this process[12,13]. Recent studies suggest that persistent infection of HBV is essential for the induction of multi-stage genetic mutations in the chromosomes through immuno-mediated injuries of hepatocytes and the resulting hyperplasia[14]. The present study demonstrated that there was synergistic effect between HBV and AFB$_1$ in human hepatocarcinogenesis, and this would offer for an animal model and cell lines for further studies on the molecular mechanism during hepatocarcinogenesis. Insight for the hepatocarcinogenesis process should come from a muhidisciplinary collaboration to explore important viral and host genes so that new approaches to diagnosis and treatment can be developed.

REFERENCES

[1] Parkin DM. The global burden of cancer. Semin Cancer Biol, 1998, 8:219-235.

[2] Ghebranious N, Sell S. Hepatitis B injury, male gender, aflatoxin, and p53 expression each contribute to hepatoeareinogenesis in transgenic mice. Hepatology, 1998, 27(2):383-391.

[3] Liu Z, Liu Y, Zeng Y. Synergistic effect of Epstein-Barr virus and tumor promoters on induction of lymphoma and carcinoma in nude mice. J Cancer Res Clin Oncol, 1998, 124(10):541-548.

[4] James C, William G. D, Adi FG, et al. Evaluation of a tetrazohum-based semiautomated colorimetric assay: assessment of chemosensitivity testing. Cancer Res, 1987, 47:936-942.

[5] Teng ZP, Zeng Y. Detection of LMP gene of Epstein-Barr virus in nasopharyngeal carcinoma by in situ hybridization with biotin labeled probes. Chinese J Virology, 1994, 10(2): 184-186.

[6] Guo XC, Wu YQ. Progress of prevention and control on viral hepatitis in China. Biomed and Environ Sci, 1999, 12: 227-323.

[7] Qian GS, Ross RK, Yu MC, et al.A followup study of urinary markers of aflatoxin exposure and liver cancer risk in Shanghai, People's Republic of China. Cancer Epidemiol Biomarkers Prev, 1994, 3:3-10.

[8] Wang LY, Hatch M, Chen C J, et al. Aflatoxin exposure and risk of hepatocellular carcinoma in Taiwan. Int J Cancer, 1996, 76:620-625.

[9] Lee SG, Rho HM. Transcription repression of the human p53 gene by hepatitis B viral X protein. Oncogene, 2000, 19(3): 468-471.

[10] Li Y, Su JJ, Qin LL, et al. Synergistic effect of hepatitis B virus and aflatoxin 131 in hepatocarcinogenesis in tree shrews. Ann Acad Med Singapore, 1999, 28(1):67-71.

[11] Lu SX, Zhang QN, Wang JB, el al. Hepatitis B virus, aflatoxin B and hepatocellular careinoma. Zhongguo Zhongliu, 1999, 8:305-306.

[12] Kim CM, Koike, Saito L, et al. HBx gene of hepatitis B virus induces liver cancer in transgenic mice. Nature, 1991, 351: 317-320.

[13] Yu DY, Moon HB, Son JK, et al. Incidence of bepatocellular carcinoma in transgenic mice expressing the hepatitis B virus X-protein. J Hepatol, 1999, 31(1):123-132.

[14] Ogden SK, Lee KC, Barton MC. Hepatitis B viral transactivator HBx alleviates p53-mediated repression of alpha-fetoprotein gene expression. J Biol Chem, 2000, 275(36):27806-27814.

[In《J Microbiol Immunol》2004, 2(3):185-190]

Construction and Characterization of Chimeric BHIV(BIV/HIV-1) Viruses Carrying the Bovine Immunodeficiency Virus Gag Gene

ZHU Yi-xin[1], LIU Chang[1], LIU Xin-lei[2], QIAO Wen-tao[1], CHEN Qi-min[1], ZENG Yi[3], GENG Yun-qi[1]

1. College of Life Sciences, Nankai University; 2. College of Life Sciences and Bioengineering, Beijing University of Technology; 3. National Institute for Viral Disease Control arid Prevention

[SUMMARY] Objective To explore the possibility of the replacement of the gag gene between human immunodeficiency virus and bovine immunodeficiency virus, to achieve chimeric virions, and thereby gain a new kind of AIDS vaccine based on BHIV chimeric viruses. Methods A series of chimeric BHIV proviral DNAs differing in the replacement regions in gag gene were constructed, and then were transfected into 293T cells. The expression of chimeric viral genes was detected at the RNA and protein level. The supernatant of 293T cell was ultra centrifuged to detect the probable chimeric virion. Once the chimeric virion was detected, its biological activities were also assayed by infecting HIV-sensitive MT4 cells. Results Four chimeric BHIV proviral DNAs were constructed. Genes in chimeric viruses expressed correctly in transfected 293T cells. All four constructs assembled chimeric virions with different degrees of efficiency. These virions had complete structures common to retroviruses and packaged genomic RNAs, but the cleavages of the precursor gag proteins were abnormal to some extent. Three of these virions tested could attach and enter into MT4 cells, and one of them could complete the course of reverse transcription. Yet none of them could replicate in MT4 cells. Conclusion The replacement of partial gag gene of HIV with BIV gag gene is feasible. Genes in chimeric BHIVs are accurately expressed, and virions are assembled. These chimeric BHIVs(proviral DNA together with virus particles)have the potential to become a new kind of HIV/AIDS vaccine.

[Keywords] gag gene; Human immunodeficiency virus; Bovine immunodeficiency virus

INTRODUCTION

The HIV epidemic continues to expand at an alarming rate and is predicted to be the worst infectious disease ever to affect human beings, and the situation in Asia is also alarming[1]. Historical experience indicates that vaccines continue to be the most cost efficient and effective intervention available for preventing infectious diseases.

Up to now, there have been 80 candidate HIV/AIDS vaccines. Forty-seven of them have completed trials, but found to be either unsafe or ineffective, while 33 of them are in ongoing trials: one in phase III, three in phase II, two in phase I/II, and the rest in phase I. These vaccines include virus-like particles, peptides, recombinant protein subunits, recombinant bacterial vectors, recombinant viral vectors, and DNA vaccines[2]. However, the chances of getting an effective HIV/AIDS vaccine with current approaches are still very negligible. We still need new vaccine strategies against HIV/AIDS[3].

The chimeric HIV might just be such a new kind of HIV/AIDS vaccine, because it can mimic the natural infection of HIV[4-6], but out of concern about safety, current chimeric SHIVs are unfit for vaccines[5-7]. Actually, they are used as challenge viruses in AIDS/rhesus models to evaluate the efficacy of HIV/AIDS vaccines. HIV-1 and SIV are so closely related phylogenetically that the chimeric virus of SIV/HIV is too dangerous to be a vaccine[5,6]. Then how about a chimeric virus between HIV and non-primates lentivirus, such as the bovine immunodeficiency virus?

Bovine immunodeficiency virus(BIV)is a lentivirus, which resembles HIV in its structural, genomic, antigenic, and biological properties[8]. Unlike HIV, BIV is a relatively mild lentivirus, and never causes severe acquired immunedeficiency syndrome in its host, the cow[9,10]. BIV seropositivity has been correlated with decreased milk production in dairy cattle, but has not been directly linked with clinical disease in naturally infected cattle[11]. Considering the similarity of genome to HIV and its low pathogenicity, BIV may be an appropriate candidate to combine with HIV to create a new kind of HIV chimeric virus-BIV.

Primary work showed the expression of BIV gag-pol gene in HIV backbone in human original MT4 cells[12]. This time we focus on the gag gene. We tried to explore the possibility of the replacement of the gag gene between human immunodeficiency virus and BIV. In doing so, a series of chimeric BHIV(BIV/HIV-1)proviruses carrying the BIV gag gene have been constructed. In order to improve the expression of chimeric genes in human cells, the

CMV promoter is introduced.

MATERIALS AND METHODS

1. Materials

Infectious cDNA of BIV127 and HIV-1 HXB$_c$2 were kept in our laboratory, and pcDNA3. 1(－)vector was from Invitrogen.

2. Methods

(1)Construction of chimeric BHIV proviral DNA Modification of pcDNA3. 1(－)vector: The pcDNA3. 1(－) plasmid was double digested with EcoRI and BamHI, then the ends were blunted with T4 DNA polymerase and self-ligated by T4 DNA ligase, so that only one SacI site remained. Then the BssHII site was removed by cutting, blunting and religating.

(2)Replacement of 5'HIV LTR U3 region by CMV promoter The fragment 1 of 5' HIV LTR R U5 and partial gag was amplified by PCR, using sense primer from HIV-1 HXB$_c$2 positions 441nt459nt(5'TCG AC-T TTT GCC TGT ACT GGG TCT3'), and anti-sense primer from HIV-1 HXB$_c$2 positions 2045-2026nt(5'TCC TTT CCA CAT TTC CAA CA3'). The fragment 2 of 3' HIV LTR and partial env was amplified by PCR, using sense primer from HIV-1 HXB$_c$2 positions 8824-8842nt(5'GTG ATT GGA TGG CCT ACT G3')and anti-sense primer from HIV-1 HXB$_c$2 positions 9719-9700nt(5'TGC TAG AGA TTT TCC ACA CT3').

Modified pcDNA3. 1(－)vector was excised with SacI, blunted, excised with ApaI, then was ligated with the PCR product of fragment 1, which was already digested with ApaI. Thus, the 5' HIV LTR U3 region was replaced by the CMV promoter of the modified pcDNA3. 1(－)vector. We got the first intermediate plasmid pCMV1.

Plasmid pCMVI was double excised with XhoI and EcoRV, which was ligated with the PCR product of fragment 2, which was already digested with XhoI. Thus, the 3' HIV LTR was transferred into the vector. We got the second intermediate plasmid pCMV2.

Plasmid pCMV2 was double digested with ApaI and XhoI, and was ligated with the 7-kb HIV ApaI-XhoI fragment, then the complete genome of HIV was transferred to the modified pcDNA3. 1(－)vector, along with the transfer of CMV promoter to the 5'HIV LTR U3 region. It was named pCHIV.

(3)Construction of pCG1 and pCG2 Chimeric gag genes of pCG1 and pCG2 were derived from C2 and C3[13]. The chimeric gag genes from C2 and C3 were excised with BssHII/ApaI, and ligated into the vector of pCHIV, which was already digested with BssHII/ApaI. So we got the complete genome of chimeric HIV in pCG1 and pCG2.

(4)Construction ofpCG3 Two rounds of PCR produced the chimeric BHIV gag fragments of pCG3. The first round PCR used BIV127 as template, and the product of the first round together with pCG1 were used as templates in the second round PCR.

(5)First round PCR sense primer 5'TAA GGT TAG GGT GAC AC3', from BIVI27 positions 741-757nt. Anti-sense primer: 5'CC-T ACA ATT CCT CTT CAA ATG3', from B1C127 positions 1963-1945nt.

(6)Second round PCR sense primer 5'TCG AC-T TTT GCC TGT ACT GGG TCT3', from HIV-1 H×B$_c$2 positions 441-459nt. Anti-sense primer was same as in the first round PCR.

(7)The complete genome of pCG3 proviral DNA was constructed as follows pCHIV was excised with ApaI, blunted, excised with BssHII, then ligated with the product of the second round PCR that was already digested with BssHII.

(8)Construction of pCG5 The proviral genome DNA was constructed hy blunt end ligation. Plasmid pCHIV was double-digested with BssHII/ApaI. The ends were blunted with T4 DNA polymerase, and then were dephosphorylated by calf intestine alkaline phosphatase. The inserted fragment was a PCR product that was already phosphorylated by T4 polynucleotide kinase. After ligation, the clone of corrected insert orientation was selected by restriction enzyme mapping.

The sense primer of the PCR was 5'CAG AAG ACT CCG GAC AG3', from BIV127 667683nt. Anti-sense primer was 5'CC-T ACA ATT CCT CTT CAA ATG3', from BIC127 19631945nt.

3. Transfection of 293T cells with BHIV proviral DNA

In a level 3 biosafety(P3) laboratory, four BHIV clones were individually transfected into 40%-50% confluence 293T cells that were grown in 10% FBS DMEM in a six-well plate by using Polyfect(Qiagen). In order to reduce the side effect of remnant proviral DNA and Polyfect, cells were washed with PBS thrice and fresh culture medium was added 24h after transfection. The cell RNA and protein were extracted 72h post-transfection by Tri reagent(Sigma).

4. Electron microscopy(EM)

To perform electron microscopy(EM), supernatants were fixed with 2.5% glutaraldehyde, followed by treatment with 4% osmium tetroxide, and then routinely processed. Samples were stained with lead citrate and uranyl acetate and then visualized by using a JEOL JEM-2000 FX transmission electron microscope.

5. Collection of chimeric BHIV virions

The culture supernatant was collected 72h post-transfection and filtered with 0.45-μm filter to remove cell fractions. The cell-free supernatant was ultra centrifuged at 30000g for 3h. The pellet was stored at -80℃.

6. Component assays of chimeric BHIV virion pellets

In Western blot, anti-BIV capsid(CA)polyclone antibody was used to detect the chimeric gag precursor and mature CA protein in these virions. Reverse transcriptase activities in these virions were assayed by Reverse Transcriptase Assay colorimetric kit(Roche). The genomic RNA in these virions were also extracted as follows: virion pellets were resuspended, DNase added to digest the remnant proviral DNA at 37℃ for 30 min, then the mixture was extracted with phenol/chloroform and RNA precipitated with ethanol.

7. Infection of MT4 with chimeric BHIV viral stock

The culture supematant was collected 72h post-transfeetion and filtered with 0.45μm filter to remove cell fractions. The cell-free supernatant was added into 5×10^6 in 5ml 10% PBS RPMI 1640 medium. After incubation at 37℃ for 18h, MT4 cells were washed thrice with PBS, then fresh medium was added and returned to incubator. After 8h, cells were again washed thrice with PBS, and then their RNA, DNA and protein were extracted by Tri reagent(Sigma).

8. Primers in PCR or RT -PCR for detecting DNA or RNA

RT-PCR was performed to detect the early(tat gene)and late(gag gene)RNA transcripts in transfected 293T cells. RT-PCR was also performed to detect the gcnomic RNA(env gene)as a representative(Tab. 1).

Tab. 1　Primers in detecting PCR or RT-PCR

Primer name	Sequence(5'-3')	Location	Product length(bp)
tatRT-PCR up	GACTCGGCTTGCTGAAG	HIV 695-711	250
tatRT-PCR low	GCTGTCTCCGCTTCTTC	HIV 5993-5977	
gagRT-PCR up	GGAGGCCAGAGCTGATAAG	BIV 1044-1062	560
gagRT-PCR low	GTCTGTGTACGGCTCCTTG	BIV 1608-1590	
envPCR up	AATGACGCTGACGGTACAGG	HIV 7826-7845	660
env PCR low	GTGCCAAGGATCCGTTCAC	HIV 8487-8469	

RESULTS

1. Four chimeric BHIV proviral DNAs were constructed

Four chimeric BHIV proviral DNAs were constructed. Both restriction enzyme mapping and DNA sequencing confirmed the sequences of these proviruses. The genomic structure of each provirus is illustrated in Fig. 1.

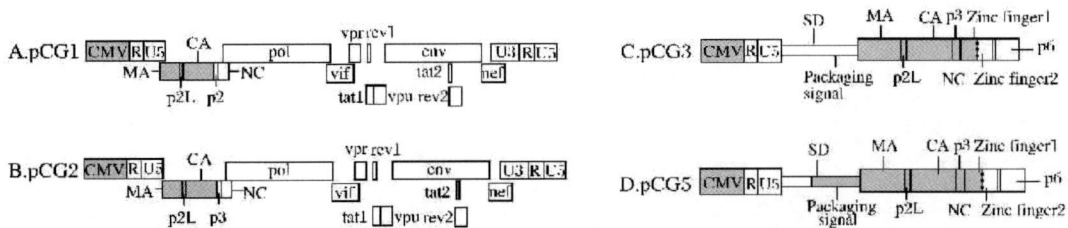

Fig. 1　The genomic structure of four chimeric BHIV DNAs. Yellow: CMV promoter; white: HIV-1 gene; blue: BIV gene

2. Early and late genes were transcribed in 293T cells

After transfection, RNA from 293T cells was extracted. The detection of early transcript of tat gene and late transcript of gag gene was performed by RT-PCR. Both early and late gene transcripts of RNA were detected in all four chimeric viruses. The results of RT-PCR are shown in Fig. 2.

3. All four chimeric gag precursors were expressed and partially cleaved in 293T cells

Western blot analysis(Fig. 3)showed that in 293T cells all four chimeric gag precursors were expressed. There was no significant difference in the amount of gag expression. All fours gag precursors were partially cleaved. There were two cleavage profiles among these four gag precursors: pCG1 belonged to one cleavage profile; pCG2, pCG3, pCG5 belonged to another. The spectrum of the latter profile was depicted on the right side of Fig. 3.

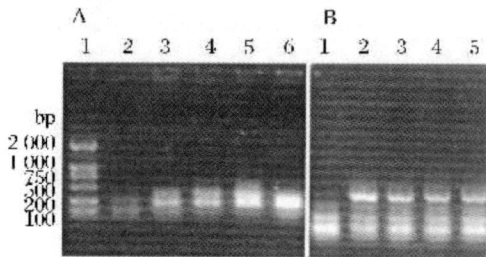

A: HIV-1 tat: 1. DL2000, 2. Negative control 3. peG 1, 4. peG2, 5. pcG3, 6. peGS; B: BIV gag: 1. Negative control, 2. pCG1, 3. pCG2, 4. pCG3, 5. pCG5

Fig. 2   RT -PCR results in 293T cells

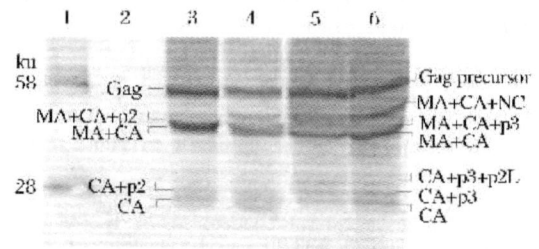

Lane 1: Marker; lane 2: 293T cell protein as negative control; lane 3: pCG1; lane 4: pCG2; lane 5: pCG3; lane 6: pCG5

Fig. 3   Western blot of 293T cells transfected by chimeric proviral DNAs. Western blot with rabbit anti-BIV CA serum

4. All four chimeric proviruses assembled virions in 293T cells

The cell-free supernatant was visualized by electron microscopy. Fig. 4 shows the results observed by EM. All four chimeric proviruses assembled virions in 293T cells. These virions have a diameter of about 100 nm, the typical scale of lentivirus. Unlike mature HIV virions, these particles do not have spindle cores, indicating that they are in the immature status.

5. Cleavage profiles of gag in chimeric virions were abnormal

The cell-free supernatant was ultra centrifuged. The pellet of viral particles was analyzed by Western blot analysis, as shown in Fig. 5. As it shows, very few gag precursors in virions were left, but the cleavage was still not complete. A large proportion of BIV CA existed in intermediate cleavage products, especially in CA+p3. A small part of BIV CA was still cut by HIV-1 protease and the products of p15 and p10 of CA were generated.

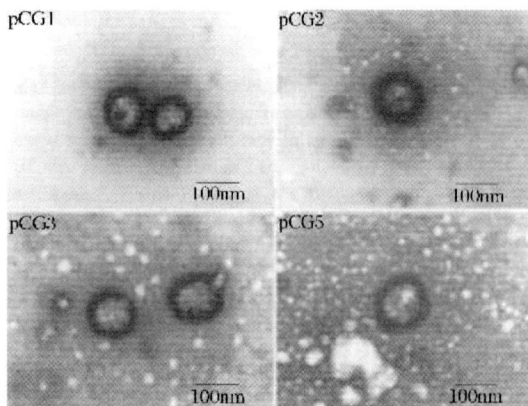

Fig. 4   Chimeric virus particles observed by EM

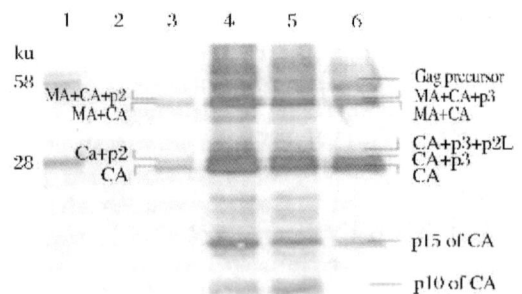

Lane 1: Marker; lane 2: 293T cell protein as negative control; lane 3: peG1; lane 4: pCG2; lane 5: peG3; lane 6: peG5

Fig. 5   Western blot of chimeric virions assembled from 293T cells after transfection. First antibody was anti-BIV CA

6. All four chimeric virions involved reverse transcriptase activities, while the RT activity of pCG1 virion was lower than the other three

The relative RT activities of four chimeric virions are shown in Fig. 6. Each measure was taken with virions centrifuged from 1ml supernatant of 293T cells. The transfection efficiency and cell confluence will also affect the release of chimeric virions, and the data of virion RT activities were semi-quantitative. We can conclude that the RT activity of pCG1 virion was lower than that of HIV positive control($P<0.01$ vs HIV), the other three do not have any significant difference from that of HIV control.

7. Genomic RNAs were packed in all four chimeric virions

Although the package signals and the package signal recognizers(mainly the nucleic capsid, NC, in gag)were different in these four chimeric virions, they all included genomic RNAs as the results of RT-PCR shown in Fig. 7.

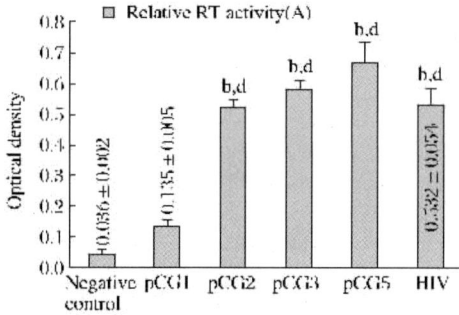

All samples are positive to negative control(°$P<0.01$ vs negative control). The RT activity of pCG1 virion was lower than the other three chimeric virions and HIV positive control(^{d}l$P<0.01$ vs pCG1)

Fig. 6 Relative reverse transcriptase activities of chimeric virions in 1ml supernatant of 293T cells($\overline{x}\pm s$, n=4)

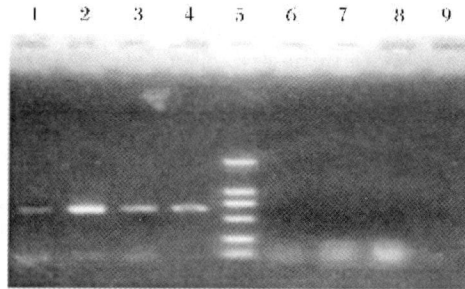

1. pCG1; 2. pCG2; 3. pCG3, 4. pCG5; 5. DL2000 marker; 6-9: Sample of pCG1, pCG2, pCG3, pCG5 RNAs without adding reverse transcriptase as negative control

Fig. 7 HIV-1 env gene RT-PCR results of chimeric virions

8. Virions of pCG2, pCG3 and pCG5 can attach and enter MT4 cells

Virions of pCG2, pCG3 and pCG5 in supernatant were incubated with human lymphocyte primary MT4 cells for 24h, then the remnant virions and culture medium were carefully eliminated. The protein of chimeric gag from virions can be detected in MT4 cells using the Western blot analysis shown in Fig. 8.

9. Virons of pCG3 can complete reverse transcription in MT4 cells

After incubation of chimeric virions with MT4 cells, we carefully eliminated the remnant virions and traced proviral DNA in the culture medium, then extracted the genomic DNA of MT4 cells. Detection of genomic DNA of chimeric virions was performed by PCR. Only in pCG3 virion infected MT4 cells we can find positive result as illustrated in Fig. 9. That means virions of pCG3 can complete reverse transcription in MT4 cells.

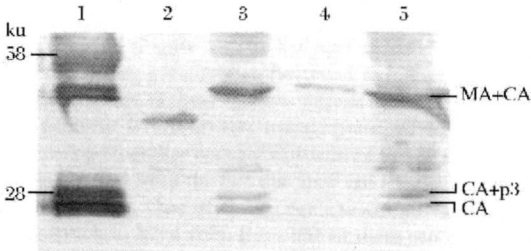

Lane 1: pCG5 virion as positive control; lane 2: MT4 cell protein as negative control; lane 3: peG2; lane 4: peG3; lane 5: pCG5

Fig. 8 Western blot of chimeric virions infecting MT4 cells. First antibody was anti-BIV CA

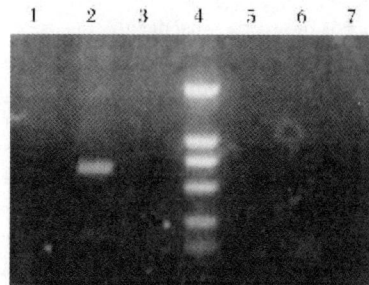

1. pCG2; 2. pCG3; 3. pCG5; 4. D12000 marker; 5-7: Culture medium of pCG2, pCG3, pCG5 infecting MT4(in last 8h)as negative control

Fig. 9 HIV-1 env gene PCR results of MT4 genomic DNA after infecting chimeric virions

DISCUSSION

The constitutionally strong promoter of CMV can replace the HIV-1 LTR U3 region and promote the RNA transcription of HIV-1. Generally speaking, the transcription efficiency of the CMV promoter is higher than that of HIV-1 LTR in human cells[14]. So, the replacement of promoter will enhance the expression of chimeric viral genes. Incidentally, the replacement took place only on the 5'LTR U3 region, not on the 3'LTR U3 region, nor any of LTR. That means the replacement only promotes the quantity of transcription, and does not change the quality of transcripts.

The expression of early genes in HIV relies on the correct post-transcriptional splicing of RNA in the nucleus of host cells[15]. In the genome of pCG4, the splicing donor comes from BIV, while the splicing receptor belongs to HIV-1. From the result of tat gene RT-PCR(Fig. 2A), we can see that the heterogeneous donor and receptor matched each other and generated correct splicing.

The chimeric gag gene as a late gene can be transcribed and translated in 293T cells. That means the early gene can work and trigger the expression of late genes[16]. The expression of gag precursor in four chimeric BHIVs was of the same magnitude, and all four chimeric BHIVs assembled virions. However, the virions assembled in pCG1 were much less than the other three. Some research pointed out that the p2 plays an important role in HIV-1 virion assembly[17-19]. The results here suggest that p3-the counterpart of p2-in BIV gag is also important in efficient assembly of BIV gag. Virions of chimeric gag(BIV gag as a major part)can still be assembled if BIV p3 is replaced by HIV-1 p2, but the assembly efficiency will be very low. This is not congruent with the result of Guo et al.[13]. We deduce that this is because of the high transcription efficiency of CMV promoter counteraeting the low assembly efficiency of pCG1 gag.

The primate lentivirus proteases have been intensively investlgated[20], anti it was found that the specificity is conserved among HIV-1, HIV-2, and SIV. For instance, synthetic HIV-2 protease deaves the gag precursor of HIV-1 with the same specificity as HIV-1 protease[21,22], and the proteolytic proeessing of the HIV-2 gag precursor is very similar to the processing of the SIVMne gag precursor[23]. However, the substrate specificity of protease between HIV-1 and the nonprimate lentivirus BIV has not been studied previously. In these experiments, the chimeric gag precursors not only in cells but also in virions were cleaved by HIV-1 protease. Among these cleaving sites in chimeric gags, some have come from HIV-1 gag, some from BIV gag, and some are even mosaics from both HIV-1 and BIV. Our results indicate that all these cleavage sites can be recognized and cleaved by HIV-1 protease although in different efficiency(Fig. 3 and 5). The relatively low cleaving efficiency may lead to the immature morphology of virions(Fig. 4).

Previous study indicated that a small percentage of the CA protein undergoes secondary proteolysis to generate additional peptides during the natural cleavage of BIV gag precursor. A 10×10^3 Cterminal peptide of CA, has been immunologically identified; another putative 16-ku N terminal peptide of CA has not been immunologically identified yet[24,25]. From Fig. 4 we can see that HIV-1 protease also can recognize and cleave this secondary alternate site inside BIV CA. Besides the alternate CA cleavage product of p10, the other putative product of a 16-ku peptide is also immunologically identified as p15. This adds to the conservative character of protease substrate specificity among lentivirus.

There are four cleavage sites within the HIV-1 gag precursor(six within chimeric gag, including the secondary alternate cleavage site inside CA), which on cleavage gives rise to the mature core proteins MA, CA, NA, and p6. (For simplicity and in the absence of specific data in our experiments, we exclude the HIV-1 gag spacer peptide of pl between NC and p6 from the discussion.) The cleaving efficiency among the four sites is different. The site of p2 NC was cleaved first, NC-p6 second, MA-CA third, and CA-p2 last[26]. Sequential cleavage of gag precursor generates certain kinds of intermediates, and from the profile of intermediates, we can deduce the cleavage sequence. In the precursor of pCG1 gag, junctions of p2NC and NC-p6 have come from HIV 1; they can surely be cleaved by HIV-1 protease efficiently. So they are the first and second cleavage sites. The junction of CA-p2 is a chimeric junction; the segment to the left of scissible bond comes from BIV, to the right of the scissible bond comes from HIV-1. It is the last site cleaved, and is responsible for the accumulation of CA+p2 intermediate(Fig. 5). In the precursor of pCG2 or pCG3 or pCG5, the p3NC junction no longer comes from HIV-1. So, the cleavage efficiency is reduced, and a new intermediate of MA+CA+NC emerged(Fig. 3). The deduced cleavage sequence of chimeric gag precursor is illustrated in Fig. 10.

The structure of these chimeric virions is complete. They have genomic RNA, reverse transcriptase, core proteins, and envelope together with gtycoprotein of gp120 and gp41(this is deduced from the fact that they can attach and enter into MT4 cells). One of them even can complete reverse transcription in MT4 cells. But none of them can replicate in MT4 cells. Because of these characteristics, they have the potential of being a new kind of HIV AIDS vaccine.

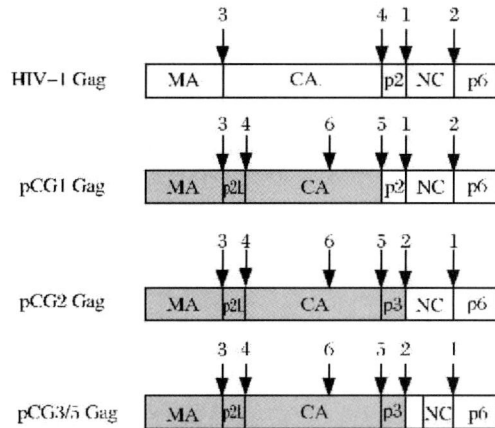

Fig. 10　Sketch map of deduced sequential cleavage of chimeric gag precursor by HIV-1 protease(pl between NC and p6 is not concerned); numbers show the sequence of the cleavage. Blue: from BIV; white: from HIV

They are relatively safe. They can express HIV antigen efficiently. They can assemble virions, and these virions can enter human lymphocytes. We anticipate that they can mimic the natural infection of HIV and stimulate the human immune system to elicit both cellular and humoral immune responses against HIVs.

In summary, the replacement of partial gag gene of HIV with BIV gag gene is feasible. Genes in chimeric BHIVs are accurately expressed, and virions are assembled. Chimeric BHIVs(proviral DNA together with virus particles)are expected to be a new kind of HIV/AIDS vaccine candidate.

ACKNOWLEDGEMENTS

We thank Liang Chen for providing the plasmid DNA of C2 and C3.

REFERENCES

[1] Roger D. HIV Surveillance, Prevention, Intervention, and treatment in Asia. The XV International HIV/AIDS Conference. New York: Guilford Press, 2004.
[2] IAVI database of AIDS vaccines in human trials, updated. Available from: URL: http://www. iavireport, org/trialsdb/defauh, asp, 14 December, 2004.
[3] erzofsky JA, Ahlers JD, Janik J, Morris J, Oh S, Terabe M, Belyakov IM. Progress on new vaccine strategies against chronic viral infections J Clin Invest, 2004, 114:450-462.
[4] Ui M, Kuwata TO lgarashi T, Ibuki K, Miyazaki Y, Kozyrev IL, Enose Y, ShimadaT, Uesaka H, Yamamoto H, Miura T, Hayami M. Protection of macaques against a SHIV with a homologous HIV-1 Env and a pathogenic SHIV89. 6P with a heterologous Env by vaccination with multiple gene-deleted SHIVs. Virology, 1999, 265:252-263.
[5] Silverstein PS, Mackay GA, Mukherjee S, Li Z, Piatak M Jr, Lifson JD, Narayan O, Kumar A. Pathogenic simian/human immunodeficiency virus SHIY(KU)inoculated into immunized macaques caused infection, but virus burdens progressively declined with time. J Virol, 2000, 74:10489-10497.
[6] Kumar A, Lifson JD, Li Z, Jia F, Mukherjee S, Adany I, Liu Z, Piatak M, Sheffer D, McClure HM, Narayan O. Sequential immunization of macaques with two differentially attenuated vaccines induced long-term virus-specific immune responses and conferred protection against AIDS caused by heterologous simian human immunodeficiency Virus SHIV89. 6 P. Virology, 2001, 279:241-256.
[7] Whitney JB, Ruprecht RM. Live attenuated HIV vaccines: pitfalls and prospects. Curt Opin Infect Dis, 2004, 17:17-26.
[8] Gonda MA. Bovine immunodeficiency virus. AIDS, 1992, 6:759-776.
[9] Gonda MA, Luther DG, Fong SE, Tobin GJ. Bovine immunodeficiency virus: molecular biology and virus-host interactions. Virus Res, 1994, 32:155-181.
[10] Carpenter S, Vaughn EM, Yang J, Baccam P, Roth JA, Wannemuehler Y. Antigenic and genetic stability of bovine immunodeficiency virus during long-term persistence in cattle experimentally infected with the BIV(R29)isolate. J Gen Viral, 2000, 81:1463-1472.
[11] McNab WB, Jacobs RM, Smith HE. A serological survey for bovine immunodeficiency-like virus in Ontario dairy cattle and association between test results, production records and management practices. Can J Vet Res, 1994, 58:36-41.
[12] Chen G, Wang S, Xiong K, Wang J, Ye T, Dong W, Wang Q, Chen Q, Geng Y, Wood C, Zeng Y. Construction and

characterization of a chimeric virus(BIV/HIV-1)carrying the bovine immunodeficiency virus gag-pol gene. AIDS, 2002, 16:123-125.

[13] Guo X, Hu J, Whitney JB, Russell RS, Liang C. Important role for the CA-NC spacer region in the assembly of bovine immunodeficiency virus gag protein. J Virol, 2004, 78:551-560.

[14] Paya CV, Virelizier JL, Michelson S. Modulation of T-cell activation through protein kinase C-or Adependent signalling pathways synergistically increases human immunodeficiency virus long terminal repeat induction by cytomegalovirus immediateearly proteins. J Virol, 1991, 65:5477-5484.

[15] Feinberg MB, Jarrett RF, Aldovini A, Gallo RC, Wong-Staal F. HTLV-Ⅲ expression and production involve complex regulation at the levels of splicing and translation of viral RNA. Cell, 1986, 46:807-817.

[16] Malim MH, Hauber J, Le SY, Maizel JV, Cullen BR. The HIV-1 rev trans-activator acts through a structured target sequence to activate nuclear export of unspliced viral mRNA. Nature, 1989, 338:254-257.

[17] Krausslich HG, Facke M, Heuser AM, Konvalinka J, Zentgraf H. The spacer peptide between human immunodeficiency virus capsid and nucleocapsid proteins is essential for ordered assembly and viral infectivity. J Virol, 1995, 69:3407-3419.

[18] Accola MA, Hoglund S, Gottlinger HG. A putative alphahelieal structure, which overlaps the capsid-p2 boundary in the human immunodeficiency virus type 1 gag precursor, is crucial for viral particle assembly. J Virol, 1998, 72: 2072-2078.

[19] Morikawa Y, Hockley D J, Nermut MV, Jones IM. Roles of matrix, p2, and N-terminal myristoylation in human immunodeficiency virus type 1 gag assembly. J Virol, 2000, 74:16-23.

[20] Pettit SC, Henderson GJ, Schiffer CA, Swanstrom R. Replacement of the P 1 amino acid of human immunodeficiency virus type 1 gag processing sites can inhibit or enhance the rate of cleavage by the viral protease. J Virol, 2002, 76:10226-10233.

[21] Wu JC, Cart SF, Jarnagin K, Kirsher S, Barnett J, Chow J, Chan HW, Chen MS, Medzihradszky D, Yamashiro D. Synthetic HIV-2 protease cleaves the gag precursor nf HIV-1 with the same specificity as HIV-1 protease. Arch Biochem Biophys, 1990, 277:306-311.

[22] Pichuantes S, Babe LM, Barr PJ, DeCamp DL, Craik CS. Recombinant HIV2 protease processes HIV1 Pr53gag and analogous junction peptides in vitro. J Biol Chem, 1990, 265:13890-13898.

[23] Henderson LE, Benveniste RE, Sowder R, Copeland TD, Schultz AM, Oroszlan S. Molecular characterization of gag proteins from simian immunodeficiency virus(SIVMne). J Virol, 1988, 62:2587-2595.

[24] Battles JK, Hu MY, Rasmussen L, Tobin GJ, Gonda MA. Immunological characterization of the gag gene products of bovine immunodeficiency virus. J Virol, 1992, 66:6868-6877.

[25] Tobin GJ, Sowder RC 2nd, Fabris D, Hu MY, Battles JK, Fenselau C, Henderson LE, Gonda MA. Amino acid sequence analysis of the proteolyric cleavage products of the bovine immunodeficiency virus gag precursor polypeptide. J Virol, 1994, 68:7620-7627.

[26] Tritch RJ, Cheng YE, Yin FH, Erickson-Viitanen S. Mutagenesis of protease cleavage sites in the human immunodefieiency virus type 1 gag polyprotein. J Virol, 1991, 65:922-930.

[In《World J Gastroenterol》2005, 11(17): 2609-2615]

Induction of Cytotoxic T Lymphocyte Respones in vivo after Immunotherapy with Dendritic Cells in Patients with Nasopharyngeal Carcinoma

ZUO Jing-min[1], ZHOU Ling[1], CHEN Zhi-jian[2], LI De-rui[2], WANG Qi[1],
CHEN Jiong-yu[2], WANG Zhan[1], YE Shu-qing[1], ZENG Yi[1]

1. State Key Laboratory for Infections Disease Prevention and Control, National Institute for Viral Disease Control and Prevention, Chinese Center for Disease Control and Prevention; 2. Tumor Hospital of Shantou University

[SUMMARY] The aim of the present study was to determine the efficacy of immunotherapy with dendritic cells to elicit EBV-specific CTL-immunity in advanced cases of EBV-positive patients with nasopharyngeal carcinoma(NPC) and to determine the safety and toxicity of this preparation. Nine cases of histologically confirmed patients with NPC undergoing treatment with radiological therapy were enrolled in this study. Dendritic cells, generated in vitro from blood monocytes of patients were cultured and matured with cytokines and then infected with recombinant adenovirus vaccine containing EBV-latent membrane protein-2(Ad-LMP2). On 9 days' cultivation of cells, the matured DCs were harvested, irradiated with ^{60}Co and then injected intradermally to patients with NPC. The injections were performed 3 times totally. After immunization, the CTL responses were assayed by means of cytotoxicity and epitope-specific IFN-γ production. The results of this trial showed that all patients could tolerate this kind of treatment without any side effect, during which marked increase of LMP2-specific CTL-responses could be demonstrated in 5 patients of this group. And the level of IgA/VCA antibody decreased in 8 of 9 patients, thus accounting for a better prognosis for these patients. All patients will be followed up for another one year. At least, the present work shows that intradennal vaccination with autologous DCs infected with recombinant Ad-LMP2 adenovirus is a safe procedure in NPC patients, in which this procedure can enhance the LMP2-specific CTL responses in patients. These data are encouraging to develop more effective vaccine strategies for the treatment of nasopharyngeal carcinoma.

[Keywords] Nasopharyngeal carcinoma(NPC); Dendritic cells; Immunotherapy; CTL-responses.

INTRODUCTION

Nasopharyngeal carcinoma(NPC) is a highly prevalent cancer in Southern China, with a yearly incidence rate between 10 and 50 per 100 000[1,2]. Currently, the treatment for NPC is radically external radiotherapy, which can cure about 80% cases during early stage. However, only 10%-40% cases during advanced stage can survive more than 5 years[3,4]. Once metastases developed, 85% of patients can not survive for more than 1 year[5]. There is therefore a need to develop additional forms of treatment for NPC.

There is considerable evidence that EBV plays an important role in the progression of NPC[6-8]. Epstein-Sarr vires(EBV) is a ubiquitous gamma-herpesvirus that can establish both latent and lytic infection. The primary EBV infection occurs mostly during childhood without obvious symptoms, but the EBV could persist in the body through the whole life. Once the EBV is animated by some inducement, it will become a pathogen of many diseases, including malignant diseases. EBV is associated with many human malignant diseases including lymphoproliferative disorder associated with immunocompromise, Burkitt's lymphoma(BE)[9], Hodgkin's disease(HD)[10], undifferentiated nasopharyngeal carcinoma(NPC), and various T-cell lymphomas[11]. The definite function of EBV in the NPC etiology is not well understood, however the existence of EBV in the tumor tissue provides a potential target for gene therapy.

The EBV proteins expressed in tumor cell are very limited. There are only several antigens of EBV, such as EBNA1, LMP1, and LMP2 which can be detected in NPC and HD[12-15]. Of these three antigens, EBNA1 contains a Gly-Ala repeat sequence, which will interrupt the presentation of this antigen to T cells through MHC class I restricted pathway[16]. LMP2 is the most frequently recognized protein by CTL. Also many MHC class I restricted epitopes of LMP2 have been identified, which are conserved during different population[17-20]. So it becomes the target of immunotherapy for NPC.

MHC class I restricted CTL plays an important role in controlling the status of EBV infection. EBV specific CTL can be present at a high level in the blood during primary infection and last for the whole life accompanying with the virus. If the level of CTL responses is reduced, for example in the transplanted patients or HIV infected individuals, some EBV-driven lymphoma proliferation will occur. But these diseases can regress when the cellular immune response is recovered after the relaxation of immunosuppression or infusion of autologous EBV-specific CTL expanded in vitro[21]. Given these observations, it is likely to target the virus-specific immune response to the EBV positive human tumors.

Adenoviruses can transfer genes into a broad spectrum of cell types. Additionally, high titers of viruses and high level of transgene expression can generally be obtained. In order to develop a NPC therapeutic vaccine, we construct the AdEasy-LMP2 containing the full-length cDNA of EBV-LMP2[22]. DCs are specialized antigen-presenting cells that can prime T cell responses, playing important roles in the anti-infection and anti-tumor processes. In 1990s, along with the establishment of method of isolation and cultivation of DC, and with the development of correlative immunology, molecular biology and tumor pathology, various means of antigen delivery to modify DCs have been used to activate T lymphocytes in vitro and in vivo[23]. Now the clinical trials of DC vaccines on malignant melanoma, renal cell carcinoma, prostate cancer and colorectal cancer are carried on extensively[24-26], and the results from these studies are encouraging. The aim of this study is to transfer recombinant adenovirus containing LMP2 gene into autologous DC and this preparation is to be used to immunize NPC patients. The safety, toxicity, and efficacy in eliciting EBV specific CTL immunity are then to be evaluated.

MATERIAL AND METHODS

1. Patients

Nine patients with ages younger than 70 years were enrolled in this study. All patients were histologically proven NPC and had a high serum IgA/VCA. The radiotherapy had been completed 6 months prior to trial. Patients were required to have adequate hepatic and renal function, and have a life expectancy of more than 6 months.

2. DC preparation

Peripheral blood mononuclear cells(PBMCs) were isolated by FicolL/Paque density gradient centrifugation. Isolated PBMCs were plated(2×10^7 cells/5ml per well)into 6-well plates(Costa, Cambridge, MA)in serum-free RPMI 1640 medium. After 2h of incubation at 37℃, nonadherent cells were removed and the adherent cells were cultured in RPMI 1640 containing 10% fetal calf serum(FCS), GM-CSF(50ng/ml)and IL-4(25ng/ml). On day 3 and day 6, half of the medium was replaced with fresh medium containing GM-CSF, IL-4. Cell differentiation was monitored by light microscope. On day 7, the DCs were collected by centrifuge in $100\mu l$ serum-free RPMI 1640, and infected by Ad-LMP2 in MOI of 1000 for 2h at 37℃. Then the DCs were cultured for another 2d in RPMI 1640 containing 10% FCS, GM-CSF(50ng/ml), IL-4(25ng/ ml)and TNF-α(20ng/ml).

On day 9, DCs were washed 3 times and resuspended in sterile saline(total volume＝0.2 ml). The expression of LMP2 on infected DCs was detected by indirect immunofluorescence staining. The purity of DCs was analyzed by immunofluorescence staining for CD80, CD83 and CD86. After the DCs were irradiated by ^{60}Co, the DCs were delivered to patients intradermally. Two further preparations of autologous antigen-pulsed DCs were produced in the same manner. The two further injections are on day 14 and day 28. The average number of DCs is about 2×10^6 each time. The immunological responses were monitored with patients' blood sample on day 56 after the first injection.

3. Intracellular stain of IFN-γ

The 5×10^5 PBMC were stimulated with mixed LMP2 specific peptides(100μg/ml, LL-WTLVV-LL, LTAG-FLIFL, LLSAWILTA, SSCSSCPLSKI, TYGPVFMCL, IEDPPFNS)for6h. The Brefeldin A(1μg/ml Sigma)was added during the last 3h. Positive controls were performed by stimulating the cells with PMA(50ng/ml, Sigma) and ionomycin(500ng/ml, Sigma). Cells were stained with a FTTC-conjugated anti-CD8. After washing, cells were fixed with4% formaldehyde/PBS for 15 min at room temperature, permeabilized in 0.5% saponin(Sigma), 2% bovine serum albumin in PBS, and stained with a PE-conjugated anti-IFN-γ(BD Pharmingen). Subsequently, cells were washed with PBS and detected by FACS.

4. Cytotoxicity assays

The suspension cells were collected after the PB-MCs were incubated in 37℃ for 2h. Part of these suspension cells were pulsed with mixed peptides(100μg/ml, LLWTLVVLL, LTAGFLIFL, LLSAWILTA, SSCSSCPLSKI, TYGPVFMCL, IEDPPFNS)for 1h to act as stimulator cells. Then the stimulate cells were incubated with autologous PBMCs in RPMI 1640 containing 10% FCS and IL-2(20 IU/ml)at the rate of 1 : 10 for 5d. The target cells were autologous PHA blast coated with the mixes peptides by exposing to 100μg/ml peptide for 2h, then washed and incubated in 96-well Vbottom plates with effector cells at effector target ratio(E : T)of 10 : 1, 20 : 1, 50 : 1. The percentage specific lysis(means of triplicate wells)was detected through LDH method(Promega).

5. Detection of IgA/VCA antibody

The B95.8 cell were stimulated by TPA for 48h, and fixed on slices. Sera of patients were diluted serially, and incubated on the slice at 37℃ for 45 min. The slices were washed by PBS for three times, and incubated with HRP conjugated anti-IgA antibody at 37℃ for 45 min. Then the slices were washed, substrate was added and the formation of color was monitored.

RESULTS

1. Expression of LMP2 in DC

The DCs were infected with Ad-LMP2 at the MOI of 1000 for 2h, and then cultured at 37℃ for another two days. After the DCs were collected by centrifuge and resuspended with saline, the DCs were incubated with anti-LMP2 rabbit serum (kindly provided by Professor Middeldorp JM, Vrije Universiteit Medical Centre, Netherlands)and FITC conjugated anti-rabbit-IgG(BD Pharmingen). After the DCs were washed, they were detected by FACS. From the result we can see, there are about 60% DCs which expressed LMP2 when they were infected with Ad-LMP2 al the MOI of 1000(Fig. 1).

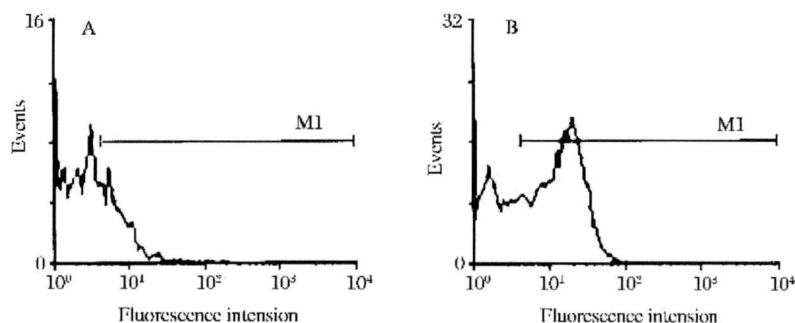

A: DCs were infected with Ad5 wild type virus, then stained with LMP2 antibody and tested through FACS. The results show that the DCs infected with wild type virus have no expression of LMP2. B: DCs were infected with Ad-LMP2, then stained with LMP2 antibody and examined by FACS. The results show that there are about 60% DCs expressing LMF2 when infected with Ad-LMP2 at the MOI of 1000.

Fig. 1 Expression of LMP2 in DC infected with Ad -LMP2

2. Adverse effects

All patients tolerated the immunization well without obvious side effects. They all completed the whole therapy. No obvious local swelling, local rigor, fever and fatigue were observed in any patients.

3. Cytotoxicity assay

To detect the LMP2 specific cytotoxicity in patients received DC immunotherapy, the patients were bled to detect the lytic activity against target cells in week 0 and week 8 through LDH method. As shown in Figs. 2 and 3, 5 immunized patients showed significant enhanced epitope-specific killing activity in week 8 compared with the result in week 0. On the other hand, no patient in the control patients showed enhanced epitope-specific killing activity. In the instance of E∶T being50∶1, the lysis rate of patient 1, 2, 4, 7 and 8 increased from 28.90% to 54.77%, 30.00% to 51.01%, 42.60% to 67.45%, 22.00% to 32.10%, 10.90% to 35.60%, respectively.

4. Flow cytometry of intracellular IFN+/CD8+ T cells

To detect the LMP2 specific cytotoxicity level in patients, the peptide-stimulated PBMC was immunostained for IFN-γ and CD8 to characterize the IFN-γ producing T cells. In the 4 patients who received IFN-γ intracellular staining assay, LMP2 specific CTL level increased markedly in 2 patients. The percentages of CD8+ cells which produced IFN-γ in response to LMP2 specific peptides in whole lymphocyte of patient 7 and 8 increased from 0.09% and 0.04% to 0.46% and0.38%(Figs. 4 and 5).

5. Detection of IgA/VCA antibody

The IgA/VCA antibody level in patients was detected in week 0 and week 8, the result showed that the antibody level of IgA/VCA decreased to below 10∶1 in 7 of 9 patients, which accounts for a good prognosis of these patients. The antibody level of other two patients did not have much changes(Fig. 6).

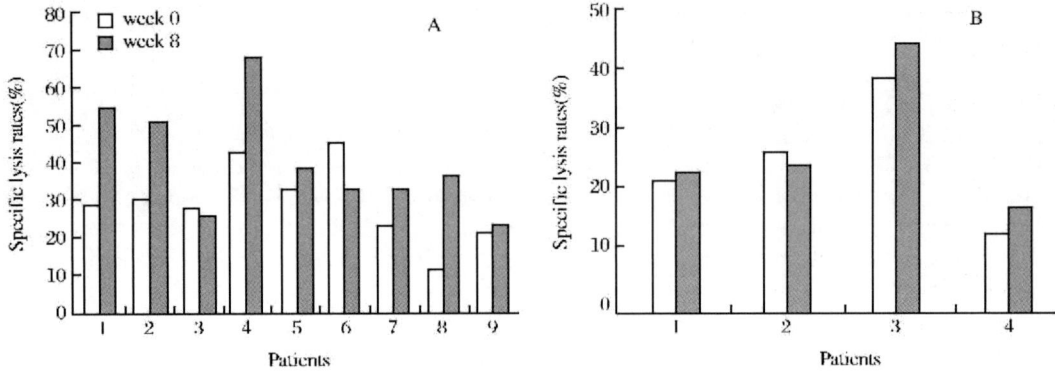

A：The PBMC of immunized patients were stimulated with mixed peptides，and autologous PHA blast coated with the mixed peptides as targets，then the specific lysis was detected at effector target ratio of 10：1，20：1，50：1. They were bled in week 0 and week 8 after immunization separately. The data being expressed as percentage specific lysis are at an effector target ratio of 50：1. B：The PBMC of control patients were tested in cytotoxicity assay as Fig. 2A. They were also bled in week 0 and week 8 separately. The data being expressed as percentage specific lysis is at an effector target ratio of 50：1

Fig. 2 Comparation of the lysis rate of CTL between pre-and post-therapy

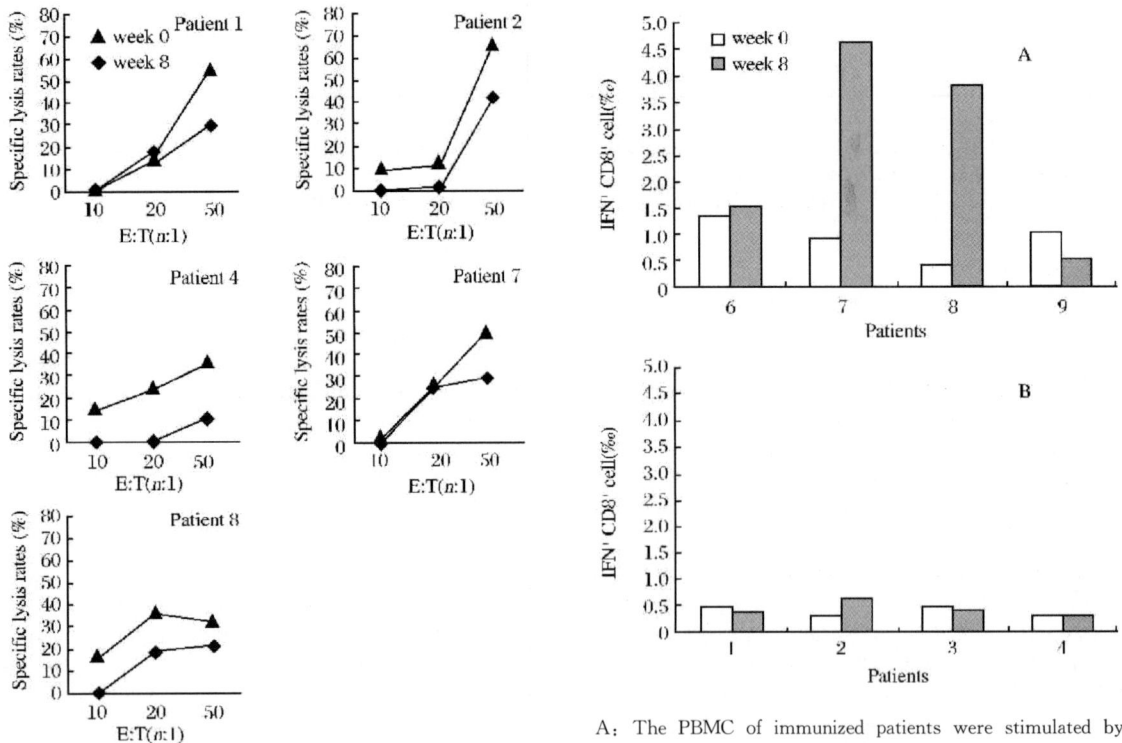

The PBMC of the 5 patients were tested in cytotoxicity assay as Fig. 2A. The data being expressed as percentage specific lysis are at an effector target ratio of 10：1，20：1 and50：1. The specific lysis between week 0 and week 8 was compared

Fig. 3 Detection of fluctuation of CTL level by LDH method

A：The PBMC of immunized patients were stimulated by mixed LMP2 specific peptides and then stained with an FTTC-conjugated anti-CD8 and PE-conjugated anti-IFN-γ，and detected by FACS. They were bled in week 0 and week 8 after immmtmization separately. B：The PBMC of control patients were tested in intracellular staining of IFN-γ as Fig. 4A. They were bled in week 0 and week 8 separately

Fig. 4 Comparison of the IFN$^+$ CD8$^+$ cell ratio between pre-and post-therapy

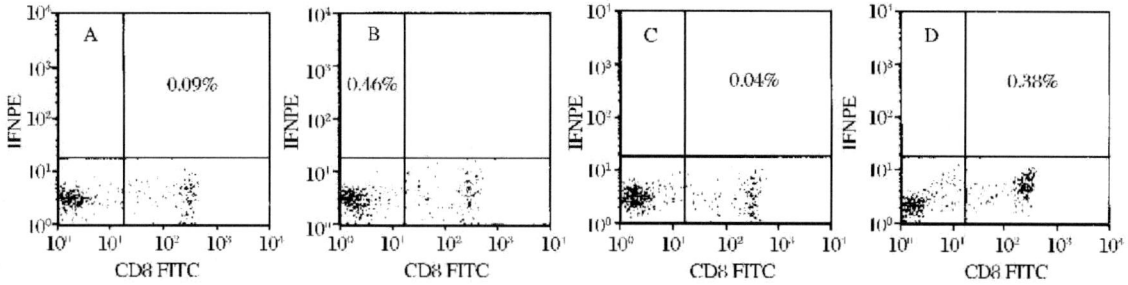

The PBMC of patient 7 and patient 8 were stimulated with mixed LMP2 specific peptides and then stained with a FITC-conjugated anti-CD8 and PE-conjugated anti-IFN-γ, and detected by FACS. They were bled in week 0 and week 8 after immunization separately. A: IFN+ CD8+ cell ratio of patient 7 prior to vaccination. B: IFN+ CD8+ cell ratio of patient 7 after 3 vaccinations. C: IFN+ CD8+ cell ratio of patient 8 prior to vaccination. D: IFN+ CD8+ cell ratio of patient 8 after 3 vaccinations

Fig. 5　Comparation of the IFN+ CD8+ cell ratio between pre-and post-therapy in patients 7 and patient 8

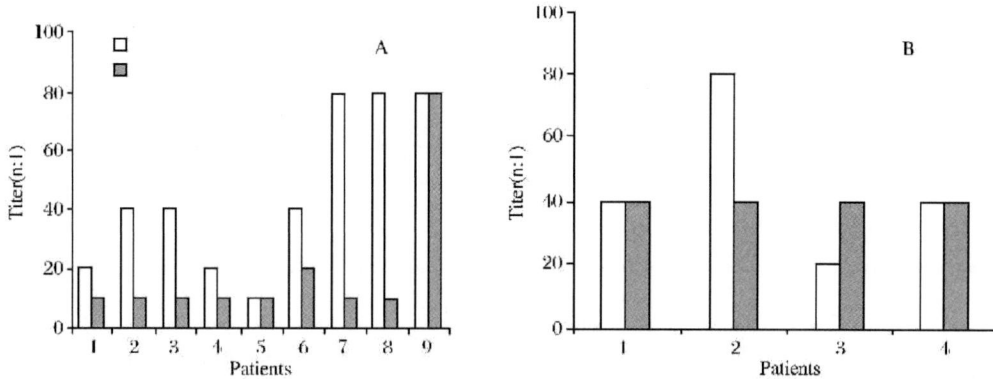

A: The serum of immunized patients were diluted serially, and incubated on the slice with TPA stimulated B95. 8 cell, and then incubated with HRP conjugated anti-IgA antibody to test the titer of IgA/VCA antibody. They were bled in week0 and week 8 after immunization separately. B: The titer of IgA/VCA antibody in control patients were tested in immunoenzyme assay as Fig. 6A. They were bled in week 0 and week 8 separately

Fig. 6　Change of the titer of IgA/VCA in patients' serum

DISSCUSION

DCs are widely distributed in the human body as the most potent antigen presenting ceils(APCs), in which the costimulating molecules, adherent molecules and MHC-molecules are highly expressed on their cell surface, and they can initiate the primary T lymphocyte-mediated responses, such as immune responses against microbes, antitumor immune responses and transplant rejection processes[27]. The studies on activation of T lymphocytes in vitro or in vivo through tumor antigen-pulsed DCs of different sources has become the focus of interest on DC tumor vaccine[28]. Vaccination therapies with DCs were found to be effective for the treatment of malignant melanoma, renal cell tumor, breast cancer and ovary cancer with encouraging results[24-26].

The studies involving the relationship between EBV and NPC and the existence of EBV in tumor tissue constitute the target for gene therapy, in which EBV-LMP2 becomes the most promising target of immunotherapy for NPC. Many workers are pursuing DC vaccine for the treatment of NPC. Lin et al had worked on the Phase I clinical trial with epitope-pulsed DC vaccine in order to evaluate the efficacy and safety of this vaccine[29]. Dendritic cells were generated in vitro from blood monocytes of NPC patients, cultured and matured with cytokines, and then pulsed with LMP2-specific HLA-restricted peptides. Twelve NPC patients were enrolled in this trial, in which each patient received 4 injections and CTL responses were assayed by intracellular staining of the epitope-specific IFN-γ and cytotoxicity. The results showed that all patients tolerated this treatment very well and the intracellular staining of IFN-γ revealed enhancement of level of LMP2-specific CTL responses in 6 patients. In addition, 2 patients treated showed partial reduction of tumor growth.

　　Recombinant adenovirus vector has many merits, including the ability to infect a broad range of mammalian cells, the actions on infection and the expressions of genes in dividing or non-dividing cells. Now, the tranduction of gene into APC by recombinant adenovirus has been regarded as a promising strategy for tumor vaccine. In the present study, although the virus used is the replication-deficient one, we also irradiated this vires with ^{60}Co for safety. It was found that the process of irradiation did not show any change in the surface markers before or after irradiation of DCs(data not shown). So the antigen-presenting function of DCs after irradiation is likely maintained. Our data also indicated that the level of LMP2-specific CTL responses was increased markedly in 5 of 9 patients. As demonstrated by LDH method, the lysis rates of cytotoxicity in these 5 patients(No. 1,2, 4, 7 and 8)increased. In addition, the percentage of CD8^{+} cells producing IFN-γ in response to the stimulation of LMP2 specific peptide in lymphocytes of patients No. 7 and 8 of 4 patients who had assayed with the intracellular staining, also increased significantly. This is in agreement with the result obtained from LDH method. At the same time, the antibody levels of IgA/VCA in these 5 patients were decreased, accounting for a better prognosis for these patients.

　　The treatment of NPC patients by using the DC vaccine modified by the recombinant adenovirus vector containing EBV-LMP2 gene is a safe procedure, because all the patients can complete the whole course of treatment without any side effects, and this kind of vaccination can induce specific CTL responses in NPC patients. However, there still existed some patients who did not show any significant response; the possible reasons for this might be the ages, general conditions of patients, and the maturation state of DCs which may influence the function of antigen presentation. Several reports suggested that compared with the healthy individuals, the dendritic cells of cancerous patients could not be cultivated to be at the full and functional state of maturation[30,31]. In the present study, there was just one patient who showed a DC maturation rate of less than 40%(data not shown). Hence, whether there is any difference between the NPC patients and the healthy individuals is still unclear. As a whole, multiple immunization may be considered to be a means to improve the efficacy of vaccines, and the exploration of more potent approaches of immunization to get more effective enhancement of specific cytoxicity is desirable in the future.

ACKNOWLEDGEMENT

This work was supported by Chinese National High-tech Program(2001AA217091).

REFERENCES

[1] Chan AT, Toe PM, Johnson PJ. Nasopharyngeal carcinoma. Ann Oncol, 2002, 13:1007-1025.
[2] Yu MC. Nasopharyngeal carcinoma: epidemiology and dietary factors. IARC Sci Publ, 1991, 105:39-47.
[3] Altun M, Fandi A, Dupuis O, Cvitkovic E, Krajina Z, Eschwege F. Undifferentiated nasopharyngeal cancer(UCNT): current diagnostic and therapeutic aspects. Int J Radiat Oncol Biol Phys, 1995, 32:859-877.
[4] Mould RF, Tai TH. Nasopharyngeal carcinoma: treatments and outcomes in the 20th century. Br J Radiol, 2002, 75: 307-339.
[5] Teo PM, Kwan WH, Lee WY, Leung SF, Johnson PJ. Prognosticators determining survival subsequent to distant metastasis from nasopharyngeal carcinoma. Cancer(Phila), 1996, 77:2423-2431.
[6] Rickinson AB, Kieff E. Epstein-Barr virus. In: Fields BN, Knipe DM, Howley PM, eds. Fields Virology. Philadelphia: Lippincott-Raven, 1996, 2397-2446.
[7] Niedohitek G. Epstein-Barr virus infection in the pathogenesis of nasopharyngeal carcinoma. Mol Pathol, 2002, 53: 248-254.
[8] Wolf H, Zurhausen H, Becker V. EB viral genomes in epithelial nasopharyngeal carcinoma cells. Nat Rew Biol, 1973, 244:245-247.
[9] Magrath I. The pathogenesis of Burkitt's lymphoma. Adv Cancer Res, 1990, 55:133-270.
[10] Deacon EM, Pallesen G, Niedobitek G, Crocker J, Brooks L, Rickinson AB, et al. Epstein-Barr virus and Hodgkin's disease: transcriptional analysis ot virus latency in the malignant cells. J Exp Med, 1993, 177:339-349.
[11] Shapiro RS, McClain K, Frizzera G, GajiPeczalska KJ, Kersey JH, Blazar BR, et al. Epstein-Barr virus associated B cell lymphoproliferative disorders following bone marrow transplantation. Blood, 1988, 71:1234-1243.
[12] Chang KL, Chen Y-Y, Shibata D, Weiss LM. Description of an in situ hybridization methodology for detection of Epstein-Barr virus RNA in paraffinem-bedded tissues, with a survey of normal and neoplastic tissues. Diagn Mol Pathol, 1992,1: 246-255.
[13] Young LS, Dawson CW, Clark D, Rupani H, Busson P, Tursz T, et al. Epstein-Barr virus gene expression in nasopharyngeal carcinoma. J Gen Virol, 1988, 69(pt 5): 1051-1065.
[14] Fahraeus R, Fu HL, Emberg I, Finke J, Rowe M, Klein G, et al. Expression of Epstein-Barr virus-encoded proteins in nasopharyngeal carcinoma, Int J Cancer, 1988, 42:329-338.
[15] Brooks L, Yao QY, Rickinson AB, Young LS. Epstein-Barr virus latent gene transcription in nasopharyngeal carcinoma

cells: coexpression of EBNA1, LMP1, and LMP2 transcripts. J Virol,1992, 66:2689-2697.

[16] Levitskaya J, Coram M, Levitsky V, Imreh S, Steigerwald-Mullen PM, Klein G, et al. Inhibition of antigen processing by the internal repeat region of the Epstein-Barr virus nuclear antigen-1. Nature, 1995, 375:685-688.

[17] Lee SP, Tiemey R J, Thomas WA, Brooks JM, Rickinson AB. Conserved CTL epitopes within EBV latent membrane protein 2: a potential target for CTL-based tumor therapy. J Immunol,1997, 158(7):3325-3334.

[18] Lee SP, Chan AT, Cheung ST, Thomas WA, CroomCarter D, Dawson CW, et al. CTL control of EBV in nasopharyngeal carcinoma: EBV-specific CTL responses in the blood and tumors of NPC patients and the antigen-processing function of the tumor cells. J Immunol, 2000, 165:573-582.

[19] Khanna R, Busson P, Burrows SR, Raffoux C, Moss D J, Nicholls JM, et al. Molecular characterization of antigen-processing function in nasopharyngeal carcinoma(NPC): evidence for efficient presentation of Epstein-Barr vires cytotoxic T-cell epitopes by NPC cells. Cancer Res, 1998, 58:310-314.

[20] Whitney BM, Chan AT, Rickinson AB, Lee SP, Lin CK, Johnson PJ. Frequency of Epstein-Barr virus-specific cytotoxic T lymphocytes in the blood of Southern Chinese blood donors and nasopharyngeal carcinoma patients. J Med Viral,2002, 67: 359-363.

[21] Rooney CM, Smith CA, Ng CY, Loftin S, Li C, Krance RA, et al. Use of gene-modified virus-spefic T lymphocytes to control Epstein-Barr virus related lympholiferation. The Lancet,1995, 345:9-13.

[22] Zuo JM, Zhou L, Wang Q, Zeng Y. The in vitro and in vivo immunogenicity of recombinant adenovirus vaccine containing EBV-latent membrane protein 2. Chinese Journal of Microbiology and Immunology, 2003, 23(6):446-449.

[23] Zhang JK. The dendritic cell and tumor immunological therapy. Shantou: The Publishing Company of the University of Shantou, 2001:65-83.

[24] Ranieri E, Kierstead LS, Zarour H. Dendritic cell/peptide cancer vaccines: clinical responsiveness and epitope spreading. Immunol Invest,2000, 29(2):121-125.

[25] Kugler A, Stuhler G, Walden P, Zoller G, Zobywalski A, Bmssart P, et al. Regression of human metastatic renal cell carcinoma after vaccination with tumor cell-dendritic cell hybrids. Nat-Med, 2000, 6(3):332-336.

[26] Bmssart P, Wirths S, Stuhler G, Reichardt VL, Kanz L, Brugger W. Induction of cytotoxic T-lymphocyte responses in vivo after vaccinations with peptide-pulsed dendritic cells. Blood,2000, 96(9):3102-3108.

[27] Banchereau J, Steinman RM. Dendritic cells and the control of immunity. Nature(Lend.), 1998,392:245-252.

[28] Nestle FO, Banchereau J, Hart D. Dendritic cells: on the move from bench to bedside. Nat Med, 2001, 7:761-765.

[29] Lin CL, Lo WF, Lee TH, Ren Y, Hwang SL, Cheng YF, et al. Immunization with Epstein-Barr Virus(EBV) peptide-pulsed dendritic cells induces functional CD8+ T-cell immunity and may lead to tumor regression in patients with EBV-positive nasopharyngeal carcinoma. Cancer Res, 2002, 62(23):6952-6958.

[30] Katsenelson NS, Shurin GV, Bykovskaia SN, Shogan J, Shurin MR. Human small cell lung carcinoma and carcinoid tumor regulate dendritic cell maturation and function. Mod Pathol, 2001,14:40-45.

[31] Inoshima N, Nakanishi Y, Minami T, Izumi M, Takayama K, Yoshino I, et al. The influence of dendritic cell infiltration and vascular endothelial growth factor expression on the prognosis of nonsmall cell lung cancer. Clin Cancer Res, 2002,8: 3480-3486.

[In《J Microbiol Immunol》2006, 4(1): 41-48]

In vitro Anti-Tumor Immune Response Induced by Dendritic Cells Transfected with EBV-LMP2 Recombinant Adenovirus

PAN Ying[1], ZHANG Jin-kun[1], ZHOU Ling[2], ZUO Jian-min[2], ZENG Yi[2]

1. Department of Onco-pathology and the Key Immunopathology Laboratory of Guangdong Province, Shantou University Medical College; 2. Institute for Viral Disease Control and Prevention, Chinese Center for Disease Control and Prevention

[SUMMARY]   Epstein-Barr virus(EBV)-associated nasopharyngeal carcinoma(NPC) is a high-incidence tumor in southern China. Latent membrane proteins 2(LMP2)is a subdominant antigen of EBV. The present study was to develop a dendritic cells(DCs)-based cancer vaccine(rAd-LMP2-DC)and to study its biological characteristics and its immune functions. Our results showed that LMP2 gene transfer did not alter the typical morphology of mature DC, and the representative phenotypes of mature DC(CD80, CD83, and CD86)were highly expressed in rAd-LMP2-DCs. The expression of LMP2 in rAd-LPM2-DCs was about 84.54%, which suggested efficient gene transfer. Transfected DCs markedly increased antigen-specific T-cell proliferation. The specific cytotoxicity against NPC cell was significantly higher than that in controls($P<0.05$), and enhanced with increased stimulations by transfected DCs. In addition, phenotypic analysis demonstrated that the LMP2-specific CTLs consisted of both CD4 + and CD8 + T cells. These results showed that development of DC-based vaccine by transfection with malignancy-associated virus antigens could elicit potent CTL response and provide a potential strategy of immunotherapy for EBV-associated NPC.

[Keywords]   Dendritic cell; Nasopharyngeal carcinoma; Epstein-Barr virus; Gene transfer; Cytotoxic T lymphocyte; Cancer vaccine

INTRODUCTION

Cytotoxic T lymphocytes(CTLs) recognize peptides derived from the intracellular breakdown of foreign antigens and present these peptides at the cell surface as a complex with major histocompatibility complex(MHC) class I molecules. Such CTLs play an important role in controlling virus infection. The virus-induced CTL response tends to focus on a few immunodominant peptide epitopes whose identities are specific for the particular MHC type of the host. This study concerns the CTL response to Epstein-Barr virus(EBV), a herpesvirus commonly associated with nasopharyngeal carcinoma(NPC). Among the EBV-associated NPC patients, the proteins of EBV expressed on tumor cells are very limited, only latent class II EBV anti-gens such as the latent EBV nuclear antigens (EBNA1)and latent membrane proteins(LMP1 and LMP2)can be detected on NPC cells. Many human leukocyte antigen(HLA)class I restricted epitopes of LMP2 have been identified and their sequences are conserved, and LMP2 is thus the most frequently recognized protein by CTLs[1]. LMP2 constitutes potentially the major target antigen for immunotherapy of NPC.

In our study, we sought to develop an efficient protocol to induce a strong LMP2-specific CTL response against tumor cells of NPC. Dendritic cells(DCs)are highly efficient and specialized antigen-presenting cells(APC) that are the only ones that can stimulate the native T cell and activate antigen-specific CTLs[2,3]. In vivo, immature DCs develop from hematopoietic progenitors and are located strategically at body surfaces, where they play a sentinel role in capturing and processing antigens.

Following antigen exposure, DCs migrate to lymphoid organs and acquire potent antigen-presenting function. Mature DCs process antigens efficiently by both MHC class I and II pathways with upregulation of cell surface adhesion molecules such as CD54(ICAMI)and of costimulatory molecules such as CD80 and CD86. DCs have demonstrated potent anti-tumor properties in a variety of experimental models[4-6].

Recently some reports showed that calcium-signaling agents could induce maturation of DCs derived from peripheral blood monocytes[7,8]. DCs activated with calcium-signaling agents, in the presence of cytokines in serum-free medium, rapidly express mature DC marker, CD83, and high levels of co-stimulatory molecules within 96 h of culture. These activated DCs can efficiently sensitize T cells to recognize tumor cells through tumor antigens expressed by tumor cells. In our study, we prepared DCs by adenoviral transfection with EBV-LPM2 and calcium ionophore treatment. The acquired DC vaccine could stimulate T cells and elicit the potent antigen-specific CTLs activity against NPC cells.

MATERIALS AND METHODS

1. **Nasopharyngeal carcinoma cell culture**: Nasopharyngeal carcinoma cell line(CNE-2) which contains LMP2 gene[9] was obtained from the Institute for Viral Disease Control and Prevention of the Chinese Center for Disease Control and Prevention(Chinese CDC). The CNE-2 cells were grown in complete RPMI medium 1640(Gibco, USA)supplemented with 10% heat-inactivated fetal calf serum(FCS, Hyclone), 2mmol/L L-glutaminc, 100 U/ml penicillin, and 100μg/ml streptomycin.

2. **Preparation of DCs**: Human peripheral blood mononuclear cells(PBMCs)were isolated from whole blood of healthy donors by Ficoll-Hypaque(d=1.077 g/ml) density-gradient centrifugation. Such PBMCs were suspended in RPMI 1640 medium supplemented with 10% heat-inactivated FCS. After incubation for 2 h at 37 ℃ in 5% CO_2, the nonadherent cells were removed. The adherent cells as monocytes were harvested and resuspended in macrophage serum-free medium(Mφ-SFM; Gibco). The monocytes were then plated in a 24-well tissue-culture plate(Costar, USA)at $2.5×10^6$ cells/well supplemented with 50 ng/ml rhGM-CSF(Peprotech, USA). This combination of Mφ-SFM and rhGM-CSF, which constitutes basal culture medium for all monocytes and DCs in this study, is henceforth referred to in the text simply as SFM/G. The monocytes were cultured for 24-48 h at 37℃ in 5% CO_2. To obtain mature DCs, the cells were treated with calcium ionophore A23187(Sigma)at a concentration of 150 ng/ml for additional 48 h. The mature DCs were then collected and were analyzed for DC typical phenotypes by fluorescence-activated cell sorter(FACS)analysis or co-cultured with T cells for sensitization assays.

3. **Preparation of adenovirus transfected DCs**: Recombinant serotype 5 adenoviruses encoding the LMP2 gene (rAd-LMP2)were obtained from the Institute for Viral Disease Control and Prevention of the Chinese CDC. The virus stocks were proliferated in human embryonic kidney(293)cells in DMEM(Gibco)supplemented with 2% heat-inactivated FCS and purified through cesium chloride(Sigma)gradient ultracentrifugations[10]. Viral particle concentration was determined by UV absorbance at 260 nm[11], and final viral titers were 10^{11} plaque-forming units (pfu).

The monocytes were cultured in SFM/G for 48h as described previously. The cells were harvested as immature DCs and were resuspended at $1×10^6$ cells/200μl in serum-free medium. The recombinant adenoviruses encoding the LMP2 gene were then added to infect immature DCs at multiplicities of infection(MOI)200. Infection was allowed to proceed for 2 h at 37 ℃. Then fresh SFM/G was added to bring the cultures to 2ml per well. One hour after adenoviruses transfection of immature DCs, calcium ionophore A23187 was added at a concentration of 150 ng/ml. Transfected cells were cultured for additional 48 h and the mature rAd-LMP2-DCs were harvested. To determine the viability of adenoviruses-infected DCs, trypan blue(Sigma)exclusion was used to determine viable cells. The expression of LMP2 protein in rAd-LMP2-DCs was analyzed by indirect immunofluorescence and FACS assays. In addition, DC phenotypes CD80, CD83, and CD86 were determined as well.

4. **Preparation of T lymphocytes**: Sterile nylon-wool isolation column(Wako, Japan)was soaked in complete RPM1 1640 medium supplemented with 10% heat-inactivated FCS, 2 mmol/L L-glutamine, 100 U/ml penicillin, and 100μg/ml streptomycin for 1 h at 37 ℃. Then the nonadherent cells isolated from peripheral blood mononuclear cells described previously were applied on the column and cultured for additional 1 h. T lymphocytes were eluted from the column with 10 ml RPMI 1640/10% FCS. Purity of about 90% was obtained with this method.

5. **Flow cytometric analysis of cell populations**: DCs were collected and resuspended in cold FACS buffer (phosphate-buffered saline with 0.2% BSA and 0.09% sodium azide). Cells were immunostained with fluorescein isothiocyanate(FITC) conjugated mouse anti-human CDS0, CD83, and CD86 antibodies(eBioscience, USA). Corresponding FITC immunoglobulin G(IgG) isotype control antibody(eBioscience, USA)was used. A total of $1×10^6$ cells were incubated overnight at 4℃ with antibodies. The cells were then washed once with FACS buffer, resuspended, and phenotyped on a FACScan(Becton-Dickinson, USA).

An intracellular staining method was used for the detection of LMP2 proteins in rAd-LMP2-DCs. Mature DCs were fixed in 2% paraformaldehyde. Cell membranes were permeated in 2% Triton X-100(Amresco, USA)and then incubated with LMP2 rabbit multiclonal antibody(obtained from Institute for Viral Disease Control and Prevention of Chinese CDC) at 4℃ overnight. After washing with PBS twice, the cells were immunostained with FITC-conjugated goat anti-rabbit IgG(Sigma)for 30 min at 37℃. The cells were then washed once with FACS buffer, resuspended, and analyzed on a FACScan.

6. **Lymphocyte proliferation assays**: Lymphocyte proliferation assays were performed by using rAd-LMP2-DCs, untransfected DCs and CNE-2 cells as stimulator cells and T lymphocytes as responder cells. Stimulator cells were incubated with Mitomycin C(MMC)at 25μg/ml at 37℃ for 30 min and then washed with PBS twice. T lymphocytes isolated from the peripheral blood mononuclear cells were plated in 96-well fiat-bottomed culture plate (Costar, USA)at $5×10^5$ cells per well. Then stimulators were added and co-cultured with responders at ratios of 1:5, 1:10,1:20, 1:50, 1:100, and 1:200 for 96 h at 37 ℃ in 5% CO_2. T cells incubated in medium alone

served as control. The cells were then incubated with 5 mg/ml metrizamide(MTT; Sigma)$20\mu l$ per well for 4 h. The supernatant was removed and $150\mu l$ dimethyl sulfoxide(DMSO; Amresco, USA)was added to each well and agitated for 10 min to fully dissolve the crystals. Absorbance was measured at 570 nm on automatic ELISA reader (TRITURUS). All determinations were carried out in triplicate and repeated four times. Stimulation index(SI)was calculated as follows: SI＝(experimental-blank)/(control-blank).

7. **Induction of CTLs by transfected DCs:** T cells were harvested by nylonwool separation as described previously. T cells(1×10^{6})were co-cultured with rAd-LMP2-DCs(5×10^{4}) in a 24-well tissue culture plate in 1ml RPMI 1640/20％ FCS at 37℃ in 5％ CO_2. IL-2 was added at a final concentration of 40 IU/ml to all wells 3 days later and every 2-3 days thereafter. Responding T cells were re-stimulated weekly for 2 weeks with transfected DC at a responder T cell-to-stimulator DC ratio of 20：1. The CTLs were then collected and used as the effector cells in CTL assays against CNE-2 cells.

8. **Cytotoxicity assays:** The target cells were placed in 96-well tissue culture plates at 1×10^{4} cells per well and co-cultured with effector cells(CTLs)at the ratio of 1：5, 1：10, and 1：20 for 48 h at 37 ℃ in 5％ CO_2. The cytotoxic activities were determined by MTT assay. Freshly prepared and filtered $20\mu l$ metrizamide(5 mg/ml)was added to each well, and the cells were continuously cultured for 4 h. The supernatant was removed and $150\mu l$ dimethyl sulfoxide was added to each well and agitated for 10 min to fully dissolve the crystals. Absorbance was measured at 570 nm on automatic ELISA reader(TRITURUS). All determinations were carried out in triplicate and repeated four times. Experiments were performed in triplicate. The percentage of specific cytotoxicity was calculated as [(experimental-minimal)/(maximal-minimal)]$\times100$. Target cells incubated in medium alone or in medium containing 1％ Triton X-100 were used to determine minimal and maximal cytotoxicity, respectively. T cells separated from the peripheral blood mononuclear cells by sterile nylonwool isolation column as described previously and the untransfected DCs were used as controls, respectively.

9. **Analysis of LMP2-specific CTLs populations:** T cells were stimulated with rAd-LMP2-DCs weekly as described previously. After two rounds of stimulations, the induced LMP2-specific CTLs were collected on day 14 and then resuspended in cold FACS buffer. Cells were immunostained with FITC/PE/PE-cyanine5 (Cy5) conjugated mouse anti-human CD4/CD8/CD3 antibodies(Jingmei Biotech, China). Corresponding mouse FITC/PE/PE Cy5 IgG isotype control antibody(Jingmei Biotech, China)was used. A total of 1×10^{6} cells were incubated with antibodies for 30 min at 37℃. The cells were then washed once with FACS buffer, resuspended, and bidimensional analyzed with a FACScan.

10. **Statistical analysis:** SPSS11. 0 was used for data variation analysis; p values less than 0. 05 were considered statistically significant.

RESULTS

1. Morphological features of rAd-LMP2-DCs

Fully morphologic differentiation of mature DCs activated by calcium ionophore required 72-96 h of culture. The rAd-LMP2-DCs retained typical morphological features of DCs(Fig. 1). While untreated PBMCs maintained their rounded, smooth surface morphology and appeared as dispersed, nonadherent cells in culture, rAd-LMP2-DCs predominantly gathered in clusters as nonadherent or loosely adherent cells with a larger cell surface and irregular shape.

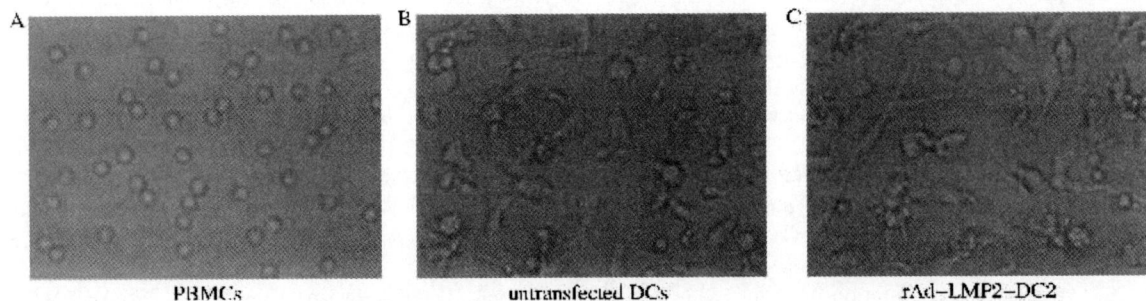

Fig. 1 Morphological characters of PBMCs(A), untransfected DCs(B), and transfected DCs(C). After 96 h culture, PBMCs were grown by suspension. DCs with or without transfection appeared similar morphology with long dendritic projection. Photomicrographs were taken with inverted phase contrast microscope under $200\times$ magnifications

2. Phenotype of transfected DCs

To determine whether mature DCs transfected with rAd-LMP2 expressed co-stimulatory molecules, mature DCs with or without rAd-LMP2 transfection were analyzed for co-stimulatory molecules(CD80 and CD86)and DC activation marker(CD83). We found these immunophenotypic alterations occurred promptly within the first 20-40h of culture with calcium ionophore A23187. Adenoviruses transfection of mature DCs did not result in significant increases or decreases in CD83, CD80, or CD86 expression. Data shown in Fig. 2 are representative of three independent experiments that produced similar results.

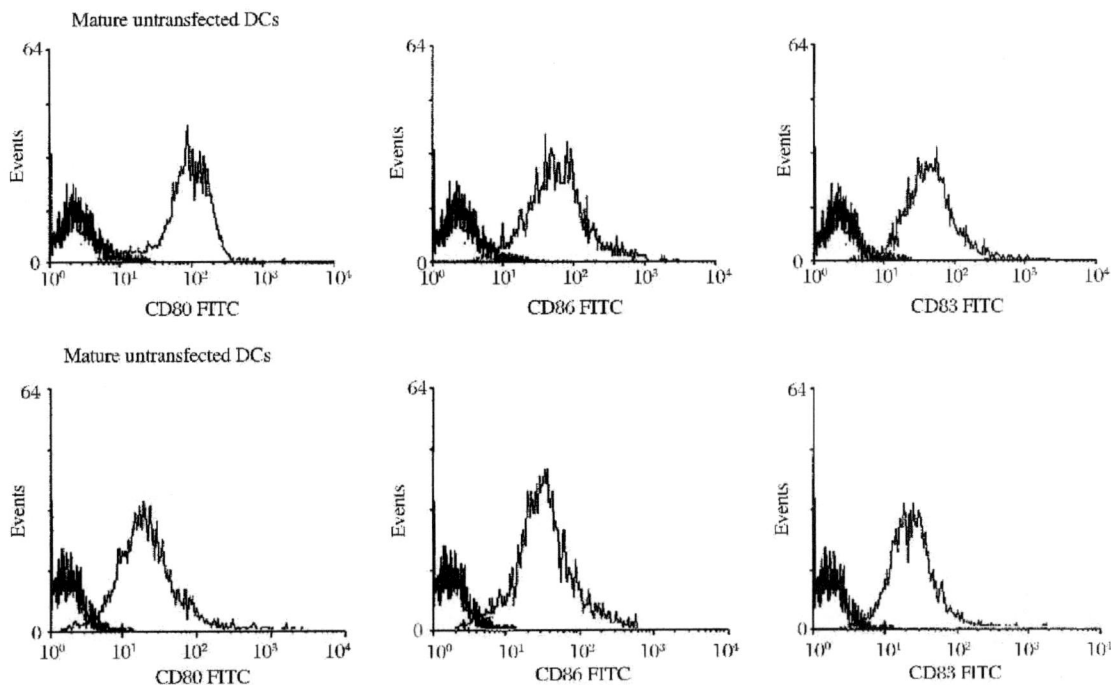

Fig. 2 Phenotype of mature DCs with or without rAd-LMP2 transfection. Cells were incubated with FITC, conjugated mAbs against CD80, CD86, and CD83. The result showed that mature untransfected DCs(top panel)with expressions of CD80, CD83, and CD86 were 86.32%, 85.73% and 86.27%, respectively; mature transfected DCs(bottom panel)were 81.54%, 87.48% and 88.37%, respectively

3. Expression of LMP2 in transfected DCs

Immature DCs were transfected with rAd-LMP2 at MOI 200 for 2h. The transfected cells were cultured in the presence of calcium ionophore and rh-GM-CSF for additional 48 h. When mature rAd-LMP2-DCs were analyzed by flow cytometry, the percentage of transfected DCs expressing LMP2 was 84.54%, which suggested efficient gene transfer(Fig. 3).

4. Stimulation of T lymphocytes by rAd-LMP2-DCs

It was found that anti-tumor T cells were generated by a single stimulation with mature DCs transfected with rAd-LMP2. The rAd-LMP2-DCs were more potent stimulators of T lymphocytes than untransfected DCs($P < 0.05$) or CNE-2 cells($P < 0.01$), respectively. The effect was enhanced with higher ratio of rAd-LMP2-DCs to T cells(Fig. 4).

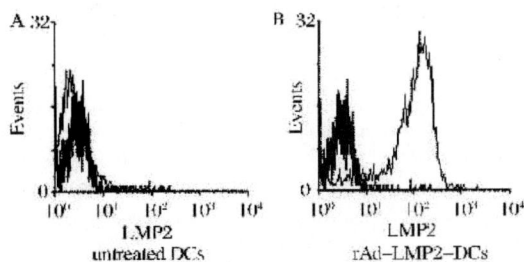

Fig. 3 Expression of LMP2 in untreated and transfected DCs. Flow cytometry indicated expression of LMP2 in rAd-LMP2-DCs(B) was 84.54 and 1.57% in untreated DCs(A)

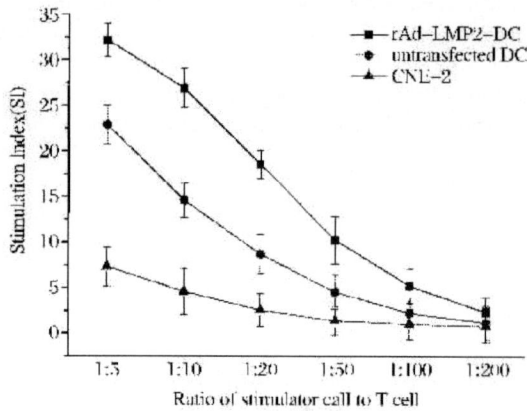

Fig. 4 T lymphocytes proliferation reaction stimulated by rAd-LMP2-DCs, untransfected DCs, and CNE-2. Mature DCs transfected with rAd-LMP2 for 48 h were collected and co-cultured with T cells for 96 h. Specific CTLs were detected by MTT assay. The results are expressed as $(\bar{x} \pm s)$ of three replicates. Data indicate that rAd-LMP2-DCs were potent stimulators of lymphocyte than untransfected DCs ($P < 0.05$)or CNE-2($P < 0.01$), respectively

5. Cytotoxicity assays

After stimulating twice with rAd-LMP2-DCs, highly LMP2-specific anti-tumor CTLs could be induced. The cytotoxic activity was enhanced with increased ratio of effector-to-target cells. MTT assay showed that cytotoxic activity in rAd-LMP2-DCs group was higher than that in untransfected DCs ($P < 0.05$) and T cell groups ($P < 0.01$), respectively(Fig. 5).

6. Effect of stimulation on cytotoxicity

T cells were stimulated by rAd-LMP2-DCs weekly. The induced CTLs were harvested as effector cells. These effector cells were used against target cells in cytotoxicity assay as previously described on day 7, 14, and 21. The results showed that LMP2-specific cytotoxicity elicited by only a single stimulation of transfected DCs was higher than those by T cell group($P < 0.01$)and untransfected DC group($P < 0.05$). Furthermore, the cytotoxicity could augment with repeated stimulations. Compared with that on day 7, the specific cytotoxicity was evidently higher on day 14 in all groups, respectively($P < 0.01$), but there was no significant difference between those on day 14 and on day 21($P > 0.05$)in untransfected DC group and rAd-LMP2-DC group(Fig. 6). The experiments indicated that two rounds of stimulation were enough to induce potent specific cytotoxicity.

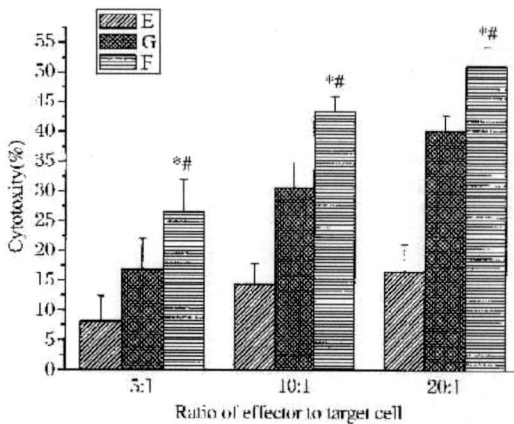

The CNE-2 cells were placed in 96-well tissue culture plates at 1×10^4 per well and co-cultured with effector cells at the ratio of $1:5$, $1:10$, and $1:20$ for 48 h. Percentage cytotoxicity($\bar{x} \pm s$) of three replicates) was determined by MTT assay. $*$ $P < 0.01$ vs. T cell group; $\#$ $P < 0.05$ vs. untransfected DC group

Fig. 5 Cytotoxicity of CTLs against nasopharyngeal carcinoma cells

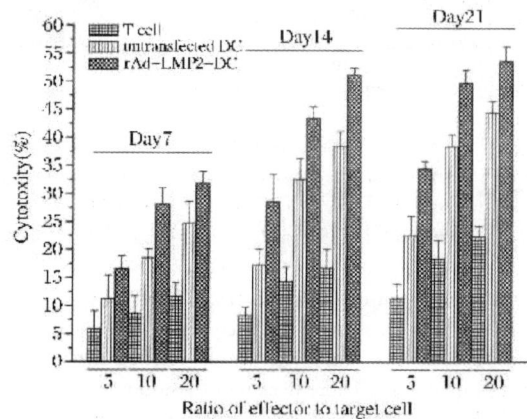

T cells were stimulated by rAd-LMP2-DCs weekly, and the induced CTLs were harvested as effector cells. These effector cells were used against target cells in cytotoxicity assay on day 7, 14, and 21. Cytotoxicity on day 14 was obviously higher than that on day 7($P < 0.01$), but there was no significant difference between those on day 14 and on day 21($P > 0.05$)

Fig. 6 Effect of different rounds of stimulation on cytotoxicity

7. Flow cytometric analysis of LMP2-specific CTLs populations

LMP2-specific CTLs induced by rAd-LMP2-DCs on day 14 were collected and analyzed with flow cytometry. We found that the CTLs consisted of CD4[+] and CD8[+] T cells simultaneously. The component of CD8[+] T cell was slightly larger than that of CD4[+] T cell(Fig. 7).

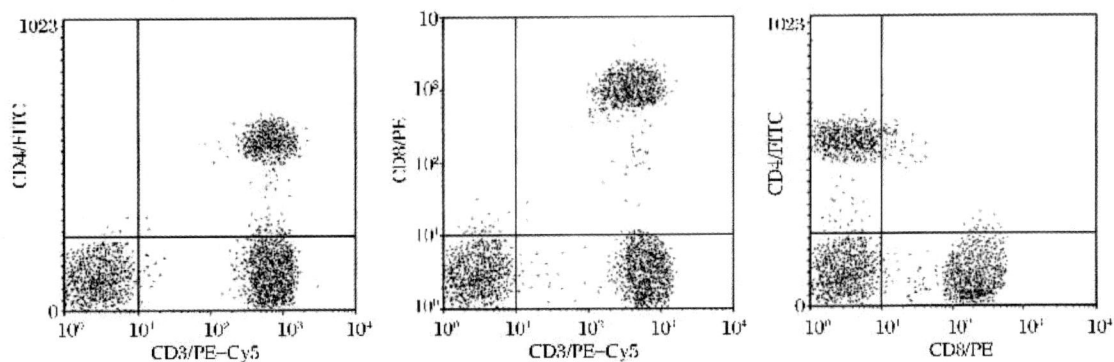

Fig. 7 Flow cytometric analysis of LMP2-specific CTLs populations. The percentage of CD3[+], CD4[+], and CD8[+] T cells was 61.73%, 36.47% and 46.18%, respectively

DISCUSSION

Recently, malignancy-associated viruses are used as potential targets for immunotherapeutic vaccines aiming to stimulate T-cell responses against viral antigens expressed in tumor cells[12-14] Here we have shown that the induction of primary antigen-specific CTL responses in vitro by human PBMCs-derived DCs adenovirally transfected with LMP2 gene, a subdominant antigen in EBV-associated NPC cells.

DCs are professional APCs that play a critical role in the activation of the immune response to antigen. Mature DCs express high levels of co-stimulatory molecules, necessary components of T cell activation by APCs, which must occur in conjunction with MHC-restricted presentation of the antigen to the T-cell receptor. The co-stimulatory molecules identified on DCs with their respective T-cell receptors are CD54, CD80, CD83, CD86, CD40 and CD40 ligand. In the present study, the co-stimulatory molecules CD80, CD86 and CD83 did not change significantly after rAd-LMP2 modification of DCs compared with untreated DCs, which demonstrated adenovirus transfection had little effect on DC maturation and antigen-presenting function.

Recent laboratory observations indicated that pharmacologic agents that mobilize intracellular calcium can be used to enhance APC functions in human PBMCs[15,16]. The phospholipase C(PLC)-calcium signaling pathway is involved in the maturation of DCs induced by the agonists such as calcium ionophore A23187. A23187 can pump extracellular calcium into the cell. The increased cytoplasmic calcium concentration induced by A23187 could cause calcium-induced calcium release from intracellular stores. On the other hand, increased cytoplasmic calcium levels may induce positive feedback that activates PLC, which causes the second messengers inositol 1, 4, 5-tri-phosphate(IP$_3$) liberating from the plasma membrane. Thus, calcium release from IP3-gated stores induces the maturation of DCs. In our study, we tried to use calcium ionophore as the main agent to generate DCs more effectively from human PBMCs and examined the characteristics of DCs including cellular morphology and APC function. Our results showed that fully morphologic differentiation of DCs activated by calcium ionophore required 72-96 h of culture, and immunophenotypic alterations occurred promptly within the first 20-40 h of culture after CI treatment, including upregulation of CD80 and CD86 expression, and de novo expression of the DC-associated activation marker CD83. Such rapid activation kinetics contrasted to the much slower activation(needed about 9-10 days)observed when PBMCs were treated with cytokine combinations such as rhGM-CSF, rhIL-4, and rhTNF-α[5,6].

Gene transfer is an attractive means to affect the immunostimulatory properties of DCs. We have used a gene-based vaccination strategy by using DCs expressing the tumor antigen to elicit a potent therapeutic anti-tumor immunity. This approach has apparent advantages over protein-or peptidebased immunization[17]. Tumor associated antigen(TAA) gene expression in DCs causes endogenous processing and presentation of multiple and/or undefined antigenic peptides independent of MHC alleles. Furthermore, specific T cell-mediated immunity may be stimulated by vaccine-involved APC without prior knowledge of responder MHC haplotypes or of relevant MHC class I-or class II-restricted peptide epitopes.

Although a variety of vectors are available for gene transfer to DCs, recombinant adenovirus is most efficient. Adenovirus vector is a highly efficient and reproducible method of gene transfer. Indeed, several studies have shown that successful adenoviral gene transfer into human DCs resulted in induction of a T-cell response against tumor[18,19]. Our results showed that the expression of LMP2 in transfected DCs reached a high level of 84.54%, which indicated efficient gene transfection.

Currently, published reports showed that malignancy-associated virus antigen could induce specific antitumor CTL. EBV is a herpesvirus commonly associated with malignancies such as Hodgkin disease(HD), T-cell lymphoma, and NPC, particularly in immunocompromised hosts. EBV elicits a strong cytotoxic T lymphocyte(CTL)response directed against a broad range of viral antigens that are involved in the control and regulation of latency and in the induction of proliferation and transformation[20]. EBV-associated NPC, a high-incidence tumor in southern China, expresses a limited set of EBV proteins. Only latent class II EBV antigens such as EBNA1 and LMP1, LMP2 can be detected on NPC cells. Among these three antigens, LMP1 is an NPC-associated viral oncogene[21], and EBNA1 is an abundant source of HLA class II-restricted CD4$^+$ T-cell epitopes that contains a Gly-Ala repeat sequence, which can interrupt the presentation of it through HLA class I-restricted subway to T cells[22,23]. LMP2 is a source of subdominant CD8$^+$ T-cell epitopes presented by HLA class I alleles common in the Chinese population[24,25]. In some studies, EBV transformed B lymphoblastoid cell lines(LCLs)have been used to induce EBV-specific CTLs. Adoptive transfer of EBV-specific CTLs has been successfully applied in the treatment of EBV associated post-transplant lymphoproliferative disease[26,27]. Nevertheless, application of this approach to EBV-associated NPC is difficult, because LCLs focus T cell expansion on immunodominant EBV antigens such as the latent EBNA3A, 3B, and 3C that are not expressed in EBV-associated NPC. On the other hand, in adoptive immunotherapy LCLs elicited only EBV-specific memory T cell responses but not native T-cell responses[28]. In our study, we demonstrated that DCs transfected with LMP2 by adenovirus vector were able to stimulate enhanced T-cell proliferation and LMP2-specific cytotoxic T-cell responses in vitro. Analyzing the populations of CTLs elicited by rAd-LMP2-DCs, we found LMP2-specific CTLs consisted of both CD4$^+$ and CD8$^+$ T cells simultaneously. Our result was similar to the reports of CTLs induced by DCs transfected with LMP2a in experiment of HD treatment[26]. The specific CTLs lysed carcinoma cells maybe by both MHC class I-and MHC class II-restricted mechanisms. In summary, the results demonstrate that vaccination using DCs simultaneously transfected with malignancy-associated virus antigens can elicit potent CTL response and provide a potential immunotherapy strategy for EBV-associated NPC.

ACKNOWLEDGEMENTS

This work was supported by the National"863"Project of China(No. 2003AA216071)and the National Natural Science Foundation of China(No. 30270520).

REFERENCES

[1] Niedobitek G, Epstein-Barr virus infection in the pathogenesis of nasopharyngeal carcinoma, J Clin Pathol, 2000, 53: 248-254.

[2] Steinman RM. The dendritic cell system and its role in immunogenicity, Ann Rev Immunol,1991, 9:271-296.

[3] Banchereau J, Steinman R. Dendritic cells and the control of immunity, Nature(Lond.),1998, 392:245-252.

[4] Tomohide T, Andrea G, Paul DR., Walter JS, Interleukin 18 gene transfer expands the repertoire of antitumor Th1-type immunity elicited by dendritic cell-based vaccines in association with enhanced therapeutic efficacy. Cancer Res,2002, 62: 5853-5858.

[5] Jenne L, Arrighi JF, Jonuleit H, et al. Dendritic cells containing apoptotic melanoma cells prime human CD8$^+$ T cells for efficient tumor cell lysis. Cancer Res, 2000, 60:4446-4452.

[6] Nouri-Shirazi M, Banchereau J, Bell D, et al. Dendritic cells capture killed tumor cells and present their antigens to elicit tumorspecific immune responses. J Immunol, 2000, 165:3797-3803.

[7] Bagley KC, Abdelwahab SF, Tuskan RG, Lewis GK. Calcium signaling through phospholipase C activates dendritic cells to mature and is necessary for the activation and maturation of dendritic cells induced by diverse agonists. Clin Diagn Lab Immunol, 2004, 11:77-82.

[8] Sadovnikova E, Parovichnikova EN, Semikina EL, et al. Adhesion capacity and integrin expression by dendritic-like cells generated from acute myeloid leukemia blasts by calcium ionophore treatment. Exp. Hematol, 2004, 32:563-570.

[9] Du HJ, Zhou L, Zuo JM, et al. A study on killing effect of cytotoxic T cell activated by LMP2 peptides in nasopharyngeal carcinoma cells. J Oncol, 2004, 10:92-94.

[10] Rosenfeld MA, Yoshimura K, Trapnell BC, et al. In vivo transfer of the human cystic fibrosis transmembrane conductance regulator gene to the airway epithelium. Cell, 1992, 68:143-155.

[11] Mittereder N, March KL, Trapnell BC, Evaluation of the concentration and bioactivity of adenovirus vectors for gene therapy. J Virol, 1996,70:7498-7509.

[12] Gottschalk S, Edwards OL, Sili U, et al. Generating CTLs against the subdominant Epstein-Barr virus LMP1 antigen for the adoptive immunotherapy of EBV-associated malignances. Blood, 2003, 101:1905-1912.

[13] Wagner HJ, Sili U, Gahn B, et al. Expansion of EBV latent membrane protein 2a specific cytotoxic T cells for the adoptive immunotherapy of EBV latency type 2 malignancies: influence of recombinant IL12 and IL15. Cytotherapy, 2003,5: 231-240.

[14] Santodonato L, Agostino GD, Nisini R, et al. Monocyte-derived dendritic cells generated after a shortterm culture with IFN-alpha and granulocyte-macrophage colony-stimulating factor stimulate a potent Epstein-Barr virusspecific CD8[+] T cell response J Immunol, 2003,170:5195-5202.

[15] Westers TM, Stam AG, Scheper RJ, et al. Rapid generation of antigen-presenting cells from leukaemic blasts in acute myeloid leukaemia, Cancer Immunol. Immunother, 2003, 52:17-27.

[16] Waclavicek M, Berer A, Oehler L, et al. Calcium ionophore: a single reagent for the differentiation of primary human acute myelogenous leukaemia cells towards dendritic cells. Br J Haematol, 2001, 114:466-473.

[17] Diebold SS, Cotten M, Koch N, Zenke M. MHC class II presentation of endogenously expressed antigens by transfected dendritic cells. Gene Ther, 2001, 8:487-493.

[18] Paul LF, Christie L, Jennifer MA, et al. Efficacy of CD40 ligand gene therapy in malignant mesothelioma. Am J Resp Cell Mol Biol,2003, 29:321-330.

[19] Jay ML, Ali M, Reiko Y, et al. Adenovirus vector-mediated overexpression of a truncated form of the p65 nuclear factor κB eDNA in dendritic cells enhances their function resulting in immunemediated suppression of preexisting murine tumors. Clin Cancer Res, 2002, 8:3561-3569.

[20] Khanna R, Burrows SR. Role of cytotoxic T lymphocytes in Epstein-Barr virus-associated diseases. Annu Rev Microbiol, 2000, 54:19-48.

[21] Burrows JM, Bromham L, Woolfit M, et al. Selection pressuredriven evolution of the Epstein-Barr virus-encoded oncogene LMP1 in virus isolates from Southeast Asia. J Virol, 2004,78:7131-7137.

[22] Munz C, Bickham KL, Subklewe M. Human CD4(+)T lymphocytes consistently respond to the latent Epstein-Barr virus nuclear antigen EBNA1. J Exp Med, 2000, 191:1649-1660.

[23] Khanna R, Tellam J, Duraiswamy J, et al.Immunotherapeutic strategies for EBV-associated malignancies. Trends Mol. Med, 2001,7:270-276.

[24] Lin CL, Lo WF, Lee TH, et al. Immunization with Epstein-Barr Virus(EBV)peptidepulsed dendritic cells induces functional CD8[+] T-cell immunity and may lead to tumor regression in patients with EBV-positive nasopharyngeal carcinoma. Cancer Res, 2002, 62:6952-6958.

[25] Taylor GS, Haigh TA, Gudgeon NH, et al. Dual stimulation of Epstein-Barr Virus(EBV)-specific CD4[+]-and CD8[+]-T-cell responses by a chimeric antigen construct: potential therapeutic vaccine for EBV-positive nasopharyngeal carcinoma. J Virol, 2004, 78:768-778.

[26] Bollard CM, Straathof KC, Huls MH, et al. The generation and characterization of LMP2-specific CTLs for use as adoptive transfer from patients with relapsed EBV-positive Hodgkin disease. J Immunother, 2004, 27:317-327.

[27] Chua D, Huang J, Zheng B, et al. Adoptive transfer of autologous Epstein-Barr virus-specific cytotoxic T cells for nasopharyngeal carcinoma. Int J Cancer, 2001, 94:73-80.

[28] Herr W, Ranieri E, Olson W, et al. Mature dendritic cells pulsed with freeze-thaw cell lysates define an effective in vitro vaccine designed to elicit EBV-specific CD4(+)and CD8(+)T lymphocyte responses. Blood, 2000,96:1857-1864.

[In《Biochemical and Biophycical Research Communication》2006, 347:551-557]

Immunogenicity of the Recombinant Adenovirus Type 5 Vector with Type 35 Fiber Containing HIV-1 Gag Gene

LIU Xin-lei[1,2], YU Shunag-qing[2], FENG Xia[2], WANG Xial-li[1], LIU Hong-mei[2],
ZHANG Xiao-mei[2], LI Hong-xia[2], ZHOU Ling[2], ZENG Yi[1,2]

1. College of Life Science and Bio-engineering, Beijing University of Technology, 2. State Key Laboratory for Infectious Disease Prevention and Control, National Institute for Viral Disease Control and Prevention, Chinese Center for Disease Control and prevention

[SUMMARY]　The immune efficiency of a recombinant adenovirus type 5 with type 35 fiber containing HIV-1gag gene (rAd5/F35-mod. gag)was investigated in BALB/c mice, in which the rAdS/F35-mod, gag was firstly identified with PCR, then transfected to 293 cells and the in vitro expression level of gag protein was determined by Western blotting and indirect immuno-fluorescent assay. Mice were immunized with intramuscular injections of rAd5/F35-mod, gag, rAd5-mod, gag or DNA and were boosted after 3 weeks. To test the effect of pre-existing anti-viral immunity on immunization, mice were also injected with Ad5-GFP vector and then immunized 4 and 7 weeks later with Ad5/F35-mod. gag vector. The P24-specific IgG antibody in sera of immunized mice was determined by ELISA and the specific cytotoxic T lymphocyte(CTL) response was assayed by intracellular cytokine staining. It was demonstrated that the rAd5/F35-mod. gag vector could express efficiently the HIV gag protein in 293 ceils in vitro and induce strong HIV-specific immune responses in vivo. The strongest CTL and serum IgG response occurred when mice were immunized twice with injection of rAd5/F35 alone, but the anti-AdS antibody after primary, infection with adenovirus could inhibit the specific immune responses induced by rAd5/F35 vector. It is concluded that single immunization with recombinant adenovirus rAd5/F35-mod, gag can induce specific CTL and serum IgG antibody responses in mice, but the immunogenicity of rAd5/F35 is comparably weaker than that of rAd5.

[Keywords]　HIV-1; AIDS vaccines; Adenoviridae

INTRODUCTION

Recombinant adenovirus(rAd)vectors are widely used for both in vitro and in vivo gene transfer. rAd-based vaccines have a number of advantages over naked DNA vaccines or vaccines based on other viruses such as poxvims or alphavims. These advantages include the ability to prepare hightiter stocks of purified virus easily and the remarkable efficiency of the Ad cell/nucleus entry process leading to high-level transgene expression. Furthermore, it is thought that Ad can provide an adjuvant effect to stimulate of antigen-specific immune responses. It has been shown in diverse in vivo models that recombinant adenovirus type 5(rAd5)has potential as a vehicle to transfer genes for HIV. However, in clinical trials of an early version of the vaccine containing a gene for the HIV gag protein, the response to the vaccine was blunted in people even with moderate levels(a titer over 1∶200)of pre-existing anti-Ad5 antibodies. In the US and Europe about one-third of the population has pre-existing immunity able to significantly reduce vaccine efficacy, and in developing countries that could be as high as 80% of the population[1,2]. The pre-existing antiviral immunity strongly influencing the efficacy of the HIV vaccine is one hurdle of using Ad5 vector. Another hurdle is the hepatocellular tropism of AdS limits the safety of this viral vector[3]. This virus uses the coxsackievirus and adenovirus receptor(CAR)as its primary attachment receptor, which confers tropism for liver parenchymal cells. In response to these two shortcomings, our laboratory has examined the immunogenicity of a replication-defective chimeric Ad5 vector with Ad type 35 fiber(rAd5/F35)(Ad35 virus was classified as subgroup B). The Ad35 fiber showed 25% amino-acid homology with the Ad5 fiber, Cell entry of Ad35 is CAR independent and may involve CD46 receptor, which expresses on most human cells[4]. In the present study, we found that the rAd5/F35 recombinants induced rather strong antigen-specific humoral and cellular immune responses in BALB/c mice.

MATERIAL AND METHODS

1. Recombinant vectors

Recombinant vectors E1, E3-deletion, replication-defective recombinant viruses were constructed by our laboratory. The recombinant virus(Ad5/F35-mod. gag, Ad5-mod. gag)was propagated and purified by vector gene technology company.

2. Expression of rAd5/F35-mod, gag in 293 cells

Human embryonic kidney cell line 293 was maintained in DMEM, supplemented with 10% bovine serum albumin. And 293 cells were infected with the rAd5/F35-mod, gag at the MOI of 10 for 2 h, and then cultured at 37℃ for another two days. Then the cells were collected, the expressed protein gag was analysed by Western blotting and immune fluorescence assay(IFA).

3. Animal immunization

Four-to 6-week old female BALB/c mice were purchased from Institute of Experimental Animal Sciences, Chinese Academy of Medical Sciences. BALB/c mice were divided into several groups with 5 in each randomly. The mice were immunized with intramuscular injection of DNA, of Ad5/F35-mod. gag or Ad5-mod. gag vector and were boosted after 3 weeks. To test the effect of pre-existing antiviral immunity on vaccination, the mice were injected intramuscularly with 8.5×10^{10} viral particles(vp) of Ad5-GFP vector and then immunized 4 and 7 weeks later with Ad5/F35-mod. gag vector. Inoculation of animals was conducted as scheduled in Tab. 1.

Tab. 1　Immunization schedule of rAd5 and rAd5/F35 vectors

Groups	0 week	4 week	7 week	8 week
1	—	PBS(100μl)	PUS(100μl)	detection of immune
2	rAd5-GFP(8.5×10^{10} vp)	rAd5/F35-gag(10^{10} vp)	rAd5/F35-gag(10^{10} vp)	detection of immune
3	—	rAdS-gag(3×10^{9} vp)	rAd5-gag(3×10^{9} vp)	detection of immune
4	—	rAdS/F35-gag(10^{10} vp)	rAd5/F35-gag(10^{10} vp)	detection of immune
5	—	DNA(100μg)	rAd5-gag(3×10^{9} vp)	detection of immune
6	—	DNA(100μg)	rAd5/F35-gag(10^{10} vp)	detection of immune

4. Intracellular cytokine staining array

Lymphocytes were isolated from the mouse spleen by EZ-Sep^T M Mouse 1 × density gradient centrifugation (Dakewe Biotech Company Limited, China). Isolated lymphocytes were cultured(2×10^{6} cells/500μl per well)into 48-well plates(Costa, Cambridge, MA)in RPMI 1640 containing 10% fetal calf serum(FCS). The cells suspension were incubated with 6μg/ml of the HIV peptide[P1(197-205): AMQMLKETI; P2(239-247): TISTLQEQI; P3 (291-300): EPFRDYVDRF]at 37℃. After 3 h, 2μg/ml monensin was added. The cells were incubated for another 10h. The cells were washed with staining buffer(1% bovine serum albumin in PBS), and stained with phycoerythrin(PE)-conjugated anti-mouse CD8 antibody(Ly-2, BD Pharmingen, USA). The cells were fixed with 4% formaldehyde/PBS for 15 min at room temperature, permeabilized in 0.3% saponin(sigma), 1% bovine serum albumin in PBS, and stained with anti-mouse IFN-γ Ab conjugated with fluorescein isothiocyanate(FITC)(BD Pharmingen, USA) at room temperature for 1 h, followed by flow cytometric analysis.

5. Detection of HIV-1-specific and Ad5-specific antibodies

The specific antibody was detected by the enzymelinked immunosorbent assay(ELISA). 96 well microtiter plates were coated with 2μg/ml of HIV P24 protein prepared by our laboratory or 10^{9} vp/ml of Ad5-LMP2 and incubated overnight at 4℃. The well were blocked with PBS containing 5% skimmed milk power for 1 h at 37℃. They were then treated with 100μl of serially diluted antisera and incubated for an additional 1 h at 37℃. The plates were washed five times with PBS containing 0.5% Tween 20 and incubated for 1 h with a 1 : 20 000 dilution of an affinity purified HRP-1a-beled anti-mouse Ab(Jackson, West Grove, Pennsylvania, US). The plates were then washed five times, developed with tetramethylbenzidine, stopped with 2 mol/L H_2SO_4, and analyzed at 450 nm/630 nm.

RESULTS

1. Detection of the recombinant adenovirus containing the gag gene

Supernatant of 293 cells infected with rAd5/F35-mod. gag was collected, proteinase K(20 mg/ml)was added into it. The supernatant was incubated in water at 55℃, and then was used as the templet of PCR. The sequences of primers were as follows(the gag sequence detection primer): 5'-GTA CCG GCT GAA GCA CAT CGT-3' (sense)and 5'-CAT CAT GAT GCT GGC GGA GTT-3'(antisense); (the fiber sequence detection primer): 5'-TGGGAGGGGGACTTACAGTG-3'(sense)and 5'-GCTTTGCTGCTGGCTACAG-3'(anti-sense). The Fig. 1 and Fig. 2 indicated that the gene gag was inserted into rAdS/F35 correctly.

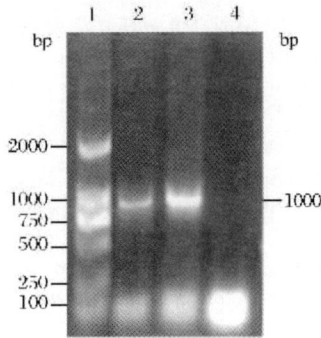

1：DL2000 DNA marker；2：PCR product of pVR-mod. gag as positive control；3：PCR product of rAd5/F35-mod. gag；4：PCR prodnet of water

Fig. 1　PCR analysis of gag

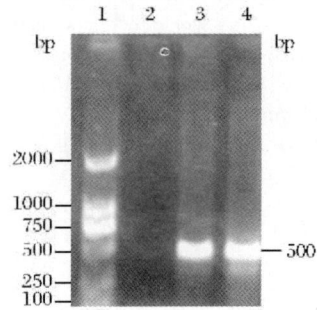

1：DL2000 DNA marker；2：PCR product of water；3：PCR product of rAd5/F35-mod，gag；4：PCR product of rAd5/F35-GFP

Fig. 2　PCR analysis of fiber

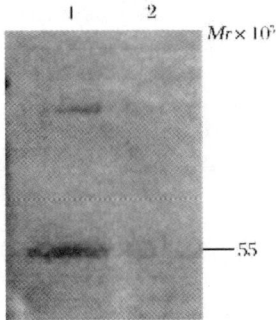

1：293 cells infected with rAd5/F35-mod，gag；2：Normal 293 Cells

Fig. 3　Western blotting analysis of expression of gag in rAd5/F35-mod，gag

2. Expression of rAd5/F35-mod・gag in 293 cells

Expression of the gag protein in rAd5/F35-mod. gag was analyzed by Western blotting. Extract protein of 293 cells transfected with rAd5/F35-mod. gag. The protein samples were subjected to SDS-PAGE and electroblotted onto nitrocellulose blotting membranes. Blots were blocked with 5% fat free milk in PBS containing 0.05% Tween 20 and probed with rabbit anti-HIV P24 polyclonal antibody prepared by our laboratory and peroxidase-conjugated goat anti-rabbit immunoglobulin. Proteins were visualized by staining with 3,3'-diaminobenzidine. The results showed that the modified gene gag in rAd5/F35-mod，gag was expressed correctly and efficiently after transfection to 293 cells(Fig. 3).

Expression of the gag protein in 293 cells infected with rAd5/F35-mod，gag was analyzed by indirect fluorescence assay. 293 cells were infected with the rAd5/F35-mod，gag at the MOI of 10 for 2h, and then cultured at 37℃ for another two days. After the 293 cells were collected by centrifugation and resuspended with saline, the 293 cells were incubated with anti-P24 rabbit serum(prepared by our laboratory), and FTTC conjugated anti-rabbit-IgG(1/160, 2 h, Jackson, West Grove, Pennsylvania, US). After cells were washed, they were detected by FIC. It was demonstrated that most 293 cells expressed gag when they were infected with rAd5/F35-mod，gag at the MOI of 10(Fig. 4).

3. Immune responses in mice after immunization

The ability of the rAd5/F35-mod，gag to trigger the activation and proliferation of antigenspecific T cells was monitored by the intracellular cytokine staining(ICS). The assay has been widely utilized to distinguish the relative contributions of CD8+ cells to the overall T-cell responses. Immunization with the rAd5/F35-mod，gag alone induced the number of HIV-specific IFN-γ-secreting CD8+ T cells more than other groups, that increased the IFN-γ-secreting CD8+ T cells to 8.828%(Fig. 5). Immunization with the rAd5-mod，gag alone is less than the effect of immunization with the rAd5/F35-mod，gag. Priming with the DNA-gag and followed by an rAd5 mod，gag boost increased the IFN-γ-secreting CD8+ T cells to 8.569%, this was significantly more than the effect of boost with rAd5/F35-mod，gag.

4. Effect of immunization on the specific serum IgG antibodies

Mice were vaccinated with rAd5/F35-mod，gag vector to explore the humoral immune response one week after the final immunization. As demonstrated by ELISA the animals immunized with 10^{10} vp of rAd5/F35-mod，gag vector developed a high-tittered anti-P24 antibody(Ab) reponse(Fig. 6).

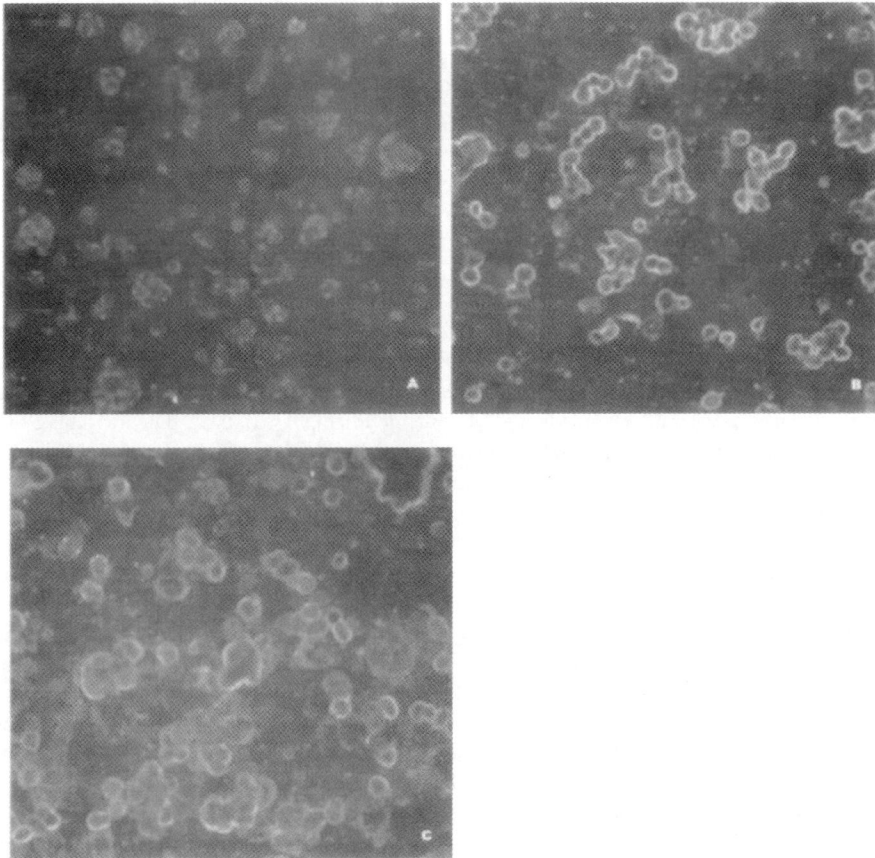

A：293 cells uninfected(×100)；B：293 cells infected with rAd5/F35-mod. gag for 48 h(×100)；
C：293 cells infected with rAd5/F35-mod. gag for 72 h(×200)

Fig. 4   IFA detection of 293 cells infected with recombinant adenoviruses rAd5/F35

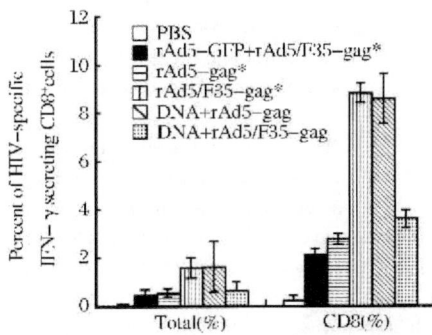

＊：Immunization with rAdS/F35-gag or rAd5-gag twice

Fig. 5   HIV-1 gag-specific，IFN-γ-secreting CD8$^+$ T cells measured by ICS

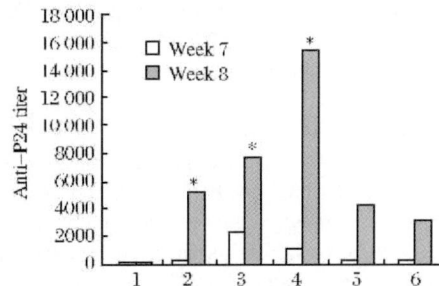

1：PBS；2：rAd5-GFP＋rAd5/F35-gag；3：rAd5-gag；4：rAd5/F35-gag；5：DNA＋rAd5-gag；6：DNA＋rAd5/F35 gag. ＊：Immunization with rAd5/F35-gag or rAd5-gag twice

Fig. 6   P24 specific antibody in immunized BALB/c mice

5. Effect of immunization on pre-existing immunity

To examine the effect of pre-existing anti-Ad5 immunity on the activity of the rAd5/F35 vector in vivo, mice were injected intramuscularly with 8.5×10^9 vp of rAd5-GFP. After 4 weeks, these animals were immunized with 10^{10} vp of rAd5/F35-mod. gag with high titers of anti-Ad5 Abs(anti-Ad5 neutralizing titer=1 ∶ 600). The HIV-specific responses were detected by ICS and ELISA after immunization. The magnitude of this response was significantly altered by preimmunization with the rAd5-GFP(Figs. 5 and 6). Although pre-existing immunity to Ad5 reduced the immune response elicited by both vectors, the rAd5/35-HIV vector was significantly less susceptible to the pre-existing Ad5 immunity than a comparable rAd5 vector. After injection with rAd5 and rAd5/F35 vector, the anti-rAd5 specific antibody titer was 1 ∶ 600 and less than 1 ∶ 100 respectively.

DISCUSSION

A practically used vaccine for HIV infection should exhibit high immunogenicity, low cost for production and low or even without pathogenicity. Under these requirements, replication-defective Ad5 may be one of the best vectors for HIV vaccine development. However, majority of human population is infected adenovirus type 5[1,2]. In addition, the neutralizing antibodies and the cellular immune responses against the Ad5 fiber capsid protein may reduce the efficacy of the Ad5 vector, when it is used as vaccine in clinical trials[2]. The switching of the serotypes of adenovirus and the substitutive use of animal adenovirus may induce partial bypass of the pre-existing immune responses to Ad5 viruses, but they would bring a few drawbacks, such as lack of knowledge about these viruses, including the tropism to human cells; the potential difficulties in the manufacture and the possibility of in vitro recombination with other human viruses leading to the development of unknown diseases.

In this study, a chimeric Ad5 vector with Ad35 fiber related to cell tropism was used, in which the rAd5/F35, similar to Ad5, had a high productive titer in tissue culture cells[5]. Nevertheless, the virus displayed cell tripism to Ad35 fiber protein[6]. Coupled with the evidence that a rAd5/F35 vector transduces human dendritic cells more efficiently as compared with the Ad5 vector[7], these findings suggest that the rAd5/F35-mod. gag vector is a promising candidate for clinical trials in humans.

In the present study, the effect of the pre-existing anti-Ad5 immunity on the rAd5/F35 vector was investigated. The effect of immunization with rAd5/F35-mod, gag twice to native mice appeared to be more prominent than that of immunization of mice that were pre-immune to adenovirus(Figs. 5 and 6). It was well known that introduction or infection with adenoviruses would induce immune responses to hexon[8], penton, and fiber protein antigen. The exchange of fiber can partially reduce inhibition of the pre-existing immunity against the parent adenovirus. Furthermore, the exchanges of other genes, including those for hexon and penton may further reduce inhibition of the pre-existing immunity against Ad5. However, researchers at Merck Co. had encountered two problems with this approach. First, the majority of these chimeric viruses lost the ability to replicate, presumably due to the structural constrains of viral capsid. Second, even though this approach allowed the viruses to overcome anti-Ad5 antibody, yet CTL reactive to other Ad5 proteins blunted the responses[9].

It was demonstrated that high titer of anti-Ad5 antibody was detected after the first immunization with rAd5, but not with rAd5/F35. This antibody could block the activity of rAd5/F35-mod. gag. Also, the effect of immunization with rAd5/F35-mod, gag twice alone was more prominent than that of immunization with rAd5-mod, gag in native mice(Figs. 5 and 6). Therefore, rAd5/ F35-mod. gag was less susceptible to the pre-existing immunity of Ad5 than a comparable rAd5-mod. gag. These results were in agreement with those data reported by other studies[10].

To examine the immunogenicity and the protective immunity of rAd5/F35 vector induced, the gene gag from HIV-1 clade B was used in the present study, because this strain of virus had been defined to be conserved in Henan province of China, and from the studies on the immunodominant epitopes, it was found that the gag gene products were the most conserved ones among the HIV-1 subtypes. Moreover, anti-gag CTL-response appeared to be inversely correlated with disease progression, suggesting that they should be considered as the first candidate to be chosen for vaccine preparation constructed aiming to induce a broad spectrum of CTL-responses[5]. The gag gene was cloned from the peripheral blood mononuclear cells(PBMCs)genome of patients infected with HIV-1 in Henan province. By analysis and alignment, the common sequence was obtained. To improve the expression level of gag protein expressed in mammalian cells, the codons of the consensus gag sequence were modified according to mammalian codon usage.

Priming with DNA-gag followed by rAd5-mod. gag boosting could induce an increase in thenumbers of the IFN-γ-producing CD8$^+$ T cells, and this was more prominent significantly than the effect of boosting with rAd5/F35-mod, gag, indicating that boosting with rAd5/F35mod, gag vector elicited slightly lower cellular immune responses and substantially lower humoral immune responses in comparison with that induced by rAd5-mod. gag. Consequently, it appears that rAd5/F35-mod. gag is less immunogenic than rAd5-mod. gag.

All together, it is evident that rAdS/F35 vector can induce strong HIV-specific immune relsponses in BALB/c mice and efficiently tranduce human dendritic cells ex vivo. Based on these observations, rAd5/F35 vectors can be used as avaluable tool for the studies of immunotherapy andvaccination.

REFERENCES

[1] Vogels R, Zuijdgeest D, Rijnsoever R, Hartkoom E, Damen I, de Bethune MP, et al. Replicationdeficient human adenovirus type 35 vectors for gene transfer and vaccination: efficient human cell infection and bypass of pre-existing adenovirus immunity. J Virol, 2003, 77:8263-8271.

[2] Barouch DH, Pau MG, Custers JH, Koudstaal W, Kostense S, Havenga M J, et al. Immunogenicity of recombinant adenovirus serotype 35 vaccine in the presence of pre-existing anti-AdS immunity. J Immunol, 2004, 172:6290-6297.

[3] Thomas CE, Ehrhardt A, Kay MA. Progress and problems with the use of viral vectors for gene therapy. Nat Rev Genet, 2003, 4:346-358.

[4] Zhang Y, Bergelson JM. Adenovirus receptors. J Virol, 2005, 79:12125-12131.

[5] Ferrari G, Kostyu DD, Cox J, Dawson DV, Flores J, Weinhold K J, et al. Identification of highly conserved and broadly cross-reactive HIV typel cytotoxic T lymphocyte epitopes as candidate immunogens for inclusion in Mycobacterium bovis BCG-vectored HIV vaccines. AIDS Res Hum Retroviruses, 2000, 16:1433-1443.

[6] Shayakhmetov DN, Papayannopoulou T, Stamatoy annopoulos G, André Lieber. Efficient gene transfer into human CD34 (+)cells by a retargeted adenovirus vector. J Virol, 2000, 74:2567-2583.

[7] Ophorst OJ, Kostense S, Goudsmit J, De Swart RL, Verhaagh S, Zakhartehouk A, et al. An adenoviral type 5 vector carrying a type 35 fiber as a vaccine vehicle: DC targeting, cross neutralization, and immunogenieity. Vaccine, 2004, 22: 3035-3044.

[8] Sumida SN, Truitt DM, Lemekert AA, Vogels R, Custers JH, Addo MN, et al. Neutralizing antibodies to adenovirus serotype 5 vaccine vectors are directed primarily against the adenovirus hexon protein. J Immunol, 2005, 174:7179-7185.

[9] Youil R, Toner TJ, Su Q, Chen M, Tang A, Bett A J, et al. Hexon gene switwh strategy for the generation of chimeric recombinant adenovims. Hum Gene Ther, 2002, 13:311-320.

[10] Xin KQ, Jounai N, Someya K, Homna K, Nizuguehi H, Naganawa S, et al. Prime-boost vaccination with plasmid DNA and a chimeric adenovirus type 5 vector with type 35 fiber induces protective immunity against HIV. Gene Ther, 2005, 12: 1769-1777.

[In《J Microbiol Immunol》2006, 4(4):306-312]

Haplotype-dependent HLA Susceptibility to Nasopharyngeal Carcinoma in a Southern Chinese Population

TANG M[1,2], ZNEG Y[3], POISSON A[4], MARTI D[4], GUAN L[5], ZHENG Y[2], DENG H[2], LIAO J[6], GUO X[3,5], SUN S[7], NELSON G[5], de The G[8], WINKLER CA[5], O'Brien SJ[1], CARRINGTON M[4], GAO X[4]

1. Laboratory of Genomic Diversity National Cancer Institute-Frederick, Frederick, MD, USA; 2. Cancer Center, Wuzhou Red Cross Hospital, Guangxi, China; 3. State Key Laboratory for Infectious Diseases Prevention and Control, Institute for Viral Disease Control and Prevention, Chinese Center for Disease Control and Prevention, Beijing, China; 4. Cancer and Inflammation Program, Laboratory of Experimental Immunology, National Cancer Institute-Frederick, Frederick, MD, USA; 5. Labolatory of Genomic Diversity SAIC-Frederick, Inc., National Cancer Institute-Frederick, Frederick, MD, USA; 6. Department of Epidemiology, Cangwu Institute for Nasopharyngeal Carcinoma Control and Prevention Guangxi, China; 7. Conservation Biology Building College of Life Sciences Peking University, Beijing, China; 8. Oncogenic Virus Epidemiology and Pathophysiology, Institute Pasteur, Paris, France

[SUMMARY] We have conducted a comprehensive case-control study of a nasopharyngeal carcinoma (NPC) population cohort from Guangxi Province of Southern China, a region with one of the highest NPC incidences on record. A total of 1407 individuals including NPC patients, healthy controls, and their adult children were examined for the human leukocyte antigen(HLA)association, which is so far the largest NPC cohort reported for such studies. Stratified analysis performed in this study clearly demonstrated that while NPC protection is associated with independent HLA alleles, most NPC susceptibility is strictly associated with HLA haplotypes. Our study also detected for the first time that A*0206, a unique A2 subtype to South and Southeast Asia is also associated with a high risk for NPC. HLA-A*0206, HLA-B*3802 alleles plus the A*0207-B*4601 and A*3303-B*5801 haplotypes conferred high risk for NPC showing a combined odds ratio(OR)of 2.6($P<0.0001$). HLA alleles that associate with low risk for NPC include HLA-A*1101. B*27. and B*55 with a combined OR of 0.42($P<0.0001$). The overall high frequency of NPC-susceptible HLA factors in the Guangxi Population is likely to have contributed to the high-NPC incidence in this region.

[Keywords] HLA; Nasopharyngeal carcinoma; Haplotype; Stratified analysis

INTRODUCTION

Nasopharyngeal carcinoma(NPC)is an epithelial malignancy caused by a combination of Epstein-Barr virus (EBV)infection and environmental factors[1-3]. Genetic predisposition also has a function in NPC susceptibility causing the observed familial aggregation[4] and distinct racial and geographical distribution of the disease incidence[5-8]. Southern China and Southeast Asia have a disproportionally high incidence of NPC. In these regions, NPC is one of the most common cancers,[9,10] but in Caucasians, it is a rare disease.[11]

Among the host genetic markers that have been associated with NPC, the class I human leukocyte antigen (HLA)genes have shown a strong and consistent association with disease risk. As it was first reported by Simons et al.[12] in a Singaporean Chinese cohort in the mid 1970s, the HLA association with NPC has been widely detected in different racial groups even though the exact HLA factors(alleles and haplotypes)associated with the disease sometimes vary among racial groups due to population-dependent HLA distributions. Populations ot Southern China and Southeast Asia share high-NPC incidence as well as common HLA characteristics. Mainland Chinese[9,13], Taiwanese[14] and Singaporean Chinese[15], NPC cohorts also show similar HLA associations, where HLA-A*11 and B*13 seem protective against NPC, and A*02(A*0207), A*33, B*46, and B*58 associate with susceptibility to this disease(Fig. 1). Other HLA loci including HLA-C and the class II loci, DR and DQ, have not shown independent associations with NPC even though certain class II alleles might be part of the extended HLA haplotypes associated with the disease as described by Hildesheim et al.[14]

Association of HLA polymorphism with human disease may indicate direct involvement of the HLA molecule in the disease pathogenesis. To date, however, there has been little in vitro or in vivo evidence that the NPC-associated HLA alleles affect differentially NPC-related EBV replica-tion on pathogenesis. The role of HLA-A and-B alleles or haplotypes that include combinations of these alleles in NPC pathogenesis remain unknown. It is possible that the associated HLA class I alleles are simply marking by linkage disequilibrium(LD)the true NPC-causing gene(s). Large-scale cohort studies exploring combinations of associated HLA alleles may provide useful insights

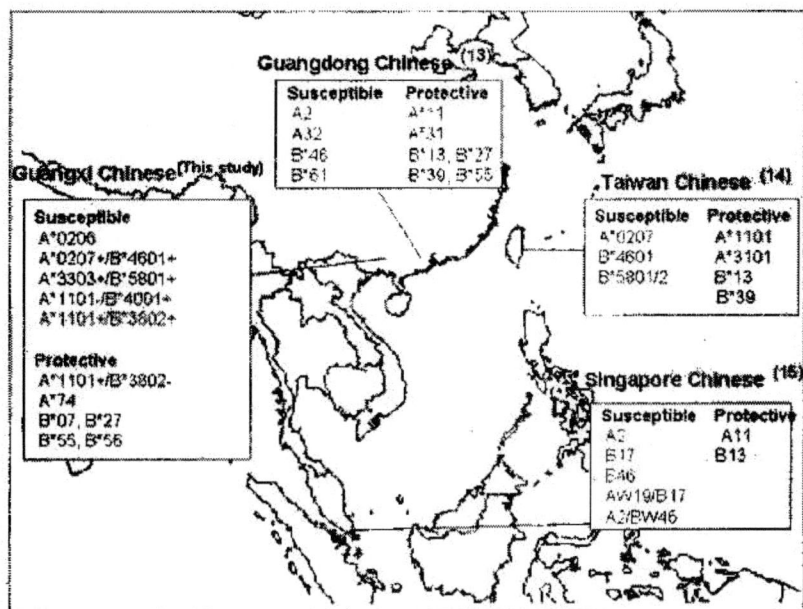

Fig. 1　HLA associations with NPC in Chinese population.

into the influence of HLA on NPC.

An early indicator of NPC development is the occurrence of immunoglobulin(Ig)A antibodies to EBV capsid antigens(EBV-IgA/VCA)[16-18]. Even though >95% of adults in the general population of all ethnic groups are healthy carriers of EBV, <2.5% are EBV-IgA/VCA antibody positive. In comparison, >95% of all NPC patients are EBV-IgA/VCA antibody positive.[10] If HLA diversity is indeed directly responsible for the individually varied NPC risks, it is plausible that the development of the EBV-IgA/VCA antibodies in EBV-positive individuals may also be affected by the HLA polymorphism.

Here, we have conducted a case-control study of an NPC cohort recruited from Guangxi Province In Southern China where the NPC incidence is as high as 25-50 cases per 10 000 individuals. DNA-based high-resolution HLA typing was performed on a total of 1407 individuals including NPC cases, matched controls, and offspring of the study subjects. This large study has allowed a comprehensive stratification of NPC-associated HLA factors and provided novel insights into the nature of the HLA association with the disease.

RESULTS

HLA typing was informative for 356 NPC patients, 287 NPC free EBV-IgA/VCA antibody positive healthy individuals, and 342 NPC free EBV-IgA/VCA antibody negative healthy individuals. Comparative analyses between the two healthy groups failed to detect any significant deviation in the frequency distribution of HLA alleles and haplotypes(Supplementary Tabs. 1 and 2), indicating that HLA polymorphism does not affect the occurrence of the EBV-IgA/VCA antibody. Therefore, in subsequent analyses, the two NPC-free groups were combined as the control group(n=629) for NPC cases.

HLA alleles showing a significant difference in frequency distribution between cases and controls are listed in Tab. 1, and full analyses are presented in supplementary Tabs. 3 and 4. For the reason of most of former NPC, HLA studies were based on serology typing, for better understanding the HLA influence in NPC, both HLA allotype and genotype were present in this table. For the HLA-A locus, 31 four-digit, alleles were detected, 12 of which had an allele frequency >1% in either the case or control group. Five alleles, A* 0206, A* 0207, A* 1101, A* 3303, and A* 7401/7402, showed a significant difference in frequency distribution between the case and control groups. After correction, however, only two alleles, A* 1101 and A* 3303, remained significant. Of the two detected A* 11 alleles, A* 1101 showed a reduced presence in patients compared with controls($P < 0.0001$), whereas the less common A* 1102 showed no difference between these groups, but due to its low frequency, it need to be confirmed in even large study cohort. Four common A* 02 subtypes, A* 0201, A* 0203, A* 0206, and A* 0207, were detected. Two of alleles, A* 0206 and A* 0207, showed an elevated frequency in patients. A* 3303 also associated with increased risk of NPC($P=0.0004$).

Tab. 1 Gene frequencies(%)of the two and four-digit HLA-A, -B, and -C alleles detected in NPC patients(n=356)and controls(n=629)

	Allele	Frequency		P-value	$P_c$value*
		NPC patients	Controls		
HLA-A	02	38.62(275)	32.75(412)	0.01	NS
	0206	5.2(37)	2.31(29)	0.0006	NS
	0207	14.89(106)	11.29(143)	0.02	NS
	11	23.74(169)	32.35(407)	0.0001	0.003
	1101	19.52(139)	29.09(366)	<0.0001	0.0003
	33	20.51(146)	14.31(180)	0.0004	0.02
	3303	20.51(146)	14.31(180)	0.0004	0.04
	74	0.14(1)	1.11(14)	0.02	NS
HLA-B	07	0.0(0)	1.03(13)	0.01	NS
	13	8.43(60)	13.04(164)	0.002	NS
	1301	7.72(55)	12.08(152)	0.002	NS
	27	0.0(0)	1.59(20)	0.001	NS
	2704	0.0(0)	1.27(16)	0.005	NS
	38	12.78(91)	9.78(123)	0.04	NS
	3802	12.64(90)	9.30(117)	0.02	NS
	39	0.28(2)	1.19(15)	0.04	NS
	40	16.29(116)	12.32(155)	0.01	NS
	4001	14.75(105)	11.05(139)	0.02	NS
	55	0.56(4)	4.21(53)	<0.0001	0.0002
	5502	0.56(4)	3.66(46)	<0.0001	0.003
	56	0.84(6)	2.23(28)	0.02	NS
	5601	0.28(2)	1.67(21)	0.006	NS
	58	19.10(136)	14.07(177)	0.003	NS
	5801	19.10(136)	14.07(177)	0.003	NS
HLA-C	0302	18.12(129)	13.43(169)	0.005	NS
	0403	0.98(7)	2.23(28)	0.05	NS
	12	1.12(8)	4.29(54)	0.0001	0.006
	1202	0.56(4)	2.23(28)	0.005	NS
	1203	0.56(4)	2.07(26)	0.01	NS
	15	1.12(8)	2.62(33)	0.03	NS

Abbreviations：HLA, human leukocyte antigen；NPC, nasopharyngeal carcinoma
* 'NS'=$P>0.05$.

Tab. 2　HLA-A/B and B/A haplotype frequencies(%) in NPC patients($n=356$)and controls($n=629$)[a]

Haplotype		Frequency		P-value*	Allele/haplotype effect[b]
		NPC patients	Controls		
(A)					
HLA-A/B					
0206	1502	1.26	0.4	0.03	Allele A*0206(S)
	Others	3.93	1.91	0.007	
0207	4601	12.22	8.59	0.01	Haplotype A*0207-B*4601(S)
	Others	2.67	2.7	NS	
1101	1301	3.79	7.07	0.003	Allele A*1101(P)
	1502	4.21	5.72	NS	
	3802	1.97	0.79	0.02	Allele offset
	4001	2.53	3.74	NS	
	4601	1.12	2.7	0.02	Allele A*1101(P)
	5101	1.4	1.43	NS	
	5401	1.4	1.03	NS	
	Others	3.09	6.6	0.0009	
3303	5801	17.13	11.29	0.0003	Haplotype A*3303-B*5801(S)
	Others	3.37	3.02	NS	
(B)					
HLA-B-A					
1301	1101	3.79	7.07	0.003	Allele A*1101(P)
	2402	1.83	2.85	NS	
	Others	2.11	2.15	NS	
3802	0203	9.41	7.07	NS	
	1101	1.97	0.79	0.03	Allele offset
	Others	1.26	1.43	NS	
4001	0203	3.23	1.59	0.02	Allele B*4001(S)
	1101	2.53	3.74	NS	
	1102	1.54	0.48	0.01	Allele B*4001(S)
	2402	4.07	3.34	NS	
	Others	3.37	1.91	NS	
5502	0203	0.42	2.07	0.004	Allele B*5502(P)
	others	0.14	1.59	0.003	
5801	3303	17.13	11.29	0.0003	Haplotype B*5801-A*3303(S)
	others	1.97	2.78	NS	

Notes: HLA, human leukocyte antigen; NPC, nasopharyngeal carcinoma.
[a] HLA-A/B haplotypes(Tab. 2A)are those containing HLA-A alleles that showed significant association with NPC in the analysis of individual alleles and HLA-B/A haplotypes(Tab. 2B)are those containing HLA-B alleles that showed significant association with NPC. Only the haplotypes with at least one allele showing significantly different gene frequencies between patients and controls are shown. Lowfrequency haplotypes(<1.0% in both groups)associated with a particular A or B allele are combined as 'others'. A*7400, which associated with protection(Tab. 1), was not found on any haplotype with a frequency of >1%, and thus is not listed. This was also the case for B*2704 and B*5601
[b] 'p'=Protective effect, 'S'=Susceptible effect
* 'NS'=$P>0.05$

Tab. 3　Effect of allelic combinations of NPC-associated HLA alleles on the disease development

Allele combination[a] A/B	NPC patients (n=356) %(n)	Controls (n=629) %(n)	OR(95% CI)	P-value*	Allele/haplotype effect
Protective					
1101/4001					Allele A*1101
−/+	19.38(69)	8.59(54)	2.56(1.76-3.72)	<0.0001	
+/−	28.37(101)	38.95(254)	0.62(0.47-0.82)	0.0008	
+/+	8.15(29)	11.92(75)	0.66(0.42-1.02)	NS	
0203/5502					Allele B*502
−/+	0.28(1)	2.54(16)	0.11(0.02-0.57)	0.009	
+/−	27.53(98)	23.37(147)	1.25(0.93-1.68)	NS	
+/+	0.84(3)	4.45(28)	0.18(0.06-0.53)	0.002	
1101/1301					Allele A*1101
−/+	5.9(21)	6.52(41)	0.9(0.52-1.55)	NS	
+/−	27.25(97)	34.02(214)	0.73(0.55-0.97)	0.03	
+/+	9.27(33)	16.85(106)	0.5(0.33-0.76)	0.001	
Susceptible					
0206/1502					Allele A*0206
−/+	13.2(47)	15.74(99)	0.81(0.56-1.18)	NS	
+/−	7.02(25)	3.66(23)	1.99(1.12-3.53)	0.02	
+/+	3.37(12)	0.95(6)	3.62(1.43-9.15)	0.007	
0207/4601					Haplotype A*0207-B*4601
−/+	7.87(28)	12.24(77)	0.61(0.39-0.96)	0.03[h]	
+/−	3.93(14)	4.93(31)	0.79(0.4-1.50)	NS	
+/+	23.31(83)	16.38(103)	1.55(1.12-2.14)	0.008	
3303/5801					Haplotype A*3303-B*5801
−/+	3.37(12)	4.45(28)	0.75(0.28-1.49)	NS	
+/−	5.06(18)	5.41(34)	0.93(0.52-1.68)	NS	
+/+	32.87(117)	21.46(135)	1.79(1.34-2.39)	0.0001	

Notes: CI, confidence interval; HLA, human leukocyte antigen; NPC, nasopharyngeal carcinoma; OR, odds ratio.
[a] '+'=positive for the allele; '−'=negative for the allele, [b] The A0207− / B4601 + signal(P=0.0325)is a weak 'protective' confirmed, the opposite of the strong susceptible haplotype A0207/B4601
* 'NS'=$P>0.05$

Fifty-five HLA-B alleles were detected, but only 14 had a frequency $>1\%$. Among the 14 B alleles, seven showed a significantly different distribution between cases and controls, including B*1301, B*2704, B*3802, B*4001, B*5502, B*5601, and B*5801. After P-value correction, however, only the decrease of B*5502 in the patient group remained significant(P corrected=0.003). Three B*27 subtypes, B*2704, B*2705, and B*2706 were detected only in the control group with a combined frequency of 1.59%(P=0.0014). B*3802, B*4001, and B*5801 were each observed more frequently among the case group but the significance disappeared after correction.

Twenty-four alleles were detected at the HLA-C locus, 13 of which had a frequency $>1\%$. Cw*0403, Cw*1202, and Cw*1203 were observed at a lower frequency in cases and Cw*0302 was the only allele showing an elevated frequency in cases. After correction, however, none of the four-digit HLA-C alleles remained significant.

Tab. 4 Protective and susceptible HLA alleles, haplotypes, and genotypes for the development of NPC

HLA factor	NPC cases($n=356$) %(n)	Controls($n=629$) %(n)	OR(95% CI)	P-value
Protective				
A*1101+/B*3802	32.58(116)	49.76(313)	0.49(0.37-0.64)	<0.0001
A*74	0.28(1)	2.07(13)	0.13(0.05-0.32)	0.03
B*07	0.0(0)	2.07(13)	0.07(0.01-0.56)	0.01
B*27	0.0(0)	3.18(20)	0.04(0.01-0.29)	0.001
B*55	1.12(4)	7.95(50)	0.13(0.05-0.32)	<0.0001
B*56	1.69(6)	4.45(28)	0.37(0.16-0.87)	0.02
Combined	34.83(124)	58.98(371)	0.37(0.28-0.49)	<0.0001
Susceptible				
A*0206	10.39(37)	4.61(29)	2.40(1.47-3.92)	0.0005
A*0207+/B*4601+	23.03(82)	16.38(103)	1.53(1.11-2.11)	0.01
A*3303+/B*5801+	32.87(117)	21.14(133)	1.83(1.37-2.44)	<0.0001
A*1101-/B*4001+	23.03(82)	14.15(89)	1.82(1.30-2.53)	0.0004
A*1101+/B*3802+	3.93(14)	1.59(10)	2.53(1.14-5.61)	0.02
Combined	73.03(260)	50.08(315)	2.70(2.05-3.56)	<0.0001

Notes: CI, confidence interval; HLA, human leukocyte antigen; NPC, nasopharyngeal carcinoma; OR, odds ratio

HLA typing was informative for 422 children of the study subjects, which enabled us to directly determine HLA haplotypes in 179 patients and 379 controls. For the remaining 177 patients and 250 controls, HLA haplotypes were assigned by population-based estimation methods. HLA-A/B haplotype frequencies were calculated on the basis of both methods of haplotype assignments. Stratification analyses were performed to determine tne nature ot the observed HLA association(Tab. 2 and 3). Tab. 2 compares the frequency distribution of all HLA-A/B (where the HLA-A allele showed individual association with NPC)and-B/A(where the HLA-B allele showed individual association with NPC)haplotypes related to individual NPC associated alleles between cases and controls to determine whether the observed allele association with NPC might be due to particular haplotypes or to an individual allele. Four of the five potentially NPC-related HLA-A alleles, A*0206, A*0207, A*1101, and A*3303, were each observed on HLA-A/B haplotypes with frequencies of >1% and were therefore included in Tab. 2A. Both the dominant A*0206-B*1502 haplotype(P=0.0278) and all other A*0206-associated haplotypes combined (P=0.0071) showed elevated frequencies in the patient group. A*0207 is predominantly associated with B*4601, and this was the only A*0207 haplotype associating with susceptibility to NPC(P=0.0095). Similarly, A*3303-B*5801 was the only A*3303 haplotype associating with NPC susceptibility(P=0.0003). The protective A*1101 allele was found on seven HLA-A/B haplotypes with frequencies >1% and these haplotypes showed inconsistent associations with NPC. A*1101-B*1301(P=0.0029), A*1101-B*4601(P=0.0198), and A*1101-B*others(P=0.0009) showed reduced frequencies in the NPC group, whereas A*1101-B*3802 haplotype(P=0.0228) showed an elevated frequency in the patient group.

Five of the seven NPC-associated HLA-B alleles composed haplotypes with frequencies>1%. The B*5801-A*3303 haplotype showed an elevated frequency in NPC patients, whereas the other B*5801 haplotypes did not. The other NPC-associated B alleles were all found on at least two common HLA-B/A haplotypes. Both B*13011 and B*3802 were significantly more common in the control group only when A*1101 was also present on these haplotypes(P=0.0029 and P=0.0228, respectively). B*4001 was associated with four haplotypes with a frequency >1%. All haplotypes containing this allele were observed more frequently in the patients(B*4001-A*0203 and B*4001-A*1102 reaching significance; P=0.0167 and P=0.0138, respectively), except for the A*1101-associated B*4001 haplotype, which was more common in the controls albeit not significantly.

Tab. 3 stratifies six common NPC-associated HLA-A/B allelic combinations to examine independent as well as collective effects of HLA alleles on NPC risk analyzed in Tab. 2. For each tested HLA-A/B phenotypic combination, the study subjects were divided into three groups: those having both of the relevant HLA-A and HLA-B alleles and those that had one, but not the other. The protective A* 1101 and the susceptible B* 4001 allele combination is included first in Tab. 3 to show the collective effect of these two offsetting NPC-associated alleles. The protective B* 5502 is in LD with A* 0203, and stratification for this allele combination showed that the protective effect of B* 5502 could be detected in the presence[odds ratio(OR)=0.18, P=0.0018]or absence(OR=0.11, P=0.0088)of A* 0203. A* 1101, which is commonly linked to the NPC-related B alleles B* 1301 and B* 4001, is the most common protective allele in the Guangxi NPC conhort. Stratified analysis showed that the A* 1101 protection was stronger when B* 1301 was also present(OR=0.5, P=0.0010; without B* 1301; OR=0.73, P=0.0280). However, B* 1301 had no effect(OR=0.9, P>0.05)in the absence of A* 1101. Remarkably, B* 4001 actually associated strongly with risk of developing NPC if A* 1101 was missing(OR=2.56, P<0.0001), but in the presence of A* 1101, the susceptibility effect of B* 4001 was completely abrogated(OR=0.66, P>0.05). The susceptibiliy effect of A* 0206 seems to be largely independent of HLA-B, though the A* 0206 and B* 1502combination was somewhat stronger(OR=3.63, P=0.0065) than that in the presence of other HLA-B alleles(OR=1.99, P=0.0184). Both A* 0207(Tab. 1)and B* 4601[14,19] were thought to be independent high-risk factors for NPC in Southern Chinese and Southeast Asia. Then, two alleles are in strong LD in the Guangxi cohort, as in most Southern Chinese populations, and the A* 0207-B* 4601 haplotype associated with susceptibility (Tab. 3). However, A* 0207 showed no effect in the absence of B* 4601, whereas B* 4601 had a weak protective effect in the absence of A* 0207(OR=0.61, P=0.0325). Finally, A* 3303 and B* 5801 forms the most common A-B haplotype in the Guangxi cohort and both alleles were associated with an elevated NPC risk(Tab. 1). Stratification of the A* 3303 and B* 5801 combination showed that the NPC effect was more strongly associated with the presence of both alleles(OR=1.79, P=0.0001)as one allele without the other had no effect.

Tab. 4 summarizes the HLA alleles and the allele combinations associated with the risk of developing NPC. HLA protection against NPC mainly involves independent allele influence except that the A* 1101 protection may be overridden by the presence of the high-risk B* 3802. The presence of one or more of the six protective factors has a frequency of 58.98% within the control group and 34.83% within the NPC patients. Together, these protective factors delivered a combined OR of 0.37(P<0.0001). NPC susceptibility, on the other hand, associates most strongly with certain allele combinations, as opposed to single alleles, with the exception of the A* 0206 effect. Ind ividual positive for any of the five high-risk factors accounted for 50.08 and 73.03% of the controls and cases, respectively. These high-risk factors showed individual ORs between 2.05 and 3.56 and a collective OR of 2.70(P<0.0001).

On tne basis of analyses shown, HLA haplotypes were classified as NPC protective(P), susceptible(S), and neutral(N), generating six genotypes. Fig. 2 shows the ORs of the six genotypes for NPC development.

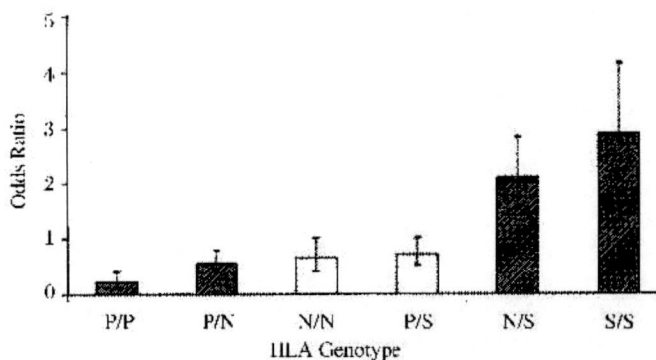

P: protective haplotype; S: susceptible haplotype; N: neutral haplotype.
Columns with a pattern indicate ORs with P values <0.05
Fig. 2 ORs of HLA genotypes for NPC development

Interestingly, neither the protective nor the susceptible genotypes seemed dominant over the other. The exact values are presented in Supplementary Tab. 5. The ORs of the remaining genotypes were distributed in a manner that was expected given that the protective and susceptible genotypes were defined in this same cohort. The validity of this scheme will be particularly interesting to test in an independent cohort.

Tab. 5 Gender and age of NPC patients and EBV-IgA/VCA positive and negative controls

	NPC patients	Controls	
		EBV-IgA/VCA positive	EBV-IgA/VCA negative
	N＝356	N＝287	N＝342
Male/female	237/119	141/146	129/213
(％male)	(67％)	(49％)	(37％)
Age	50.09±10.83	45.69±8.90	46.87±10.24
EBV-IgA/VCA	95.50％	100％	0％

Abbreviations: EBV, Epstein-Barr virus; NPC, nasopharyngeal carcinoma.

The influence of HLA genotypes on NPC risk was analyzed by comparing all individual genotypes in HLA-A and-B loci separately and the compound genotypes of HLA-A and B. Two HLA-A, six HLA-B genotypes and six HLA-A-B compound genotypes were significantly associated with either elevated NPC risk or protection. These genotypes all involve at least one allele showing a higher risk or protection for the disease.

DISCUSSION

Southern China has a disproportionally high incidence of NPC compared with other parts of the world. The study population from Wuzhou City of Guangxi Province in Southern China holds, perhaps, the highest recorded NPC incidence.[9,10] Apart from unique environmental factors(mainly traditional diet), our data support a role for genetic predisposition contributing to the high-disease incidence. The results from this study confirm and extend previously reported HLA, and NPC associations in Southern Chinese populations,[12-14,19] such as the protective effect associated with HLA-A* 1101 and susceptibility effects associated with B* 0207, A* 3303, and B* 5801. This study provides further insights into the nature of the HLA association with NPC, such as the observation that the dominant A* 11 protection can be entirely attributed to the major subtype A* 1101. The other A* 11 subtype detected in this population, A* 1102, did not show any protective effect even though the two A* 11 subtypes differ by only a single amino acid in position 19 outside of the peptide-binding groove.

Our stratified analyses demonstrated that a proportion of the HLA-associated NPC susceptibility is likely to be haplotype-dependent in this cohort(Tab. 3). In earlier cohort studies from Southern China[13] and Taiwan,[14] the A* 0207-B* 4601 allele combination was consistently associated with a high-NPC risk, but there are contradictory reports on whether the two alleles have independent effects. In our study cohort, two major high-risk HLA-A/B allele combinations, A* 0207-B* 4601 and A* 3303-B* 5801, were identified. Patients with either of these two allele combinations accounted for half of the NPC cohort and susceptibility conferred by these HLA-A/B combinations was strictly dependent on the presence of both alleles. The alleles comprising both pairs are in strong LD, forming the two most common HLA-A/B haplotypes in the Guangxi population.

Haplotype-dependent disease associations may indicate one of the two possibilities:(1)the two alleles on the haplotype are behaving in an epistatic manner to reach functional synergy or(2) the disease-associated HLA haplotype is tracking an unidentified disease locus present on that specific haplotype. An example of the former is that the structural stability of the HLA-DQ αβ dimer is affected by the type of DQA and DQB alleles carried on HLA haplotypes, which in turn influences the risk of insulin-dependent diabetes mellitus(IDDM)[20]. Functional synergy between HLA-A and -B molecule and any potential clinical relevance such synergy may have, however, are yet to be established. In terms of the alternative HLA marker model, there are no data that unequivocally support or refute the hypothesis in NPC studies, despite efforts to identify non-HLA disease genes in the extended MHC region[21,22]. Still, direct involvement of HLA molecules in NPC pathogenesis, including that involving the causative EBV infection, also lacks functional data support. Interpretations of the present results tend to support the locus tracking hypothesis in that there is evidence for(1)a lack of HLA association with the occurrence of IgA antibodies to EBV IgA/VCA, a well-known precursor of NPC,(2)haplotype-dependent but allele-independent disease susceptibility, and(3)the lack of association of A* 1102 despite its identical peptide-binding structure sbared with the well-documented protective A* 1101 allele[14]. Furthermore, distinct population-specific HLA alleles associate with susceptibility to NPC, which is unexpected if HLA is directly involved in disease pathogenesis.

In contrast to the haplotype-dependent but allele-independent susceptibility exhlited by the two major high-risk haplotypes A* 0207-B* 4601 and A* 3303-B* 5801, the dominant protective effect conferred by A* 1101 did not show a clear haplotypic dependence. In fact, most A* 1101-linked A/B haplotypes showed a trend of underrepresentation in the case group except the one linked with the susceptible B* 3802. A* 1101 seems to protect against other viral infections as well. For example, A*1101 may confer protection against AIDS through restriction of immunodominant HIV peptide,[23,24] but the structural and functional basis for its direct involvement in NPC pathogenesis has not been thoroughly explored. The detected allele and haplotype associations with NPC seem to be independent of HLA genotypes as genotypes showing significant ORs are essentially those with least two copies of NPC-associated alleles or haplotypes. Also, no particular genotypes showed stronger association than individual alleles or haplotypes.

Another noteworthy HLA association observed in the Guangxi NPC cohort is an opportune'complete'protection of B*27 against disease development. B*27 was detected with a typical frequency in the control group (1.59%), but was completely absent in the patient group(OR=0.04, P=0.001). Earlier cohort studies from Southern China and Taiwan have also detected B*27 as a low-risk allele though the protection was never'complete'[14,19,25]. B*27 is well known for its high-risk association with the inflammatory autoimmune disease ankylosing spondylitis and it confers protection against AIDS progression apparently through its peptide-binding properties for immunodominant HIV epitopes.[26] Perhaps B*27 is also involved in EBV-related pathogenesis, impacting the risk of NPC development. Given the low frequency of B*27 in the study population, however, the absence of B*27 in the patient group should be confirmed in larger replication cohort studies.

The overall HLA profile of a population is likely to influence the incidence of HLA-associated diseases. An example is the correlation between the rates of IDDM incidence and the frequency distribution of the IDDM associated HLA-DQ and DR alleles in world populations[27] The NPC incidence in a population may also correlate positively witn the frequencies of NPC-susceptible HLA alleles and haplotypes of the population. The two dominant susceptible HLA haplotypes, A*0207-B*4601 and A*3303-B*5801, are the two most common HLA-A/B haplotypes in Guangxi and together they account for 20% of the total haplotype frequency of the study Wuznou population, which is one of the highest in Far East Asian populations. Overall, the susceptible HLA factors were found in about half of the individuals in the Wuzhou population, which is also one of the highest. Therefore, the unusually high presence of NPC-associated HLA alleles and haplotypes may partly explain the disproportionally high-NPC incidence in Southern China and Southeast Asia.

MATERIALS AND METHODS

Study cohorts

NPC cases and controls were recruited from Wuzhou City and Cangwu County of Guangxi Province.[10] All study subjects were of Han ethnic origin. Informed consent was obtained from all study participants. An effort was made to enroll triads consisting of a proband(either NPC patient or NPC-free but EBV-IgA/VCA antibody positive), an unaffected spouse and an adult child. The case group included 356 unrelated patients with biopsy-confirmed NPC. The mean age was 50.1 years(range 19-80), 95.5% of them being EBV-IgA/VCA antibody positive. Two groups of control were the case's spouse or geographically matched residents who were NPC free at the time of study enrollment. An antibody to EBV capsid antigen(EBV-IgA/VCA) were confirmed by serologic testing at the time of study enrollment. One group was positive(n=287) and the other negative(n=342) for the EBV-IgA/VCA antibody. The mean age was 45.7 and 46.9, respectively, for the antibody positive and negative groups. The controls were matched to the cases by age, ethnicity, and geographic residence(Tab. 5). In addition, 422 adult children of the study subjects in the case and control groups were recruited to allow elucidation of HLA haplotypes, but they were excluded in all other analyses.

Detection of EBV-IgA/VCA antibody

The presence of the EBV-IgA/VCA antibody was detected using the immunoperoxidase assay as described earlier.[28] EBV positive B95-8 cells fixed on slides were incubated with multiple dilutions of the testing serum followed by incubation with antihuman IgA horseradish peroxidase and staining with diaminobenzidine. Testing sera with a staining titer of 1:10 or higher dilution were considered positive for the EBV-IgA/VCA antibody.

HLA typing

HLA class I alleles were characterized using a PCR-SSOP(sequence-specific oligonucleotide probe)typing protocol developed by the 13th International histocompatibility Workshop.[29] Briefly, the gene fragment spanning exon 2, intron 2, and exon 3 was amplified using locusspecific primers for HLA-A, -B, and -C separately. The PCR products were immobilized on nylon membranes and hybridized with a panel of p^{32}-labeled oligonucleotide(19 mers)matching all known sequence variations of the HLA genes. Typing results were interpreted by SSOP hybridization patterns based on sequences of known HLA alleles. Typing ambiguities were resolved by sequencing exons 2 and 3 completely. For sequencing analysis, the PCR product of HLA-A, -B, or -C was used as the template for the sequencing reaction. For each of the HLA genes, two sequencing reactions(one for exon 2 and one for exon 3) were performed using exon-specific sequencing primers. The sequencing analysis was per formed using the ABI Big Dye Terminator Cycle Sequencing Kit and AB13730×1 DNA analyzer(Applied Biosystems, Foster City, CA,

USA). HLA alleles were assigned on the basis of the sequence database of known alleles with the help of the AS-SIGN software developed by Conexio Genomies(Conexio Genomics, Perth City, WA, Australia). Ambiguous heterozygous genotypes were resolved by additional PCR and sequencing procedures using allele-specific PCR primers to selectively amplify only one of the two alleles.

Statistical analyses

HLA allele frequeneies were calculated based on observed genotypes, and HLA-A and -B haplotype frequencies were estimated using one of the two methods: (1) unambiguous assignment based on familial segregation for the cases and controls using recruited spouse and child genotype data or(2)indirect assignment based on maximum likelihood estimation for the study subjects without recruited family members. For the latter, the haplotypic analysis was performed using the BLOCKHEAD genetic analysis software developed by George Nelson in the Laboratory of Genomic Diversity, National Cancer Institute.

The effect of HLA alleles on the development of NPC and EBV-IgA/VCA antibody was evaluated by computing ORs and 95% confidence intervals as well as exact P-values using the FREQ procedure of the SAS 9. 1 software(The SAS Institute, NC, USA). A correction of 0. 5 was applied on every cell of the 2×2 table that contains a zero. The analyses were performed at four-digit and two-digit resolution levels separately. P-value was calculated by X^2-test for eaeh allele and was corrected by multiplying the number of all detected alleles. Significance was considered at $P < 0.05$. Both uncorrected and corrected P-values were presented in our tables. Stratified analyses were applied to evaluate the effect of haplotypes of HLA-A and -B that contained alleles showing individual significant associations with NPC risk.

ACKNOWLEDGEMENTS

This project has been funded in whole or in part with federal funds from the National Cancer Institute, National Institutes of Health, under Contract No. HHSN261200800001E. The content of this publication does not necessarily reflect the views or policies of the Department of Health and Human Services, nor does mention of trade names, commercial products, or organizations imply endorsement by the US Government. This Research was supported in part by the Intramural Research Program of the NIH, National Cancer Institute, Center for Cancer Research.

REFERENCES

[1] Brown TM, Heath CW, Lang RM, et al. Nasopharyngeal cancer in Bermuda. Cancer, 1976, 37:1464-1468.

[2] Yu MC, Garabrant DH, Huang TB, et al. Occupational and other non-dietary risk factors for nasopharyngeal carcinoma in Guangzhou, China. Int J Cancer, 1990, 45:1033-1039.

[3] Guo X, Johnson RC, Deng H, et al. Evaluation of non-viral risk factors for nasopharyngeal carcinoma in a high-risk population of Southern China. Int J Cancer, 2009, 124:2942-2947.

[4] Coffin CM, Rich SS, Dehner LP. Familial aggregation of nasopharyngeal carcinoma and other malignancies. A clinicopathologic description. Cancer, 1991, 68:1323-1328.

[5] Jeannel D, Hubert A, de Vlathaire F, et al. Diet, living conditions and nasopharyngeal carcinoma in Tunisia-a case-control study. Int I Cancer, 1990, 46:421-425.

[6] Laramore GE, Clubb B, Quick C, el al. Nasopharyngeal carcinoma in Saudi Arabia: a retro spective study of 166 cases treated with curative intent. Int J Radiat Oncol Biof Phtls, 1988, 15:1119-1127.

[7] Johansen LV, Mestre M, Overgaard J. Carcinoma of the nasopharynx: analysis of treatment results in 167 consecutively admitted patients. Head Neck, 1992, 14:200-207.

[8] Lee AW, Foo W, Mang O. Changing epidemiology of nasopharyngeal carcinoma in Hong Kong over a 20-year period(1980-99): an encouraging reduction in both incidence and mortality. Int Cancer, 2003, 103:680-685.

[9] Lu SJ, Day NE, Degos L, et al. Linkage of a nasopharyngeal carcinoma susceptibility locus to the HLA region. Nature, 1990, 346:470-471.

[10] Guo XC, Scott K, Liu Y, et al. Genetic factors leading to chronic Epstein-Barr virus infection and nasopnaryngeal carcinoma in South East China: study design, methods and feasibility. Hum Genomics, 2006, 2:365-375.

[11] Burt RD, Vaughan TL, McKnight B, et al. Associations between human leukocyte antigen type and nasopharyngeal carcinoma in Caucasians in the United States. Cancer Epidemiof Biomarkers Prey, 1996, 5:879-887.

[12] Simons MJ, Wee GB, Chan SH, et al. Immunogenetic aspects of nasopharyngeal carcinoma(NPC) III. HL-a type as a genetic marker of NPC premsposition to test the hypothesis that Epstein-Barr virus is an etiological factor in NPC. IARC Sci Publ, 1975: 249-258.

[13] Hu SP, Day NE, Li DR, et al. Further evidence for an HLA-related recessive mutation in nasopnaryngeal carcinoma among the Chinese. BR J Cancer, 2005, 92:967-970.

[14] Hildesheim A, Apple RJ, Chen CJ, et al. Association Of HLA class I and II alleles and extended haplotypes with nasopharyngeal carcinoma in Taiwan. J Natl Cancer Inst, 2002, 94:1780-1789.

[15] Chan SH, Day NE, Kunaratnam N, et al. HLA and nasopharyngeal carcinoma in Chinese-a further study. Int J Cancer, 1983, 32:171-176.

[16] Henle G, Henle W. Epstein-Barr virus-specific IgA serum antibodies as an outstanding feature of nasopharyngeal carcinoma. Int J Cancer,1976, 17:1-7.

[17] Zeng Y, Zhang LG, Li HY, et al. Serological mass survey for early detection of nasopharyngeal carcinoma in Wuzhou City, China. lnt J Cancer,1982, 29:139-141.

[18] Zeng Y, Zhang LG, Wu YC, et al. Prospective studies on nasopharyngeal carcinoma in EpsteinBarr virus lgA/VCA antibody-positive persons in Wuzhou City, China. Int J Cancer, 1985,36:545-547.

[19] Wu SB, Hwang SJ, Chang AS, et al. Human leukocyte antigen(HLA)frequency among patients with nasopharyngeal carcinoma in Taiwan. Anticancer Res, 1989, 9:1649-1653.

[20] Kwok WW, Schwarz D. Nepom BS, et al. HLA -DQ molecules from alpha-beta heterodimers of mixed allotype. J Immunol, 1988, 141:3123-3127.

[21] Lu CC, Chen Jc, Tsai ST, et al. Nasopharyngeal carcinoma-susceptibility locus is localized to a 132 kb segment containing HLA-A using high-resolution microsatellite mapping. Int J Cancer, 2005, 115:742-746.

[22] Ooi EE, Ren EC, Chan SH. Association between microsatellites within the human MHC and nasopharyngeal carcinoma, Int J Cancer, 1997, 74:229-232.

[23] Beyrer C, Artenstein AW. Rugpao S, et al. Epidemiologic and biologic characterization of a cohort of human immunodeficiency virus type 1 highly exposed, persistently seronegative female sex workers in northern Thailand. Chiang Mai HEPS Working Group. J Infect Dis, 1999, 179:59-67.

[24] Fukada K, Tomiyama H, Chujoh Y, et al. HLA-A∗1101-restricted cytotoxic T lymphocyte recognition for a novel epitope derived from the HIV-1 Env protein. Aids, 1999, 13:2597-2599.

[25] Yu MC, Huang TB, Henderson BE. Diet and nasopharyngeal carcinoma: a case-control study in Guangzhou, China. Int J Cancer, 1989, 43:1077-1082.

[26] Gao X, Bashirova A, Iversen AK, et al. AIDS restriction HLA allotypes target distinct intervals of HIV-1 pathogenesis. Nat Med, 2005, 11:1290-1292.

[27] Bao MZ, Wang JX, Dorman JS, et al. HLADQ beta non ASP-57 allele and incidence of diabetes in China and the USA. Lancet 1989, 2:497-498.

[28] Cevenini R, Donati M, Rumpianesi F, et al. An immunoperoxidase assay for the detection of specific IgA antibody in Epstein-Barr vieua infections. J Clin Pathol, 1984, 37:440-443.

[29] Gao X, Nelson GW, Karacki P, et al. Effect of a single amino acid change in MHC class I molecules on the rate of progression to AIDS. N Engl J Med, 2001, 344:1668-1675.

[In《Genes and immunity》2010:1-9]

The Principal Genetic Determinants for Nasopharyngeal Carcinoma in China Involve the HLA Class I Antigen Recognition Groove

Minzhong Tang[1,2,3], James A. Lautenberger[4], Xiaojiang Gao[5,6], Efe Sezgin[2], Sher L. Hendrickson[7], Jennifer L. Troyer[8], Victor A. David[2], Li Guan[8], Carl E. Mcintosh[8], Xiuchan Guo[8,9], Yuming Zheng[3], Jian Liao[10], Hong Deng[3], Michael Malasky[8], Bailey Kessing[4], Cheryl A. Winkler[8], Mary Carrington[5], Guy dé The[11], Yi Zeng[1,9*], Stephen J. O'Brien[2*]

1 College of Life Science and Bio-Engineering, Beijing University of Technology, Beijing, China, 2 Laboratory of Genomic Diversity, National Cancer Institute, Frederick, Maryland, United States of America, 3 Wuzhou Health System Key Laboratory for Nasopharyngeal Carcinoma Etiology and Molecular Mechanism, Wuzhou Red Cross Hospital, Guangxi, China, 4 BSP-CCR Genetics Core, Frederick National Laboratory for Cancer Research, Frederick, Maryland, United States of America, 5 Cancer and Inflammation Program, Laboratory of Experimental Immunology, SAIC-Frederick, Frederick National Lab, Frederick, Maryland United States of America, 6 Ragon Institute of MGH, MIT, and Harvard, Boston, Massachusetts, United States of America, 7 Department of Biology, Shepherd University, Shepherdstown, West Virginia, United States of America, 8 Laboratory of Genomic Diversity, SAIC-Frederick, NCI-Frederick, Frederick, Maryland, United States of America, 9 State Key Laboratory for Infectious Diseases Prevention and Control, Institute for Viral Disease Control and Prevention, Chinese Center for Disease Control and Prevention, Beijing, China, 10 Department of Epidemiology, Cangwu Institute for Nasopharyngeal Carcinoma Control and Prevention, Guangxi, China, 11 Oncogenic Virus Epidemiology and Pathophysiology, Institute Pasteur, Paris, France

[ABSTRACT] Nasopharyngeal carcinoma(NPC)is an epithelial malignancy facilitated by Epstein-Barr Virus infection. Here we resolve the major genetic influences for NPC incidence using a genome-wide association study(GWAS), independent cohort replication, and high-resolution molecular HLA class I gene typing including 4,055 study participants from the Guangxi Zhuang Autonomous Region and Guangdong province of southern China. We detect and replicate strong association signals involving SNPs, HLA alleles, and amino acid(aa)variants across the major histocompatibility complex-HLA-A, HLA-B, and HLA-C class I genes($P_{HLA-A-aa-site-62} = 7.4 \times 10^{-29}$; $P_{HLA-B-aa-site-116} = 6.5 \times 10^{-19}$; $P_{HLA-C-aa-site-156} = 6.8 \times 10^{-8}$ respectively). Over 250 NPC-HLA associated variants within HLA were analyzed in concert to resolve separate and largely independent HLA-A-B, and -C gene influences. Multivariate logistical regression analysis collapsed significant associations in adjacent genes spanning 500kb(OR2H1, GABBR1, HLA-F, and HCG9)as proxies for peptide binding motifs carried by HLA-A* 11 : 01. A similar analysis resolved an independent association signal driven by HLA-B* 13 : 01, B* 38 : 02, and B* 55 : 02 alleles together. NPC resistance alleles carrying the strongly associated amino acid variants implicate specific class I peptide recognition motifs in HLA-A and -B peptide binding groove as conferring strong genetic influence on the development of NPC in China.

Citation: Tang M, Lautenberger JA, Gao X, Sezgin E, Hendrickson SL, et al.(2012)The Principal Genetic Determinants for Nasopharyngeal Carcinoma in China Involve the HLA Class I Antigen Recognition Groove. PLoS Genet 8 (11): e1003103, doi:10. 1371/journal.pgen. 1003103

Editor: Marshall S. Horwitz, University of Washington, United States of America

Received July 7, 2012; Accepted September 19, 2012; Published November 29, 2012

Funding: This project has been funded in whole or in part with federal funds from the Frederick National Laboratory for Cancer Research, National Institutes of Health, under contract HHSN261200800001E, N01-CO-12400; Guangxi science and technology grant, China(114003A-49); and Wuzhou science and technology grant, China(201102062). The funders had no role in study design, data collection and analysis, decision to publish, or preparation of the manuscript.

Competing Interests: The authors have declared that no competing interests exist.

* E-mail: zengy@public.bta.net.cn(Y Zeng); Igdchief@gmail.com(SJ O'Brien)

INTRODUCTION

Nasopharyngeal carcinoma(NPC)is an epithelial malignancy with highly variable incidence rates around the world. An estimated 84,400 incident cases of NPC and 51,600 deaths occurred in 2008 with the highest incidence in South-Eastern Asia, relative to the Americas, Europe, Africa, and Central and Eastern Asia[1]. An early indicator of NPC development is the occurrence of immunoglobulin(Ig) A antibodies to Epstein-Barr virus(EBV) capsid antigens(EBV-IgA/VCA).[2,3] NPC incidence for individuals expressing IgA/VCA antibodies were 31.7 times higher than the incidence in the age matched general population.[4] Linkage and family studies indicated that genetic predisposition also plays an important role in NPC onset and susceptibility.[5,6] Among host genetic markers implicated as associated with NPC, the highly variable class I human leukocyte antigen(HLA) genes on chromosome 6(6p21.3) have shown a strong and consistent association with NPC risk.[7,8,9,10,11,12,13]_ENREF_7 HLA class I association studies across mainland China[11,13], Taiwan[10,12], and Singapore[8] have consistently demonstrated that HLA-A* 11 and B* 13 are associated with NPC resistance, while A* 02(A* 02:07), A* 33, B* 46 and B* 58 are associated with increased NPC susceptibility(Tab. S1). Genome-wide association studies(GWAS) have been applied to numerous complex diseases to implicate common risk variants through well powered genetic studies[14,15,16]. Recent GWAS also affirmed a strong HLA influence on NPC incidence and implicated four additional nonHLA genes, however extensive linkage disequilibrium across the gene dense HLA region have confounded identification of the causal association gene(s).[17,18,19]

To refine and extend these reports, we explore here the operative factors of genetic association for this disease in a comprehensive four step study utilizing: 1) A GWAS utilizing 591,458 SNPs resolved by Affymetrix 6.0 genotyping platform to identify gene regions associated with NPC; 2) SNP genotyping to replicate the top signals in a second independent NPC cohort; 3) High resolution HLA molecular genotyping to identify specific alleles and haplotypes associated with NPC; and 4) Amino acid variant analysis to fine map the major genetic determinants associated with this disease. The analyses demonstrates that two independent association signals, specifying peptide binding grove motifs in HLA-A and in HLA -B drive the signals tracked by scores of SNP and amino acid variants that are association proxies for the HLA class I NPC association.

Author Summary

NPC is a deadly throat cancer in China that is dependent on EBV infection. Here, we performed a 1 M SNP genomewide association study using a large cohort of Chinese study participants at risk for NPC. Although several putative gene regions show significant associations, the strongest statistical signals involved scores of variants within the HLA region on chromosome 6. HLA poses a formidable association-genetics challenge because of extensive linkage disequilibrium, rather low allele frequencies, and multiple physically close interacting genes of diverse function. We examined over 250 NPC-HLA associated variants detected with sequence-based nucleotide alleles and amino acid variants. The multiple associations were collapsed to implicate causal signals by multivariate logistical regression to resolve allele association interaction. One operative variant was identified as the HLA-A* 11:01 allele motif, specifically in the peptide binding groove, which recognizes invading antigens; a second involved two aa sites with HLA-B tracking B* 13:01 and B* 55:02 alleles. We synthesize these new and previous discoveries to help resolve the important gene influences on this disease.

RESULTS

We performed a GWAS with 1104 southern Chinese individuals from NPC-phase II study cohorts[20,21] (See Materials and Methods)using the Affymetrix Genome-Wide SNP 6.0 genotyping platform. After SNP-and sample-base quality control(Tab. S2), 591, 458 SNPs genotyped in 1043 study participants(567 cases and 476 controls; Tab. S3, line I). Principal components analysis confirmed that all samples came from individuals of Southern Chinese ancestry(Figs. S1, S2, S3, S4, S5). A quantile-quantile plot of the observed p-values showed a clear deviation from the null distribution which suggested that the most significant lower pvalues are smaller than those expected by chance and likely reflect genetic association(Fig. S6). The GWAS allele associations suggested a strong influence in the HLA-A region of chromosome 6 and weaker signals on chromosome 16 and 17(Fig. 1A).

Twenty-four SNPs(Tab. S4)with p-values less than 5×10^{-5} in 16 association tests(Tab. S5)and sixteen previous GWAS reported NPC associated SNPs (Tab. S6) and were selected for replication. Replication SNP genotyping was conducted in an independent Chinese cohort that included 356 NPC cases and 629 controls(Tab. S3, line II). Six of 40 SNPs that showed genomewide significant NPC association and replication were within 500 kb of each other in the MHC region of chromosome 6 (Tab. 1, Tab. S7). The most significant SNP rs417162 ($P_{combined} = 1.1 \times 10^{-11}$, OR=0.61)is located within the HLA-A locus, while four additional replicated SNPs were within adjacent genes, GABBR1 and HCG9.

A fine-grain view of the pattern of GWAS SNPs around the HLA-A locus is illustrated in Fig. 1B. An extensive cluster of associated HLA-A region SNPs that approach or exceed genomewide association threshold p-values ($P < 10^{-8}$)is apparent within 500 kb including associations in the adjacent HCG9 and GABBR1 genes(Fig. 1C). The strong linkage disequilibrium(LD)across the HLA region is well known, which raises the question whether these HLA region associations represent single, multiple independent, or LD-proxy driven associations.

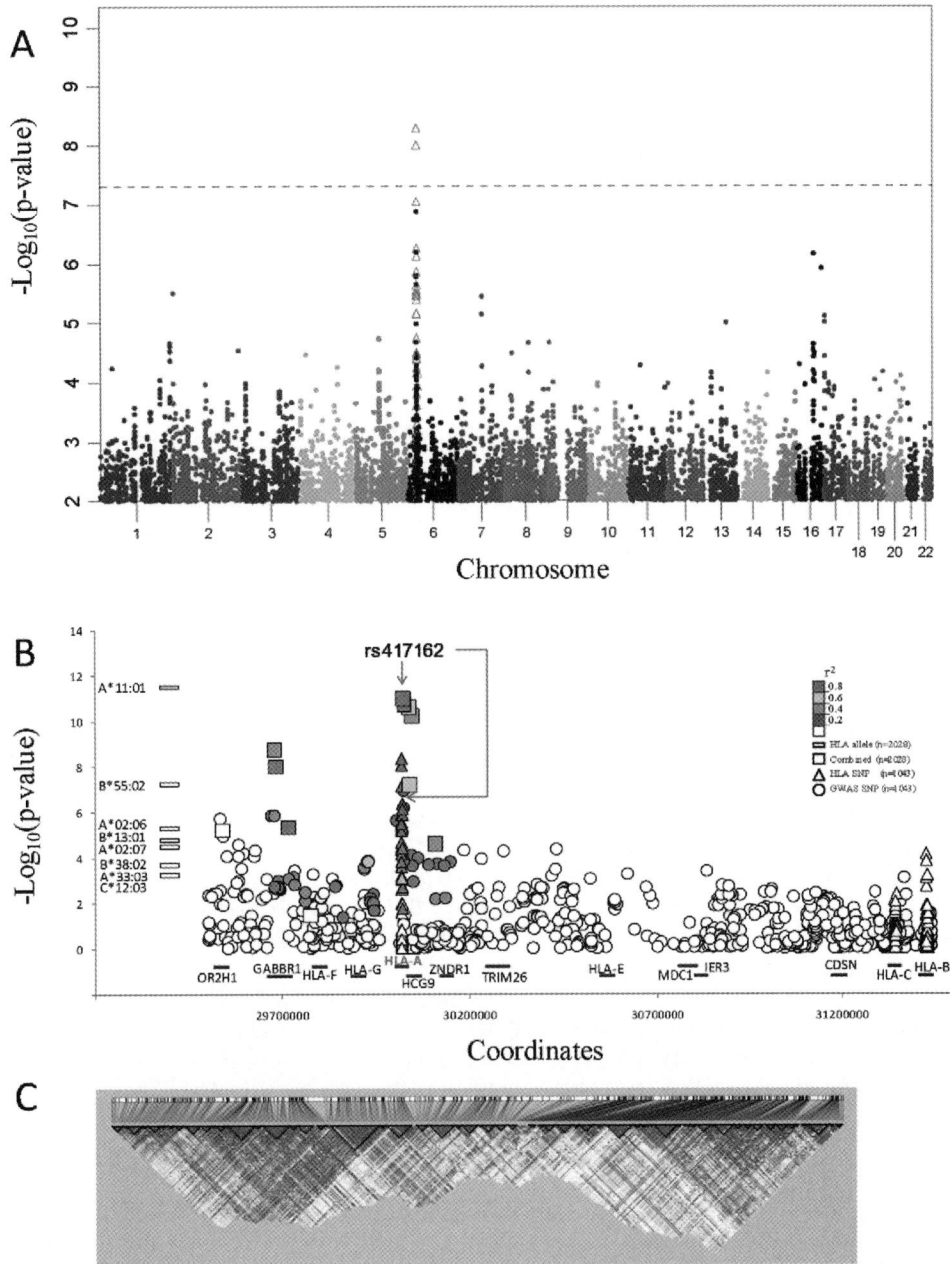

Fig. 1 NPC associations of GWAS and Taqman validation. A.) Manhattan plot of GWAS P value association results of 591, 458 SNP allele genotypes versus chromosome coordinate position(N＝1043 study participants; Row I in Tab. S3). Association p-values(-$\log_{10}$ transformed)are calculated by logistic regression in additive logistic model and plotted by genomic position. Association p-values for HLA SNP that were assessed by HLA sequence base typing for the same 1043 individuals are indicated by open red triangles(see text). B.) NPC association signal for significant HLA alleles (left)and included SNP variants on Chromosome 6. The -$\log_{10}$ p values, calculated with the logistic regression model, in GWAS and combined association tests are shown, SNPs are ordered according to the location on chromosome 6 HLA-A region. Color coded indicate the LD value(r^2)of each variant with the most significant SNP rs417162. C.) Disequilibrium coefficient values for SNPs genotyped in the HLA region for NPC GWAS(N＝1043), generated with the use of Haploview software.

doi: 10.1371/journal.pgen.1003103.g001

Tab. 1 GWAS and validation of SNPs association data in two independent NPC cohorts.

SNP name	Gene	Chr.	MA[†]	GWAS(N=1,043)			Validation(N=985)			Combined(N=2,028)	
				MAF[‡]	P-value	OR(95% CI)	MAF	P-value	OR(95% CI)	P-value	OR(95% CI)
rs417162	HLA-A	6	C	0.26/ 0.37	1.13E-07	0.58 (0.48-0.71)	0.26/ 0.35	3.75E-05	0.63 (0.50-0.78)	1.05E-11	0.63 (0.53-0.75)
rs2517713*	HLA-A	6	G	0.26/ 0.37	3.03E-07	0.57 (0.46-0.71)	0.26/ 0.35	2.61E-05	0.62 (0.50-0.78)	1.63E-11	0.60 (0.52-0.70)
rs9260734*	HCG9	6	A	0.22/ 0.32	5.90E-07	0.57 (0.45-0.71)	0.21/ 0.32	1.32E-05	0.59 (0.47-0.75)	2.63E-11	0.59 (0.50-0.69)
rs5009448*	HCG9	6	T	0.26/ 0.35	1.09E-05	0.63 (0.51-0.77)	0.24/ 0.35	4.43E-07	0.56 (0.45-0.70)	6.40E-11	0.61 (0.53-0.71)
rs2267633	GABBR1	6	G	0.17/ 0.26	1.43E-06	0.58 (0.47-0.73)	0.17/ 0.24	2.77E-04	0.63 (0.49-0.81)	1.89E-09	0.61 (0.52-0.72)
rs29230*	GABBR1	6	C	0.17/ 0.25	2.37E-05	0.60 (0.47-0.76)	0.17/ 0.24	6.02E-04	0.65 (0.50-0.83)	9.48E-09	0.61 (0.52-0.72)

*：Replication SNPs that not included in Affymetrix Genome-Wide SNP Array；

†：MA, Minor allele；

‡：MAF, Minor allele frequencies；

doi：10.1371/journal.pgen.1003103.t001

To characterize the HLA association with NPC in finer detail, high-resolution molecular HLA genotyping was performed on 4055 study participants; 1043 subjects in the discovery cohort, 985 subjects in the replication cohort, and 2027 subjects that comprise the remainder of cohort(Tab. S3).[20,21] NPC cases, controls with EBV-IgA/VCA positive, and controls with EBV-IgA/VCA negative were examined for association of HLA alleles and HLA haplotypes with NPC risk and EBV IgA/VCA antibody status. Three HLA alleles, A*11:01, B*38:02 and B*55:02 showed the most significant association with NPC($P=1.7\times10^{-19}$, $P=7.0\times10^{-11}$, and $P=1.6\times10^{-10}$ respectively; Tab. 2). In addition to the strong HLA-A and -B associations, there was a moderate association of HLA-C*12:02 allele as well($P=4.3\times10^{-5}$; Tab. 2). NPC associated HLA-A-B-C haplotypes which included HLA allele combinations from Tab. 2 were also apparent(Tab. S8).

Functional variation of different MHC molecules to bind peptides and activate effector cells in the immune system underlies their association with disease.[22,23]_ENREF_18 To identify the specific site driving the NPC HLA associations, HLA gene sequence was translated to identify amino acid variants using a web-based software of the Immunology Database and Analysis Portal(ImmPort)system[24]. Genetic association of 284 detected HLA amino acid variant within the three HLA class I genes implicated the most significant NPC association of glutamine (Gln, Q)at amino acid position 62 of HLA-A gene($P=1.2\times10^{-24}$, OR=0.59; Fig. 2A; Tab. S9 and S10)which marks HLA-A*11, however there are 25 additional amino acid sites I in HLA-A that also show exceed genome wide significance($P<$_ENREF_1810^{-8}; Fig. 2A). The HLA-B signal centered on amino acid Leucine(Leu, L)at amino acid position -16 and 116($P=1.7\times10^{-13}$ and 2.4×10^{-13}, OR=0.65 and 0.63; Tab. S10), which marks B*13:01 and B*55:02. A far less significant association was observed for the amino acid residue Tryptophan (Trp, W)at amino acid position 156 for HLA-C($P=1.4\times10^{-9}$, OR=0.47;). Amino acid residues that correspond to the antigenic peptide binding groove residues showed the strongest association(See color code in Fig. 2A-2C)suggesting that the peptide binding groove and function are major genetic factors for NPC risk.

Tab. 2. Gene frequencies(%) of the HLA-A, -B, and -C alleles detected and association analysis(N=4,055).#

Allele Name	Amino Acid Binding Motifs*	Allele Frequencies			NPC vs. Control		NPC VS. EP. Controls		NPC VS. EN. Controls	
		NPC Patients (N=1405)	EP. Controls† (N=1288)	EN. Controls‡ (N=1362)	OR(95% CI)	P Value	OR(95% CI)	P Value	OR(95% CI)	P Value
HLA-A										
02:03§	.[LV]......[LI]	15.80(444)	10.87(280)	15.01(409)		Ns	1.52(1.29-1.79)	4.49E-07		Ns
02:06	.[VQ]......[VS]	2.62(139)	2.21(57)	3.01(82)		Ns	1.91(1.38-2.65)	1.00E-04		Ns
02:07	.[L-]......[VL]	16.48(463)	13.32(343)	11.56(315)	1.38(1.21-1.57)	1.52E-06		Ns	1.49(1.28-1.74)	3.98E-07
11:01	.[YT]......[K-]	20.25(569)	30.12(776)	29.11(793)	0.59(0.53-0.66)	1.72E-19	0.57(0.50-0.65)	1.43E-16	0.61(0.53-0.69)	3.13E-14
33:03	[DE].L......[R-]	17.69(497)	15.76(406)	12.37(337)	1.36(1.19-1.54)	3.14E-06		Ns	1.57(1.35-1.84)	1.01E-08
HLA-B										
13:01	.[-]......[-]	8.04(226)	12.27(316)	10.87(296)	0.66(0.56-0.77)	4.52E-07	0.62(0.51-0.74)	3.15E-07	0.71(0.59-0.86)	3.16E-04
27:04	R[R-]......[LF]	0.53(15)	0.97(25)	1.69(46)		Ns		Ns	0.31(0.17-0.55)	8.56E-05
38:02	.[-]......[-]	12.21(343)	6.83(176)	8.48(231)	1.67(1.43-1.94)	6.96E-11	1.88(1.55-2.28)	1.96E-10	1.51(1.26-1.80)	5.90E-06
46:01	.[MI]......[YF]	19.18(539)	17.97(463)	14.46(394)		Ns		Ns	1.39(1.21-1.60)	4.77E-06
55:02	.[P-]......[AV]	1.00(28)	3.38(75)	3.67(100)	0.27(0.18-0.40)	1.57E-10	0.28(0.18-0.43)	7.38E-09	0.26(0.17-0.40)	5.02E-10
58:01	.[TS]......[WF]	16.65(468)	15.49(399)	12.22(333)	1.47(1.26-1.71)	2.38E-04		Ns	1.43(1.23-1.67)	1.47E-06
HLA-C										
01:02		22.03(619)	21.35(550)	17.99(490)		Ns		Ns	1.28(1.12-1.46)	2.16E-04
03:02		16.37(460)	15.22(392)	11.97(326)	1.28(1.12-1.46)	2.05E-04		Ns	1.48(1.26-1.73)	1.30E-06
07:02		21.64(608)	16.89(435)	19.38(528)	1.25(1.11-1.40)	1.84E-04	1.37(1.19-1.58)	1.65E-05		Ns
12:02		0.93(26)	1.59(41)	2.83(77)	0.41(0.27-0.63)	4.28E-05		Ns	0.31(0.20-0.49)	4.14E-07
12:03		0.78(22)	2.14(55)	1.76(48)	0.41(0.25-0.65)	1.47E-04	0.37(0.22-0.62)	1.37E-04		Ns

*: Amino acid motifs from Lund et al., 2004.

†: EP. controls, the controls of NPC free and EBV IgA/VCA antibody positive.

‡: EN. controls, the controls of NPC free and EBV IgA/VCA antibody negative.

§: Allele also showed significant in the comparison of EP. controls VS. EN. controls, $P=7.81E-06$, OR=0.69(0.59-0.81).

#: A preliminary analysis of HLA association in phase I was previously reported(Tang et al., 2010). Now, HLA associations with phase I and phase II(See Materials and methods)are presented separately in Tab. S12.

doi: 10.1371/journal.pgen.1003103.t002

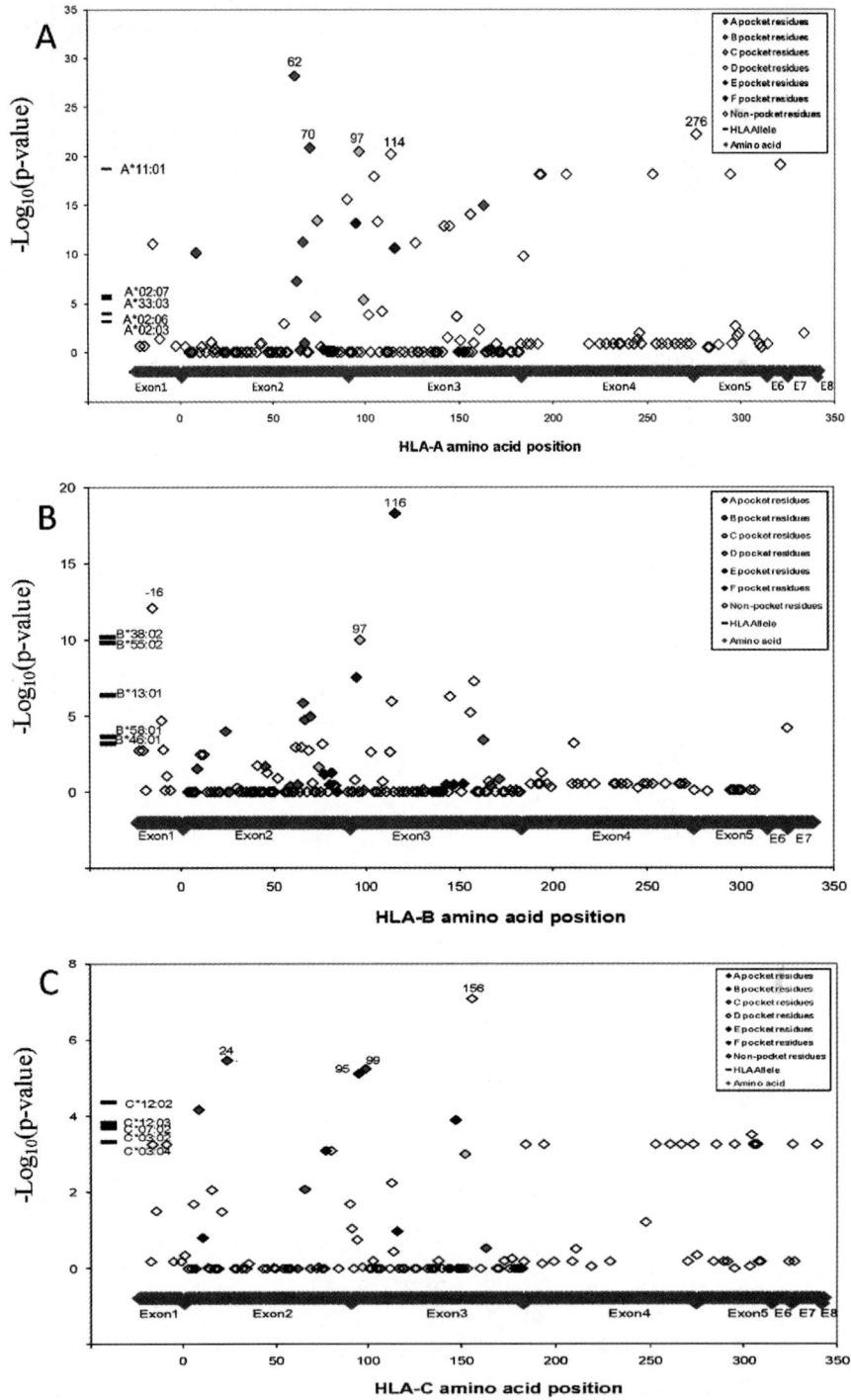

Fig. 2 NPC associations of HLA alleles and amino acid variants. A. NPC associations of alleles and amino acid variants at HLA-A locus; B. NPC associations of alleles and amino acid variants at HLA-B locus; C. NPC associations of alleles and amino acid variants at HLA-C locus. Genetic association of HLA alleles and amino acid sites were calculated(N=4055 study participants; Line V in Tab. S3). For amino acid positions with more than two alleles, p-value for the omnibus test that tests all amino acid alleles simultaneously(with>1 degrees of freedom)for association to control.

doi: 10. 1371/journal.pgen. 1003103.g002

Given the plethora and complexity of HLA genetic associations plus the extensive LD within HLA, we attempted to resolve which HLA region SNPs and aa-variants represent proxy variants for one or more functional sites(i.e. they were tracking by LD) and which represent independent(non-LD)association signals using a multivariate logistic regression analyses[25]. Strongly associated aa-variants(Fig. 2 and in Tabs. S9 and S10; e.g HLA-A-62Gln) were analyzed in a multivariate logistical regression analysis adjusting statistically for non-random influence of each of the adjacent aa-variants(Fig. 3; also in Tab. S11). A dramatic reduction of association p-value significance for the strongest HLA-A aa variant, HLA-A-62Gln, is observed when this model is adjusted for adjacent aa-variants within and about the HLA-A gene but are not diminished by adjusting for variants in HLA-B or HLA-C. Thus, we conclude that there is a single association signal in HLA-A tracked by several dozen proxy aa/SNP variants within the HLA-A region. When HLA-A*11:01 is the index allele, the extreme NPC association signal is diminished to 0. 1-0. 01 by HLA-A aa variants as well as each SNP in the genes adjacent to HLA-A locus(See Fig. 3B and HLA-A*11:01 column in Tab. S11). This multivariate dependence plus the knowledge that HLA-A*11:01 carries the five strongly significant associated aa variants (62Gln, 276Leu, 114Arg, 70Gln, and 97Ile) in the peptide binding groove and reaches the highest significance in allele level would support the conclusion that the causal association is driven by the HLA-A*11:01 allele(Tab. 2, Tab. S10, Fig. S7).

A multivariate logistical regression analysis for HLA-B variants indicates that HLA-B associations are independent from the HLA-A signals and driven by two amino acid sites in strong LD with each other(HLA-B; -16Leu and 116Leu; $P=1.7 \times 10^{-13}$ and 2.4×10^{-13})(Fig. 3C and Tab. S9). The most significant HLA-B signal is located at amino acid position 116(Fig. 2B). The amino acid variant HLA-B-116Leu is present in the two strongly associated protective HLA-B alleles B*13:01 and B*55:02, but the encoded amino acid in the associated suscetible allele HLA-B*38:02 is Phenylalanine(Tab. S9). It is also relevant that the same location of HLA-B amino acid position 116 has also been definitively implicated as the single aa site that drives high susceptibility of the HLA-B*35 association with very rapid AIDS progression in HIV-1 infected European Americans.[26,27] It seems that this variant influences HLA peptide repertoire recognition and/or presentation for both HIV and EBV infections. The amino acid substitution in the heavy chain at position 116 could abolish the ability of P9 picket of HLA-B*35:01 to bind tyrosine but preferentially accommodate smaller hydrophobic residues such as methionine, valine, or leucine at the carboxy-terminal anchor had been shown by peptide-binding assays.[28]

The HLA-C signal is ten logs weaker than HLA-A or HLA-B and is diminished slightly by adjusting for HLA-A or HLA-B variants(Fig. 3E, Tab. S11). Further, the most significant HLA-C alleles(HLA-C*03:02 and -C*12:02)track HLA-A and -B alleles in the haplotype analyses(Tab. S8), suggesting the HLA-C association are likely proxies of the stronger HLA-B and -A associations. We interpret these cumulative data as suggestive that there are two robust independent HLA association signals with NPC development: HLA-A including at least five amino acid position in 62Gln, 70Gln, 97Ile, 114Arg and 276Leu carried by HLA-A*11:01 and HLA-B including the -16Leu and 116Leubearing alleles.

Our GWAS analysis also provided an opportunity to inspect regions of the genome outside HLA that had been implicated in previous NPC studies. The results(Tab. S6 and Tab. 1) offer strong supportive confirmation of SNPs in the HLA-A gene region (including the adjacent HCG9, and GABBR1 genes)as suggested by previous GWAS.[18,19] However, our SNP replication(Tab. S6) and multivariate logistical regression analysis(Fig. 3; Tab. S11) indicate that all these associations are by and large proxies for the primary functional aa variants association in our cohort. We also replicated the TNFRSF19, MDS1-EV11, CDNK2A/2B gene associations[19] in our cohort($P=1.5 \times 10^{-5}$; 5.0×10^{-5} and 5.6×10^{-3} respectively)although these genes did not achieved genome wide significance(Tab. S6). The ITGA9 association reported by Ng et al[14] was not replicated in our cohort(Tab. S6).

DISCUSSION

We present and interpret a 1 M SNP GWAS, in subjects from Guangxi Zhuang Autonomous Region and Guangdong province of southern China, where perhaps the highest recorded NPC incidence has been found.[3,4,20,21] Multiple genome wide significant association signals were evident with the HLA gene region and in a few other chromosomal regions(Fig. 1A). Because the HLA region is complex and displays extennsive LD, we sought to resolve the causal association signals with several different approaches. These included replication in an independent cohort from the same area, sequence based gene typing of the HLA-A, -B and -C genes, and analysis of sequence based nucleotide alleles as well as 284 amino acid site variants across the HLA genes(Fig. 2). We compared association signals of SNPs, aa variants, HLA-alleles defined by molecular typing and associated HLA -A, -B and C haplotypes. To resolve the operative variants from proxies that track signals by LD, we enlisted a multivariate logistical regression of alleles and site variants with the strongest signals(Fig. 3, Tab. S11). Finally we revisited and attempted replication in our cohort reports from other NPC gene associations including GWAS recently published, [17,18,19] (TNFRSF19 -CHR 13, MDS1-EVI1-CHR3, and CDNK2A/2B-CHR 9; Tab. S6)affirming gene influence that are important in this disease.

In the present study, two independent powerful association signals within the HLA region were resolved for NPC, amidst a background of scores of adjacent associated LD-proxy variants. The first influence involved the HLA-A*11:01 allele sequence and function, specifically in the peptide binding groove, which recognizes invading antigens. This conclusion derives from several lines of evidence: 1) HLA-A*11:01 is a common allele in the populations($F=0.25$)and is the only"protective" allele with genome wide significant HLA-A signal(OR$=0.59$; $P=1.7 \times 10^{-19}$; Tab. 1)the strongest of all HLA alleles. 2) HLA-A*11:01 is included in the significantly associated protective HLA haplotypes(Tab. S8); 3) 100% of associated SNPs and aa variants about HLA-A, including those in adjacent genes, namely the HCG9, and GABBR1 loci, are proxies HLA-A*11:01(Fig. 3; Tab. S11); 4)

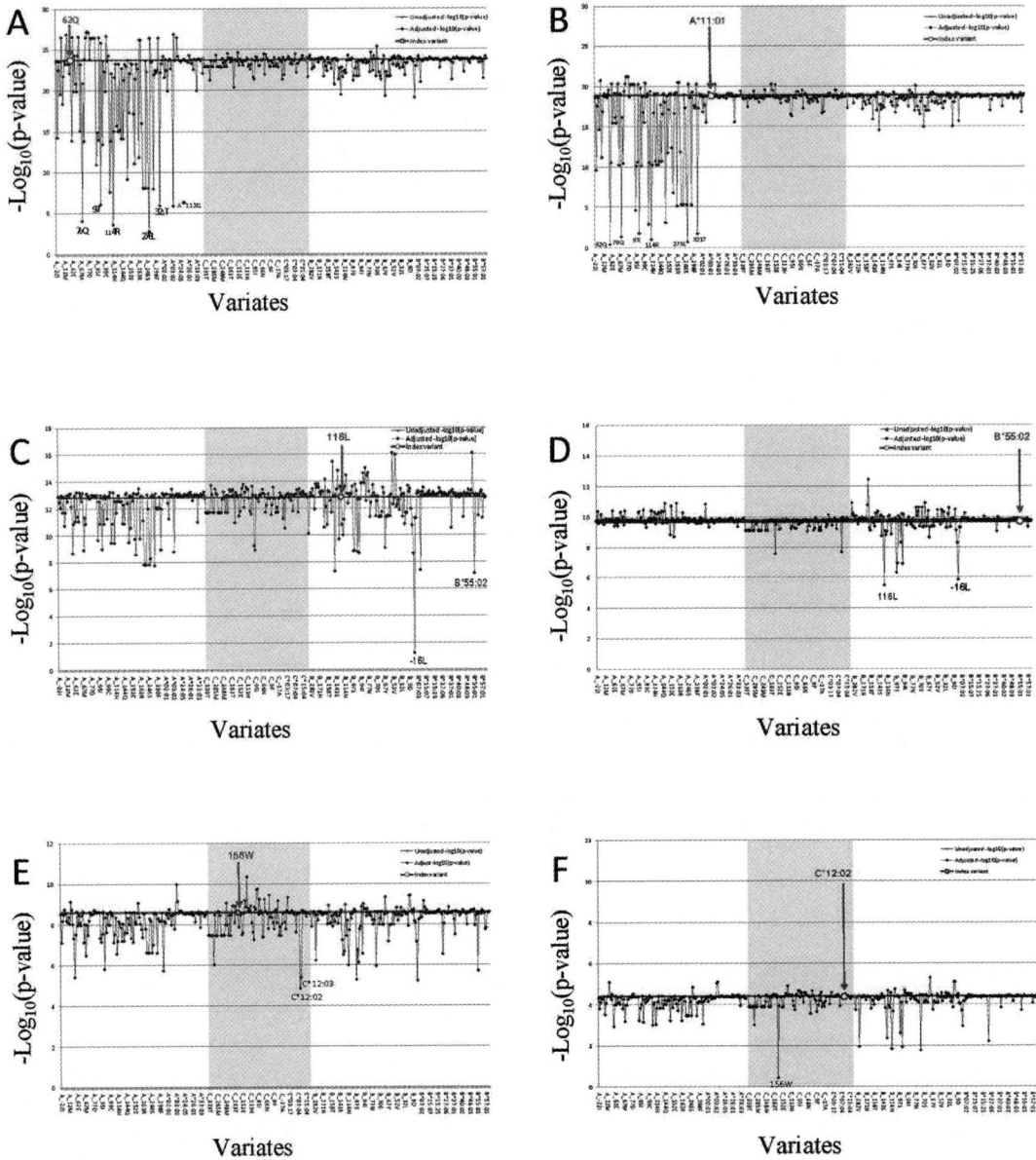

Fig. 3 Proxy variant analysis for the strongest aa-variants or HLA allele in HLA-A, in HLA-B, and in HLA-C. Genetic association of each HLA amino acid variant was calculated. Study participants in both phase I and phase II (N = 4055 study participants; Line V in Tab. S3). Multivariate conditional logistic regression analysis was performed to compute amino acid variants (A, C, and E) or HLA alleles (B, D, and F) association p-value. The HLA typing data set (N = 4055 study participants; Line V in Tab. S3) were used PLINK to examine the residual effect of index amino acid variant or HLA allele while using other amino acid variant or HLA allele as a covariate, and we adjusted the results for age and gender. The index amino acid variant or HLA allele was marked with bold red font. The red line indicated unadjusted $-\log_{10} p$ of index. Three HLA class I genes regions were separated by light blue block of HLA-C gene between HLA-A and HLA-B. The X-axis is amino acid or HLA allele covariate, ranking by their coordinate. HLA alleles were group together ranking by allele names in each HLA class I gene locus. The Y-axis is the $-\log_{10} p$ of index variant adjust by covariate. Independent variants should not change the adjusted p-values from the strong unadjusted values of the index variant, while LD-proxies would reduce their p-values appreciably depending upon the strength of LD.

doi: 10.1371/journal.pgen.1003103.g003

HLA-A*11:01 carries five strongly significant associated aa variants(62Gln, 276Leu, 114Arg, 70Gln, and 97Ile) in its peptide binding groove(Tab. S10). Taken together, the HLA-A association is centered on HLA-A*11:01 allele function and tracked by internal and closely linked proxy aa and SNP variants.

It may also be relevant that the sequence of HLA-A*11:01 allele($F=0.25$ in this population)differs by only one amino acid residue(Lys19Glu)from that of the HLA-A*11:02 allele($F=0.04$), yet HLA-A*11:02 shows no apparent association with NPC onset. Both HLA-A*11:01 and HLA-A*11:02 alleles share a unique peptide binding motif signature of".[YT]...[K-]"(Tab. 2)and an identical sequence within the defined residues of the antigen recognition site.[23] Since the only Lys19Glu residue difference between the two HLA-A*11 alleles is outside the peptide binding region, the possibility of an alternative mechanisms for NPC pathogenesis, e.g. HLA-A/KIR innate immunity involvement[29] or dendritic cell interaction,[30] should be considered and explored in future studies.

We further demonstrate an independent HLA-B signal derived from three representative alleles, two protective alleles(B*13:01 and B*55:02)and a susceptible allele B*38:02. Both HLA-A and -B associations involve functional variants in the antigenic recognition site. The strongest HLA-B aa site implicated is identical to the single aa sire that mediates HLA-B*35 rapid AIDS progression reported previously.[26,27,30] All the NPC associations were genome wide significant in one or more analyses, replicated internally in independent Guangxi cohorts and externally in other genetic association studies in Asia. Our study demonstrates a powerful genetic influence on NPC onset in Chinese people, implicates explicit HLA alleles, peptide recognition motifs, and aa variants that confer strong genetic influence on the development of NPC in China. HLA disease associations are likely to involve multiple mechanisms. A recent study in HIV disease showed that allelic diversity of HLA-C can cause variation in the level of surface expression of the HLA-C molecule, which in turn affects viral load control and disease progression[31], perhaps through both HLA-restricted CTL responses and HLA/KIR-mediated NK cell activities. The functional basis for HLA associations with NPC should be explored fully, now that the genetic basis of this disease is well-characterized, in hopes of explaining the complex HLA association with NPC in the Chinese population.

MATERIALS AND METHODS

Ethics statement

This study were approved by institutional ethics review committees at the relevant organizations, and conducted with the IRB approval(NIH IRB-02-C-N056). Informed consent was obtained from all study participants.

Study cohorts

A total of 4055 study subjects(1405 NPC cases and 2650 controls, Tab. S3)were recruited in two independent collection phases: phase I -April 2000 to June 2001 and phase II-November 2004 to October 2005, from the Guangxi autonomous region and Guangdong province of southern China.[20] All study subjects were of Han ethnic origin and reside in the catchment area of the Xijiang River. IgA antibodies to EBV capsid antigen(EBV-IgA/ VCA)were confirmed by serologic testing for all the subjects at the time of study enrollment. In phase I, the case group included 356 unrelated patients with biopsy-confirmed NPC. The mean age was 50.1 years(range 19-80), 95.5% of them were EBV-IgA/VCA antibody positive. Controls included case spouses or geographically matched residents who were NPC free at the time of study enrollment. An additional 422 adult children of the study subjects were enrolled for haplotype inference and for quality control assessment, but they were excluded in association analyses. In phase II, the case group included 1049 unrelated patients with biopsy-confirmed NPC. The mean age was 46.3 years(range 1077), 96.3% of them were EBV-IgA/VCA antibody positive. Two distinct NPC-free control groups were included: one group was positive(N=1001)and the other negative(N=1020)for the EBVIgA/VCA antibody. The mean ages were 46.1 and 46.6, for the antibody positive and negative controls groups. All study subjects were self-reported Guangxi or Guangdong provincial ancestry for either maternal or paternal ancestry for at least three generations.

Genome-wide SNPs genotyping

A total of 598 NPC cases and 506 controls were randomly selected from phase II enrollment cohort for GWAS analysis. DNA was extracted from whole blood by traditional phenol/ chloroform method with phase Lock Gel tube(Qiagen, MaXtract High Density, catalog ♯ 129065). The genome-wide genotyping experiments were conducted by using the Affymetrix GenomeWide SNP Array 6.0 genotyping platform. 325 nanograms of DNA per sample were prepared for both Sty 1 and Nsp 1 restriction enzyme digestion for this assay, genotyping in according to the manufacturer's instructions.

Quality control

Patient DNA. Genotyping analysis of GWAS samples was performed in Genotyping Console 3.0.2 for first-pass quality control. The contrast quality control(CQC) metrics were computed by the Affymetrix software. We attempted to ascertain genotypes for 1,104 NPC study subjects. 11 samples failed genotyping or were removed because of failing CQC(<0.4)or call rate(<90%). An additional 17 samples failed to meet further QC filters which included heterozygosity $<=25\%$ and at least one enzyme specific CQC value(Nspl or Styl)>1.24 samples were removed because the genotypes determined in the GWAS were discordant with genotypes previously determined by the Laboratory of Genomic Diversity for candidate gene studies. The gender of the samples was determined from the heterozygosity of X chromosome SNPs(Affymetrix and PLINK software)and by the ratio of the mean intensity of the copy number probes on the Y chromosome to the mean intensity of a subset of copy number probes on the X chromosome(Affymetrix software). Four samples were removed because the gender determined from the genotypes was discordant with the gender provided by the cohort. Identity by descent(IBD) statistics computed using PLINK software were used to detect cryptic familial relationships. Four first degree relationships were observed(3 full sib pairs and 1 parent-offspring pair). For each of these pairs, the sample with the lowest call rate was removed. A fifth sample was removed because the IBD statistics were consistent with that individual having a first cousin relationship with five other subjects. After sample filtering, a number of 1043 subjects were remained for further analyses(Tab. S2).

SNPs. Genotypes were ascertained for the 934,968 SNPs on the Genome-wide SNP 6.0 platform using the command line option of Affymetrix software. NetAffx version 30 was used for SNP annotation. This data set uses map positions based on the NCBI Build 36.1/UCSC hg18 human genome assembly. Unsupported SNPs, QC SNPs, non-autosomal SNPs, and remaining redundant SNPs were identified from the annotation data set and removed. Genotypes from 8 CEPH and 10 NPC mother/father/ offspring trios were checked for errors in Mendelian inheritance using PLINK software. SNPs having 2 or more errors in either group of samples were rejected. Per-SNP call rate, Hardy Weinberg test statistics, and minor allele frequencies were computed for 1,043 NPC study samples(see Tab. S2A)using PLINK software. SNPs not meeting the criteria shown in the table were removed (Tab. S2B).

Replication genotyping

Validation and replication genotyping of significant SNPs from our GWAS and from other studies was performed using the ABI Taqman genotyping assays by design in accordance with the manufacturer's instructions. The sequence detection software(SDS2.2, Applied Biosystems, Foster City, CA, USA)was used for allelic discrimination and confirmed the good quality of genotyping.

HLA typing

High resolution HLA molecular typing was performed for all 1,405 unrelated NPC cases and 2,650 unrelated controls from both enrollment cohorts. HLA class I alleles were characterized using a PCR-SSOP (sequence-specific oligonucleotide probe) typing protocol developed by the 13th International Histocompatibility Workshop[32] for the first enrollment study cohort(N=985), and using a DNA sequence-based typing(SBT) protocol in the second enrollment study cohort(N=3070). The sequencing analysis was performed using the ABI Big Dye Terminator Cycle Sequencing Kit and the ABI3730xl DNA analyzer(Applied Biosystems, Foster City, CA). HLA alleles were assigned on the basis of the sequence database of known alleles with the help of the ASSIGN software developed by Conexio Genomics(Conexio Genomics, Western Australia, Australia). Ambiguous heterozygous genotypes were resolved by additional PCR and sequencing procedures using allele-specific PCR primers to selectively amplify only one of the two alleles.

Haplotype of HLA-A, HLA-B and HLA-C allelic combinations were assessed using 422 children of the phase I study subjects in 179 patients and 379 controls. Based on expectation maximization algorithm to generate maximum likelihood estimation haplotype, we observed 90% accuracy on HLA-A-B-C haplotypes, 91% on HLA-A-B and HLA-A-C haplotypes, and 99% on HLA-B-C haplotypes. For the remaining NPC cases and controls, HLA haplotypes were assigned by population-based estimation methods of PROC HAPLOTYPE in SAS/Genetics package.

HLA amino acid variant definition

Because the most significant NPC associated SNPs is located on the HLA class I region(see Results), an amino acid analysis was carried out to evaluate the role of functional relative amino acid residues in HLA associations. From our high resolution HLA genotyping results, we were able to define corresponding amino acid sequences for all study subjects. The amino acid variants in HLA class I genes were defined by using web-based software of the Immunology Database and Analysis Portal(ImmPort)system[24].

Proxy SNP-variant analysis

We have used the method of testing each variant for reduced-pvalues in multi-variants models resulting from co-linearity of variants to recognize LD and independence of signals in the association of NPC with HLA-A, -B and -C. Multicollinearity in logistic regression models is a result of strong correlations between variables. The existence of multicollinearity(high r^2)between variants inflates the variances of the parameter estimates. That will likely result in lowered p-values for a given SNP that was determined to be in significant association with NPC when tested signally. We used a reduction in significance as an indicator that two variants were in strong LD, and therefore not independent signals as has been done by recent authors[18]. This gives us a general idea about independence of the signals within HLA and adjacent genes within the context of the disease association. However, we recognize that although multicollinearity may lower magnitudes of regression coefficient estimates and resulting pvalue significance in cases of LD, this method may be subject to error such as when a rare SNP on a haplotype does not have a large effect on the model. These methods are provided as an indicator of independence, but not as a definitive measure in our understanding of the disease.

Statistical analysis

We performed logistic regression model analysis for all SNPs passing the quality control filters, using a Cochran-Armitage trend, co-dominant, dominant, recessive, and allelic model taking the number of copies of the rare allele 0, 1 or 2, as the explanatory variable. The comparisons were conducted between NPC cases and NPC free controls, NPC cases and NPC-free but EBV-IgA/VCA antibody positive controls(EP controls), NPC cases and NPC-free but EBV-IgA/VCA-antibody negative controls(EN controls), EP controls and EN controls respectively. Population structure/ stratification was assessed using the Principal Components Analysis(PCA)module of Eigensoft software[33]. Study samples were first run together with HapMap individuals of European, African, and Asian descents to identify any potential admixed individuals. Later, PCA analyses of only the study samples were conducted Initially all autosomal SNPs that passed the quality control filters were used to estimate the contribution of each SNP to the top ten eigenvectors. Previously reported correlated genome regions[19] (such as on chromosomes 6, 8, and 11)were observed and excluded from the following PCA analyses. Moreover, to avoid any confounders due to LD among the SNPs, the genotype data was pruned to 90 K independent SNPs distributed throughout the genome by PLINK prior to the PCA analyses. The logistic regression analysis performed using PLINK[25], controlling for gender, age and the first three eigenvectors; the significance was evaluated using the log likelihood test. SNPs were sorted according to the lowest P-value in a combined set of samples in one of these models. The chi-square tests were used for testing case-control association for allele effects. HLA allele frequencies were calculated based on observed genotypes; HLA-A, -B and -C haplotype were assigned based on maximum likelihood estimation using the SAS/Genetics HAPLOTYPE procedure. The effect of HLA alleles on the development of NPC and EBV-IgA/VCA antibody was evaluated by computing odds ratios(OR)and 95% confidence intervals(CI)using logistic regression. For HLA allele and haplotype test, P values were calculated by logistic regression and then corrected by the Bonferroni, which was multiplied by the number of all detected alleles or haplotypes. Significance was considered at $P < 0.05$ after correction.

SUPPORTING INFORMATION

Fig. S1 Plots of principal components from the PCA for genetic matching. Plot of the first two PCs from the PCA(N=1043 study participants; Row I in Tab. S3)and 206 HapMap individuals, including 57 Yoruba in Ibadan, Nigeria(YRI), 44 Japanese in Tokyo, Japan(JPT), 45 Han Chinese in Beijing, China(CHB)and 60 CEPH(Utah residents with ancestry from northern and western Europe)(CEU).

（TIF）

Fig. S2 Plots of principal components from the PCA for genetic matching. Plot of the first two PCs from the PCA(N=1043 study participants; Row I in Tab. S3), 44 Japanese in Tokyo, Japan(JPT), and 45 Han Chinese in Beijing, China(CHB).

（TIF）

Fig. S3 Plots of the first two principal components from the PCA of 1,043 NPC study samples for genetic matching.

（TIF）

Fig. S4 Plot of the first and third PCs from the PCA of 1,043 NPC study samples for genetic matching.

（TIF）

Fig. S5 Plots of the second and third PCs from the PCA of 1,043 NPC study samples for genetic matching.

（TIF）

Fig. S6 Quantile-quantile plot showing the distribution of observed statistic by allelic test for association of each SNP with NPC.

（TIF）

Fig. S7 Schematic overview of the structure of HLA-A*11:01 in complex with SARS nucleocapsid peptide. The α1-helix is shown in blue; α2-helix is shown in purple; β-pleated sheet is shown in lightblue. The significantly associated exposed positons of the peptide in the binding groove are shown in red with label indicated. Green balls in the binding groove indicate SARS nucleocapsid peptide K[T]FPPTEP[K], notice the P2 and P9 residues with red. The crystal structure of 1X7Q[13] was download from PDB database(http://www.pdb.org/pdb/home/ home. do).(a) Top view,(b)P2 residueThreonine(Thr, T)in peptide bingding groove,(c)P9 residue Lysine(Lys, K)in peptide binding groove. All figures were prepared with PyMOL[14].

（TIF）

Tab. S1 NPC associated classical HLA class I alleles.

（DOCX）

Tab. S2 Sample and SNP filtering for this study.

（DOCX）

Tab. S3 Summary of samples used in GWAS, replication and HLA analysis.

（DOCX）

Tab. S4 GWAS Results（N＝1,043 subjects）using different test combinations and genetic models for 24 SNPs with the lowest p values.

（DOCX）

Tab. S5 List of 16 genetic association tests.

（DOCX）

Tab. S6 Replication of previously reported NPC associated GWAS SNPs and candidate genes in these cohorts.

（DOCX）

Tab. S7 40 GWAS and validation of SNPs association data in two independent NPC cohorts.

（DOCX）

Tab. S8 Significant explicit and imputed haplotype NPC association analysis.

（DOCX）

Tab. S9 Association results for the amino acid residues in each of the classical HLA loci in all study subjects.

（DOCX）

Tab. S10 The five most significant NPC associated amino acid in each HLA class I locus.

（DOCX）

Tab. S11 Multivariate logistic regression analysis for significant variant and HLA class I alleles.

（DOCX）

Tab. S12 HLA-A, -B and -C allele association analysis separated into in phase I and II analyses.

（DOCX）

ACKNOWLEDGMENTS

We would like to acknowledge Lisa Garland, Mary McNally, and David Wells for the excellent technical assistance and Joan Pontius and Marilyn Raymond for invaluable statistical advice. We are also grateful to all colleagues at the Wuzhou Red Cross Hospital for their excellent assistance in recruiting subjects.

AUTHOR CONTRIBUTIONS

Conceived and designed the experiments: Y Zeng, G dé The, SJ O′Brien, X Gao. Performed the experiments: M Tang, JL Troyer, CE Mcintosh, M Malasky, L Guan, X Guo. Analyzed the data: M Tang, E Sezgin, SL Hendrickson, X Guo, JA Lautenberger, VA David, CA Winkler, M Carrington, X Gao. Contributed reagents/materials/analysis tools: Y Zheng, J Liao, H Deng. Wrote the paper: M Tang, E Sezgin, SL Hendrickson, X Gao. Clinic and genotype data management: B Kessing.

REFERENCES

[1] Jemal A, Bray F, Center MM, Ferlay J, Ward E, et al. (2011) Global cancer statistics. CA Cancer J Clin 61: 69-90.

[2] Henle G, Henle W (1976) Epstein-Barr virus-specific IgA serum antibodies as an outstanding feature of nasopharyngeal carcinoma. Int J Cancer 17:1-7.

[3] Zeng Y, Zhang LG, Li HY, Jan MG, Zhang Q, et al. (1982) Serological mass survey for early detection of nasopharyngeal carcinoma in Wuzhou City, China. Int J Cancer 29:139-141.

[4] Zeng Y, Zhang LG, Wu YC, Huang YS, Huang NQ, et al. (1985) Prospective studies on nasopharyngeal carcinoma in Epstein-Barr virus IgA/VCA antibodypositive persons in Wuzhou City, China. Int J Cancer 36:545-547.

[5] Ng WT, Yau TK, Yung RW, Sze WM, Tsang AH, et al. (2005) Screening for family members of patients with nasopharyngeal carcinoma. Int J Cancer 113:998-1001.

[6] Coffin CM, Rich SS, Dehner LP (1991) Familial aggregation of nasopharyngeal carcinoma and other malignancies. A clinicopathologic description. Cancer 68:1323-1328.

[7] Simons MJ, Wee GB, Chan SH, Shanmugaratnam K, Day NE, et al. (1975) Immunogenetic aspects of nasopharyngeal carcinoma (NPC) III. HL-a type as a genetic marker of NPC predisposition to test the hypothesis that Epstein-Barr virus is an etiological factor in NPC. IARC Sci Publ: 249-258.

[8] Chan SH, Day NE, Kunaratnam N, Chia KB, Simons MJ (1983) HLA and nasopharyngeal carcinoma in Chinese-a further

study. Int J Cancer 32:171-176.

[9] Lu SJ, Day NE, Degos L, Lepage V, Wang PC, et al.(1990)Linkage of a nasopharyngeal carcinoma susceptibility locus to the HLA region. Nature 346:470-471.

[10] Hildesheim A, Apple RJ, Chen CJ, Wang SS, Cheng YJ, et al.(2002)Association of HLA class I and II alleles and extended haplotypes with nasopharyngeal carcinoma in Taiwan. J Natl Cancer Inst 94:1780-1789.

[11] Hu SP, Day NE, Li DR, Luben RN, Cai KL, et al.(2005)Further evidence for an HLA-related recessive mutation in nasopharyngeal carcinoma among the Chinese. Br J Cancer 92: 967-970.

[12] Yu KJ, Gao X, Chen CJ, Yang XR, Diehl SR, et al.(2009)Association of human leukocyte antigens with nasopharyngeal carcinoma in high-risk multiplex families in Taiwan. Hum Immunol 70:910-914.

[13] Tang M, Zeng Y, Poisson A, Marti D, Guan L, et al.(2010)Haplotypedependent HLA susceptibility to nasopharyngeal carcinoma in a Southern Chinese population. Genes Immun 11: 334-342.

[14] Reilly MP, Li M, He J, Ferguson JF, Stylianou IM, et al.(2011)Identification of ADAMTS7 as a novel locus for coronary atherosclerosis and association of ABO with myocardial infarction in the presence of coronary atherosclerosis: two genome-wide association studies. Lancet 377:383-392.

[15] Seshadri S, Fitzpatrick AL, Ikram MA, DeStefano AL, Gudnason V, et al.(2010) Genome-wide analysis of genetic loci associated with Alzheimer disease. JAMA 303:1832-1840.

[16] YangJJ Plenge RM(2011)Genomic technology applied to pharmacological traits. JAMA 306:652-653.

[17] Ng CC, Yew PY, Puah SM, Krishnan G, Yap LF, et al.(2009)A genome-wide association study identifies ITGA9 conferring risk of nasopharyngeal carcinoma. J Hum Genet 54:392-397.

[18] Tse KP, Su WH, Chang KP, Tsang NM, Yu CJ, et al.(2009)Genome-wide association study reveals multiple nasopharyngeal carcinoma-associated loci within the HLA region at chromosome 6p21. 3. Am J Hum Genet 85: 194-203.

[19] Bei JX, Li Y, Jia WH, Feng BJ, Zhou G, et al.(2010)A genome-wide association study of nasopharyngeal carcinoma identifies three new susceptibility loci. Nat Genet 42:599-603.

[20] Guo XC, Scott K, Liu Y, Dean M, David V, et al.(2006)Genetic factors leading to chronic Epstein-Barr virus infection and nasopharyngeal carcinoma in South East China: study design, methods and feasibility. Hum Genomics 2:365-375.

[21] Guo X, Johnson RC, Deng H, Liao J, Guan L, et al.(2009)Evaluation of nonviral risk factors for nasopharyngeal carcinoma in a high-risk population of Southern China. International Journal of Cancer 124:2942-2947.

[22] Bjorkman PJ, Saper MA, Samraoui B, Bennett WS, Strominger JL, et al.(1987) The foreign antigen binding site and T cell recognition regions of class I histocompatibility antigens. Nature 329:512-518.

[23] Lund O, Nielsen M, Kesmir C, Petersen AG, Lundegaard C, et al.(2004) Definition of supertypes for HLA molecules using clustering of specificity matrices. Immunogenetics 55: 797-810.

[24] Karp DR, Marthandan N, Marsh SG, Ahn C, Arnett FC, et al.(2010)Novel sequence feature variant type analysis of the HLA genetic association in systemic sclerosis. Hum Mol Genet 19:707-719.

[25] Purcell S, Neale B, Todd-Brown K, Thomas L, Ferreira MA, et al.(2007) PLINK: a tool set for whole-genome association and population-based linkage analyses. Am J Hum Genet 81:559-575.

[26] Gao X, Nelson GW, Karacki P, Martin MP, Phair J, et al.(2001)Effect of a single amino acid change in MHC class I molecules on the rate of progression to AIDS. N Engl J Med 344:1668-1675.

[27] Thammavongsa V, Schaefer M, Filzen T, Collins KL, Carrington M, et al.(2009) Assembly and intracellular trafficking of HLA-B* 3501 and HLA-B* 3503. Immunogenetics 61:703-716.

[28] Steinle A, Falk K, Rotzschke O, Gnau V, Stevanovic S, et al.(1996)Motif of HLA-B* 3503 peptide ligands. Immunogenetics 43:105-107.

[29] Bashirova AA, Thomas R, Carrington M(2011)HLA/KIR restraint of HIV: surviving the fittest. Annu Rev Immunol 29: 295-317.

[30] Huang J, Goedert JJ, Sundberg EJ, Cung TD, Burke PS, et al.(2009)HLA-B* 35-Px-mediated acceleration of HIV-1 infection by increased inhibitory immunoregulatory impulses. J Exp Med 206:2959-2966.

[31] Kulkarni S, Savan R, Qi Y, Gao X, Yuki Y, et al.(2011)Differential microRNA regulation of HLA-C expression and its association with HIV control. Nature472: 495-498.

[32] Hurley C(2005)IHWG Technology Core Joint Report: Hansen JA, Dupont B, editors: Immunobiology of the Human MHC: Proceedings of the 13th International Hisotcompatibility Workshop and Conference, Fred Hutchinson Cancer Research.

[33] Price AL, Patterson NJ, Plenge RM, Weinblatt ME, Shadick NA, et al.(2006) Principal components analysis corrects for stratification in genome-wide association studies. Nat Genet 38: 904-909.

Phylogenetic and Temporal Dynamics of Human Immunodeficiency Virus Type 1 CRF01_AE in China

Jingrong Ye[1,2,3]🕭, Ruolei Xin[1]🕭, Shuangqing Yu[3]🕭, Lishi Bai[1]🕭, Weishi Wang[4]🕭, Tingchen Wu[1]🕭, Xueli Su[1], Hongyan Lu[1], Xinghuo Pang[1], Hong Yan[2], Xia Feng[3]*, Xiong He[1]*, Yi Zeng[2,3]*

1 Beijing Center for Disease Prevention and Control, Beijing, China, 2 College of Life Science and Bio-engineering, Beijing University of Technology, Beijing, China, 3 State Key Laboratory for Infectious Diseases Prevention and Control, National Institute for Viral Disease Control and Prevention, China Center for Disease Prevention and Control, Beijing, China, 4 Program of Pharmacology and Toxicology, University of Toronto, Toronto, Canada

[ABSTRACT]   To explore the epidemic history of HIV-1 CRF01_AE in China, 408 fragments of gag gene sequences of CRF01_AE sampled in 2002-2010 were determined from different geographical regions and risk populations in China. Phylogenetic analysis indicates that the CRF01_AE sequences can be grouped into four clusters, suggesting that at least four genetically independent CRF01_AE descendants are circulating in China, of which two were closely related to the isolates from Thailand and Vietnam. Cluster 1 has the most extensive distribution in China. In North China, cluster 1 and cluster 4 were mainly transmitted through homosexuality. The real substance of the recent HIV-1 epidemic in men who have sex with men(MSM) of North China is a rapid spread of CRF01_AE, or rather two distinctive natives CRF01_AE. The time of the most recent common ancestor(tMRCA) of four CRF01_AE clusters ranged from the years 1990. 9 to 2003. 8 in different regions of China. This is the first phylogenetic and temporal dynamics study of HIV-1 CRF01_AE in China.

Citation: Ye J, Xin R, Yu S, Bai L, Wang W, et al.(2013)Phylogenetic and Temporal Dynamics of Human Immunodeficiency Virus Type 1 CRF01_AE in China. PLoS ONE 8(1): e54238. doi: 10. 1371/journal.pone. 0054238
Editor: Paul Sandstrom, National HIV and Retrovirology Laboratories, Canada
Received July 19, 2012; Accepted December 10, 2012; Published January 24, 2013

Funding: This study was supported by China megaprojects in infectious diseases(2012ZX10001-005 and 2012ZX10001-002). The funders had no role in study design, data collection and analysis, decision to publish, or preparation of the manuscript.
Competing Interests: The authors have declared that no competing interests exist.
* E-mail: fengxia621@126.com(XF); hexiong200@sina.com(XH); basketball 197602 @ hotmail.com(YZ)
🕭 These authors contributed equally to this work.

INTRODUCTION

China is the world's most populous country, where the human immunodeficiency virus type 1(HIV-1)epidemic is still increasing. At the end of 2011, the estimated number of people living with HIV in China was 780,000. Women accounted for 28. 6% of these cases. Prevalence among the population as a whole was 0.058%; Of the total number of people living with HIV, 154,000 were cases of Acquired Immune Deficiency Syndrome (AIDS). It is estimated that there were 48,000 new cases of HIV in 2011, and that the prevalence among the population as a whole was 0.057%. HIV/ AIDS is also the leading cause of death from infectious diseases in China, accounting for an estimated 28,000 deaths in 2011. Sexual transmission continues to be the primary mode of transmission, and homosexual transmission is also increasing rapidly. Of the780,000 people estimated to be living with HIV in 2011, the percentage of infected cases through sexual transmission was 63. 9% in which 46. 5% were infected through heterosexual transmission and 17. 4% through homosexual transmission. The percentage of infected cases through intravenous drug user(IDU) was 28. 4%. Among the 48,000 new cases estimated for 2011, heterosexual transmission accounted for 52. 2%, homosexual transmission 29. 4%, and IDU accounted for 18. 0% of cases[1].

HIV-1 CRF01_AE is the earliest circulating recombinant form(CRF)among those identified to date. They represent a putative subtype of A/E recombinant that was originated from Central Africa but spreading epidemically in Asia.[2] CRF01_AE plays important role in regional epidemics and is responsible for 5% of cases in the world.

The majority(83%) of CRF01_AE was found in South and Southeast Asia, whereas 9% in East Asia. In Cambodia, Thailand, and Vietnam, CRF01_AE is responsible for more than 95% of the infections[3]. CRF01_AE was first identified from the women who had returned to Yunnan province, China from Thailand after involving in commercial sex works in late 1994[4]. Later, CRF01_AE strains were found in injecting drug users(IDUs)from Guangxi province in 1996[5].

In the recent years, HIV-1 CRF01_AE spreads rapidly since the early 2000s in China. The recent molecular epidemiology survey in Beijing identified HIV-1 CRF01_AE(40.4%)as the most dominant strains. In men who have sex with men(MSM), CRF01_AE was accounted for 56.8% of all infections(unpublished data).The factors associated with the rapid increase of CRF01_AE in China are not completely known, but in certain regions where it has been introduced, CRF01_AE has overtaken other HIV-1 strains introduced earlier. The rapid spread of CRF01_AE in many regions of China including Beijing, Guangxi, Guangdong, Jiangxi, Hunan and Hainan has drawn particular attention[6-9]. Recent studies suggested that Hong Kong CRF01_AE epidemic likely derived from multiple origins with 3 separate transmission clusters identified[10]. In Guangxi region also there were multiple introductions of CRF01_AE strains and a peculiar CRF01_AE monophyletic lineage distinct from other CRF01_AE viruses was identified[11]. However, the genetic characteristics of CRF01_AE in other parts of China remained mysterious.

By combining phylogenetic analyses and a Bayesian coalescentbased approach, the phylogenetic relationships of CRF01_AE isolates from China were studied in order to provide more understanding on the epidemic growth model of HIV-1 CRF01_AE virus.

RESULTS

1. Study subjects

A total of 408 CRF01_AE gag gene(836-1486 nt, HXB2) sequences isolated from 27 provinces of China during the year 2002-2010 were used in this study. 186 cases were newly characterized from ongoing molecular epidemiology studies mainly in Beijing, the capital city of China, and 222 cases were obtained from the Los Alamos HIV sequence database(www.hiv.lanl.gov) from previously published reports. The clinical and demographic characteristics of the 186 HIV-1 CRF01 _ AE Infectors reported by our laboratory were as follows: mean age was 32.0(2-69) years and 91.9%(171 of 186)were male. The predominant route of transmission was MSM in(64.0%,119 of 186)of the subjects, while the remaining were heterosexual(25.8%, 48 of 186), IDUs(3.2%, 6 of 186), Mother to child transmission(0.5%, 1 of 186), and blood transmission(0.5%,1 of186). Median CD4 count was 328 cells/mm3 (Tab. 1). The province of origin and sampling year of the 222 CRF01_AE sequence are listed in Tab. 2. Geographically, the 408 CRF01 _ AE gag gene sequences originated from different regions of China are as follows: the North China(Beijing n=67, Hebei n=33, Shanxi n=1, Inner Mongolia n=2); Northeast China(Liaoning n=60, Jilin n=5, Heilongjiang n=5); East China(Shanghai n=1, Jiangsu n=5, Zhejiang n=5, Anhui n=2, Fujian n=14, Jiangxi n=2, Shandong n=7); South Central China(Henan n=9, Hubei n=2, Hunan n=2, Guangdong n=1, Hainan n=1 Guangxi n=144); Southwest China(Chongqing n=2, Sichuan n=14, Yunnan n=4); Northwest China(Shannxi n=3, Gansu n=5, Ningxia n=2, Xinjiang n=1); Unknown(n=7)(Tab. 3).

Tab. 1 Demographic and clinical information for the 186 HIV-1 CRF01_AE Infectors reported by our laboratory.

	Overall(186)
Age[median(range)], yrs	32(2-69)
gender n(%)	
male	171(91.9)
famale	15(8.1)
Risk factors n(%)	
Hetero	48(25.8)
MSM	119(64.0)
IDUs	6(3.2)
Mother to child	1(0.5)
Blood	1(0.5)
Unknown	11(5.9)
Median CD4 count(cells/mm^3)	328
Range of sampling date	2006-2010
Province	
Beijing	67(36.0)
Hebei	24(12.9)
Henan	9(4.8)
Sichuan	14(7.5)
Other 23 Province	72(38.7)

doi:10.1371/journal.pone.OO54238.t001

Tab. 2　Sampling information for the 222 HIV-1 CRF01_AE sequences obtained from the Los Alamos HIV sequence database.

	Overall(222)
Province	
Fujian	12(5.4)
Guangxi	144(64.9)
Hebei	9(4.1)
Jiangsu	1(0.5)
Liaoning	56(25.2)
Range of sampling date	2002-2010

doi：10.1371/journal.pone.0054238.t002

Tab. 3　Distribution of CRF01_AE isolates(cluster 1 to 4)in different regions of China

Region	overall	cluster 1	cluster 2	cluster 3	cluster 4	other
North China	103	75	5	3	18	2
Beijing	67	46	4	2	13	2
Hebei	33	26	1	1	5	
Shanxi and Inner Mongolia	3	3				
Northeast China	70	12	2	4	48	4
Liaoning	60	5	2	4	46	3
Jilin and Heilongjiang	10	7			2	1
East China	36	20	1	5	3	7
Fujian	14	1	1	4	1	7
Shandong	7	7				
Zhejiang, Anhui, Jiangxi, Shanghai, Jiangsu	15	12		1	2	
South Central China	161	14	68	70	2	7
Guangxi	146	7	66	67		6
Henan	9	2	1	3	2	1
Hubei, Hunan, Guangdong, Hainan	6	5	1			
Southwest China	20	12	2	1	3	2
Sichuan	14	8	2	1	2	1
Chongqing and Yunnan	6	4			1	1
Northwest China	11	7			3	1
Shanxi, Gansu, Ningxia, Xinjiang	11	7			3	1
Unknown	7	6			1	
Total	408	146	78	87	78	19

doi：10.1371/journal.pone.0054238.t003

2. Molecular Epidemiology of the HIV-1 CRF01_AE Infection in China

A phylogenetic tree was reconstructed using NJ method with 418 gag sequences, consisting of 408 China sequences and 10 CRF01_AE reference sequences isolated in Thailand, Vietnam, Cyprus, Japan and Hong Kong. The tree demonstrated 19 out of 408 China sequences(4.7%)which were scattered among each other while the

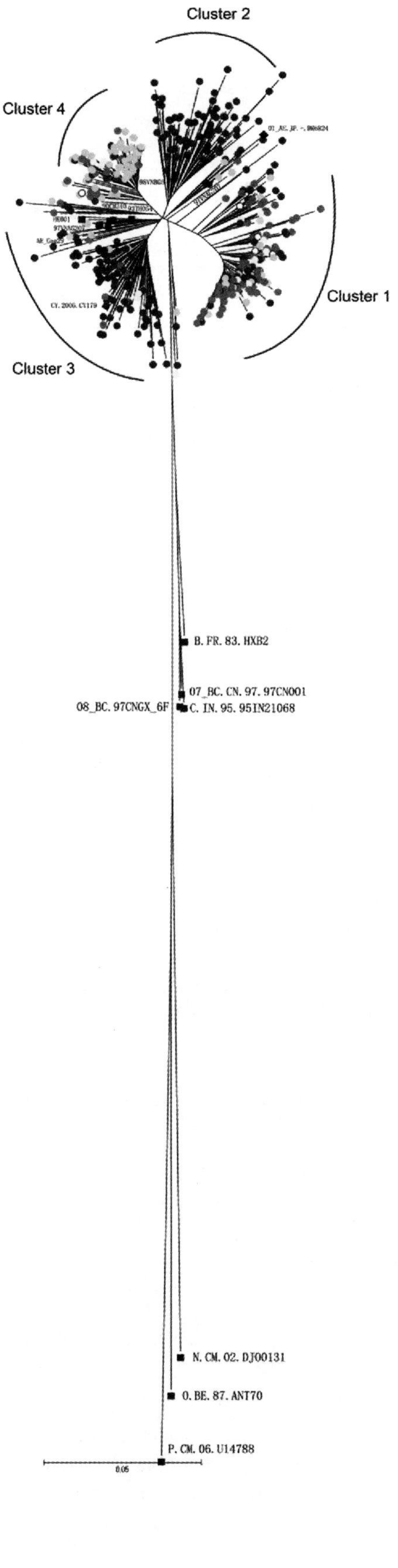

Fig. 1　Phylogenetic tree analysis of Chinese HIV-1 CRF01_AE gag gene sequences. The phylogenetic tree was constructed using neighbor-joining methods(Mega 4. 0)for the gag region. Samples of North China, Northeast China, South Central China, East China, Southwest China and Northwest China are shown by red, green, blue, purple, yellow and cyan solid circles in the tree. The empty circle indicate unknown. The black solid squares indicate reference sequences from the Los Alamos HIV sequence database. doi:10. 1371/journal.pone. 0054238.g001

other 389 sequences were segregated into four major distinct clusters(indicated as cluster 1 to 4)with bootstrap value above 70％ and more than 20 members(Fig. 1). Among the 4 clusters, cluster 1 had 146 members that isolated from North China(75), Northeast China(12), East China(20), South Central China(14), Southwest China(12)and Northwest China(7). the epidemic information of 127 individuals which was available, the median age range was 31. 6(20-62)years, 124 were males and 3 were females. Heterosexual(18. 1％, 23 of 127)and MSM(71. 7％,91 of 127)accounted for the major transmission routes for these isolates. For cluster 2, 78 sequences were mainly isolated from South Central China(84. 6％, 66 of 78)and 12 people from other province of China. This cluster also contains one sequence(98VNBG5)from Vietnam. Cluster 3 included 87 sequences mainly from Guangxi(77. 0％, 67 of 87)and were found to cluster with 7 reference sequences isolated from HIV-1-infector in Thailand(90CM240, 93TH054, 93TH051, TH. 2006. AE _ Gag29)-Vietnam(97VNHCM319), Cyprus(CY. 2006. CY179)and Hong Kong(HK. 2004. HK001). Cluster 4 included 78 sequences mainly from Northeast China(61. 5％,48 of 78)and North China(23. 1％, 18 of 78), the 33 infectors of which the epidemic information was available, were all male with the median age of 31. 4(20-61)years, 23 belonged to the MSM risk group, whereas 9 were infected through heterosexual contacts. Phylogenetic analyses of the viral gag genes showed that clusters 2 and 3 were closely related to the strains identified in Thailand and Vietnam, suggesting that the two clusters have close genetic relationships with these strains. The CRF01_AE sequences in cluster 1 and cluster 4 were different from those belonging to Thailand and Vietnam. These two clusters were pure Chinese CRF01_AE clusters which do not contain any foreign strains. As far as the transmission routes were concerned in North China, the cluster 1 and cluster 4 were mainly transmitted by homosexual, cluster 2 by heterosexual, and cluster 3 by combined methods including heterosexual, homosexual and IDUs(Tab. 4). The Maximum Clade Credibility with time scale(MCC)tree of six region of China were included in this study as shown in Fig. S1, S2, S3, S4, S5, S6.

3. Regional distribution of HIV-1 CRF01_AE in China: Analysis by Region

Marked differences were found between the six region in China. Tab. 3 gives the details of the distribution of HIV-1 CRF01_AE within each region. For the North China, 72.8% (75 of 103) of CRF01_AE infections were caused by cluster 1, with smaller proportions of infections caused by cluster 4 (17.5%, 18 of 103), cluster 2 (4.9%, 5 of 103) and cluster 3 (2.9%, 3 of 103) strains (Tab. 4). While, in Northeast China, the dominant CRF01_AE strains were cluster 4 (68.6%, 48 of 70) and cluster 1 accounts for 17.1% (12 of 70). In South Central China, the most prevalent CRF01_AE strains were cluster 3 (43.5%, 70/161) and cluster 2 (42.2%, 68/161). In East China, Southwest China and Northwest China, the epidemic of CRF01_AE is dominated by cluster 1, which was found to be responsible for 55.6% (20 of 36), 60.0% (12 of 20) and 63.6% (7 of 11) of all infections, respectively.

Tab. 4 Demographic and clinical information for patients infected with CRF01_AE virus in North China.

	Overall(103)	cluster 1(75)	cluster 2(5)	cluster3(4)	cluster 4(18)
Age[median(range)], yrs	33.7(20-69)	33(20-62)	31.4(25-45)	46(27-69)	34.4(20-61)
gender n(%)					
Male	98(95.1)	74(98.7)	4(80.0)	2(50.0)	18(100.0)
Female	5(4.9)	1(1.3)	1(20.0)	2(50.0)	
Risk factors n(%)					
Heterosexual	23(22.3)	11(14.7)	5(100.0)		7(38.9)
MSM	73(70.9)	60(80.0)		2(50.0)	11(61.1)
IDUs	2(1.9)	1(1.3)			
Blood	1(1.0)			1(25.0)	
Unkown	4(3.9)	3(4.0)		1(25.0)	
Median CD4 count(cells/mm³)	316	337	168	181	386
Range of sampling date	2006-2010	2006-2010	2006-2010	2007-2009	2006-2010

doi:10.1371/journal.pone.0054238.t004

4. Date of Origin of the Four HIV-1 CRF01_AE Strains in China

The four taxons identified were used for the tMRCA calculations. The mean estimated evolutionary rate for four clusters in different regions ranged from 2.31×10^{-3} to 3.34×10^{-3} substitutions site^{-1} year^{-1} under the relaxed exponential clock model (Tab. 5). The Bayes factor analysis showed that the relaxed exponential clock model was strongly supported by other model for this dataset. The estimated dates of introduction of cluster 1 into different regions were as follows: 1990.9 into East China, 1992.7 into North China and Southwest China, 1998.8 into South Central China, 2003.8 into Northeast China. Cluster 2 into South Central China was dated back to 1998.0. Cluster 3 has an estimated tMRCA around 1997.9 in South Central China. The median estimation of the tMRCA for the cluster 4 in North China and Northeast China were 1998.8 and 1995.3, respectively (Tab. 5). This is in agreement with previous epidemiological investigations on the first report of CRF01_AE in the middle of 1990s in China.

Tab. 5 Estimated Substitution Rates and Dates for Transmission Clusters.

Region	Bayesian Coalescent*	
	Rate of evolution	tMRCA
North China		
Cluster 1	2.31×10^{-3}	1992.7(1989.5-1995.9)
Cluster 4	3.17×10^{-3}	1998.8(1998.1-1999.5)
Northeast China		
Cluster 1	2.46×10^{-3}	2003.8(2003.3-2004.3)

（续 表）

Region	Bayesian Coalescent[*]	
	Rate of evolution	tMRCA
Cluster 4	3.29×10^{-3}	1995.3(1995.1-1995.5)
East China		
Cluster 1	2.89×10^{-3}	1990.9(1987.9-1993.9)
South Central China		
Cluster 1	2.56×10^{-3}	1998.8(1997.2-1999.4)
Cluster 2	3.34×10^{-3}	1998.0(1996.0-2000.0)
Cluster 3	2.86×10^{-3}	1997.9(1996.12-1998.7)
Southwest China		
Cluster 1	2.77×10^{-3}	1992.3(1990.3-1994.3)

[*] Estimates of the mean evolutionary rate(μ, substitutions.site^{-1}. year^{-1})and the median time of the most recent common ancestor(tMRCA)for the different clusters(95% high posterior density in parentheses).

doi:10.1371/journal.pone.0054238.t005

5. Epidemic history of of HIV-1 CRF01_AE cluster 4 in Northeast China

Bayesian skyline plot(BSP)analysis was also used to infer the estimation of the effective population size at the time of CRF01_AE epidemics in Northeast China, for the as sampling time span was ranged from 2002-2010.The demographic history from the gag BSP identified three epidemic growth phases(Fig. 2), an initial slow growth phase until the year 2002, followed by an exponential growth phase till 2005, followed by a stationary phase, approaching the present time.

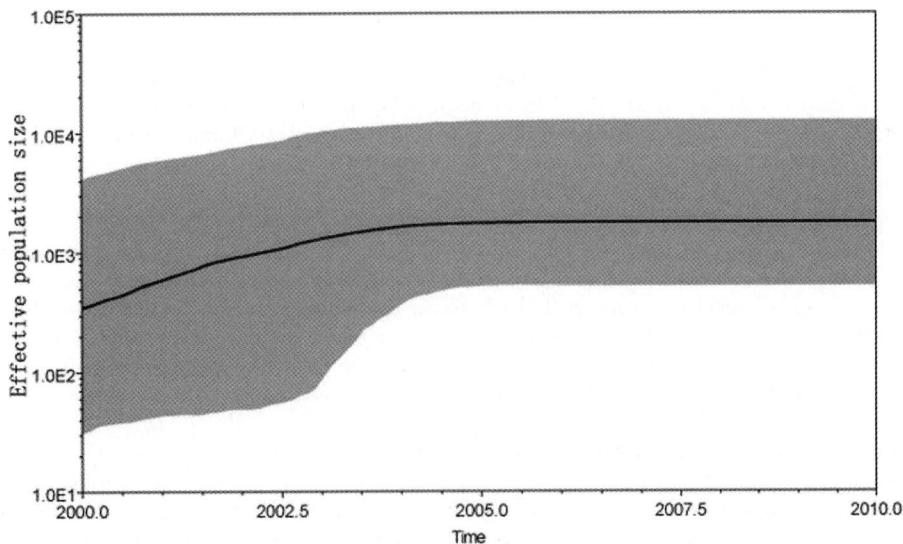

Fig. 2 Baysian skyline plot was estimated to reconstruct the demographic history of CRF01_AE cluster 4 in Northeast China. The x axis is the time in units of years, and the y axis is equal to the effective population size. The thick solid line is the mean estimates, the 95% HPD credible region is showed by blue areas.

doi:10.1371/journal.pone.0054238.g002

DISCUSSION

To the best of our knowledge, this is the first nationwide phylodynamic study depicting the spatiotemporal dynamics of HIV-1 CRF01_AE in China and to trace the tMRCA of the CRF01_AE strains. The analyses using phylogenetic reconstruction and coalescence inference indicate that the spread of CRF01_AE in China involved at least 4 viral lineages. Cluster 1 strains play a visible role in the CRF01_AE epidemic in China, and cause a significant proportion of infections in Southwest China(60%), East China(55.6%), Northwest China(63.6%), and especially in North China(72.8%). Both cluster 2 and cluster 3 are found mainly in South Central China and are responsible for about 42.2% and 43.5% of infections, respectively. Cluster 4 was prevalent in Northeast China (68.6%)and North China(17.5%).

The tMRCA of cluster 1 ranged from 1990.9 to 2003.8 in different regions of China. The CRF01_AE cluster 2 lineage likely entered the South Central China around 1998.0. The cluster 3 CRF01_AE epidemic in South Central China was probably established around 1997.6. Cluster 4 was dated back to 1995.3 and probably introduced later into neighboring North China region around 1998.8. Cluster 4 was a latest cluster that was mainly confined to Northeast China and North China. But it remained unclear whether the isolate spread to other regions.

Previous studies have defined the tMRCA of the two clades of CRF01_AE strains from Viatnam in 1989.8 and 1997.5, respectively[12,13].A recent report regarding the tMRCA of HIV-1 CRF01_AE in Hong Kong dates back to late 1980s and late 1990s[10]. In this study, the time of origination of the China HIV-1 CRF01_AE was defined as from 1990.9 to 2003.8.This evidence suggested that CRF01_AE strain might begin to circulate in mainland China at nearly the same time as Hong Kong. Our results also conform the long time assumption that CRF01_AE in China was originated from Southeast Asia. Zeng H et al. identified three HIV-1 CRF01_AE variants in Guangxi province in 293 CRF01_AE samples recruited between 2009 and 2010, of which one was novel strain distinct from other CRF01_AE viruses[11]. Indeed, nearly all of these strains in Guangxi were included in the current study and the strains mostly belong to cluster 2 and cluster 3.

Nonetheless, a comment should be made about the limitation of the data acquisition in this study. Although the entire China CRF01_AE gag sequences from NCBI GenBank were included when this study was initiated, the number of the sequences was relatively small, especially for East China, Southwest China, and Northwest China, until more archival specimens from these regions were retrieved and thoroughly analyzed, the complex dissemination of CRF01_AE lineages were interpreted with caution.

MATERIALS AND METHODS

1. Ethics Statement

This study was approved by the Committee on Human Research at the Beijing Center for Disease Prevention and Control(Beijing CDC)and written inform consents were obtained from all participants.

2. Study Population

In total, 408 CRF01_AE gag gene sequences sampled within the China during 2002-2010 were obtained(GenBank accession numbers are JF759957-JF760203), including 186 from the molecular epidemiology research conducted in Beijing and 222 for which province of origin and sampling year were known, from Los Alamos HIV sequence database. The patient epidemiological information including age, gender, ethnicity, place of birth, route of infection, and CD4 cell count were also collected.

3. Sequence Alignment and Phylogenetic Tree Analysis

The 408 local CRF01_AE gag sequences were aligned with 10 HIV-1 CRF01_AE reference sequences isolated from Thailand, Vietnam, Cyprus, Japan and Hong Kong using Vector NTI 8.0 software(Invitrogen, USA). Multiple alignments were performed automatically by BioEdit with minor manual adjustments. A phylogenetic tree based on gag sequence was constructed with Kimura 2-Parameter model and Neighbor-Joining(NJ)method, using MEGA 4. The bootstrap test was performed with 1,000 replications[14]. Reference sequences of different subtypes (B, C) and CRFs(CRF07_BC, CRF08_BC) strains were downloaded from HIV-1 Los Alamos Database as outgroup sequences.

4. Estimation of the Transmission History of CRF01_AE in China

The evolution rate, time of most recently common ancestor(tMRCA), and demographic historT of the CRF01_AE strains circulating in mainland China were inferred using Bayesian Markov chain Monte Carlo(MCMC) method in BEAST version 1.4.8.The Relaxed Clock: Uncorrelated Exponential model was tested in combination with four different coalescent tree priors('Constant Size';'Exponential Growth','Logistic Growth'and'Bayesian Skyline')under an HKY nucleotide substitution model with heterogeneity among sites modeled with a gamma distribution and invariant sites. For each model the MCMC chain was run for 20,000,000 steps and sampled every 2,000 steps. The first2,000,000 steps of each run were discarded as burn-in. The resulting log-files were analyzed in Tracer v.1.6.2 and the Bayes Factor was calculated to compare molecular clock models, using marginal likelihood as implemented in Tracer v.l.5. The Maximum Clade Credibility with time scale(MCC)tree was obtained by TreeAnnotator vl.6.1 with a burn-in of the first hundred trees[15-17].

SUPPORTING INFORMATION

Fig. S1 Bayesian phylogenetic tree of HIV-1 CRF01_AE gag sequences isolated from North China.

（PDF）

Fig. S2 Bayesian phylogenetic tree of HIV-1 CRF01_AE gag sequences isolated from Northeast China.

（PDF）

Fig. S3 Bayesian phylogenetic tree of HIV-1 CRF01_AE gag sequences isolated from East China.

（PDF）

Fig. S4 Bayesian phylogenetic tree of HIV-1 CRF01_AE gag sequences isolated from South Central China.

（PDF）

Fig. S5 Bayesian phylogenetic tree of HIV-1 CRF01_AE gag sequences isolated from Southwest China.

（PDF）

Fig. S6 Bayesian phylogenetic tree of HIV-1 CRF01_AE gag sequences isolated from Northwest China. Colors indicate the geographic location of sampling as

follow: cluster 1 in red, cluster 2 in green, cluster 3 in purple and cluster 4 in blue.

（PDF）

ACKNOWLEDGMENTS

We thank the entire laboratory members of Beijing Center for Disease Prevention and Control, College of Life Science and Bio-engineering, Beijing University of Technology and the National Institute for Viral Disease Control and Prevention of China for their support in carrying out this project.

Author Contributions

Conceived and designed the experiments: JY XF XH YZ. Performed the experiments: JY RX SY LB WW TW XS HL. Analyzed the data: JY XP HY. Contributed reagents/materials/analysis tools: JY RX XF. Wrote the paper: JY XF.

REFERENCES

[1] Ministry of Health of the People's Republic of China, UNAIDS, WHO(2012) China 2011 AIDS Epidemic Report. Chin J AIDS STD 18:1-5.(in Chinese).

[2] Murphy E, Korber B, Georges-Courbot MC, You B, Pinter A, et al.(1993) Diversity of V3 region sequences of human immunodeficiency viruses type 1 from the central African Republic. AIDS Res Hum Retroviruses 9:997-1006.

[3] Hemelaar J, Gouws E, Ghys PD, Osmanov S(2006)Global and regional distribution of HIV-1 genetic subtypes and recombinants in 2004. AIDS 20:W13-23.

[4] Cheng H, ZhangJ, Capizzi J, Young NL, Mastro TD(1994)HIV-1 subtype E in Yunnan, China. Lancet 334:953-954.

[5] ChenJ, Young NL, Subbarao S, Warachit P, Saguanwongse S, et al.(1999)HIV type 1 sutypes in Guangxi province,China,1996. AIDS Res Hum Retroviruses15:81-84.

[6] Ye JR, Yu SQ, Lu HY, Wang WS, Xin RL, et al.(2012)Genetic diversity of HIV type 1 isolated from newly diagnosed subjects(2006-2007)in Beijing, China. AIDS Res Hum Retroviruses 28:119-123.

[7] Li L, Liang S, Chen L, Liu W, Li H, et al.(2010)Genetic characterization of 13 subtype CRF01_AE near full-length genomes in Guangxi, China. AIDS Res Hum Retroviruses 26:699-704.

[8] Cheng CL, Feng Y, He X, Lin P, Liang SJ, et al.(2009)Genetic characteristics of HIV-1 CRF01_AE strains in four provinces, southern China. Chin J Epidemiol 30:720-725.(in Chinese).

[9] Deng W, Fu P, Bao L, Vidal N, He Q, et al.(2009)Molecular epidemiological tracing of HIV-1 outbreaks in Hainan island of southern China. AIDS 23:977-985.

[10] Chen JH, Wong KH, Li P, Chan KC, Lee MP, et al.(2009)Molecular epidemiological study of HIV-1 CRF01_AE transmission in Hong Kong. J Acquir Immune Defic Syndr 51:530-535.

[11] Zeng H, Sun Z, Liang S, Li L, Jiang Y, et al.(2012)Emergence of a New HIV Type 1 CRF01_AE Variant in Guangxi, Southern China. AIDS Res Hum Retroviruses 28:1352-1356.

[12] Liao H, Tee KK, Hase S, Uenishi R, Li XJ, et al.(2009)Phylodynamic analysis of the dissemination of HIV-1 CRF01_AE in Vietnam. Virology 391:51-56.

[13] Bontell I, Cuong DD, Agneskog E, Diwan V, Larsson M, et al.(2012) Transmitted drug resistance and phylogenetic analysis of HIV CRF01_AE in Northern Vietnam. Infect Genet Evol 12:448-452.

[14] Xin R, He X, Xing H, Sun F, Ni M, et al.(2009)Genetic and temporal dynamics of human immunodeficiency virus type 1 CRF07_BC in Xinjiang, China. J Gen Virol 90:1757-1761.

[15] Drummond AJ, Rambaut A(2007)BEAST:Bayesian evolutionary analysis by sampling trees. BMC Evol Biol 7:214.

[16] Chen JH, Wong KH, Chan KC, To SW, Chen Z et al.(2011)Phylodynamics of HIV-1 subtype B among the men-having-sex-with-men(MSM)population in Hong Kong. PLoS One 6:e25286.

[17] Neogi U, Bontell I, Shet A, De Costa A, Gupta S, et al.(2012)Molecular epidemiology of HIV-1 subtypes in India: origin and evolutionary history of the predominant subtype C. PLoS One 7:e39819.

Haplotype-dependent HLA Susceptibility to Nasopharyngeal Carcinoma in a Southern Chinese Population

M Tang[1,2], Y Zeng[3], A Poisson[4], D Marti[4], L Guan[5], Y Zheng[2], H Deng[2], J Liao[6],
X Guo[3,5], S Sun[7], G Nelson[5], G de Thé[8], CA Winkler[5], SJ O'Brien[1], M Carrington[4] and X Gao[4]

[1]Laboratory of Genomic Diversity National Cancer Institute-Frederick, Frederick, MD, USA; [2]Cancer Center, Wuzhou Red Cross Hospital, Guangxi, China; [3]State Key Laboratory for Infectious Diseases Prevention and Control, Institute for Viral Disease Control and Prevention, Chinese Center for Disease Control and Prevention, Beijing, China; [4]Cancer and Inflammation Program, Laboratory of Experimental Immunology, National Cancer Institute-Frederick, Frederick, MD, USA; [5]Laboratory of Genomic Diversity SAIC-Frederick, Inc., National Cancer Institute-Frederick, Frederick, MD, USA; [6]Department of Epidemiology, Cangwu Institute for Nasopharyngeal Carcinoma Control and Prevention, Guangxi, China; [7]Conservation Biology Building, College of Life Sciences, Peking University, Beijing, China and [8]Oncogenic Virus Epidemiology and Pathophysiology, Institute Pasteur, Paris, France

[ABSTRACT]　We have conducted a comprehensive case-control study of a nasopharyngeal carcinoma(NPC) population cohort from Guangxi Province of Southern China, a region with one of the highest NPC incidences on record. A total of 1407 individuals including NPC patients, healthy controls, and their adult children were examined for the human leukocyte antigen(HLA) association, which is so far the largest NPC cohort reported for such studies. Stratified analysis performed in this study clearly demonstrated that while NPC protection is associated with independent HLA alleles, most NPC susceptibility is strictly associated with HLA haplotypes. Our study also detected for the first time that A*0206, a unique A2 subtype to South and Southeast Asia is also associated with a high risk for NPC. HLA-A*0206, HLA-B*3802 alleles plus the A*0207-B*4601 and A*3303-B*5801 haplotypes conferred high risk for NPC showing a combined odds ratio(OR)of 2.6($P<0.0001$). HLA alleles that associate with low risk for NPC include HLA-A*1101, B*27, and B*55 with a combined OR of 0.42($P<0.0001$). The overall high frequency of NPC-susceptible HLA factors in the Guangxi population is likely to have contributed to the high-NPC incidence in this region.

Genes and Immunity(2010)11,334-342; doi:10.1038/gene.2009.109; published online 14 January 2010

[Keywords]　HLA; nasopharyngeal carcinoma; haplotype; stratified analysis

INTRODUCTION

Nasopharyngeal carcinoma(NPC)is an epithelial malignancy caused by a combination of Epstein-Barr virus (EBV)infection and environmental factors.[1-3] Genetic predisposition also has a function in NPC susceptibility causing the observed familial aggregation[4] and distinct racial and geographical distribution of the disease incidence.[5-8] Southern China and Southeast Asia have a disproportionally high incidence of NPC. In these regions, NPC is one of the most common cancers,[9,10] but in Caucasians, it is a rare disease.[11]

Among the host genetic markers that have been associated with NPC, the class I human leukocyte antigen (HLA)genes have shown a strong and consistent association with disease risk. As it was first reported by Simons et al.[12] in a Singaporean Chinese cohort in the mid 1970s, the HLA association with NPC has been widely detected in different racial groups even though the exact HLA factors(alleles and haplotypes) associated with the disease sometimes vary among racial groups due to population-dependent HLA distributions. Populations of Southern China and Southeast Asia share high-NPC incidence as well as common HLA characteristics. Mainland Chinese,[9,13] Taiwanese,[14] and Singaporean Chinese[15] NPC cohorts also show similar HLA associations, where HLA-A*11 and B*13 seem protective against NPC, and A*02(A*0207), A*33, B*46, and B*58 associate with susceptibility to

Correspondence: Professor Y Zeng, State Key Laboratory for Infectious Diseases Prevention and Control, Institute for Viral Disease Control and Prevention, Chinese Center for Disease Control and Prevention, Beijing 100052, China.
E-mail: zengy@public.bta.net.cn or Dr M Carrington, Cancer and Inflammation Program, Laboratory of Experimental Immunology, PO Box B, Bldg 560, Room 21-89, Frederick, MD 21702, USA.
E-mail: carringt@ncifcrf.gov
Received 13 July 2009; revised 19 October 2009; accepted 12 November 2009; published online 14 January 2010

this disease(Fig. 1). Other HLA loci including HLA-C and the class II loci, DR and DQ, have not shown independent associations with NPC even though certain class II alleles might be part of the extended HLA haplotypes associated with the disease as described by Hildesheim et al.[14]

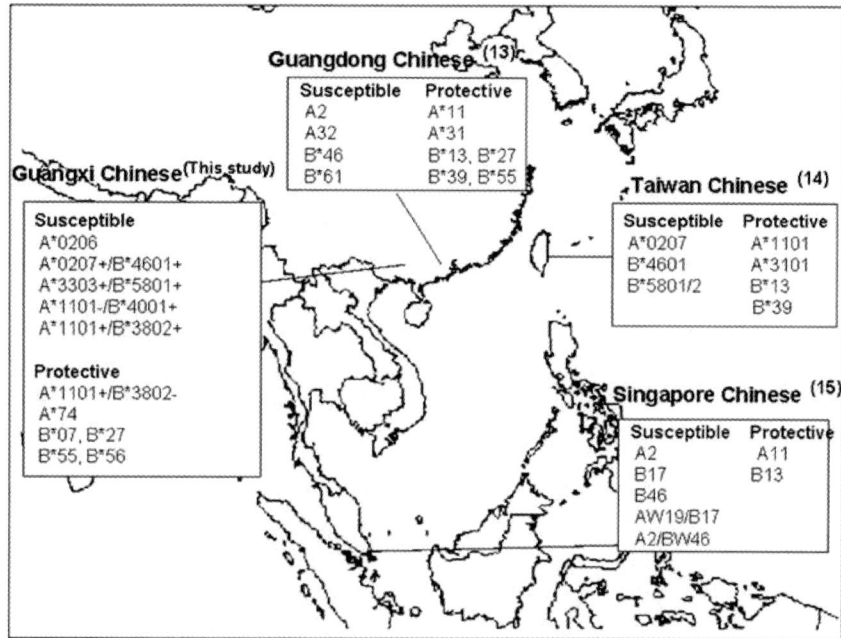

Fig. 1　HLA associations with NPC in Chinese population.

Association of HLA polymorphism with human disease may indicate direct involvement of the HLA molecule in the disease pathogenesis. To date, however, there has been little in vitro or in vivo evidence that the NPC-associated HLA alleles affect differentially NPC-related EBV replication on pathogenesis. The role of HLA-A and -B alleles or haplotypes that include combinations of these alleles in NPC pathogenesis remains unknown. It is possible that the associated HLA class I alleles are simply marking by linkage disequilibrium(LD)the true NPC-causing gene(s). Large-scale cohort studies exploring combinations of associated HLA alleles may provide useful insights into the influence of HLA on NPC.

An early indicator of NPC development is the occurrence of immunoglobulin(Ig)A antibodies to EBV capsid antigens(EBV-IgA/VCA).[16-18] Even though $>95\%$ of adults in the general population of all ethnic groups are healthy carriers of EBV, $<2.5\%$ are EBV-IgA/VCA antibody positive. In comparison, $>95\%$ of all NPC patients are EBV-IgA/VCA antibody positive.[10] If HLA diversity is indeed directly responsible for the individually varied NPC risks, it is plausible that the development of the EBVIgA/VCA antibodies in EBV-positive individuals may also be affected by the HLA polymorphism.

Here, we have conducted a case-control study of an NPC cohort recruited from Guangxi Province in Southern China where the NPC incidence is as high as 25-50 cases per 10 000 individuals. DNA-based high-resolution HLA typing was performed on a total of 1407 individuals including NPC cases, matched controls, and offspring of the study subjects. This large study has allowed a comprehensive stratification of NPC-associated HLA factors and provided novel insights into the nature of the HLA association with the disease.

RESULTS

HLA typing was informative for 356 NPC patients, 287 NPC free EBV-IgA/VCA antibody positive healthy individuals, and 342 NPC free EBV-IgA/VCA antibody negative healthy individuals. Comparative analyses between the two healthy groups failed to detect any significant deviation in the frequency distribution of HLA alleles and haplotypes(Supplementary Tabs. 1 and 2), indicating that HLA polymorphism does not affect the occurrence of the EBV-IgA/VCA antibody. Therefore, in subsequent analyses, the two NPC-free groups were combined as the control group(N=629)for NPC cases.

Tab. 1 Gene frequencies(%)of the two and four-digit HLA-A,-B, and -C alleles detected in NPC patients(N=356)and controls (N=629)

| | Allele | Frequency | | P-value | P$_c$-value* |
		NPC patients	Controls		
HLA-A	02	38.62(275)	32.75(412)	0.01	NS
	0206	5.2(37)	2.31(29)	0.0006	NS
	0207	14.89(106)	11.29(143)	0.02	NS
	11	23.74(169)	32.35(407)	0.0001	0.003
	1101	19.52(139)	29.09(366)	<0.0001	0.0003
	33	20.51(146)	14.31(180)	0.0004	0.02
	3303	20.51(146)	14.31(180)	0.0004	0.04
	74	0.14(1)	1.11(14)	0.02	NS
HLA-B	07	0.0(0)	1.03(13)	0.01	NS
	13	8.43(60)	13.04(164)	0.002	NS
	1301	7.72(55)	12.08(152)	0.002	NS
	27	0.0(0)	1.59(20)	0.001	NS
	2704	0.0(0)	1.27(16)	0.005	NS
	38	12.78(91)	9.78(123)	0.04	NS
	3802	12.64(90)	9.30(117)	0.02	NS
	39	0.28(2)	1.19(15)	0.04	NS
	40	16.29(116)	12.32(155)	0.01	NS
	4001	14.75(105)	11.05(139)	0.02	NS
	55	0.56(4)	4.21(53)	<0.0001	0.0002
	5502	0.56(4)	3.66(46)	<0.0001	0.003
	56	0.84(6)	2.23(28)	0.02	NS
	5601	0.28(2)	1.67(21)	0.006	NS
	58	19.10(136)	14.07(177)	0.003	NS
	5801	19.10(136)	14.07(177)	0.003	NS
HLA-C	0302	18.12(129)	13.43(169)	0.005	NS
	0403	0.98(7)	2.23(28)	0.05	NS
	12	1.12(8)	4.29(54)	0.0001	0.006
	1202	0.56(4)	2.23(28)	0.005	NS
	1203	0.56(4)	2.07(26)	0.01	NS
	15	1.12(8)	2.62(33)	0.03	NS

Abbreviations: HLA, human leukocyte antigen; NPC, nasopharyngeal carcinoma.
'NS'=P>0.05.

Tab. 2 HLA-A/B and B/A haplotype frequencies(%)in NPC patients(N=356)and controls(N=629)[a]

| Haplotype | | Frequency | | P-value* | Allele/haplotype effect[b] |
		NPC patients	Controls		
(A)					
HLA-A/B					
0206	1502	1.26	0.4	0.03	Allele A*0206(S)
	Others	3.93	1.91	0.007	

Haplotype		Frequency		P-value[a]	Allele/haplotype effect[b]
		NPC patients	Controls		
0207	4601	12. 22	8. 59	0. 01	Haplotype A* 0207-B* 4601(S)
	Others	2. 67	2. 7	NS	
1101	1301	3. 79	7. 07	0. 003	Allele A* 1101(P)
	1502	4. 21	5. 72	NS	
	3802	1. 97	0. 79	0. 02	Allele offset
	4001	2. 53	3. 74	NS	
	4601	1. 12	2. 7	0. 02	Allele A* 1101(P)
	5101	1. 4	1. 43	NS	
	5401	1. 4	1. 03	NS	
	Others	3. 09	6. 6	0. 0009	
3303	5801	17. 13	11. 29	0. 0003	Haplotype A* 3303-B* 5801(S)
	Others	3. 37	3. 02	NS	
(B)					
HLA-B-A					
1301	1101	3. 79	7. 07	0. 003	Allele A* 1101(P)
	2402	1. 83	2. 85	NS	
	Others	2. 11	2. 15	NS	
3802	0203	9. 41	7. 07	NS	
	1101	1. 97	0. 79	0. 03	Allele offset
	Others	1. 26	1. 43	NS	
4001	0203	3. 23	1. 59	0. 02	Allele B* 4001(S)
	1101	2. 53	3. 74	NS	
	1102	1. 54	0. 48	0. 01	Allele B* 4001(S)
	2402	4. 07	3. 34	NS	
	Others	3. 37	1. 91	NS	
5502	0203	0. 42	2. 07	0. 004	Allele B* 5502(P)
	others	0. 14	1. 59	0. 003	
5801	3303	17. 13	11. 29	0. 0003	Haplotype B* 5801-A* 3303(S)
	others	1. 97	2. 78	NS	

Abbreviations：HLA，human leukocyte antigen；NPC，nasopharyngeal carcinoma.

[a]HLA-A/B haplotypes(Tab. 2A) are those containing HLA-A alleles that showed significant association with NPC in the analysis of individual alleles and HLA-B/A haplotypes(Tab. 2B)are those containing HLA-B alleles that showed significant association with NPC. Only the haplotypes with at least one allele showing significantly different gene frequencies between patients and controls are shown. Lowfrequency haplotypes($<1.0\%$ in both groups)associated with a particular A or B allele are combined as 'others'. A* 7400, which associated with protection(see Tab. 1), was not found on any haplotype with a frequency of $>1\%$, and thus is not listed. This was also the case for B* 2704 and B* 5601.

[b]'p'=Protective effect，'S'= Susceptible effect.

[c]'NS'=$P>0.05$.

HLA alleles showing a significant difference in frequency distribution between cases and controls are listed in Tab. 1, and full analyses are presented in Supplementary Tabs. 3 and 4. For the reason of most of former NPC, HLA studies were based on serology typing, for better understanding the HLA influence in NPC, both HLA allotype and genotype were present in this table. For the HLA-A locus, 31 four-digit alleles were detected, 12 of which had an allele frequency $>1\%$ in either the case or control group. Five alleles, A* 0206, A* 0207, A* 1101, A* 3303, and A* 7401/7402, showed a significant difference in frequency distribution between the case and control groups. After correction, however, only two alleles, A* 1101 and A* 3303, remained significant. Of the two detected A* 11 alleles, A* 1101 showed a reduced presence in patients compared with controls ($P < 0.0001$), whereas the less common A* 1102 showed no difference between these groups, but due to its low frequency, it need to be confirmed in even large study cohort. Four common A* 02 subtypes, A* 0201, A* 0203, A* 0206, and A* 0207, were detected. Two of alleles, A* 0206 and A* 0207, showed an elevated frequency in patients. A* 3303 also associated with increased risk of NPC($P = 0.0004$).

Tab. 3　Effect of allelic combinatioNS of NPC-associated HLA alleles on the disease development

Allele combination[a] A/B	NPC patients (N=356) %(n)	Controls(N=629) %(n)	OR(95% CI)	P-value*	Allele/haplotype effect
Protective					
1101/4001					Allele A* 1101
−/+	19. 38(69)	8. 59(54)	2. 56(1. 76-3. 72)	<0. 0001	
+/−	28. 37(101)	38. 95(254)	0. 62(0. 47-0. 82)	0. 0008	
+/+	8. 15(29)	11. 92(75)	0. 66(0. 42-1. 02)	NS	
0203/5502					Allele B* 5502
−/+	0. 28(1)	2. 54(16)	0. 11(0. 02-0. 57)	0. 009	
+/−	27. 53(98)	23. 37(147)	1. 25(0. 93-1. 68)	NS	
+/+	0. 84(3)	4. 45(28)	0. 18(0. 06-0. 53)	0. 002	
1101/1301					Allele A* 1101
−/+	5. 9(21)	6. 52(41)	0. 9(0. 52-1. 55)	NS	
+/−	27. 25(97)	34. 02(214)	0. 73(0. 55-0. 97)	0. 03	
+/+	9. 27(33)	16. 85(106)	0. 5(0. 33-0. 76)	0. 001	
Susceptible					
0206/1502					Allele A* 0206
−/+	13. 2(47)	15. 74(99)	0. 81(0. 56-1. 18)	NS	
+/−	7. 02(25)	3. 66(23)	1. 99(1. 12-3. 53)	0. 02	
+/+	3. 37(12)	0. 95(6)	3. 62(1. 43-9. 15)	0. 007	
0207/4601					Haplotype A* 0207-B* 4601
−/+	7. 87(28)	12. 24(77)	0. 61(0. 39-0. 96)	0. 03[b]	
+/−	3. 93(14)	4. 93(31)	0. 79(0. 41-1. 50)	NS	
+/+	23. 31(83)	16. 38(103)	1. 55(1. 12-2. 14)	0. 008	
3303/5801					Haplotype A* 3303-B* 5801
−/+	3. 37(12)	4. 45(28)	0. 75(0. 28-1. 49)	NS	
+/−	5. 06(18)	5. 41(34)	0. 93(0. 52-1. 68)	NS	
+/+	32. 87(117)	21. 46(135)	1. 79(1. 34-2. 39)	0. 0001	

Abbreviations: CI, confidence interval; HLA, human leukocyte antigen; NPC, nasopharyngeal carcinoma; OR, odds ratio.
[a] '+'=positive for the allele; '−'=negative for the allele.
[b] The A0207-/B4601+ signal($P = 0.0325$)is a weak 'protective' confirmed, the opposite of the strong susceptible haplotype A0207/B4601.
* 'NS'=$P > 0.05$.

Tab. 4 Protective and susceptible HLA alleles, haplotypes, and genotypes for the development of NPC

HLA factor	NPC cases(N=356) %(n)	Controls(N=629) %(n)	OR(95% CI)	P-value
Protective				
A* 1101+/B* 3802	32.58(116)	49.76(313)	0.49(0.37-0.64)	<0.0001
A* 74	0.28(1)	2.07(13)	0.13(0.05-0.32)	0.03
B* 07	0.0(0)	2.07(13)	0.07(0.01-0.56)	0.01
B* 27	0.0(0)	3.18(20)	0.04(0.01-0.29)	0.001
B* 55	1.12(4)	7.95(50)	0.13(0.05-0.32)	<0.0001
B* 56	1.69(6)	4.45(28)	0.37(0.16-0.87)	0.02
Combined	34.83(124)	58.98(371)	0.37(0.28-0.49)	<0.0001
Susceptible				
A* 0206	10.39(37)	4.61(29)	2.40(1.47-3.92)	0.0005
A* 0207+/B* 4601+	23.03(82)	16.38(103)	1.53(1.11-2.11)	0.01
A* 3303+/B* 5801+	32.87(117)	21.14(133)	1.83(1.37-2.44)	<0.0001
A* 1101/B* 4001+	23.03(82)	14.15(89)	1.82(1.30-2.53)	0.0004
A* 1101+/B* 3802+	3.93(14)	1.59(10)	2.53(1.14-5.61)	0.02
Combined	73.03(260)	50.08(315)	2.70(2.05-3.56)	<0.0001

Abbreviations: CI, confidence interval; HLA, human leukocyte antigen; NPC, nasopharyngeal carcinoma; OR, odds ratio.

Fifty-five HLA-B alleles were detected, but only 14 had a frequency >1%. Among the 14 B alleles, seven showed a significantly different distribution between cases and controls, including B* 1301, B* 2704, B* 3802, B* 4001, B* 5502, B* 5601, and B* 5801. After P-value correction, however, only the decrease of B* 5502 in the patient group remained significant(P corrected=0.003). Three B* 27 subtypes, B* 2704, B* 2705, and B* 2706 were detected only in the control group with a combined frequency of 1.59%(P=0.0014). B* 3802, B* 4001, and B* 5801 were each observed more frequently among the case group but the significance disappeared after correction.

Twenty-four alleles were detected at the HLA-C locus, 13 of which had a frequency >1%. Cw* 0403, Cw* 1202, and Cw* 1203 were observed at a lower frequency in cases and Cw* 0302 was the only allele showing an elevated frequency in cases. After correction, however, none of the four-digit HLA-C alleles remained significant.

HLA typing was informative for 422 children of the study subjects, which enabled us to directly determine HLA haplotypes in 179 patients and 379 controls. For the remaining 177 patients and 250 controls, HLA haplotypes were assigned by population-based estimation methods. HLA-A/B haplotype frequencies were calculated on the basis of both methods of haplotype assignments. Stratification analyses were performed to determine the nature of the observed HLA association(Tabs. 2 and 3). Tab. 2 compares the frequency distribution of all HLA-A/B (where the HLA-A allele showed individual association with NPC) and -B/A(where the HLA-B allele showed individual association with NPC)haplotypes related to individual NPC-associated alleles between cases and controls to determine whether the observed allele association with NPC might be due to particular haplotypes or to an individual allele. Four of the five potentially NPC-related HLA-A alleles, A* 0206, A* 0207, A* 1101, and A* 3303, were each observed on HLA-A/B haplotypes with frequencies of>1% and were therefore included in Tab. 2A. Both the dominant A* 0206-B* 1502 haplotype(P=0.0278)and all other A* 0206-associated haplotypes combined (P=0.0071)showed elevated frequencies in the patient group. A* 0207 is predominantly associated with B* 4601, and this was the only A* 0207 haplotype associating with susceptibility to NPC(P=0.0095). Similarly, A* 3303-B* 5801 was the only A* 3303 haplotype associating with NPC susceptibility(P=0.0003). The protective A* 1101 allele was found on seven HLA-A/B haplotypes with frequencies >1% and these haplotypes showed inconsistent associations with NPC. A* 1101-B* 1301(P=0.0029), A* 1101-B* 4601(P=0.0198), and A* 1101-B* others(P =0.0009)showed reduced frequencies in the NPC group, whereas A* 1101-B* 3802 haplotype(P=0.0228) showed an elevated frequency in the patient group.

Five of the seven NPC-associated HLA-B alleles composed haplotypes with frequencies >1%. The B* 5801-A* 3303 haplotype showed an elevated frequency in NPC patients, whereas the other B* 5801 haplotypes did not. The other NPC-associated B alleles were all found on at least two common HLA-B/A haplotypes. Both B* 1301 and B* 3802 were significantly more common in the control group only when A* 1101 was also present on these haplotypes($P=0.0029$ and $P=0.0228$, respectively). B* 4001 was associated with four haplotypes with a frequency >1%. All haplotypes containing this allele were observed more frequently in the patients(B* 4001-A* 0203 and B* 4001-A* 1102 reaching significance; $P=0.0167$ and $P=0.0138$, respectively), except for the A* 1101-associated B* 4001 haplotype, which was more common in the controls albeit not significantly.

Tab. 3 stratifies six common NPC-associated HLA-A/ B allelic combinations to examine independent as well as collective effects of HLA alleles on NPC risk analyzed in Tab. 2. For each tested HLA-A/B phenotypic combination, the study subjects were divided into three groups: those having both of the relevant HLA-A and HLA-B alleles and those that had one, but not the other. The protective A* 1101 and the susceptible B* 4001 allele combination is included first in Tab. 3 to show the collective effect of these two offsetting NPC-associated alleles. The protective B* 5502 is in LD with A* 0203, and stratification for this allele combination showed that the protective effect of B* 5502 could be detected in the presence(odds ratio(OR)$=0.18$, $P=0.0018$)or absence(OR$=0.11$, $P=0.0088$)of A* 0203. A* 1101, which is commonly linked to the NPC-related B alleles B* 1301 and B* 4001, is the most common protective allele in the Guangxi NPC cohort. Stratified analysis showed that the A* 1101 protection was stronger when B* 1301 was also present(OR$=0.5$, $P=0.0010$; without B* 1301; OR$=0.73$, $P=0.0280$). However, B* 1301 had no effect(OR$=0.9$, $P>0.05$)in the absence of A* 1101. Remarkably, B* 4001 actually associated strongly with risk of developing NPC if A* 1101 was missing(OR$=2.56$, $P<0.0001$), but in the presence of A* 1101, the susceptibility effect of B* 4001 was completely abrogated(OR$=0.66$, $P>0.05$). The susceptibility effect of A* 0206 seems to be largely independent of HLA-B, though the A* 0206 and B* 1502 combination was somewhat stronger(OR$=3.63$, $P=0.0065$)than that in the presence of other HLA-B alleles (OR$=1.99$, $P=0.0184$). Both A* 0207(Tab. 1)and B* 4601[14,19] were thought to be independent high-risk factors for NPC in Southern Chinese and Southeast Asia. The two alleles are in strong LD in the Guangxi cohort, as in most Southern Chinese populations, and the A* 0207-B* 4601 haplotype associated with susceptibility(Tab. 3). However, A* 0207 showed no effect in the absence of B* 4601, whereas B* 4601 had a weak protective effect in the absence of A* 0207(OR$=0.61$, $P=0.0325$). Finally, A* 3303 and B* 5801 forms the most common A-B haplotype in the Guangxi cohort and both alleles were associated with an elevated NPC risk(Tab. 1). Stratification of the A* 3303 and B* 5801 combination showed that the NPC effect was more strongly associated with the presence of both alleles(OR$=1.79$, $P=0.0001$) as one allele without the other had no effect.

Tab. 4 summarizes the HLA alleles and the allele combinations associated with the risk of developing NPC. HLA protection against NPC mainly involves independent allele influence except that the A* 1101 protection may be overridden by the presence of the high-risk B* 3802. The presence of one or more of the six protective factors has a frequency of 58.98% within the control group and 34.83% within the NPC patients. Together, these protective factors delivered a combined OR of 0.37($P<0.0001$). NPC susceptibility, on the other hand, associates most strongly with certain allele combinations, as opposed to single alleles, with the exception of the A* 0206 effect. Individual positive for any of the five high-risk factors accounted for 50.08% and 73.03% of the controls and cases, respectively. These high-risk factors showed individual ORs between 2.05 and 3.56 and a collective OR of 2.70($P<0.0001$).

On the basis of analyses shown, HLA haplotypes were classified as NPC protective(P), susceptible(S), and neutral(N), generating six genotypes. Fig. 2 shows the ORs of the six genotypes for NPC development. Interestingly, neither the protective nor the susceptible genotypes seemed dominant over the other. The exact values are presented in Supplementary Tab. 5. The ORs of the remaining genotypes were distributed in a manner that was expected given that the protective and susceptible genotypes were defined in this same cohort. The validity of this scheme will be particularly interesting to test in an independent cohort.

The influence of HLA genotypes on NPC risk was analyzed by comparing all individual genotypes in HLA-A and -B loci separately and the compound genotypes of HLA-A and -B. Two HLA-A, six HLA-B genotypes and six HLA-A-B compound genotypes were significantly associated with either elevated NPC risk or protection. These genotypes all involve at least one allele showing a higher risk or protection for the disease.

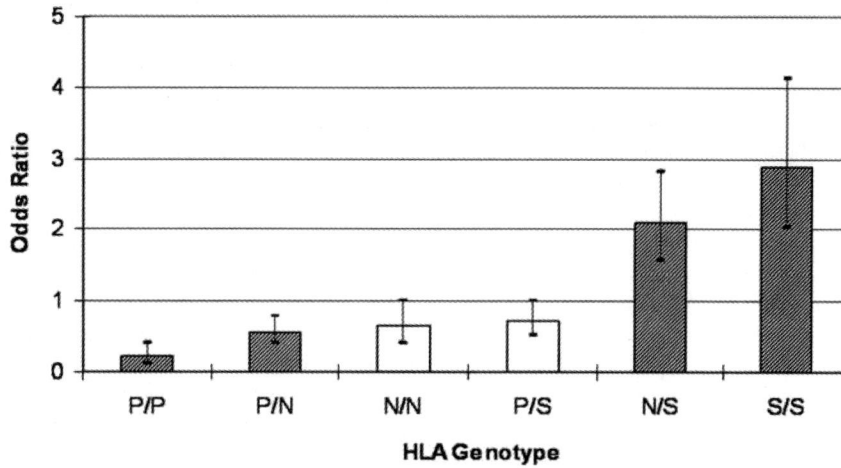

P: protective haplotype; S: susceptible haplotype; N: neutral haplotype. Columns with a pattern indicate ORs with P values <0.05.

Fig. 2 ORs of HLA genotypes for NPC development.

Tab. 5 Gender and age of NPC patients and EBV-IgA/VCA positive and negative controls

	NPC patients	Controls	
		EBV-IgA/ VCA positive	EBV-IgA/ VCA negative
	N＝356	N＝287	N＝342
Male/female	237/119	141/146	129/213
(％ male)	(67％)	(49％)	(37％)
Age	50.09±10.83	45.69±8.90	46.87±10.24
EBV-IgA/VCA	95.50％	100％	0％

Abbreviations: EBV, Epstein-Barr virus; NPC, nasopharyngeal carcinoma.

DISCUSSION

Southern China has a disproportionally high incidence of NPC compared with other parts of the world. The study population from Wuzhou City of Guangxi Province in Southern China holds, perhaps, the highest recorded NPC incidence.[9,10] Apart from unique environmental factors(mainly traditional diet), our data support a role for genetic predisposition contributing to the highdisease incidence. The results from this study confirm and extend previously reported HLA and NPC associations in Southern Chinese populations,[12-14,19] such as the protective effect associated with HLA-A* 1101 and susceptibility effects associated with B* 0207, A* 3303, and B* 5801. This study provides further insights into the nature of the HLA association with NPC, such as the observation that the dominant A* 11 protection can be entirely attributed to the major subtype A* 1101. The other A* 11 subtype detected in this population, A* 1102, did not show any protective effect even though the two A* 11 subtypes differ by only a single amino acid in position 19 outside of the peptide-binding groove.

Our stratified analyses demonstrated that a proportion of the HLA-associated NPC susceptibility is likely to be haplotype-dependent in this cohort(Tab. 3). In earlier cohort studies from Southern China[13] and Taiwan,[14] the A* 0207-B* 4601 allele combination was consistently associated with a high-NPC risk, but there are contradictory reports on whether the two alleles have independent effects. In our study cohort, two major high-risk HLA-A/B allele combinations, A* 0207-B* 4601 and A* 3303-B* 5801, were identified. Patients with either of these two allele combinations accounted for half of the NPC cohort and susceptibility conferred by these HLA-A/B combinations was strictly dependent on the presence of both alleles. The alleles comprising both pairs are in strong LD, forming the two most common HLA-A/B haplotypes in the Guangxi population.

Haplotype-dependent disease associations may indicate one of the two possibilities: (1) the two alleles on the haplotype are behaving in an epistatic manner to reach functional synergy or (2) the disease-associated HLA haplotype is tracking an unidentified disease locus present on that specific haplotype. An example of the former is that the structural stability of the HLA-DQ αβ dimer is affected by the type of DQA and DQB alleles carried on HLA haplotypes, which in turn influences the risk of insulin-dependent diabetes mellitus (IDDM).[20] Functional synergy between HLA-A and -B molecules and any potential clinical relevance such synergy may have, however, are yet to be established. In terms of the alternative HLA marker model, there are no data that unequivocally support or refute the hypothesis in NPC studies, despite efforts to identify non-HLA disease genes in the extended MHC region.[21,22] Still, direct involvement of HLA molecules in NPC pathogenesis, including that involving the causative EBV infection, also lacks functional data support. Interpretations of the present results tend to support the locus tracking hypothesis in that there is evidence for (1) a lack of HLA association with the occurrence of IgA antibodies to EBV-IgA/VCA, a well-known precursor of NPC, (2) haplotypedependent but allele-independent disease susceptibility, and (3) the lack of association of A* 1102 despite its identical peptide-binding structure shared with the well-documented protective A* 1101 allele.[14] Furthermore, distinct population-specific HLA alleles associate with susceptibility to NPC, which is unexpected if HLA is directly involved in disease pathogenesis.

In contrast to the haplotype-dependent but alleleindependent susceptibility exhibited by the two major high-risk haplotypes A* 0207-B* 4601 and A* 3303-B* 5801, the dominant protective effect conferred by A* 1101 did not show a clear haplotypic dependence. In fact, most A* 1101-linked A/B haplotypes showed a trend of underrepresentation in the case group except the one linked with the susceptible B* 3802. A* 1101 seems to protect against other viral infections as well. For example, A* 1101 may confer protection against AIDS through restriction of immunodominant HIV peptides,[23,24] but the structural and functional basis for its direct involvement in NPC pathogenesis has not been thoroughly explored.

The detected allele and haplotype associations with NPC seem to be independent of HLA genotypes as genotypes showing significant ORs are essentially those with least two copies of NPC-associated alleles or haplotypes. Also, no particular genotypes showed stronger association than individual alleles or haplotypes.

Another noteworthy HLA association observed in the Guangxi NPC cohort is an opportune 'complete' protection of B* 27 against disease development. B* 27 was detected with a typical frequency in the control group (1.59%), but was completely absent in the patient group (OR = 0.04, P = 0.001). Earlier cohort studies from Southern China and Taiwan have also detected B* 27 as a low-risk allele though the protection was never 'complete.'[14,19,25] B* 27 is well known for its high-risk association with the inflammatory autoimmune disease ankylosing spondylitis and it confers protection against AIDS progression apparently through its peptide-binding properties for immunodominant HIV epitopes.[26] Perhaps B* 27 is also involved in EBV-related pathogenesis, impacting the risk of NPC development. Given the low frequency of B* 27 in the study population, however, the absence of B* 27 in the patient group should be confirmed in larger replication cohort studies.

The overall HLA profile of a population is likely to influence the incidence of HLA-associated diseases. An example is the correlation between the rates of IDDM incidence and the frequency distribution of the IDDM-associated HLA-DQ and DR alleles in world populations.[27] The NPC incidence in a population may also correlate positively with the frequencies of NPC-susceptible HLA alleles and haplotypes of the population. The two dominant susceptible HLA haplotypes, A* 0207-B* 4601 and A* 3303-B* 5801, are the two most common HLA-A/B haplotypes in Guangxi and together they account for 20% of the total haplotype frequency of the study Wuzhou population, which is one of the highest in Far East Asian populations. Overall, the susceptible HLA factors were found in about half of the individuals in the Wuzhou population, which is also one of the highest. Therefore, the unusually high presence of NPC-associated HLA alleles and haplotypes may partly explain the disproportionally high-NPC incidence in Southern China and Southeast Asia.

MATERIALS AND METHODS

Study cohorts

NPC cases and controls were recruited from Wuzhou City and Cangwu County of Guangxi Province.[10] All study subjects were of Han ethnic origin. Informed consent was obtained from all study participants. An effort was made to enroll triads consisting of a proband (either NPC patient or NPC-free but EBV-IgA/VCA antibody positive), an unaffected spouse and an adult child. The case group included 356 unrelated patients with biopsy-confirmed NPC. The mean age was 50.1 years (range 19-80), 95.5% of them being EBV-IgA/VCA antibody positive. Two groups of control were the case's spouse or geographically matched residents who were NPC free at the time of study enrollment. An antibody to EBV capsid antigen (EBV-IgA/VCA) were confirmed by serologic testing at the time of study enrollment. One group was positive (N=287) and the other negative (N=342) for the EBV-IgA/

VCA antibody. The mean age was 45.7 and 46.9, respectively, for the antibody positive and negative groups. The controls were matched to the cases by age, ethnicity, and geographic residence (Tab. 5). In addition, 422 adult children of the study subjects in the case and control groups were recruited to allow elucidation of HLA haplotypes, but they were excluded in all other analyses.

Detection of EBV-IgA/VCA antibody

The presence of the EBV-IgA/VCA antibody was detected using the immunoperoxidase assay as described earlier.[28] EBV positive B95-8 cells fixed on slides were incubated with multiple dilutions of the testing serum followed by incubation with antihuman IgA horseradish peroxidase and staining with diaminobenzidine. Testing sera with a staining titer of 1 : 10 or higher dilution were considered positive for the EBV-IgA/VCA antibody.

HLA typing

HLA class I alleles were characterized using a PCR-SSOP (sequence-specific oligonucleotide probe) typing protocol developed by the 13th International histocompatibility Workshop.[29] Briefly, the gene fragment spanning exon 2, intron 2, and exon 3 was amplified using locusspecific primers for HLA-A, -B, and -C separately. The PCR products were immobilized on nylon membranes and hybridized with a panel of P^{32}-labeled oligonucleotide (19 mers) matching all known sequence variations of the HLA genes. Typing results were interpreted by SSOP hybridization patterns based on sequences of known HLA alleles. Typing ambiguities were resolved by sequencing exons 2 and 3 completely. For sequencing analysis, the PCR product of HLA-A, -B, or -C was used as the template for the sequencing reaction. For each of the HLA genes, two sequencing reactions (one for exon 2 and one for exon 3) were performed using exon-specific sequencing primers. The sequencing analysis was performed using the ABI Big Dye Terminator Cycle Sequencing Kit and ABI3730xl DNA analyzer (Applied Biosystems, Foster City, CA, USA). HLA alleles were assigned on the basis of the sequence database of known alleles with the help of the AS-SIGN software developed by Conexio Genomics (Conexio Genomics, Perth City, WA, Australia). Ambiguous heterozygous genotypes were resolved by additional PCR and sequencing procedures using allele-specific PCR primers to selectively amplify only one of the two alleles.

Statistical analyses

HLA allele frequencies were calculated based on observed genotypes, and HLA-A and -B haplotype frequencies were estimated using one of the two methods: (1) unambiguous assignment based on familial segregation for the cases and controls using recruited spouse and child genotype data or (2) indirect assignment based on maximum likelihood estimation for the study subjects without recruited family members. For the latter, the haplotypic analysis was performed using the BLOCKHEAD genetic analysis software developed by George Nelson in the Laboratory of Genomic Diversity, National Cancer Institute.

The effect of HLA alleles on the development of NPC and EBV-IgA/VCA antibody was evaluated by computing ORs and 95% confidence intervals as well as exact P-values using the FREQ procedure of the SAS 9.1 software (The SAS Institute, NC, USA). A correction of 0.5 was applied on every cell of the 2×2 table that contains a zero. The analyses were performed at four-digit and two-digit resolution levels separately. P-value was calculated by x^2-test for each allele and was corrected by multiplying the number of all detected alleles. Significance was considered at $P < 0.05$. Both uncorrected and corrected P-values were presented in our tables. Stratified analyses were applied to evaluate the effect of haplotypes of HLA-A and -B that contained alleles showing individual significant associations with NPC risk.

CONFLICT OF INTEREST

The authors declare no conflict of interest

ACKNOWLEDGEMENTS

This project has been funded in whole or in part with federal funds from the National Cancer Institute, National Institutes of Health, under Contract No. HHSN261200800001E. The content of this publication does not necessarily reflect the views or policies of the Department of Health and Human Services, nor does mention of trade names, commercial products, or organizations imply endorsement by the US Government. This Research was supported in part by the Intramural Research Program of the NIH, National Cancer Institute, Center for Cancer Research.

REFERENCES

[1] Brown TM, Heath CW, Lang RM, Lee SK, Whalley BW. Nasopharyngeal cancer in Bermuda. Cancer 1976; 37: 1464-1468.

[2] Yu MC, Garabrant DH, Huang TB, Henderson BE. Occupational and other non-dietary risk factors for nasopharyngeal carcinoma in Guangzhou, China. Int J Cancer 1990; 45:1033-1039.

[3] Guo X, Johnson RC, Deng H, Liao J, Guan L, Nelson GW et al. Evaluation of non-viral risk factors for nasopharyngeal carcinoma in a high-risk population of Southern China. Int J Cancer 2009; 124:2942-2947.

[4] Coffin CM, Rich SS, Dehner LP. Familial aggregation of nasopharyngeal carcinoma and other malignancies. A clinicopathologic description. Cancer 1991; 68:1323-1328.

[5] Jeannel D, Hubert A, de Vathaire F, Ellouz R, Camoun M, Ben Salem M et al. Diet, living conditions and nasopharyngeal carcinoma in Tunisia-a case-control study. Int J Cancer 1990;46: 421-425.

[6] Laramore GE, Clubb B, Quick C, Amer MH, Ali M, Greer W et al. Nasopharyngeal carcinoma in Saudi Arabia: a retrospective study of 166 cases treated with curative intent. Int J Radiat Oncol Biol Phys 1988; 15:1119-1127.

[7] Johansen LV, Mestre M, Overgaard J. Carcinoma of the nasopharynx: analysis of treatment results in 167 consecutively admitted patients. Head Neck 1992; 14:200-207.

[8] Lee AW, Foo W, Mang O, Sze WM, Chappell R, Lau WH et al. Changing epidemiology of nasopharyngeal carcinoma in Hong Kong over a 20-year period(1980-99): an encouraging reduction in both incidence and mortality. Int J Cancer 2003; 103:680-685.

[9] Lu SJ, Day NE, Degos L, Lepage V, Wang PC, Chan SH et al. Linkage of a nasopharyngeal carcinoma susceptibility locus to the HLA region. Nature 1990; 346: 470-471.

[10] Guo XC, Scott K, Liu Y, Dean M, David V, Nelson GW et al. Genetic factors leading to chronic Epstein-Barr virus infection and nasopharyngeal carcinoma in South East China: study design, methods and feasibility. Hum Genomics 2006; 2: 365-375.

[11] Burr RD, Vaughan TL, McKnight B, Davis S, Beckmann AM, Smith AG et al. Associations between human leukocyte antigen type and nasopharyngeal carcinoma in Caucasians in the United States. Cancer Epidemiol Biomarkers Prev 1996; 5: 879-887.

[12] Simons MJ, Wee GB, Chan SH, Shanmugaratnam K, Day NE, de-The G. Immunogenetic aspects of nasopharyngeal carcinoma(NPC)III. HL-a type as a genetic marker of NPC predisposition to test the hypothesis that Epstein-Barr virus is an etiological factor in NPC. IARC Sci Publ 1975;249-258.

[13] Hu SP, Day NE, Li DR, Luben RN, Cai KL, Ou-Yang T et al. Further evidence for an HLA-related recessive mutation in nasopharyngeal carcinoma among the Chinese. Br J Cancer2005; 92: 967-970.

[14] Hildesheim A, Apple RJ, Chen CJ, Wang SS, Cheng YJ, Klitz W et al. Association of HLA class I and II alleles and extended haplotypes with nasopharyngeal carcinoma in Taiwan. J Natl Cancer Inst 2002; 94:1780-1789.

[15] Chan SH, Day NE, Kunaratnam N, Chia KB, Simons MJ. HLA and nasopharyngeal carcinoma in Chinese-a further study. Int J Cancer 1983; 32:171-176.

[16] Henle G, Henle W. Epstein-Barr virus-specific IgA serum antibodies as an outstanding feature of nasopharyngeal carcinoma. Int J Cancer 1976; 17:1-7.

[17] Zeng Y, Zhang LG, Li HY, Jan MG, Zhang Q, Wu YC et al. Serological mass survey for early detection of nasopharyngeal carcinoma in Wuzhou City, China. Int J Cancer 1982; 29:139-141.

[18] Zeng Y, Zhang LG, Wu YC, Huang YS, Huang NQ, Li JY et al. Prospective studies on nasopharyngeal carcinoma in Epstein-Barr virus IgA/VCA antibody-positive persons in Wuzhou City, China. Int J Cancer 1985; 36:545-547.

[19] Wu SB, Hwang SJ, Chang AS, Hsieh T, Hsu MM, Hsieh RP et al. Human leukocyte antigen(HLA)frequency among patients with nasopharyngeal carcinoma in Taiwan. Anticancer Res 1989; 9:1649-1653.

[20] Kwok WW, Schwarz D, Nepom BS, Hock RA, Thurtle PS, Nepom GT. HLA-DQ molecules form alpha-beta heterodimers of mixed allotype. J Immunol 1988; 141:3123-3127.

[21] Lu CC, Chen JC, Tsai ST, Jin YT, Tsai JC, Chan SH et al. Nasopharyngeal carcinoma-susceptibility locus is localized to a 132 kb segment containing HLA-A using high-resolution microsatellite mapping. Int J Cancer 2005;115:742-746.

[22] Ooi EE, Ren EC, Chan SH. Association between microsatellites within the human MHC and nasopharyngeal carcinoma. Int J Cancer 1997; 74:229-232.

[23] Beyrer C, Artenstein AW, Rugpao S, Stephens H, VanCott TC, Robb ML et al. Epidemiologic and biologic characterization of a cohort of human immunodeficiency virus type 1 highly exposed, persistently seronegative female sex workers in northern Thailand. Chiang Mai HEPS Working Group. J Infect Dis 1999; 179:59-67.

[24] Fukada K, Tomiyama H, Chujoh Y, Miwa K, Kaneko Y, Oka S et al. HLA-A* 1101-restricted cytotoxic T lymphocyte recognition for a novel epitope derived from the HIV-1 Env protein. Aids 1999; 13: 2597-2599.

[25] Yu MC, Huang TB, Henderson BE. Diet and nasopharyngeal carcinoma: a case-control study in Guangzhou, China. Int J Cancer 1989; 43:1077-1082.

[26] Gao X, Bashirova A, Iversen AK, Phair J, Goedert JJ, Buchbinder S et al. AIDS restriction HLA allotypes target distinct intervals of HIV-1 pathogenesis. Nat Med 2005; 11:1290-1292.

[27] Bao MZ, Wang JX, Dorman JS, Trucco M. HLA-DQ beta nonASP-57 allele and incidence of diabetes in China and the USA. Lancet 1989; 2: 497-498.

[28] Cevenini R, Donati M, Rumpianesi F, Moroni A, Paolucci P. An immunoperoxidase assay for the detection of specific IgA antibody in Epstein-Barr virus infections. J Clin Pathol 1984; 37:440-443.

[29] Gao X, Nelson GW, Karacki P, Martin MP, Phair J, Kaslow R et al. Effect of a single amino acid change in MHC class I molecules on the rate of progression to AIDS. N Engl J Med 2001; 344:1668-1675.

[In:《Genes and Immunity》2010,11:334-342]

三、曾毅院士学术年表

曾毅院士中文论文目录

[1] 黄东英,曾毅,梁旻若.广州市鼠类带出血性钩端螺体调查的初步报告.微生物学报,1957,5(3):232-238.

[2] 中国医学科学院病毒学系脊髓灰白质炎组(曾毅,戴莹,王见南).1957年至1959年我国某些城市脊髓灰白质炎病毒的分离和鉴定.中华医学杂志,1961(1):55-57.

[3] 黄桢祥,诸福棠,贾秉谊,林家传,曾毅.麻疹减毒活疫苗的研究.中华医学杂志,1961(6):346-351.

[4] 曾毅,邓裕美.应用血凝抑制试验检查脊髓灰质炎病毒抗体.中华医学杂志,1961(6):355-357.

[5] 顾方舟,曾毅,毛江森,刘宗芳,王见南.7岁以下小儿口服脊髓灰质炎三型混合减毒活疫苗的血清学反应.中华医学杂志,1961(7):423-428.

[6] 刘宗方,曾毅,毛江森,顾方舟.北京市城区和郊区农村健康居民脊髓灰白质炎中和抗体的调查.中华医学杂志,1961(7):429-431.

[7] 曾毅,毛江森.人羊膜细胞培养方法的研究.微生物学报,1963,9(1):48-52.

[8] 曾毅,邓德美,黄桢祥.影响麻疹病毒血凝素滴度的某些因素的探讨.微生物学报,1963,9(3):267-271.

[9] 曾毅,张竟芳,顾方舟.国产胎盘球蛋白中肠道病毒(ECHO和coxsackie)中和抗体的测定.中华儿科杂志,1963(1):21-23.

[10] 曾毅,李以莞,刘宗方,阚履珍,顾方舟.中药对脊髓灰质炎病毒和其他肠道病毒的作用.中华医学杂志,1964,50(8):521-524.

[11] 曾毅,王政,顾方舟.红血球对Echo 6 D'Amori毒株和脊髓灰质炎病毒的吸附及其与血凝的关系.微生物学报,1964,10(3):357-362.

[12] 曾毅,王政,顾方舟.不同细胞对Echo 6 D'Amori毒株的血凝能力改变的影响.微生物学,1965,11(1):125-131.

[13] 曾毅,王政,顾方舟.传代细胞对Echo病毒的敏感性及对其血凝能力改变的影响.微生物学报,1965,11(3):335-339.

[14] 曾毅,朱家鸿,谷淑燕.人腺病毒18型诱发细胞转化的研究.中国医学,1965(11):125.

[15] 中国医学科学院病毒研究所,中国医学科学院日坛医院(免疫协调组曾毅,王来记,张吕先,白金芬).病毒治疗癌性胸腹水疗效初步总结.肿瘤工作简报,1971年12月第15期.

[16] 中国医学科学院肿瘤防治研究所病毒室，中国医学科学院流行病防治研究所肿瘤组电镜室，中山医学院肿瘤研究所病因研究室微生物教研组电镜室（曾毅，等）从鼻咽癌组织培养建立类淋巴母细胞株和分离巨细胞病毒.中华耳鼻喉科杂志，1978(1)：14-18.

[17] 中山医学院微生物教研组，中国医学科学肿瘤防治所病毒室，中国医学科学院流行病防治研究所肿瘤组，广东中山县肿瘤防治队.鼻咽癌病人和鼻咽黏膜病变患者血清中 EB 病毒补体结合抗体水平的调查研究.中华耳鼻喉科杂志，1978(1)：19-25.

[18] 朱家鸿，曾毅，丘福禧.流行性乙型脑炎病毒的溶血性及不同株的溶血性、血凝性及毒力比较.微生物学报，1978，18(1)：59-65.

[19] 中国医学科学院，北京工农兵医院耳鼻咽喉科（曾毅，等）.鼻咽癌病人的 EB 病毒免疫球蛋白 G 和 A(IgG 和 IgA)抗体的测定.微生物学报，1978，18(3)：253-258.

[20] 广东中山县肿瘤防治队，中山医学院微生物学教研组，中山医学院肿瘤研究所，中山医学科学院肿瘤防治研究所病毒室，中国医学科学院流行病防治研究所肿瘤组（曾毅，等）.北京市正常人群血清中 EB 病毒补体结合抗体水平的调查研究.中华耳鼻喉科杂志，1978(1)：23-25.

[21] 南方五省鼻咽癌防治研究协作组（闫华庆，吴阴棠，潘启超，黄小芒，胡孟璇，曾毅）.我国南方五省鼻咽癌流行病学的初步调查研究.肿瘤防治研究，1978，(3)：24-32.

[22] 中国医学科学院，中山医学院（曾毅，等）.人体鼻咽癌上皮样细胞株和梭形细胞株的建立.中国科学，1978(1)：113-118.

[23] 中国医科院病毒所，卫生部生物制品所，卫生部生物制品检定所（曾毅，等）.北京某鸡场鸡胚带鸡白血病病毒情况的调查研究.生物制品通讯，1979，8(3)：107-110.

[24] 中国医学科学院病毒学研究所肿瘤病毒组（曾毅，等）.鸡淋巴白血病病毒对母鸡免疫及其对鸡胚带病毒的初步调查研究.生物制品通讯，1979，8(3)：111-114.

[25] 朱家鸿，丘福禧，曾毅.感染流行性乙型脑炎病毒的组织培养中的血凝素和血凝抑制物.病毒学集刊，1979(1)：21-27.

[26] 曾毅，刘育希，刘纯仁，陈三文，韦继能，祝积松，载惠炯.应用免疫酶法和免疫放射自显影法普查鼻咽癌.中华肿瘤杂志，1979，1(1)：2-7.

[27] 刘育希，曾毅，董温平，曹桂茹.应用免疫酶法测定鼻咽癌病人的免疫球蛋白 A 抗体.中华肿瘤杂志，1979，1(1)：8-11.

[28] 曾毅，商铭，刘纯仁，程一瞿，杜瑞生，李新章，甘宝文，胡明杰，陈明，何士勒，沐桂潘.我国八个省市鼻咽癌病人 EB 病毒壳抗原的免疫球蛋白 A 抗体的测定.中华肿瘤杂志，1979，1(2)：81-83.

[29] 刘纯仁，商铭，曾毅，韩春生，载惠炯，胡银玲，曹桂茹，董温平.免疫放射自显影法的建立及其在测定鼻咽癌病人 EB 病毒特异性 IgA 抗体中的应用.科学通报，1979，24(15)：715-720.

[30] 吴冰，吴玉清，李以莞，曾毅，吴旻，赵志辉，龚翠红.不同来源带 EB 病毒的淋巴瘤和类

淋巴母细胞株巨 A 染色体的研究.中华肿瘤杂志,1979,1(2):91-95.

[31] 刘纯仁,商铭,曾毅,古惠炯,杜瑞生.应用免疫放射自显影法测定鼻咽癌病人唾液中的 EB 病毒 IgA/VCA 抗体.中华医学检验杂志,1979,2(4):197-198.

[32] 曾毅,刘育希,韦继能,祝积松,蔡绍霖,王培中,钟建明,李瑞成,潘文俊,黎而介,谭碧芳.鼻咽癌的血清学普查.中国医学科学院学报,1979(2):123-126.

[33] 谷淑燕,曾毅.类淋巴母细胞株简化培养液的研究.中华医学检验杂志,1979,2(3):132-133.

[34] 钟建明,曾毅,刘育希,韦继能,皮国华,祝积松,莫永坤,成积儒.鼻咽癌病人和正常人唾液中 EB 病毒 IgA/VCA 抗体的测定.中华流行病学杂志,1980,1(4):225-226.

[35] 李新章,周英伟,胡晞棠,曾毅.鼻咽癌患者血清中 EB 病毒早期抗原(EA)的抗体检测试验.中华耳鼻喉科杂志,1980,15(2):71-74.

[36] 曾毅,皮国华,赵文平.检查 EB 病毒核抗原的抗补体免疫酶法的建立.中国医学科学院学报,1980,2(2):134-135.

[37] 曾毅,皮国华,张钦,沈淑静,赵明伦,马姣莲,董翰基.应用抗补体免疫酶法检查鼻咽癌细胞和鼻咽部上皮细胞中的 EB 病毒核抗原.中国医学科学院学报,1980,2(4):220-223.

[38] 林毓纯,赵文平,曾毅,刘存仁,胡银玲.鼻咽癌病人淋巴细胞对鼻咽癌上皮样细胞株(CNE)的体外细胞毒性反应.中华肿瘤杂志,1981,3(1):1-4.

[39] 谷淑燕,曾毅,宋献文,罗天锡.人肉瘤细胞株的建立及其抗原性的研究.中华微生物学和免疫学杂志,1981,1(3):170-173.

[40] 王培中,邓洪,吴淑华,王兰芝,曾毅,侯云德.人 α-干扰素治疗鼻咽癌一例报告(简报).中国医学科学院学报,1981(1):78.

[41] G dethe,曾毅.EB 病毒与人类疾病的关系.广西医学,1981(5):35-38.

[42] 曾毅,张吕先,朱家鸿,谷淑燕.人腺病毒 18 型诱发细胞转化的研究.病毒学集刊,1982(1):167-169.

[43] 范江,曾毅,张绍基,许吉林,龚美东,涂丽珍.宫颈癌高发区和低发区正常妇女和宫颈癌病人的单纯疱疹病毒 I 型、II 型抗体测定.中华微生物学和免疫学杂志,1982,2(4):240-243.

[44] 曾毅,钟建明,G. deThe,吴淑华,侯云德,苗学谦.干扰素对 B95-8 细胞自发 VCA-EA 抗原和 Raji 细胞 EA 抗原诱发的促进作用.中华微生物学和免疫学杂志,1982,1(3):142-144.

[45] 曾毅,兰祥英.应用豚鼠 C3 抗体作免疫酶试验.中华微生物学和免疫学杂志,1982(2):110.

[46] 范江,曾毅,刘延富.应用免疫酶法检测宫颈癌病人单纯疱疹病毒 I、II 型的 IgA 和 IgG 抗体.中国医学科学院学报,1982,4(1):50-52.

[47] 谷淑燕,曾毅.一株人肉瘤细胞对 8-氮鸟便嘌呤的抵抗和在细胞杂交中的应用.中华微生

物学和免疫学杂志，1982，2（1）：41-43.

[48] 曾毅，张芦光，李景源，江民康，张钦，吴映成，黄以树，苏桂荣.广西梧州市居民的鼻咽癌血清学普查.癌症，1982（1）：6-8.

[49] 曾毅，周海媚，徐世平.维生素甲衍生物对EB病毒早期抗原诱发的抑制作用.中国医学科学院学报，1982，4（4）：251-253.

[50] 曾毅，沈淑静，邓洪，马姣莲，张钦，祝积松，潘文俊，成积儒，谭碧芳.应用抗补体免疫酶法从IgA/VCA抗体阳性者中检查早期鼻咽癌.中国医学科学院学报，1982，4（4）：254-255.

[51] 张思仲，吴荫棠，曾毅，L. Zech，G. Klein.鼻咽癌上皮样细胞株的细胞遗传学的研究Ⅰ CNE-1细胞株染色体的结构异常和标记染色体.癌症，1982（3）：157-159.

[52] 林毓纯，崔惠云，胡银铃，商铭，秦德兴，蔡伟民，曾毅，赵文平.鼻咽癌的细胞免疫及其HLA的限制.中华肿瘤杂志，1982，4（4）：254-256.

[53] 田野，曾毅，刘延富.宫颈癌患者单纯疱疹病毒的分离与鉴定.癌症，1982（2）：118-120.

[54] 田野，曾毅，刘延富.应用抗补体免疫酶法检查宫颈癌脱落细胞中单纯疱疹病毒抗原.癌症，1982（4）：239-240.

[55] 谷淑燕，曾毅，叶树清.抵抗8-氮鸟便嘌呤的CNf-A细胞株的建立.中国医学科学院学报，1982，4（6）：363-366.

[56] 谷淑燕，赵文平，曾毅，唐慰平，赵明伦，邓惠华，李昆.从低分化鼻咽癌病人建立鼻咽癌上皮细胞株.癌症，1983，2（2）：70-72.

[57] 曾毅，钟建明，李来云，王培中，邓洪，马益如，祝积松，潘文俊，刘育希，韦继能，成积儒，莫永坤，黎而介，谭碧芳.广西苍梧县EB病毒IgA/VCA抗体阳性者的追踪观察.肿瘤防治研究，1983，10（1）：23-26.

[58] 黎而介，谭碧芳，曾毅，王培中，钟建明，邓洪，祝积松，韦继能，潘文俊.EB病毒VCA/IgA抗体水平与鼻咽黏膜病变的关系.中华病理学杂志，1983，12（1）：9-11.

[59] 祝积松，潘文俊，钟建明，李来云，曾毅，江民康，方仲.苍梧县水上居民的鼻咽癌血清学普查.肿瘤防治研究，1983，10（3）：189-190.

[60] 沈淑静，陈秋波，张钦，马姣莲，黄大香，林福荣，胡云贵，曾毅.抗补体免疫酶法检查鼻咽癌及有关鼻咽脱落细胞的进一步研究.湛江医学院学报，1983（1）：34-37.

[61] 谷淑燕，H.Wolf，曾毅.EB病毒核酸片段与嗜菌体DNA重组方法的研究.重组核酸的获得和鉴定.癌症，1983，2（3）：129-132.

[62] 张思仲，高秀坤，曾毅.人体低分化鼻咽癌上皮样细胞株CEN-2的细胞遗传学研究.遗传学报，1983，10（6）：498-503.

[63] 谷淑燕，Hans Wolf，曾毅.EB病毒核酸片段重组于噬菌体M13mp8方法的研究——Ⅱ.制备敏感的核酸杂交实验的探针.中华微生物学和免疫学杂志，1984，4（5）：281-285.

[64] 曾毅，张钦，张芦光，李锦源，贾精医.应用酶标记葡萄球菌A蛋白抗补体免疫酶法检测

EB 病毒核抗原.肿瘤防治研究，1984，11(3):142-143.

[65] 皮国华，Desgranges C，BaornKamn GW，沈淑静，曾毅，deThe G.测定鼻咽部脱落细胞中 EBV/DNA 和核抗原方法的比较.中国医学科学院学报，1984，6(2):124-127.

[66] 皮国华，曾毅，焦伟.应用 X 线胶片免疫放射自显影法测定鼻咽癌病人血清中的 EB 病毒 IgA/EA 抗体.癌症，1984，3(3):169-171.

[67] 曾毅.鼻咽癌.中国医学科学年鉴.1984:185-190.

[68] 曾毅，龚翠红，江民康，方仲，张芦光，李锦源.应用免疫放射自显影法测定鼻咽癌病人的 EB 病毒 EA/IgA.中华微生物学和免疫学杂志，1984，4(1):45-47.

[69] 曾毅，钟建民，莫永坤，苗学谦.中草药对 Raji 细胞 EB 病毒早期抗原的诱发作用.中国医学科学院学报，1984，6(2):84-87.

[70] 崔运昌，汪美先，王伯沄，隋延仿，曾毅.人鼻咽癌上皮样细胞系的单克隆抗体(简报).第四军医大学学报，1984，5(3):209-212.

[71] 谷淑燕，Wolf H，曾毅.用生物素标记 DNA 检查肿瘤细胞中的 EB 病毒核酸.癌症，1984，3(4):233-236.

[72] 曾毅，张芦光，吴映成，黄以树，黄乃琴，李锦源，王运保，江民康，方仲，蒙尼妮.广西梧州市 EB 病毒 IgA/VCA 抗体阳性者的追踪观察.病毒学报，1985，1(1):7-11.

[73] 谷淑燕，Wolf，曾毅.间接核酸杂交方法的建立.病毒学报，1985，1(1):70-74.

[74] 曾毅，等.土壤中含 EB 病毒诱导物的检测.病毒学报，1985，1(2):122-124.

[75] 谷淑燕，曾毅，等.用碘标记核酸检查鼻咽癌上皮细胞中的 EB 病毒基因.病毒学报，1985，1(2):126-129.

[76] 兰祥英，曾毅，日沼赖夫.应用明胶凝集颗粒试验检测人群中 T 细胞白血病病毒抗体.病毒学报，1985，1(2):181-182.

[77] 曾毅，苗学谦，等.芫花酯乙和黄芫花提出液对 EB 病毒早期抗原的诱导和促进 EB 病毒对淋巴细胞转化的研究.病毒学报，1985，1(3):229-232.

[78] 夏恺，曾毅，吴中明.酶标记抗人 IgA 单克隆抗体及其在 Epstein-Barr 病免疫酶技术中的应用.病毒学报，1985，1(3):289-291.

[79] 曾毅，蓝祥英，王必璨，范江，陈文杰，杨天楹，梁晋金，许贤芬，王毓銮，隋延方，胡仁义，Hinuma Y.成人 T 淋巴细胞白血病病毒抗体的血清流行病调查.病毒学报，1985，1(4):344-348.

[80] 王必常，曾毅，Tsuchie H，Kurimura T，Hinuma Y.应用间接免疫荧光试验检测我国正常人和白血病病人血清中嗜 T 淋巴细胞Ⅲ型病毒抗体.病毒学报，1985，1(4):391-392.

[81] 曾毅，江民康，方仲，蒙绮妮.应用滤纸全血作 EB 病毒 IgA 抗体测定.癌症，1985，4(4):230-231.

[82] 崔运昌，汪美先，曾毅.一种筛选上皮样细胞表面抗原单克隆抗体的 ELISA.中华微生物学和免疫学杂志，1985，5(2):110-114.

[83] 皮国华，曾毅，张芦光.IgA/VCA 抗体阴性人群鼻咽部细胞中 EB 病毒核酸的研究.中华微生物和免疫学杂志，1985，5(1):45-48.

[84] 胡垠玲，曾毅.几种中草药提对淋巴细胞的促转化作用.中华肿瘤杂志，1985，7(6):417-419.

[85] 倪芝瑜，曾毅，夏恺，等.广西常见的五种具激活 EB 病毒早期抗原作用植物.宁波师范学院学报，1985，3(1):134-137.

[86] 区宝祥，曾毅.EB 病毒与鼻咽癌病因和发病学的研究.人民卫生出版社，1985:12-29.

[87] 夏恺，曾毅，龚翠红.分泌抗人 IgA 单克隆抗体(McAb)杂交瘤细胞株的建立.癌症，1986，5(2):183-186.

[88] 唐慰萍，黄培根，赵明伦，廖少玲，曾毅.了哥王对大鼠实验性鼻咽癌的促发作用.临床与实验病理学杂志，1986，2(2):34-36.

[89] 曾毅，皮国华，江民康，方仲，赵全璧，陶仲强，韦继能，黎而介，王培中，韦瑞环，古世堂，涂志明，江锡民，邓洪.罗城仫佬族自治县鼻咽癌血清学普查.广西医学，1986，8(2):79-81.

[90] 钟建明，莫永坤，倪芝瑜，黄长春，成积儒，唐苍庭，曾毅.苍梧县环境促 EB 病毒物质的研究.广西医学，1986，8(3):145-146.

[91] 胡银玲，曾毅，伊藤洋平.巴豆油、黄芫花和了哥王对兔乳头瘤病毒诱发的兔乳头瘤的促进作用.病毒学报，1986，2(1):81-82.

[92] 曾毅，王必璩，汤德骧，周绍聪，范江，张钦，郑锡文.血友病患者血清中淋巴腺病病毒/人 T 细胞Ⅲ型病毒抗体检测.病毒学报，1986，2(2):97-100.

[93] 纪志武，曾毅等.人精液对 Raji 细胞中 Epstein-Barr 病毒早期抗原的诱导.病毒学报，1986，2(2):182-183.

[94] 曾毅.艾滋病病原-淋巴腺病病毒/人 T 细胞Ⅲ型病毒.病毒学报，1986，2(2):190-196.

[95] 曾毅，王嫣，叶树清，苗学谦，钟建明.中成药乙醚提取液对 Raji 细胞的 Epstein-Barr 病毒早期抗原的诱导.病毒学报，1986，2(4):306-309.

[96] 胡银玲，曾毅.丁酸钠促进 EB 病毒对淋巴细胞转化的研究.癌症，1986，5(3):243-246.

[97] 崔运昌，隋延防，刘雪松，王伯云，汪美先，曾毅.人鼻咽癌细胞的单克隆抗体.免疫学杂志，1986，2(3):187-192.

[98] 隋延仿，王伯潭，崔运昌，汪美先，曾毅.抗人鼻咽癌细胞单克隆抗体免疫荧光组织化学观察.中华医学杂志，1986，66(12):739-741.

[99] 谷淑燕，Hans Wolf，曾毅.碘标记核酸方法的建立及在检查 EB 病毒核酸中的应用.中华肿瘤杂志，1986，8(2):107-110.

[100] 谷淑燕，韩日才，司静懿，江民康，李昆，舒明炎，王申五，赵文平，H. wolf，H. Zur Hausen，曾毅.宫颈癌中乳头瘤病毒核酸的检测.病毒学报，1986，2(3):260-262.

[101] 皮国华，曾毅，G de-The，方仲，赵全璧.检查 Epstein-Barr 病毒 IgA/EA 抗体的 ELISA

法.病毒学报，1987，3(1):81-85.

[102] 杜滨，曾毅，H. Wolf.鼻咽癌患者血清中抗 Epstein-Barr 病毒早期和晚期膜抗原抗体的检测.病毒学报，1987，3(1):92-94.

[103] 皮国华，曾毅，余世荣，方仲，赵全璧.抗人 IgA 多克隆抗体 ELISA 法的建立和应用.病毒学报，1987，3(2):177-180.

[104] 皮国华，曾毅，方仲，赵全璧，余世荣，H. Wolf.血清中 Epstein-Barr 病毒膜抗原 IgA 抗体检测法的改进及应用.病毒学报，1987，3(2):181-185.

[105] 孙瑜，陈敏海，肖红，刘汉燕，陈晓，曾毅，伊藤洋平.黄芫花及桐油提取物对 2 型单纯疱疹病毒诱癌的促进作用.病毒学报，1987，3(2):131-133.

[106] 皮国华，曾毅，叶树清，方仲.用改进的测定 Epsstein-Barr 病毒早期抗原 IgA 的方法为 2054 人检查鼻咽癌.病毒学报，1987，3(3):236.

[107] 皮国华，谷淑燕，江民康，叶树清，赵文平，曾毅，H. Wolf.用重组痘苗病毒感染动物细胞表达的 Epstein-Barr 病毒膜抗原检查 IgA/MA 抗体.病毒学报，1987，3(4):388-392.

[108] 曾毅，杜滨，苗学谦，M Mackett，JR Arrand.用 PO_4 细胞为靶细胞检测人血清中 Epstein-Barr 病毒 IgA/MA 抗体以诊断鼻咽癌.病毒学报，1987(3):396-397.

[109] 司静懿，李昆，韩日才，曾毅，等.人乳头瘤病毒和人子宫颈鳞状上皮细胞癌关系的超微结构与基因分子.中国医学科学院学报，1987，9(4): 264-270.

[110] 曾毅.鼻咽癌的检测和早期诊断.中华耳鼻咽喉科杂志，1987，22(3): 145-147.

[111] 钟建明，成积儒，莫永坤，唐苍庭，曾毅.含激活 EB 病毒的土壤及其生长的青菜促 EB 病毒物质的研究.癌症，1987，6(1):35-37.

[112] 钟建明，成积儒，莫永坤，唐苍庭，曾毅.苍梧县周木村环境促 EB 病毒物质的研究.癌症，1987，6(4):292-293.

[113] 孙瑜，陈敏海，张有新，曾毅.中草药黄芫花和桐油提取物对实验性宫颈癌的促进作用.中华肿瘤杂志，1987，9(5): 345-347.

[114] 范江，于恩庶，曾毅，等.一例华人艾滋病患者血清人免疫缺陷病毒抗体检测.中华医学杂志，1987，67(8): 469.

[115] 崔运昌，朱勇，曾毅，等.用 EBV-杂交瘤技术制备肾综合征出血热病毒的人单克隆抗体.第四军医大学学报，1987，8(1): 封 4.

[116] 崔运昌，现朱勇，高磊，安献禄，甄荣，曾毅.肾综合征出血热病毒的人单克隆抗体的产生和初步鉴定.解放军医学杂志，1987，12(4): 248-251.

[117] 隋延仿，王伯沄，崔运昌，汪美先，曾毅.抗人鼻咽癌细胞单克隆抗体相关抗原免疫荧光定位观察.中华肿瘤杂志，1988，10(2): 95-97.

[118] 唐慰萍，黄培根，赵明伦，蔡琼珍，廖少玲，曾毅.黄芫花提取物对大鼠实验性鼻咽癌的促发作用.癌症，1988，7(3): 171-173.

[119] 谷淑燕，江民康，赵文平，任贵方，曾毅，侯云德，Hans Wolf.表达乙型肝炎病毒表面抗

原和 Epstein-Barr 病毒膜抗原的双价痘苗病毒的组建.病毒学报，1988，4(1)：1-7.

[120] 曾毅，G. deThe，Y. Hinuma.应用明胶颗粒凝集试验检测人免疫缺陷病病毒（HIV-1）抗体.病毒学报，1988，4(1)：65-68.

[121] 曾毅，王必瓒，郑锡文，苏崇鳌，等.艾滋病的血清流行病学调查研究.中华流行病学杂志，1988，9(3)：138-140.

[122] 倪芝瑜，黄长春，陆小鸿，曾毅，钟建明.激活 Raji 细胞早期抗原植物的研究.广西植物，1988，8(3)：291-296.

[123] 曾毅，王必嫦，邵一鸣，赵尚德，苗学谦.我国首次从艾滋病病人分离到艾滋病毒.中华流行病学杂志，1988，9(3)：135-137.

[124] 孙瑜，李新志，王志洁，张有新，曾毅.某些环境促癌因素的实验研究(I乌柏与了哥王对 HSV2 诱癌的促进作用).病毒学杂志，1988(2)：153-156.

[125] 纪志武，曾毅.乌柏、射干和巴豆油对 3-甲基胆蒽诱发小白鼠皮肤肿瘤的促进作用的研究.癌症，1989，8(5)：350-352.

[126] 袁方，曾毅.可表达 EB 病毒核抗原的鼻咽癌/淋巴瘤细胞杂交株.南京医学院学报，1989，9(3)：219.

[127] 范江，曾毅，M.Motz，H.Wolf.EB 病毒壳抗原在大肠杆菌中的表达及纯化.中国医学科学院学报，1989，11(5)：380-387.

[128] 袁方，K.Takada，曾毅.用转染 EB 病毒基因片段的真核细胞检测鼻咽癌病人的抗 EB 病毒核抗原-1(EBNA)抗体.病毒学报，1989，5(2)：168-171.

[129] 杨嘉林，曾毅等.EB 病毒在原发型干燥综合征发病中的作用.中华医学杂志，1989，69(12)：707-708.

[130] 袁方，曾毅，H.Wolf，高田寒三.抗 EB 病毒核抗原 I 型单克隆抗体的研制和应用.中华微生物学和免疫学杂志，1989，9(3)：198-202.

[131] 邵一鸣，韩孟杰，曾毅.人免疫缺陷病毒蛋白蛋白印迹法的改进.病毒学报，1990，6(2)：184-188.

[132] 邵一鸣，曾毅，韩孟杰，Wolf. H.艾滋病血清学诊断方法-免疫斑点法的建立.病毒学报，1990，6(3)：250-255.

[133] 韩汝晶，F.Huang，E.Kiell，曾毅.鼻咽癌病人 EB 病毒 EBNA-2A 及 EBNA-LP IgG 和 IgA 抗体的测定.病毒学报，1990，6(3)：228-232.

[134] 金传芳，Wolf H，曾毅.应用纯化的重组 Epstein-Barr 病毒早期抗原建立检测鼻咽癌病人血清 IgA/EA 抗体的 ELISA 方法.病毒学报，1990，6(3)：256-261.

[135] 纪志武，李洪波，H. Wolf，曾毅.Epstein-Barr(EB)病毒早期抗原 P138 P54 的重组与表达.病毒学报，1990，6(4)：316-327.

[136] 蓝祥英，曾毅，D.V.Ablashi，M.Yavad，C.Zompetta，R.Gallo.北京人血清中嗜人 B 淋巴细胞病毒抗体的检测.病毒学报，1990，6(4)：373-374.

［137］纪志武，曾毅，王培中，谭会珍.鼻咽癌病人和其他鼻咽部疾病病人鼻咽部厌氧菌代谢产物对类淋巴母细胞 Raji 细胞和 P3HR-1 细胞中 EB 病毒抗原诱导作用.癌症，1990，9（1）：1-3.

［138］王哲，曾毅.人免疫缺陷病毒血清学诊断免疫酶法的建立及其应用.中华流行病学杂志，1990，11（4）：243-246.

［139］孙瑜，刘朝奇，王志洁，李志新，曾毅.人精液和阴道杆菌滤液在诱发小鼠宫颈癌中的作用.中华肿瘤杂志，1990，12（6）：401-403.

［140］王哲，曾毅.应用桥联酶免疫技术检测艾滋病毒抗体.病毒学杂志，1990（3）：291-293.

［141］杨天楹，曾毅，吕联煌，等.中国的成人 T 细胞白血病.中华血液学杂志，1990，11（9）：488.

［142］杨嘉林，何祖根，曾毅，等.原发性干燥综合征肾小管酸中毒于 EB 病毒感染的相关性.中华内科杂志，1991，30（3）：151-153.

［143］杨嘉林，曾毅，等.EB 病毒与干燥综合征的病因关系.中华医学杂志，1991，71（3）：131-135.

［144］王哲，曾毅，孙新华，等.HIV-1 抗体检测初筛试剂质量评价.中华流行病学杂志，1991，12（6）：369-373.

［145］王哲，强来英，曾毅.检测 HIV-1 抗体的合成肽 ELISA 试剂盒的制备及应用.中国生物制品学杂志，1991，4（3）：125-128.

［146］刘朝奇，孙瑜，曾毅，姚学军，鲁德银.人精浆、厌氧菌培养液和 HSV-2 协同诱导小鼠宫颈癌过程中机体免疫学变化.中华微生物和免疫学杂志，1991，11（1）：36.

［147］纪志武，方仲，曾毅.用重组 Epstein-Barr 病毒早期蛋白 P83 为抗原检测鼻咽癌病人血清中 IgA 抗体.病毒学报，1991，7（3）：269-271.

［148］王哲，曾毅.带有 HIV 抗原的 MT-4A 细胞株的建立和应用.病毒学报，1991，7（3）：277-281.

［149］郑锡文，曾毅，王哲，林旭东，等.云南瑞丽县 225 例吸毒者行为及 HIV 感染危险因素初步调查分析.中华流行病学杂志，1991，12（1）：12-14.

［150］邵一鸣，陈筝，曾毅，马英，段一娟.从云南艾滋病病毒（HIV）感染者分离 HIV.中华流行病学杂志，1991，12（3）：129-135.

［151］刘朝奇，黄树林，孙瑜，曾毅，姚学军，鲁德银.精浆、厌氧菌培养液及单纯疱疹 II 型对癌基因的激活作用.中华医学杂志，1991，71（6）：352-353.

［152］孙瑜，刘朝奇，鲁德银，曾毅.人精液、厌氧菌培养液在 HSV-2 诱导宫颈癌中的作用.中国病毒学，1992，7（1）：11-15.

［153］李稻，曾毅，纪志武，方仲，G. Pearson.鼻咽癌血清中 Epstein-Barr 病毒早期抗原特异性抗体的 IgA 类抗独特型抗体的检测.病毒学报，1992，8（1）：26.

［154］曾毅，钟建明，叶树清，倪芝瑜，苗学谦，莫永坤.诱导 Epstein-Barr 病毒早期抗原表达的

中草药和植物的筛选.病毒学报，1992，8(2):158-162.

[155] 邓洪，曾毅，黄乃琴，黄玉英，黎跃，苏辉民，钟汉桑，练英熙，王培中，G.de The.广西梧州市鼻咽癌现场10年的前瞻性研究.病毒学报，1992，8(1)：32-37.

[156] 纪志武，钟建明，曾毅.火殃筋、铁海棠、扭曲藤和红背叶对3-甲基胆蒽诱发小白鼠皮肤肿瘤作用.癌症，1992，11(2)：120-122.

[157] 曾毅，Jean-claude Nicolas，Guy Schwaab，Guy de The，Bernard Clausse，Thomas Tursz，Irene Joab.Epstein-Barr病毒相关疾病的IgG/Z抗体检测.病毒学报，1992，8(3)：218-222.

[158] 蓝祥英，曾毅，王得新，冯子敬，汤美华，纪燕，于庚庚，李昆.一株释放逆转录病毒样颗粒的人恶性T淋巴细胞株的建立.病毒学报，1992，8(2)：187-190.

[159] 何士勤，土育成，曾毅，等.C型逆转录病毒抗原测定技术的建立及其临床应用.中华医学检验杂志，1992，15(1):12-14.

[160] 何士勤，秦克旺，方征，曾毅，等.C型逆转录病毒与人类白血病病因的探讨，人兽共患病杂志，1992，8(1)：11-12.

[161] 何士勤，张天堃，曾毅，等.C型逆转录病毒和自身免疫病的关系.中国人兽共患病杂志，1992，8(6)：13-14.

[162] 洪明理，蓝祥英，章东，冯子敬，王得新，曾毅.一株来自脑炎患者的类C型逆转录病毒形态学研究.电子显微学报，1992，11(5)：375-376.

[163] 谷淑燕，唐慰平，曾毅，赵明伦.从低分化鼻咽癌建立上皮细胞株.癌症，1993(2)：70-73.

[164] 曾毅.鼻咽癌的控制和预防.中国肿瘤，1993，2(5)：24-25.

[165] 王哲，曾毅，孙新华.HIV检测实验室质量评估方法建立及应用.中华流行病学杂志，1993，14(3)：139-143.

[166] 邵一鸣，曾毅，等.中国及国外某些地区HIV感染者血清HIV-1gp120 V3肽反应的比较研究.中华微生物学和免疫学杂志，1993，13(1)：1-5.

[167] 蓝祥英，曾毅，王得新，陈筝，何士勤，郭树森，欧阳美馨，杜滨.人嗜T淋巴细胞Ⅰ型病毒与神经系统疾病关系的研究.病毒学报，1993，9(4)：382-385.

[168] 纪志武，K.Takada，李保民，叶淑清，曾毅.EB病毒Zebra基因(BZLF1)在大肠杆菌中的表达.病毒学报，1994，10(1)：14-18.

[169] 陈卫平，李扬，王惠，曾毅.抗癌基因Rb在大肠杆菌中的表达.病毒学报，1994，10(1)：19-23.

[170] 陈卫平，黄振录，韦荣干，李扬，刘时才，黎而介，曾毅.p53蛋白在鼻咽癌组织中的过量表达.病毒学报，1994，10(1)：72-74.

[171] 陈卫平，李扬，余升红，周微雅，王培中，曾毅.鼻咽癌组织中P53基因249位点未发现突变.病毒学报，1994，10(1)：75-76.

[172] 李稻，曾毅，Cochet Chantal，Joab Irene.鼻咽癌病人血清中IgG/Zebra抗体的ELISA法

检测.病毒学报,1994,10(1):78-80.

[173] 纪志武,K. Takada,李保民,曾毅.采用病毒受体基因转移技术建立 EB 病毒细胞感染模型.病毒学报,1994,10(2):154-158.

[174] 滕智平,曾毅.应用生物素标记探针进行细胞原位杂交检测人鼻咽癌细胞株中的 EB 病毒LMP 基因.病毒学报,1994,10(2):184-186.

[175] 蓝祥英,曾毅,章东,洪明理,王得新,张永丽,冯子敬,汤美华,冯宝章.带有逆转录病毒的恶性 T 淋巴细胞株的建立.病毒学报,1994,10(3):209-215.

[176] 赵永森,曾毅,徐克沂,李兴旺.从一名国内感染的艾滋病人分离人免疫缺陷病毒(HIV).病毒学报,1994,10(3):216-220.

[177] 邵一鸣,赵全壁,王斌,陈筝,苏玲,曾毅,赵尚德,张家鹏,段一娟,Wolfgang Hell,Hans Wolf.我国云南德宏地区 HIV 感染者 HIV 毒株膜蛋白基因的序列测定和分析.病毒学报,1994,10(4):291-299.

[178] 陈国敏,何士勤,王柠,张永利,曾毅.用聚合酶链反应检测 T 细胞白血病/淋巴瘤中HTLV-I 前病毒 DNA.病毒学报,1994,10(4):366-368.

[179] 陈耀全,林京来,曾福全,李泽琳,曾毅,马林.2′,3′-双脱氧-3′-叠氮- 5-甲基-2-N-烷基异胞苷的合成及抗 HIV-1 活性.科学通报,1994,39(24):2247-2249.

[180] 周玲,曾毅,H.Wolf.Epstein-barr 病毒膜抗原 gp250/350 在 CHO 细胞中高表达的初筛.中华实验和临床病毒学杂志,1994,8(4):375-376.

[181] 邓洪,曾毅,王培中,李秉均,雷一鸣,刘启福.广西鼻咽癌预防研究(综述).广西科学,1994,1(4):61-66.

[182] 曾毅.遗传因素环境因素及 EB 病毒在鼻咽癌发生中作用的研究.中国肿瘤,1995,4(3):24-25.

[183] 余升宏,陈卫平,李扬,曾毅.鼻咽癌组织中 Epstein-barr 病毒潜伏感染膜蛋白基因片段的克隆及分析.病毒学报,1995,11(1):10-14.

[184] 苏玲,滕智平,赵全壁,曾毅.高分化及低分化鼻咽癌细胞株中 Epstein-Barr 病毒潜伏感染膜蛋白(LMP1)基因的原位杂交与克隆及序列分析.病毒学报,1995,11(2):114-118.

[185] 段振峰,滕智平,曾毅.人 T 细胞白血病病毒 I 型 env 基因的克隆与表达.病毒学,1995,11(3):228-233.

[186] 纪志武,Kenzo,Takada,李保民,曾毅.Epstein-Barr 病毒核抗原 II(EBNA2)重组质粒pSG5-EBNA2-Hyg 的构建及其在哺乳动物传代细胞中的表达.病毒学报,1995,11(3):265-270.

[187] 纪志武,Kenzo,Takada,李保民,叶树清,曾毅.Epstein-Barr 病毒潜伏膜蛋白(LMP)基因在哺乳动物传代细胞中的表达.病毒学报,1995,11(4):305-311.

[188] 李保民,纪志武,刘振声,曾毅.EB 病毒诱导永生化人上皮细胞发生恶性转化.病毒学报,1995,11(4):371-373.

[189] 陈国敏，薛守贵，张永利，林惠添，董德华，林星，魏礼康，陈武，曾毅.我国福建省福清地区 HTLV-1 无症状携带者体内 HTLV-1 病毒核酸的检测.病毒学报，1995，11(4)：374-376.

[190] 曾毅.艾滋病和艾滋病毒的现状和研究进展(综述).中华实验和临床病毒学杂志，1995，9(4)：383-387.

[191] 滕智平，朱托夫，段一娟，张家鹏，曾毅，David D. Ho.我国云南瑞丽市区 HIV 分子流行病学分析.中国性病艾滋病防治，1995，1(1)：1-5.

[192] 焦伟，周薇雅，张兴，王培中，黎而介，黄立国，陆胜经，曾毅，于庚庚，滕智平.人鼻咽癌肝转移灶裸鼠移植瘤模型的建立(CNT-1)及特性的研究.广西医学，1995，17(1)：10-12.

[193] 邓洪，赵正保，张政，皮至明，李秉均，廖建，黎而介，李可能，胡良芳，银佑长，王培中，曾毅.广西21市县338868人鼻咽癌血清学普查.中华预防医学杂志，1995，29(6)：342-343.

[194] 周玲，李晓利，张晓梅，刘海鹰，曾毅，I.Demt，R.Wagher，H.Wolf.应用重组质粒 pAM-HBs Ag 在果蝇细胞中表达乙型肝炎病毒表面抗原及基因免疫的初步研究.中华实验和临床病毒学杂志，1995，9(4)：322-326.

[195] 孙伟，肖俊，兰祥英，张永利，曾毅.类风湿病与人类6型疱疹病毒感染的研究.中华实验和临床病毒学杂志，1995，9(1)：59-61.

[196] 邓洪，周日晶，黄仁养，卢志荛，何伟军，黄志英，韦德才，胡达兴，黎卫东，赖达森，李嘉瑞，雷一鸣，曾毅.梧州地市100704人鼻咽癌普查.当代肿瘤学杂志，1995，2(2)：92-94.

[197] 曾毅.鼻咽癌病因研究，中国肿瘤，1996，5(5)：8.

[198] 梁俊峰，薛田，曹伟，蔡国平，邓昌学，周玲，曾毅.基因枪介导的 HBsAg 基因免疫.科学通报，1996，41(9)：840-842.

[199] 薛守贵，陈国敏，林惠添，张永利，董德华，曾毅，林星，魏礼康.福建部分沿海地区嗜人 T 细胞病毒 I 型血清流行病学调查及病毒携带者的临床研究.中华实验和临床病毒学杂志，1996，10(1)：42-45.

[200] 纪志武，Kenzo Takada，李保民，谈浪逐，曾毅.风湿性关节炎与 Epstein-barr 病毒关系的研究.中华实验和临床病毒学杂志，1996，10(1)：56-61.

[201] 曾毅.艾滋病和艾滋病毒的现状和研究进展.中华实验和临床病毒学杂志，1996，10(1)：96-100.

[202] 马一盖，李振玲，陈国敏，廖军鲜，董彭春，徐韶华，张永利，刘永生，龙红，王银平，李挺，王质彬，蒋玉玲，曾毅.5例不典型嗜人 T 细胞病毒 I 型相关性成人 T 细胞白血病/淋巴瘤的发现.中华实验和临床病毒学杂志，1996，10(2)：104-109.

[203] 刘振声，李保民，刘彦仿，王锦玲，Irene Joab，曾毅.头颈肿瘤组织中 Epstein-barr 病毒

编码的 RNAs 原位杂交检测.中华实验和临床病毒学杂志,1996,10(2):163-165.

[204] 臧卫东,纪志武,谈浪逐,李保民,曾毅.Epstein-barr 病毒核抗原 II(EBNA2)基因免疫的初步研究.中华实验和临床病毒学杂志,1996,10(3):222-224.

[205] 钟建明,曾毅,廖建,李秉钧,潘文俊,严壮南,韦继能,王培中,黎而介.Epstein -barr 病毒 IgA/VCA 抗体变动规律和鼻咽癌发病的关系.中华实验和临床病毒学杂志,1996,10(3):225-228.

[206] 李保民,纪志武,刘振声,曾毅.Epstein-barr 病毒在人上皮细胞中的增殖和表达.中华实验和临床病毒学杂志,1996,10(4):340-343.

[207] 刘振声,李保民,滕智平,曾毅.鼻咽癌细胞株中 Epstein-barr 病毒编码的 RNAs 的检测.中华实验和临床病毒学杂志,1996,10(4):349-350.

[208] 赵全壁,管永军,段一娟,杨映全,曾毅,邵一鸣.1995 年云南瑞丽人免疫缺陷病毒的生物学特性.中华实验和临床病毒学杂志,1996,10(4):364-367.

[209] 王斌,邵一鸣,陈筝,赵全壁,苏玲,韩峰,曾毅.云南瑞丽长期静脉吸毒人群免疫缺陷病毒 I 型感染者毒株 envV3 区序列测定.中华实验和临床病毒学杂志,1996,10(4):387-388.

[210] 刘振声,李保民,刘彦仿,曾毅.EB 病毒与促癌物协同作用诱发人鼻咽癌恶性淋巴瘤和未分化癌的研究.病毒学报,1996,12(1):1-8.

[211] 邵一鸣,管永军,赵全壁,曾毅,张家鹏,张勇,段一娟,杨贵林,Josef Kostler,Hans wolf.1995 年云南瑞丽 HIV1 毒株的基因变异和分析.病毒学报,1996,12(1):9-17.

[212] 王斌,邵一鸣,曾毅.HIV-1 SF2 株 env 基因(120)在大肠杆菌中的表达.病毒学报,1996,12(1):18-22.

[213] 纪志武,Kenzo Takada,谈浪逐,李保民,叶树清,曾毅.Epstein-Barr 病毒 BCRF1 基因重组质粒的构建及其在真核细胞中的表达.病毒学报,1996,12(4):323-329.

[214] 李保民,刘振生,纪志武,曾毅.Epstein-Barr 病毒反义 LMP1 基因对鼻咽癌细胞 CNE2 株生长的抑制.病毒学报,1996,12(4):330-334.

[215] 段震峰,滕智平,纪志武,陈国敏,张永利,曾毅.人嗜 T 淋巴细胞白血病病毒 I 型(HTLV-1)核心蛋白(p24)基因的克隆及在大肠杆菌中的表达.病毒学报,1996,12(4):381-384.

[216] 刘术侠,刘彦勇,王恩波,曾毅,李泽琳.Keggin 结构钨磷酸错杂多蓝的合成及抗 HIV-1 活性研究.高等学校化学学报,1996,17(8):1188-1190.

[217] 刘术侠,李白涛,王恩波,曾毅,李泽琳.新型穴状结构阴离子[NaSb9W21O86]18-杂多蓝的合成及抗 HIV-1 活性.科学通报,1997,42(15):1622-1626.

[218] 刘术侠,王力,王恩波,曾毅,李泽琳.钨钛磷稀土杂多酸盐合成及抗 HIV-1 活性研究.中国稀土学报,1997,15(1):59-63.

[219] 管永军,陈钧,邵一鸣,赵全壁,曾毅,张家鹏,段一娟,Josef Kostler Hans Wolf.云南

瑞丽人免疫缺陷病毒感染者 gp120 基因 C2-V3 区的序列测定和亚型分析.中华实验和临床病毒学杂志,1997,11(1):8-12.

[220] 杨锦华,陈国敏,余秀葵,庄春兰,郑璇,庄坚,陈慎奔,廖传红,张永利,曾毅.广东省人群中嗜 T 细胞病毒 I 型感染的血清流行病学调查及其与人类疾病的关系.中华实验和临床病毒学杂志,1997,11(1):56-58.

[221] 刘海鹰,周玲,邓洪,周维雅,J. Middeldorp,曾毅.用合成肽抗原检测 Epstein-Barr 病毒抗体.中华实验和临床病毒学杂志,1997,11(1):87-88.

[222] 刘振声,邓永江,李家喜,丁华野,郭志祥,曾毅.Epstein-Barr 病毒潜伏膜蛋白在喉癌组织中的表达.中华实验和临床病毒学杂志,1997,11(2):153-155.

[223] 赵峰,刘海鹰,周玲,蔡伟明,杜滨,叶树清,曾毅.重组 rAAV-LMP 诱导的特异性细胞毒 T 细胞对 LMP 阳性靶细胞的识别与杀伤.中华实验和临床病毒学杂志,1997,11(3):247-251.

[224] 周玲,刘海鹰,王汉明,曾毅.含有 Epstein-Barr 病毒膜抗原的 DNA 疫苗接种诱生细胞免疫的初步研究.中华实验和临床病毒学杂志,1997,11(3):291-292.

[225] 张晓梅,周玲,刘海鹰,曾毅.HBsAg 基因免疫条件优化的比较.中华实验和临床病毒学杂志,1997,11(3):293.

[226] 孙荷,陈国敏,杜文慧,欧阳小梅,庞月婵,何有明,张君芬,张永利,曾毅.新疆南疆地区嗜人 T 淋巴细胞病毒 I 型血清流行病学调查.中华实验和临床病毒学杂志,1997,11(4):366-368.

[227] 周玲,王汉明,刘海鹰,曾毅.含有 Epstein-Barr 病毒膜抗原的重组表达质粒及其基因免疫.病毒学报,1997,13(1):41-46.

[228] 王汉明,周玲,张晓梅,曾毅,H Wolf.Epstein-Barr 病毒 BLRF2 基因重组质粒的构建及其在真核细胞中的表达.病毒学报,1997,13(1):75-78.

[229] 刘淑红,陈荷新,陈家童,陈启民,耿运琪,C Wood,秦贞奎,赵祥平,侯艳梅,曾毅.牛免疫缺陷病毒(BIV)92044 毒株的分离及鉴定.病毒学报,1997,13(4):357-364.

[230] 李保民,纪志武,刘振声,曾毅.Epstein-Barr 病毒诱导永生化人上皮细胞恶性转化.病毒学报,1998,14(2):133-138.

[231] 纪志武,臧卫东,谈浪逐,曾毅.Epstein-Barr 病毒潜伏膜蛋白(LMP)基因免疫的初步研究.病毒学报,1998,14(2):139-143.

[232] 周玲,刘海鹰,柯越海,王汉明,马林,曾毅.重组含有 Epstein-Barr 病毒潜伏膜蛋白 1(LMP1)基因的杆状病毒在昆虫细胞中的表达.病毒学报,1998,14(3):210-214.

[233] 柯越海,汪家权,曾毅.重组 HIV-1 逆转录酶的纯化与活性研究.病毒学报,1998,14(4):315-320.

[234] 滕智平,冯加武,王爱霞,王自春,余红,徐莲芝,C. Wood,耿运琪,曾毅.在 AIDS 病人和非 AIDS 的卡波西肉瘤病人中检测 HHV-8 基因和抗体.中华实验和临床病毒学杂志,

1998，12(1)：87-88.

[335] 陈少湖，刘祖宏，张稳定，李丽珠，岑山，谈浪逐，沈忠英，曾毅.揭阳地区食管癌和贲门癌与人乳头状瘤病毒的关系.中华实验和临床病毒学杂志，1998，12(4)：382-383.

[336] 刘海鹰，周玲，曾毅.检测 Epstein-Barr 病毒特异性细胞毒性 T 淋巴细胞方法的建立及其初步研究.中华实验和临床病毒学杂志，1998，12(4)：357-360.

[337] 韩立群，方芳，高进，曾毅.鼻咽癌亚系细胞中 EB 病毒 LMP-1 基因的检测.中华病理学杂志，1998，27(3)：230.

[338] 孙荷，陈国敏，杜文慧，欧阳小梅，张明涛，王兰婷，张永利，曾毅.新疆阿勒泰地区人类嗜 T 淋巴细胞病毒 I 型血清流行病学调查.中华实验和临床病毒学杂志，1999，13(1)：85-86.

[339] 滕智平，李德贵，高连胜，曾毅.人类免疫缺陷病毒 I 型包膜糖蛋白 gp41 的基因重组表达.中华实验和临床病毒学杂志，1999，13(2)：113-116.

[340] 沈忠英，岑山，蔡维佳，滕智平，沈健，胡智，曾毅.人乳头状瘤病毒 18 型 E6E7 基因诱导人胚食管上皮永生化.中华实验和临床病毒学杂志，1999，13(2)：121-123.

[341] 沈忠英，沈健，蔡维佳，岑山，曾毅.人乳头状瘤病毒 18 型 E6E7 基因诱导胎儿食管永生化上皮的生物学特征.中华实验和临床病毒学杂志，1999，13(3)：209-212.

[342] 王自春，曾毅.人类获得性免疫缺陷病毒 I 型内壳蛋白 P24 在大肠埃希菌中的表达与纯化.中华实验和临床病毒学杂志，1999，13(4)：386-388.

[343] 马一盖，陈国敏，汪晨，徐韶华，郦筱能，曾毅.中国人成人 T 细胞白血病/淋巴瘤 12 例临床分析.中华内科杂志，1999，38(4)：251-254.

[344] 沈忠英，蔡维佳，沈健，许锦阶，岑山，滕智平，胡智，曾毅.人乳头状瘤病毒 18 E6E7 和 TPA 协同诱发人胚上皮细胞恶性转化的研究.病毒学报，1999，15(1)：1-6.

[345] 王自春，滕智平，袁静明，曾毅.人类免疫缺陷病毒 II 型跨膜蛋白在大肠杆菌中的表达.病毒学报，1999，15(2)：188-191.

[346] 杨成勇，蔡伟民，沈倍奋，曾毅.鼻咽癌患者 EB 病毒潜伏膜蛋白(LMP1)的特异性细胞免疫研究.病毒学报，1999，15(3)：193-198.

[347] 陈国敏，曾毅.人疱疹病毒 8 型 kg330 基因片段的检出与 Kaposi 肉瘤的关系.病毒学报，1999，15(3)：275-276.

[348] 周薇雅，周玲，曾毅.EB 病毒潜伏感染膜蛋白特异性 T 淋巴细胞.中国肿瘤，1999,8(6)：288-289.

[349] 曾毅.艾滋病和艾滋病毒的发现及其起源(一).中国性病艾滋病防治，1999，5(6)：285-287.

[350] 曾毅.艾滋病和艾滋病毒的发现及其起源(二).中国性病艾滋病防治，2000，6(6)：55-60.

[351] 李泽琳，曾毅.天花粉蛋白对人类免疫缺陷病毒及其他病毒的抑制作用.见:汪猷，金善炜.天花粉蛋白.北京:科学出版社(第 2 版),2000：272-278.

[352] 杜文慧，陈国敏，孙荷，曾毅.新疆地区普通人群中人疱疹病毒8型IgG抗体的调查报告.中华实验和临床病毒学杂志，2000，14(1)：44-46.

[353] 管永军，刘海鹰，朱跃科，周玲，杜宾，曾毅.重组HIV-1腺病毒伴随病毒的构建及表达.中华实验和临床病毒学杂志，2000，14(4)：322-324.

[354] 朱伟严，周玲，姚家伟，曾毅.EB病毒潜伏膜蛋白2重组逆转录病毒的构建及表达.中华实验和临床病毒学杂志，2000，14(4)：342-344.

[355] 沈忠英，陈晓红，沈健，蔡维佳，陈炯玉，黄天华，曾毅.人乳头状瘤病毒诱导人胚食管上皮永生化细胞恶性转变.病毒学报，2000，16(2)：97-101.

[356] 管永军，朱跃科，刘海鹰，周玲，曾毅.中国HIV-1流行毒株的DNA疫苗的初步研究.病毒学报，2000，16(4)：322-326.

[357] 周玲，姚家伟，陈志坚，周薇雅，李德锐，A. Rickinon，曾毅.免疫斑点法检测特异性EBV潜伏膜蛋白2合成肽的细胞毒T淋巴细胞.中华实验和临床病毒学杂志，2000，14(4)：384-385.

[358] 邓洪，曾毅，王培中，李秉均，雷一鸣，郑裕明，黄碧珍.鼻咽癌血清学早期诊断的应用研究.中国肿瘤，2000，9(11)：500.

[359] 曾毅，吴尊友.遏制艾滋病在中国流行.中国科学院院刊，2000(2)：115-119.

[360] 周玲，姚庆云，Steve. Lee，A. Rickinon，曾毅.鼻咽癌病人和正常人群中EB病毒特异性T细胞对靶抗原的识别和应答.病毒学报，2001，17(1)：7-10.

[361] 王琦，周玲，姚家伟，陈志坚，李德锐，周微雅，曾毅.中国不同人群中T细胞对EB病毒潜伏膜蛋白2的识别.中国肿瘤，2001，10(12)：707-708.

[362] 许丽艳，沈忠英，李恩民，蔡唯佳，沈健，李淳，洪超群，陈炯玉，曾毅.HPV18 E6E7基因诱发的人胎儿食管上皮永生化和恶性转化细胞端粒长度和端粒酶活性.癌变、畸变、突变，2001，13(3)：137-140.

[363] 沈忠英，陈铭华，蔡唯佳，沈健，陈炯玉，洪超群，曾毅.丁酸钠对食管永生化上皮细胞增殖、分化和凋亡的作用.中华病理学杂志，2001，30(2)：121-124.

[364] 郭秀婵，盛望，张永利，黄燕萍，T Ooka，曾毅.EB病毒BARF1基因协同TPA诱发猴肾上皮细胞恶性转化的研究.中华实验和临床病毒学杂志，2001，15(4)：321-323.

[365] 兰祥英，郭秀婵，周玲，张永利，沈忠英，曾毅.乙肝病毒和黄曲霉素协同作用在裸鼠体内诱发人胎肝细胞癌变的研究.病毒学报，2001，17(3)：200-204.

[366] 郭秀婵，兰祥英，周玲，滕智平，张永利，陈炯玉，沈忠英，曾毅.乙肝病毒和黄曲霉素协同作用诱发人肝细胞癌细胞株的建立.病毒学报，2001，17(3)：205-209.

[367] 王书晖，熊鲲，刁丽榕，陈国敏，王全忠，陈君民，耿运琪，曾毅.BHIV gag-pol基因在MT4细胞中的表达.南开大学学报，2001，34(4)：86-90.

[368] 黄燕萍，郭秀婵，何祖根，曾毅.EB病毒诱导胸腺恶性T细胞淋巴瘤的研究.病毒学报，2001，17(4)：289-294.

［369］ 刘雁征，吴小兵，周铃，伍志坚，侯云德，曾毅.含 HIV-1 gag，gagV3 基因的重组腺病毒伴随病毒的构建及其免疫原性的研究.病毒学报，2001，17(4)：328-331.

［370］ 陈志坚，李德锐，周玲，曾毅.三株人鼻咽癌 scid 小鼠移植瘤的建立及特性研究.中华实验和临床病毒学杂志，2001，15(4)：324-326.

［371］ 沈忠英，许丽艳，陈铭华，蔡维佳，陈炯玉，洪超群，沈键，曾毅.人乳头状瘤病毒诱导食管上皮永生化细胞的双相分化.病毒学报，2001，17(3)：210-214.

［372］ 叶涛，王琦，陈国敏，张骅，闫芳，王天宇，马金石，李泽琳，曾毅.胆红素衍生物体外抗HIV-1 的初步研究.中华实验和临床病毒学杂志，2002，16(1)：66-68.

［373］ 黄燕萍，郭秀婵，何祖根，曾毅.EB 病毒诱导的胸腺恶性 T 细胞淋巴瘤细胞体外长期培养的研究.病毒学报，2002，18(1)：34-38.

［374］ 朱伟严，周玲，王琦，姚家伟，曾毅.EB 病毒潜伏膜蛋白 2 DNA 疫苗的构建及其免疫效果的研究.中华微生物学和免疫学杂志，2002，22(2)：185-190.

［375］ 贾俊岭，周玲.EB 病毒 II 型隐形感染免疫反应与 NPC 的免疫治疗.中国肿瘤，2002，11(10)：597-599.

［376］ 孙荷，姚梅，陈国敏，杜文慧，曾毅.乌鲁木齐地区 HIV 感染人群中人类疱疹病毒 8 型IgG 抗体调查.中华实验和临床病毒学杂志，2002，16(2)：195.

［377］ 郭秀婵，叶梁，张永利，曾毅，等.国产蜂胶对肝癌细胞体外杀伤作用的研究.中国肿瘤，2002，11(7)：431-432.

［378］ 郭秀婵，杜海军，何安光，张永利，李红霞，曾毅.我国北方地区鼻咽癌患者 EB 病毒LMP1 基因缺失分析.病毒学报，2002，18(4)：307-311.

［379］ 沈忠英，沈健，蔡唯佳，陈炯玉，曾毅.人永生化食管上皮细胞恶性转化的验证.中华肿瘤学杂志，2002，24(2)：107-109.

［380］ 沈忠英，沈健，蔡唯佳，陈铭华，吴贤英，郑瑞明，曾毅.丁酸钠对人乳头状瘤病毒诱导的永生化食管上皮恶性转化的促进作用.中华病理学杂志，2002，31(4)：327-330.

［381］ 洪少林，王家壁，李平川，周玲，司静懿，许雪梅，郭秀婵，曾毅.尖锐湿疣病变的人乳头瘤病毒 6 型 L1 序列多肽性分析.病毒学报，2002，18(2)：102-107.

［382］ 王书晖，熊鲲，杨怡姝，朱义鑫，夏秋雨，陈国敏，王金忠，陈启民，耿运琪，曾毅.BIV在人源细胞 MT-4 中的活性.中国病毒学，2002，17(4)：354-357.

［383］ 张拥军，郭秀婵，张永利，赵健，沈忠英，曾毅.腺病毒伴随病毒介导 HPV16E6E7 基因转化人胚食管组织.病毒学报，2003，19(1)：1-5.

［384］ 左建民，周玲，王琦，曾毅.含 EBV-LMP2 基因重组腺病毒疫苗的构建及其诱导 CTL 应答的初步探讨.中华微生物学和免疫学杂志，2003，23(6)：446-449.

［385］ 贾俊岭，周玲，左建民，王琦，曾毅.去除致癌基因的 EB 病毒潜伏膜蛋白 1 重组腺病毒的构建及其免疫效果研究.病毒学报，2003，19(3)：245-248.

［386］ 左建民，周玲，曾毅.EB 病毒潜伏膜蛋白 2 的研究回顾.中华实验和临床病毒学杂志，

2003，17(3)：296-299.

[387] 杜海军，周玲，曾毅.EB病毒中早期表达的癌基因——BARF1.国外医学病毒学分册，2003，10(6)：172-174.

[388] 岑山，腾智平，张月，沈忠英，许锦阶，杜宾，曾毅.腺病毒伴随病毒表达载体表达人乳头瘤病毒18型E6E7基因构建及其转化作用的鉴定.中华实验和临床病毒学杂志，2003，17(1)：5-9.

[389] 汤敏中，郑裕明，郭秀婵，张永利，曾毅.鼻咽癌患者EBV LMP1基因C端区的缺失突变及序列分析.中华实验和临床病毒学杂志，2003，17(1)：35-38.

[390] 杨怡姝，陈国敏，董温平，陈启民，耿运琪，曾毅.嵌合人/牛免疫缺陷病毒cDNA的构建及其在MT4细胞中的活性分析.中华实验和临床病毒学杂志，2003，17(2)：143-145.

[391] 何祖根，黄燕萍，郭秀婵，林冬梅，周玲，曾毅.T细胞淋巴瘤中EB病毒感染情况的研究.中华实验和临床病毒学杂志，2003，17(3)：229-233.

[392] 赵健，曹泽毅，孙耘田，廖秦平，杜海军，曾毅.人乳头状瘤病毒16型与促癌物TPA协同作用诱发人胚口腔细胞恶性转化研究.中华实验和临床病毒学杂志，2003，17(3)：234-236.

[393] 王自春，滕智平，张晓光，郭秀婵，袁静明，曾毅.利用新型表达载体一步获得HIV-1核壳蛋白P24纯品.中华微生物学和免疫学杂志，2003，23(5)：375-379.

[394] 孙荷，陈国敏，王兰婷，加娜尔，朱丽红，杜文慧，曾毅.新疆乌鲁木齐及阿勒泰地区围产母婴人疱疹病毒8型感染的调查.中华围产医学杂志，2003，6(1)：21-23.

[395] 姚家伟，周玲，王琦，左建民，曾毅.EB病毒潜伏膜蛋白2重组腺病毒的构建及其免疫效果的研究.中国肿瘤，2003，12(1)：45-47.

[396] 赵健，曹泽毅，周玲，曾毅.多胺对Raji细胞中Epstein-Barry病毒早期抗原的诱导.中国肿瘤，2003，12(3)：177-178.

[397] 赵健，曹泽毅，廖秦平，周玲，曾毅.阿司匹林对宫颈癌细胞系Caski的生长抑制作用.中国妇产科临床杂志，2003，4(1)：37-39.

[398] 赵健，曹泽毅，廖秦平，杨怡姝，周玲，曾毅.腺病毒伴随病毒表达载体表达人乳头状瘤病毒16型E6/E7基因的构建及应用.中国妇产科临床杂志，2003，4(4)：286-289.

[399] 李平川，张晓光，周玲，曾毅.用甲醇酵母表达经基因优化的HPV6型L1蛋白.中华实验和临床病毒学杂志，2003，17(4)：310-315.

[400] 李平川综述，周玲，曾毅审校.HPV疫苗研究现状.肿瘤基础与临床，2003，1(1)：39-42.

[401] 李恩民，许丽艳，蔡唯佳，熊华淇，沈忠英，曾毅.SHEEC食管癌细胞中NGAL基因的功能.生物化学与生物物理学报，2003，35(3)：247-254.

[402] 王微，赵春惠，黄春，吴昊，赵大伟，袁春旺，杨露绮，曾毅，马大庆，袁云娥，刘忠齐.螺旋CT、X线胸片和热断层(TTM)对SARS诊断价值的评价.香山科学会议论文集，北京：香山科学会议，2003.

[403] 左建民，周玲，王琦，曾毅.EBV-LMP2 基因密码子优化对其蛋白表达及免疫效果的影响.现代免疫学杂志，2004，24(4)：301-304.

[404] 曾毅，许华.宣传教育与干预是遏制艾滋病流行最有效手段.医学论坛杂志，2004，25(1)：1-6.

[405] 杨怡姝，陈国敏，陈启民，耿运琪，曾毅.嵌合人/牛免疫缺陷病毒 cDNA(pHBIV-2)传染性克隆的构建及其生物学活性.病毒学报，2004，20(2)：138-142.

[406] 冯霞，余双庆，陈国敏，左建民，周玲，曾毅.含密码子优化型 HIV-1gp120 基因重组腺病毒的构建及其免疫效果研究.中华实验和临床病毒学杂志，2004，18(2)：113-117.

[407] 张拥军，郭秀婵，张永利，赵健，沈忠英，曾毅.逆转录病毒载体介导 HPV16 E6E7 基因转化人胚食管纤维细胞的研究.中华实验和临床病毒学杂志，2004，18(3)：223-226.

[408] 刘雁征，周玲，王琦，叶树清，李红霞，曾毅.HIV DNA 疫苗与重组腺病毒伴随病毒联合免疫效果的研究.中华实验和临床病毒学杂志，2004，18(3)：251-254.

[409] 杜海军，周玲，左建民，王琦，李红霞，曾毅.EBV-LMP2 多肽所激活的特异性 CTL 对鼻咽癌细胞杀伤活性的研究.肿瘤学杂志，2004，10(2)：92-94.

[410] 杜海军，周玲，左建民，付华，王琦，李红霞，曾毅.EBV-LMP2 多肽激活的特异性 CTL 抑制同 HLA-的鼻咽癌移植瘤的形成.中国肿瘤生物治疗，2004，11(3)：157-160.

[411] 余双庆，冯霞，陈国敏，龚非，周玲，曾毅.HIV-1 B 亚型 gp120 基因密码子优化前后免疫原性的比较.病毒学报，2004，20(3)：214-217.

[412] 沈忠英，岑山，滕智平，蔡唯佳，沈健，陈炯玉，陈志坚，李德锐，曾毅.人乳头状瘤病毒协同 60 钴照射促进食管上皮细胞恶性转化.病毒学报，2004，20(3)：225-229.

[413] 李泽琳 王仲民 刘学周 张泽书 王哲 马士文 陈春华 薛晓玲 温瑞兴 岳彦超 朱新朋 曾毅.祛毒增宁胶囊治疗艾滋病的疗效观察.中华实验和临床病毒学杂志，2004，18(4)：305-307.

[414] 冯霞，余双庆，陈国敏，吴小兵，左建民，董温平，周玲，曾毅.含 HIV-1gp120 基因的重组腺相关病毒和重组腺病毒疫苗联合免疫的研究，中华实验和临床病毒学杂志，2004，18(4)：312-315.

[415] 程绍辉，梁明华，李泽琳，张霆，张珑，马洪涛，刘哲伟，曾毅.焦磷酸测序技术在确认北京严重急性呼吸综合征(SARS)病毒株并检测基因突变中的应用.病毒学报，2005，21(3)：168-172.

[416] 左建民，周玲，杜海军，付华，王琦，曾毅.含 EBV-LMP2 基因重组腺病毒修饰的树突状细胞疫苗体内外特异性抗瘤作用的研究.病毒学报，2005，21(3)：235-237.

[417] 郭秀婵.B 病毒感染及防治.病毒学报，2005，21(6)：481-484.

[418] 邓洪，曾毅，等.488683 人鼻咽癌普查基础方案分析，肿瘤学杂志，2005，25(2)：152-154.

[419] 朱义鑫，刘畅，乔文涛，陈启民，耿运琪，曾毅.替换 HIV-1 衣壳蛋白基因 SHIV 的构建

及其活性测定.中国病毒学，2005，20(4)：346-351.

[420] 付华，周玲，吴小兵，杜海军，左建民，王琦，曾毅.EBV-LMP1 重组腺病毒疫苗的研究及与 Ad-LMP2 疫苗联合免疫效果的探讨.中国免疫学杂志，2005，21：7-11.

[421] 付华，周玲，曾毅.新一代腺病毒载体研究进展.中华实验和临床病毒学杂志，2005，19(2)：190-193.

[422] 任军，周玲，曾毅.BRLF1-EBV 的一种立即早期基因的研究进展.中国肿瘤，2005，14，(6)：372-375.

[423] 李岚，杨怡姝综述，李泽琳，曾毅审校.HIV-1 Vif 与机体内在抗病毒因子 APOBEC3G 的研究进展.国外医学病毒学分册，2005，12(5)：143-146.

[424] 欧阳雁玲，李泽琳，曾毅.RNA 干扰在抗 HBV 感染中作用的研究进展.中华实验和临床病毒学杂志，2005，19(3)：297-299.

[425] 曾毅，李昆，沈忠英.病毒与肿瘤.见：张天泽，徐光炜：肿瘤学.沈阳：辽宁科学技术出版社，2005：92-115.

[426] 周玉柏，周玲，吴小兵，曾毅.腺病毒载体介导密码子优化型 HPV 16 L1 基因在哺乳动物细胞中的高效表达及病毒样颗粒的装配.病毒学报，2006，22(2)：101-106.

[427] 马晶，郭秀婵，曾毅.HIV 抗体检测技术研究进展.病毒学报，2006，22(2)：156-158.

[428] 滕智平，张萍，秦效英，潘秀英，郝乐，徐红，史惠琳，江滨，曾毅，陆道培.内源性逆转录病毒长末端重复序列在嗜酸性粒细胞增多症的基因表达及核苷酸序列分析.病毒学报，2006，22(3)：209-213.

[429] 郭秀婵，曾毅.禽流感病毒 H5N1 对卫生工作人员的危险.疾病监测，2006，21(3)：162-166.

[430] 曾毅.宣传教育与干预是控制艾滋病流行的主要策略.海峡预防医学杂志，2006，12(1)：1-4.

[431] 王湛，周玲，吴小兵，卢觅佳，宣尧仙，左建民，李峰，王琦，叶树清，曾毅.Ad-LMP2 重组腺病毒疫苗在恒河猴体内免疫效果的研究.中华实验和临床病毒学杂志，2006，20(2)：63-65.

[432] 沈忠英，滕智平，沈健，蔡唯佳，陈铭花，岑山，陈炯玉，曾毅.亚硝基吡啶对人乳头状瘤病毒诱导对食管上皮永生化细胞的促癌作用.中华实验和临床病毒学杂志，2006，20(2)：81-83.

[433] 郭秀婵，O'BRIEN Stephen J，WINKLER Cheryl，SCOTT Kevin，HUTCHESON Holli，DAVID Victor，KESSING Bailey，郑裕明，廖建，刘彦，GUY de The，曾毅.4 号染色体短臂微卫星多态性与鼻咽癌相关性的研究.遗传，HEREDITAS(Beijing)，2006，28(7)：783-790.

[434] 柳丽丽，钟儒刚，曾毅.微囊藻毒素及其毒性研究进展.卫生研究，2006，35(2)：247-249.

[435] 柳丽丽，钟儒刚，曾毅.微囊藻毒素污染及其促肝癌作用研究进展.卫生研究，2006，35

（3）：377-379.

[436] 柳丽丽，叶树清，钟儒刚，曾毅.微囊藻毒素 MC-LR 对 Raji 细胞中 Epstein-Barr 病毒早期抗原的诱导.武汉科技大学学报（自然科学版），2006，29（4）：422-424.

[437] 吕传臣，马雪梅，曾毅.人类免疫缺陷病毒 HIV 检测技术的研究进展.临床和实验医学杂志，2006，5（4）：421-423.

[438] 岑山，张月，许锦阶，沈忠英，曾毅.佛波酯和人乳头瘤病毒在细胞恶性转化作用中的协同效应.中华实验和临床病毒学杂志，2006，20（3）：260-262.

[439] 张晓梅，钟建明，汤敏中，张晓光，廖建，郑裕明，邓洪，曾毅.EBV4 型 IgA/VCA IgA/EA IgG/EA IgG/ZEBRA 抗体在鼻咽癌普查好早期诊断中的应用.中华实验和临床病毒学杂志，2006，20（3）：263-265.

[440] 李岚，杨怡姝，张晓光，张晓梅，李泽琳，曾毅.HIV-1 病毒感染因子基因克隆、表达、纯化及其抗体制备的研究.中华实验和临床病毒学杂志，2006，20（4）：305-307.

[441] 马晶，郭秀婵，张晓光，张晓梅，曾毅.HIV P66 蛋白的表达、纯化及活性检测.病毒学报，2006，22（5）：364-368.

[442] 杜海军，赵健，周玲，王琦，李红霞，曾毅.EB病毒 LMP1 C-端序列缺失对细胞增殖的影响.病毒学报，2006，22（6）：440-444.

[443] 任军，张晓梅，张晓光，李红霞，周玲，曾毅.以 Rtac2/3 为抗原用于鼻咽癌病人检测的初步研究.中华微生物学和免疫学杂志，2006，26（11）：1057-1059.

[444] 郭秀婵，O'BRIEN Stephen J，曾毅.宿主遗传多态性与 HIV/AIDS 感染和进展的关系.科学通报，2006，51（23）：2705-2713.

[445] 杨怡姝，李岚，李泽琳，曾毅.激光扫描共聚焦显微镜 APOBEC3G 蛋白的亚细胞定位.病毒学报，2007，23（1）：16-20.

[446] 刘新蕾，余双庆，冯霞，王小利，刘红梅，张晓梅，李红霞，周玲，李泽琳，曾毅.含 HIV-1 gag 基因的重组腺病毒 5 型与 35 型嵌合病毒免疫效果研究.中华实验和临床病毒学杂志，2007，21（1）：5-7.

[447] 杨松梅，周玲，曾毅.免疫治疗 EBV 相关肿瘤的研究进展.中华实验和临床病毒学杂志，2007，21（1）：94-96.

[448] 白立石，王开利，周广恩，孟宾，刘颜成，曾毅.相同来源 HIV-1Env、Gag 基因序列变异和宿主基因多态性与疾病进展关系的分析.中华实验和临床病毒学杂志，2007，21（2）：153-155.

[449] 莫武宁，周玲，吴小兵，王湛，唐安洲，黄光武，余双庆，王琦，叶树清，杜海军，曾毅.Ad5F35-LMP2 重组腺病毒免疫效果的研究.中华实验和临床病毒学杂志，2007，21（3）：226-228.

[450] 李岚，杨怡姝，李泽琳，曾毅.细胞免疫成分 TRIM5a 和 APOBEC3G 抗 HIV-1 作用机制的研究进展（综述）.中华实验和临床病毒学杂志，2007，21（3）：299-300.

［451］ 刘红梅，余双庆，冯霞，刘新蕾，董小岩，吴小兵，曾毅.1 型和 2 型外壳蛋白构建的 AAV 载体携带 HIV-1gag 诱导免疫反应的比较研究.病毒学报，2007，23(3)：177-182.

［452］ 莫武宁，周玲，吴小兵，王湛，唐安洲，黄光武，曾毅.Ad5F35-LMP2 重组腺病毒的构建及鉴定.中国免疫学杂志，2007，23(3)：251-255.

［453］ 任会均，张锦堃，周玲，左建民，魏锡云，曾毅.冻融人树突状细胞基因疫苗体外抗肿瘤免疫效应.中华肿瘤防治杂志，2007，14(12)：884-887.

［454］ 金芳，白立石，李红霞，辛天义，任海英，周玲，曾毅.HIV/AIDS 家庭社会心理状况调查.中国公共卫生，2007，23(9)：1038-1039.

［455］ 白立石，刘启浩，金芳，李红霞，任海英，周玲，曾毅.HIV-1 感染者家庭慢性病现况及发病因素分析.中国公共卫生，2007，23(9)：1057-1059.

［456］ 马晶，张晓光，张晓梅，郭秀婵，曾毅.HIV-1 整合酶蛋白的表达、纯化及复性研究.中华微生物学和免疫学杂志，2007，27(10)：928-933.

［457］ 张北川，曾毅，许华，李秀芳，周生建，李辉，廖留妹，张晓梅.中国部分城市 2004 年 1389 例男男性接触者艾滋病高危行为及其相关因素调查.中华流行病学杂志，2007，28(1)：32-36.

［458］ 欧阳雁玲，李泽琳，曾毅.中药提取物人衔草对乙型肝炎病毒的抑制作用.世界华人消化杂志，2007，15(4)：394-398.

［459］ 曾毅.艾滋病的预防与控制.中华实验和临床病毒学杂志，2007，21(1)：1.

［460］ 杨怡姝，王润田，张晓光，李泽琳，曾毅.国产 HIV-1 p24 抗原检测试剂盒的评价.中华实验和临床病毒学杂志，2007，21(1)：8-10.

［461］ 曾毅.艾滋病的预防与控制.见：路甬祥.科学与中国——院士专家巡讲团报告集(第四辑).北京大学出版社，2007：233-246.

［462］ 吕岫华、刘伟、李泽琳、曾毅.抗 HIV/AIDS 中药免疫与病毒关系的研究.中华中医药，2007，22(4)：250-252.

［463］ 李岚，杨怡姝，李泽琳，曾毅.人 APOBEC3G 基因克隆、表达、纯化及多克隆抗体制备.北京工业大学学报，2008，34(2)：197-203.

［464］ 李淑英，李颖，王立东，吴晓舟，周玲，赵晓瑜，刘宏图，曾毅.应用聚合酶链反应检测食管癌组织中人乳头瘤病毒.中华实验和临床病毒学杂志，2008，22(4)：251-253.

［465］ 莫武宁，周玲，王湛，唐安洲，黄光武，曾毅.Ad5F35-LMP2 重组腺病毒修饰 DC 体外诱导特异性 T 细胞免疫的研究.中华实验和临床病毒学杂志，2008，22(4)：254-256.

［466］ 张晓光，戚其平，马晶，张晓梅，王自春，李红霞，曾毅.高效表达重组 HIV-1 gp41 及在尿液检测中的应用.中华实验和临床病毒学杂志，2008，22(4)：308-310.

［467］ 冯霞，余双庆，刘红梅，刘新蕾，王小利，周玲，曾毅.HIV-1 B 亚型 gag 基因密码子优化及其免疫原性的研究.病毒学报，2008，24(3)：190-195.

［468］ 周玉柏，李泽琳，周玲，盛望，马洪涛，曾毅.表达 HPV16 L1 抗原的 1 型重组 AAV 载体

免疫效果的研究.病毒学报，2008，24（4）：300-304.

［469］周玉柏，周玲，李泽琳，盛望，曾毅.含密码子优化型HPV16 L1基因重组腺病毒的构建及其免疫效果的研究.中华实验和临床病毒学杂志，2008，22（1）：18-20.

［470］杜海军，周玲，刘宏图，王琦，詹少兵，贾志远，毛乃颖，曾毅.北京地区儿童EB病毒感染的血清学调查.中华实验和临床病毒学杂志，2008，22（1）：30-32.

［471］周玉柏，李泽琳，周玲，盛望，马洪涛，曾毅.含HPV16L1基因重组腺病毒和1型重组AAV载体联合免疫效果的研究.中华实验和临床病毒学杂志，2008，22（6）：416-418.

［472］杨松梅，王湛，周玲，杜海军，莫武宁，曾毅.携带EBV-LMP2基因的DNA疫苗、腺相关病毒疫苗和腺病毒疫苗免疫小鼠的特异性细胞免疫应答.中国科学C辑：生命科学，2009，39（4）：342-345.

［473］冯霞，杨海儒，余双庆，周玲，李红霞，李泽琳，曾毅.河南省有偿供血者HIV-1外膜蛋白env基因序列分析及表型预测.病毒学报，2009，25（2）：88-94.

［474］张磊，曾毅.Balb/c 3T3细胞体外转化实验及其在环境致癌物检测上的应用.卫生研究，2009，38（2）：226-232.

［475］杜鹏，陈国敏，李泽琳，曾毅.河南地区HIV-1毒株Gag基因抗原表位特征及准种特点研究.中华实验和临床病毒学杂志，2009，23（1）：20-22.

［476］赵蕊，张磊，钟儒刚，周玲，曾毅.293细胞检测致癌物的应用研究.中华实验和临床病毒学杂志，2009，23（1）：47-49.

［477］詹少兵，钟建明，麦稚平，叶树清，周玲，曾毅，廖建.鼻咽癌血清学检测方法的改进.中华实验和临床病毒学杂志，2009，23（1）：65-67.

［478］周媛，滕智平，曾毅.新城疫病毒作为疫苗载体的研究进展.中华实验和临床病毒学杂志，2009，23（1）：79-80，封三.

［479］詹少兵，麦稚平，谭珍连，钟建明，叶树清，周玲，廖建，曾毅.生物素——链霉亲和素放大免疫酶法在鼻咽癌血清学检测中的应用.中国肿瘤，2009，18（5）：396-398.

［480］李淑英，李颖，沈立萍，吴晓舟，赵晓瑜，周玲，刘宏图，曾毅.人乳头瘤病毒与食管癌病原学关系的Metallic分析.中华实验和临床病毒学杂志，2009，23（2）：85-87.

［481］赵晓瑜，李淑英，李颖，王晓莉，李玉兰，吴晓舟，周玲，刘宏图，曾毅.保定地区食管癌患者癌组织中人乳头瘤病毒感染的检测.中华实验和临床病毒学杂志，2009，23（2）：91-93.

［482］杨海儒，冯霞，余双庆，张晓光，张晓梅，陈国敏，李泽琳，曾毅.HIV-1 C亚型Gp120蛋白表达、纯化及其抗体制备的研究.中华实验和临床病毒学杂志，2009，23（2）：94-96.

［483］张晓光，李魁彪，马晶，王乃福，张晓梅，桑云虎，董婕，徐红，曾毅.含H5N1-HA基因重组腺病毒疫苗的构建及其诱导免疫应答的初步探讨.中华实验和临床病毒学杂志，2009，23（2）：97-99.

［484］张磊，赵蕊，钟儒刚，周玲，李德昌，吴永宁，曾毅.BALB/c 3T3细胞转化实验的优化及

其在致癌物协同作用研究中的应用.中华实验和临床病毒学杂志，2009，23(2)：121-123.

[485] 刘平，李泽琳，曾毅.检测人 APOBEC3G 与 HIV-1 病毒感染因子的新方法及原理(综述).中华实验和临床病毒学杂志，2009，23(4)：319-320，封三.

[486] 李淑英，杜海军，王湛，周玲，赵晓瑜，曾毅.EB 病毒感染与胃癌患者临床病理特征相关性的 Meta 分析.中国科学(C 辑：生命科学)，2009，39(9)：891-897.

[487] 马晶，张晓光，陈红，李魁彪，张晓梅，张柯，杨亮，徐红，舒跃龙，谭文杰，曾毅.含有人 H5N1 流感病毒 NA 基因的重组腺病毒候选疫苗株在小鼠体内诱发细胞免疫反应.病毒学报，2009，25(5)：327-332.

[488] 余双庆，冯霞，刘红梅，杨海儒，李红霞，曾毅.表达 HIV-1 gag 基因的重组 AAV2/1 和 Ad5 疫苗免疫原性比较.中华实验和临床病毒学杂志，2009，23(6)：421-423.

[489] 李连芹，陈春玲，曹泽毅，廖秦平，杜海军，詹少兵，周玲，曾毅.过氧化物还原酶 3 在宫颈病变中的表达特点.中华实验和临床病毒学杂志，2009，23(6)：443-445.

[490] 马晶，张晓光，李魁彪，张晓梅，王敏，白天，杨亮，徐红，舒跃龙，曾毅.含有 H5N1 NA 基因重组腺病毒疫苗在小鼠体内的免疫效果研究.中华实验和临床病毒学杂志，2009，23(6)：449-451.

[491] 杜海军，周玲，曾毅.鼻咽癌的临床免疫治疗.中华实验和临床病毒学杂志，2009，23(6)：502-503.

[492] 王乃福，马晶，张晓光，张晓梅，白天，王敏，温乐英，王大燕，舒跃龙，周玲，曾毅.H5N1-NP 蛋白的原核表达及与宿主蛋白相互作用的初步研究.中华实验和临床病毒学杂志，2010，24(1)：27-29.

[493] 周媛，贾润清，滕智平，张晓梅，曾毅.NDV LaSota 株 P、NP 蛋白基因表达载体的构建及鉴定.中华实验和临床病毒学杂志，2010，24(1)：62-64.

[494] 杨怡姝，王小利，李泽琳，曾毅.新型内在抗病毒分子—Tetherin.病毒学报，2010，26(1)：71-75.

[495] 余双庆，冯霞，刘红梅，杨海儒，李红霞，曾毅.表达 HIV-1 gp120AAV2/1 在小鼠和恒河猴体内的免疫原性.病毒学报.病毒学报，2010，26(2)：115-120.

[496] 尉秀霞，杜海军，周玲.EB 病毒潜伏膜蛋白 1 诱导细胞免疫的研究进展中华实验和临床病毒学杂志，2010，24(1)：77-78.

[497] 王湛，马晶，周玲，张晓光，杜海军，杨松梅，曾毅.EBV-LMP2 蛋白的表达和初步纯化.中华实验和临床病毒学杂志，2010，24(3)：168-170.

[498] 王湛，周玲，杜海军，叶树青，尉秀霞，周玲，曾毅.不同时间 EBV-LMP2 重组腺病毒体内细胞免疫效果研究.中国医药指南，2010，(18)：78-79.

[499] 王湛，孙云霞，周玲，吴伟娜，李洪贞，杜海军，左从林，周玲，曾毅.EBV-LMP2 重组腺病毒体内细胞免疫效果及分布研究.中国医药指南，2010，16：66-69.

[500] 杨亮，张晓梅，张晓光，马晶，王敏，温乐英，王大燕，白天，舒跃龙，钱永华，曾毅.多重 RT-

PCR 结合反向杂交技术检测多种流感病毒方法的研究.中华实验和临床病毒学杂志，2010，24(5):383-385.

[501] 桑云虎，张晓梅，张晓光，李学仁，乐家昌，曾毅.免疫旋转生物传感器高灵敏检测 HIV-1 p24 抗原方法的研究.中华实验和临床病毒学杂志，2010，24(4)：305-307.

[502] 叶景荣，卢红艳，白立石，曾毅.北京地区流行的 HIV-1 CRF01_AE 株基因特征研究，中华流行病学杂志，2010，31(11)：1231-1234.

[503] 莫武宁，王湛，周玲，詹少兵，唐安洲，黄光武，曾毅.A5F35-LMP2 重组腺病毒修饰 DC 体内特异性抗瘤作用的研究.中华实验和临床病毒学杂志，2010，24(4):270-272.

[504] 杜鹏，陈国敏，李泽琳，曾毅.HIV-1 毒株 V3 环顶端四肽多态性及原发耐药性研究.中华实验和临床病毒学杂志，2010，24(5):321-323.

[505] 杨海儒，张凌斐，冯霞，余双庆，庄著伦，李红霞，曾毅.表达 HIV-1 B 亚型 env 基因的质粒 DNA 及腺病毒载体疫苗的免疫原性研究.中华实验和临床病毒学杂志，2010，24(6)：415-417.

[506] 赵健，张晓光，陈锐，毕惠，王旭，刘桂文，姚殿昕，曾毅，廖秦平.高危型人乳头状瘤病毒 DNA 检测方法在宫颈疾病中的临床意义.中华实验和临床病毒学杂志，2010，25(2)：149-151.

[507] 叶景荣，郭蕾，白立石，辛若雷，卢红艳，余双庆，曾毅.北京市性传播 HIV-1 感染者流行毒株 gag 基因序列测定和亚型分析.中华微生物学和免疫学杂志，2011,31(2):136-139.

[508] 叶景荣，辛若雷，卢红艳，白立石，曾毅.北京市 50 例 HIV/AIDS 病人 CCR5 CXCR4 HLA-DR 和 CD38 表达与疾病进展关系.中国艾滋病性病，2011，17(3):287-290.

[509] 叶景荣，郭蕾，卢红艳，辛若雷，曾毅.北京市未经抗病毒治疗的 HIV 感染者耐药突变流行性调查.中华医学杂志，2011，91(21):1453-1456.

[510] 李淑英，张科，杜海军，王湛，慈雅丽，王新燕，周玲，曾毅.携带 BARF1 基因的人胃上皮细胞株的建立.中国人兽共患病学报，2011，27(5):407-410.

[511] 李淑英，张科，杜海军，王湛，李旭坤，慈雅丽，王新燕，张秀军，周玲.BARF1 基因真核表达载体 PIRES2-EGFP/BARF1 的构建及鉴定.辽宁师范大学学报（自然科学版），2011，34(1):98-101.

[512] 王湛，尉秀霞，周玲，杜海军，叶树清，曾毅.EB 病毒 LMP2-LMP1Δ 融合基因免疫效果的初步研究.中国病毒病杂志，2011，Vol.1(1):5-10.

[513] 赵健，张晓光，陈锐，毕惠，王旭，刘桂文，姚殿昕，曾毅，廖秦平.高危型人乳头状瘤病毒 DNA 检测方法在宫颈疾病中的临床意义.中华实验和临床病毒学杂志，2011，25(2)：149-151.

[514] 吴青青，陈国敏，曾毅，杨清，徐越，徐水洋，骆淑英，吴方，许云峰.浙江省个体经商人员艾滋病相关知信行现状及影响因素研究.中国健康教育，2011，27(8):592-595.

[515] 李淑英，李劲涛，杜海军，王湛，朱丽，周玲，曾毅.EB 病毒 BARF1 基因对人胃上皮细胞

恶性转化的作用.第三军医大学学报，2011，33（19）：2025-2028.

[516] 李芸，杨柳，杨玲，陈丹瑛，冯霞，余双庆，李泽琳，曾毅.Ad5-HIVgag 免疫的食蟹猴中腺病毒中和抗体与 Gag 特异性细胞免疫反应的研究.中华实验和临床病毒学杂志，2011，25(6):413-415.

[517] 杨柳、李芸、杨玲、张凌斐、冯霞、余双庆、陈丹瑛、李泽琳、曾毅.rAd5 和 rAAV2/1 载体疫苗诱导载体特异性和外源基因特异性免疫反应的研究.中华实验和临床病毒学杂志，2011,25(6):431-433.

[518] 马树波，陈国敏，曾毅.北京市昌平区大学生艾滋病哨点监测结果分析.实用预防医学，2011，18(12)：2416-2418.

[519] 魏秀霞，王湛，周玲，杜海军，叶树清，曾毅.携带 EBV-LMP1Δ 基因的 DNA 疫苗和腺病毒疫苗联合免疫效果研究.中国病毒病杂志，2012,2(4):250-254.

[520] 杜海军，王湛，尉秀霞，周玲，马晶，冯霞，叶树清，曾毅.肌肉免疫 DC-EBV-LMP2 诱导免疫应答的研究.中国医药指南杂志，2012,10(30):1-3.

[521] 汪慧敏，徐柯，余双庆，丁林林，罗海艳，冯霞，Robin Flinko，George K. Lewis，邵继荣，管永军，曾毅.利用 B 细胞培养和 RT-PCR 技术从我国 HIV-1 感染者中筛选膜蛋白特异性单克隆抗体的初步研究.病毒学报，2012,28(4):358-365.

[522] 尚诚彰，陈国敏，张怀渝，曾毅.HIV-1 毒株 gag 和 pol 基因区抗原表位及耐药性突变分析.病毒学报，2012,23(4):351-357.

[523] 郭飞飞，陈国敏，曾毅.26 例有偿献血员 HIV-1 基因分型与变异特征.中华实验和临床病毒学杂志，2012，26(1)：37-39.

[524] 闫晓，马晶，张晓梅，常战军，刘建勋，兰琳，徐兰英，张胜勇，白建敏，钱建华，张晓光，曾毅.河南省某市 HIV 感染者基因型耐药横断面调查.中华实验和临床病毒学杂志，2012，26(3)：165-167.

[525] 曲鹏，李劲涛，王立东，曾毅，楚秀生.安阳地区不同食管鳞癌标本 HPV 感染率的比较研究.中华实验和临床病毒学杂志，2012,26(1):34-36.

[526] 武双，李劲涛，钟儒刚，曾毅.比较两种细胞转化实验对多环芳烃致癌性的评价能力.中华实验和临床病毒学杂志，2012,26(5)：359-361.

[527] 武双，李劲涛，钟儒刚，曾毅.人乳头状瘤病毒16型 E6E7 基因与 MCA 和 TPA 协同诱导细胞恶性转化的实验研究.山东医药，2012，52(17)：35-37.

[528] 汤敏中，李军，蔡永林，郑裕明，廖建，曾洪，O'BRIEN Stephen，曾毅.应用鼻咽癌家系资料评估 HLA 三座位单倍型软件推算方法.中华实验与临床病毒学杂志，2012，26(4)：288-290.

[529] 汤敏中，蔡永林，郑裕明，曾毅.人类白细胞抗原与鼻咽癌的相关性研究进展.遗传，2012，34(12):1505-1512.

[530] 黄湘滢,余双庆,程湛,叶景荣,徐柯,冯霞,曾毅.利用磁珠分选和单细胞 RT-PCR 筛选

HIV-1 Env 特异性单克隆抗体的研究.中华实验与临床病毒学杂志，2013，27（2）：123-125.

[531] 郝彦哲，滕智平，曾毅.HIV 基因治疗概况及最新进展.中华实验与临床病毒学杂志，2013，27（2）：156-158.

[532] 詹少兵、张晓光、李红霞、曾毅.筛选 HIV-1P24 蛋白适配子的一种简便的 SELEX 方法.中华实验和临床病毒学杂志，2013，27（3）：218-220.

[533] 詹少兵、曾毅.SELEX 技术及近年研究进展，病毒学报，2013，29（5）：573-577.

[534] 李劲涛，周福有，董温平，王立东，曾毅.一株人乳头瘤病毒阳性的新的食管癌细胞系的建立及鉴定.病毒学报，2013，29（2）：119-125.

[535] 郝彦哲，滕智平，杨怡姝，孙晓娜，马晶，金孝华，曾毅.慢病毒介导双 shRNA 表达对 HIV 的抑制作用研究.病毒学报，2013，29（2）：126-131.

[536] 叶景荣，苏雪丽，余双庆，辛若雷，郝明强，卢红艳，冯霞，贺雄，曾毅.北京地区 2006-2010 年女性 HIV-1 感染者流行毒株分子特征研究，中华流行病学杂志，2013，34（1）：49-52.

[537] 叶景荣，董晓根，卢红艳，郝明强，苏雪丽，辛若雷，余双庆，冯霞，闫红，贺雄，曾毅.北京市 HIV-1 B'-C 重组型分子流行特征分析.中华医学杂志，2013，93（29）：2301-2304.

[538] 杜海军，王湛，尉秀霞，周玲，叶树清，曾毅.DC-LMP2 与 rAd-LMP2 所诱导的细胞免疫应答效果研究.中华实验与临床病毒学杂志，2013，27（6）：437-439.

[539] 聂凯，滕智平，曾毅，马学军.力环介导等温扩增技术研究进展及其在病原检测中的应用.中华实验和临床病毒学杂志，2013，27（4）：316-318.

[540] 徐柯，胥少华，冯霞，余双庆，曾毅.IL-15 基因佐剂对 HIV-1B 亚型 gp160DNA 及腺病毒载体疫苗的免疫效果的影响.病毒学报，2014，30（1）：62-65.

[541] 陈丹瑛，何小周，汪孟冉，余双庆，徐柯，李秦剑，曾毅，冯霞.含密码子优化的 SIV gag 基因的 DNA 疫苗与 rAd5 疫苗构建及免疫原性评价.中华实验和临床病毒学杂志.2014，28（1）：17-19.

[542] 全艳艳，杜海军，曾毅.EBNA1 在鼻咽癌发生中细胞免疫应答的研究.中华实验与临床病毒学杂志，2014，28（1）：73-75.

[543] 徐柯，冯霞，余双庆，曾毅，胥少华.慢病毒介导白介素 IL15 在人树突状细胞中表达研究.中华实验和临床病毒学杂志.2014，28（2）：132-134.

[544] 汪孟冉，陈丹瑛，何小周，叶景荣，余双庆，徐柯，曾毅，冯霞.HIV-1B/C 重组型外膜蛋白 env 基因序列分析及表型预测.中华实验和临床病毒学杂志.2014，28（3）：203-205.

[545] 陈丹瑛，汪孟冉，何小周，叶景荣，余双庆，李秦剑，徐柯，曾毅，冯霞.HIV-1 中国流行株 CRF01-AE env 基因改造及其重组 DNA 疫苗的构建.中华实验和临床病毒学杂志.2014，28（3）：227-229.

[546] 全艳艳，李红霞，张丽霞，王湛，周玲，曾毅，杜海军.含 EB 病毒核心抗原 1 重组腺病毒的构建.病毒学报，2014，30（4）：429-435.

曾毅院士英文论文目录

[1] Zeng Yi. Tranformation of golden hamster cells by adenovirus type 5. China Medicine, 1966, 1:10.

[2] Laboratory of Tumor Viruses of Cancer Institute, Laboratory of Tumor Viruses of Institute of Epidemiology, Department of Radiotherrapy of Cancer Institute, and Laboratory of cell biology of Cancer Institute, Chinese Academy of Medical Sciences; Laboratory of Electron Microscope, Department of Microbiology, and Laboratory of Pathogenesis, Chung Shan Medical College Establishment of an Epithelioid Cell Line and a Fusiform Cell Line from a Patient with Nasopharyngeal Carcinoma Scientia Sinica, 1978, 21 (1):127.

[3] Zeng Yi, Liu YX, Liu CR, Chen SW, Wei JN, Zhu JS, Zai HJ. Application of an Immunoenzymatic Medthod and an immunradioautographic Method for a Mass Survey of Nasopharyngeal Carcinoma. Intervirology, 1980, 13(3):162-168.

[4] Department of Microbiology and Cancer Hospital, Zhongshan Medical College, Guangzhou, Department of Virology, Cancer Institute and Department of Tumor Viruses, Institute of Virology, Chinese Academy of Medical Sciences, Beijing and Cancer Institute of Zhongshan County, Guangdong Investigation of Epstein-Barr Virus complement-fixing antibody levels in sera of Patients with Nasopharyngeal Carcinoma and Nasopharyngeal Mucosal Hyperplasia. Chinese Medical Journal, 1980, 93(6): 359-363.

[5] Wu Bing, Wu YQ, Li YW, Zeng Y, Wu M, Zhao AH, Gong CH. Study of Giant Group A Marker Chromosome in Several Burkitt's Lymphoma and Lymphoblastoid Cell Lines with Epsrein-Barr Virus From Different Origins. Chinese Medical Journal, 1980, 93(6): 400-406.

[6] Zeng Yi, Shen Shujing, Pi Guohua, Ma Jianlian, Zhang Qin, Zhao Minglun. Anticomplement Immunoenzymatic Method of Detecting Epstein-Barr Nuclear Antigen in Nasopharyngeal Carsinoma Cells and Nornal Epithelial Cells. Chnese Medical Journal, 1981, 94(10): 663-668.

[7] Zeng Yi, Shen SJ, Pi GH, Ma JL, Zhang Q, Zhao ML, Dong HJ. Application of Anticomplement Immunoenzymatic Method for the Detection of EBNA in Carcinoma Cells and Normal Epithelial Cells from the Nasopharynx 11th Int. Symp. Nasopharyngeal Carcinoma, Dusseldorf, West Germany. Carcer Campaign, vol. 5-Sp139 Nasopharyngeal

Carcinoma,1981：237-245.

[8] Pi GH，Zeng Y，Zhao WP，Zhang Q. Development of an Anticomplement Immunoenzyme test for detection of EB Virus Nuclear Antigen(EBNA) and Antibody to EBNA. J Immunological Methods，1981，44(1)：73-78.

[9] Zeng Yi，Zhu HM，Xu SP. Inhibitory Effect of Retinoids on Epstein-Barr Vrius Induction in Raji Cells. Intervirology，1981，16(1)：29-32.

[10] Zeng Y. Serological studies on nasopharyngeal carcinoma and cervical cancer in China 《Herpesvirus》 Hiroshi Shiota，Yung Chi Cheng William H.Prusoff eds，1981：380-388.

[11] G. deThe，Desgrang C，Zeng Y，Wang PC，Bornkamm GW，Zhu JS，Shang M. Search for pre-cancerous lesions and EBV markers in the Nasopharyng of IgA positive individuals. Grandman et al(eds) cancer campaign vol 5. Nasopharyngeal carcinoma Gustar Fischer stuttgart NY，1981：111-117.

[12] Zeng Y，Zhang LG，Li HY，Jan MG，Zhang Q，Wu YC，Wang YS，Su GR. Serological Mass Survey for Early Detection of Nasopharyngeal Carcinoma in Wuzhou City，China. International J. Cancer，1982，29(2)：139-141.

[13] Desgrange C，Bormkamm GW，Zeng Y，Wang PC，Su JS，Shang M，deThe G. Detection of EBV DNA internal Repearts in the Nasopharyngeal mucesa of Chinese with IgA/EBV specific antibodies. Int J cancer，1982，29(1)：87-91.

[14] Zeng Y，Zhong JM，deThe G，Wu SH，Hou YT，Xiao XQ. Enhancement of Spontaneous VCA and EA Induction in B95-8. Cells and EA Induction in Raji Cells Treated with Human Leukocyte Interferon. Intervirology，1982，18(1-2)：33-37.

[15] Zhang SH，Zeng Y，Lore Zech L，Geoge Klein. Cytogenetic Studies on An Epithelioid Cell Line Derived from Nasopharyngeal Carcinoma. Hereditas，1982，97(1)：23-28.

[16] Zeng Y，Zhong JM，Li LY，Wang PZ，Tang H，Ma YR，Zhu JS，Pan WJ，Liu XX，Wei ZN，Chan JY，Mo YK，Li EJ，Tan BF. Follow-up studies on Epstein-Barr virus IgA/VCA antibody positive persons in Zang Wu county China. Intervirology，1983，20(4)：190-194.

[17] Zeng Y，Zhong JM，Mo YK，Miao XC. Epstein-Barr Virus early antigen induction in Raji cells by Chinese medicinal herbs. Intervirology，1983，19(4)：201-204.

[18] deThe G，Zeng Y. Nasopharyngeal carcinoma can antiviral interventions be contemplated to prevent this cacer? 13Th international cancer congress. Prog Clin Biol Res，1983，132B：37-47.

[19] Ito Y，Ohigashi H，Koshimizu K，Zeng Y. EB Virus activating principle in the ether extracts of soils collected from under plants which contain activce diterpene ester. Cancer letter，1983，19(2)：113-117.

[20] Zhang SH，Gao XK，Zeng Y，et al. Cytogenetic Studies on and Epithelial Cell Line Derived from Poorly Differntiated Nasopharyngeal Carcinoma. Int J. Cancer，1983，31(5)：587-590.

[21] Pi GH，C Desgrange，GW Bornkamm，Shen SJ，Zeng Y，G deThe. Comparative Evaluation of Various Techniques to Detect EBV DNA in Exfoliated Nasopharyngeal Cells. Ann. Virol，1983，134：21-32

[22] Zeng Yi，Gong CH，Jan MG，Fun z，Zhang LG，Li HY. Detection of Epstein-Barr Virus IgA/EA Antibody for Diagnosis of Nasopharyngeal Carcinoma by Immunoautoradiography. Int J. Cancer，1983，31：599-601.

[23] Zeng Y，Gong CH，Jan MG，Zhang LG，Fun Z. Brief Communication：Detection of EB Virus IgA/EA Antibody for Diagnosis of Nasopharyngeal Carcinoma By Immunoautoradiography Nasopharyngeal Carcinoma 《Nasopharyngeal Carcinoma Current Concepts》U. Prasad，D.VAblashi，P.H.Levine. G.R.Pearson. eds，1983：137-140.

[24] Gu SY，Tan WP，Zeng Y，Zhao WP，Li K，Deng HH，Zhao ML. Brief communication：Establishment of an epithelial cell line from patients with poorly differentiated nasopharyngeal carcinoma 《Nasopharyngeal Carcinoma Current Concepts》U. Prasad，D. VAblashi，P.H.Levine.G.R.Pearson. eds，1983：273-276.

[25] G.de The，Y.Zeng，C.Desgranges，G.H.Pi The existence of Pre-nasopharyngeal carcinoma Conditions Should allow preventive interventions 《Nasopharyngeal Carcinoma Current Concepts》U. Prasad，D. VAblashi，P. H. Levine. G. R. Pearson. eds，1983：365-374.

[26] C.Desgranges，G.H.Pi，G.W.Bornkamm，C.Legrand，Y.Zeng，G.deThe. Presence of EBV-DNA Sequences in Nasopharyngeal Cells of Individuals Without IgA-VCA Antibodies Int.J.Cancer，1983，32(5)：543-545.

[27] Zeng Yi，Shen Shujing，Deng Hong，Ma Jiaolian，Zhang Qin，Zhu Jisong，Cheng Jiru. Early Nasopharyngeal Carcinoma among IgA/VCA antibody Positive Individuals Detected by Antixomplement immunoenzymatic Method Chinese Med.J，1984，97(3)：155-157.

[28] Zeng Yi，Lan XY，Fang J，et al. HTLV-I antibody in China. Lancet，1984，1(8380)：799-800.

[29] Zeng Yi，Miao XC，B. Jaio，Li HY，Ni H Y and Yo Hei Ito. Epstein-Barr Virus Activation in Raji Cells with other extracts of soil from different areas in China. Cancer Letters，1984，23(1)：53-59.

[30] Zeng Y，Ji ZW，Ito Y. Epstein-Barr Virus activation by Human Semen Principle：Synergistic effect of culture fluids of Bacteria Isolated from Patients with Carcinoma of Uterine

Cervix. Cancer Letters, 1985, 28(3):311-315.

[31] Y.Zeng, L.G.Zhang, Y.C.Wu, Y.S.Huang, N.Q.Huang, J.Y.Li, Y.B.Wang, M.K. Jiang,Z.Fang, N.N.Meng. Prospective Studies on Nasopharyngeal Carcinoma in Epstein-Barr Virus IgA/VCA Antibody-Positive Persons in Wuzhou City,China. Int. J. Cancer, 1985, 36(5):545-547.

[32] Zeng, Y. Seroepidemiological Studies on Nasopharyngeal Carcinoma in China. In: G. Klein., Wein house. Advance in Cancer Research. S.eds Academic Press, Inc. 1985, 44: 121-139.

[33] Zeng Yi and G.de The. Nasopharyngeal Carcinoma:Early Detection and IgA-Related pre-NPC Condition.Achievements and Prospecives 《Epstein-Barr Virus and Associated Diseases》P.H.Levine, D.V.Ablashi,G.R.Pearson,and S.D.Kottaridis eds, 1985: 151-163.

[34] Y.Ito, H.Tokuda, H.Ohigashi, K.Koshimizu and Y.Zeng Epstein-Barr Virus-Activating Substance(s) from Soil《Epstein-Barr Virus and Associated Diseases》P.H.Levine, D.V. Ablashi,G.R.Pearson,and S.D.Kottaridis eds, 1985: 383-391.

[35] Li Ej, Tan BF, Zeng Y, Wang PC, Zhong JM, Deng H, Zhu CS, Wei JN, Pan WJ. Nasopharyngeal Mucosal Changes in EB Virus VCA-IgA Antibody Positive Persons. Chinese Medical Journal, 1985, 98(1): 25-30.

[36] Pi GH, Zeng Y, de The G. ELISA for the Detection of Nasopharyneal Carcinoma Using IgA Antibodies to EBV Early Antigen. Ann. Inst. Pasteur/Virol, 1985, 136: 131-140.

[37] Zeng Yi, Fan J, Zhang Q, Wang PC, Tang DJ, Zhon SC, Zheng XW, Lui DP. Prospective Studies on Nasopharyngeal Carcinoma and Epstein-Barr Virus inducers. Cancer of the liver, Esophagus and Nasopharyngeal Carcinoma. Gustav Wagner, Zhang Y H.(eds) Springer-verlag, 1986: 164-169.

[38] Zeng Y, Fan J, Zhang Q, Wang PC, Tang DJ, Zhon SC, Zheng XW, Liu DP. Detection of Antibody to LAV/HTLV III in sera from hemophiliacs in China. AIDS Research, 1986, 2(s1): 147-150.

[39] Zeng Y, Pi GH, Deng H, Zhang JM, Wang PC, Wolf H, De Thé G. Epstein-Barr Virus seroepidemiology in China. AIDS Research, 1986, 2(1): 7-4.

[40] Zhu X X, Zeng Y, H Wolf. Detection of IgG and IgA Antibodies to Epstein-Barr Virus Membrane Antigen in Sera from Patients with Nasopharyngeal Carcinoma and from Normal Individuals. Int J Cancer, 1986, 37(5): 689-691.

[41] G. deThe, Zeng Y. Population screening for EBV markers Toward improvement of Nasopharyngeal Carcinoma control. The Epstein-Barrvirus. Epstein, MA, BG Achong(eds) william Heinemann Medical Books, 1986: 237-248.

[42] H.Wolf, M. Motz, S. Modrow, W. Jilg, R. Seibl, R. Kuhbeck, J. Fan, Y. Zeng. Ep-

stein-Barr Virus and Nasopharyngeal Carcinoma.Contr. Oncol.,(Karger, Basel), 1987, 24：142-157.

[43] B.McKnight，S.T.Lu，L.Ju，N.E.Day，L.Degos,V.Lepage，S.H.Chan，U.Prasad，J.H. C.Ho，M.J.Simons，Y.Zeng，and G.de-The. A Preliminary Analysis of HLA Studies on Multiple NPC Cases among Siblings from the People's Republic of China，Hong Kong，Singapore，and Malaysia《Epstein-Barr Virus and Human Disease》P. H. Levine，D. V. Ablashi，M.Nonoyama，G.R.Pearson，and R.Glaser eds，1987：25-29.

[44] Chan KH，YiP TC，Choy D，Chan CW，Zeng Y，MH Ng. Evaluation of Monoclonal Antibodies for the Detection of Exfoliative Nasopharyngeal Carcinoma Cells. Int J Cancer，1987，39(4)：455-448.

[45] H.Wolf，M. Motz，R. Kuhbeck，W. Jilg，J.Fan，G.H.Pi，Y. Zeng. Development of a Set of EBV-Specifec Antigenns with Recombinant Gene Technologyfor Diagnosis of EBV-Related Malignator Nonmalignant Diseases 《 Epstein-BarrVirus and Human Disease》P.H.Levine，D.V.Ablashi，M.Nonoyama,G.R.Pearson,and R.Glaser eds，1987：179-182.

[46] G.deThe，Zeng Y. Epidemiology of Nasopharyngeal Carcinoma with Special Reference to early detection and Pre-NPC conditions. Cancer of the liver，Esophagus，and Nasopharyngeal Carcinoma. Gustav Wagner，Zhang Y H.(eds) springer-verlag，1987：147-151.

[47] Zeng Yi. EB Virus and Nasopharyngeal Carcinama《Etiology and Pathogenesis of Nasopharyngeal Carcinama》Zeng Yi，Ou Baoxiang ed，1987：18-47.

[48] Zeng Y.，H.Wolf，K.Takada，J.R.Arrand G.de The. Detection of EBV Specific IgA Antibodies to EA，MA and EBNA-1 Recombinant Proteins in NPC Patients and Controls. 《Epstein-Barr Virus and Human Disease 1988》 Humana Press Clifton. New Jersey，1988：309-313.

[49] Shao Y. M.，S Poirier，H.Oshima，C. Malaveille，Zeng Y.，G. deThe，H.Bartsch，Epstein-Barr Virus activation in Raji Cells by extract of preserved food from NPC high risk arears. Carcinogenesis，1988，9(8)：1455-1457.

[50] Tang WP，Huang PG，Zhao ML，Liao SL，Zeng Y. Wikstroemia Indica promotes development of nasopharyngeal carcinoma in rats initiated by dinitrosopiperazine. J. Cancer Res. Clin. Oncol，1988，114(4)：429-431.

[51] Zeng Y.,Zhang J.M. Aetlogical Studies on Nasopharyngeal Carcinoma in China《Current Topics in Medical Virology—Invited Papers from the First Asia-Pacific Congress of Medical Viroilogy Singapore 6-11 November 1988》Y.C.Chan ed World Scientific，1989：92-102.

[52] S Poirier，G Bouvier，C Malaveille，H Ohshima，Shao YM，A Hubert，Zeng Y，G de-

The and H Bartsch. Volatile nitrosamine levels and genotoxicity of food samples from high-risk areas for nasopharyngeal carcinoma before and after nitrosation. Int J Cancer, 1989, 44(6): 1088-1094.

[53] Zeng Y. Nasopharyngeal Carcinoma. Advances in Mark's disease Reaearch(S. Kato et al eds) 1989: 2-3.

[54] Zeng Yi. EB virus inducers, Tumor promoters and nasopharyngeal carcinoma EB virus Symposion. Oxford, 1989.

[55] Edward Littler, Zeng Y. Diagnosis of Nasopharyngeal Carcinoma using the Epstein-Barr Virus coded DNase, Membrane antigen and Thymidine Kinase. Annual Report, 1990, 337(8743):685-689.

[56] Lu SL, Nicholas E Day, Degos L, Lepage Y, Hung PC, Chan SHM, Mcknight B, Easton D, Zeng Y, deThe G. Linkage of a nasopharyngeal carcinoma susceptibility locus to the HLA region. Nature, 1990, 346(8743):470-471.

[57] Edward Littler, Sally A. Baylis, Yi Zeng, Margaret J. Conway, Michael Mackett, John R. Arrand. Diagosis of Nasopharyngeal Carcinoma by means of Recombinant Epstein-Barr Virus Proteins. Lancet, 1991, 337(8743): 685-689.

[58] Q. Y. Yao, M Rowe, AJ Morgan, CK Sam, U Prasad, H Dang, Y Zeng and Rickinson AB. Salivary and Serum IgA Antibodies to the Epstein-Barr Vrius Glycoprotein gp340: Incidence and Potential for Virus Neutralization. Int J Cancer, 1991, 48(1): 45-50.

[59] Irene Joab, Jean-Claude Nicolrs, Guy Schwaab, Guy. deThe, Bernard Clause, Michel Perricaudet, Yi Zeng. Detection of anti-Epstein Barr Virus Transactivator Zebra) Antibodies in Sera from Patients with Nasopharyngeal Carcinama. Int J Cancer, 1991, 48(5): 647-649.

[60] Jiangyi Si, Kun Lee, icai Han, Zeng Yi, et al. A research for the relationship between human papillomavirus and human uterine cervical carcinoma. J. The identification of viral genome and subgenomic sequences in biopsies of Chinese patients. Cancer Res Clin Oncol, 1991, 117(5): 454-459.

[61] Jiangyi Si, Kun Lee, Wei Zhang, Zeng Yi, et al. A research for the relationship between human papillomavirus and human uterine cervical carcinoma. II Molecular genetic and ultrastructural study on the transforming activity of recombinant retrovirus containing human papillomavirus type 16 subgenomic sequences. J Cancer Res Clin Oncol, 1991, 117(5): 460-472.

[62] Liu Chaoqu, Sen Yu, Zeng Yi and Huang Shuling. Studies on Mouse Cervical Carcinoma Co-induced by Seminal Plasma, Culture Fluid of Anaerobic Bacteria and/or HSV-2. Virus Information Exchange News letter, 1991, 8:83.

[63] Zeng Yi. HIV Infection and AIDS in China. AIDS Research, 1992, 6(1-2): 1-5.

[64] Chen WP, Lee Y, Wang H, Yu GG, Jiao W, Zhou WY, Zeng Y. Suppression of human nasopharygeal carcinoma cell growth in nude mice by the wide-type P53 gene. J Cancer Res Clin Oncol, 1992, 119(1): 46-48.

[65] Zeng Yi, Deng H, Zhong JM, Huang NQ, Li PJ, Pan WJ, Huang YY, Li Y, Wang PZ, G deThe. A 10-year Prospective Study on Nasopharyngeal Carcinoma in WuZhou City and ZangWu County, GuangXi, China. The Epstein-Barr Virus and Associated Disease, 1993, 225: 735-741.

[66] Yi Zeng, Hiroshi Ohshima, Guy Bouvier, Pascal Roy, Zhong Jianming, Bingjun Li, Lsabelle Bruet, Guy de The and Helmut Bartsch. Urinary excretion of nitrosamino acids and nitrate by inhabitants of high-and low-risk arera for nasopharyngeal carcinoma in southern China. Cancer Epidemiology, Biomarkers and Prevention, 1993, 2(3): 195-200.

[67] Chen WP, Lee Y, Wang H, Yu GG and Zeng Y. Antioncogenes in nasopharyngeal carcinoma tissues. The Epstein-Barr Virus and Associated Disease, 1993, 225: 533-537.

[68] Deng H, Pi ZM, Tan BF, Zeng Y, Lei YM, Zhao ZB, Wang PZ, Li BJ, Pan WJ, Zhong ZY and Wu JY. Nasopharyngeal Carcubina serological survey in 21 cities and counties in three provinces of south China Proceeding of the international cancer congress (Rai, R, S, eds) New Delhi India 30, 1994, oct-5 nov: 1015-1019.

[69] Y.M. Zheng, P Tuppin, A Hubert, D Jeannel, YJ Pan, Y Zeng, G de The. Enviromental and dietary risk factors for nasophryngeal carcinoma: a case-control study in Zangwu county, Guangxi, China. Br. J. Cancer, 1994, 69(3):508-514.

[70] Lan XY, Zeng Y, Zhang D, Hong ML, Wang DX, Zhang YL, Feng ZJ, Tang MH and Feng BZH. Establishment of a Human Malignant T Lymphoma Cell Line Carrying a Retrovirus-like Particles with RT Activity. Biomedical and environmental sciences, 1994, 7(1): 1-12.

[71] Zeng Yi, Zhong Jan Ming, Ye Shu Qing, Ni Zhi Yu, Miao Xue Qian. Screening of Epstein-Barr Virus Early Antigen Expression Inducers from Chinese Medicinal Herbs and Plants. Biomedical and Enviromental Science, 1994, 7(1):50-55.

[72] Deng H, Zeng Yi, Lei Yiming, Zhao Zengbao, Wang Peizhong, Li Bingjun, Pi Zhiming, Tan Bifang, Zheng Yuming, Pan Wenjun, Zhong Zhengyi, Wu Jueyan. Sero-epidemiological survey of nasopharyngeal carcinoma in 21 cities of south China. Chinese medical journal, 1995, 108(4): 300-303.

[73] Teng Zhiping, Tadamasa Ooka, Doll P Huang, Yi Zeng. Detection of Epstein-Barr DNA in well and poorly differentiated Nasopharyngeal carcinome cell lines. Virus Genes,

1996，13(1)：53-60.

[74] Bao-min Li，Zhi-wu Ji，Zhen-Sheng Liu，Yi Zeng. Epstein-Barr virus in synergy with tumor-promoter- induced malignant transformation of immortalized human epithelial cells. J cancer Res clin oncol，1997，123(8)：441-446.

[75] Nancy S. SUNG，Rachel H. Edwards，Francoise Seillier-Moiseiwttsch，Ashley G. Perkins，Yi Zeng，Nancy Raab-Traub. Epstein-Barr virus strain variation in nasopharyngeal carcinoma from the endemic and non-endemic regions of China. Int J Cancer，1998，76(2)：207-215.

[76] Virginie Grunewald，Mathilde Bonnet，Sylvie Boutin，Timothy Yip，Hechmi Louzir，Massimo Levrero，Jean Marie Seineurin，Martine Raphael，Robert Touitou，Dominique Martel-Renoir，Chantal Cochet，Anne Durandy，Patrtrice Andre，W Lau，Yi ZengY，I Joab. Amino-acid change in the Epstein-Barr-virus ZEBRA protein in undifferentiated nasopharyngeal carcinomas from Europe and North Africa. Int J Cancer，1998，75(4)：497-503.

[77] Liu Zheng Seng，Yanfang Liu，Yi Zeng. Synergistic effet of Epstein-Barr Virus and Tumor Promoters on Induction of Lymphoma and Carcinoma in Nude Mice. J Cancer Res Clin Oncol，1998，12(10)：541-548.

[78] Shen-ZY，Tan-LJ，Cai-WJ，Shen-J，Chen-C，Tang-XM，Zheng-MH. Arsenic trioxide induces apoptosis of esophageal carcinoma in vitro. Int J Mol Med，1999，4(1)：33-37.

[79] Zeng Yi，Wu Zunyou. Control of AIDS Epidemic in China Bulletin of the Chinese Academy of Sciences，2000，14(2)：106-111.

[80] Zhongying Shen，Shan Cen，Shen J，Cai WJ，Xu JJ，Teng ZP，Hu Z，Zeng Y. Study of immortalization and malignant transformation of human embryonic esophageal epithelial cells induced by HPV18E6E7. J Cancer Res Clin Oncol，2000，126(10)：589-594.

[81] Shen ZY，Xu LY，Chen XH，Cai WJ，Shen J，Chen JY，Huang TH and Zeng Y. The genetic events of HPV-immortalized esophageal epithelium cells. Int J Mol Med，2001，8(5)：537-542.

[82] Shen ZY，Xu LY，Li C，Cai WJ，Shen J，Chen JY，Zeng Y. A comparative study of telomerase activity and malignant phenotype in multistage carcinogenesis of esophageal epithelial cells induced by human papillomavirus. Int J Mol Med，2001，8(6)：633-639.

[83] Chen HB，Chen L，Zhang JK，Shen ZY，Su ZJ，Cheng SB，Chew EC. Human papillomavirus 16 E6 is associated with the nuclear matrix of esophageal carcinoma cells. World J Gastroenterol，2001，7(6)：788-791.

[84] Joint working group report of Aids/Infectious Diseases PMP and mother and child PMP Mother to child transmission of HIV-antiretroviral therapy and therapeutic vaccine：A

scientific and community challenge 412-418, 2001 Series Editor: A Zichichi International seminar on Nuclear War-26th Session, 2001.

[85] Shen ZY, Hu SP, Shen J, Lu LC, Tang CZ, Kuang ZS, Zeng Y. Detection of Human Papillomavirus in Esophageal Carcinoma. J Med Virol, 2002, 68(3): 412-416.

[86] Shen ZY, Xu LY, Li EM, Cai WJ, Chen MH, Shen J, Zeng Y. Telomere and telomerase in the initial stage of immortalization of esophageal epithelial cell. World J Gastrointerol, 2002, 8(2): 357-362.

[87] Shen ZY, Xu LY, Li EM, Shen J, Zheng RM, Cai WJ, Zeng Y. Immortal phenotype of the esophageal epithelial cells in the process of immortalization. Int J Mol Med, 2002, 10 (5): 641-646.

[88] Shen ZY, Xu LY, Chen MH, Shen J, Cai WJ, Zeng Y. Progressive transformation of immortalized esophageal epithelial cells. World J Gastroenterol, 2002, 8(6):976-981.

[89] G Biberfeld, F Buonaguro, A Lindberg, G de The., Z Y, and R Zetterstrom. Prospects of vaccination as a means of preventing mother-to-child transmission of HIV-I. Acta Padiatr, 2002, 91(2): 241-243.

[90] Guomin Chen, Shuhui Wang, Kun Xiong, Jinzhong Wang, Tao Ye, Wenping Dong, Qi Wang, Qimin Chen, Yunqi Geng, Charles Wood and Yi Zeng. Construction and characterization of a chimeric virus(BIV/HIV-1) carrying the bovine immunodeficiency virus gag-pol gene. AIDS, 2002, 16(1):123-125.

[91] Xiong XD, Xu LY, Shen ZY, Cai WJ, Luo JM, Han YL, Li EM. Identification of differentially expressed proteins between human esopahgeal immortalized and carcinomatous cell lines by two-dimensional electrophoresis and MALDI-TOF-mass spectrometry. World J Gastroenterol, 2002, 8(5):777-781.

[92] Shen ZY, Shen J, Li QS, Chen CY, Chen JY, Zeng Y. Morphological and functional changes of mitochondria in apoptotic esophageal carcinoma cells induced by arsenic trioxide. World J Gastruenterol, 2002, 8(1):31-35.

[93] Shen ZY, Shen WY, Chen MH, Shen J, Cai WJ, Zeng Y. Nitric oxide and calcium ions in apoptotic esophageal carcinoma cells induced by arsenite. World J Gastroenterol, 2002, 8(1):40-43.

[94] Shen ZY, Shen WY, Chen MH, Shen J, Cai WJ, Zeng Y. Mitochondria, calcium and nitric oxide in the apoptotic pathway of esophageal carcinoma cells induced by As203. Int J Mol Med, 2002, 9(4):385-390.

[95] Shen ZY, Shen J, Chen MH, Wu XY, Wu MH, Zeng Y. The inhibition of growth and angiogenesis in heterotransplanted esophageal carcinoma via intratumoral injection of arsenic trioxide. Oncol Rep, 2003, 10(6):1869-1874.

[96] Shen ZY, Xu LY, Li EM, Li JT, Chen MH, Shen J, Zeng Y. Ezrin, actin and cytoskeleton in apoptosis of esophageal epithelial cells induced by arsenic trioxide. Int J Mol Med, 2003, 12(3): 341-347.

[97] Shen ZY, Shen WY, Chen MH, Shen J, Zeng Y. Reactive oxygen species and antioxidants in apoptosis of esophageal cancer cells induced by As2O3. Int J Mol Med, 2003, 11(4): 479-484.

[98] Shen ZY, Xu LY, Chen MH, Li EM, Li JT, Wu XY, Zeng Y. Upregulated expression of Ezrin and invasive phenotype in malignantly transformed esophageal epithelial cells. World J Gastroenterol, 2003, 9(6):1182-1186.

[99] Shen ZY, Xu LY, Chen MH, Cai WJ, Shen J, Ceng JY, Zeng Y. Cytogenetic and molecular genetic changes in malignant transformation of immortalized esophageal epithelial cells. Int J Mol Med, 2003, 12(2): 219-224.

[100] Shen ZY, Cen S, Xu LY, Cai WJ, Chen MH, Shen J, Zeng Y. E6/E7 genes of human papilloma virus type 18 induced immortalization of human fetal esophageal epithelium. Oncol Rep, 2003, 10(5):1431-1436.

[101] Shen ZY, Xu LY, Li EM, Cai WJ, Shen J, Chen MH, Cen S, Tsao SW, Zeng Y. The multistage process of carciogenesis in human esophageal epithelial cells induced by human papillomavirus. Oncol Rep, 2004, 11(3): 647-654.

[102] Zhong-Ying Shen, Yuan Zhang, Jiong-Yu Chen, Ming-Hua Chen, Jian Shen, Wen-Hong Luo and Yi Zeng. Intratumoral injection of arsenic to enhance antitumor efficacy in human esophageal carcinoma cell xenografts. Oncology Reports, 2004, 11(1): 155-159.

[103] Xiuchan Guo, Xiangying Lan, Ling Zhou, Zhiping Teng, Yongli zhang, Zhongying Shen and Yi Zeng. Malignant Transformation of Human Embryonic Liver Cells Induced by Hepatitis B Virus and Aflatoxin B. J Microbiol Immunol, 2004, 2(3):185-190.

[104] Zeng Yi, Xu Hua, and Zhang Jiaxi. Infectious Diseases in China. AIDS in Asia(Edited by Yichen Lu andMax Essex) Kluwer Academic/Plenum Publishers, New York, 2004: 295-305.

[105] Francisco M. De La Vega, Hadar Isaac, Andrew Collins, Charles R. Scafe, Bjarni V. Halldorsson, Xiaoping Su, Ross A. Lippert, Yu Wang, Marion Laig-Webster, Ryan T. Koehler, Janet S. Ziegle, Lewis T. Wogan, Junko F. Stevens, Kyle M. Leinen, Sheri J. Olson, Karl J. Guegler, Xiaoqing You, Lily H. Xu, Heinz G. Hemken, Francis Kalush, Mitsuo Itakura, Yi Zeng, et al. The linkage disequilibrium maps of three human chromosomes across four populations reflect their demographic history and a common underlying recombination pattern. Genome Research, 2005, 15(4): 454-462.

[106] Yi-Xin Zhu, Chang Liu, Xin-Lei Liu, Wen-Tao Qiao, Qi-Min Chen, Yi Zeng, Yun-Qi

Geng. Construction and characterization of chimeric BHIV(BIV/HIV-1) viruses carrying the bovine immunodeficiency virus *gag* gene. World J Gastroenterol, 2005, 11(17): 2609-2615.

[107] Hua XU, Yi ZENG, Allen F ANDERSON. Chinese NGOs in action against HIV/AIDS. Cell Research, 2005, 15(11-12): 914-918.

[108] Xiu Chan Guo, Kevin Scott, Yan Liu, Michael Dean, Victor David, George W. Nelson, C. Johnson, Holli H. Dilks, James Lautenberger, Bailey Kessing, Janice Martenson, Li Guan, Shan Sun, Hong Deng, Yuming Zheng, Guy de The, Jian Liao, Yi Zeng, et al. Genetic Factors leading to Chronic Epstein Barr virus Infection and Nasopharyngeal Carcinoma in Southeast China: Study Design, Methods and Feasibility. Human Genomics, 2006, 2(6): 365-375.

[109] Jian Min ZUO, Ling ZHOU, Zhi Jian CHEN, De Rui LI, Qi WANG, Jiong Yu CHEN, Zhan WANG, Shu Qing YE and Yi ZENG. Induction of cytotoxic T lymphocyte respones in vivo after immunotherapy with nasopharyngeal carcinoma. J Microbiol Immunol, 2006, 4(1): 41-48.

[110] Ying Pan, Jinkun Zhang, Ling Zhou, Jianmin Zuo, Yi Zeng. In vitro anti-tumor immune response induced by dendritic cells transfected with EBV-LMP2 recombinant adenovirus. Biochemical and Biophysical Research Communications, 2006, 347(3): 551-557.

[111] Yue-Qing Li, Ze-Lin Li, Wei-Jie Zhao, Rui-Xing Wen, Qing-Wei Meng, Yi Zeng. Synthesis of stilbene derivatives with inhibition of SARS coronavirus replication. European Journal of Medicinal Chemistry, 2006, 41(9): 1084-1089.

[112] Xin-Lei Liu, Shuang-Qing Yu, Xia Feng, Xiao-Li Wang, Hong-Mei Liu, Xiao-Mei Zhang, Hong-Xia Li, Ling Zhou, Yi Zeng. Immunogenicity of the recombinant adenovirus type 5 vector with type 35 fiber containing HIV-1 gag gene. J Microbiol Immunol, 2006, 4(4):306-312.

[113] Wei-Hua Jia, Qi-Hong Huang, Jian Liao, Weimin Ye, YY Shugart, Qing Liu, Li-Zhen Chen, Yan-Hua Li, Xiao Lin, Fa-Lin Wen, Hans Olov Adami, Yi Zeng and Yi Xin Zeng Trends in incidence and mortality of nasopharyngeal carcinoma over a 20-25 year period(1978/1983-2002)in Sihui and Cangwu counties in southern China. BMC Cancer, 2006 (6): 178.

[114] Zeng Yi. Strategy for AIDS Prevention and Treatment. Virologica Sinica, 2007, 22(6): 419-420.

[115] Shen ZY, Zeng Y, Qing BQ. Human papillomavirus and esophageal squanmous cell carcinoma. In:《New Research on Esophageal Cancer》. Editor: Antonio Carminati. Chapter-2. Nova Science Publishers, 2007: 95-130.

[116] Xiuchan Guo, StephenJ.O Brien, Yi Zeng, W.Nelson, Cheryl A. Winkler GSTM1 and GSTT1 gene Deletions and the Risk for Nasopharyngeal Carcinoma in Han Chinese. Cancer Epidemiol Biomarkers Prev, 2008, 17(7): 1760-1763.

[117] Shuangqing Yu, Xia Feng, Tsugumine Shu, Tetsuro Matano, Mamoru Hasegawa, Xiaoli Wang, Hongtao Ma, Hongxia Li, Zelin Li, Yi Zeng. Potent specific immune responses induced by prime-boost-boost strategies based on DNA, adenovirus, and Sendai virus vectors expressing gag gene of Chinese HIV-1 subtype B. Vaccine, 2008, 26(48): 6124-6131.

[118] Lan LI, Yi-shu YANG, Ze-lin LI and Yi ZENG. Prokaryotic Expression and Purification of HIV-1 Vif and hAPOBEC3G, Preparation of Polyclonal Antibodies. VIROLOGICA SINICA, 2008, 23(3): 173-182.

[119] Xia Feng, Shuang-qing YU, Tsugumine Shu, TetsuroMatano, ManoruHasegawa, Xiao-li Wang, Hong-tao MA, Hong-xia LI and Yi Zeng. Immunogenicity of DNA and Recombinant Sendai Virus Vaccines Expressing the HIV-1gag Gene. VIROLOGICA SINICA, 2008, 23(4): 295-304.

[120] Lan LI, Yi-shu YANG, Ze-Lin LI and Yi ZENG. Prokaryotic Exssion and Purification of HIV Vif and hAPOBEC3G Preparation of Polyclonal Antibodies Virologica Sinica, 2008, 23(3): 173-182.

[121] Zhang DH, Shen ZY, Zhang QY, Xu LY, Li EM, Zeng Y. Current detection of human papillomavirus in esophageal squamous cell carcinoma. Current Topics in Virology Vol. 7. Ref. No. RT/VR/78 2008.

[122] Xiuchan Guo,Randall C. Johnson, Hong Deng, Jian Liao, Li Guan, George W.Nelson, Mingzhong Tang, Yuming Zheng, Guy de The, Stephen J. O'Brien, Cheryl A.Winkler and Yi Zeng. Evaluation of nonviral risk factors fornasopharyngealcarcinoma in high-risk population of Southern China. Int J Cancer, 2009, 124(12): 2942-2947.

[123] MO Wu-ning, Tang An-zhou, Zhou Ling, HUANG Guang-wu, WANG Zhan and Zeng Yi. Analysis of Epstein-Barr virus DNA load, EBV-LMP2 specific cytotosic T-lymphocytes and levels of CD4[+]CD25[+] T cells pn patients with nasopharyngeal carcinomas positive for IgA antibody to EBV viral capsid antigen. Chinese Medical Journal, 2009, 122 (10): 1173-1178.

[124] M Tang, Y Zeng, A Poisson, D Marti, L Guan, Y Zheng, H Deng, J Liao, X Guo, S Sun, G Nelson, G de The, CA Winkler, SJ O'Brien, M Carrington and X Gao. Haplotype-dependent HLA susceptibility to nasopharyngeal carcinoma in a Southern Chinese population. Genes and Immunity, 2010, 11(4): 334-342.

[125] Xiuchan Guo, Yi Zeng, Hong Deng, Jian Liao, Yuming Zheng, Ji Li, Bailey Kessing,

Stephen J O'Brien. Genetic Polymorphisms of CYP2E1, GSTP1, NQO1 and MPO and the Risk of Nasopharyngeal Carcinoma in a Han Chinese Population of Southern China. BMC Resarch Notes, 2010 (3): 212.

[126] Shuang-qing YU, Xia FENG, Tsugumine Shu, Tetsuro Matano, Mamoru Hasegawa, Xiaoli WANG, Hong-xia LI, Zelin LI, Rugang ZHONG, Yi ZENG. Comparison of the Expression and Immunogenicity of Wild-Type and Sequence-Modified HIV-1 gag Genes in a Recombinant Sendai Virus Vector. Current HIV Research, 2010, 8(3): 199-206.

[127] Li Shuying, Du Haijun, Wang Zhan, ZhouLing, Zhao Xiaoyu and ZengYi. Meta-analysis of the relationship between Epstein-Barr virus infection and clinicopathological features of patients with gastric carcinoma. Science china: Life Sciences, April, 2010, 53(4): 524-530.

[128] M Tang, Y Zeng, A Poisson, D Marti, L Guan, Y Zheng, H Deng, J Liao, X Guo, S Sun, G Nelson, G de The, CA Winkler, SJ O'Brien, M Carrington and X Gao. Haplotype -dependent HLA susceptibility to nasopharyngeal carcinoma in a Southern Chinese population. Genes and Immunity, 2010, 11(4): 334-342.

[129] Ke Zhang, Jin-Tao Li, Shu-Ying Li, Li-Hua Zhu, Ling Zhou, Yi Zeng. Integration of human papillomavirus 18 DNA in esophageal carcinoma 109 cells. World Journal of Gastroenterology, 2011, 17(37): 4242-4246.

[130] Jing-rong Ye, Ruo-lei Xin, Li-shi Bai, Hong-yan Lu, Shuang-qin Yu, Yi Zeng. Sequence analysis of the gag-pol gene of Human Immunodeficiency Virus Type 1 of Inersubtype(B'/C) Recombinant Strain in Beijing, China. AIDS Research and Human Retroviruses, 2011, 27(3):331-337.

[131] Wang Zhan, Yang Songmei, Zhou Ling, Du Haijun, Mo Wuning, Zeng Yi. Specific cellular immune responses in mice immunized with DNA, adeno-associated virus and adenoviral vaccines of Epstein-Barr virus-LMP2 alone or in combination. Science China(Life Science), 2011, 54(3): 1-4.

[132] Jing-rong Ye, Shuang-qing Yu, Hong-yan Lu, Wei-shi Wang, Ruo-lei Xin, and Yi Zeng. Genetic Diversity of HIV Type 1 Isolated from Newly Diagnosed Subjects(2006-2007) in Beijing, China. AIDS Research and Human Retroviruses, 2012, 28(1): 119-123.

[133] Jing-rong Ye, Hong-yan Lu, Wei-shi Wang, Ruo-lei Xin, Shuang-qing Yu, Ting-chen Wu, Yi Zeng, and Xiong He. The Prevalence of Drug Resistance Mutations Among Treatment-Naïve HIV-Infected Individuals in Beijing, China. AIDS Research and Human Retroviruses, 2012, 28(4): 418-423.

[134] Jian Zhao, Xiaoguang Zhang, Jing Ma, Guiwen Liu, Dianxin Yao, Weiyuan Zhang, Ji-

andong Wang, Lihui Wei, Yun Zhao, Yi Zeng, Qinping Liao. Clinical performance characteristics of the Cervista HPV HR test kit in cervical cancer screening in China. J Low Genit Tract Dis, 2012, 16(4):358-363.

[135] Lingfei Zhang, Liu Yang, Xia Feng, Zhu-lun Zhuang, Shuangqing Yu, Ling Yang, Hongxia Li, Xianghui Yu, Wei Kongc, Yi Zeng. Combined Immunization of Mice with DNA、rMVA and rAd5 Expressing HIV-1 Structural Genes from Different Subtypes. Current HIV research, 2012, 10(5): 498-503.

[136] Minzhong Tang, James A. Lautenberger, Xiaojiang Gao, Efe Sezgin, Sher L. Hendrickson, Jennifer L. Troyer, Victor A. David, Li Guan, Carl E. Mcintosh, Xiuchan Guo, Yuming Zheng, Jian Liao, Hong Deng, Michael Malasky, Bailey Kessing, Chery A. Winkler, Mary Carrington, Guy de' The, Yi Zeng, et al. The Principal Genetic Determinants for Nasopharyngeal Carcinoma in China Involve the HLA Class I Antigen Recognition Groove. PLOS Genetics, 2012, 8(11): 1003103.

[137] Jingrong Ye, Ruolei Xin, Shuangqing Yu, Lishi Bai, Weishi Wang, Tingchen Wu, Xueli Su, Hongyan Lu, Xinghuo Pang, Hong Yan, Xia Feng, Xiong He, Yi Zeng. Phylogenetic and Temporal Dynamics of Human Immunodeficiency Virus Type 1 CRF01_AE in China. PLOS ONE, 2013, 1(8): 54238.

[138] Hongwei Liu, Jintao Li, Mingkun Diao, Zhenhai Cai, Jun Yang, and Yi Zeng. Statistical Analysis of Human Papillomavirus in a Subset of Upper Aerodigestive Tract Tumors. Journal of Medical Virology, 2013, 85(10): 1775-1785.

[139] Fang Zhang, Zhiping Yang, Minjun Cao, Yinsheng Xu, Jintao Li, Xuebin Chen, Zhi Gao, Jing Xin, Shaomei Zhou, Zhixiang Zhou, Yishu Yang, Wang Sheng, Yi Zeng. MiR-203 suppresses tumor growth and invasion and down-regulates MiR-21 expression through repressing Ran in esophageal cancer. Cancer Lett. 2014, 342(1): 121-129.

曾毅院士主要获奖奖项

1.成果、论文及著作获奖奖项

[1] 高分化鼻咽癌细胞株的建立(CNE-1).全国科学大会奖.1978年.

[2] 鼻咽癌防治研究.全国科技大会奖.1978年.

[3] 测定EB病毒免疫球蛋白(VCA-IgA)抗体方法的建立及其在鼻咽癌诊断和普查中的应用.第一完成人.中国医学科学院科技一等奖.1978年.

[4] 测定EB病毒免疫球蛋白(VCA-IgA)抗体方法的建立及其在鼻咽癌诊断和普查中的应用.第一完成人.卫生部1980年甲级科技成果奖.1980年.

[5] 应用抗补体免疫酶法检测鼻咽癌细胞和鼻咽部上皮细胞中的EB病毒核抗原.第二完成人.广东省高等教育局科技成果二等奖.1981年.

[6] 人体部分肿瘤细胞株的建立及生物学特性,鼻咽癌低分化细胞株建立.第二完成人.卫生部乙级科技成果奖.1984年.

[7] 核酸重组和标记新方法的建立及在EB病毒核酸研究中的应用.第二完成人.卫生部乙级科技成果奖.1985年.

[8] 核酸重组和标记新方法的建立及在EB病毒核酸研究中的应用.第二完成人.卫生部乙级科技成果奖.1985年.

[9] 建立一种筛选上皮细胞表面抗原单克隆抗体的酶免疫吸附试验.第四完成人.第四军医大学科学技术进步三等奖.1985年.

[10] 鼻咽癌前瞻性现场研究及早期诊断技术的建立和应用.第一完成人.卫生部科技进步二等奖.1988年.

[11] 鼻咽癌早期诊断技术的建立和应用及前瞻性现场的研究.第一完成人.国家科技进步三等奖.1988年.

[12] 艾滋病的血清流行病学调查和病毒分离研究.第一完成人.卫生部科技进步三等奖.1989年.

[13] 艾滋病毒抗体检测免疫酶试剂盒.第一完成人.中国预防医学科学院科技进步二等奖.1990年.

[14] EB病毒IgA/VCA,IgA/EA抗体测定试剂盒.第一完成人.全国医药科技成果展览会优秀奖.1990年.

[15] 鼻咽癌早期诊断、前瞻性研究及病因的研究.第一完成人.陈嘉庚医药科学奖.1991年.

[16] 浙江省艾滋病感染者监测与防治的综合研究.第三完成人.浙江省科技进步二等奖.1991年.

[17] HTLV-1在中国的血清流行病学调查.第一完成人.中国预防医学科学院科学技术二等奖. 1994年.

[18] 促癌物的调查及其与化学致癌因素在致癌中的协同作用.第一完成人.中国预防医学科学院科学技术三等奖.1994年.

[19] 遗传因素、环境因素及EB病毒在鼻咽癌发生中作用的研究.第一完成人.卫生部科技进步二等奖.1995年.

[20] 遗传因素、环境因素及EB病毒在鼻咽癌发生中作用的研究.第一完成人.国家科委自然科学/发明三等奖.1996年.

[21] 我国人群中HTLV1病毒血清流行病学调查及其与人类疾病关系的研究.第二完成人.卫生部科技进步三等奖.1996年.

[22] 云南瑞丽流行区艾滋病毒的生物学和分子生物学跟踪研究.第二完成人.卫生部科技进步二等奖.1996年.

[23] EB病毒在鼻咽癌细胞的存在及其促癌物在鼻咽癌发生中的协同作用.第一完成人.卫生部科技进步二等奖.1997年.

[24] 云南瑞丽流行区艾滋病毒的生物学和分子生物学跟踪研究.第四完成人.国家科委自然科学/发明三等奖.1997年.

[25] EB病毒在鼻咽癌细胞的存在及其与促癌物在鼻咽癌发生中的协同作用.第一完成人.国家科委科技进步三等奖.1998年.

[26] 鼻咽癌血清学早期诊断成果推广及应用研究.广西壮族自治区医药卫生科学技术进步二等奖.2000年.

[27] 鼻咽癌血清学早期诊断成果推广及应用研究.广西壮族自治区科技进步三等奖.2000年.

[28] 世纪的警告.院士科普丛书.国家科技进步二等奖.2005年.

[29] 我国既往有偿供血人群艾滋病流行病学与控制策略研究.第二完成人.中华医学会科技进步一等奖.2008年.

[30] 我国既往有偿供血人群艾滋病流行病学与控制策略研究.第二完成人.北京市科技进步二等奖.2009年.

[31] 中国艾滋病重大疫情与关键技术研究及应用.第二完成人.中华医学科技二等奖.2013年.

2.主要科学贡献奖及荣誉

[1] 国家有突出贡献中青年科学家,中华人民共和国人事部、国家科学技术委员会颁发, 1984年.

[2] 在"鼻咽癌'六五'国家科技攻关项目"(课题负责人)中成果显著,特予表彰(奖金6万元), 国家计委、国家科委、国家财政部、国家经济委员会、国务院电子振兴领导小组办公室、国务院重大技术装备领导小组办公室联合颁发,1985.

[3] 政府特殊津贴,中华人民共和国国务院颁发,1990年.

[4] 中国预防医学科学院病毒所艾滋病研究与检测中心（中心的负责人）获"小西奖"，中国环球性病艾滋病基金会，1992年.

[5] 科技贡献一等奖，中国预防医学科学院病毒学研究所，1993年.

[6] 荣誉职工称号，中国预防医学科学院病毒学研究所颁发，1993年.

[7] 预防控制艾滋病性病先进个人，卫生部疾病控制司、中国预防性病艾滋病基金会，1996年.

[8] 优秀研究生指导教师称号，中国预防医学科学院颁发，1997年.

[9] 柯麟医学奖，中山医科大学广东省柯麟医学教育基金会，1998年.

[10] 全国预防与控制艾滋病性病先进个人，国家卫生部、公安部、教育部、广播电影电视总局，1999年.

[11] 艾滋病防治贡献奖，英国 Belly-Martin 基金会，2006年.

[12] 公共卫生与预防医学发展贡献奖，中华预防医学会，2008年.

[13] 公共卫生终身成就奖，美国马里兰大学人类研究所，2012年.

第三部分

大师风范

巍巍科山不老松

——记中国科学院资深院士曾毅教授

英国伯明翰大学肿瘤研究所　姚庆云

在祖国巍峨的科学高峰上，有一棵苍劲挺拔的不老松，他就是中国科学院资深院士曾毅教授。

曾教授今年 84 岁，这样的高龄，照理早可以在家颐养天年，然而曾教授至今还担任北京工业大学生命科学院院长、病毒病预防控制所院士实验室主任。每天早出晚归，全天工作，忙时还要加班加点，究竟是什么力量支撑他如此奋斗不息呢？

1929 年 3 月 8 日，曾毅出生于广东省揭西县一个商人家庭，从小聪颖过人，热衷读书，5 岁入小学，14 岁进入梅县东山中学读高中，该校以教学质量高闻名，叶剑英元帅就曾是这所学校的学生。当时交通不便，由揭西到梅县要步行 3 天，虽然是在校住读，但寒暑假都要走路回家。中学毕业时他立志学医，1946 年年仅 17 岁的他就远离家乡，由汕头乘货轮去上海读大学，货轮上没有床位，晚上只能睡甲板上或货物堆上，遇到下雨得找地方躲雨，十分艰苦，就是这样颠簸了好几天才到上海。1946 年先进入复旦大学，1947 年进入上海第一医学院。青少年时期的艰苦生活锻炼了曾毅不怕困难，刻苦耐劳的品质和毅力。"文革"期间，不少人都选择逍遥度日，曾教授却冒着走"白专道路"的风险，每天骑 4 小时的自行车，往返于家里、研究所、医院之间，坚持科研工作，曾毅就是有这么一股拼劲。

1952 年曾毅毕业于上海第一医学院，当时新中国成立不久，卫生条件还很差，看到脊髓灰质炎、伤寒、霍乱等传染病流行，夺去不少宝贵的生命，震撼了他年轻的心，他决心要在预防和控制疾病方面做出贡献，而不仅仅是医治单个病人，于是便进入了微生物学高级师资培训班，从此进入了微生物和病毒学研究领域，一干就是六十多年，成为国内外著名的医学病毒学家。

六十多年来，曾教授研究的范围很广，涉及多种肿瘤病毒和艾滋病病毒，而其中最突出的贡献是 EB 病毒和鼻咽癌的研究。

1964 年英国学者 Epstein 和 Barr 发现了一种新的疱疹病毒，以发现者的姓氏命名为 EB 病毒。1968 年 Old 等报道了鼻咽癌病人的血清中 EB 病毒抗体增高，这一发现吸引了曾教授的特别关注，鼻咽癌是中国广东、广西发病率最高的恶性肿瘤之一，于是曾毅就全力投入了 EB 病毒的研究。他检测了大量病人的血清抗体，证实鼻咽癌病人血清中有一种特异性的 EB 病毒 IgA/VCA.EA 抗体可用以诊断鼻咽癌。当时国际上都是采用免疫荧光法来做血清抗体测定，但荧光显微镜价格昂贵，以致无法广泛应用，经过反复摸索与实验，曾教授成功地建立了免疫酶检测法，该方法只要使用普通光学显微镜，简单易行，适合在全国推广。最初的血清学检测，只是用于门诊鼻咽癌病人的诊断,这些门诊病人多数已经是晚期病例,确诊后的治愈率低。因此,他毅然决定:应该走出实验室,到鼻咽癌高发区去做 EB 病毒血清学普查,这样不仅在学术上可以进一步了解 EB 病毒感染在鼻咽癌发病中的作用,更重要的是有可能发现一些早期病人,使这些病人得到及时治疗,从而提高治愈率。他的想法得到了广西壮族自治区领导的大力支持,卫生厅隋副厅长亲自带队,到鼻咽癌高发区苍梧县去实地调查,并在几天内就提供了五间房建立了实验室,随后又在梧州市成立了肿瘤研究所,支持和配合这项工作。

经过一番紧锣密鼓的准备之后,1977 年在广西的梧州和苍梧开展了大规模的血清学普查工作。曾毅是普查工作的组织者和领导者,也是业务培训班的主讲人,工作繁忙,与当地科研人员深入工厂和农村,发动群众进行血清学普查。由于要从每人的耳垂或手指上取几滴血来检查,有的群众不理解,有一位中年妇女居然说:"你们要取我的血,我就跳河",说完真的跳到河里,好在河水不深,工作人员把她从水中拉上来,好言相劝,反复说明普查可以早期发现,早期诊断鼻咽癌,最终还是说服了她,取了几滴血。有的人检查出 IgA 抗体,自认为身体健康,不愿进行临床复查,经说服后检查出早期癌,治疗后完全治愈。有的不愿临床复查,后来发展成晚期癌。经过多年的努力,在广西苍梧、梧州两地,普查了三十多万人。进行这样大规模的 EB 病毒血清学普查工作,是国际上首例。

后来在广西卫生厅领导的支持下在全广西推广普查数十万人,发现了一批 EB 病毒 IgA/VCA 抗体阳性的早期鼻咽癌病人。使鼻咽癌的早期诊断率从原来的 $20\%\sim30\%$ 提高到 80% 以上,这些早期病人,由于诊断治疗及时,提高了治愈率,挽救了很多病人的生命。普查后对抗体阳性者进行 20 年追踪,最迟的可以在普查后 18 或 19 年出现鼻咽癌,即可以在 20 年内预测鼻咽癌发生的可能性。

曾教授的工作,得到了国际上高度的评价,Epstein 教授在其专著"EB 病毒"一书中称:"这些卓越的新进展,是应用病毒血清学方法进行普查诊断人类癌症的第一个例子"。

在进行 EB 病毒血清学普查的同时,曾毅也同步进行了实验室的研究,早在 1976 年就在国际上首次建立了鼻咽癌高分化细胞株,普遍认为此型鼻咽癌与 EB 病毒无关;1980 年又建立了低分化细胞株。应用 PCR 技术和原位杂交法,首次证明高分化癌细胞也有 EB 病毒的 DNA,即不同分化类型的鼻咽癌都与 EB 病毒有关。

通过大规模的现场血清学普查和环境致癌物和促癌物的检查,结合实验室的研究成果,曾毅提出了以 EB 病毒感染为主因,环境中致癌和促癌因素协同,遗传易感性为基础的鼻咽癌多病因假说,这一假说在实验中得到证实。他首次证明 EB 病毒感染胎儿鼻咽部黏膜上皮细胞,在环境促癌物的协同作用下能诱发正常细胞癌变。Epstein 教授审阅该文稿后指出:"这确实是第一次证明 EB 病毒在促癌物的协同作用下诱发上皮细胞癌变",并认为"完全同意曾毅对中国鼻咽癌病因的看法"。此外,曾毅还进行了 EB 病毒疫苗的研究,该疫苗已获得国家药监局批准正在进行临床试验。

2014 将是 EB 病毒发现 50 周年,为了纪念这一重要的发现,有关方面决定 2014 年 3 月在英国牛津大学召开一次国际学术会议,并要出版一本《EB 病毒研究 50 年》的专著,谈到这 50 年的研究历史,必然要涉及对 EB 病毒研究做出过杰出贡献的科学家,其中也包括了曾教授,为此该书主编 Rickinson 教授委托我专程到北京采访了曾教授。

曾教授不仅是中国科学院院士,还是法兰西国家医学科学院外籍院士,俄罗斯医学科学院外籍院士,集诸多光环于一身的他并没有在荣誉面前止步不前,在我们的访谈中,他说:"要走的路还长,还有很多急需要研究和解决的问题,目前重点工作是抗 EB 病毒和艾滋病病毒疫苗的研发"。八十四岁高龄的曾教授毫无退休之意,他表示光阴如流,岁月不再,年龄大了就更要珍惜时光,争分夺秒。

曾教授是一位老科学家,同时也是一位老革命家,早在新中国成立前,作为一名青年大学生,他就冒着生命危险,秘密地参加了学生运动。今天,他在祖国科学事业上,忘我劳动,锲而不舍的奉献精神,向人们展现出的正是一位老共产党员的高尚情操。

2013 年 10 月 18 日

本文作者:姚庆云,英籍华人,英国伯明翰大学肿瘤研究所高级研究员。

科学青春永驻

中国疾病预防控制中心病毒病所　邵一鸣　周　玲

曾毅院士在病毒学、肿瘤学和艾滋病防治研究中建树良多，这些研究成果多次获得国家和部委科技进步奖，以及诸如陈嘉庚奖等社会科技奖项。深厚的科学造诣和对我国医学科学的杰出贡献，使曾先生在1993年当选为中科院院士，之后又被推选为法国和俄罗斯国家医学科学院外籍院士。2012年被马里兰大学人类病毒研究所授予"公共卫生终身成就奖"。

曾先生之所以能取得这样的学术成就，推动祖国医学事业的进步，与他具备的科学大家的优秀素质分不开。作为曾先生三十多年的学生，我们体会最深刻的是他探寻真理的科学精神，不受限于教条的创新思维和勇于实践、善于钻研的科学态度。曾先生对学科发展方向具有敏锐的洞察力，加之他不断追求创新的强烈意识，使得他能针对重要的医学需求，整合众多科学方法和技术手段，通过不断的试验、失败、再试验直至成功。更为可贵的是，他的研究从不止步于发表论文，而是不惜花费更多的时间和精力，推动其应用于临床，使病人能分享到科学的成果，成为最终受益者。

正是这种对探知科学真理的强烈欲望和为发展我国预防医学事业的高度责任感，激励着曾毅院士走过了六十多年的风风雨雨，成就了我国一代肿瘤病毒学和艾滋病防治医学的科学大师。

今天，曾毅院士和夫人李泽琳教授以八十多岁高龄仍每天工作在艾滋病和肿瘤防治科研的第一线，他们的精神和行动鞭策着我国年轻一代科学家更加努力工作，早日实现把我国建成创新型国家的科技强国梦。我们衷心祝愿曾院士和夫人身体健康，科学青春永驻，科学精神永存。

本文作者

邵一鸣，中国疾病预防控制中心性病艾滋病预防控制中心病毒与免疫研究室主任，教授，中国疾病预防控制中心性病艾滋病预防控制中心首席专家；兼任卫生病毒部艾滋病专家咨询委员会副主任委员，中华微生物学会病毒学专业委员会主任委员，联合国世界卫生组织（WHO）全球艾滋病规划署顾问（1980年）。

周玲，中国疾病预防控制中心病毒病预防控制所肿瘤室主任，教授。

鸿儒硕学　高瞻远瞩

中国疾病预防控制中心性病艾滋病预防控制中心　吴尊友

曾毅院士从事肿瘤病毒学、艾滋病病毒学研究和肿瘤与艾滋病防治研究 60 年来发表的中、英文科技论文 560 余篇,本书选集了 52 篇,反映了他在医学病毒学领域和肿瘤与艾滋病防治方面做出的卓越贡献。

《曾毅院士集》体现了他在两个重要领域的科学成就。一个领域是病毒相关肿瘤病因研究和诊断与防治,另一个领域是艾滋病的病毒学、诊断与防治。这些论文都见证了曾毅院士是我国在肿瘤病毒研究和艾滋病病毒研究及其防治领域的开拓者。

针对我国南方鼻咽癌发病率高的问题,曾毅院士首先提出病毒为其病因的科学假设,并进行积极探索,发现并描述了 EB 病毒与鼻咽癌发生的因果关系。他首先研制出鼻咽癌的普查和早期诊断方法,并将这一简单易行的早期诊断方法在鼻咽癌高发区的人群中广泛推广应用,提高了鼻咽癌的早期诊断率,使得他们能够及早得到治疗,减少了病死率。这一系列研究成果和科学论文的发表,使得曾毅院士成为该领域最具权威的专家。曾毅院士的科学论文不仅发表在国内、外科学技术期刊上,更是把科学防治鼻咽癌这篇大文章写在了人民群众的健康上。

当 1981 年世界上报道首例艾滋病病人时,曾毅院士就开始关注这一新的疾病。虽然中国报道第一例艾滋病病人是在 1985 年,但曾毅院士从 1984 年已在我国首次开展艾滋病病毒和艾滋病的研究,并证明 1982 年人类免疫缺陷病毒(HIV)就已经随着进口血液制品从美国传入我国,1983 首次感染我国公民。这一研究揭示,艾滋病病毒在美国报道艾滋病的第二年就已经进入中国。这比绝大多数人把中国 1985 年报道从美国来华旅游的第一例艾滋病病人作为艾滋病进入中国的时间,提前了 3 年。

在艾滋病流行早期,我国的艾滋病感染者都是零星入境的感染者,研究工作及寻找研究对象都比较困难。1987 年,曾毅院士首先报道分离到我国第一个 HIV-1 毒株。当时,艾滋病血清学诊断试剂几乎全部依赖进口,曾毅院士研制了 HIV 蛋白印迹快速诊断试剂盒,并获得卫生部的生产批文。特别是在 1995 年初,我国一些地方在单采血浆献血员中发现艾滋病感染,他研制的快速蛋白印迹诊断试剂盒,在全国广泛应用,对于吸毒者及在短时间内及时了解单采血浆污染造成艾滋病传播的范围,掌握艾滋病疫情,控制疫情进一步蔓延扩散,起到了重要的作用。

曾毅院士不仅是一位资深的病毒学专家,更是一位有着重要影响的公共卫生专家。他以科学家的敏锐和睿智,积极呼吁通过加强预防艾滋病宣传教育,控制艾滋病流行。由曾毅院士牵头组织 6 名院士和国内专家撰写"关于呈报'关于迅速遏止艾滋病在我国蔓延的呼吁'的报告""关于全面加强艾滋病宣传教育和行为干预的建议"和"关于我国艾滋病疫苗研发策略的建议",有力地推动了我国艾滋病防治工作的开展。

曾毅院士是一位积极向党和国家领导人建言献策的科学家。2003年,当"非典"在我国流行造成严重社会危害时,在国务院组织召开的一次专家座谈会上,曾毅院士当面直言,无论是防控的难度,还是造成的社会危害和影响,"非典"与艾滋病相比,简直就是小巫见大巫。曾院士的坦言,引起了国家对艾滋病防治工作的高度重视,极大地推动了一系列艾滋病防治重要措施的出台和实施,为扭转我国艾滋病防治工作的被动局面做出了重要贡献。

曾毅院士的这些突出工作,获国家和部级科技成果奖30余项。1991年获陈嘉庚医药科学奖,2006年获英国Belly-Martin基金会艾滋病防治贡献奖,2012年获美国马里兰大学人类病毒研究所"公共卫生终身成就奖",2013年获中华医学科技奖二等奖。

《曾毅院士集》的出版,不仅是对他本人科研和防治工作的总结,更为年轻一代疾病控制科研和防疫人员提供了完整、系统学习老一辈专家严谨的工作作风和勇于探索的科学精神的机会。这也是我国公共卫生领域的一份重要科技文献。

毅者人生

——访医学病毒学家曾毅院士

中国卫生人才杂志记者 孙 馨

初见曾毅院士,你很难相信他已经是一位耄耋之年的老人,他精神矍铄,和年轻人一样充满干劲。

曾毅有过许多头衔:医学病毒学家、中国科学院院士、法国国家医学科学院外籍院士、俄罗斯医学科学院外籍院士、美国马里兰大学医学院兼职教授、中国预防医学科学院院长、北京工业大学生命科学与生物工程学院院长;美国马里兰大学公卫终身成就奖、贝利·马丁奖、陈嘉庚医药科学奖、国家科技进步奖和卫生部科技进步奖、国家杰出贡献中青年科学家、政府特殊津贴……但他从来就把奖励和荣誉看得很淡。他说,成绩不是终点,而意味着新的起点和新的开始。

一次选择,一生努力
"这里更需要我。"

毅者,果决,志向坚定而不动摇也。

认识曾毅的人都说,他人如其名——勇往直前、不懈奋斗,执着追求、百折不挠,顾全大局、刚正不阿。

1952年,曾毅毕业于上海第一医学院(复旦大学上海医学院前身),虽然很想成为一名临床医师,但曾毅响应政府号召,作为一名基础学科的教师,培养医学人才,他说:"研究微生物,做好疾病预防工作可以帮助很多人,这里更需要我。"

那时候新中国百废待兴,曾毅和很多青年人一样充满理想和干劲。1952年毕业后他留校参加"高级师资培训班"。怀着"服从分配,到祖国最需要的地方去"的理想,1953年和17名年轻人奔赴海南岛,筹建海南医专。虽然台风肆虐,环境恶劣,但每个人都怀着一颗火热的心……可惜强台风损毁了简易的校舍,最终领导决定暂停办学,所有人撤回广州,曾毅被分配到当时的华南医学院(中山大学中山医学院前身)。

1956年调任北京时,曾毅进入中央卫生研究院(中国医学科学院前身)病毒系,师从我国著名的病毒学家黄祯祥先生,开始脊髓灰质炎病毒的研究。1961年开始研究麻疹病毒,在国内首先应用血凝抑制试验检测麻疹病毒抗体,以检测麻疹疫苗的免疫效果。

1959年组织上选派曾毅留苏深造,曾毅觉得应该趁此机会到国外学习新的领域,在他看来,很多动物肿瘤是由病毒引起的,人的肿瘤也应该由病毒引起。他从1961年开始研究肿瘤病毒。

初涉新领域,科研工作很难一帆风顺,曾毅始终以顽强的毅力和脚踏实地的努力来应对。从

1973年起,他开始研究有"广东癌"之称的我国高发恶性肿瘤——鼻咽癌与EB病毒的关系。1974年,作为"文革"期间稀少的留学生,曾毅赴英国格拉斯哥病毒研究所研究肿瘤病毒,回国后他开始研究鼻咽癌,重点是应用血清学诊断鼻咽癌,在国际上首次建立了鼻咽癌细胞株,证明高分化细胞株也带有EB病毒;曾毅的研究团队与广西壮族自治区人民医院、苍梧县鼻咽癌防治所及梧州市肿瘤研究所组成了协作组,在广西各级政府的领导下,开展了30多年的血清学普查,取得了很好的效果,并建立了简便、有效的鼻咽癌血清学诊断方法。免疫酶试剂盒于1990年获卫生部批准生产的证书。该试剂盒检查了46.8万人,早期诊断率为87.2%。能提前18年预测鼻咽癌发生的可能性,使鼻咽癌患者早期诊断率从20%～30%提高到80%～90%,及时挽救了很多人的生命。EB病毒发现者Epstein教授称"这项显著的新进展是应用病毒血清学方法进行普查诊断人类癌症的第一个例证"。今年,广西壮族自治区政府已经启动在全自治区开展鼻咽癌、肝癌筛查的健康惠民工程,这是以人为本,保障人民健康的重大举措。曾毅领导的团队还研究了遗传因素与鼻咽癌发生的关系,发现了一些易感基因和保护基因。此外,还研究了环境中的促癌物质,从1963种中成药和植物中发现有52种有激活EB病毒的促癌物;还发现了人体内的厌氧杆菌产生的丁酸也具有促癌作用;动物实验证明,EB病毒在促癌物和丁酸的协同作用下,首次诱发出鼻咽癌。Epstein教授对此项发现也完全赞同,认为这是国际上第一次证明病毒诱发上皮细胞癌变。这些研究对鼻咽癌病因和疫苗的研制有重要意义。EB病毒Lmp2疫苗已获国家药监局批准,正在临床试验,已完成Ⅰ期临床试验,证明了疫苗是安全的。应用疫苗感染病人树突细胞免疫常规治疗的鼻咽癌病人,获得了较好的免疫反应。曾毅的团队希望通过早期诊断和疫苗防治,降低病死率,控制鼻咽癌的发生。

摒弃浮躁,百炼成钢
"细推物理须行乐,何用浮名绊此身。"

在病毒学领域摸爬滚打61年的曾毅很喜欢杜甫的诗句。在他眼中,如果没有求真务实的精神,刻苦钻研的禀性,淡漠物欲的心境,敢为人先的气概,就会永远与科学研究无缘。以鼻咽癌研究为例,相关工作持续了40年。"既然选择了艰苦的基础研究工作,就要经受坐冷板凳的煎熬,要有'十年磨一剑'的耐力。"他如是说。

1984年,曾毅又启动了艾滋病病毒研究,年过半百开始新的创业。自1981年国际上首次报道艾滋病后,曾毅就意识到这是一个重型传染病,预测病毒必然会传播到我国,关键在于加强防范。他一方面密切关注国内外的研究动向,另一方面积极开展调查研究,为我国艾滋病防控提供依据。当时相关研究刚刚起步,实验环境和设备都很缺乏,但他丝毫没有考虑个人的安危,首当其冲,身体力行。在那份敬业精神的感召下,短期内科研团队取得了累累硕果:1984年开展了艾滋病的血清学检测,证明中国城乡人群尚未发现HIV感染者。1985年与浙江医科大学合作,检查了该省18例用过进口Ⅷ因子制剂的血友病患者,查出4例艾滋病病毒抗体阳性,证实了早在1982年艾滋病病毒已随进口血液制品传入我国。1986年分离出我国第一株艾滋病病毒(HIV-1AC株),研制出诊断试剂盒,获得国家批件,为我国深入研究病毒的特性、制备诊断试剂和研制疫苗创造了条件。现正在继续研究抗艾滋病药物和疫苗,同时开展了大量艾滋病的宣传教育工作。

曾毅谦虚地将研究工作的成绩归结于和他先后共事过的合作者、同事和学生们的努力工作。他说,重大创新一定要靠协作,协作的前提是共赢,一个人能做的事是很有限的。此外,对医学科学研究,"不能盲目跟风,要摒弃急功近利、急于求成的浮躁心态,认准了方向就要用尽全力去做。"曾毅总结道。

耆年硕德,相濡以沫
"感谢夫人一直以来紧密合作和相互帮助"

2009 年,曾毅院士八十华诞,时任中国科学院院长路甬祥发来贺信。其中"热爱祖国,献身科学,为人正直,治学严谨"的评价,十分中肯。

和很多老一辈医学科学家一样,"文革"中曾毅也遇到种种磨难,但逆境的磨砺并没有使他丧失信仰,而进一步锻造了终生受用的坚毅和求实精神。

他缓缓地讲述那段经历,"其中不得不提到一个人,就是夫人一直以来默默地帮助和支持。"

其实对夫人,他一直饱含歉意。在 60 多年前的上医校园,曾毅邂逅了自己的终身伴侣李泽琳,二人风雨相伴。他既自豪又抱歉:"夫人是很成功的药学家,青蒿素的主要研究者之一,也是第一批派往英国进修的科研人员。她是我事业上的好搭档,也在家庭生活上付出很多很多。"

如今曾毅院士的生活依然忙碌,也几十年如一日的简单。不仅在生活上与夫人相濡以沫,更在事业上携手共进——两人从 1987 年开始进行抗艾滋病毒药物研究,已进入临床研究阶段,已获 9 项国内外专利,特别是来北京工业大学后,负责和参与了多项抗艾滋病药物的研究开发。

2002 年,73 岁的曾毅被邀来到北京工业大学,组建北京工业大学生命科学与生物工程学院,一干又是十年。其间夫人仍在默默支持,在病毒与药理研究室的建设、运行以及研究生培养方面倾注心血。平时二人的研究领域各有侧重,默契的合作带来的高效率,常常事半功倍。

忙碌一辈子,如今曾毅院士的生活有了新的重心。"学生们的成长是我最在意的事。我已经84 岁了,还能再干几年? 我要与时间赛跑,把经验让更多人传承下去。"说到这里,他目光坚定地看向远方。

[中国卫生人才杂志　2013 年 06 期,18-19]

曾毅:只为挽救更多生命

中国科学报记者　王　庆

马里兰大学"公共卫生终身成就奖"首次颁给了美国国外的科学家,曾毅也是首位获得该奖项的中国科学家。

50多年来,曾毅的工作始终围绕着一个主题——与病毒作战。

一个月前度过85岁生日的曾毅院士,在接受《中国科学报》专访的前一天,刚刚从英国参加"EB病毒发现50周年"学术会议回来。

集中科院院士、法国和俄罗斯国家医学科学院外籍院士等多个头衔于一身,"空中飞人"的生活对他来说已是家常便饭。目前,曾毅院士担任北京工业大学生命科学与生物工程学院院长、中国疾病预防控制中心病毒病预防控制所院士实验室主任。

50多年来,他的工作始终围绕着一个主题——与病毒作战。

2012年,在国际病毒研究学界享有盛誉的马里兰大学人类病毒研究所授予曾毅"公共卫生终身成就奖"。该所所长 Gallo 说:"曾毅教授将基础研究成功地应用于临床,取得了开创性的成就,我们都非常尊敬他。"

该奖旨在表彰为科学研究和公共卫生事业作出突出贡献的科学家。那一年,马里兰大学"公共卫生终身成就奖"首次颁给了美国以外的科学家,曾毅也是首位获得该奖项的中国科学家。

抓捕鼻咽癌背后的元凶

20世纪50年代末,一个想法反复在曾毅的脑海中闪现:"动物的癌症很多是由病毒引起的,从进化的角度来看,人的癌症也可能是由病毒引起的。"于是他开始研究病毒与癌症的关系。"肿瘤是很难早期诊断的,一旦证明是由外来的病毒引起,肿瘤细胞一定有病毒的核酸及蛋白的存在,这有利于早期诊断和治疗。"

随后,鼻咽癌进入了他的视野。鼻咽癌在我国南方数省,尤其是广西和广东发病率很高,且该病具有早期难以被觉察的特点,发现症状再去诊治的大部分患者都已到了晚期。

1968年,国际学界发现,鼻咽癌病人的血清中常有 EB 病毒 IgG 抗体。这启发了曾毅,他便开始着重研究鼻咽癌与 EB 病毒的关系,开展了血清学诊断的研究。

当时国外都采用免疫荧光法来做血清抗体测定,这种方法需用价格昂贵的荧光显微镜来检查,难以在中国推广。经过研究,曾毅终于在1976年建立了免疫酶检测法。借此方法,用普通光学显微镜即可检查 EB 病毒。

1977年,曾毅带着自己创立的这种新型血清学检查方法,赴广西与当地医疗卫生单位组成鼻咽癌协作组,开展了大规模的血清学普查工作。

在当时的社会环境下,除了科研工作本身的压力,曾毅还不得不面对来自民众的不解甚至排斥。当地人很害怕鼻咽癌,认为是不治之症且害怕传染,甚至有的家庭出现鼻咽癌病人就送到山里,搭个帐篷,每天送饭吃,直到死亡。

检查鼻咽癌须从每人的耳垂或手指上取几滴血,很多当地居民害怕被检查出患有这种"不治之症"。

"当时有一家人,男主人因肝癌刚刚故去,他妻子一开始拒绝接受检查,说万一我查出来鼻咽癌,那我们一家子都完了。"曾毅回忆道,"我就向她解释,恰恰相反,查出来是早期就容易治疗了,正是为了救你一家。"

还有更极端的。有一位中年妇女居然说:"你们要取我的血,我就跳河。"说完真的跳到河里去。从河里将其救起后,曾毅耐心向她解释"抽血检查可以早期发现,早期诊断鼻咽癌",最终才说服了她。

截至2005年,在曾毅多年的推动下,广西共普查了467 957人,查出188例鼻咽癌病人,早期病人占87.2%,使鼻咽癌的早期诊断率从原来的20%～30%提高到85%以上。这些早期患者,由于诊断治疗及时,提高了治愈率,很多生命得以挽救。

颇具戏剧性的是,多年前一位王姓年轻工程师看到报纸上的消息,将血滴在纸上寄给曾毅,经检查为抗体阳性。于是曾毅建议他立刻来北京并得到确诊和治疗,及时挽救了他的生命。多年后,当曾毅前往北工大出任生命科学与生物工程学院院长时,那位工程师也在该校任教。他看到曾毅的名字,激动地找到当年的"救命恩人"再次致谢。

除了患者的感激,曾毅的工作还得到国际学界的高度评价,EB病毒发现者之一、英国病毒学家Epstein在其专著《EB病毒》一书中称曾毅的"这些卓越的新进展,是应用病毒血清学方法进行普查诊断人类癌症的第一个例子"。

此外,曾毅于1976年就在国际上首次建立了鼻咽癌高分化细胞株,1980年又建立了低分化细胞株,并且首次证明高分化癌细胞也有EB病毒的DNA,即不同分化类型的鼻咽癌都与EB病毒有关。

经多年调查研究,曾毅还提出了以EB病毒感染为主因,环境中致癌物和促癌物起协同作用,以遗传易感性和机体免疫力为基础的鼻咽癌多病因假说,这一假说在实验中也得到证实。

坎坷求知路

香港大学微生物系主任吴文翰认为:"称曾毅教授为当今癌症预防与控制领域的领导人物之一,是毫无争议的。"

在他看来,曾毅在早期诊断病毒肿瘤特别是鼻咽癌方面的不朽贡献,为学界提供了一个迄今为止最有说服力的证据,即鼻咽癌是可以被有效控制的。

"在进行比较后,我们对此贡献的意义会更感惊讶,因为早期和晚期鼻咽癌治疗的预后是完全不一样的。"吴文翰表示,"用此方法(曾毅创立的检测方法)在普查中发现的鼻咽癌多数是早期的,而没有普查的鼻咽癌绝大多数已处于晚期。"

虽获业界赞誉,但曾毅的科研之路从一开始却并非坦途。

1929 年 3 月,曾毅出生在广东省揭西县。高中时,为了到教育质量更好的学校求学,每学期开学时,他要步行三天才能赶到学校上学。

17 岁时,他背井离乡,由汕头坐货轮去上海读大学,货轮上没有床位,晚上只能睡在露天的甲板上或货物堆上,遇到下雨更是难熬。

"当时我想考上海医学院。"曾毅回忆道,"但赶到上海时已经错过了考试的日子,只能先考到复旦大学。"

次年,他如愿考入上海医学院。不过随后他还得面对科学之外的压力甚至磨难。

由于积极参加学生运动,在新中国成立前一个月曾毅和同学们被关进了牢房。一天夜里,一位临时代管的青年军战士来找曾毅等人要便服,提醒说:"看管你们的是'飞行堡垒',因临时有事被调走了,他们回来会枪毙你们的,趁半夜赶紧逃吧。"曾毅和同学们由此逃过一劫。为了躲避再次被抓捕,曾毅等甚至在当时上海医学院附属医院——上海第八人民医院的太平间里藏了几天。

新中国成立不久,由于当时简陋的卫生条件,伤寒、霍乱、脊髓灰质炎等传染病流行,不少人因此丧命或致残。这些亲眼所见深深震撼了年轻的曾毅。他发自内心地希望在病毒研究领域有所建树。

然而"文革"期间,因为新中国成立前家里开过织布作坊,曾毅遭到批斗,但他觉得这个阶段总会熬过去,始终没有停止学习和钻研业务。

抗击艾滋先行者

在科研方面,曾毅一直力求保持开阔的视野和敏感的嗅觉。

1981 年,远在大洋彼岸的美国报道了一种新的传染病——艾滋病。曾毅听到这个消息后的第一反应是,这种疾病极可能与病毒有关,才会有这样严重的传播情况,并预测这种疾病一定会威胁到我国。

当时,中国已经开始对外开放,各国人员往来逐渐频繁,"传染病是没有国界的",曾毅开始对这一疾病保持高度警惕。

1984 年,曾毅在国内开始了艾滋病的血清学检测工作。从城市和乡村获得的所有样本,检查结果都为阴性,这似乎暗示病毒还没有进入中国。但曾毅问自己:"中国普通人群确实没有感染,但是高危人群有没有感染?有没有用过美国血液的?"

根据调查,他发现美国 Armour 公司和 Alpha 公司于 1982 年曾将一些血液制品——第 8 因子赠送给了我国某医院,1983—1985 年,这些血液制品被输给了一批血友病患者。曾毅找到了接受过这些血液制品的患者,在 19 位使用 Armour 公司第 8 因子的患者中查出了 4 例艾滋病病毒感染者。这是我国第一次发现艾滋病通过血液感染,并且证实早在 1982 年艾滋病病毒就已经随着美国的血液制品传入中国。

1986 年,一名美国患者在中国因艾滋病死亡。得到消息后,曾毅立即赶赴昆明,采来了血样,并着手分离病毒。这本来应该在 P3 实验室(生物安全防护三级实验室)中进行,但由于当时并没有这种实验室,曾毅就在北京一间简陋的实验室内,在普通的接种柜里面,戴上手套分离病毒。

他成功分离出了我国第一株艾滋病病毒 HIV—IAC 株,确认了早期我国艾滋病病毒属于 B 型。随后,他又迅速用分子生物学的方法做出了快速诊断试剂,并经卫生部批准,使得我国在早期就拥有了自己的诊断试剂。

不仅如此,他还深入河南等地调查艾滋病通过卖血途径传播的问题,多次上书中央提出艾滋病防治对策,致力于抗艾滋病药品和疫苗的研制,并敢于揭示艾滋病传播的真实情况。

由于曾毅认真的调查可能会给地方政府带来压力,甚至有地方官员向当地配合曾毅调查的医务人员施压:"以后不要与曾毅往来,他已经被撤职了。"曾毅有时不得不像"地下党"似的进行暗访。

2009 年,曾毅院士八十大寿之际,时任中国科学院院长路甬祥高度评价曾毅"热爱祖国,献身科学,为人正直,治学严谨"。

采访中,秘书进来跟曾毅商量,考虑到他的年纪,最好再出差时派人陪同。曾毅则说服秘书不要担心,"别耽误其他人的工作陪我了,出差我自己去就行"。

如今,他依旧马不停蹄。接下来他又将赴广西出差。"两天跑两个地方,学术上我能帮点忙的,一般不好意思拒绝"。

[中国科学报　2014 年 4 月 4 第 9 版人物周刊]

快乐老人的预防哲学

中国科学报记者　王　庆

记者：你刚刚从英国出差回来，如此奔波应该很辛苦，但看你气色、状况都不错，有什么锻炼或者保健秘诀吗？

曾毅：这些年，我到国外过海关的时候，有时海关工作人员低头瞧瞧护照，再抬头看看我的相貌，然后问我到底多少岁了？不少人都觉得我不像八十多，也就六十多。

其实我没什么养生秘诀，工作挤占了绝大部分时间。凭着这些年积累的经验和能力，有些科研工作能往前推一步是一步。

在办公室和各个实验室之间走来走去可能起到了一定的锻炼作用吧。我觉得"乐观"是自己多年来保持旺盛工作精力的最大秘诀，用乐观的态度面对困难。

记者：其实你的科研领域强调预防，某种意义上也是研究和提醒大众怎么保持健康。

曾毅：可以这么说。很多病毒传染都是公众缺乏公共卫生知识引起的。大家一定要提高公共卫生意识，正确认识各种病毒，做好免疫防治，做到早发现、早治疗。

记者：比如鼻咽癌？

曾毅：是的，早发现、早治疗仍是挽救患者生命和提高生命质量的最有效手段。遗憾的是，到门诊来诊断的病人70％～80％都是晚期。鼻咽癌早期的治疗很简单，95％的病人只要使用放疗、化疗就可以治好。但如果鼻咽癌到了中晚期，治愈率分别下降到了70％和50％。

记者：在鼻咽癌早期，患者为什么容易忽视？

曾毅：由于鼻咽癌早期没有明显的症状，因而不容易被发现。随着肿瘤的发展，肿瘤部位的黏膜发生溃破、感染，而出现涕血等症状；肿瘤阻塞鼻后孔和咽鼓管咽口时，就会出现鼻塞、耳鸣、听力下降和头痛等症状。鼻咽癌的恶性度较高，很容易出现颈部转移，且常常由于肿瘤向鼻咽黏膜下发展，鼻咽部没有明显的肿瘤，而颈部已有肿块，或向颅底发展，侵犯脑神经，出现相应的症状。鼻咽癌的病人往往是有了明显的自觉症状，或颈部有了很大的肿块才到医院看病，这时约70％的病人已属于晚期，难于治愈，病死率很高。

记者：所以早期诊断和预防就显得很重要？

曾毅：鼻咽癌的血清学早期诊断方法很简便，而且非常安全。用消毒针刺破手指头采血，经免疫酶法检测，即可判断结果。如果没有抗体，一般在5年内都可以放心了。如果检出抗体，就可能查出早期鼻咽癌。这时应该对鼻咽黏膜可疑处取活检做组织病理学检查，看有无鼻咽癌细胞。如果没有癌细胞，则根据抗体滴度高低定期检查。

［中国科学报　2014年4月4第9版人物周刊］

A Controversial Bid to Thwart the "Cantonese Cancer"

Jia Hepeng

Zeng Yi has spent 3 decades probing a connection between Epstein-Barr virus and nasopharyngeal cancer. A new vaccine should show whether he is on the right track

NANNING, CHINA—In the coming weeks, scientists here plan to launch the first clinical trial of a vaccine that aims to mobilize the immune system to prevent nasopharyngeal cancer(NPC). It is the climax of one researcher's quest to decipher a disease that kills as many as 13,000 Chinese each year—more than 10 times the fatalities in the rest of the world combined.

Zeng Yi, a 78-year-old virologist at the Institute for Viral Disease Control and Prevention of the Chinese Center for Disease Control and Prevention in Beijing, earned fame for revealing a link between Epstein-Barr virus (EBV) infection and NPC. Based on this insight, Zeng initiated screening programs to detect NPC at an early stage. Along the way, he crossed swords with skeptics— and prevailed. Colleagues admire his indefatigable character. "Without Zeng's work, we would not have today's achievements in NPC control and treatment," says Tang Bujian, chair of the Guangxi Society of Cancer Control in Nanning.

Cancer became the number one killer in China in 2005(see sidebar), and the government has begun paying more attention to prevention, says Qi Guoming, vicechair of the Chinese Medical Association and a former top health official in charge of epidemic control. That's why, Qi says, the government is ready to back a $1.2 million trial of a preventative vaccine that builds on Zeng's work. Some experts laud the attempt. "Targeting the one risk factor shared by virtually all patients with NPC—that is, EBV—seems like a reasonable approach," says Ellen Chang, an epidemiologist at Northern California Cancer Center in Fremont.

Not everyone is convinced. The link between EBV and NPC is too shaky to focus on a vaccine, argues Yao Kaitai, an oncologist at Southern Medical University in Guangzhou. EBV's carcinogenic role, he says, "is not as decisive as the links between hepatitis viruses and liver cancer and between human papilloma virus and cervical cancer."

Zeng disagrees. "Our experiments prove the EBV can induce cancer and that our vaccine is effective."

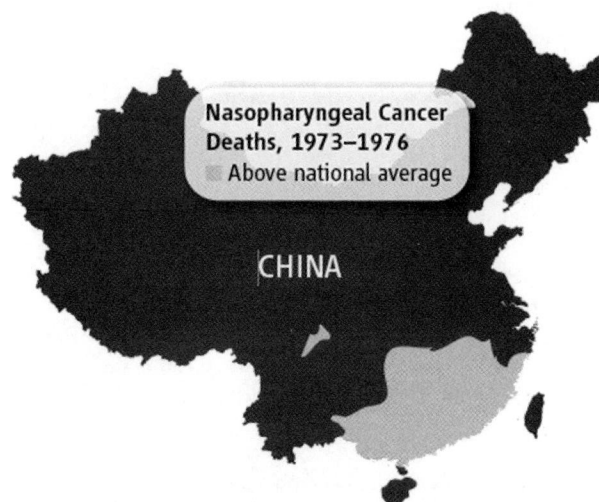

Southern scourge.
Nasopharyngeal cancer hits Cantonese-speaking parts of China harder than other regions.

Early clues

Every year in China, as many as 40,000 people are diagnosed with NPC. For many, it's a death sentence: The 5-year survival rate is less than 50%. In much of the world, NPC is rare, with less than one case per 100,000 people, on average. But in southern China's Cantonese-speaking Guangdong Province and Guangxi Zhuang Autonomous Region, the incidence is 15 to 25 cases per 100,000. NPC is called the "Cantonese cancer."

Although Zeng is a Guangdong native, he paid scant attention to NPC until 1973, when he came across a report about high levels of immunoglobulin G(IgG) in the serum of an NPC patient. Zeng knew that IgG can be a marker of EBV infection. "My instinct told me that there would be a relationship between EBV infection and NPC," he says.

Zeng started probing which antigens are elevated in NPC patients. He zeroed in on EBV-specific IgA/virus capsid antigen(IgA/VCA), another marker of EBV infection. Levels of IgA/VCA are high in nasopharyngeal epithelial cells of NPC patients, he found, suggesting that antigen levels rise with NPC onset. Although early-stage NPC can be treated effectively with radiation therapy, at the time only 20% to 30% of cases were caught at that stage. Screening for EBV biomarkers, Zeng reasoned, could increase the success rate. But there was a hitch: More than 90% of people worldwide are infected with EBV sometime in their lives. Which ones would develop NPC?

The answer occurred to Zeng after a serendipitous field trip. In 1977, Zeng was invited to Nanning, the capital of Guangxi, to lecture on cancer. Afterward, health officials coaxed Zeng to visit an NPC hot spot: Wuzhou in Guangxi's mountainous southeast. "Cancer patients were sleeping in the streets, waiting for beds in the hospital," says Deng Hong, former director of Wuzhou Oncology Institute. A few months later, Zeng persuaded health practitioners to screen for IgA/VCA levels in the serum of people in Cangwu County, near Wuzhou. In 1977 and 1978, screening 23,711 people turned up 1308 with high biomarker levels, of whom 15, after examination of their nasopharyngeal tissue, were diagnosed with NPC. "The facts strongly suggested that EBV infection is at least one cause of NPC," Zeng says.

But direct proof—and a mechanism—has been elusive. "We highly appreciated [Zeng's] NPC screening, but at the time the scientific community was not fully convinced that EBV really caused NPC," says Hans Wolf, a microbiologist at the University of Regensburg in Germany who thinks EBV is involved—but not the whole story. Labs failed to infect cultured human nasopharyngeal epithelial cells with EBV.

"The ubiquitous presence of EBV antibodies worldwide was not seen to be specific enough to prove a causal relationship," Wolf says.

Faced with skepticism about his proposed EBV infection-NPC link, Zeng searched for potential environmental triggers of the disease. Intriguingly, he and his colleagues found that 52 herbs in traditional Chinese medicine contain compounds that activate EBV in cell culture. Of these herbs, 45 are planted and used in Guangdong and Guangxi, including Liaogewang(Radix Wiksteroemiae), which is widely prescribed for inflammation. Although EBV may be relatively benign in most people, its effects might be altered by such herbs, Zeng argues. Genetic factors could also play a role, as southern Chinese are much more likely to contract NPC than other population groups, even after they move elsewhere.

In 1996, Zeng proposed that EBV infection, abetted by environmental factors, causes NPC in people with genetic susceptibility and frail immune systems. That year, Zeng's lab performed a critical experiment. His group infected human fetal nasopharyngeal tissue, which is vulnerable to viral infection, with EBV. Next, they transplanted the infected tissue into mice and fed them tumor promoters extracted from Guangdong herbs. Three months later, tumors appeared in transplanted fetal tissue that expressed EBV genes and antigens but not in fetal tissue without the tumor promoters.

Despite successes in the lab, NPC screening has faltered. "Doctors were reluctant to spend their time" on a venture from which they couldn't turn a profit, says Deng. In 2006, he moved to a Guangzhou hospital to promote voluntary EBV antibody screening, which costs less than $1 thanks to an immunoenzyme test Zeng developed. Still, health workers have found it difficult to persuade people to spend a small sum to look for a disease they are unlikely to contract. "We would not give up," Zeng says. "Without identifying antibody-positive people, our tremendous efforts would be in vain."

Taking their best shot

Zeng's new tack is a vaccine. The idea is to prevent the cancer by blocking an EBV gene called latent membrane protein 2(LMP2) that integrates itself into human DNA and can trigger NPC in susceptible people, says Zhou Ling, chief scientist of the NPC vaccine project at the Chinese Centers for Disease Control and Prevention. A plasmid encoding the LMP2 gene should elicit a cellular and humoral immune response, which in turn should tamp down LMP2 expression.

The plan is to launch a safety trial in 30 cancer patients by the end of 2008, pending approval from China's State Food and Drug Administration. If the 1-year trial is a success, and if funds are available, the vaccine will be given to 300 volunteers who test positive for the IgA/VCA antibody but don't have cancer at Shantou University Medical School in Guangdong and Guangxi People's Hospital in Nanning.

Some argue that large-scale vaccination against NPC is economically unjustified. "The cost is too high to immunize 100,000 people just to prevent 10 to 20 cancers," says Zhao Ping, director of the Cancer Institute and Hospital of the Chinese Academy of Medical Sciences in Beijing. Others contend that the science itself is too weak. "Much more work is needed to repeatedly prove the causal link between EBV and NPC," says Yao.

Zeng Yixin, director of the State Key Laboratory of Oncology at Sun Yat-sen University in Guangzhou, says, "A vaccine, no matter for EBV infection or for blocking NPC initiation, has been a dream for many labs in the field, but the evidence for using LMP2 to induce a strong immune response specific to NPC is not sufficient."

Wolf, for one, is in Zeng's corner. His team planned to test a similar preparation in the late 1990s, but the project was abandoned after funds failed to materialize. A vaccine, Zeng hopes, might someday make NPC just as rare among Cantonese speakers as it is in most other regions of the world.

[SCIENCE,2008, 321: 1154-1155]

第四部分

社会影响

普查人类癌症的第一个例证
The First Example of Mass Screening for a Human Cancers

Anthony Epstein

The characteristic serological responses to EBV infection shown by patients with undifferentiated NPC, in particular the high titres of IgA to EBV viral capsid antigen(VCA) and early antigen(EA), are well known. Now, tests for these antibodies are being used on a large scale to screen populations with a high incidence of the tumour both for early tumour detection and to identify and follow prospectively individuals marked as high-risked cases by their serological profiles(Zeng et al., 1982, 1983a, b; Chapter 9). This remarkable new development represents the first example of mass screening based on viral serology for the detection of a human cancer (Chapter 9).

［Quoted from M. A. Epstein in the *The Epstein-Barr Virus*, *Recent Advances*. M. A. Epstein and B. G. Achong(eds) Willian Hememann, London, 1986, Chapter 1.］

EB 病毒发现者国际著名肿瘤专家 Epstein 教授对我国建立和应用病毒血清学方法进行鼻咽癌早期诊断和前瞻性研究的评价:

现已熟知鼻咽癌病人对 EB 病毒的感染有特殊的血清学反应,特别是有高滴度的 EB 病毒 IgA/VCA 和 IgA/EA 抗体。现在测定这些抗体的方法,正在鼻咽癌高发区人群中广泛应用于早期诊断,并对这些有血清学指标的高危人群进行前瞻性的观察(曾毅等 1982,1983a,1983b 本书第九章 1986)。这项显著的新进展是应用病毒血清学方法进行普查诊断人类癌症的第一个例证。

这是首次证明 EB 病毒可以在体内诱发实验性癌症

——Anthony Epstei 教授给曾毅院士的一封信

Dear Yi,

Thank you for you letter of 15 February 1955; I would have answered sooner but it has taken me some days to find out from my friends in Paris exactly what your plans were and where I should send my reply.

As you can imagine, I was most interested in the experiments you describe and the fascinating results obtained. How was the TPA administered which made the EBV/293 cells carcinogenic in nude mice? And the same question applies to the EBV/ foetal epithelial cells which gave lymphomas in the nude mice or carcinomas if TPA was administrated with butyric acid. I think you are right in saying that this is the first time that EBV has been shown to cause experimental carcinomas in vivo under the influence of TPA and butyrates, but I am sure you know of the related in vivo experiment by Osato and his group(Aya et al., Lancet 337:1190, 1991) in which TPA treated EBV-infected lymphoid cells showed translocations of chromosome 8 and c-myc activation after treatment, and the ability to cause lymphomas on injection in nude mice—a somewhat similar story.

I completely agree with your suggested interactions of EBV, TPA, and butyric acid in human in China. The late professor Ito from Kyoto did a great deal of work on phorbol ester-containing plants in China before he died and contributed a chapter on this in "The Epstein-Barr Virus: recent advances".(eds Epstein& Achong, 1986)

Do please continue to keep me informed of these significant investigations and do not hesitate to send me your mss. I should be delighted to see them.

I hope your travels went well and that your various meetings proved worthwhile. I expect to visit China twice this year but will only be in Beijing in November. Hopefully we may have an opportunity to meet then.

With my thanks again and warm greetings.

Your sincerely

Anthony Epstein

尊敬的曾毅教授：

　　您 1955 年 2 月 15 日的来信已经收到。我本来是要早点回复您的,在这之前,我花了一些时间从我巴黎的朋友那里得到您的地址和您的行程。

　　您可以想象得到,我对您所描述的实验和获得的十分吸引人的结果非常感兴趣,即肿瘤多肽抗原(TPA)对感染了 EBV 的 293 细胞在裸鼠体内如何形成癌变以及在 TPA 和丁酸的协同作用下,感染了 EB 病毒的人胎上皮细胞在裸鼠中诱发淋巴瘤和鼻咽癌的反应。我完全赞同这是首次证明在促癌物 TPA 和丁酸的协同作用下,EB 病毒可以在体内诱发实验性癌症。不过,我想您也知道 Osato 和他的实验室曾进行过相关的体内实验:用 TPA 作用于 EB 病毒感染的淋巴细胞后,可以使 8 号染色体易位,c-myc 活化。将其注射到裸鼠体内后能诱导淋巴瘤。这与您的实验有一些相同点。

　　我完全同意您的意见,在中国人中 EBV、TPA 和丁酸相互作用。日本京都的 Ito 教授生前对中国含佛波酯类的植物做过大量的研究,1986 出版《EB 病毒的最新研究》(由 Epstein 和 Achong 编写)中有一章是关于他在这方面的研究。

　　请和我保持联系并告知我最新的进展。我非常高兴能看到您在这方面的研究成果。

　　希望您这次旅行愉快。也希望您参加的这些会议能对您有所帮助。今年我将两次访问中国,十一月份会去北京。非常期待能有机会和您见面。

　　谢谢! 祝好!

安东尼·爱普斯坦

对鼻咽癌细胞中 EB 病毒标记的阐述是举世无双的

——德国慕尼黑大学 Hans Wolf 教授对曾毅课题组
鼻咽癌研究工作的评价

To whom it may concern

Evaluation of a prospective study on early diagnoses of Nasopharyngeal Carcinoma in the field.

I have been working with Epstein Barr Virus and its association with Nasopharyngeal Carcinoma since 1970. In this time I have followed very closely the progress in many fields and aspects involved enormous progress has been made.

However, a central issue, the practical impact of measuring virus associated parameters such as EBV specific antibodies was long missing and has now been demonstrated in the recent few years by the group of Professor Zeng Yi.

This work found world wide unanimous acceptance and represents the outstanding highlight of patient oriented basic research not only in the field of EBV but of general tumorvirology. The findings are of greatest impact by themselves because they allowed the detection of the respective antibodies as early as 5 years before the onset of the disease and as much as 92% of the patients could be identified as tumor leaves in very early stages as compared to 30% in serologically uncontrolled populations.

This is of greatest significance because these patients in early stages can be cured with high probability(above 70%—90%). The design and consequent evaluation of this study is unique in the world and is already becoming a reference of outstanding importance for all scientists working in the field. Moreover these works laid the fundaments for future developments and justify the enormous investments in new technologies involving genetically engineered products. A field where the group of Professor Zeng Yi is now also entering with consequence and enthusiasm. The work deserves highest scientific rating and praise.

München, 28. Nov. 1985

Hans Wolf

　　我自 1970 年起，一直在从事 EB 病毒及其相关的鼻咽癌的研究工作，也一直密切地注视着该领域及有关方面的进展。现在确实取得了许多进展，但在一个关键问题上——一个在实际工作中急待解决的测定 EB 病毒标记如病毒特异性抗体方面的工作却长期缺欠。现在这一问题已被曾毅教授的研究小组近几年的工作阐明了。

　　这项工作得到了世界范围的承认，并代表着不仅仅是 EB 病毒而且是整个肿瘤病毒领域的、面向病人的基础研究的一项杰出的成就。这一发现本身具有十分重大的实际意义，因为其可在发病 5 年前就检查出特异性抗体。并且查出的病人中，92％是早期鼻咽癌，而不经此血清学检查的病人，仅有 30％是早期的。这一点之所以极为重要，是因为早期鼻咽癌病人的治愈率可达 70％～90％。该研究的设计及其最终结果的评价均是举世无双的，这已成为该领域所有科学家研究工作的一项非常重要的参考。另外这项研究还为将来在基因工程等新技术方面的发展和投资的判断打下了基础。曾毅教授的小组正在以极大的热情和智慧投入这个研究领域。

　　这项研究属于最高级别的科学成果，应得到最高的赞誉。

Hans Wolf

1985 年 11 月 28 日于慕尼黑

德国雷根斯堡大学卫生与微生物研究所　所长

　　本文作者：Hans Wolf 教授是德国慕尼黑大学 Pettenkofer 研究所分子肿瘤病毒研究室主任、雷根斯堡大学卫生与微生物研究所所长，他是肿瘤研究中第一个发现鼻咽癌细胞中含有 EB 病毒 DNA 的专家。

当代医学上的一个里程碑

——香港大学微生物系主任吴文翰教授对鼻咽癌早期诊断工作的评价

To WHOM IT MAY CONCERN

Few will dispute that Prof. Zeng Yi is amongst the leaders in cancer control and prevention. His monumental work on early detection of nasopharyngeal carcinoma specifically and on virus associated cancers in general has been widely publicized in professional journals reviews as well as in mass media in different countries. The methods he developed and subsequently perfected provides the most cost effective and reliable means, for early detection of the disease. Concurrent with the laboratory studies, the application of the evolving methodology for mass screening and the subsequent impact of this effort on a large population provide the most convincing evidence today that NPC, an ethnic malignant disease of China, can be effectively controlled. This accomplishment is the more startling when compared with situation elsewhere; whereas the disease was almost exclusively diagnosed at its early stages among the screened population, the larger majority of the cases diagnosed elsewhere are already at the later stages. The difference between the two situation is a substantially different prognosis following treatment.

In my long personal and professional association with the man behind this effort, it is quire apparent that such an accomplishment requires not only the ability of an outstanding scientist but also that of an exceptional administrator. Only with these abilities combined, do we expect a fact that can be rightly regarded as a mile stone in modern medicine.

His current interest in early intervention is a logical extension of his work to date on early detection. The results accumulating on the aspects regarding environmental promotors and on EBV vaccine holds out great promise and I look forward to the day when this effort lead us to an effective strategy for control of this disease.

M.H. Ng
Professor of Microbiology
and Head of Department

Januart 11th 1986

称曾毅教授为当今癌症预防与控制领域的领导人物之一，是毫无争议的。他在早期诊断病毒相关肿瘤特别是鼻咽癌方面不朽的贡献，不仅在专业期刊上广泛发表，同时也被新闻界广泛报道。由他建立并使之完善的方法，提供了一项最有效、最可靠的早期诊断鼻咽癌的技术。该技术在现场普查中的应用以及其在广大人群中产生的巨大作用，再加上实验室研究工作，为我们提供了一个迄今为止最有说服力的证据，即作为中国的一个与人种有关的肿瘤——鼻咽癌，是可以被有效地控制的。在进行比较后，我们对此贡献的意义会更感惊讶，因为早期与晚期鼻咽癌治疗的预后是完全不一样的，用此方法在普查中发现的鼻咽癌几乎无一例外的是早期的，而在其他地方诊断的鼻咽癌绝大多数已处于晚期。

在我与做出上述成就的教授的私人及工作交往中，深深体验到，这一成就的取得，不仅需要有杰出科学家的素质，而且还需要有超群的管理才能。能做到集二者于一身，还不能被公正地誉为当代医学上的一个里程碑吗？

曾教授的兴趣现在已经转移到如何干预早期鼻咽癌的进一步发展方面。这是他在早期诊断方面做出的工作的一个合乎逻辑的扩展。有关环境致癌因子及 EB 病毒疫苗方面不断积累着资料，显示出光明的前景。我期待着，经这方面的努力而找到一条有效控制鼻咽癌的途径的这一天的到来。

香港大学微生物系主任

吴文翰教授

1986 年 1 月 11 日于香港

曾毅教授的贡献值得国际、国内科学界的承认和赞扬

——法国国家科学中心 Guy Blaudin DE-THE 教授对鼻咽癌研究工作的评价

Following my visit to the Institute of Virology in Beijing on November 18, 1985, I wish to stress the paramount interest of the work of Prof. Zeng Yi. The follow-up sero-epidemiological studies which have been conducted under his direction in both Wuzhou and Cangwu in the Guangxi Autonomous Region, are of the utmost value and relevance to both the pathogenesis of nasopharyngeal carcinoma and the control of this major killing disease.

Prof. Zeng Yi and his team in Beijing and in the Guangxi Autonomous Region have made two major achievements in cancer research and cancer prevention.

The first was to show that a simple test detecting IgA antibodies to EBV/VCA and later to EBV/EA can detect this tumor at very early stages, when this cancer can be cured by radiotherapy, in a high percentage of individuals.

The second was, through prospective studies of IgA/VCA positive individuals, to show that this antibody marker defines a subgroup of the population at immediate risk for developing this cancer. He showed that an increase in IgA/VCA titers conveys a 18% risk of developing NPC within three years. Thus all efforts of prevention should be directed on the small group of pre-cancerous individuals.

The achievements of Pr. Zeng Yi merit the recognition of both the national and international communities.

Professor Guy Blaudin DE-THE
Director of Research at CNRS

Lyon, le November 29, 1985

　　我于1985年11月18日访问了北京的病毒学研究所。我愿在此强调一下曾毅教授的研究工作的重大意义。在他的领导下进行的广西壮族自治区梧州、苍梧血清流行病学追踪观察,对鼻咽癌这一主要致死性疾病的发病机制及控制均有至关重要的价值。

　　曾毅教授及其在北京、广西的研究队伍,在肿瘤研究和预防方面做出了两项重要贡献。

　　第一,他们建立了一种检测抗EB病毒壳抗原的IgA抗体(IgA/VCA)的方法,以后又进一步发展了测定抗EB病毒早期抗原IgA抗体(IgA/EA)的方法。应用这些方法可以查出极早期的鼻咽癌病人。经过放射治疗,多数早期病人可被治愈。

　　第二,经过对IgA/VCA阳性人群的前瞻性调查研究,发现用此抗体为指标,可确定出一组有患鼻咽癌高度危险性的人群。他阐明在IgA/VCA抗体滴度升高者中有18%的人可能在3年内患鼻咽癌。因此所有预防鼻咽癌的努力应针对这一小部分癌前期病人。

　　曾毅教授的这些贡献得到了国际、国内科学界的承认和赞扬。

法国巴斯德研究所

法国科学院院士

Guy Blaudin De-THE 教授

1985年11月29日于里昂

　　注:Guy Blaudin De-THE教授是法国国家科学中心肿瘤、病毒、免疫和流行病学室主任,国际病毒性肿瘤协会秘书长。

中国科学院贺信

尊敬的曾毅先生：

欣逢您八十华诞，我谨代表中国科学院、中国科学院学部主席团并以我个人的名义向您致以最诚挚的祝贺和良好的祝愿！对您几十年来为推动祖国科技事业的发展所做出的重要贡献表示崇高的敬意！

作为我国著名医学病毒、肿瘤病毒和艾滋病病毒学家，您在鼻咽癌的早期诊断和鼻咽癌病毒病因研究方面做出了卓越贡献，建立了一系列鼻咽癌的血清学诊断方法，提前 5～18 年预测鼻咽癌发生的可能性，使鼻咽癌病人早期诊断从 20%～30% 提高到 80%～90%，挽救了大批病人的生命。您肯定了 EB 病毒在鼻咽癌发生中的作用，不仅证明 EB 病毒与鼻咽癌有关，还首次证明高分化癌也与 EB 病毒有关。探讨了环境因子和遗传因素与鼻咽癌的关系，提出了"在鼻咽癌的发生上，遗传因素是基础，EB 病毒起重要作用，可能是启动作用，环境中的促癌物、致癌物起协同作用"。自 1984 年起，您长期从事分子流行病学、疫苗和抗艾滋病药物的研究，为推动我国对艾滋病的检测和防治研究做出了重要贡献。

您热爱祖国，献身科学，为人正直，治学严谨。衷心恭祝您生日快乐，健康长寿，阖家幸福！

中国科学院院长

路甬祥

中国科学院学部主席团执行主席

二○○九年三月八日

第五部分

人生风采

● 科研工作 ●

曾毅在广西壮族自治区苍梧县对当地医务人员进行鼻咽癌血清学普查的培训（1977年）

曾毅院士在广西壮族自治区人民医院举办"艾滋病病毒流行性控制"和"EB病毒疫苗"的专题讲学（2005年）

曾毅院士（右二）在广西壮族自治区人民医院指导工作，左一为院党委书记张法灿，右一为常务副院长林辉（2006年）

曾毅院士在全国"预防与控制艾滋病性病学研讨会"上做专题报告

曾毅院士（左二）访问云南大学"禁毒防艾研究与援助中心"，并与校长何天淳及专家就该中心的建设与科研工作进行了深入交流（2011年）

曾毅院士在中南民族大学为该校师生做"艾滋病流行和防治新进展"的学术报告和"病毒与癌症"的专题讲座（2012年）

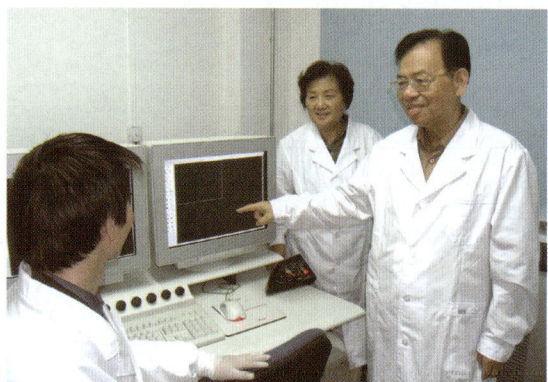

曾毅院士（右一）在实验室指导工作（2006年）

曾毅院士在P3实验室工作

曾毅院士（一排右三）与中国疾病预防控制中心病毒病所同仁合影

● 国际交流 ●

曾毅留学英国（1974—1975年）

曾毅（左二）陪同美国华盛顿大学微
生物系主任、免疫学家G. Person教授
及夫人访问广西苍梧县鼻咽癌普查现
场（1980年）

曾毅（右）陪同国际著名EB病毒专
家、哈佛大学传染病研究室Ellit kieff
教授访问广西苍梧县鼻咽癌防治所
（1982年）

曾毅（右二）陪同日本东京都大学医学院院长Y.Ito教授（右一）访问广西壮族自治区苍梧县鼻咽癌普查现场（1983年）

日本著名病毒专家Hinuma教授（左三）率日本代表团与曾毅教授（左二）合作，在新疆调查HTLV-1在中国的流行情况（1983年）

曾毅（左）应邀访问美国芝加哥大学，与微生物系主任E.Kieff教授（中）和法国病毒学家T.Ooka博士（右）合影（1983年）

日本东京都大学病毒所所长Hinuma教授来华与曾毅（左二）合作研究成人T细胞白血病病毒在中国的流行病学（1985年）

曾毅（右三）协助广西壮族自治区建立了"梧州市肿瘤研究所"，积极开展鼻咽癌普查工作。法国科学院院士Guy de The（右二）和Hueber博士（右五）访问梧州市苍梧县血清学普查出的早期鼻咽癌患者（1985年）

曾毅（左）拜访2008年诺贝尔奖获得者、法国Zur Hansen教授（1986年）

曾毅（左）应邀访问德国慕尼黑大学微生物系并与H.wolf教授合影（1987年）

曾毅（左三）应邀访问以色列耶路撒冷大学微生物系，与系主任Y.Becker教授（左一）及家人合影（1991年）

曾毅（右一）向阿尔及利亚默罕默德医生（右二）传授鼻咽癌血清学普查和诊断技术（1992年）

美国国立卫生研究院（NIH）Ablashka教授访问广西壮族自治区苍梧县鼻咽癌现场，与曾毅院士（左）合影（1993年）

中国预防医学科学院病毒学研究所聘请EB病毒发现者 Tony Epstein 教授（左）为名誉教授，曾毅院士为其颁布发证书（1994年）

诺贝尔奖获得者、法国著名学者L.Montagnier（中）应邀来华参加"中国艾滋病防治研讨会"并做专题报告，期间曾毅院士（右）和夫人陪同其游览长城（1995年）

曾毅院士（前排右二）在"国际鼻咽癌防治高级论坛暨广西鼻咽癌现场防治研究三十周年学术研讨会"上（2007年）

在广州举行的国际"鼻咽癌的研究进展"学术报告会上，曾毅院士（一排右四）、法国巴斯德研究所De The院士（一排左四）、美国NIH O'Brien院士（一排左六）与参会代表合影（2007年）

● 重要时刻 ●

曾毅（右）获陈嘉庚医药科学奖，诺
贝尔奖获得者丁肇中教授为其颁发奖
状（1991年）

曾毅院士（右）当选为俄罗斯医学科学院
外籍院士，院长为其授予证书（1995年）

"中国艾滋病防治基金会"会长曾毅
院士（右八）在广西壮族自治区组织
和主持了"艾滋病防治展览会"，自
治区副主席李振潜（右九）参加开幕
式并讲话（1997年）

曾毅院士（左）当选为法国医学科学院外籍院士，并接受让·弗朗索瓦·马太院长授予的证书（2003年）

2003年11月，中国疾病预防控制中心病毒病预防控制所肿瘤病毒室与中国疾病预防控制中心性病艾滋病预防控制中心为曾毅院士举办了"肿瘤病毒研究工作40年、艾滋病病毒研究工作20年回顾暨学术报告会"，100多位国内外专家和国家科技部、卫生部领导参加了会议（从左至右：邵一鸣教授、曾毅院士、周玲教授）

曾毅院士（左）获美国马里兰大学"公共卫生终身成就奖（2012年）

● 珍贵合影 ●

中央组织部组织中国科学院和中国工程院部分院士在吉林休假合影，前排左四、左三为曾毅院士与夫人（1994年）

中国科学院第十二次院士大会上生物学部院士合影，三排左十为曾毅院士（2004年）

曾毅院士（左）参加国庆60周年庆典，在天安门观礼台上留影（2009年）

曾毅院士（左一）参加中国合格评定国家认可委员会（CNAS）资深顾问座谈会（2014年）

● 幸福生活 ●

曾毅院士与夫人李泽琳教授

曾毅与夫人李泽琳教授在瑞士（1981年）

曾毅院士与家人在一起